CROSS CURRENCY SWAPS

edited by
Carl R. Beidleman
DuBois Professor of Finance
Lehigh University
Bethlehem, Pennsylvania

BUSINESS ONE IRWIN
Homewood, Illinois 60430

© RICHARD D. IRWIN, INC. 1992

This publication is designed to provide accurate and authoritative information in regard to the subject matter covered. It is sold with the understanding that neither the author nor the publisher is engaged in rendering legal, accounting, or other professional service. If legal advice or other expert assistance is required, the services of a competent professional person should be sought.

From a Declaration of Principles jointly adopted by a Committee of the American Bar Association and a Committee of Publishers.

Project editor: Jean Roberts
Production manager: Diane Palmer
Jacket designer: Renée Klyczek-Nordstrom
Production Services: Publication Services
Typeface: 11/13 Times Roman
Printer: R. R. Donnelley & Sons Company

Library of Congress Cataloging-in-Publication Data

Cross currency swaps / edited by Carl R. Beidleman.
    p.   cm.
    Includes index.
    ISBN 1-55623-316-7
    1. Swaps (Finance)   2. Foreign exchange futures.   3. Cash
management.   I. Beidleman, Carl R.
HG3851.C75   1991
332.4′ 5—dc20

CIP 91-15377
CIP

Printed in the United States of America
1 2 3 4 5 6 7 8 9 0 DOC 8 7 6 5 4 3 2 1

To Inge

PREFACE

The first edition of *Financial Swaps* was written in 1984 and published in 1985. It was a solo effort based extensively on discussions with financial intermediaries and users of financial swaps. The book was an attempt to document the evolution of swaps, the rationale for their development, and the applications for which they were useful financial instruments. At that time financial swaps were in their infancy. Markets were not yet fully developed, documentation was not standardized, pricing was fee based rather than spread based, liquidity was limited, and most players were quite far down on the learning curve.

When it came time to consider revision of the book, I played with the idea of reworking the book myself and producing a second edition that built on and updated the first—a practice employed successfully by many authors. Review of the developments in financial swaps that had transpired since the appearance of the first edition, however, made me quickly realize that a single writer could no longer do justice to the topic: the markets had moved too far; applications had become too comprehensive; modifications to basic instruments had transformed their uses in many ways; pricing and portfolio risk management had become more sophisticated and efficient; and credit risk, regulatory concerns, accounting, and taxation issues had reached new levels of complexity. Hence, I decided to rely on my understanding of the subject and my association with scholars and practitioners in the field of swaps to assemble a body of material that could adequately treat this burgeoning subject. The result has taken the form of two volumes, each concerned with a major subset of financial swaps. This book, *Cross Currency Swaps*, treats issues concerned with altering cash flows in multiple currencies. It was preceded a year earlier by a companion volume, *Interest Rate Swaps*, which dealt with altering interest flows in a common currency.

Cross currency swaps have flourished in the recent overall surge of financial activity. Despite the fact that the full range of material integral to this subject is unusually far-reaching, I have attempted to gather in this volume the basic knowledge intrinsic to the success-ful deployment of cross currency swaps. The book examines most of the factors responsible for the rapidly growing interest in cross cur-rency swaps. Part 1 begins with the basics of cash-flow management, moves quickly into the role of swaps in the menu of modern finan-cial instruments, and describes basic terminology, applications, and instruments. It then covers variations to basic instruments that give them unique features for arbitrage and hedging applications.

This material is followed, in Part 2, with extensive material on widely diverse applications of currency swaps. Parts 3 and 4 cover valuation and conceptual issues that should be of special interest to students of the rapidly growing field of financial engineering. Much of the material found in these sections represents advanced thinking on the valuation of streams of cash flows and on the conceptual rela-tionships between currency swaps and related financial instruments. These are the areas in which financial innovation is currently mak-ing its greatest strides and which should therefore appeal most to advanced thinkers seeking a better understanding of modern financial products. The final section, Part 5, covers regulation, accounting, and taxation—issues sometimes thought to be peripheral but which are in fact essential. A final chapter looking forward to the next generation of swappers rounds out the book.

I am pleased with both the capabilities of the chapter contributors and the quality of their manuscripts. They are competent professionals in their respective sectors of financial swaps. The book is intended to provide a foundation and framework upon which serious swap-pers and financial engineers can build. It will also provide a useful guide for the uninitiated, as well as a handy reference for experienced swappers. It should prove useful to financial managers and portfolio managers, whose function is to source or manage funds. CEOs and corporate directors should also find it useful in developing an un-derstanding of the effective management of exchange-rate risk and capital market arbitrage. Analysts and executives of international fi-nancial intermediaries should use it frequently as they seek to manage their own balance sheets or offer advice and service in assisting clients in matters of asset and liability management.

The book should also be useful for advanced undergraduate and MBA courses in international financial management, for banking and executive seminars concerned with foreign exchange risk management and arbitrage, and as a resource volume for financial intermediaries and general business practitioners. Finally, commercial and investment banks, institutional investors, international organizations, and others who face cash flows denominated in foreign currencies will find *Cross Currency Swaps* a valuable aid in training sessions for employees and clients.

Acknowledgment of assistance in extensive undertakings such as this can never be complete. I am, of course, especially grateful to the individual chapter contributors, who have done a remarkable job in covering the material that was assigned to them. I wish to express my appreciation to Richard W. Barsness, Dean of the College of Business and Economics at Lehigh University, for establishing the environment in which efforts such as this can reach fruition. I am grateful to many members of the community of investment and merchant bankers and to users of currency swaps for generously sharing their perceptions of the development of the swapping process. I also wish to thank Janice Schaeffer, who assisted remarkably with the administrative burden that underlies any enterprise of this sort.

The editorial and production staffs at BUSINESS ONE Irwin, who were thoughtful and helpful throughout the process leading to the publication of this book, made it a more enjoyable undertaking.

Finally, I thank my wife, Inge, for her confidence and encouragement during the ongoing process that led to the completion of these works. She alone remembers when it all began.

Any errors of omission or commission that remain are mine.

Carl R. Beidleman

THE CONTRIBUTORS

Carl A. Batlin is managing director in charge of risk management research at Manufacturers Hanover Trust Company. He has also worked at Chase Manhattan and Chemical Banks and as professor of finance at the University of Michigan. He holds a Ph.D. in financial economics from Columbia University and has published articles on various financial topics in a number of academic and trade journals.

Carl R. Beidleman joined the Lehigh University faculty in 1967 and was awarded the Allen C. DuBois Distinguished Professorship in Finance in 1975. In 1983 he was appointed the first chairman of the newly organized Department of Finance. A graduate of Lafayette College, Dr. Beidleman earned the M.B.A. degree at Drexel University and the Ph.D. at the Wharton School, University of Pennsylvania. He is a member of the boards of directors of the Martin Guitar Corp., Independence Bancorp Inc., and Bucks County Bank and Trust Co., and he has served as a consultant to commercial banks, legal counsel, and industrial firms.

Keith C. Brown is the Allied Bancshares Centennial Fellow and an assistant professor of finance at the Graduate School of Business, University of Texas at Austin. He received his M.S. and Ph.D. degrees in financial economics from the Krannert Graduate School of Management at Purdue University. He specializes in teaching investments and capital markets courses at the M.B.A. and Ph.D. levels. From June 1987 to July 1988 he was based in New York as a senior consultant to the Corporate Professional Development Department of Manufacturers Hanover Trust Company. He has also lectured extensively in executive development programs. In August 1988 he received his charter from the Institute of Chartered Financial Analysts. In addition, Mr. Brown has published articles in a variety of economic journals.

Frederick D. S. Choi is Research Professor of International Business at New York University's Stern School of Business. He served as chairman of NYU's Area of Accounting, Taxation and Business Law from 1983–86 and is former director of the Vincent C. Ross Institute of Accounting Research. Professor Choi has contributed more than 50 articles to scholarly and professional journals and is the author or coauthor of 10 books on the subject of international accounting and financial control. He is the recipient of five literature awards from the National Association of Accountants, and his textbook, *International Accounting*, with G. Mueller, was recently awarded the Wildman Gold Medal by the American Accounting Association. He is currently serving as editor-in-chief of a new specialist journal, *The Journal of International Financial Management and Accounting*, published in the spring of 1989. He has served as a consultant to multinational companies, international accounting firms, financial organizations, and academic institutions and is a frequent lecturer in executive development programs in the United States and abroad.

Vincent Cirulli is vice president in charge of equity derivatives at Citibank in New York. He formed this trading desk in 1990, focusing on index options and equity swaps for the U.S. and Japanese markets. Prior to this he managed a trading desk dealing in non–U.S.-dollar-denominated caps and swaptions and ran this business for three years. In the past six years he has traded a range of derivative products, specializing in new products and structured transactions. Mr. Cirulli holds a bachelor of science degree in finance from Iona College in New Rochelle, New York.

Daniel P. Cunningham is a partner in the law firm of Cravath, Swaine & Moore and was the firm's resident London partner from 1986 through 1990. His corporate finance practice includes rate and currency swaps, mergers and acquisitions, and receivables finance. Mr. Cunningham participated in the preparation of standard master agreement forms for interest rate and currency swaps by the International Swap Dealers Association Documentation Task Force. He received his A.B. degree from Princeton University in 1971 and graduated from Harvard Law School in 1975. He was an editor of the *Harvard Law Review*.

Ravi E. Dattatreya is a Senior Vice President at Sumitomo Bank Capital Markets, Inc. He received his master's degree from the University of Wisconsin at Madison and his doctorate in Operations Research from the University of California at Berkeley. He later joined Goldman, Sachs & Co., where he worked on the development of the now commonly accepted parametric approach to fixed income securities. Before joining Sumitomo Bank Capital Markets, Dr. Dattatreya was Director of the Financial Strategies Group at Prudential-Bache Securities. He is a coauthor (with Frank Fabozzi) of *Active Total Return Management of Fixed Income Portfolios* (Probus Publishing, 1989). He is an editor or coeditor of several books, including *The Handbook of Derivative Products* (Probus Publishing, 1991) and *Fixed Income Analytics* (Probus Publishing, 1991). He is also the series editor for the Institutional Investor Monograph Series in Finance. Dr. Dattatreya is a member of the editorial advisory board of *The Journal of Portfolio Management* and *The International Journal of Mortgage-Backed Securities*.

David F. DeRosa is a vice president of Alliance Capital Management L.P., where he is a specialist in derivative and synthetic securities and foreign exchange. He received his A.B. and his Ph.D. from the University of Chicago.

Donna J. Fletcher is a visiting professor in finance at Lehigh University. Upon receiving her doctorate from Lehigh in June 1991, she joined the finance faculty at Bentley College in Waltham, Massachusetts. Professor Fletcher is a certified public accountant and worked in public accounting and investment banking prior to completing her graduate studies in finance.

George Handjinicolaou is an executive director of Security Pacific Hoare Govett Limited, with responsibility for derivative products in Europe. He joined Security Pacific's swap group in New York in 1986, and since the spring of 1987 he has been the head of European market-making activities in derivative products in London. Before joining Security Pacific he was with the World Bank, where he was instrumental in building the World Bank's swap program and implementing several innovative borrowings. Prior to that, Dr. Handjinicolaou taught finance at New York University and Baruch College of the City University of

New York and has also worked at Salomon Brothers and Josephthal & Co. Inc. in New York. He holds a B.A. in economics from the University of Athens and an M.B.A. and a Ph.D. in economics and finance from New York University.

Peter L. Harnik is director and manager of the swaps and derivatives department of UBS Phillips & Drew International, Ltd., Tokyo. He has been in Tokyo since 1986, originally serving as deputy representative for the Union Bank of Switzerland, Zurich's Capital Markets Group, Tokyo Representative Office. Before joining the UBS group, he spent 11 years at Irving Trust where he directed their entry into the swaps business and, prior to that, held positions in treasury trading and management and international corporate banking in New York, Miami, and Tokyo. He received his bachelor's degree from Williams College and his masters in international affairs from Columbia University.

Benjamin Iben is vice president for General Re Financial Products Corporation. He was vice president for Swaps and Foreign Exchange Research, Manufacturers Hanover Trust Co. He graduated with honors in economics from the University of California, Berkeley, and did graduate work at the Graduate School of Business of the University of Chicago, where he completed the M.B.A. with a specialization in finance. During this time he was an exchange student at ESC, Paris, France. His early career included work at the Federal Reserve Bank of San Francisco, where, as a research associate, he focused on the relationships among market concentration, profitability, and new entry. In his recent work, he designed and implemented zero coupon-based pricing and hedging systems for swap products and was responsible for monitoring exposure of all interest rate options positions.

Cal Johnson is a vice president in the Bond Portfolio Analysis (BPA) Group at Salomon Brothers. After joining Salomon in 1980, he spent four years in quantitative equity research before moving to fixed-income research. As a member of the BPA Hedge Group since 1984, he has worked on a wide variety of valuation and hedging problems and has written articles on synthetic assets, fixed-income options and futures, and interest rate swaps. He holds a B.S. in mathematics from the California Institute of Technology and a Ph.D. in mathematics from the University of Massachusetts.

Suresh E. Krishnan is currently vice president for international fixed-income research at Merrill Lynch. His responsibilities cover global asset-liability management, international fixed-income trading strategies, global bond indices, and currency risk management. Prior to joining Merrill Lynch, he was a senior consultant to Manufacturers Hanover Trust, Bank of America, and Chase Manhattan Bank. He has also served as a faculty member at Pennsylvania State University and the University of Michigan. He received his doctorate in international finance from the University of Michigan.

David Lawrence is a vice president in the global finance sector of Citicorp Investment Bank Limited in London. He is the senior research analyst for Europe and the divisional risk manager, with responsibility for the development of new risk management processes, procedures, and systems. He was the principal author of the bank's *Risk Management Manual*, which set out new risk management controls that are now used to manage the business globally throughout Citicorp. Since 1976, Mr. Lawrence has worked in many different areas of Citibank, including the Consumer Bank, the Institutional Bank, and the Investment Bank. Before joining Citicorp, he was a senior consultant in computer sciences and a university fellow in computing. He holds an M.A. in physics from Cambridge University, a D.Phil. in nuclear physics from Oxford University, and an M.B.A. from the University of New South Wales.

Alicja K. Malecka is a first vice president for Deutsche Bank Capital Corporation in New York. Since returning from the Far East in 1990, she has managed the marketing of swaps and derivative products to Japanese corporate customers. From 1982 to 1990 Ms. Malecka worked in Japan and Hong Kong establishing and managing the Swap Group and the Yen Swap Book for DB Capital Markets (Asia). She previously established the Swap Department and the Foreign Exchange Advisory Service for Chemical Bank throughout Asia. Prior to her Asian assignment, she was a managing consultant of Chemical Bank's FEAS headquarters in New York. Ms. Malecka has a master's degree in economics from the State University of New York at Stony Brook, an M.B.A. in international finance from DePaul University in Chicago, and an undergraduate degree in international trade from the Main School of Planning in Warsaw.

Ian Mordue is assistant general manager of financial engineering at the Investment Bank subsidiary of the Australia and New Zealand (ANZ) Banking Group. A science graduate from the University of Newcastle majoring in pure mathematics and applied mathematics, Mr. Mordue has worked for transnationals and governments in operations research and management science. He has spent the past 11 years in the finance sector, where he has been involved in the swaps market since its inception in Australia.

Kari R. Nars is director of finance for the government of Finland. He is in charge of all financing and liability management operations, both in the domestic and international markets. Before joining the Ministry of Finance, Mr. Nars worked as an economist with the International Monetary Fund, full-time director in charge of international operations at the Central Bank of Finland, and executive managing director of the Bank of Helsinki. In addition, he has held directorships in several corporations and financing institutions and is presently cochairman of the international top-borrowers club, the Government Borrowers Forum. He has published several books and numerous articles on economic subjects, specializing in international financing and hedging against currency risks. Mr. Nars holds a Dr.Sc. degree in economics from the Helsinki School of Economics.

Philip G. Nehro is a vice president of Alliance Capital Management L.P., where he specializes in fixed-income and derivative and synthetic securities. Mr. Nehro was formerly with the sales and trading division of Salomon Brothers Inc. He received his A.B. and M.B.A. degrees from the University of Detroit and completed studies at the Graduate School of Banking of the University of Wisconsin.

Alan Pryor is Executive Vice President of Deutsche Bank Capital Corporation with responsibility for swaps and derivative products. He was formerly a Vice President in International Capital Markets at Citibank. He received his M.A. in Economics from the University of Michigan in 1974.

James R. Ramsey is currently the chief state economist for the commonwealth of Kentucky and the executive director for the commonwealth of Kentucky's Office of Financial Management and Economic

Analysis. In these positions, Dr. Ramsey has responsibility for the investment of the state's $1.7 billion portfolio, the issuance and administration of the state's 28 debt-issuing authorities, and the revenue-estimating function of state government. Dr. Ramsey is also an adjunct professor at the University of Kentucky and has done consulting work and training programs for numerous corporations and state and local governments. He has served as director of investments for Republic Savings Bank and is on the board of trustees of the Churchill Tax Free Fund, the board of trustees of the Kentucky Retirement System, and the board of directors of MedEcon Securities Inc.

Vembar K. Ranganathan is a principal in the Interest Rate and Currency Risk Management Group of Security Pacific National Bank (SPNB). He is a senior marketing officer providing debt strategy services to corporations in the Midwest. Prior to joining SPNB in 1984, he was a vice president at Citibank's North American Investment Bank, where he specialized in exchange rate forecasting and basis swaps. Beginning his banking career in 1970 at Citibank, Hong Kong, Mr. Ranganathan served for seven years as a senior economist, covering the Asia-Pacific region. He has an M.B.A. from New York University, and a M.Phil. in economics from Columbia University and has published several articles on exchange rates, international trade, and Asian economies. He is also the author of *Interest Rate Trends and Comparisons*, published by SPNB, now in its fifth edition.

Janet L. Showers is a director of research of Salomon Brothers and the manager of the Hedge Group in the Bond Portfolio Analysis Department. Her major responsibilities include the quantitative analysis of fixed-income and foreign exchange hedging products, the development of hedging strategies for asset and liability problems, and new product development. The group is also responsible for the development of valuation models of government bonds, corporate bonds, and high-yield debt, including the analysis of bonds with embedded options and option pricing models. She joined Salomon in 1983 after holding various positions at Bell Telephone Laboratories and at the Chase Manhattan Bank. Dr. Showers holds a Ph.D. in operations research from Columbia University, an M.S. in operations research from Stanford University, and a Sc.B. in applied mathematics from Brown University.

Donald J. Smith is an associate professor of finance and economics at the School of Management, Boston University. He received his M.B.A. and Ph.D. degrees in economic analysis and policy at the School of Business Administration, University of California at Berkeley. He specializes in teaching money and capital markets and futures and options courses at the undergraduate and M.B.A. levels. He has published widely in academic and practitioner-oriented journals. From August 1986 to August 1987 he was a senior consultant to the Corporate Professional Development Department of Manufacturers Hanover Trust Company.

Barry W. Taylor is counsel to The First National Bank of Chicago. He specializes in swaps and derivatives and has authored several articles on the subject. Mr. Taylor received his J.D. degree from Northwestern University School of Law and holds an A.B. degree from the University of Illinois.

Raj E. S. Venkatesh is currently an Analyst in the Product Analysis Group at the Chase Manhattan Bank, N.A. He received his Ph.D. in Metallurgical Engineering from New Mexico Institute of Mining and Technology, Socorro. He has previously worked at E.F. Hutton and Dean Witter Reynolds and is the author of several published articles. His current research interests are in option pricing models and other derivative products.

Vijaya Venkatesh is a capital markets analyst at Credit Lyonnais, New York. Her responsibilities include the analysis and development of the management reporting system for swaps, and the evaluation, implementation, and maintenance of the systems for swaps, money market instruments, and mortgage- and asset-backed securities. After her graduate studies in engineering and science management at the University of Alaska, she joined the Financial Strategies Group at Security Pacific National Bank, New York. Prior to joining the financial industry, she worked as a research engineer at Conoco, Inc. She has authored and coauthored several publications.

Samuel C. Weaver earned a Ph.D. in finance and economics from Lehigh University in 1985. Prior to joining Hershey Foods as manager of Corporate Financial Analysis (1984), he was an assistant professor of finance at Elizabethtown College and was a consultant to Hershey Foods. In 1988, he became a member of the board of directors of the Financial Management Association and was recently listed in *Who's Who in Finance* (1989). Additionally, he is a certified management accountant and an adjunct professor in the M.B.A. program at Lehigh University.

Michael Wood is a Senior Manager in the International Financial Markets Division of Dresdner Bank AG, Frankfurt. He has worked in international finance since 1975, being actively involved in the syndication of international loans until 1982, working for Westdeutsche Landesbank Girozentrale, Düsseldorf, and thereafter in the interest rate and currency swaps market. In 1986 he joined Dresdner Bank AG in Frankfurt to assist in setting up the bank's swaps trading and marketing group. His present responsibilities cover the documentation of capital market instruments, including the documentation of swaps and their derivative products. He was educated at Harrow School in England and holds a Master of Arts degree in Modern Languages from Oxford University.

CONTENTS

PART 1
GENERIC CROSS CURRENCY SWAPS

1 Characteristics of Cash Flows, Foreign Exchange Risk, and
   Forerunners of Currency Swaps   3
   Carl R. Beidleman, Lehigh University, Bethlehem, Pennsylvania

2 The Place of Currency Swaps in Financial Markets   28
   *George Handjinicolaou, Security Pacific Hoare Govett Ltd,
   London*

3 Currency Swaps: Quotation Conventions, Market Structures
   and Credit Risk   63
   *Keith C. Brown, The University of Texas at Austin
   Donald J. Smith, Boston University*

4 Development of the Cross Currency Swap Market   91
   Michael Wood, Dresdner Bank AG, Frankfurt

5 Standardized Swap Definitions and Documentation   112
   *Daniel P. Cunningham, Cravath, Swaine & Moore, New York
   Michael Wood, Dresdner Bank AG, Frankfurt*

6 Structural Variations in Currency Swaps   140
   *Raj E. S. Venkatesh, Chase Manhattan Bank, N.A., New York
   Vijaya E. Venkatesh, Credit Lyonnais, New York
   Ravi E. Dattatreya, Sumitomo Bank Capital Markets, Inc.,
   New York*

PART 2
APPLICATIONS OF SWAPS

7 Capital Market Applications of Cross Currency Swaps   155
   Peter L. Harnik, Union Bank of Switzerland, Tokyo

8 Asset-Based Cross Currency Swaps   178
   Suresh E. Krishnan, Merrill Lynch, New York

9 Forward Currency Swaps: An Instrument for Managing
   Interest Rate and Currency Exposure   195
   Janet L. Showers, Salomon Brothers Inc., New York

10   Cross Currency Swaptions   218
     Vincent J. Cirulli, Citibank, New York

11   Government Use of Cross Currency Swaps   238
     Kari Nars, Finland Ministry of Finance, Helsinki
     James R. Ramsey, Office of Financial Management
     and Economic Analysis, Commonwealth of Kentucky
     Carl R. Beidleman, Lehigh University, Bethlehem, Pennsylvania

12   Hedging Economic Risks Using Currency Swaps   259
     Vembar K. Ranganathan, Security Pacific National Bank,
     New York

13   Equity-Linked Cross Currency Swaps   276
     David F. DeRosa, Alliance Capital Management L.P., New York
     Philip G. Nehro, Alliance Capital Management L.P., New York

14   The Function of Tokyo in the Cross Currency Swap Market   293
     Alicja K. Malecka, Deutsche Bank Capital Corp., New York

PART 3
VALUATION OF SWAPS

15   Currency Swap Pricing and Valuation   331
     Cal Johnson, Salomon Brothers Inc., New York
     Janet L. Showers, Salomon Brothers Inc., New York

16   The Role of Currency Swaps in Integrating World Capital Markets   364
     Donna J. Fletcher, Lehigh University, Bethlehem, Pennsylvania
     Carl R. Beidleman, Lehigh University, Bethlehem, Pennsylvania

17   The Role of Covered Interest Arbitrage in the Pricing of Cross
     Currency Swaps   400
     Benjamin Iben, General Re Financial Products Corporation,
     New York

PART 4
CONCEPTUAL RELATIONSHIPS

18   Risk Management of a Swap Portfolio   419
     David E. Lawrence, Citicorp Investment Bank Ltd., London

19   Relationships between Cross Currency Swaps and
     Interest Rate Swaps   432
     Carl A. Batlin, Manufacturers Hanover Trust Company,
     New York

20   Using Financial Engineering to Create Long-Date Forward
      Foreign Exchange (LDFX) Transactions, Cross Currency
      Annuity Swaps, and Currency Swaps with Notional Principals   453
      *Ian Mordue, Australia and New Zealand
      Banking Group Limited, Melbourne*
21   Contrasting Short-Date and Long-Date Cross Currency
      Swap Decisions   481
      *Samuel C. Weaver, Hershey Foods Corporation,
      Hershey, Pennsylvania*

PART 5
PERIPHERAL ISSUES

22   Credit Exposure, Regulation and Capital Requirements   513
      *Alan M. Pryor, Deutsche Bank Capital Corporation,
      New York*
23   Are Swaps Futures?   533
      Barry W. Taylor, The First National Bank of Chicago
24   Accounting and Taxation for Currency Swaps   554
      Frederick D.S. Choi, New York University
25   Innovations, New Dimensions, and Outlook for
      Cross Currency Swaps   582
      *Carl R. Beidleman, Lehigh University,
      Bethlehem, Pennsylvania*

Index   605

PART 1

GENERIC CROSS CURRENCY SWAPS

CHAPTER 1

CHARACTERISTICS OF CASH FLOWS, FOREIGN EXCHANGE RISK, AND FORERUNNERS OF CURRENCY SWAPS

Carl R. Beidleman
Lehigh University
Bethlehem, Pennsylvania

INTRODUCTION

In its broadest and simplest context, finance may be thought of as a study of cash flows. Each of the myriad applications of finance deals with the movement of funds toward or away from an entity. As we examine cross currency swaps, we should place them properly in context as part of a set of financial instruments that can be employed to deal with a broader set of financial issues. This can be accomplished by (1) focusing on the characteristics of cash flows and evaluating the alternative means available to modify or manage an entity's (or firm's) cash flows and (2) briefly reviewing the financial instruments that have been used for these purposes and from which the currency swap evolved.

THE CHARACTERISTICS OF CASH FLOWS

In a purely domestic context, the fundamental characteristics of a cash flow are limited to just four: (1) the size of the flow, (2) its direction (in or out), (3) its timing, and (4) its quality, or degree of

3

uncertainty. These characteristics may seem extremely simplistic considering the multitrillion-dollar magnitude of the financial services industry; nonetheless, domestic cash flows can be defined by *size, direction, timing,* and *quality.* Whether we consider credit analysis, project finance, security valuation, capital markets, insurance, portfolio management, stripped securities, risk assessment, or even the current exotics (i.e., financial futures, options on securities, options on indices, and options on futures), these four attributes of cash flows constitute the foundation for financial analysis and decision making.

In nondomestic applications, a fifth characteristic may enter the picture—the *currency* of the cash flow. The currency of a cash flow warrants attention when it differs from the currency in which the financial results are to be measured. Although questions of foreign exchange exposure surface frequently when transactions cross national borders, some international transactions can be conducted exclusively in terms of home currency. You can, for example, denominate an international transaction in your home currency or conduct international financing or investing in the Euromarket with your home currency.

It is not possible, however, to have an international commercial transaction denominated in the home currency of both parties. Moreover, Euromarkets are not always available or appropriate for all international financial or investment transactions. Hence, many large and small transactions have been arranged in what is a foreign currency from the point of view of one of the parties to the transaction. This additional currency characteristic rounds out the fundamental components of the nature of cash flows. Since financial management is concerned with the efficient management of cash flows, examining the available ways to modify the characteristics of cash flows so as to make them more amenable to the needs or preferences of financial managers is desirable.

MODIFYING THE CHARACTERISTICS
OF CASH FLOWS: FINANCIAL ENGINEERING

Expectations for cash flows constitute the fundamental components of analytical input for all financial decisions. In developing expected cash flows for an international course of action, each analyst must specify the five characteristics outlined above. Cash flow forecasts may not be easily formulated for many financial ventures, especially those in which the quality or uncertainty of the flows is so large that it seriously reduces the accuracy of the size or timing of the flows. In extreme cases even the direction of the expected flow may be unclear. Examples of such high risk may be associated with state-of-the-art investment projects involving new products, processes, or markets.

Despite the uncertainty of many financial decisions, a very large set of financial actions exists for which the quality of the underlying cash flows is remarkably high and the uncertainty connected with the flows is quite low (in some cases approaching zero). Cash flows of this sort are, of course, associated with fixed income or debt securities, where highest quality flows (near-zero risk) are related to the obligations of the central government. Situations such as these lend themselves readily to financial engineering or the rearrangement of the cash flows in order to better suit the preferences of the user.

In situations that involve high-quality cash flows, the underlying size, direction, and timing may be readily altered in the bond, bank loan, or money markets by implementing appropriate borrowing or investment strategies. Provided that active capital markets exist, straightforward portfolio changes can be made that shift the size, direction, and timing of expected cash flows to a revised but equivalent configuration as prescribed by the financial managers.

When evaluating the quality characteristic of expected cash flows, little can be done to alter the underlying risk profile of project, equity, or even low-grade, debt-related cash flows. However, as a result of recent innovations in financial instruments, modifications can be made, if desired, in the quality of interest payments on certain classes of debt instruments. These innovations involve the use of the recently developed financial instruments known as *interest rate swaps* and *cross currency swaps*. These instruments together with financial futures, options, and options on futures form the basis for the arrangement and rearrangement of cash flows that is rapidly becoming known as financial engineering.

INTEREST RATE SWAPS

An *interest rate swap* provides a convenient means of altering certain aspects of the quality characteristic of expected cash flows. Its primary objective is to exchange floating-rate interest payments for fixed-rate payments in the same currency, or vice versa. In the past most contractual interest payments were fixed over the life of a debt instrument. However, as a result of innovations in financial instruments, many debt issues in recent years call for interest or coupon payments that float or are revised every three or six months. The rolling over or continued renewal of short-term borrowings would also fit into this category. The basis for these revisions is some well-understood market rate such as the London Interbank Offer Rate (LIBOR), some short-term Treasury rate, commercial paper rate, prime rate, or some other index of rates. Such instruments are often called *floating-rate notes (FRNs)*.

Because the interest rate floats with market rates, floating-rate interest flows are less certain (and of lower quality) than the certain nature (high quality) of the coupon flows of fixed-rate instruments. Using currently available documentation, this question of quality or risk of the coupon cash flows can be altered by swapping the floating-rate coupon with a borrower who may be more willing to face a floating interest cost in return for having his fixed-rate coupon serviced by another party. Hence, an interest rate or coupon swap may be defined as an exchange of a coupon or interest payment stream of one configuration for another coupon stream with a different configuration on essentially the same principal amount. Moreover, a type of interest rate swap called a "basis swap" provides for the exchange of coupons on one floating-rate instrument for coupons on another floating-rate instrument, where the interest rate on each side of the swap floats on a different basis. These swaps would be done to alter the quality of the coupon cash flows and to make them more compatible with the floating-rate preferences of specific debt security issuers or investors.

Investors or issuers of fixed- or floating-rate securities are now able to swap their coupon receipts or payments as their preferences dictate. Instruments currently available to accomplish these objectives, descriptive characteristics, and their applications are covered in detail in a companion volume to this book, *Interest Rate Swaps*.

CROSS CURRENCY SWAPS

The currency in which cash flows are denominated is important because it may significantly alter the ultimate cash flows to the decision makers after conversion to their home currencies. If the currency of the cash flows is other than the home currency of the decision makers, and if that foreign currency may be expected to fluctuate in terms of the home currency, the home currency value of the residual cash flows may be seriously altered. This condition may be more onerous the further the expected foreign currency flows are from the present; cash flows with time horizons of 10 or 15 years can be seriously affected. Given all the forces that influence exchange rates, projecting cash flows so far out in time is extremely difficult to do with any degree of confidence. Nevertheless, long-term financial decisions involving cash flows that are denominated in foreign currencies over many years must still be made.

As in the case of coupon exchanges, instruments that enable participants to cover long-date foreign exchange risk have been developed. In this context, "long date" is taken to mean beyond one year, and in many cases implies periods of 7 to 10 years. The menu of instruments is somewhat broader than in interest rate swaps, but the substance of the arrangement is essentially the same. In a cross currency swap, each party exchanges one currency for another on day 1 on some notional principal amount, with an agreement to service the interest payments on the counterparty's debt and to reverse the initial exchange at a specified time and at the original exchange rate. Cross currency swap agreements may consist of a stream of currency in each period, say semiannual, as may be necessary to service the interest payments or receipts on an obligation in foreign currency together with an exchange of funds at maturity, or they may provide for only an exchange of an annuity of interest payments on the notional principal. Many applications exist for currency exchanges, and various instruments have been devised to accommodate the intricacies of alternative applications.

Cross currency swaps had their origin in the development of an instrument to hedge foreign exchange risk. They have since found extensive applications as an arbitrage instrument and have also been used as a speculative vehicle. In order to understand their evolution as a vehicle for hedging exchange-rate risk, the following background material should prove helpful.

FOREIGN EXCHANGE RISK

Since the emergence of flexible exchange rates in the early 1970s, changes in the economic fundamentals have been quickly reflected in the exchange rates of most of the actively traded currencies. As a result, recent volatility in inflation and interest rates among countries has produced wide swings in exchange rates. These fluctuations have significantly increased the exchange-rate risk faced by participants in international trade and investment. This volatility in exchange rates is not expected to subside markedly in the near future. Unless properly managed, this uncertain exchange-rate environment can lead to sizable gains or losses on routine foreign exchange transactions.

The high volume of short-term commercial and financial transactions has led to the development of efficient instruments and markets in forward exchange, where firms can avoid the exchange-rate risk encountered in short-term international transactions. An example using actual exchange rates illustrates the management of the exchange rate risk typically encountered in short-term foreign transactions.

Example: Currency Exposure

An American firm wished to procure raw material parts in Canada and placed an order for parts costing 10,000 Canadian dollars (C$) on June 15, 1990. The parts were shipped on July 2 and invoiced with terms net 30 days, payment to be made in Canadian currency. On July 2 the Canadian dollar was selling for US$0.8591. The American buyer knew his cost in Canadian dollars but faced an uncertain cost in his home currency if the Canadian dollar were to appreciate or depreciate (i.e., change in value in terms of the U.S. currency). If the Canadian unit appreciated, the buyer would face a higher cost in U.S. dollars; conversely, if the Canadian dollar floated downward against the U.S. dollar, the buyer would get a windfall gain.

A number of choices were available to the American firm. It could do nothing and simply bear the risk of changes in exchange rates, acknowledging that adverse outcomes in exchange rates might eliminate its operating margins. Since it had insufficient expertise in forecasting changes in exchange rates, it might wish to hedge this risk in the forward currency markets. Another alternative would be to purchase the foreign exchange on July 2 at the spot rate of US$0.8591/C$ and invest the funds in Canada until the invoice was due or simply pay the bill in advance. These last two alternatives would entail either incurring management costs in Canada or losing interest for the credit period. They are seldom used in practice.

The choices reduced to covering in the forward currency market or bearing the risk of exchange-rate changes. Fortunately, forward markets in active currencies such as the Canadian dollar have developed over the years, and the American firm could easily find forward quotes for Canadian dollars for delivery in 30 days against U.S. dollars. On July 2, a representative quote was US$0.8554/C$ for 30 days, reflecting a discount of US$0.0037/C$ or an annualized forward discount of 5.17 percent. Because of the discount implicit in the quote, the buying firm could both hedge its foreign exchange risk position *and* save 5.17 percent (annualized) on the cost of the parts. Evidently, the participants in the forward markets expected the Canadian dollar to depreciate against its U.S. equivalent and were willing to offer Canadian dollars for future delivery at a lower price than was offered for spot or current delivery.

Using the forward currency market, the American firm could have locked in a fixed cost for its parts and fully side-stepped the risk of exchange-rate changes if it chose to do so. As it turned out, the American firm would have been wise to hedge because the Canadian dollar did not depreciate over the subsequent 30 days as expected but, in fact, rose to US$0.8675/C$ on August 1, 1990. The appreciation in this one month was 0.98 percent over its July 2 value, and, had the firm not hedged, it would have had to pay US$0.8675/C$ times C$10,000 or US$8,675 for what it could have hedged for US$8,554. This misjudgment represented a real loss of 1.41 percent for *not* hedging. This difference in cost could have had a significant impact on the firm's final operating profits.

The foreign exchange risk encountered in short-term commercial and financial transactions in major currencies can readily be hedged in the forward currency markets offered by major banks or in currency futures markets such as the International Monetary Market of the Chicago Mercantile Exchange or the London International Financial Futures Exchange. Forward currency positions have generally been available in reasonable size from commercial banks through periods of up to six months. For maturities beyond six months, however, the volume of transactions decreases markedly. Some volume can now be transacted based on open quotations beyond one year, but the bulk of these transactions are swap related.

FORERUNNERS OF SWAPS

The fundamental role of long-date currency cover is to create *both* a long-term liability in a currency in which an undesired actual or planned long-term asset position exists *and* a corresponding asset in an alternative currency in which it is desirable to denominate assets. All the applications of long-date currency cover are the result of one party's wanting to convert the denomination of some of its planned or actual liabilities to another currency. In this section we examine the nature of the various instruments that historically have been available to provide such cover.

A number of alternative methods have evolved to accommodate the need for long-date currency cover. Some of these are simple to understand but often difficult or impossible to implement. Our discussion of the various means available to establish long-date currency cover begins with conceptually simple methods and proceeds to the more complex, but more popular, methods currently receiving the attention of increasing numbers of international financial managers. In this process we also see how modern means of obtaining long-date cover have evolved from the earlier, more rudimentary methods and examine limitations of each.

Foreign Currency Debt

Recall that the essential element of long-date cover is the creation of a term liability denominated in an undesired, say foreign, currency, which is offset by a term asset in a desired home currency. Given this objective, the most straightforward means of establishing long-date currency cover has been to sell foreign debt for the desired term, convert the proceeds to the home currency, and invest them in home currency debt instruments that mature on the same date as the foreign debt. A flowchart of the underlying cash flows of foreign currency debt instrument is shown in Figure 1.

Despite its conceptual simplicity, this "do-it-yourself" method has a number of significant disadvantages in that many firms are unwilling or unable to undertake it and many foreign capital markets are not sufficiently developed to accommodate it. Firms tend to be either reluctant or unable to inflate their balance sheets by borrowing in one currency and investing in another. They are also aware that this practice generally has an adverse effect on financial ratios and that it

FIGURE 1

Cash Flows Associated with a Foreign Currency Debt Placement

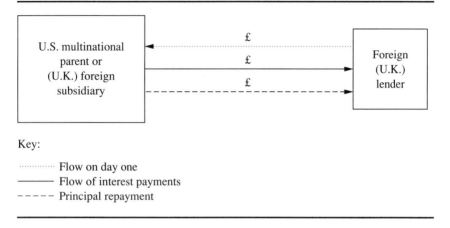

Key:

·········· Flow on day one
———— Flow of interest payments
– – – – – Principal repayment

may, in extreme cases, affect borrowing costs and lenders' willingness to extend additional credit.

The cost of obtaining long-date cover using foreign currency debt, when available, is the interest differential between the foreign loan rate and the domestic investment rate plus the transaction costs associated with borrowing, converting, and investing. Note, however, that the interest differential between the currencies is a cost common to all forms of long-date cover regardless of the nature of the instrument or its legal arrangement. Moreover, it is the interest differential that establishes the basis for negotiation of the actual pricing terms of more complex arrangements.

Currency-Collateralized Loans

Traditionally, enterprising international banks evaluate their global relationship with a customer and accommodate the customer's major needs for foreign exchange financing. Under these arrangements, a firm may be able to finance a foreign subsidiary by placing its home currency on deposit with its bank and having a foreign branch of that bank extend a credit to a subsidiary in another country and currency. In this case the bank assumes an exchange risk on the transaction as an inherent part of doing business in each country. The bank will undoubtedly offset its foreign exchange exposure against its own liability position in that currency (its so-called "book") or against other foreign exchange liabilities, or it may seek new foreign currency liabilities to restore a balanced currency position. Such currency-collateralized loans with bank participation are particularly attractive in countries where the capital markets are not well developed or where alternative sources of local finance may not be available. A flowchart of the underlying cash flows of a currency-collateralized loan is shown in Figure 2.

This two-step, cash-collateralized foreign exchange loan was the precursor of the *parallel loan* or *back-to-back (BTB) loan*. These instruments were developed to formalize the cash-collateralized, foreign exchange bank loan and extend its use to combinations of nonbank parties, each seeking long-date cover. In a sense the cash-collateralized foreign exchange loan is a BTB loan with a bank, entered into for the purpose of transferring liquidity from one currency to another. In the process the borrower also establishes a term liability in the (undesired) foreign currency. The bank either assumes this new foreign exchange asset exposure against its existing

FIGURE 2
Cash Flows Associated with a Currency-Collateralized Loan

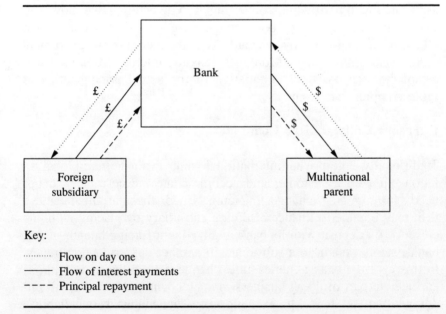

Key:

.... Flow on day one
———— Flow of interest payments
- - - - Principal repayment

liabilities or quickly seeks to lay it off against new liabilities (deposits) that its foreign branch is able to attract. In this way the bank is able to fill the global needs of its customer and price the loan and deposit to make a profit after full provision for its currency exposure. These concepts form the basic logic for parallel or BTB loans, which can be used with or without bank participation.

Parallel Loans and Back-to-Back Loans

Parallel and BTB loans are essentially similar economic and legal devices to which certain participants in long-date cover have attached special distinctions. Because of their great similarity, they are treated jointly here, and certain distinctions that have been made between them are subsequently highlighted.

Like a currency-collateralized loan, a parallel or BTB loan establishes a term liability in an undesired currency by borrowing the currency on day 1 from a (foreign) counterparty and promising to pay interest and principal in the (undesired) currency in which natural cash flows are generated by a foreign affiliate. However, to collateralize this arrangement, the domestic party concurrently lends available surplus liquidity in its desired (home) currency directly to its (foreign) counterparty or counterparty affiliate. The primary role of parallel or BTB loans is to transfer surplus liquidity from one currency to another. Implementation relies on a mirror-image match by two parties with excess liquidity in one currency and capital requirements in another currency for like amounts and periods. Unless a third party is prepared to assume the credit risk of each primary party, their credit standings must be similar and usually quite high. Because of their role in transferring liquidity from currency to currency, parallel or BTB loans are not useful as a primary financing strategy. They merely provide for transfer of liquidity from currency to currency while hedging the long-date exchange risk associated with an (undesired) foreign currency.

The instruments for parallel or BTB loans provide for two separate loan agreements, one for each currency, with an interest rate applicable to each. In two-party loans, the mutual agreements are between the two primary parties, who may on-lend the funds to their respective foreign subsidiaries. Three- or four-party loans provide for the direct lending of the funds to foreign subsidiaries of one or both of the parents. Flowcharts of the underlying cash flows in two-, three-,

FIGURE 3
Cash Flows Associated with a Two-Party Parallel Loan

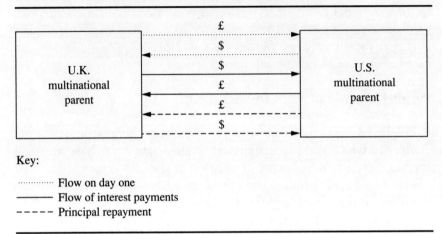

Key:

.... Flow on day one
———— Flow of interest payments
– – – – Principal repayment

and four-party parallel loans are shown in Figures 3, 4, and 5, respectively.

Another variation provides for cross-lending, say, dollars by a U.S. parent to the U.S. subsidiary of a U.K. parent matched by the cross-lending of sterling by the U.K. parent to a British subsidiary of the U.S. parent. A flowchart of the underlying cash flows in a four-

FIGURE 4
Cash Flows Associated with a Three-Party Parallel Loan

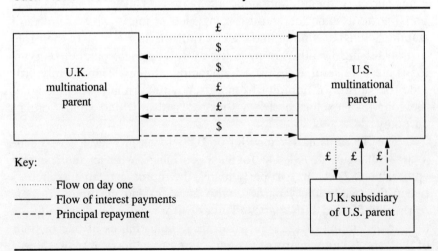

Key:

.... Flow on day one
———— Flow of interest payments
– – – – Principal repayment

FIGURE 5
Cash Flows Associated with a Four-Party Parallel Loan

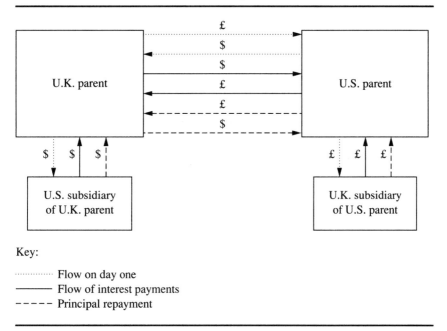

Key:

············· Flow on day one
————— Flow of interest payments
– – – – Principal repayment

party cross-lending parallel loan is shown in Figure 6. Separate loan agreements are required with interest rates appropriate for the term and risk of each loan in its respective currency.

Security Provisions
Unlike the effective security arrangements that exist in cash-collateralized loans, the question of inadequate security in parallel or BTB loans may be significant. For one thing, cash-collateralized loans involve a bank as one party to the agreement, and banks are prepared to assess and assume reasonable credit risk for a fee. Parallel and BTB loans, on the other hand, may be done without a bank to intermediate the respective credit risks of the parties. In this case the parties are frequently ill-equipped to assess, much less assume, each other's credit risk.

At least four approaches have been employed to resolve this problem of credit risk in parallel or BTB loans:

1. The *right of offset* is, of course, the most obvious. It provides that if one party defaults on interest or principal, the coun-

FIGURE 6
Cash Flows Associated with a Four-Party Cross-Lending Parallel Loan

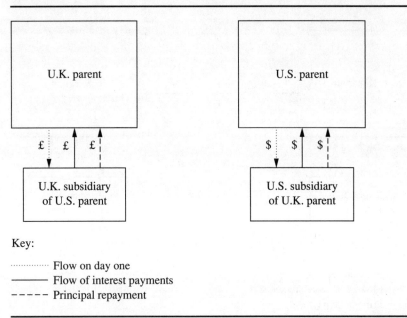

Key:

··············· Flow on day one
————— Flow of interest payments
– – – – – Principal repayment

terparty is relieved of its obligations under the counterloan. Although an offset agreement appears to resolve most of the credit exposure, it is not absolute and may not even be operational in some cases. For example, as exchange rates change with time, the security value of the depreciating currency loan will be insufficient to offset the value of the appreciating currency loan. The result is an element of credit risk exposure even where a right of offset exists.

The operational effectiveness of the right of offset is open to question. In three- and four-party loans, the loans may have been made to subsidiaries of the counterparty rather than to the counterparty directly. Although such agreements may frequently call for the guarantee of the foreign parent, some question still arises if the subsidiary party in an unguaranteed loan goes into bankruptcy. In the case of two-party loans with additional on-lending to subsidiaries or affiliates, the question of a possible failure of a parent, with the subsidiary surviving, further clouds the legal right of offset.

2. *Topping up* of the loan denominated in the depreciating currency to its original value in terms of the appreciating currency whenever a currency devalues by, say, 5 or 10 percent has also resolved this vexing problem in many instances. However, topping up can cause additional problems if the receiving party has no use for the added foreign currency or if it must report the topping-up payment as taxable income.

3. Attempts to *match the credit risk* of the parties (e.g., avoiding pairing an AAA-rated credit with a BBB-rated credit) is another approach to the problem of inadequate security. When this is done by AAA-rated credits, each party's concern over credit risk is diminished.

4. A safer approach to the problem of credit risk, and one that has been used by many participants, is to resort to *specialists in credit risk* to assume this risk for the primary parties. This involves bringing in a bank, whose normal business is to evaluate and assume credit risk, to intermediate the loans for one or both parties. A flowchart that reflects the cash flows when a bank assumes the credit risk in a parallel loan is shown in Figure 7.

Bank compensation for assuming this risk ranges from 0.1 to 0.5 percent per annum, depending on the credit status of the parties and whether the bank, in fact, takes a principal

FIGURE 7
Cash Flows Associated with a Parallel Loan When a Bank Intermediates the Credit Risk for Both Parties

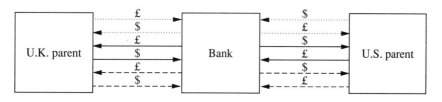

Key:

··········· Flow on day one
——— Flow of interest payments
– – – – – Principal repayment

position between them. This fee is usually lower than a bank's typical letter-of-credit fee because the availability of offset reduces the aggregate exposure to only that which may result from the devaluation of one of the currencies. Devaluations, while significant in the past, would not be expected to exceed, say, 30 percent of the value of the loan in the currencies of most countries. Moreover, any devaluation loss would, of course, apply to only one side of the combined loan package.

Parallel and Back-to-Back Loans Contrasted

The terms *parallel loan* and *back-to-back loan* are names for essentially the same instrument. Although certain distinctions have been made by participants in these transactions and by active intermediaries, general agreement as to the suggested variations does not exist. For example, BTB loans are regarded by some as specifically including the right of offset, whereas parallel loans are not. There is also a tendency to call a paired four-party cross-loan arrangement between parents and unrelated subsidiaries a parallel loan, and a two-party agreement, whether or not the funds are on-lent to subsidiaries, a BTB loan. It appears, however, that these distinctions have been made more for arbitrary classification purposes than for conceptual reasons.

Because of the more general acceptance of alternative instruments that have recently become available, the four-party parallel loan is now more or less obsolete except where exchange controls make it imperative. As noted, the right of offset in a loan is unclear in the event of default. Moreover, four-party loans lack flexibility and are more difficult to draft than alternative means of obtaining long-date cover. A two-party parallel or BTB loan is legally safer and more flexible because, if the subsidiary fails, its parent normally is obliged to make the loan good. However, as a result of additional innovations that occurred in 1976, the application of an old-line long-date currency swap to commercial transactions provided a more preferable arrangement for most applications of long-date currency cover at the time.

Old-Line Currency Swap

Like parallel and BTB loans, the old-line currency swap was a currency exchange agreement that provided for the transfer of currencies between counterparties on day 1 and the reversal of the flows at the maturity of the swap, normally at the same rate of exchange. In a sense, it was a spot or current market currency transaction coupled with an agreement to reverse the transaction at maturity. Unlike a loan agreement, there was no interest payment by either side. Instead, the provider of the stronger currency normally paid a fee to the provider of the weaker currency. This fee compensated for the expected changes in exchange rates over the life of the swap. The size of the fee was negotiable by the parties; however, such negotiations invariably began with the interest differential between interbank deposits in the two currencies of approximately the same term as that of the swap. A flowchart of the underlying cash flows in an old-line currency swap is shown in Figure 8.

The introduction of the old-line commercial swap in 1976 was a milestone in the development of long-date currency cover. It fulfilled the cover objectives of earlier instruments but removed a number of significant legal and accounting impediments. The concept itself was not new; currency swaps had existed among central banks for decades. Although not an economic or financial invention, the old-line commercial currency swap was an important legal innovation since it provided better security in the event of default than was available

FIGURE 8
Cash Flows Associated with an Old-Line Currency Swap

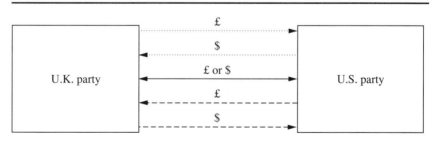

Key:

·············· Flow on day one

————— Annual fee in either direction,
                depending on the interest differential

— — — — Flow at maturity

through the questionable right of offset employed with parallel or BTB loans.

The genius of the old-line currency swap rested in its legal basis. Whereas the legal basis for parallel or BTB loans relied on security law and the broad question of offset was unclear, the legal basis for the old-line currency swap was rooted in contract law, where the rights of the parties were clearly understood. That is, under contract law, if one party did not perform, the contract was breached, and it became unnecessary for the other party to perform its obligation. This removed the legal question about the right of offset and vastly improved the flexibility of the available long-date currency cover. Moreover, simplified standardized documentation has been developed for the old-line currency swap, which employed a single agreement rather than two agreements or documents as in parallel loans.

Currency swaps also have accounting and tax advantages over loans. Since they are not loans, swaps are not normally required to be included on a firm's balance sheet. Rather, they are disclosed only in the notes to the statements. Although most firms net their parallel or BTB loans on their balance sheets, this practice is dubious and subject to criticism by the strictest of public accountants. And, although the tax-deductible status of interest seems clear in the case of loans, the status of topping-up payments remains in doubt. In the case of old-line currency swaps, firms have been successful in deducting the fees associated with the swaps.

Forward Currency Contracts

Forward (outright) currency contracts are similar to old-line currency swaps, but they provide for no funds transfer on day 1. That is, a forward contract provides only for a forward or future currency exchange at a specified future date and at a specified exchange rate. A flowchart of the underlying cash flows in a forward exchange agreement is shown in Figure 9.

It is, of course, quite possible to simulate a forward contract by using an old-line currency swap and moving funds in the current or spot market to reverse the spot flow if this is desired. Normally there is no annual payment between the parties in the case of a forward contract. Instead, a forward exchange rate, which usually differs from the spot rate on day 1, is negotiated. The starting basis for the

FIGURE 9

Cash Flows Associated with a Forward Exchange Agreement

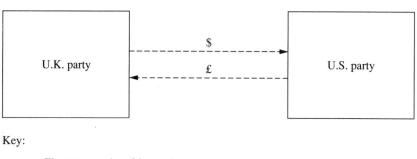

Key:

– – – – – Flow at maturity of forward
          exchange agreement

long-date forward rate negotiation begins with the differential in similar term interest rates on interbank deposits in the two currencies. For example, the theoretical five-year forward rate (F_5) for a forward contract for currencies A and B would be based on the spot rate on day one (S_0), where S_0 is defined in terms of units of currency A per unit of currency B, and the respective five-year interest rates on interbank deposits denominated in each currency, i_{5a} and i_{5b}:

$$F_5 = S_0 \left(\frac{1 + i_{5a}}{1 + i_{5b}} \right)^5 \qquad (1)$$

More generally, for year n,

$$F_n = S_0 \left(\frac{1 + i_{na}}{1 + i_{nb}} \right)^n \qquad (2)$$

The calculation shown in Equations (1) and (2) provides for a downward adjustment or discount in the forward rate from the current spot rate in those currencies with a higher domestic interest rate, and vice versa. This theoretical basis for pricing long-date forward contracts is similar to that used in short-term forward contracts in that it is based on interest differentials between the two currencies. Like its short-term analogue, it assumes that the market is efficient for term deposits and that forward premiums or discounts on a currency are based on interest differentials. These assumptions, while quite appropriate for short-term markets in the popular currencies, may not hold up empirically in long-date maturities or in many of the exotic currencies. Hence, there is latitude for negotiation of long-date forward dates.

Although found most commonly in long-date forward contracts, the use of a forward discount or premium instead of an annual fee has also been employed in long-date currency swap agreements. The underlying logic and negotiating strengths that apply to long-date forward contracts are identical to those applied in long-date currency swaps.

The forward contract was, by far, the most popular of all the instruments available for long-date currency cover. Prior to the advent of the modern cross currency swap, approximately 75 percent of all long-date currency cover had been implemented by forward currency contracts. This result was due to the high degree of flexibility of these swaplike agreements plus the absence of a need for funds-flow requirements prior to maturity.

Even though no funds were transferred until maturity, a risk on nonperformance remained. This risk could be managed by dealing only with strong credits, or it could be passed by bringing in a bank to intermediate the credit risk. Like currency swaps, forward currency agreements need not be reflected on a firm's financial statements except for disclosure in the notes.

The simplicity of forward contracts also improved their understanding by higher levels of management and reduced the difficulty in obtaining approval from boards of directors and other supervising bodies. And the absence of funds flow prior to maturity made it somewhat easier to find matching counterparties. Applications that require debt service in a foreign currency could be accommodated by a stream of forward contracts, further increasing their attractiveness at the time.

Issuing contracts to highly creditworthy firms and using bank intermediation for credit risk reduced to negligible levels the potential loss due to nonperformance. Forward contracts also conformed perfectly in arbitrage applications where the need for long-date cover was essential in order to reduce a firm's world cost of capital or increase an investor's all-in rate of return after the cost of hedging cash flows in an undesired currency. The suitability of forward contracts also applied with equal force to those instances where a party was hedging an existing net asset exposure or other known long-date transaction or translation exposure.

Modern Cross Currency Swaps

During the early and mid-1980s the marketplace for old-line currency swaps evolved from a type of shadow market, where quotations represented only indications of price and few deals were done without the knowledge of firm counterparties to take the other side of the swap, to a modern market in which quotations are firm and market makers are prepared to warehouse swaps and carry inventory positions as needed. This process was aided by the increased volumes of currency swap transactions and by the standardized documentation that was developed by the International Swap Dealers Association (ISDA). The transition to modern cross currency swaps was also stimulated by the concurrent progress that was being made by the interest rate swaps market, which began in 1982 and developed into a mature market much more rapidly than did the market for cross currency swaps.

The transition that occurred required the adoption of marketwide standards and conventions. This process followed many of the conventions recently evolved in the interest rate swaps market. One major change entailed the revised convention in cross currency swaps that the standard, or plain vanilla, swap would include interest flows as well as initial and terminal flows of the notional principal of the swap. This meant that a modern cross currency swap's cash flows could perfectly match the cash flows of a traditional bond. The standardization process went further in that the basic swap would entail non–U.S. dollar (N$) fixed-rate periodic cash flows (interest) to be paid/received against U.S. dollar (US$) floating-rate periodic cash flows that were pegged to the London Interbank Offer Rate (LIBOR); that is, fixed N$ flows were swapped against floating US$ flows along with an initial and terminal interchange of notional principal.

The mechanics, conventions, flow diagrams, and market structures of standard cross currency swaps are covered in detail in Chapter 3 and will not be duplicated here. Similarly, the ISDA standardized swap documentation and definitions are presented in Chapter 5. It is important at this stage to understand that significant changes have taken place in the mechanics and conventions in swapland such that the modern cross currency swap, now tailored to match a fixed- or floating-rate bond, has been designed to better accomplish the hedging, arbitrage, and even speculative applications that come before it than was the old-line swap. Moreover, to the extent that swappers wish to alter the features of a standardized swap, many variations are possible as described in Chapter 6 and successive chapters.

BASIC APPLICATIONS
OF CROSS CURRENCY SWAPS

Cross currency swaps, like other instruments employed by financial engineers to alter the characteristics of cash flows, have three major application sets. Cross currency swaps can be used to improve the match between the parties to a debt contract based on their underlying currency preferences in order to hedge their balance sheet exposure. Other hedging applications include the squaring up of the currency denomination of its assets and liabilities in order to better insulate a firm from the ravages of exchange-rate risk.

Cross currency swaps can also be used to arbitrage opportunities that arise from differential credit-risk premiums in the fixed- and floating-rate markets. Other arbitrage applications arise in the use of swaptions to arbitrage the differential pricing of option premiums in the bond and swap-option markets. These applications will be covered in detail in Chapters 7 through 14.

In addition to risk-management, or hedging, applications and arbitrage applications, cross currency swaps can be used in trading, or speculative, applications. Little has been written about this last set of applications because they entail a significant risk posture in that the view on exchange rates that drives the swap strategy may turn out to be wrong. Basically, cross currency swaps enable a speculator who believes that exchange rates will fall to enter into a swap agreement to receive dollars and pay foreign exchange (FX) rates on a given notional principal. If the speculator's view was that exchange rates would rise, he would want to receive FX and pay dollars throughout the swap period. Although the volume of speculative swaps is not known and little has been written on them, it would be naive to believe that it was negligible. Given the risks involved, it would appear that the bulk of such applications lie in the shorter range of the swap maturity spectrum.

ORGANIZATION OF THE BOOK

In the foregoing introductory material, I have attempted to identify the characteristics of financial flows and to illustrate how certain of them may be altered to suit the needs or preferences of financial managers. I have also briefly described how cross currency swaps may be used to accomplish these objectives. These tasks are discussed in great detail as the book progresses. In the balance of this chapter, I provide a preview of the material that lies ahead and its order of presentation.

The book is divided into five parts. In the balance of this part, accomplished academics and practitioners who are presently involved in cross currency swap activity present the generic aspects of interest rate swaps. The next chapter was prepared by the director of swaps activity of the London office of Security Pacific, Hoare Govett, Ltd. In it he describes the place of swaps among financial market instruments by focusing on the environmental and comparative advantage factors that have led to the emergence of swaps. Then in the next chapter, two academics with prior experience in the New York financial market cover the basics of plain vanilla swaps. This is followed by a chapter on the development and standardization of the swap market written by a well-prepared German banker, who then collaborates in the next chapter with an ISDA attorney to present standardized definitions and documentation on cross currency swaps that have been accepted by the industry. In the following chapter, three swap practitioners who are on the swap desks of a trio of New York multinational banks offer a thorough development of the variations to basic swaps, with applications provided throughout.

Part 2 covers applications of swaps. Each chapter describes a set of applications in detail and is well provided with case studies and examples that illustrate each specific application. The first two chapters in Part 2 deal with capital market– or liability-oriented applications and asset-based applications. They were written by research and strategy professionals at prominent investment banks. The next five chapters cover more specific applications of cross currency swaps, including options on swaps, equity-linked swaps, and the extension of swaps to non–U.S. dollar applications. They were written by extremely capable personnel, most of whom are actively involved on the swap desks of the New York or Tokyo offices of large international merchant banks or are swap users. The final chapter in Part 2 deals with the role of the rapidly expanding Tokyo market in the evolution of currency swaps. It is written by a professional from a German commercial bank who has had extensive experience in Tokyo as well as other financial centers.

In Part 3 we examine the critical material that deals with the valuation of interest rate swaps. The first chapter is an essential piece on the pricing of cross currency swaps. It is followed by a chapter that examines the contribution of cross currency swaps to the integration of the capital markets around the world. The next chapter highlights a critical dimension to the swap (and bond) valuation process: that of using zero-coupon pricing rather than traditional bond pricing to value the fixed-rate side of a cross currency swap. It was written by a financial strategy associate of a large U.S. insurance company.

Part 4 covers conceptual relationships among swaps and other interest rate derivative products. We first examine the ways in which a swap market maker can manage the risk of its swap portfolio, relying on much of the material on zero-coupon pricing and duration analysis presented in Part 3. This work was done by a very successful U.S. commercial bank that developed these concepts for the management of its own warehouse of swaps. This work is followed by a chapter, written by a strategist at another prominent U.S. commercial bank, that considers the linkages between the two most common types of swaps (interest rate and cross currency) and identifies their common foundations and conceptual relationships. The next chapter considers conceptual variations to currency swaps—including long-date forward contracts, annuity-only swaps, and cross currency swaps without notional principals, in which the principal is not at risk. It is written by an Australian strategist of some renown. The last chapter in this part deals with the relationships and assumptions that are necessary for a strip of short-date forward contracts to equate to the long-date cover that is obtainable from a cross currency swap. It was drafted by a practitioner who understands the role of swaps in his own set of Treasury operations.

Certain peripheral issues are covered in Part 5, which begins with a chapter covering the very topical question of cross currency swap credit exposure and capital requirements. It is followed by a chapter, written by a noted corporate attorney, that carefully contrasts swaps with futures from a conceptual and regulatory perspective. Accounting and taxation of swaps encompass a wide area that has numerous ramifications that differ in many countries of the world. These concepts are covered in the next chapter, by an astute professor who has long been active in accounting for financial transactions. Here he has attempted to summarize the accounting and tax implications inherent in undertaking a cross currency swap strategy. Finally, in the last chapter I have tried to identify the ways in which the swap market has evolved and innovated during its brief lifespan. I attempt to catalog some of the new and pending dimensions of the market and provide some outlook for what may lie ahead. As it has turned out, the evolution of the market has far exceeded anything that any of us could have expected in its short existence, so that any attempt to forecast its future prospects may be little more than frivolous or naive.

CHAPTER 2

THE PLACE OF CURRENCY SWAPS IN FINANCIAL MARKETS

George Handjinicolaou
Security Pacific Hoare Govett Ltd
London

INTRODUCTION

Among the most successful of the innovations in financial techniques that have taken place over the course of the 1980s have been currency and interest rate swaps. First made famous by the World Bank–IBM currency swaps in 1981, markets for swaps have developed beyond the expectations of the users and banks who put together the first swap transactions. Swaps are essentially agreements between two counterparties to exchange cash flows (usually exchanges of interest obligations but also of principal, in the case of currency swaps), undertaken for the mutual benefit of the parties concerned. Depending upon the type of cash flows exchanged, swaps are classified into *interest rate, currency,* and *cross currency interest rate* swaps. In an interest rate swap the parties exchange fixed-rate for floating-rate cash flows in the same currency. In a currency swap the parties exchange cash flows expressed in different currencies, whereas in a cross currency interest rate swap the parties transform both the currency and the type of cash flows exchanged.

From the few structured proprietary transactions that were first put together in the late 1970s, an enormous market has developed during the 1980s. According to surveys conducted by ISDA (the International Swap Dealers Association), an estimated $2.5 trillion in interest rate and currency swaps were outstanding at the end of 1989.

The development of swaps as a technique of finance has been particularly rapid over the past few years, even though the technique has been available for some time. Why this phenomenal growth?

The reasons for this development are complex, but by and large they rest on the volatility of interest rates and exchange rates and on the dramatic changes that have taken place in the world financial markets over the past 10 to 15 years. The increased volatility, combined with deregulation in a number of capital markets has led to an explosion of financial innovation. These developments have brought the various capital markets around the world much closer, opening up new investment and funding opportunities. Swaps have been one of the most successful of the innovations arising from this process. Most importantly, the growth of the swap market has been fed, and at the same time reinforced, by the above developments. Today, many participants around the globe, including financial institutions and corporate, supranational, and sovereign entities, utilize swaps for asset/liability management purposes. By combining the issuance of debt in accessible markets with an interest rate and/or currency swap, borrowers can create synthetic liabilities that cost less than traditional financing, while investors can create synthetic assets that yield more than conventional investments of the same risk class. For example, a borrower of Swiss francs who wants U.S. dollars can swap liability with a borrower of U.S. dollars who wants Swiss francs, and in the process both parties can reduce their borrowing costs. Fixed-rate borrowers can exchange their funds for floating-rate liabilities and vice versa.

An important feature of the cash flow exchanges involved in swaps is that they offer a way to hedge risk, whether foreign exchange risk, interest rate risk, or both. In the interest rate area, swaps offer the means of matching the maturity and price characteristics of liabilities (e.g., floating and short-term) with the characteristics of assets to reduce interest rate risk. Savings and loans, for example, can "swap" their variable-rate deposit liabilities into fixed-rate, long-term capital market liabilities to match their long-term assets, such as mortgages, through a swap of interest streams with a counterparty whose funding requirements demand variable rate borrowings. Each party can obtain the type of financing it needs through the other party. Such opportunities have led to an explosion in the use of interest rate swaps. It is estimated that at the end of 1989 the outstanding notional amount of interest rate swaps contracts exceeded $1.5 trillion. This compares with an estimated volume of $1.0 trillion in 1988, $170 billion in 1985, and zero in 1981. Most importantly, although the swap market first emerged in, and was primarily limited to, the U.S. dollar markets and a couple of other currencies (pound sterling, Swiss franc), over the last two to three years new interest rate swap markets have emerged in all the other major international reserve currencies (i.e., Japanese yen, Deutschemarks) as well as in the currencies of emerging capital markets such as French francs; European Currency Units (ECUs); Australian, New Zealand, and Hong Kong dollars; Belgian francs; Danish and Swedish kroner; Spanish pesetas; and Italian lire.

In the currency area, swaps are important in reducing the risks associated with trade finance and asset/liability management in international business more effectively than more traditional hedging alternatives. For the importer or exporter with foreign currency payables or receivables, swaps offer advantages in increased certainty and lower cost over such alternatives as offshore funding, leads or lags in payments, or short-term hedges in the forward foreign exchange markets. Swaps, moreover, accomplish these purposes without the destabilizing effects on the foreign exchange market or the added capital market access requirements associated with the comparatively awkward techniques previously available. It is estimated that an additional $0.9 trillion in currency swaps was outstanding the end of 1989, as compared with the few transactions (perhaps a few hundred million dollars) that first took place in the 1979–1980 period. In addition, the growth of this market segment has been further boosted by the emergence of interest rate swap markets in many capital markets around the world.

Table 1 presents information about the relative size of the various swap markets around the world.

The demand for hedging was a necessary condition for the emergence and further growth of swaps. But by itself it would not have been sufficient to support the rapid growth that has taken place in this market. The sufficient conditions came in the form of two major factors: first, an environment that was conducive to the development of the swap market, an environment charaterized by financial deregulation, innovation, and increasing globalization; second, the presence of market participants who were willing to stand on the other side of such hedging transactions. Such participants either came in as parties with complementary hedging or were attracted by the arbitrage opportunities that the hedgers, in search of liquidity, were creating.

TABLE 1
Estimated Volume of Outstanding Swaps (End of 1989—US$ billions)

	Interest Rate	Currency	Total	Percent
U.S. dollars	993,746	354,166	1,347,912	56.82%
Japanese yen	128,022	201,145	329,167	13.88
Deutschemarks	84,620	53,839	138,459	5.84
Pounds sterling	100,417	33,466	133,883	5.64
Australian dollars	67,599	61,768	129,367	5.45
Swiss francs	28,605	64,823	93,428	3.94
Canadian dollars	29,169	32,580	61,749	2.60
ECUs	18,998	39,948	58,946	2.48
French francs	42,016	8,435	50,451	2.13
Dutch guilders	5,979	10,132	16,111	0.68
New Zealand dollars	444	5,818	6,262	0.26
Belgian francs	835	2,997	3,832	0.16
Hong Kong dollars	2,149	583	2,732	0.12
Total	1,502,600	869,699	2,372,299	100.00%

Source: International Swap Dealers Association (ISDA).

Arbitrage has been the other prime motivation for using swaps. And, although the initial economic need satisfied through swaps was hedging, it is arbitrage that has glorified the swap markets.

The themes of this chapter are volatility, hedging, innovation, arbitrage, and comparative advantage and how they were combined to lead to the creation and growth of such an enormous market as the swap market. The objectives of this chapter are twofold: first, to provide a description and an analysis of the factors that led to the emergence, growth, and development of the swap market; second to provide a framework within which the concepts of hedging and arbitrage of swaps can be visualized and analyzed within the context of the overall financial markets. In this respect it serves as a "big picture" chapter for swaps by focusing on the economics that drive a swap. Finally, it highlights the important role played by the currency swap markets in global finance.

The remainder of the chapter is organized into five sections. The first section focuses on the factors that have led to the emergence of swaps. It starts by exploring the dual origin of the currency swap market, namely the forward foreign exchange market and the capital markets. Then it moves on to argue that the increased volatility in interest rates and foreign exchange rates has been the major reason for the emergence of swaps. The collapse of the Bretton Woods agreement and the shift in the implementation of the monetary policy in the United States in controlling money supply were the two events that led to the increased volatility. The hedging needs and the demands of asset/liability management are touched upon.

The second section turns to the factors that have contributed significantly to the growth and development of the swap market by focusing on the impact of factors such as deregulation, innovation, and increased globalization on the financial markets. These concepts serve as the platform for introducing the sufficient conditions for the development of the swap markets.

The focus of the third section is on the use of swaps as a tool for taking advantage of the arbitrage opportunities that became available as a result of all the changes in the world financial markets over the past two decades. The concept of the *comparative advantage,* borrowed from the theory of international trade, is the analytical tool used to facilitate the presentation. A few examples illustrate the deployment of swaps as a tool for capturing gains emanating from firms acting upon their financial comparative advantage. The nature of arbitrage and its utilization for lowering the cost of borrowing or enhancing asset returns is also illustrated through these examples. The implications of this arbitrage activity are also explored.

The fourth section highlights the critical role played by the currency swap markets in integrating capital markets around the world.

The last section summarizes the chapter and draws its conclusions.

FACTORS THAT HAVE CONTRIBUTED TO THE EMERGENCE OF SWAPS

Although the exact date of the appearance of the first swap is still debated, it is generally acknowledged that swaps first appeared in the late 1970s. With the benefit of hindsight one can see that the emergence of swaps in that period was not accidental. The 1970s (and in this respect the 1980s) will be remembered as a period during which the financial landscape was reshaped. The enormous changes in the world financial markets have been enormous and have been caused by a number of factors, from fundamental changes in the underlying economic environment to changes due to advances in regulation, technology, and communications. The objective of this section is to focus on the origins of the currency swap markets by pointing out the dual character of these markets, comprising a forward foreign exchange element and a capital market element. It continues by describing the context within which these instruments emerged, namely, an unprecedented increase in the volatility of interest rate and exchange rate levels. An overview is given of the economic and financial environment that prevailed in the early 1970s and the developments that led to the increases in volatility that we have experienced in recent years.

The Origin of the Currency Swap Market

Currency swaps arose from the desire of many market participants, primarily multinational corporations operating in many different countries, to protect cash flows associated with assets and liabilities from adverse foreign exchange developments and thus protect their earnings. Until the early 1970s, the short-dated forward foreign exchange market had been the primary vehicle available to corporations for hedging their payments and receipts denominated in currencies other than their own. Although this market enabled participants to hedge only short-term cash flows (up to one year), it was sufficient because most of the cash flows were indeed of short-term nature (trade receivables and payables), and the risk exposure caused by hedging longer maturity cash flows (longer than one year) by rolling over short-term forward foreign exchange positions was tolerable given the reasonable level of foreign exchange stability offered by the Bretton Woods system.

However, several developments took place in the late 1970s. First, fueled by the unprecedented world economic expansion following World War II, international trade, liquidity, and capital mobility were expanding rapidly, leading to transactions with payments and receipts stretching over longer periods of time. Second, as explained in detail later, volatility in foreign exchange rates increased following the collapse of the Bretton Woods agreement. These developments created a need for new hedging instruments covering maturities longer than the 6 to 12 months that traditionally had been offered in the interbank forward exchange market. Financial institutions responding to such needs started offering gradually longer and longer maturities. Responding to market demand, sophisticated foreign exchange dealers began to extend their short-term hedging services in the forward foreign exchange market by providing hedging for periods longer than one year. However, such service was offered only sporadically to selected clients and was generally kept from the public arena because it was correctly viewed as proprietary. Furthermore, such transactions gave rise to significant risks for the banks offering them because offsets were not easily obtainable and hedging instruments were not available.

By the late 1970s only a few banks were involved in forward foreign exchange contracts for maturities longer than one year. As such, they were considered the exception to the rule and did not represent a major market development. However, the employment of such techniques started gaining momentum in the late 1970s as volatility picked up considerably both in interest and exchange rates. It was the desire on the part of many institutions to hedge existing assets and liabilities from such exchange fluctuations that led to the extension of the maturities beyond one year to as long as five and seven years in the forward market.

Another factor that helped in the acceleration of the above developments was the emergence and rapid growth of the Eurodeposit markets. These markets were traditionally the outlets utilized by the banks for offsetting risk undertaken in the forward foreign exchange market, because a forward foreign exchange transaction is equivalent to a simultaneous borrowing and investment in the respective currencies. The growth of this market, fueled by the recycling of the so-called "petrodollars," further enhanced the banks' ability to hedge such forward positions and made them more eager to offer such products.

The major push for the growth of the currency swap, however, came when market participants came up with the wide array of imaginative applications of the hedging characteristics of these instruments. Astute players realized the potential of these instruments as tools for obtaining the desired type of liability (or asset). It was in this phase of market development that currency swaps in their present form took off. In the late 1970s a number of U.S. dollar–based corporations with offshore operations, anticipating a strengthening of the dollar after almost a decade of continuous depreciation, started converting some of their nondollar assets back into U.S. dollars, thus "locking in" exchange gains because of the strong performance of these currencies vis-à-vis the U.S. dollar. That is, they were selling the nondollar currencies (and buying U.S. dollars) forward. By doing so they offered hedging alternatives to other entities that, coming from a different perspective, had the desire to create U.S. dollar liabilities using nondollar funding.

It was at this point that the capital market element entered the currency swap market. In a typical transaction, an entity would raise nondollar funding (e.g., through a Swiss franc–denominated bond issue, or a DM bond issue in the Euromarkets) and through a series of long-dated forward transactions or simply a currency swap would convert the funding into U.S. dollars at substantial savings. Such transactions were the natural counterparties to the U.S. dollar–based corporations that were hedging their nondollar assets or asset cash flows. It was at this stage that the currency swap structure as we observe it today (which involves exchanges of interest rate and principal cash flows associated with respective borrowing obligations) gained momentum at the expense of the more traditional methods employed in the forward foreign exchange market. The familiarity of market participants with the concept of interest flows, as well as their previous experience with similar structures, such as parallel and back-to-back loans, exerted an important influence in the way the market evolved. An even more important reason for the tilting of the market toward the currency swap structure, however, was the liquidity created in the longer end of the market (i.e., the 5- to 10-year segment) by the abundant supply of capital market transactions (bond issues) in that market segment.

The currency swap market today reflects its historical origins by being dominated in the short end of the market (up to two years) by money market activities while capital market activities are the predominant factor in influencing the longer end of the market (longer than two years).

The World Economic Environment in the 1970s

If one were to have taken a snapshot of the world financial markets as we were entering the 1970s, the following observations would have been made.

First, developed financial markets (in the sense of the word used today) existed only in the United States and to some extent in Europe, centered around the so-called Euromarkets. In the United States, the size of the economy, the prosperity of the postwar period, a well-established legal and regulatory framework, and a "promarket" philosophy combined with a stable political system allowed the development of a wide spectrum of large liquid markets that served as efficient vehicles for transferring funds from the investors to the borrowers. Even in the United States, however, the various market segments were not integrated into a single market in which pressures in one segment were relieved by offsetting movements of funds from the other segments. The emergence of the Euromarkets, on the other hand, had its origins in a series of events (large U.S. balance of payments deficits, reluctance on the part of several countries to deposit money in the United States, and tax considerations) that led over a period of time to the creation of large pools of U.S. dollars abroad, outside the U.S. system, that were deposited primarily with London-based financial institutions. Over time, a network of markets emerged, ranging from deposits to securities, through which funds changed hands without being subject to the supervisory, regulatory, and tax-imposing arms of any monetary authority. Domestic financial markets in other countries were in an embryonic stage, isolated from one another and closely regulated by national authorities. Nonresident access to these capital markets was tightly controlled while the scope of instruments available to borrowers and investors was very limited.

Second, the primary vehicle for transferring financial flows from investors to borrowers was by means of traditional commercial banking instruments, mostly syndicated loans; securities played a comparatively modest role. Lending in the form of medium-term (five to seven years of maturity), U.S. dollar–denominated floating-rate syndicated loans was the main form of channeling such resources.

Finally, most international financial transactions were conducted in U.S. dollars, because of the critical role of the U.S. dollar as the linchpin of the international financial system. Governed by the Bretton Woods agreement, the values of all the currencies of the western world were pegged to the U.S. dollar, which in turn had a fixed price vis-à-vis gold. Thus, the U.S. dollar in effect was the international medium of exchange as well as the main reserve currency.

During this period two major events took place that unraveled the environment described earlier and led to the sequence of events that changed the financial landscape. The first was the collapse of the Bretton Woods agreement in 1971, and the second was the change in 1979 in the conduct of the U.S. monetary policy from targeting interest rates to controlling money supply. These two events account for most of the unprecedented levels of volatility in interest rates and foreign exchange rates over the past 15 years.

The Collapse of the Bretton Woods Agreement

The year 1971 marked the end of the international monetary system as it had functioned since the Bretton Woods agreement of 1944. Under this system, the U.S. dollar had been the linchpin of the system because of fixed price vis-à-vis gold, and the values of all western currencies were pegged in relation to the dollar. As a result, exchange rates were fixed, and the countries involved agreed to manipulate their economic policies in such a way as to maintain these rates. This system ended when the convertibility of the U.S. dollar was suspended in August of 1971. The dollar was no longer convertible into gold, and foreigners would no longer be able to turn their dollars to the U.S. Treasury and exchange them for gold. Exchange rates were no longer fixed; instead they "floated"—that is, they were determined by free market forces. The major casualty of these developments was the U.S. dollar, which, given the overhang of U.S. dollars worldwide, started a long period of sustained depreciation lasting until the end of the 1970s. During the same period, the demand for other "hard" currencies to take the place of the U.S. dollar as an international reserve currency led to significant appreciation in the values of such currencies as the Deutschemark, the Swiss franc, and the Japanese yen.

The changes in the values of these currencies had a significant impact on both the internal and external sectors of the various economies around the world. For example, the devaluation of the U.S. dollar meant that its purchasing power changed dramatically. Importing goods into the U.S. cost more, affecting the domestic price level; at the same time, higher-valued imports and lower-valued exports widened the external trade deficit. Most importantly, since the U.S. dollar was de facto the international reserve currency, most international trade was denominated in U.S. dollars, thus increasing worldwide the effect of the weaker U.S. dollar on inflation and trade accounts. Revenues of firms associated with exports and/or imports fluctuated dramatically; the valuation of official reserves, mostly in

U.S. dollars, was negatively affected, and commodity prices started following the price of gold.

In 1972, signs of worldwide inflation began to emerge, with a 50 percent increase in commodity prices due to poor harvests. In November 1973 came the oil price "shock," which was largely precipitated by the oil-producing countries' reaction to reduced oil export revenues (since oil prices were denominated in U.S. dollars). What followed was tremendous variation in inflation rates among countries as different countries adopted different economic policies for tackling the "wealth effects" caused by the major transfer of economic power from the oil-consuming to the oil-producing countries. The resulting differences in interest rates and price levels among countries and the varying balance of payments accounts added another source of currency fluctuation to an already volatile environment.

Since then, volatility has been a new feature with which participants in the international economic system have had to cope. An appreciation of the magnitude of the economic changes induced by the collapse of the Bretton Woods agreement and the resulting divergence of exchange rates can be gained by looking at Figure 1, which shows

FIGURE 1
Exchange Rate Fluctuations Over the Period of 1971–1989 (Monthly Data, January 1970 to August 1989)

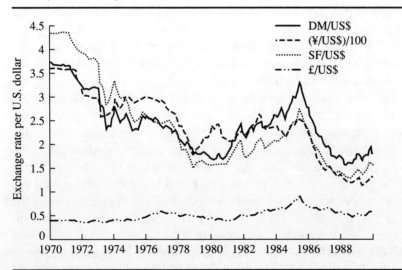

Source: Security Pacific Hoare Govett Limited.

how widely the value of the main trading currencies has fluctuated against the U.S. dollar between January 1970 and August 1989.

Almost all parties have felt the volatility of exchange rates and interest rates. Not only have exporters and importers suffered from the exchange rate volatility, but also foreign investors and those who borrowed overseas. As a result, almost all participants active in the international financial markets have felt a keen need for protection. Exporters, international corporations, and importers all require hedging vehicles to be able to compete. Exporters want assurance of the value of the currency they will be paid in, and importers want to safeguard the amount they will be required to pay. Multinational corporations want to protect their activities in different parts of the globe. Because they provided protection against currency fluctuations, currency swaps were one of the strategies the marketplace came up with for protecting participants from the increased foreign exchange uncertainty.

Controlling Money Supply as a Means of Conducting Monetary Policy

As discussed in the previous section, the first signs of prolonged interest rate uncertainty are traceable to the breakdown of the Bretton Woods agreement. However, interest rate volatility became a permanent feature of the financial landscape in 1979, when the U.S. Federal Reserve Board, responding to the lack of confidence in the U.S. dollar internationally and to mounting inflationary pressures domestically, changed the way it was conducting monetary policy by focusing on the control of the money supply instead of targeting interest rates in the hope of bringing monetary growth under control. The results were dramatic: interest rates in the United States reached unprecedented levels. Most importantly, under the policy of controlling money supply, interest rates became a residual policy-making tool, resulting in greater movements in interest rates than at any time in the postwar period.

The change in the conduct of U.S. monetary policy had repercussions beyond the U.S. dollar markets, and resulted in wider fluctuations in the levels of interest rates in other countries. The pursuit of independent monetary policies in the various European countries and Japan was made more difficult by the effects of floating exchange rates; monetary authorities had to make a choice between domestic

(domestic interest rates and inflation) or international (exchange rate) objectives. To protect their currencies, most monetary authorities allowed their domestic rates to be influenced by interest rate levels in the United States, which led to worldwide interest rate increases.

The extent of the volatility in the levels of interest rates in the major economies around the world is illustrated by Figure 2, which portrays the movement of short-term interest rates (six-month LIBOR) in selected currencies from January 1980 to August 1989.

As inflationary expectations were sweeping the economy, raising funds (particularly fixed-rate funds) became exceedingly difficult for corporations, financial institutions and even the U.S. Treasury. Savers were reluctant to invest in long-term financial assets that were losing value rapidly; they expressed a preference for short-term, floating-rate investments, which offered protection against such losses. Such developments led to the emergence of variable-rate funding. However, borrowing entities such as industrial corporations, which traditionally are in need of long-term fixed-rate funding in order to finance the

FIGURE 2

Fluctuations in the Six-Month LIBOR Rates, 1980–1989 (Monthly Data, January 1980 to August 1989)

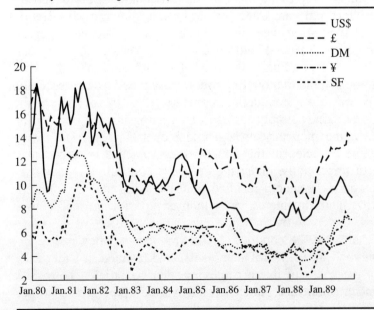

Source: Security Pacific Hoare Govett Limited.

acquisition and/or construction of long-lived assets such as plant and equipment, were exposed by variable-rate funding to significant interest rate risks arising from mismatches in their assets (long-term, fixed-rate producing) and their liabilities (short-term, variable-rate). Similarly, for deposit-accepting financial institutions where credit risk has been traditionally the most important risk and therefore the most important determinant of earnings, the new environment led to the emergence of a new class of risk called spread income risk—that is, the risk of being squeezed between the rate they were earning on their assets (which were either fixed or floating) and their liabilities (which, again, were either fixed or floating).

As a consequence of this volatility, the management of interest rate risk became much more important. Interest rate swaps came about as a means for hedging such interest rate risk. For example, industrial corporations, because of their access to funding (e.g., bank funding tied to the prime interest rate and/or short-term markets such as commercial paper), were in a position to convert such funding into fixed rate funding by hedging it through interest rate swaps. Financial institutions were able to reduce the sensitivity of their liabilities to interest rate fluctuations and thus protect themselves from rising interest rates by transforming floating-rate liabilities into fixed-rate liabilities. Most importantly, interest rate swaps have enabled institutions to manage more effectively the choice between fixed- and floating-rate liabilities and protect themselves from interest rate fluctuations, or even to use such fluctuations to lock in profits.

Investors have also benefited from the emergence of interest rate swaps. The versatility and flexibility of interest rate swaps make them ideal for combination with other assets to create packages that offer higher return for the same level of risk and, more generally, create assets that have the desirable risk/return profile. As explained later, one of the first uses of interest rate swaps was the packaging of fixed-rate bonds with an interest rate swap to create floating-rate assets (by swapping out the fixed stream of coupon payments for floating) that yielded significantly more than other floating-rate assets of the same risk class.

Of course, interest rate swaps were not the only tool for managing risk. Other asset/liability management tools included financial futures contracts, options, and other over-the-counter products. Yet the interest rate swap is perhaps the most flexible and versatile of all the instruments available for hedging interest rate risk.

FACTORS THAT HAVE CONTRIBUTED
TO THE GROWTH AND DEVELOPMENT
OF SWAPS

The extreme volatility of interest and foreign exchange rates that prevailed in the late 1970s provided the fertile environment for the emergence of swaps. However, the swap market would not have grown to its current size if a number of other developments had not taken place. In particular, trends such as deregulation, innovation, and globalization through advances in technology, communications, and transportation have been critical in shaping the new environment and thus have contributed to the development of swaps and other derivative products. Although these trends emerged separately, in their evolution they fed one another and are now closely intertwined, affecting and reinforcing one another.

Financial Deregulation

Financial deregulation has been the principle factor in the emergence and acceleration of financial innovation and in the trend toward closely linked capital markets around the globe. Deregulation opened new markets and increased the choices available to borrowers and investors by bringing into the market new instruments and structures for composing or decomposing risk and thus creating assets and liabilities with desirable risk profiles. Most of the innovation has taken place in markets outside the United States, largely because of the steps taken toward financial deregulation in several key countries. The trend was set in the Euromarkets, which have been operating in a regulatory vacuum beyond the reach of any tax and monetary authority. These markets attracted large amounts of funds that in turn were offered to investors who preferred anonymity and no tax burden. The emergence and dynamic growth of these markets and the gravity they exerted on international money flows in the 1970s and early 1980s induced several monetary authorities to rewrite the regulations they had been building to control capital flows with the intent of diverting such flows back to their local markets. What we have observed over the past 10 years has been an effort by several key countries with developed capital markets, particularly Japan, Germany, Switzerland, and Britain, to prevent such overshadowing by liberalizing their financial markets.

In the United States a critical step in this direction was the abolishment of the 30 percent withholding tax on coupon payments of U.S. dollar–denominated bond issues issued by U.S. corporations and held by foreign investors. Similar steps were taken in Germany, first with the removal of the 25 percent withholding tax imposed on domestic Deutschemark investments held by foreigners (offsetting the advantage offered to investors holding Euro-DM–denominated investments). The next step was opening the Euro-DM bond market by eliminating the mandatory queue for Euro-DM bond issues and by allowing foreign institutions with a banking presence in Germany to lead-manage such issues. Finally, authorities permitted the issuance of nontraditional bonds issues, such as FRNs, zero-coupon bonds, and dual-currency issues, which enhanced the appeal of the Deutschemark to the international investors. Similar considerations led the Swiss and Dutch authorities to proceed in 1990 with reforms to partially deregulate the Swiss franc and Dutch guilder bond markets. In the United Kingdom, radical changes in the structure of the equity and bond markets took place in 1986, transforming the existing market structures along the lines of the U.S. prototype, in which securities firms could act as both principals and agents.

At the same time, in the equity markets, the system of minimum commissions was eliminated. The consolidation of the principal and agent functions led to increased competition among the many market participants (including several non-British entities) and an increased need for innovation as a competitive weapon.

Finally, major changes took place in Japan. Market forces were allowed to determine interest rates in the domestic markets, replacing a vast array of administered rates. Access to Samurai and Euroyen markets that was formerly restricted to supranational and sovereign credits became available to most market participants, and restrictions on currency swaps and forward foreign exchange transactions were lifted.

What has followed has been more or less predictable. Many of the innovations that had been initiated in the Euromarkets started appearing in several domestic markets. For example, the past 10 years have seen the issuance of the first Japanese yen and Deutschemark floating-rate notes (FRNs), the emergence of the first zero-coupon bonds in Switzerland, Germany, and the United Kingdom, the issuance of dual-currency bonds, and the issuance of foreign currency–denominated bonds in domestic markets. In turn, the appearance of new instruments accelerated the arbitrage process through swaps (as explained later) by making it possible to capture arbitrage profits that otherwise would only be observable. This large-scale financial deregulation had a significant effect on the development of the swap market. By eliminating tax considerations, it induced parties to make decisions based on fundamental economics, thereby improving the allocation of funds. Elimination of restrictions regarding the type of instruments available enhanced the menus available to both investors and borrowers. Finally, deregulation has encouraged swap activity, which in turn has increased market efficiency by facilitating the process of transferring funds from the saving surplus to the deficit surplus economic units.

Financial Innovation

Broadly speaking, innovation is spurred when market participants respond to changes in the surrounding economic environment and to competitive pressures by introducing new techniques, new instruments, and, more generally, new ways of transferring funds from investors to borrowers. The innovation process, by its very nature, creates funding and investment opportunities for the various financial market participants that otherwise would not have been possible. It allows borrowers to obtain financing at reduced cost, compared with traditional techniques. At the same time, the process of composing and decomposing risk that is embedded in the innovative techniques also creates more alternatives for investors by offering yield improvements compared with similar risk assets. Apart from swaps, examples of such major innovations that have taken place over the past 15 years include the emergence of markets for FRNs, options, and futures and the trend towards securitization.

The significance of the FRN as a financial innovation was that it gave a further impetus to the growth of the swap market. It has enabled borrowers to further decompose the funding decision from the decision as to the form and type of their liabilities (i.e., fixed or floating). At the same time, it enabled investors to expand the universe of instruments that would typically be considered as investment choices. For example, a bank wishing to expand its floating-rate asset portfolio now routinely considers asset swaps (i.e., packages of fixed-rate bonds that, together with interest rate or currency swaps, emulate the risk profile of a floating-rate asset) among its choices.

The emergence of options and futures, whether foreign exchange or interest rate, was another response by market participants to the excess volatility of the last decade. Like swaps, these new instruments provide borrowers and investors with more choice and flexibility in managing their assets and liabilities. Furthermore, the growth of these instruments, particularly in countries other than the United States (the United Kingdom, France, Germany, Australia) has indirectly led to development and further liquidity in local swap markets, as swap warehouse managers are more able to hedge their risks. The explosive growth in these markets in the late 1980s is an indication of how the management of risk has evolved.

Another financial innovation has been the trend toward securitization, the process by which funds that once were channeled from investors to borrowers through some sort of intermediation, are instead channeled directly through the issuance of publicly offered tradeable securities. Securitization has taken several forms. First, an increasing variety of high-quality assets has been used to collateralize such instruments (including assets such as credit card receivables and automobile loans). In addition, by cleverly packaging such assets, new types of securities, such as the Collateralized Mortgage Obligations (CMOs), have emerged, with cash flows resembling those of traditional bonds (semiannual payments as opposed to the monthly payments on GNMAs and floating-rate structures). Furthermore, an increasing number of high-quality borrowers, such as highly rated corporates and sovereign entities, have been securitizing their borrowings. These entities, which traditionally have used bank credit as their main source of borrowed funds, have been bypassing intermediating institutions, raising funds directly through the issuance of securities. The emergence and rapid growth of the FRN and Eurocommercial markets are prime examples. Again, this process has enabled borrowers to further decompose the funding decision from the decision as to the form and type of their liabilities (i.e., fixed or floating) and enhance their ability to lower borrowing costs by employing swap-related debt management techniques. At a broader level, it has intensified the competition between commercial banks (the traditional suppliers of loans) and the securities houses (the beneficiaries of securitization), inducing the former to work off their comparative advantage (their strong balance sheets) in order to reclaim the lost business.

Globalization of Financial Markets

The third important factor that has been critical in the growth and development of the swap market has been the growing trend toward increased internationalization, or globalization, of financial markets. This term is used to describe the trend toward financial integration of the various capital markets around the globe. The globalization of financial markets is the product of deregulation and innovation, combined with rapid technological advances in computing and communications.

Deregulation has brought down many of the barriers, in the form of taxes or restrictions and controls, that had prevented the free flow of capital. Innovation has provided the tools with which the bridging of the various capital markets could be accomplished. Advances in computing allow quick comparison of the various alternatives offered, and advances in communications have brought together physically distant markets. In this respect swaps are the perfect example of an innovation that has contributed significantly to an integrated international capital market. The interest rate swap markets are integrally linked to the local money and capital markets. At the same time, the interest rate swap markets are intimately linked with their currency swap sectors, which in turn make up an international web of satellite markets to form an efficient mechanism for transmitting changes in one market to the others. The whole process has received a tremendous boost from the rapid advances in communications and computer technology. These advances have led to a collapse of the constraints of time and distance, permitting the immediate exchange of information and intensifying competition among the various financial centers.

The result has been that the major borrowers and investors no longer perceive their borrowing and investment opportunities within the framework of their local markets. They seek the best terms by borrowing and investing in all the major (and minor) financial centers of the world, whether in Europe, the United States, or Japan. Issuers and investors have a wider range of currencies, instruments, and markets from which to choose, and their ability to arbitrage across markets has been enhanced. As a result, the role of financial institutions and the capital markets is being redefined. The distinction between investment and commercial banks in the United States and Japan is becoming more and more blurred, and both kinds of banks are reorienting themselves internationally. In this environment, financial institutions from every major country compete with one another to attract the business of entities that need to raise funds (whether corporate or sovereign credits) or that need to invest excess cash. In the process they continuously invent new ways of transferring funds that give an edge to the borrowers, or the investors, or the financial institutions themselves, and sometimes, if the new ways are true innovations, to all of the above.

This is all good news for the international economy, because markets have become more efficient. As such, they better fulfill their role as the mechanism for distributing investments and savings among the various economic units. The result has been greater efficiency in the real economy and the creation of more and more demand for products such as swaps.

THE USE OF CURRENCY SWAPS AS AN ARBITRAGE TOOL

The previous discussion focused on the conditions that necessitated the appearance of the currency and interest rate swaps as a tool for commercial and financial hedging. The need for hedging vehicles was a necessary condition for the development of swaps, but it was not a sufficient one. The important factor behind currency swaps has been the motivation to take advantage of arbitrage opportunities that exist because of capital market inefficiencies. Such arbitrage has attracted a great deal of attention in the financial press, which has glorified the use of swaps, and has been a main selling point used by banks in convincing many corporations and financial institutions to enter the swap market. This section addresses the issue of how currency swaps help in capturing arbitrage gains. This is explained within the context of the theory of comparative advantage, which is well established in economics. Finally, we address the issue of where these arbitrage opportunities come from.

The Liability Currency Swap Arbitrage

Swaps can be used to capture arbitrage gains in many different ways. However, the use of swaps as an arbitrage tool in connection with fund raising has done the most to popularize the technique. To illustrate just how this advantage comes about and how it can be exploited through a swap, we will start by taking a look at an example of currency swap arbitrage in connection with creating a new liability. Using typical funding cost spreads that borrowers might face in two different capital markets, we identify the economics that underlie these transactions and demonstrate how the arbitrage gain arises and how it can be captured with the help of swaps.

Let's consider a Fortune 500 U.S. industrial firm with a BBB credit rating that wishes to raise $150 million in 10-year, fixed-rate funds in order to finance the acquisition of another company. Given its BBB credit rating, the firm can borrow 10-year funds in the U.S. dollar market at a fixed rate of 11.50 percent. The company does not have immediate access to the U.S. fixed-rate bond market because of its weak credit rating and the fact that it has tapped the fixed-rate bond market frequently over the past few years. Unable to proceed without paying a premium over the usual cost of funds, the treasurer of the firm contacts his investment banker and asks for suggestions to lower the cost of borrowing.

At the same time, the investment banker is aware that an international institution with access to the international capital markets and a better credit rating (its obligations have been rated AAA by Standard & Poor's and Moody's) wants to take advantage of the favorable market conditions to raise medium-term funding in Swiss francs. If this institution were to decide to access the Swiss fixed-rate market directly, it could raise the funds at an all-in cost of 7.50 percent. The institution, however, is exploring alternatives for reducing the cost of such borrowings. Given its AAA credit rating, the institution could access the U.S. dollar bond market and raise the amounts at an all-in cost of 9.50 percent, because it is well regarded in the U.S. dollar market and has not tapped the U.S. bond rate market recently, and therefore can obtain favorable borrowing terms. An inquiry with the banker's syndicate desk reveals that the BBB firm has never tapped the Swiss market before and therefore could command a "scarcity value" premium leading to an all-in cost of 8.50 percent for 10-year fixed-rate funds. The relative borrowing costs of the two entities in the two markets are shown in Table 2.

Careful examination of the relative funding costs of the two firms reveals some interesting points.

First, as one would expect, Firm AAA, being a better credit risk, has an absolute advantage in both markets since it can raise funds at a lower cost than Firm BBB.

Second, although Firm AAA has an absolute advantage in both markets, its relative advantage is in the U.S. dollar fixed-rate market since it can borrow at a cost 200 basis points lower than that of Firm BBB. By comparison, Firm AAA's borrowing advantage over Firm BBB's in the Swiss franc fixed market is only 100 basis points. That is, Firm AAA's comparative financial advantage, which can arise from any one of the market inefficiencies discussed later, is thus in the Swiss franc fixed-rate market. Similarly, Firm BBB, disadvantaged in both markets, has less of a disadvantage in the Swiss franc market, where its borrowing disadvantage vis-à-vis Firm AAA is only 100 basis points (as opposed to 200 basis points in the U.S. dollar fixed-rate market).

Third, the difference in funding costs between the two companies in the two markets is not identical. In the U.S. dollar market the difference in costs is 2.00 percent while in the Swiss franc market the difference is 1.00 percent. That is, the credit premium between the two firms, which is defined as the difference (spread) in their funding costs in the two markets, is different. Investors in the U.S. dollar market assess the difference between the two credits to be worth 200 basis points, whereas investors in the Swiss franc market assess it to be 100 basis points. This difference gives rise to a classic arbitrage

TABLE 2
Relative Borrowing Costs in Two Markets

	U.S. Dollar Fixed-Rate Market	Swiss Franc Fixed-Rate Market
Firm AAA	9.50%	7.50%
Firm BBB	11.50%	8.50%
Credit spread	200 bp	100 bp
Arbitrage	100 bp	

situation since an otherwise identical item (the credit difference between the firms) has different prices in two different markets.

If the arbitrage difference were to be captured, it would be possible for one or both firms to lower their funding costs. As in any other arbitrage opportunity, this can be accomplished by selling the item (the credit spread) in the more expensive market and buying it back in the cheaper market. We mentioned that Firm AAA has a comparative advantage in the U.S. dollar market, while Firm BBB has a comparative advantage in the Swiss franc market. If each firm issues in the market where it can borrow at the lowest relative cost and then exchanges payments through a currency swap, both borrowers can lower their borrowing costs. Given that the current spot exchange rate between the U.S. dollar and Swiss franc is US$1 = SF2.00, the recommended steps for each firm are presented in Table 3.

The net effect of the above transaction is that Firm AAA ends up with a Swiss franc funding (proceeds and interest payment in Swiss francs), and Firm BBB ends up with a dollar funding (proceeds and interest payments in U.S. dollars). It is clear that the level of payments made between the two firms is critical to the success of this structure. If the two firms were to simply pass on their respective borrowing costs, the structure would not work. Firm AAA would never enter the agreement, because the Swiss franc rate funds would cost the firm 8.50 percent, while it could obtain the same funds at 7.50 percent on its own—that is, 100 basis points cheaper. And Firm BBB would have U.S. funds at 9.50 percent, 200 basis points less than it would have to pay in a direct borrowing. Clearly, such an arrangement would not be sustainable. The typical outcome is that the parties

TABLE 3
Steps Necessary to Lock In Arbitrage Gain

Firm AAA	Firm BBB
Raise US$150 million at 9.50%	Issue SF200 million at 8.50%
Deliver US$ proceeds to Firm BBB	Deliver SF proceeds to Firm AAA
Receive fixed-rate US$ payments from BBB	Receive fixed-rate SF payments from AAA
Make fixed-rate SF payments to BBB	Make fixed-rate US$ payments to AAA

divide their differences in borrowing costs in the two markets. This is often accomplished according to the relative bargaining strength of the borrowers. Firm AAA, the stronger credit, and the one that can borrow at the lowest cost in both markets, will take most of the savings but will share some of the savings with Firm BBB to induce it to enter into the transaction. (In addition, a portion of the savings will go to the intermediating bank, since it is highly unlikely that Firm AAA would accept Firm BBB as a direct counterparty.)

In this case, there is a net cost savings of 100 basis points to be divided (an easy way to calculate the net savings is by observing that Firm BBB benefits by 200 basis points while Firm AAA loses 100 basis points if interest payments are simply exchanged). To complete the example, assume that Firm AAA obtains 75 basis points of savings and Firm BBB gets the remaining 25 basis points. A final minor technical point is how these savings will be delivered to each party. For simplicity, assume that Firm AAA gets the 75 basis point savings in the form of lower fixed interest rate payments that it receives from Firm BBB. Figure 3 shows how these arrangements are finalized.

This transaction benefits both parties. Firm AAA has been able to raise Swiss franc funds at 75 basis points below cost (6.75 percent compared with its direct cost of 7.50 percent). Firm BBB has been

FIGURE 3
Swap Payment Structure

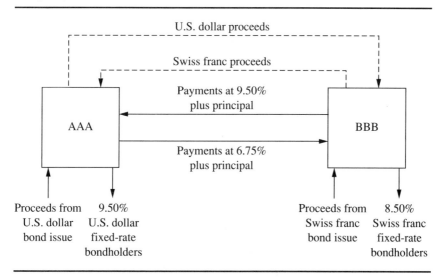

able to obtain U.S. dollar funds at 25 basis points below cost (at 11.25 percent compared with its direct cost of 11.50 percent). The cost savings for each party resulting from swap payments are shown in Table 4.

By exploiting its financial comparative advantage, Firm AAA has been able to transform its advantage in accessing the U.S. dollar fixed-rate bond market into a cost-effective way of creating a Swiss franc liability of similar maturity. Firm BBB has done the reverse.

This example has been instrumental in demonstrating a few common elements that form the basic principles of swap activity in connection with borrowing arbitrage:

- In order for a currency swap to lead to arbitrage gains for one or both parties, at least one party must have an advantage in at least one market. Arbitrage gains occur only if each party borrows in the market where it has the comparative advantage.
- The total arbitrage gain available to both parties reflects the comparative advantage of the two issuers in the two markets. If one party has an absolute advantage in both markets, the total arbitrage gain is the difference between the differential borrowing costs. If each party has an advantage in only one market, the total arbitrage gain available is equal to the sum of the comparative advantages.

TABLE 4
Cost after the Currency Swap

Firm AAA		Firm BBB	
Receives from Firm BBB		Pays to Firm AAA	
(US$)	9.50%	(US$)	9.50%
Pays to bondholders (US$)	9.50	Pays to bondholders (SF)	8.50
Pays to Firm BBB		Receives from Firm AAA	
(SF)	6.75	(SF)	6.75
Net cost of SF debt	6.75	Net cost of US$ debt	11.25*
Direct cost of SF debt	7.50	Direct cost of US$ debt	11.50
Net savings	0.75	Net savings	0.25

* Note that the savings to Firm BBB are subject to foreign exchange risk, since a portion of its 11.25% U.S. dollar debt is in Swiss francs (the difference between 8.50% and 6.75%). In practice, however, the intermediating bank can hedge this risk on behalf of Firm BBB, and thus "lock in" the 0.25% savings.

- Finally, the allocation of arbitrage gains depends on the relative bargaining strengths of the two parties involved.

The Asset Currency Swap Arbitrage

The preceding example is an accurate representation of the conditions prevailing in the early 1980s and demonstrates the first use of swaps as an arbitrage instrument. Currency swaps were popularized on the liability side of the business; the term used initially was *liability* swaps. Furthermore, the large arbitrage gains achievable though combinations of borrowings and currency swaps highlight the high public profile of swap activity. However, arbitrage opportunities also exist on the asset side. In fact, shortly after the appearance of the liability swaps, the first asset packages involving interest rate and currency swap arbitrage were put together.

In the typical asset swap, the investor (typically a bank) is interested in obtaining a variable-rate asset that yields a margin over LIBOR, which roughly represents the cost of funds in the interbank market. A bank, by acquiring an asset yielding a spread over LIBOR (say 25 basis points) and financing it at LIBOR, locks in the spread. The typical source of such assets are the FRNs and/or the syndicated loans market. Another way of creating a floating-rate asset is to buy fixed-rate assets (e.g., fixed-rate bonds) and swap the fixed-income receipts for floating payments based on LIBOR through an interest rate or currency swap. Because the interest rate at which fixed payments made under the swap is less than the interest rate at which fixed payments are received from the fixed-rate asset, a spread over LIBOR is created. If this spread over LIBOR is higher than what is achievable by directly buying an FRN or a syndicated loan of the same issuer, the asset package (the fixed-rate bonds plus the interest rate swap) are preferable. The following example is typical of the so-called "asset-swap" activity, which continues today. Table 5 portrays the yields that we observe on the secondary market values of the obligations of Firm

TABLE 5
Relative Yields in Various Markets

Fixed Rate	Floating Rate	Swap Rate
10.50%	US$ LIBOR + 15 bp	10.25%

XXX in the fixed-rate and floating-rate markets in the same currency (say U.S. dollars). The table also shows the yield on the fixed-rate leg of an interest rate swap of similar maturity.

The reader may observe that these three markets are not in equilibrium with one another because combinations of two of them result in a package of similar risk but with different return from the third market. For example, if the holder of fixed-rate bonds enters into an interest rate swap in which it makes fixed-rate payments and receives six-month LIBOR, it can create a floating-rate package with a spread of 25 basis points over LIBOR, which is higher than the spread of 15 basis points observed in the floating-rate paper of the same issuer.

A similar example can be constructed involving nondollar fixed-rate bonds (e.g., ECU fixed-rate bonds) and a currency swap. Table 6 portrays such a situation. Again, it is possible to combine the purchase of the ECU fixed-rate bonds with a currency swap in which the investor pays the fixed rate and receives US$ LIBOR plus a spread that is higher than the spread over LIBOR observed in the floating-rate market. Note that in this case the currency swap is merely a way of converting from ECUs to dollars. It is discrepancies of this nature that can be exploited through asset interest rate and currency swap arbitrage. Table 7 and Figure 4 show the arrangement of such combinations.

This is another example of how interest rate and currency swaps have been used (and are being used) to capture arbitrage gains.

The Sources of Arbitrage Activity

The examples used to demonstrate how swaps can be used as a tool for capturing arbitrage profits also show how real corporations are able not only to change the currency in which their liabilities are denominated, but to lower their borrowing costs in the process. In the previous section, we argued that the benefit of lower costs derives

TABLE 6
Relative Yields across Markets for Firm XXX's Securities

ECU Fixed-Rate Market	US$ Floating-Rate Market	ECU Currency Swap Rate
10.50%	LIBOR + 15 bp	10.25%

TABLE 7
Investor Yield Enhancement after the Interest Rate
or Currency Swap

Receives from fixed-rate bonds (ECU or US$)	10.50%
Pays to swap counterparty CCC	10.50
Receives from swap counterparty CCC	LIBOR + 25 bp
Net return from floating-rate asset	LIBOR + 25 bp
Direct return from floating-rate asset	LIBOR + 15 bp
Yield enhancement	0.10%

from the utilization of a firm's comparative advantage in particular markets. In this section, we explore the sources of this comparative advantage.

Capital markets exist for the purpose of efficiently channeling funds from economic units with excess funds (savers) to economic units in need of funds (borrowers). Interest rates are the means by which an equilibrium is achieved between the supply of funds by the savers and the demand of funds by the borrowers in each capital

FIGURE 4
Asset Swap Structure

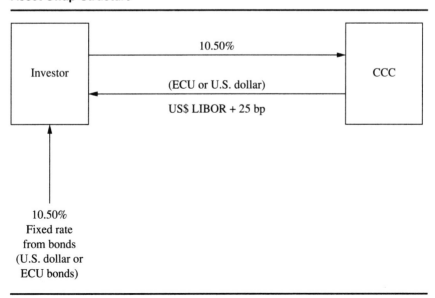

market. The levels of interest rate determined in this way in the various markets are related to one another. The forward exchange markets, for example, relate and reflect the interest rate levels between two currency markets. If markets were perfect, a firm would not have an advantage in raising funds in a particular capital market and/or in a particular currency. Interest rate parity would ensure that the cost would be identical, regardless of the currency in which the borrowing is denominated. In practice, however, markets are neither perfect nor totally integrated. When finance theorists talk about perfect markets, they assume that these markets have the following characteristics:

- Markets are frictionless (no transaction costs, taxes, divisible assets, or regulations).
- Markets are informationally efficient; that is, information is costless and available to everybody.
- There is perfect competition, so that everybody is a price taker (no individual can affect the price).
- Economic units are rational and are allowed to maximize their wealth.

If any of these conditions is violated, then inefficiencies appear in the system, creating comparative advantage that can be exploited through arbitrage. Following the above classification inefficiencies can be categorized as follows: regulatory constraints, imperfect information, imperfect competition, and portfolio saturation.

First, regulatory constraints or frictions create cost differentials, which the market, to the extent that it can, tries to exploit. One form that these constraints take is the imposition by the monetary authorities of controls that limit access to the capital markets. The monetary authorities of most countries do not permit, or permit in a constrained manner, nonresidents to enter their capital markets. Their control can take the form of refusing entry outright, restricting access to certain maturities, imposing formal or informal queuing systems, requiring the approval by capital markets committees, or simply enforcing gentlemen's agreements that reflect some of the above. Strictly speaking, there is not a single national market that is totally free from access controls. The Eurodollar market (because of the lack of any formal regulations) and the market in ECU bonds (because ECUs are not the currency of any country) are exceptions. Every other market is subject to some form of access control. The result is that there are issuers with access to certain currencies and issuers with no access at all.

Firms that have access to a particular currency (whether domestic or nonresident) in effect generate the comparative advantage for themselves because of their monopoly situation that has been created by the regulation of the market.

Another way that access to the market is regulated is through the imposition of various taxes, usually in the form of withholding taxes. In virtually every country in the world, investment income in one way or another is subject to taxes, and this gives investors the incentive to pay a premium for the opportunity to avoid being subject to taxes. For example, bearer bonds (in which the identity of the investor is not revealed) in the Eurobond market are placed at yields lower than those of their domestic markets. All of these factors cause yield discrepancies and, therefore, are typically sources of comparative advantage. In light of the developments that have taken place in the world financial markets over the 1980s, it is not surprising that the availability of arbitrage has been diminishing over the same time period.

A second source of comparative advantage is informational inefficiencies. If markets were perfect and every participant in every market possessed the same information, then corporations would be evaluated identically and thus raise funds at the same credit risk premiums. However, in practice, market participants in, say, the Benelux countries, are not totally familiar with top-credit U.S. corporations in the U.S. capital market. Similarly, U.S. investors may not be familiar with top-credit European corporations. The result is that two issuers (say, one German and one U.S. corporation) of identical credit standing might face different risk premiums in raising funds in the U.S. and the German capital markets. In particular, the German corporation may have an advantage vis-à-vis the U.S. corporation in the German market while the opposite might be true for the U.S. corporation in the U.S. market. Therefore, imperfect information is an additional source of comparative advantage. Again, with advances in communications and information technology the source of such arbitrage has been diminishing.

A third source of comparative advantage may be the noncompetitive financial structures that exist in several countries. For example, in most European countries, the financial systems are dominated by the banking sector, which in turn is dominated by a handful of large banks (the three big banks in Switzerland, Deutsche Bank in Germany, the four large clearing banks in the United Kingdom, two or three large banks in the Netherlands). These structures do not allow the market-clearing process to work efficiently, resulting in interest rate levels that may deviate substantially (lower or higher) from competitively driven market interest rates, which, in turn, leads to arbitrage opportunities.

A more recent source of comparative advantage, stemming again from the lack of perfect competition, is swap intermediation costs. As detailed elsewhere in this book, swaps expose the user to the risk that the counterparty in the swap transaction may become insolvent and thus stop serving its swap obligations. To avoid this risk, most players in the swap market will not deal with lesser-quality counterparties directly; instead, they put a bank in the middle, which, for an intermediating fee, in effect substitutes itself for the lesser credit in the transaction. If the bank does not properly assess the risk involved and as a result charges a smaller fee, then in effect the bank creates comparative advantage. In a perfectly competitive environment, credit risk assessment should not differ according to whether the assessment takes place by the public in the bond markets, or by the credit analysts in the insurance companies or commercial banks.

Finally, another source of creating cost differentials among issuers with identical credit standings is the lack of diversification in individual portfolios. If flows of funds are controlled and investors' choices are constrained, then the portfolios of investors in particular markets may become saturated. The primary reason for this is again the restricted access to the various markets that forces investors in these markets to hold suboptimally diversified portfolios—that is, portfolios in which "local" securities are held in proportions higher than efficient diversification would suggest. Investors in these currencies or markets want to diversify their portfolios to include a broader range of international credits. The result is that these investors are willing to pay a premium to hold securities underrepresented in their portfolios; at the same time, they need a yield inducement to hold securities overrepresented in their portfolios. Thus, depending on the relative volume of their respective borrowings and the frequency with which they go to a particular market, borrowers of identical credit quality may pay markedly different rates of interest. A prime example of portfolio saturation is the case of the World Bank in the Swiss capital market in the mid-1980s. The Swiss capital market has been a major source of funds for the World Bank over the past 20 years. As a result, World Bank bonds were overrepresented in the portfolios of the Swiss franc market investors and the credit spread of the World Bank vis-à-vis other, less creditworthy issuers worsened substantially. This gave rise to large amounts of swap activity in which the World Bank sourced Swiss francs at substantial savings. Scarcity value and portfolio saturation are important determinants in pricing new issues and cause yield differentiation for identical credits. Therefore, they are a source of comparative advantage.

IMPLICATIONS OF CURRENCY SWAP ACTIVITY FOR FINANCIAL MARKETS

The discussion of the previous section highlighted the several factors that lead to the creation of financial comparative advantage. The discussion also pointed out that comparative advantage arises from inefficiencies that are created primarily by regulators and/or policy makers. These inefficiencies introduce temporary or long-term differences in credit spreads, which, through the vehicle of swaps, can be exploited to reduce borrowing costs and/or increase asset returns.

Even more important in this respect is the role played by the currency swap market, which, in effect, serves as linkage among the intermediate financial markets. This can be appreciated by the fact that most currency swaps are done (at the most basic level) against US$ LIBOR. With the advent of swaps we now have a globally integrated marketplace, in which pressures in one market are felt literally throughout the system, and the very existence of arbitrage ensures consistency of pricing across markets. Figure 5 shows how the various markets are now integrated through interest rate and currency swaps.

Arbitrage activity, apart from being beneficial for the parties involved, benefits financial markets in general by improving the markets' ability to distribute funds from savings units to borrowing units more efficiently. The improvements in market efficiency gained through arbitrage activity take various forms. First, swaps serve as linkage among the various markets. Before the appearance of swaps, fixed-rate and floating-rate markets were isolated from one another. Market participants would move from one market to the other on the basis of their expectations about the level and/or shape of the yield

FIGURE 5
Schematic Presentation of Market Linkages and Integration

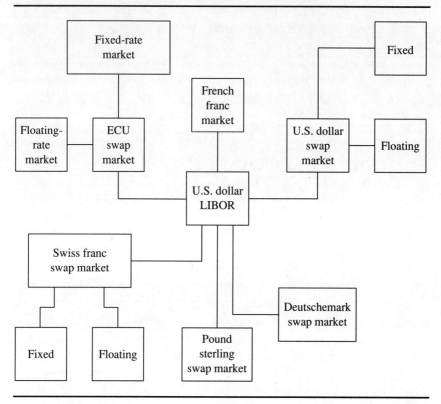

curve. Funds would flow from one market to the other only to the extent that expectations changed. With the advent of the swaps market, participants do not have to restrict themselves to the market in which they have chosen to borrow or invest. Instead, having formed an opinion about future interest rates, they now have the ability to look at both markets simultaneously in search of the best deal. For example, a borrower who wants to raise fixed-rate funds considers not only the fixed-rate market but also the combination of floating-rate funding with an interest rate swap. This process ensures consistency of pricing between the fixed- and floating-rate markets and helps alleviate pressures that might build in the various market segments.

Another example of market integration resulting from swap-driven arbitrage can be seen in asset swaps. As discussed earlier, floating-rate investors actively consider among their alternatives packages of fixed-rate bonds and interest rate swaps. By doing so they ensure that the yields prevailing in the secondary markets are consistent with those in the primary market. For example, if the yields prevailing in the secondary fixed-rate market are higher than those in the primary market, market participants would buy the higher-yielding bonds and combine them with interest rate swaps to create packages yielding a spread over six-month LIBOR in excess of that obtained by buying newly issued fixed-rate bonds and combining them with interest rate swaps, or by buying seasoned FRNs or new FRNs. Again, the process brings efficiency to the market in that new issues are priced in a manner that is consistent with the secondary markets.

Arbitrage of this nature continues even today, although the arbitrage gains achievable have become much less because of market integration. In fact, one reason swap markets have emerged in various parts of the world is in pursuit of arbitrage opportunities in markets which, because of their size or lack of sophistication, such opportunities still exist. Moreover, processes like these, taking place in all the financial markets where interest rate swap markets have developed, have led to efficiencies in a number of domestic financial markets around the world. These markets have been further integrated through the existence of the cross currency swap market. In the same way that interest rate swaps ensure pricing consistency among market segments within a particular financial market, cross currency swaps ensure pricing consistency across financial markets in different currencies. Developments of this nature have pushed the globalization of the financial markets even further, creating a global marketplace composed of a series of interlinked markets. Events affecting a particular market are transmitted through swaps throughout the global network of markets.

Clearly, the new global environment has implications for the conduct and the efficiency of the monetary policies of the various countries around the world. The actions of the monetary authorities in one country, particularly if it is a reserve currency country, are transmitted to the other financial markets around the world, thus affecting the monetary variables in other countries and offsetting or reinforcing actions taken by the local monetary authorities. As a result, there is an increased need for cooperation among the key monetary authorities around the world to coordinate closer their policies in an increasingly interlinked global marketplace.

SUMMARY AND CONCLUSIONS

The objective of this chapter was to provide a description of the environment that has led to the emergence of the swap market within the context of financial markets. In doing so, the changes that have taken place in the world financial markets over the past 10 to 15 years were described. We saw that this period was characterized by an unprecedented increase in the volatility of foreign exchange and interest rates. The collapse of the Bretton Woods agreement, the oil crisis, and the subsequent divergence in the monetary policies of the leading western countries, and of the United States in particular, were identified as the major sources of the volatilities that provided the necessary conditions for the emergence of swaps as a prime hedging instrument.

In addition to an increasingly volatile environment, a number of other factors have significantly contributed to the growth and development of the swap market. Within this context, the trends toward deregulation, financial innovation, and global market integration were discussed.

Finally, the important role of swap-driven arbitrage was discussed, focusing on the benefits and implications of this activity, concluding that market participants have benefited and, as a result, capital markets have become more efficient in channeling funds from investors to borrowers.

CHAPTER 3

CURRENCY SWAPS: QUOTATION CONVENTIONS, MARKET STRUCTURES, AND CREDIT RISK

Keith C. Brown
The University of Texas at Austin
Donald J. Smith
Boston University

The past two decades have given rise to an unprecedented awareness of the need for corporations to manage their foreign exchange exposure. Without a doubt, the largest single factor contributing to this heightened concern has been the dramatic increase in the levels of both interest rate and exchange rate volatility. Starting with the abandonment of the Bretton Woods fixed-exchange-rate system in 1973 and continuing with the Federal Reserve Bank's "deregulation" of interest rates in 1979, a confluence of economic events has exacerbated the risks borne by a company having an unanticipated surplus or deficit of any particular currency on its balance sheet. For example, Rawls and Smithson (1989) document that the volatility of the Japanese yen/U.S. dollar exchange rate experienced more than a sevenfold increase after 1973. Not surprisingly, therefore, the last several years have also witnessed the creation of myriad financial innovations expressly developed to mitigate this risk exposure. Prominent among these new products and strategies is the currency swap agreement.

As it is usually structured, a currency swap involves the periodic exchange of cash flows between two parties in much the same manner as an ordinary interest rate swap.[1] The two transactions are similar in that both typically require counterparties to make periodic cash settlement payments, one based on a fixed interest rate and the other based on a floating reference rate, such as LIBOR (London Inter-bank Offered Rate). Compared with the interest rate swap, however, the currency swap contract is a more complicated financial structure since the cash flows are denominated in two different currencies. The biggest difference this makes for the most basic, or *plain vanilla,* currency swap transaction is that the two counterparties also transfer principal amounts. This scheduled exchange of principals, and its in-evitable credit risk, is one of the factors that has limited the growth of currency swaps relative to the interest rate swap market. In fact, whereas the market for all swaps had grown to an estimated $1.3 trillion by the end of 1988 (*The Economist,* November 4, 1989), a survey conducted by the International Swap Dealers Association (ISDA) in-dicated that cross currency swaps accounted for only about 20 percent of the total. From the absolute magnitude of these numbers, though, it is clear that currency swaps constitute a large and thriving financial market.

Our objective in this chapter is to explain the economic funda-mentals and market conventions associated with currency swap trans-actions. Although the currency swap market began as a means of circumventing capital outflow restrictions, it has rapidly evolved to become a major tool in both the management of risk and the creation of innovative financial structures. We will start our examination with an overview of the historical development and trading structure of the swap market. We then review the industry pricing conventions and provide a numerical example to calculate settlement cash flows for the most commonly traded variety of currency swap. Following this, we demonstrate how the plain vanilla "fixed/floating" rate transaction can be transformed into a "fixed/fixed" rate scheme and suggest two alternative interpretations of the basic swap agreement: (1) a portfolio of capital market transactions and (2) a series of long-dated foreign exchange (FX) forward contracts. The credit risk in a currency swap is then analyzed with a detailed numerical example by calculating the

---

[1]For a survey of the structures, applications, and credit risk in the interest rate swap market, see Brown and Smith (1990). For further background on swaps, see Beidleman (1985), Felgren (1987), Walmsley (1988), Marshall and Kapner (1990), or Smith, Smithson, and Wilford (1990).

mark-to-market, or *replacement cost,* value of the transaction at the time of default. Credit risk is shown to be asymmetric between the two counterparties because of the design of the transaction itself, leading to the potential problem of a "default timing option." Finally, the roles of cross default and netting provisions in currency swap documentation are discussed as ways of dealing with this asymmetric credit risk.

HISTORICAL BACKGROUND
AND MARKET STRUCTURE

The origin of the currency swap market can be traced to the system of *parallel loans* and *back-to-back loans.* As the name implies, a parallel loan involves two companies entering into simultaneous lending agreements with one another in two different currencies. As this arrangement was usually structured, a multinational company headquartered, say, in the United States would lend dollars to the U.S. subsidiary of a foreign-based parent firm while having its own overseas subsidiary borrow in the currency unit of the foreign company. A back-to-back loan agreement, on the other hand, would take place directly between the respective parent companies. The primary benefit of either of these transactions is that it allows both corporate entities to correct an imbalance in the FX exposure on their balance sheets. For instance, if the foreign-based firm had a shortage of dollars relative to its own currency, the parallel loan transaction would correct this problem by allowing for the periodic transfer of currencies at a fixed rate of exchange. Although a comparable series of currency exchanges could be established through the use of FX forward contracts, the advantage of the parallel loan system—particularly for companies based in the United Kingdom—was that it avoided governmental restrictions on direct currency transfers.

As appealing as the parallel and back-to-back loan agreements were in the management of currency risk, however, they both suffered from a potentially costly flaw. Since each of the counterparties in these structures actually borrows funds from the other, both are exposed to the possibility that the other counterparty might default on its obligation to repay. Although such a risk exists with any loan agreement, what makes this situation more tenuous is that the counterparty that did not default may still be obligated to repay its borrowing even after the cash flows had stopped coming in from the other party. That is, it is unclear if one counterparty would have the right to suspend debt repayments in the event of a default by the other. Of course, this problem is more likely to occur under the parallel loan system than with back-to-back loans since in the former arrangement the two parent firms are not borrowing money directly from one another. The currency swap transaction reduces this exposure substantially because, by design, it is closer to a sequence of currency *purchases and sales* rather than a sequence of currency lendings and borrowings. In this manner, settlement payments can be easily "set off" if a default does occur. Beyond this, currency swaps also are a more cost-efficient structure in that a single document replaces two separate loan agreements—each with its attendant placement fees—and does so without altering the debt-equity ratios of the respective counterparties.

It is interesting to note that the development of the currency swap market began in the mid-1960s and hence preceded the ascent of the interest rate swap market by a number of years. This is because the FX risk exposures that gave rise to the use of currency swaps are sensitive to both interest rate and exchange rate movements, and the latter was effectively deregulated before the former. It is generally acknowledged that the first large-scale, widely publicized currency swap was transacted in 1981 between IBM and the World Bank, with Salomon Brothers serving as the market maker. IBM had previously issued Deutschemark and Swiss franc debt and apparently had left its currency exposure uncovered. Then, as the U.S. dollar subsequently strengthened, IBM desired to lock in its fortuitous exchange gains. At the same time, World Bank debt was experiencing saturation in the same markets. The Bank was able to reduce its cost of funds by issuing dollar-denominated bonds and then, via the currency swap with IBM, effectively converting the debt to its desired Deutschemark and Swiss franc obligations. (A detailed example of this type of "financial engineering" is provided later.) From IBM's perspective, the swap provided the long-term currency cover it needed to capitalize on the appreciation of the U.S. dollar. These transactions illustrate that swap market participants can have quite different motives for entering the agreement.[2]

---

[2]See Beidleman (1985) for examples of the many motivations and applications of currency swaps in international corporate finance.

Today currency swaps are executed for virtually every currency associated with a major capital market, including U.S. dollars, Hong Kong dollars, Swiss francs, Deutschemarks, yen, pounds sterling, Canadian dollars, Australian dollars, and European currency units (ECU). Further, it is possible to obtain a swap involving any two of these currencies on either a fixed or a floating rate basis, although it should be noted that an ISDA survey reported that in the first half of 1989 more than 85 percent of all transactions had U.S. dollars on one side of the deal. The same survey also noted that even though swaps are done with maturities as long as 10 years, the most rapidly growing segment of the market is for maturities shorter than 2 years. This is at least partially due to the new capital adequacy requirements imposed on the money-center commercial and investment banks that serve as the main market makers for the industry, since shorter-term swaps involve less risk. Principal amounts range anywhere from the equivalent of $5 million to $100 million.

Finally, like interest rate swaps, the currency swap market developed from one that was primarily broker-oriented into one that is now dealer-oriented. That is, the first currency swaps tended to be organized (as in the case of the IBM–World Bank deal) by brokers who would simply "match" the needs of the two counterparties in exchange for a swap arrangement fee. This allowed the market maker to avoid having to commit its own capital to the transaction, even if it meant that the client might experience a delay in implementing the desired position. As end users began to demand better execution, however, these market makers increasingly found themselves actively involved in the transaction as dealers who "warehoused" one side of a swap transaction (and hedged the inherent price risk) until a second counterparty could be found. This development had broad ramifications, as it meant that the ultimate end users of the swap were exposed to the credit risk of the dealer rather than to each other's risk. Consequently, a market maker with a high credit quality quickly found itself with a competitive advantage when pricing deals in both the primary and secondary swap markets. The secondary market for currency swaps has now become sufficiently active that, except for long-dated agreements that are still matched, market makers routinely quote prices on "half deals." As confirmation of this, the ISDA survey documents that fewer than 2 percent of all swaps done in the first six months of 1989 were executed on a brokered basis.

CURRENCY SWAP
QUOTATION CONVENTIONS

There are two factors that make the plain vanilla currency swap a more difficult transaction to analyze than a single-currency interest rate swap of comparable maturity. First, as noted earlier, currency swaps almost always require an actual exchange of principal at the origination and termination dates of the deal (i.e., the principal amount is not merely notional). Second, since two different currencies are involved, the interest rates defining the transaction can be quoted on either a fixed or a floating rate basis in either currency. Assuming that the U.S. dollar is one of the two currencies involved in the swap, there are four possible quotation scenarios: (1) a fixed rate in foreign currency versus a fixed rate in U.S. dollars, (2) a fixed rate in foreign currency versus a floating rate in U.S. dollars, (3) a floating rate in foreign currency versus a fixed rate in U.S. dollars, and (4) a floating rate in foreign currency versus a floating rate in U.S. dollars. Although all of these cases are used in practice, the predominant convention in the market is the second, that is, to quote a fixed rate in a foreign currency against a floating rate in U.S. dollars.[3]

Exhibit 1 illustrates the transactions in a standard currency swap. Notice that there are two distinct types of exchanges: principal on both the origination and maturity dates and "coupon" interest on the intervening settlement dates (and also on the maturity date). In the currency swap market, it is customary to base both principal exchanges on the spot market FX rate prevailing at the date of initiation regardless of subsequent FX rates. The floating-rate side of the coupon exchanges is tied typically to U.S. dollar LIBOR as the reference rate and usually is quoted *flat,* or without adjustment. The actual level of the dollar cash flow paid by counterparty B on each settlement date is determined by multiplying the prevailing LIBOR by the U.S. dollar

---

[3] Although they have become the market standard, currency swaps involving a fixed rate for a foreign currency and a dollar-based floating rate were once sufficiently novel as to be labeled CIRCUS swaps, with the acronym standing for "combined *i*nterest *r*ate and *c*urrency *s*wap." Also, agreements employing floating rates for both currencies are often referred to as *basis* swaps.

EXHIBIT 1
Basic Currency Swap Mechanics

At origination:

On each settlement date (including the maturity date):

At maturity:

principal amount. Similarly, the periodic cash flow that counterparty A is obligated to pay can be established as the product of the quoted fixed rate and the foreign currency–based principal amount.

Exhibit 2 lists some representative swap quotes for various maturities and currencies as of June 10, 1988. For comparative purposes, quotes for plain vanilla, fixed/floating interest rate swaps denominated exclusively in U.S. dollars are also presented. There are several in-

EXHIBIT 2
Representative Market Quotes for June 10, 1988,
for Fixed-Rate Foreign Currency Swaps versus U.S. Dollar LIBOR

		Swap Maturity				
Currency		2 years	3 years	5 years	7 years	10 years
Yen	Bid	4.78%	4.85%	5.10%	5.25%	5.36%
	Ask	4.84	4.92	5.16	5.32	5.42
Sterling	Bid	9.65	9.83	9.85	9.98	10.02
	Ask	9.75	9.93	9.95	10.08	10.12
Swiss franc	Bid	3.48	3.79	4.33	4.50	4.78
	Ask	3.52	3.85	4.38	4.55	4.85
Deutschemark	Bid	4.68	4.98	5.65	6.18	6.60
	Ask	4.78	5.08	5.75	6.28	6.70
U.S. dollar	Bid	8.65	8.89	9.20	9.46	9.67
	Ask	8.72	8.93	9.26	9.52	9.73

Source: Globecon.

teresting things to observe in this display. First, notice that since it is assumed that the floating-rate side of a swap is based on U.S. dollar LIBOR quoted flat, the market maker's bid-ask spread is built into the fixed-rate side of the market. As with single-currency interest rate swaps, the bid (ask) quote refers to the fixed rate the dealer is willing to pay (receive) in the swap transaction. For instance, in exchange for receiving U.S. dollar LIBOR on a five-year pound sterling swap, the dealer would be willing to pay a bid rate of 9.85 percent. Conversely, the same dealer would demand a sterling-based rate of 9.95 percent in exchange for the payment of U.S. dollar LIBOR. Second, across all of the different currencies and maturities, the bid-ask spread never exceeds 10 basis points. Since this spread represents the market maker's profit margin, it is clear that even though the market for currency swaps is not as large as that for interest rate swaps, it is nevertheless quite competitive. Third, notice that as the maturity of the swap lengthens, the level of the fixed rate rises. At any time there will exist a term structure of swap rates (or *swap yield curve*) unique to each currency, in this case upward-sloping in each market. Finally, it should be noted that it is not possible to directly compare all of the fixed rates listed in Exhibit 2 for a given maturity since different currencies use different rate quotation standards. For instance, the rates quoted for yen, sterling, and U.S. dollars assume semiannual payments and an "actual/365" day count, whereas those for Swiss francs and Deutschemarks assume annual payments and a "30/360" day count.[4]

To see how these quotation conventions translate into an exact set of cash flows over the life of the swap, consider the position of company XYZ, which has agreed to pay the dealer's offer rate of 9.95 percent on a five-year sterling swap against the receipt of six-month U.S. dollar LIBOR. Suppose that after reaching an initial agreement, the company and the swap market maker confirm the details of their transaction as follows:

Initiation (or trade) date: June 10, 1988
Termination date: June 10, 1993
Principal amounts: £20 million and US$36.4 million
Fixed-rate payer: Company XYZ
Fixed rate: 9.95 percent in pounds sterling
                               (semiannual bond basis)
Fixed-rate receiver: Swap dealer
Floating rate: Six-month LIBOR in U.S. dollars
                               (money market basis)
Settlement dates: June 10 and December 10
                               each year
LIBOR determination: Determined in advance,
                               paid in arrears

In this transaction the principal amounts to be exchanged at the inception and termination of the deal were calculated on the basis of the actual June 10, 1988, dollar/pound exchange rate of $1.82/pound. Notice also that although the sterling fixed rate of 9.95 percent and the U.S. dollar floating rate of LIBOR are both expressed on a semiannual basis, they are not directly comparable since the latter is based on an assumed 360-day year. Therefore, different formulas are needed for calculating the fixed-rate and floating-rate settlement payments.

---

[4]For a more complete description of the various interest rate quotation conventions, as well as the appropriate conversion formulas, see Antl (1986).

These are given as:

$$\text{Fixed-rate settlement payment} = 0.0995 \times \frac{\text{Number of days}}{365} \times £20 \text{ million}$$

and

$$\text{Floating-rate settlement payment} = \text{LIBOR} \times \frac{\text{Number of days}}{360} \times \$36.4 \text{ million}$$

where "number of days" represents the actual number of days between settlement dates. Once these temporal values have been established, the complete sequence of sterling-based fixed payments can be determined. The dollar-based floating payments, however, depend on future levels of LIBOR and can only be calculated six months in advance (e.g., the June 10, 1989, floating payment would have been based on the six-month LIBOR prevailing on December 10, 1988). Exhibit 3 gives a complete set of initial exchange and subsequent

EXHIBIT 3
Swap Cash Flows from Fixed-Rate Payer's Perspective (in millions)

Settlement Date	Number of Days	Assumed Current U.S. Dollar LIBOR	Fixed-Rate Payment	Floating-Rate Receipt
Initial exchange of principal:				
6/10/88	—	8.25%	($36.4)	(£ 20.0)
Coupon exchanges:				
12/10/88	183	8.50	£ 0.998	$ 1.527
6/10/89	182	8.75	0.992	1.564
12/10/89	183	9.00	0.998	1.619
6/10/90	182	9.25	0.992	1.656
12/10/90	183	9.50	0.998	1.712
6/10/91	182	9.75	0.992	1.748
12/10/91	183	9.50	0.998	1.804
6/10/92	183	9.25	0.998	1.758
12/10/92	183	9.00	0.998	1.712
Final coupon and principal exchange:				
6/10/93	182	—	0.992	1.656
			20.000	36.400

swap payments and receipts from the perspective of company XYZ, the fixed-rate payer, for an assumed LIBOR series. Since they are denominated in two different currencies, these payments and receipts are not reduced to a net basis—as they would in an interest rate swap—but could be actually paid in that manner after the appropriate translation at the respective spot market FX rates.

CREATING A "FIXED/FIXED" CURRENCY SWAP

Although the "fixed foreign currency versus floating U.S. dollar" convention is typical of the manner in which currency swaps are quoted by dealers, it is not necessarily the most useful way to package the cash flows for the ultimate end user. What if, for instance, counterparty B in Exhibit 1 had wanted to pay a *fixed* rate in U.S. dollars, instead of floating-rate LIBOR, in exchange for the receipt of a fixed rate in the foreign currency? In such a case, the "fixed/floating" industry quotation standard is not consistent with the "fixed/fixed" swap the end user desires. Fortunately, this is easily resolved by combining a "fixed/floating" currency swap with a "fixed/floating" U.S. dollar interest rate swap. To see how this works, suppose that counterparty B wants to enter into a five-year swap agreement in which it will pay a fixed rate in U.S. dollars and receive a fixed rate in pounds sterling. Using the rate quotes in Exhibit 2, this can be accomplished by the following two transactions with the swap market maker:

1. Pay U.S. dollar LIBOR in exchange for receiving the sterling bid rate of 9.85 percent.
2. Receive U.S. dollar LIBOR in exchange for paying the dollar ask rate of 9.26 percent.

Notice that since the second of these swaps involves only dollar-based cash flows, physical exchange of principal at origination and maturity is required only for the first. Exhibit 4 provides a graphical display of the sequence of exchanges that will occur on the settlement dates.

The key point to recognize from the preceding discussion is that by supplementing the conventional currency swap with a plain vanilla interest rate swap, the structure can be easily configured to offer a more desirable pattern of cash flows to the end user. In fact, since

EXHIBIT 4
**Creating a Five-Year, U.S. Dollar versus Sterling Fixed/Fixed Currency
Swap** (payments on settlement dates)

"Receive fixed sterling and pay U.S. dollar LIBOR" currency swap:

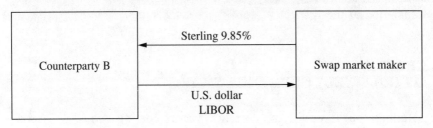

"Pay fixed dollar and receive U.S. dollar LIBOR" interest rate swap:

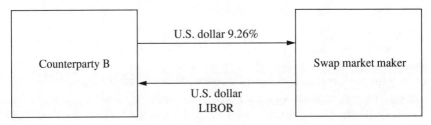

Net transaction: "receive fixed sterling and pay fixed dollar" currency swap:

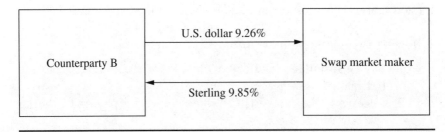

both of the hypothetical swap transactions in Exhibit 4 were done with
the same market maker, both counterparties are likely to regard the
net transaction as a single position to minimize documentation and
bookkeeping. Similarly, the swap dealer will probably quote such a
deal in a "prepackaged" form. That is, regardless of how it books the
transaction internally, the market maker is likely to offer counterparty

B a quote of "pay U.S. dollar 9.26 percent and receive sterling 9.85 percent" directly rather than as two separate agreements.[5]

A CURRENCY SWAP APPLICATION

An archetypal example of a "fixed/fixed" currency swap involves a corporation issuing debt in one currency and then using a swap to transform that debt into another currency. Suppose that a U.S. dollar–based firm issues five-year, par-value Euroyen bonds in the amount of ¥5 billion. The bonds pay an annual coupon of 5 percent, or ¥250 million. The corporation then enters a five-year currency swap with a commercial bank counterparty to convert the cash flows to U.S. dollar funding.[6] The corporation initially receives $40 million in exchange for the ¥5 billion, based on the current spot exchange rate, which is taken to be ¥125/dollar. Then, on each annual coupon payment date, the firm receives ¥250 million and pays $4 million. At maturity the firm receives ¥5.25 billion (principal plus the final coupon payment) and pays $44 million. Exhibit 5 portrays the overall transaction in box-and-arrow format. The upper panel shows the cash flows at origination (date 0), the middle panel at the intermediate coupon payment dates (dates 1–4), and the lower panel at maturity (date 5).

A currency swap that is attached to a capital market instrument is usually motivated by an apparent arbitrage opportunity. For any number of possible reasons, the cost of funds via the swap appears to be lower than by a direct debt obligation. The reasons are varied: taxes, regulations, saturation of one investor base and strong appeal in another, or subsidized financing. The key point is that any reduction in the *all-in cost of funds,* that is, inclusive of brokerage fees and underwriting commissions, must be sufficient to compensate for the credit risk inherent in the currency swap. Although such arbitrage

---

[5]It is also possible to combine two currency swaps having different fixed rates against LIBOR to form a "fixed/fixed" swap that does not involve U.S. dollars at all. For example, using the quotes in Exhibit 2, a "pay Swiss franc 4.38 percent and receive U.S. dollar LIBOR" five-year swap could be combined with a "receive Deutschemark 5.65 percent and pay U.S. dollar LIBOR" five-year swap from the same market maker to create a "pay Swiss franc 4.38 percent and receive Deutschemark 5.65 percent" agreement.

[6]The counterparty need not be a bank, but in many swap transactions a commercial bank stands as the intermediary between the ultimate corporate end users. See Brown and Smith (1988) for a discussion of the motivations for banks to operate in these markets.

EXHIBIT 5
Yen/Dollar Fixed/Fixed Currency Swap

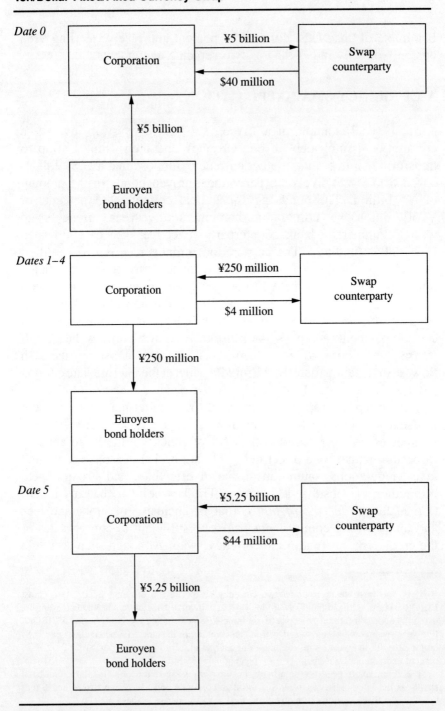

Date 0

Corporation → ¥5 billion → Swap counterparty

Swap counterparty → $40 million → Corporation

Euroyen bond holders → ¥5 billion → Corporation

Dates 1–4

Swap counterparty → ¥250 million → Corporation

Corporation → $4 million → Swap counterparty

Corporation → ¥250 million → Euroyen bond holders

Date 5

Swap counterparty → ¥5.25 billion → Corporation

Corporation → $44 million → Swap counterparty

Corporation → ¥5.25 billion → Euroyen bond holders

opportunities do appear from time to time, especially in the more thinly traded currencies, the general efficiency of the global financial marketplace acts to close these "windows." That is, exploitation of the opportunity itself eventually leads to further rate adjustments that tend to eliminate the arbitrage advantage. But the first mover can often enjoy a significant gain. Currency swaps can also be used as hedging or speculative transactions, whether or not they are attached to a specific asset or liability. A swap could be entered to intentionally increase or decrease the user's exposure to a particular currency, depending on the decision maker's view on future interest and FX rates.

A Capital Market Interpretation of the Currency Swap Example

A useful way to view a currency swap is a cash flow diagram. Exhibit 6 illustrates, from the corporation's perspective, how the swap transforms the original yen debt issue into U.S. dollar funding. Cash inflows to the corporation are above the time line; outflows from the corporation are below. Yen amounts are represented by the shaded boxes, dollar amounts by the open boxes. The upper panel shows the scheduled cash flows on the Euroyen note issue. The middle panel shows the spot market FX transaction and the currency swap. Netting the inflows and outflows for each date leads to fixed-rate U.S. dollar funding, shown in the lower panel.

The middle panel in Exhibit 6 is the source of the capital market interpretation of a currency swap. The cash flows are the same as if the corporation had issued a 10 percent fixed-rate, five-year $40 million bond at par value (the open-box cash flows) and, at the same time, bought a 5 percent fixed-rate, five-year ¥5 billion bond also at par value (the shaded-box cash flows). In sum, a "pay fixed dollars and receive fixed yen" currency swap is equivalent to a short position in a U.S. dollar bond and a long position in a yen bond. That, combined with the initial short position in the Euroyen note, results in a net short position in a dollar bond—in other words, synthetic fixed-rate U.S. dollar funding.

In lieu of a currency swap, the corporation could enter these prescribed capital market transactions using, for example, parallel or back-to-back loans. However, there are certain efficiencies to the swap. First, it is an off-balance-sheet transaction given current U.S.

EXHIBIT 6
Cash Flow Representation of a Synthetic Fixed-Rate Dollar Bond

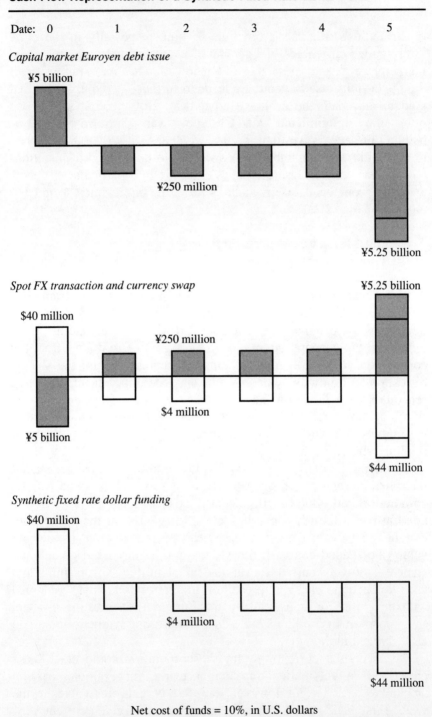

Net cost of funds = 10%, in U.S. dollars

accounting practices, so the corporation's debt-equity ratio is unchanged. Second, the underwriting fees and commissions of a capital market debt issue are avoided. Third, and most important, the currency swap minimizes the credit risk to the corporation, as discussed earlier.

An FX Forward Market Interpretation of the Currency Swap Example

The currency swap also can be viewed as a series of FX forward transactions at pre-agreed exchange rates. As a preliminary, however, suppose that there exists a long-dated FX forward market at rates consistent with *interest rate parity,* which implies that there are no obvious covered interest arbitrage opportunities. That series of forward rates would be as follows:

Spot	¥125/$
One-year forward	¥119.318/$
Two-year forward	¥113.895/$
Three-year forward	¥108.718/$
Four-year forward	¥103.776/$
Five-year forward	¥99.059/$

This assumes a five-year 10 percent interest rate in dollars, a five-year 5 percent interest rate in yen, and a spot market exchange rate of ¥125/dollar. The forward rates are based on a forward premium on yen (or discount on the dollar) of 4.545 percent, calculated as $(0.05 - 0.10)/1.10 = -0.04545$. Then $119.318 = 125 \times (1 - 0.04545)$, $113.895 = 119.318 \times (1 - 0.04545)$, and so forth.

The transactions in the middle panel of Exhibit 6 appear to be *one* spot market exchange at date 0 and *five* "off-market" forward market exchanges at dates 1–5. The implicit transactions are:

Date	Type of Contract	Implicit Exchange Rate	Principal
0	Spot	¥125/$	$40 million
1	One-year forward	¥62.5/$	$4 million
2	Two-year forward	¥62.5/$	$4 million
3	Three-year forward	¥62.5/$	$4 million
4	Four-year forward	¥62.5/$	$4 million
5	Five-year forward	¥119.318/$	$44 million

The fifth-year transaction is a composite of $4 million at ¥62.5/dollar and $40 million at ¥125/dollar. The given rate of ¥119.318/dollar is the weighted average: (¥62.5/dollar) (4/44) + (¥125/dollar) (40/44).

The corporation, as the payer of dollars and receiver of yen on the currency swap, has entered a contract in which it *sells* yen at the spot market rate at date 0, agrees to *buy* yen forward at a "worse-than-expected" exchange rate at dates 1–4, and then agrees to *buy* yen at a "better-than-expected" rate at date 5. On the first four coupon payment dates the corporation exchanges $4 million for ¥250 million—an implicit exchange rate of ¥62.5/dollar. Compared to the forward rates that would be consistent with interest rate parity, which range from ¥119.318/dollar to ¥103.776/dollar, the rates imbedded in the swap are clearly unfavorable. However, at the maturity date the corporation exchanges $44 million for ¥5.25 billion. That implicit exchange rate, ¥119.318/dollar, is better than the rate implied by interest rate parity, which would be ¥99.059/dollar. Moreover, the final transaction is based on $44 million, and the four others are based on only $4 million.

Notice that the corporation could choose to issue the Euroyen note and buy the required amounts of yen in the forward market. In reality, however, trading in FX markets tends to be focused on three- to six-month contracts and is quite thin after one to two years forward. Nevertheless, given the assumed forward rates and interest rate parity, the corporation could convert to U.S. dollar funding, as shown in Exhibit 7. Note that the cost of funds, calculated as the internal rate of return, is again 10 percent. The only difference is that the currency swap structure provides for level coupon payments, whereas the FX forward structure requires increasing dollar payments, rather like a deep-discount "step-up" coupon bond. The payments increase each period in line with the forward discount on the dollar.

CREDIT RISK ON A CURRENCY SWAP

The credit risk on a currency swap, although always less than the risk on a parallel or back-to-back loan structure, can still be substantial. The amount of the loss if the counterparty defaults will depend on the number of remaining payments, the level of interest rates in each currency, and the exchange rate at the time of default. These factors

EXHIBIT 7
Cash Flow Representation Using FX Forward Transactions

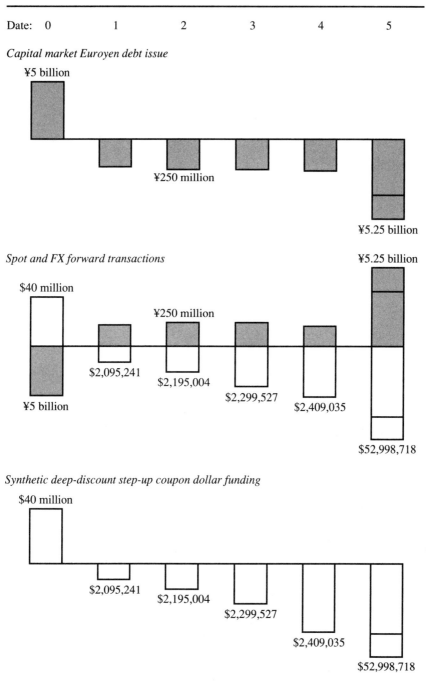

Date: 0   1   2   3   4   5

Capital market Euroyen debt issue

¥5 billion

¥250 million

¥5.25 billion

Spot and FX forward transactions

¥5.25 billion

$40 million

¥250 million

¥5 billion

$2,095,241

$2,195,004

$2,299,527

$2,409,035

$52,998,718

Synthetic deep-discount step-up coupon dollar funding

$40 million

$2,095,241

$2,195,004

$2,299,527

$2,409,035

$52,998,718

Net cost of funds = 10%, in U.S. dollars

are summarized by the mark-to-market value of the swap. Before examining an example of this calculation, it is useful to discuss some of the characteristics of the credit risk on swap transactions.

One should distinguish *potential* from *actual* credit risk. Potential credit risk is a forward-looking assessment of possible movements in interest and exchange rates and the likelihood that the counterparty will experience financial distress. Unlike a funding transaction, potential credit risk on a swap is always bilateral. Each counterparty must assess the credit risk of the other and consider that risk in the pricing of the swap. For banks, this often involves the inability to require the same set of restrictive covenants as on loan documents. For instance, restrictions limiting the sale of particular assets or requiring the maintenance of certain financial ratios might be hard to negotiate when the counterparty could ask the same of the bank.

Actual credit risk is the immediate loss that results if the counterparty defaults. This risk is zero at origination, assuming the swap reflects current market rates. Presumably, the corporation could enter a new currency swap with identical terms with another market maker if the original counterparty were to walk away from the deal. This, of course, neglects any up-front legal and administrative costs. The credit loss would be zero since the swap at origination has an economic value of zero. Note that the swap does have a valued role in the context of the corporation's financial structure. Having issued the Euroyen notes, to continue the previous example, the corporation has reduced exposure to currency risk since, by assumption, it has dollar-based revenues. But as a separate transaction, the swap does not have economic value in that it could not be sold to a third party for a profit.

After origination, the actual credit risk will shift toward one side of the transaction as interest and exchange rates change. However, the actual credit risk is always unilateral in that a swap is a "zero-sum game." One side's loss is the other side's gain; the swap can have positive economic value to only one counterparty at a time.

Actual credit risk is based on current market interest and exchange rate data. The economic value in dollars of the currency swap to the corporation is the present value of the remaining yen inflows, which are evaluated at the relevant interest rate in yen and converted to dollars at the spot market exchange rate, less the present value of the dollar outflows, which are evaluated at the relevant interest rate in dollars. This can be summarized as:

$$V_t = \frac{(PV_¥)_t}{(¥/\$)_t} - (PV_\$)_t$$

where V_t is the economic value, $PV_¥$ and $PV_\$$ are the present values of the yen and dollar flows, and $¥/\$$ is the exchange rate, all as of time t. The economic value of the swap to the corporation's counterparty at time t is simply the negative of V_t.

As seen in the equation, V_t will increase when $PV_¥$ increases or when $¥/\$$ or $PV_\$$ decreases. Since the nominal cash flows are known in advance, the factors that affect the present values are the relevant interest rates in each currency.[7] Recall that the currency swap can be interpreted as the corporation having bought a yen bond and sold a dollar bond. The value of a long position in a yen bond is heightened when yen interest rates fall or the yen appreciates against the dollar. The value of a short position in a dollar bond is heightened when dollar interest rates rise. Therefore, in terms of actual credit risk, the corporation in the example is exposed to a weaker dollar, higher rates in the dollar market, and lower rates in the yen market. When the economic value of a swap increases, its actual credit risk increases, since an economic loss would be suffered if the counterparty were to default.

The equation also suggests why a "fixed/fixed" currency swap has more credit risk than the "fixed/floating" or "floating/floating" varieties. A floating-rate instrument by design removes exposure to interest rate changes. For instance, if the swap were for a fixed rate in yen against U.S. dollar LIBOR, the $PV_\$$ term should remain at (or very close to) par value. Then the swap entails exposure only to the yen interest rate and the exchange rate. In the extreme, the economic value of a "floating/floating" currency swap, say, U.S. dollar

---

[7]Actually, the value will depend on the entire term structure of interest rates. Here, for simplicity, we assume that the term structures in each currency are flat, so that a single interest rate summarizes the market.

LIBOR versus Deutschemark LIBOR, deviates from zero only due to exchange rate fluctuations.

A numerical example will clarify the calculation of economic value. Suppose that at date 1, immediately *prior* to the initial exchange of ¥250 million and $4 million, the yen has appreciated to ¥120/dollar, four-year dollar interest rates are 11 percent, and four-year yen rates are 4.5 percent. Note that the relevant time to maturity on interest rates is now four years. Then V_1 is calculated as:

$$(PV_¥)_1 = ¥250 \text{ M} + \frac{¥250 \text{ M}}{1.045} + \frac{¥250 \text{ M}}{(1.045)^2} + \frac{¥250 \text{ M}}{(1.045)^3} + \frac{¥5,250 \text{ M}}{(1.045)^4}$$

$$= ¥5,339,688,142$$

$$(PV_\$)_1 = \$4 \text{ M} + \frac{\$4 \text{ M}}{1.11} + \frac{\$4 \text{ M}}{(1.11)^2} + \frac{\$4 \text{ M}}{(1.11)^3} + \frac{\$44 \text{ M}}{(1.11)^4}$$

$$= \$42,759,022$$

$$V_1 = \frac{¥5,339,688,142}{¥120/\$} - \$42,759,022$$

$$= \$1,738,379$$

where M represents millions. Since $V_1 > 0$, the swap has positive economic value to the corporation, and its loss would be over $1.7 million if the counterparty were to default. Notice that even if the corporation itself were in financial distress, it would not default on the swap. Instead, the corporation would seek to sell the swap to a third party (subject to the approval of the counterparty, since there is potential credit risk) to capture some or all of that economic value. The swap has become an asset that maintains its value only if the corporation continues to meet the terms of the agreement.

The *mark-to-market* valuation used in the preceding analysis is essentially equivalent to a *replacement swap* methodology. Suppose that on date 1 the counterparty does default just prior to the initial exchange. The immediate need for ¥250 million can be satisfied on the spot FX market for a purchase price of $2,083,333 at the going rate of ¥120/dollar. To cover the remaining outflows on the Euroyen note, the corporation would need to enter a new, replacement currency swap. As of date 1, four-year currency swaps presumably are available for receipt of a yen rate of 4.5 percent and payment of a dollar rate of 11 percent, since those are the assumed current coupon rates on par-value bonds. The corporation, however, needs 5 percent in yen and therefore is willing to pay a somewhat higher rate in dollars than 11 percent. Assume that the terms agreeable to the new counterparty are for the corporation to receive yen payments of ¥250 million on dates 2–4 and ¥5,250 million on date 5, and to make dollar payments of $4,824,240 on dates 2–4 and $46,490,907 on date 5. That turns out to be 5 percent in yen and 11.5782 percent in dollars, based on a principal of $41,666,667 (or ¥5 billion).[8]

Compared to the orginal swap, the corporation has a net gain of $1,916,667 ($4,000,000 − $2,083,333) on date 1; a net loss of $824,240 ($4,824,240 − $4,000,000) on dates 2, 3, and 4; and a net loss of $2,490,907 ($46,490,907 − $44,000,000) on date 5. The net present value of those dollar cash flows, as of date 1 and evaluated at 11 percent, is $1,738,379. That equals V_1, the mark-to-market value calculated.

The Timing of Default and the Asymmetry of Credit Risk Exposure

The example just presented demonstrates that the credit risk on the currency swap from the perspective of the corporation increases as the yen interest rate falls, as the dollar interest rate rises, and as the yen appreciates against the dollar. Given the assumptions, the loss would be over $1.7 million if the corporation's counterparty were to default prior to the initial exchange. Notice, however, that the counterparty would not default prior to the initial exchange if there were any way to defer the event of default itself until *after* that transaction. Clearly, the counterparty gains by completing the date 1 transaction as agreed. The corporation is scheduled to pay $4 million in exchange for ¥250

---

[8]The new four-year, fixed/fixed plain vanilla currency swap would be 4.5 percent in yen versus 11 percent in U.S. dollars, based on an exchange rate of ¥120/dollar. In order to receive 5 percent rather than 4.5 percent, the corporation will have to pay more than 11 percent. The value of those additional 50 basis points in yen is approximately 57.82 basis points in U.S. dollars. That approximation is calculated as the present value of a four-year annuity of 50 basis points discounted at 4.5 percent. Then that present value is converted to a four-year annuity of 57.82 basis points per year by using 11 percent as the discount factor. This approximation technique for converting a value of a basis point across currencies assumes flat yield curves in each market.

million, in effect buying yen at an off-market rate of ¥62.5/dollar rather than at the on-market rate of ¥120/dollar. The counterparty could buy the ¥250 million on the spot market for $2,083,333 and enjoy an immediate cash inflow of $1,916,667. Therefore, the date 1 effective credit risk on the swap from the corporation's perspective is seriously understated at $1,738,379. Since there is no economic incentive for the counterparty to default prior to the exchange, the credit risk is more aptly stated at $3,655,046—the value of the swap immediately *after* the initial transaction.[9]

The presence of a "default timing option" complicates the analysis of the credit risk on a currency swap. To see an extreme case of this, suppose that the counterparty holds only the currency swap and that it can choose to default at any time. As shown, it would complete the initial exchange, selling yen at an "overvalued" exchange rate of ¥62.5/dollar when the market rate is ¥120/dollar. Then the decision to default would be deferred until date 2, since there is no rational reason to "prematurely" exercise the default option. Instead, it can wait and observe market rates at date 2 at no cost. The choice to default before or after the second scheduled exchange again will depend on the spot market exchange rate relative to ¥62.5/dollar. If it can continue to sell "overvalued" yen, it will complete the terms of the agreement, delivering the ¥250 million in exchange for $4 million (i.e., not defaulting).

This process will continue until the final exchange, at date 5. Since that payment contains the reexchange of principal, the implicit forward exchange rate is ¥119.318/dollar. If the spot rate on previous dates has remained above ¥62.5/dollar, the counterparty would not have defaulted since each exchange resulted in a net gain. But the counterparty would default if the date 5 spot market exchange rate is below ¥119.318/dollar. Using the series of forward rates consistent with interest rate parity as measures of future spot market exchange rates, the likelihood of default by the counterparty is seen to be very small on dates 1 to 4 (since the dollar is expected to be stronger than ¥62.5) and then large on date 5 (since the dollar is expected to be weaker than ¥119.318).

---

[9]This amount can be found by removing the ¥250 M and $4 M terms from the calculations of $(PV_¥)_1$ and $(PV_$)_1$ in the preceding equation and then solving for V_1.

This demonstrates the essential *asymmetry* in the credit risk on a "fixed/fixed" currency swap. Given that the swap can be interpreted as a series of off-market implicit FX forward contracts, one side buys and the other sells an "overvalued" currency on all the settlement dates except the final one, when the roles are reversed. In the example, the counterparty is very unlikely to default at any time prior to the final exchange date. In contrast, the corporation represents a credit risk on dates 1 to 4 from the perspective of the counterparty, but much less so on date 5. Therefore, the credit risk on a currency swap is due to the *design* of the contract as well as to the stochastic nature of interest and FX rates. In particular, the design includes a single fixed exchange rate (representing the exchange of coupon flows) for each of the settlement dates.

Another way of interpreting this credit risk asymmetry is that the implicit FX forward contracts that make up the currency swap do not have zero expected values at origination. Although the sum of the expected values is zero (hence, the economic value is zero at origination), the first four exchanges are positive to the counterparty and the fifth is negative. Since there is no incentive to default on a contract that has positive value, the time profile of potential credit risk differs for the two counterparties to the swap. For the corporation, the risk that the other party defaults is concentrated at date 5; for the bank counterparty, the risk that the corporation defaults is spread over dates 1 to 4. Notice that the asymmetry is fundamentally due to the different levels of interest rates in the two currencies and increases with that difference. In general, exchanges prior to maturity will have positive (negative) expected values to the payer (receiver) of the lower-rate currency, and the final exchange at maturity will have a negative (positive) expected value.

The idea of a default timing option is that there might be circumstances when it is strategic for a firm to defer or advance the event of default. Notice that for a traditional debt instrument there is not likely to be a similar economic advantage to deferring default. Although there may be scenarios where postponing bankruptcy itself is advantageous given legal costs and reentry barriers, there is no apparent motive to continue payments on a particular debt obligation once bankruptcy proceedings have begun. In fact, creditors would no doubt insist that payments *not* be made to maintain a financial liability (other than, perhaps, to employees and some critical suppliers). A currency swap, however, is an exchange agreement that, with some fortuitous shifts in market interest and FX rates, can transform itself from a liability into an asset. A debt instrument, however, is always a liability. Thus, a swap that has positive economic value, or one that has negative economic value but an immediate positive cash inflow (as in the preceding numerical example), will be honored, and all creditors would concur with that decision.

Counterparties to currency swaps typically deal with the possibility of this default timing option by including a *cross-default* clause in the documentation. This extends the specified events of default beyond nonexecution of the contract itself. For example, the swap is clearly in default if the corporation does not deliver the $4 million on date 1 or if the counterparty does not deliver the ¥250 million. A cross-default clause would typically include nonpayment of any other contractual obligation, such as on borrowings or bankruptcy proceedings being filed against the party. If the cross-default clause were operative prior to date 1 on the currency swap in the example, the corporation could be exonerated from completing the unfavorable exchange and exacerbating its loss (from approximately $1.7 million to $3.6 million). Notice that this clause would not help if the counterparty had no other business beyond the swap, but in practice that is rare.

A very similar clause often included in swap documents is a *netting* requirement, which is used if there are multiple agreements between the counterparties, as is common for major corporations and commercial and investment banks. This prevents a counterparty from "cherry-picking" in bankruptcy proceedings, that is, honoring swaps that have positive economic value (or currently positive cash inflows) and defaulting on those that have negative values. All swap transactions between the two parties would be combined, so that offsetting exposures would cancel.

SUMMARY AND CONCLUSIONS

Currency swaps evolved over the decade of the 1980s from customized, broker-oriented transactions to much more standardized, dealer-oriented contracts. Market makers now quote rates for a number of currencies, usually in the format of the foreign fixed rate versus U.S. dollar LIBOR. Applications of currency swaps range from exploitation of an arbitrage opportunity arising from some (perhaps temporary) mispricing across international capital markets to actively managing FX risk exposure. Swaps now compete with exchange-traded FX futures and over-the-counter FX forwards as instruments for currency risk management. The latter products can be viewed as substitutes for short-term maturities under a year or two. For longer-term maturities, however, currency swaps extend the market for risk management since the other products are either nonexistent or thinly traded at such levels.

The credit risk on a currency swap results from the stochastic nature of interest and foreign exchange rates as well as from the design of the agreement itself. That is, even if future market rates could be accurately predicted, there would still be credit risk. Moreover, there would still be asymmetric credit risk, especially if there is a difference in the levels of interest rates between the two currencies. This is because a plain vanilla "fixed/fixed" currency swap can be interpreted as a series of implicit off-market FX forward contracts. The forward rates are "off-market" in that they differ from the forward rates implied by interest rate parity. The asymmetry arises because the exchanges prior to maturity tend to have positive expected value to the payer of the lower-rate currency, and the final exchange at maturity tends to have positive expected value to the payer of the higher-rate currency. Therefore, the timing of credit risk exposure is asymmetric — one party is mostly concerned about the early exchanges, the other about the final one.

In principle, the credit risk on a swap could be reduced by periodic mark-to-market valuation and settlement. However, the swap market in recent years has prospered in large part because of its flexibility and ease of operational management. That is in part because of the absence of margin accounts and mark-to-market settlement. Commercial banks, which are already heavily in the credit business, have assumed the role of intermediaries to bear the credit risk themselves and to be compensated in the bid-ask pricing of the swaps. Therefore, mark-to-market settlement has not been widely used except with notably weak counterparties.

Collateral and credit enhancements, such as standby letters of credit, can also be used to manage credit risk. However, there are limits to the use of these requirements since the credit risk on a swap is bilateral. Unlike the case for a debt instrument, each counterparty weighs the credit risk of the other. One cannot ask for restrictive covenants without having to agree to the same. Collateral and credit enhancements are usually used only when there is a significant imbalance in the relative credit standings of the two counterparties.

REFERENCES

Antl, B. "Yield Calculation Principles," in *Euromoney Swap Finance,* vol. 1 (B. Antl, ed). London: Euromoney Publications, 1986, pp. 97–103.

Beidleman, Carl R. *Financial Swaps.* Homewood, Ill.: Dow Jones-Irwin, 1985.

Brown, Keith C., and Donald J. Smith. "Recent Innovations in Interest Rate Risk Management and the Reintermediation of Commercial Banking," *Financial Management,* Winter 1988, pp. 45–58.

Brown, K., and D. Smith. "Plain Vanilla Swaps: Market Structures, Applications, and Credit Risk," in *Interest Rate Swaps* (C. Beidleman, ed.). Homewood, Ill.: Business One Irwin, 1990, pp. 61–96.

Felgren, Steven D. "Interest Rate Swaps: Use, Risk, and Prices," *New England Economic Review,* November/December 1987, pp. 22–32.

Marshall, John F., and Kenneth Kapner. *Understanding Swap Finance.* Cincinnati: South-Western, 1990.

Rawls, S., and C. Smithson. "The Evolution of Risk Management Products," *Journal of Applied Corporate Finance,* vol. 1, no. 4, Winter 1989, pp. 18–26.

Smith, Clifford W., Jr., Charles W. Smithson, and D. Sykes Wilford. *Managing Financial Risk.* New York: Harper & Row, 1990.

Walmsley, J. *The New Financial Instruments.* New York: John Wiley & Sons, 1988.

CHAPTER 4

DEVELOPMENT OF THE CROSS CURRENCY SWAP MARKET

Michael Wood
Dresdner Bank AG
Frankfurt

INTRODUCTION

The cross currency swap as we know it today is a product used world-wide by banks and corporations and forms an integral part of the international capital markets. In contrast to other, more traditional banking products such as loans and deposits, the swap has only recently become a standard financial service. It is not possible to pinpoint when this occurred, since it is the result of a continuous development process. In retrospect, however, we can observe certain milestones and thereby obtain a better understanding of the characteristics of this product and of the current state of the cross currency swap market.

In view of the similarities between the forward foreign exchange market and the cross currency swap market, it is necessary to define at the outset what is meant by the term *cross currency swap*. Taking the ISDA (International Swap Dealers Association) definition (as used for the ISDA market survey statistics), "a Currency Swap is a transaction between two Counterparties involving periodic interest exchanges calculated on the Notional Principal of two currencies (and usually involving one or more exchanges of principal amounts of the two currencies)." In a forward foreign exchange transaction, the interest payments are in effect compounded and netted out at the final exchange of capital so that the forward exchange rate is quoted at either a premium or a discount to the spot rate.

This distinction between a cross currency swap and a forward currency contract, based on the timing of the interest payments, is somewhat artificial since in practice the markets are closely linked. For example, a zero-coupon currency swap is in effect a forward foreign exchange transaction. A fixed/fixed currency swap can also be synthetically created—although the exact cash flows will be slightly different—through the use of a consecutive series of forward foreign exchange transactions. Because of these links, some banks handle their long-term forward foreign exchange business and their cross currency swap business in the same trading area.

The observations that follow on the standardization and development of the currency swap market relate to currency swap transactions as defined here.

BEGINNINGS

The swap technique, exchanging one currency or commodity for another at a given date and reexchanging these currencies or commodities at a fixed later date, goes back many years. Currency and gold swaps have been carried out by central banks for some time. These were usually of a short-term nature, with the aim of obtaining liquidity in the acquired currency, often with a view to intervention on the foreign exchange markets. Such short-term currency swaps have been practiced for some time also in the foreign exchange markets, where arbitrage between the short-term money markets and the forward foreign exchange market is often the driving force.

Long-term Forward Foreign Exchange Transactions

In the 1970s some longer-dated forward foreign exchange transactions were arranged that were linked to capital market or credit operations. Examples are the swaps between Bos Kalis Westminster NV and ICI Finance Ltd., the U.S. dollar/French franc swap arranged for the Republic of Venezuela to meet the French franc financing obligations in connection with the construction of the Caracas rail system, and the swap arranged in connection with a Deutschemark–Eurobond issue for RoyLease.

However, only a few of these deals became publicly known; details of these transactions are not generally available even today, and the parties' motivation for entering into these transactions is consequently a matter for speculation.

Parallel Loans

Accompanying the development in the foreign exchange market were transactions arranged, although motivated by entirely different reasons, in the parallel and back-to-back loan markets. These were generally long-term agreements involving the lending and borrowing of capital amounts together with intermediate payments of interest. Through the parallel loan construction, U.S. dollar liquidity for example, could be provided for a UK subsidiary, in effect by using the parent company's own liquidity:

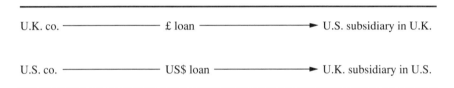

U.K. co. ——————— £ loan ———————————► U.S. subsidiary in U.K.

U.S. co. ——————— US$ loan ———————————► U.K. subsidiary in U.S.

During the time of exchange controls in the United Kingdom, such constructions were often used to avoid acquiring investment dollars through the foreign exchange market, which would have incurred the added cost of the investment premium. Since the investment premium at that time represented a substantial cost, parties were willing to pay significant front-end fees to arrangers able to provide suitable partners and with the necessary expertise in producing the documentation. Such arrangers, who could earn between 0.5 and 1 percent flat on a transaction, were traditionally the UK merchant banks and stockbrokers. Commercial banks at this stage were probably aware of such business but were almost certainly not actively involved in it.

IBM/World Bank Swap

The major milestone in the development of the cross currency swap market was the transaction arranged in August 1981 by Salomon Brothers between IBM and the World Bank. This transaction has been extensively commented on, since it contained many new features. Perhaps the most important aspect of all was the timing of this particular transaction, which came at a turning point in the history of capital markets.

Background

During the previous decade the international banking industry had been busy recycling OPEC deposits through the syndicated loan market to industrialized and developing countries. In 1981, however, Mexico announced that it was suspending the repayment of principal on its outstanding international debt. Poland had already entered into rescheduling negotiations with its bank creditors. It was relatively clear that if Mexico was having difficulty meeting its payment obligations, other countries in Latin America would be in a similar situation, and it seemed probable that other countries worldwide would also be affected.

In other words, within a relatively short time, a major part of international lending business came to a total standstill. Commercial bank lenders were faced with (1) the real possibility that even short- and medium-term debt would be on their balance sheets for a long period of time, thus adversely affecting their liquidity ratios; (2) the fact that fee income from these loans had dried up; and (3) the prospect that many staff employed in the syndicated loan market would have to be redeployed. Under these circumstances banks were looking for future business that, ideally, would not affect their balance sheet ratios and that would in addition provide fee or margin income.

It was against this background that the details of the IBM/World Bank swap emerged.[1]

Significance

The swap between IBM and the World Bank was the first transaction in which the details and the motivation behind the swap were made public. Swap transactions previously had remained confidential: arrangers had no interest in propagating "trade secrets." In this particular instance, the World Bank appeared to be keen to publicize

---

[1]Fuller details of the IBM/World Bank swap are contained in David Bock's article in the *Euromoney* Special Financing Report *Swap Financing Techniques*, 1984, pp. 135–140.

the transaction and to establish itself as a major participant in the swap market in order to assist its refinancing program.

Also of significance is the fact that this was not a typical back-to-back or parallel loan construction between companies seeking to find ways around regulatory restrictions; it was a transaction involving top-quality issuers in the capital markets.

Last but not least, this was the first time that a currency swap was used to arbitrage between capital markets, that is, where a capital market issue was done solely for the purpose of swapping into another currency. Interestingly, this swap involved two different motives, both of which were to play a major part in subsequent currency swaps: the World Bank's objective to achieve the best possible rate on its debt, and IBM's management of its currency exposure. (Through the swap IBM hedged its existing Swiss franc and Deutschemark debt into U.S. dollars and at the same time realized a profit through the appreciation of the dollar against these currencies since the time this debt was originally issued.)

The techniques used for valuing and constructing the cash flows for this transaction are basically the same techniques as those employed today.

Benefits

Commercial banks were quick to exploit the benefits implicit in this transaction:

- The currency swap transaction would avoid direct impact on the balance sheet. Forward FX contracts are usually noted off the balance sheet, and under the then-current supervisory regulations, only on-balance-sheet items entailed capital requirements. Such off-balance-sheet items did not require any additional capital, either in respect to any credit exposure risk or in respect to on-balance-sheet liquidity ratios.
- This swap technique opened the possibility for banks to issue medium- and long-term debt in the capital markets, swapping this subsequently into the floating-rate funds that they desired—usually based on six-month LIBOR (London Interbank Offered Rate)—to match their floating-rate assets. Such transactions could be arranged to provide floating-rate funds at an attractive margin under LIBOR. In these early days it was not uncommon for the swap to produce funding for the bank

at costs of 0.5 percent p.a. (per annum) or more below LIBOR. Indeed, under certain circumstances (for example, by issuing in the Euro-Australian dollar bond market) margins in excess of 0.75 percent p.a. were achieved.

- By being able to raise medium- and long-term debt through capital market issues, banks could extend the maturity of their liabilities, which traditionally had been based on short-term deposits, and thereby improve their liquidity ratios.
- The close connection between currency swaps and capital market transactions opened up possibilities for banks to generate fee income from the capital markets, reinforcing the tendency for transactions to move from the syndicated loan market to the international bond markets.

To summarize: The World Bank/IBM transaction pointed the way for banks to earn margin income and at the same time manage their balance sheet ratios, and for corporations to raise attractively priced funds and/or actively manage their currency exposure.

Under these circumstances, the back-to-back and parallel loan constructions, which usually had the disadvantage of affecting the balance sheet, receded into the background, since the same cash flow effect could be created through a currency swap. The subsequent abolition of UK exchange controls also reduced the rationale behind the parallel loan market.

Cross Currency Swap Structure Evolution

The cash flow of a typical cross currency swap (for example, Swiss francs against U.S. dollars) would be as follows:

Initial exchange	A ——————— SF capital ——————— ► B	
	B ——————— US\$ capital ——————— ► A	
Subsequent exchanges of interest and capital	A ——————— US\$ interest and US\$ capital ——————— ► B	
	B ——————— SF interest and SF capital ——————— ► A	

The fundamental structural difference between a cross currency swap and a long-dated forward exchange contract—the physical exchange of interest amounts during the life of the swaps—created new possibilities for the participants:

- Interest amounts need not be defined at the outset; they could be based on a variable-rate formula (e.g., six-month LIBOR). The cross currency interest rate swap was born.
- The interest payments could be constructed and linked exactly to match the payments corresponding to the underlying capital market transactions. With the intermediate interest payments fully matched and, hence, with no risk of change in the actual reinvestment or borrowing rates, it was possible to extend the maturity of currency swaps out to 10 or even 15 years, the only limitations being the maturities available in the capital market and the creditworthiness of the swap counterparty.

GROWTH AND STANDARDIZATION

Within a couple of years following the IBM/World Bank transaction, the basic economic parameters for the cross currency swap market were established.

Users

The main users were (1) commercial banks interested in raising long-term funds in whatever capital market offered the best arbitrage possibilities at the time and (2) corporate counterparties interested either in obtaining funds from markets not usually available to them or in managing their foreign currency exposure.

Detailed statistics of the early market are not generally available. Transactions were generally arranged on a one-off basis, with an investment bank seeking to find suitable counterparties with matching interests.

In view of the attractive arrangement fees available, commercial banks soon moved into this area, setting up swap groups that worked closely with the capital market departments to identify arbitrage opportunities for potential issuers and to provide the necessary counterparties. Such transactions often involved the identification of a number of counterparties—four or five not being uncommon—and a number of capital market transactions, so that considerable expertise was required to bring all parties to the point of completion at the same time. Usually, transactions were arranged on a "matched" basis, with all the cash flows between the counterparties involved matching out more or less exactly. This expertise and the information about counterparties' particular interests at any one time was of definite competitive advantage, as reflected in the salaries and status of the individuals responsible for such "swap groups."

Arbitrage in Capital Markets

Deregulation of numerous national capital markets opened up new markets for the issuance of securities, some of which have been driven almost wholly by the growing currency swap market. (The linkage between the currency swap market and the primary capital markets for new issues is covered in detail in Chapter 7.)

Multileg Transactions, or Cocktail Swaps

Since, in general, the issuing institutions usually had no use for the funds in their original form, these were swapped in various "legs" into the currency and interest form required.

To swap out of fixed-rate Australian dollars, for example, into floating-rate Deutschemarks, a number of transactions would typically have to be arranged, since it was highly improbable that two counterparties with these exact complementary requirements would be in the market at the same time. However, a number of counterparties might be available that wished to swap one of these currencies against six-month LIBOR U.S. dollars (which soon became the recognized pivot in the currency swap market, in the same way that the dollar functions as the pivot for the forward foreign exchange market). Such a transaction would then be arranged in stages:

>   Partner 1:   Cross currency swap:
>   Fixed-rate Australian dollars into
>   LIBOR U.S. dollars

Partner 2: Cross currency swap:
LIBOR U.S. dollars into fixed-rate
Deutschemarks

Partner 3: Interest rate swap:
Fixed-rate Deutschemarks into floating-rate
Deutschemarks

There are, of course, a number of possible variations on this. Instead of the swap with partner 2, if no such partner were available, the LIBOR U.S. dollars could be swapped into fixed-rate dollars via an interest rate U.S. dollar swap and then, via the forward foreign exchange market, into fixed-rate Deutschemarks.

Central Role of LIBOR U.S. Dollars
There were a number of reasons, still valid today, why the currency swap market pivoted on U.S. dollar LIBOR:

- Liquidity can always be invested and rolled over in the interbank deposit market at a LIBOR-based rate. Even though, depending on the credit risk involved, the deposit may be effectively priced at a margin under LIBOR, for example, at LIBID (London Interbank Bid Rate), the interest basis can be assumed to be LIBOR. Alternatively, funds may be invested in a Floating Rate Note, which also is priced by reference to LIBOR. The amount of credit risk the investor is willing to bear, and hence the margin he is prepared to forgo, depends on personal preferences. Any margin over or under LIBOR would be taken into account in calculating the overall economic result of the transaction.
- Conversely, swap counterparties, even those with lesser credit ratings, are normally able to obtain liquidity at a LIBOR-based rate. Again, any margin over or under LIBOR would be brought into the calculation of the overall result.
- The interbank Eurodollar market is the market with the least chance of regulatory interference. That is, apart from commercial considerations of liquidity or credit risk, the market perceives little risk of governmental regulations covering, for example, the level of interest, minimum reserves, or withholding taxes.

An acronym was soon coined for joint currency and interest rate swap transactions, perhaps with the complexity of some of the structures in mind: CIRCUS(Combined Interest Rate and CUrrency Swap).

Swaps as Tools for Currency Management

It is, even in retrospect, not possible to define exactly when the use of currency swaps was extended from the arbitrage of the capital markets to cover asset swaps and the currency management of existing assets and liabilities. A major factor may well have been the extreme currency volatility of the period, giving rise to substantial gains in foreign currency debt and, by the same token, creating possibilities for losses. In addition, accounting regulations in the United States (FASB *Statement No. 8* and *Statement No. 52*) compelled U.S.-based companies to consider the effect of currency movements on their balance sheets and profit-and-loss accounts. A number of U.S. dollar/Deutschemark currency swaps, for example, were transacted for non–Deutschemark–based counterparties during 1983 and 1984 to convert their liabilities arising out of Euro–Deutschemark bond issues—which, because of existing Bundesbank regulations, could not be swapped at the time of issue—into dollars, allowing them to realize the exchange profit on these borrowings.

It was also well known that some French issuers active in the international markets were using currency swaps to actively manage their currency exposure arising out of their foreign currency borrowings.

CONSTRAINTS

Serious constraints to the growth of the currency swap market began to appear in the mid-1980s. These stemmed basically from the transition of the market from one based on a small number of individual, high–profit margin transactions, to a market utilizing fairly standard economic techniques and with considerable potential for further growth. These factors were the same as those affecting the interest rate swap market.

The constraints in the main centered around (1) documentation and definitions of frequently used terms (e.g., *LIBOR*), (2) the ready availability of counterparties, and (3) credit questions. These constraints were resolved by the market in different ways, depending on whether the elements to be addressed constituted a part of a standardized product or could be best solved by banks individually, thus creating a competitive advantage.

Aside from the basic economic structure of the currency swap, standardization was primarily achieved through creating a uniform documentation and by establishing common definitions for terms.

Documentation and Definitions

In the early days of the cross currency swap market, record keeping was usually based on the capital and loan market philosophy of a complete set of documentation for each transaction. It was not unusual for the documentation of transactions arranged on the telephone in a matter of minutes to be completed months later. Documentation backlogs were substantial since each transaction had to be individually negotiated, a task made worse by the fact that there was no common agreement on how many of the substantive issues should be resolved.

The problem became so serious that, almost simultaneously in London and in New York, working groups of bankers and their lawyers were set up to develop a standardized set of documentation. As a result the British Bankers' Association interest rate swap (BBAIRS) terms were established in London in 1985, and in the same year the working party in New York—which had formed into the ISDA—produced the 1985 Code of Swaps. Whereas the BBAIRS terms were not developed further, the documentation group of the ISDA continued to improve and extend the documentation process.

A major drawback of the 1985 code was that, even though it provided useful standardized definitions, swap parties still had to complete separate contracts for each transaction. This work was rationalized still further in a radical move by the development of swap master agreements containing all the major standardized provisions. (A fuller description of the development of swap documentation and definitions, together with the text of the current ISDA Interest Rate and Currency Exchange Agreement, can be found in Chapter 5 of this book.)

Availability of Counterparties

Even though a relatively efficient informal system of matching counterparties had developed during the first half of the 1980s, by 1985 to 1986 it was clear that such a system had numerous constraints. In particular, the need to execute transactions quickly, without being dependent on the availability of a counterparty, became crucial. In a transparent, public capital market, the time span or "window" for new issue arbitrage opportunities became smaller and smaller, sometimes lasting only a few hours. For currency swaps to be effective in the management of an existing currency exposure, the need to lock in an exchange rate in a volatile FX environment meant that currency swap transactions had to be executable immediately.

Warehousing Swaps

The market's solution to the problem of the availability of counterparties was for banks to take on the role of principal, warehousing swaps on their own books until the other side was put in place. (The risk and techniques involved in warehousing swaps and ultimately running a portfolio of swaps are discussed in detail in Chapter 18 of this book.)

This development fundamentally changed the nature of the market. Expertise in matching counterparties and negotiating terms was no longer the key to success, since a market maker could provide a price at any time, as well as take on uneven cash flows. The market then developed into a traders' market, with the market makers' profits achieved through the bid-offer spreads made to the rest of the market and through the skillful risk management of the swap position or inventory. Even though relatively few banks actually make markets in currency swaps, the transparency of the market is such that prices today do not differ substantially and quotes for large amounts can be obtained easily.

Liquidity

The liquidity for currency swaps is, however, less than that for pure interest rate swaps. This may be based on the fact that a currency swap is not as easy to hedge as an interest rate swap. Most market makers in cross currency swaps probably hedge themselves against movements in foreign exchange rates by executing a short swap for three or six months in the more liquid short-term foreign exchange market, which can be offset easily when the other side of the longer-dated cross currency swap is found. This technique, however, still leaves the market maker with an interest rate exposure from the short-term rates implicit in the foreign exchange swaps versus the longer-term rates of the currency swaps.

In addition, if the hedge position needs to be rolled over, the succeeding short-term swap will in all probability be based on a different foreign exchange rate due to rate movements. This will create either a cash surplus or a shortfall at the beginning of the second rollover period, with a corresponding shortfall or surplus at the end of this period. This cash position must be either invested or refinanced and, in any case, will affect the balance sheet. In addition, it may give rise to an interest rate mismatch due to differences in the interest rates applicable to these short-term funds versus the interest rates of the currency swaps just mentioned. (The reader is referred to Chapter 21 for a more complete discussion of this rollover risk.)

Credit Questions

Credit risk is one of the factors preventing the currency swap from becoming a totally standardized product. A major attraction of the cross currency swap is that it extends foreign currency hedging to long maturities. Against this, however, must be set the corresponding disadvantage that credit questions—and, hence, the standing of the particular counterparty—play a critical role in transactions with such long maturities. In other words, the product may in itself offer a good solution to a long-term hedging problem, but this will be of no use if there are no acceptable counterparties with whom to conclude the transaction. Most banks set limits for currency swaps up to five years; beyond this period only exceptionally good-quality names have access to the currency swap market. Various solutions have been proposed for extending the availability of the market to less established names: a regular marking to market, the provision of collateral, or the creation of a swap clearinghouse. To date, however, none of these has provided a generally valid solution to the problem.

Marking to Market
The marking of a currency swap to market—in effect, not unlike variation margin payments on futures contracts—involves either intermediate cash payments or the provision of securities. In either case, the

administrative costs have to be taken into account as well as the interest effect of the intermediate cash flows, which cannot be ascertained in advance.

Collateral

The provision of collateral is, in some areas, part of normal swap business and can provide a solution to the problem of credit in particular instances. A long-dated currency swap would, however, require collateral for over 30 percent of the nominal amount of the swap[2] to be posted, theoretically at least, for the lifetime of the swap, for the risk to be approximately covered.

Clearinghouse

Discussions concerning a clearinghouse for swaps have been going on for some time. However, at the time of this writing, no workable solutions to the problems that this would pose have emerged.

Capital Costs

In addition to the default risk inherent in currency swaps, commercial banks will in the future have to count the cost of providing capital for their currency swaps in calculating the profitability of transactions. Here again the ISDA played an instrumental role in defining the methodology for measuring the exposure risk against a swap counterparty.

Based on the recommendations of the Cooke report[3] for calculating swap exposure risk, an idea of the costs incurred by having to provide capital against cross currency swaps can be obtained as follows:

The first step is to calculate the credit-equivalent exposure arising out of the cross currency swap. Banks may use one of two methods to calculate this:

Method 1

The sum of the mark-to-market value of each swap, if positive,[4] plus

---

[2] The Cooke Method 2 risk calculation for a 10-year currency swap works out to 32 percent.

[3] Committee on Banking Regulations and Supervisory Practices, *International Convergence of Capital Measurement and Capital Standards,* July 1988.

[4] That is, if a loss would arise on default by the counterparty.

1 percent of the notional amount of each swap with a residual maturity of less than one year, plus

5 percent of the notional amount of each swap with a residual maturity of one year or more.

Method 2

2 percent of the notional amount of each swap with an original maturity of less than one year, plus

5 percent of the notional amount of each swap with an original maturity of one year and less than two years, plus

For each swap with an original maturity of two years or more, 3 percent of the notional amount for each additional year.

The credit-equivalent amount calculated according to one of these methods is then weighted according to the category of counterparty, for example:

Commercial companies[5]	50%
Banks incorporated in OECD countries	20%
OECD governments and central banks	0%

The minimum capital required to support the net credit-equivalent amount (i.e., after weighting) is arrived at by applying the minimum capital ratio employed by the bank. The Cooke report envisages a minimum capital ratio of 8 percent (of which no more than 4 percent may consist of supplementary capital, such as subordinated debt) by the end of 1992.

A 10-year on-market cross currency swap with a corporate counterparty with a notional amount of US$100 million would, at the outset, therefore require capital of:

$$US\$100,000,000 \times 5\% \times 50\% \times 8\% = US\$200,000$$

by method 1, or

$$US\$100,000,000 \times 32\% \times 50\% \times 8\% = US\$1,280,000$$

---

[5]Since counterparties in the swap market have generally been first-class names, the Cooke report accepts that a lower risk weighting for swap corporate counterparties is justifiable. Central banks will, however, keep this issue under review.

under method 2. (A more detailed description of capital requirements is contained in Chapter 22 in this book.)

The actual cost of supporting this capital will vary from bank to bank since, despite the widespread application of the Cooke report recommendations, the actual capital costs for each bank—and hence the pricing targets—are by no means standardized. They depend on:

- The method the bank uses for calculating the credit equivalent (method 1 or 2).
- The bank's actual exposure at market rates (method 1).
- The maturity of the transaction (method 2) and the status of the counterparty.
- Any exposure netting arrangements the bank may have with its counterparty.[6]
- To what extent the bank is subsidizing capital costs on currency swaps with more profitable interest rate swap business.
- The actual costs of raising new capital or servicing existing capital, which in turn depend on the level of individual share prices, equity reserves, and the ratio of core capital to "tier 2" capital, among other things.

Even though it is not possible to exactly quantify these costs for the market as a whole, it is accepted that the imposition of such capital costs will increase effective costs in the currency swap market and, as a result, reduce activity driven by pure arbitrage considerations. The ruling will also clearly benefit good-name counterparties, which either can operate outside the regulatory framework (such as subsidiaries of nonbank organizations) or have access to relatively cheap sources of capital.

PRESENT SITUATION

The currency swap market at present is made up of both specialized, high-margin transactions and relatively low-margin, standardized products.

---

[6]At the time of writing, discussions are taking place with bank supervisory authorities to allow exposure netting for capital purposes under certain circumstances.

Specialization

The trend toward specialization arises from:

1. *Credit risk and capital costs:*
   a. The counterparty credit risk inherent in longer-dated currency swaps, leading to individual credit arrangements between the parties concerned.
   b. The regulatory requirements for capital to be held against each currency swap, which impose on the commercial bank players an additional nonstandard cost factor.
2. *Hedging risk:* The fact that the "warehousing" of a currency swap requires protection against interest rate and foreign exchange rate movements. Although it is possible to construct hedges that achieve this, parts of the hedge structure may involve capital costs for hedging the full maturity and may involve cash positions that impact the balance sheet and income statement.
3. *Valuation risk:* The difficulties often encountered in practice in valuing currency swaps, especially where the terms of the transaction are substantially off-market. (A full treatment of the pricing of currency swaps is contained in Chapter 15.) Since the full capital value of a cross currency swap is subject to variation depending upon foreign exchange movements, the importance of the discount or reinvestment rate and valuation method used in determining the size of the present value payment is critical. The discount or reinvestment rates rest on certain assumptions that may not actually exist in the form of risk-free investment or borrowing possibilities. In practice, valuation of a currency swap is a relatively time-consuming procedure, and a standard, benchmark procedure has not yet evolved in the marketplace.
4. *Liquidity:* In practice, the liquidity of the secondary market is somewhat restricted. Trades do take place, but these are effectively limited by the acceptability of the counterparty name and the evaluation difficulties.

Given these factors, a number of market participants see in the currency swap business an area in which to earn higher profit margins based on their professional expertise and their good credit standing.

Moving away from the simple cross currency swap, they concentrate on specialized swap structures that may involve three or four different currencies and the use of long-dated foreign exchange options. The cash flows of such structures have usually been created on a one-off basis to match the particular cash flow of an individual party at a particular time. A few banks capitalize on their good credit standing by specializing in the long-dated currency swap market, arranging deals that may extend as long as 15 years.

Actual information on the profit margins achievable in such transactions is, of course, not generally available. They are arranged on a bilateral, private basis, and only a small number of banks are actively involved in this market, possess the necessary technical know-how, and have active relationships with the relevant counterparties.

Standardization

The trend toward standardization arises in part out of:

1. *Profit:* More and more prospective participants will seek to join a market where they perceive the returns to be attractive. It is possible that firms will seek higher-margin business to compensate for the generally diminishing returns from "plain vanilla" high-volume interest rate swap business.
2. *Transfer of expertise:* The necessary expertise was previously confined to only a few organizations. This will, over time, become available throughout the marketplace. This will occur through the physical transfer of personnel with new banks wishing to start up in the business and offering a premium for the acquisition of know-how, through seminars such as those run by ISDA and independent seminar organizations, and through publications in the financial press. There seems to be no reason, therefore, why warehousing and valuation techniques should not become common knowledge and thus part of the standards in the currency swap market, in the same way that they are now commonplace in the interest rate swap market.
3. *Mitigation of credit risk:* How credit risk can be mitigated through various devices. Even though some may be cumbersome and difficult to administrate, the higher transaction

costs can be justified if the deals show an appropriate profit margin.

   a. Collateral arrangements. In view of the documentation standardization developed in the swap market, it is not inconceivable that the market could, if the need arose, also produce standardized collateral documentation. Such collateral could, for example, take the form of "topping up" by the provision of cash or bonds when the exposure reaches a certain pre-agreed level.

   b. The development of payment netting arrangements to reduce the settlement risk inherent in foreign exchange transactions. Typically one party will have to pay, for example, yen in Tokyo before receiving the corresponding amount in U.S. dollars in New York some hours later. At present, commercial and central banks are working to achieve payment netting on a global basis by using computer systems to net out balances between groups of banks. In addition, parties in the cross currency swap market often set out special arrangements in their swap agreements with the aim of minimizing the payment settlement risk. For example, they may provide for escrow or trustee accounts to be set up through which the payments are to be made, or they may agree to reduce the settlement risk on the final exchange at maturity by paying only the difference between the two currency amounts, leaving each party to cover itself in the spot foreign exchange market for the remainder.

   c. Exposure netting provisions in the documentation. These would allow for currency swap credit exposure to be netted against other currency swaps and off-balance sheet transactions.

LOOKING FORWARD

The growth rates of the currency swap market up till now have lagged significantly behind those of the interest rate swap market. This phenomenon can be seen vividly in Exhibits 1 and 2. It may be due to the alternatives available in the long-term foreign exchange market,

EXHIBIT 1
Interest Rate and Cross Currency Swaps: Notional Principal Outstanding
(in billion U.S.$)

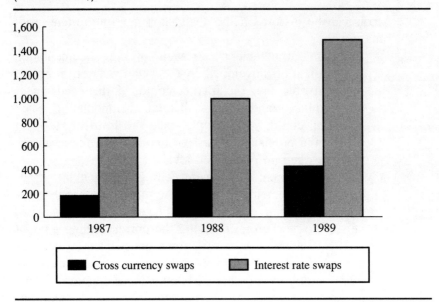

Source: International Swap Dealers Association

EXHIBIT 2
**Interest Rate and Cross Currency Swaps: Number of Contracts
Outstanding** (in thousands)

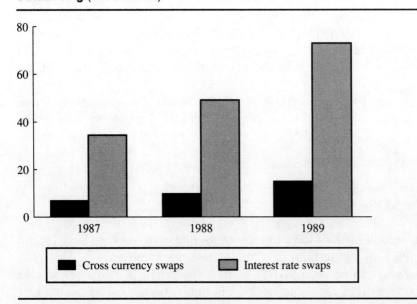

Source: International Swap Dealers Association

the volume figures of which are not included in the ISDA currency swap market statistics. Other causes may be the alternative use of interest rate swaps in asset swap constructions and the relative lack of demand from financial institutions for this specific product. (Financial institutions generally are interested in currency swaps only as a means of arbitraging new issues for funding purposes; foreign exchange positions arising out of day-to-day trading or strategic considerations are usually handled through other instruments.) The standardization so far has come about as the result of the increased volume; where volume figures are low and expected to remain so, the need for standardization is not pressing.

At the time of writing, there does not appear to be enough demand potential to warrant further standardization development in the currency swap. The ISDA standards in the documentation and in the definitions of terminology employed are generally sufficient to cover most of the range of the currency swap transactions in the market at present.

CHAPTER 5

STANDARDIZED SWAP DEFINITIONS AND DOCUMENTATION

Daniel P. Cunningham
Cravath, Swaine & Moore
New York

Michael Wood
Dresdner Bank AG
Frankfurt

EARLY SWAP DOCUMENTATION

In the early days of the cross currency swap there was no clear, common understanding of the legal status of swap payments; therefore, documenting a swap transaction meant entering new territory. Such swap agreements were drafted individually for each transaction and went under a variety of names, such as "Forward Payment Agreement," "Currency Exchange Agreement," or "Foreign Currency Conversion Agreement."

Precedents for some clauses existed in cross-border loan documentation. For example, events of default and representations and warranties were borrowed from loan agreements, and some of the early agreements were indeed drafted as parallel loans. This treatment did not, however, take into account either the character of these swap transactions as mutual exchanges or the intention of the parties that these deals should not appear on their balance sheets as loans.

The drafters of these early swap agreements had been used to working primarily in capital and loan market documentation, which is based on a one-way flow of funds. The documentation of these agreements has two aims: first, to protect against disbursing funds to a defaulting borrower; and second, to achieve the best possible position for the lender if the borrower is unable to repay the debt. Many drafters of early swap agreements therefore had little practical experience in negotiating agreements covering a series of reciprocal payments.

To make matters even more difficult, there was no common agreement on how crucial questions, such as the risk of the imposition of withholding taxes, should be resolved between the parties, or how, for example, in the absence of a liquid market with prices readily available, damages on the default of a party should be calculated. In practice, damages were often calculated using alternative sources of borrowing and re-investment as reference points. This was not ideal, because markets did not provide easily identifiable benchmark sources for reference, and because there was an anomaly in calculating the value of an off-balance sheet deal by referring to cash transactions. Such cash transactions, which would appear on a bank's balance sheet, impact on balance sheet ratios and therefore do not replicate exactly the economic effect of a swap, which does not appear on a balance sheet.

As a result, documentation backlogs quickly became substantial. The time and effort employed in drafting a complete new agreement for each deal was out of proportion to the resources available.

THE BBAIRS[1] TERMS

In order to solve the documentation problem the market set up informal working groups of bankers and their lawyers in New York and London, in order to develop a standardized system of documentation. The British Bankers' Association (BBA) working party commenced work in October 1984, and by September 1985 had produced standardized terms for interest rate and currency swaps,[2] forward rate agreements,[3] and foreign exchange options. These terms were designed to apply to each individual transaction, but, because they were contained in a published booklet, they could be incorporated simply by reference rather than reprinted for each transaction.

---

[1]British Bankers' Association Interest Rate Swaps
[2]"BBAIRS" terms
[3]"FRABBA," Forward Rate Agreement British Bankers' Association terms

To enhance market acceptability, the emphasis was placed on simplicity. Credit questions were thus not addressed, and the withholding tax arrangements paralleled the usual tax provisions in cross-border loan documentation. The question of the definition of a party's loss in the event of the other party's bankruptcy was neatly solved by leaving it to the non-defaulting party to determine its own loss.

The terms were drafted specifically with short-term instruments (up to two years) in mind and were deemed to govern all transactions in the London market unless expressly agreed otherwise. Nonetheless, because of the terms' simplicity, many counterparties in the continental European market have used them for swaps with maturities beyond two years.

BBAIRS Reference Rates

As part of these terms, standardized reference pages for LIBOR were introduced. Previously, LIBOR had been fixed by reference to the Reuters LIBOR page for U.S. dollar LIBOR rates. Rates for nondollar currencies had to be obtained by telephone from reference banks. The latter was a time-consuming approach, and was always open to criticism for being uncertain and inaccurate. Screen quotations, on the other hand, provided the market with a quick and transparent source. This method was developed by the BBA, which publishes rates obtained daily from eight banks of a group of 12 designated reference banks. The rates cover U.S. dollars, pounds sterling, Deutschemarks, Swiss francs, and Japanese yen for maturities from 1 to 12 months. Of particular assistance is the record of past fixings maintained by the BBA.

ISDA

In May 1984, a group of 10 major swap dealers met in New York to discuss the possibilities for standardizing market conventions and terminology. This group formed the initial membership of the International Swap Dealers Association, which is today the recognized industry body for the swap profession.

The 1985 Code of Swaps

The most immediately apparent success of the ISDA was its production of standardized documentation, beginning with the 1985 Code of Standard Wording, Assumptions and Provisions for Swaps. Unlike the BBAIRS approach, which was to provide a uniform set of documentation for the market and to provide a complete contract for the parties involved in both interest rate and currency swaps, the 1985 ISDA code was restricted to U.S. dollar interest rate swaps. It was also designed to provide users with standard definitions (e.g., how cash flows were to be calculated), which could be incorporated in short form into the relevant agreements. The 1985 code reflects different market views by offering a "menu" technique by which parties can choose from preformulated definitions (e.g., floating-rate options) for the calculation of damages and payments on default.

In 1986 the ISDA code was revised to incorporate more definitions, reflect the increasing use of master agreements, and extend its usefulness to cross-border transactions.

SWAP MASTER AGREEMENTS

The ISDA code, while providing useful definitions, nonetheless required swap parties to complete separate contracts for each swap transaction. In order to simplify this cumbersome process, the market began in the mid-1980s to develop master agreements, with the aim of setting out provisions for swaps between the parties in a one-time master agreement that could be standardized or that would be applicable to all transactions. The documentation of the individual transaction could then be a simple telex or letter confirming the economic details, which could be produced quickly and easily. When drafting a master agreement, it was a relatively simple exercise to extend its terms to cover all types of swaps, including interest rate and currency swaps.

Despite the incorporation of definitions, these master agreements were often lengthy and complicated, and a reader would frequently need to refer to the relevant code (which might or might not be subsequently amended). Although the major market players were able to conclude master agreements among themselves, it proved to be time-consuming and expensive for other players to negotiate master agreements individually, since there was no set format and no standard market practice for handling such crucial clauses as termination events, default, withholding taxes, and the definition of losses or damages.

In view of the volume of business being transacted and the still-growing backlog of documentation, the market began in the second half of 1986 to develop a standard master agreement to cover all international swap transactions. Working parties from banks in local markets developed master agreements for local transactions. A small group of German banks, for example, produced in January 1987 the first version of a master agreement for interest rate and currency swaps for use between counterparties inside Germany and governed by German law.

THE ISDA MASTER AGREEMENTS

In 1987 the ISDA developed comprehensive Master Agreements for interest rate swaps[4] and currency swaps.[5] The ISDA also produced a separate definitions booklet,[6] to be used with the Interest Rate and Currency Exchange Agreement. The booklet contained comprehensive definitions of the most commonly used currencies and interest rates and the calculation methods most often used to expedite the documentation of actual transactions. Although the Interest Rate and Currency Exchange Agreement and the Definitions booklet were specifically designed for use in cross-border transactions and they rapidly gained general market acceptance, with the result that in international currency swap transactions these have now become the standard documentation form.

The agreements place less emphasis on the menu approach than the codes. The ISDA master agreements include a "complete" set of representations, events of default, and termination provisions. Certain events of default and termination events (for example, cross-default, credit event upon merger), however, require parties to "opt in" and to specify certain operative definitions. To facilitate these choices, as well as any other agreed changes to the standard form text, the ISDA master agreements include *schedules*. Parties using the ISDA master agreements set out all revisions to the printed text and all required

---

[4]Interest Rate Agreement ©ISDA 1987.
[5]Interest Rate and Currency Exchange Agreement ©ISDA 1987.
[6]1987 Interest Rate and Currency Definitions.

choices in the schedules. In this way, parties (and their lawyers) who are familiar with the standard form need only examine the schedule with the desired changes, and the negotiation process is thus simpler and quicker.

The full text of the Interest Rate and Currency Exchange Agreement and the Schedule can be found at the end of this chapter.

STANDARDIZATION IN THE ISDA AGREEMENTS

Not only were the 1987 ISDA forms a much-needed solution to the documentation problem, but they have also contributed to the standardization of the currency swap market itself. The ISDA technique of taking a snapshot of the most common practices and terms in the swap market and incorporating these into the agreements or into the definitions has resulted in the even wider acceptance of such practices or terms as market standards. This has occurred even though parties are free to agree on other terms. In conflict situations or in situations where, for example, traders are uncertain as to how to agree on a business day rule, the obvious answer is to use the ISDA form as the reference. Standardized practices have even evolved for the optional credit provisions. Thus cross-default and credit event upon merger are almost always included in documentation as a matter of principle. The exact wording of the cross-default clause and the definition of what constitutes a credit event upon merger are often negotiated on a case-by-case basis, although even here standardized variations can be observed.

The questions of no-default early termination of swaps, insolvency, and calculation of damages, which had plagued earlier drafters of agreements, have now been standardized. Briefly, the agreements provide for early termination in a no-default situation (imposition of taxes, illegality) and also in the case of a default by one party either in its obligations under the agreement or under other swap agreements or because of insolvency. Payments on termination or damages on the default of one party are calculated according to market replacement values. This major advance has been the result of the ongoing development of the market and the corresponding increase in swap liquidity, which make it no longer necessary to refer to borrowing or investment alternatives.

Bearing in mind the worldwide range of counterparties in many different jurisdictions using these forms and the complexity and variety of terms and practices in the swap market, the degree of standardization achieved by the ISDA in the 1987 forms is commendable. Since they were first published only one addition has been made to the Interest Rate and Currency Exchange Agreement, namely the Alternative Tax Clauses. The definitions, which contain only a very few minor technical inaccuracies, have generally been used as the basis for documenting the individual terms of interest rate and currency swaps. In 1989 the ISDA published an addendum to its master agreement for documentation of interest rate, caps, collars, and floors. In 1990 the ISDA published a second addendum to its master agreement for documentation of swap option transactions. For an overview of the ISDA cross currency swap documentation, see Exhibit 1.

In early 1991 ISDA published a revision to the definitions that corrects these inaccuracies and that includes new definitions to reflect the growth in the market covering new currencies such as the Spanish peseta and the Scandinavian currencies. The revised definitions also include the provisions developed by the ISDA during 1989 and 1990 to facilitate the documentation of collar, cap, floor, and swap options transactions. Finally, the revised definition also includes certain provisions for commodity swaps.

This chapter concludes with the full text of the 1987 ISDA Interest Rate and Currency Exchange Agreement.

EXHIBIT 1
Overview of ISDA Documentation for
Cross Currency Swaps

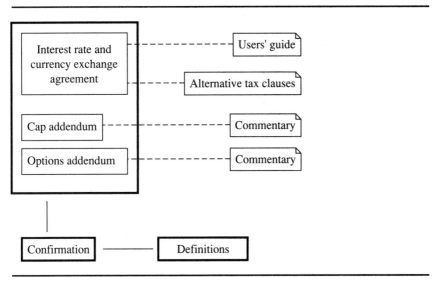

International Swap Dealers Association, Inc.

INTEREST RATE

AND

CURRENCY EXCHANGE AGREEMENT

Dated as of...

.... and ....

have entered and/or anticipate entering into one or more transactions (each a "Swap Transaction"). The parties agree that each Swap Transaction will be governed by the terms and conditions set forth in this document (which includes the schedule (the "Schedule")) and in the documents (each a "Confirmation") exchanged between the parties confirming such Swap Transactions. Each Confirmation constitutes a supplement to and forms part of this document and will be read and construed as one with this document, so that this document and all the Confirmations constitute a single agreement between the parties (collectively referred to as this "Agreement"). The parties acknowledge that all Swap Transactions are entered into in reliance on the fact that this document and all Confirmations will form a single agreement between the parties, it being understood that the parties would not otherwise enter into any Swap Transactions.

Accordingly, the parties agree as follows:–

1. **Interpretation**

(a) *Definitions.* The terms defined in Section 14 and in the Schedule will have the meanings therein specified for the purpose of this Agreement.

(b) *Inconsistency.* In the event of any inconsistency between the provisions of any Confirmation and this document, such Confirmation will prevail for the purpose of the relevant Swap Transaction.

2. **Payments**

(a) *Obligations and Conditions.*

    (i) Each party will make each payment specified in each Confirmation as being payable by it.

    (ii) Payments under this Agreement will be made not later than the due date for value on that date in the place of the account specified in the relevant Confirmation or otherwise pursuant to this Agreement, in freely transferable funds and in the manner customary for payments in the required currency.

    (iii) Each obligation of each party to pay any amount due under Section 2(a)(i) is subject to (1) the condition precedent that no Event of Default or Potential Event of Default with respect to the other party has occurred and is continuing and (2) each other applicable condition precedent specified in this Agreement.

(b) *Change of Account.* Either party may change its account by giving notice to the other party at least five days prior to the due date for payment for which such change applies.

(c)   *Netting.* If on any date amounts would otherwise be payable:–

(i)   in the same currency; and

(ii)   in respect of the same Swap Transaction,

by each party to the other, then, on such date, each party's obligation to make payment of any such amount will be automatically satisfied and discharged and, if the aggregate amount that would otherwise have been payable by one party exceeds the aggregate amount that would otherwise have been payable by the other party, replaced by an obligation upon the party by whom the larger aggregate amount would have been payable to pay to the other party the excess of the larger aggregate amount over the smaller aggregate amount.

If the parties specify "Net Payments — Corresponding Payment Dates" in a Confirmation or otherwise in this Agreement, sub-paragraph (ii) above will cease to apply to all Swap Transactions with effect from the date so specified (so that a net amount will be determined in respect of all amounts due on the same date in the same currency, regardless of whether such amounts are payable in respect of the same Swap Transaction); *provided that,* in such case, this Section 2(c) will apply separately to each Office through which a party makes and receives payments as set forth in Section 10.

(d)   *Deduction or Withholding for Tax.*

(i)   *Gross-Up.* All payments under this Agreement will be made without any deduction or withholding for or on account of any Tax unless such deduction or withholding is required by any applicable law, as modified by the practice of any relevant governmental revenue authority, then in effect. If a party is so required to deduct or withhold, then that party ("X") will:–

(1)   promptly notify the other party ("Y") of such requirement;

(2)   pay to the relevant authorities the full amount required to be deducted or withheld (including the full amount required to be deducted or withheld from any additional amount paid by X to Y under this Section 2(d)) promptly upon the earlier of determining that such deduction or withholding is required or receiving notice that such amount has been assessed against Y;

(3)   promptly forward to Y an official receipt (or a certified copy), or other documentation reasonably acceptable to Y, evidencing such payment to such authorities; and

(4)   if such Tax is an Indemnifiable Tax, pay to Y, in addition to the payment to which Y is otherwise entitled under this Agreement, such additional amount as is necessary to ensure that the net amount actually received by Y (free and clear of Indemnifiable Taxes, whether assessed against X or Y) will equal the full amount Y would have received had no such deduction or withholding been required. However, X will not be required to pay any additional amount to Y to the extent that it would not be required to be paid but for:–

(A)   the failure by Y to comply with or perform any agreement contained in Section 4(a)(i) or 4(d); or

(B)   the failure of a representation made by Y pursuant to Section 3(f) to be accurate and true unless such failure would not have occurred but for a Change in Tax Law.

(ii)   *Liability.* If:–

(1)   X is required by any applicable law, as modified by the practice of any relevant governmental revenue authority, to make any deduction or withholding in respect of which X would not be required to pay an additional amount to Y under Section 2(d)(i)(4);

(2)   X does not so deduct or withhold; and

(3)   a liability resulting from such Tax is assessed directly against X,

then, except to the extent Y has satisfied or then satisfies the liability resulting from such Tax, Y will promptly pay to X the amount of such liability (including any related liability for interest, but including any related liability for penalties only if Y has failed to comply with or perform any agreement contained in Section 4(a)(i) or (d)).

(e)   *Default Interest.* A party that defaults in the payment of any amount due will, to the extent permitted by law, be required to pay interest (before as well as after judgment) on such amount to the other party on demand in the same currency as the overdue amount, for the period from (and including) the original due date for payment to (but excluding) the date of actual payment, at the Default Rate. Such interest will be calculated on the basis of daily compounding and the actual number of days elapsed.

3. Representations

Each party represents to the other party (which representations will be deemed to be repeated by each party on each date on which a Swap Transaction is entered into and, in the case of the representations in Section 3(f), at all times until the termination of this Agreement) that:–

(a)   *Basic Representations.*

(i)   *Status.* It is duly organised and validly existing under the laws of the jurisdiction of its organisation or incorporation and, if relevant under such laws, in good standing;

(ii)   *Powers.* It has the power to execute and deliver this Agreement and any other documentation relating to this Agreement that it is required by this Agreement to deliver and to perform its obligations under this Agreement and any obligations it has under any Credit Support Document to which it is a party and has taken all necessary action to authorise such execution, delivery and performance;

(iii)   *No Violation or Conflict.* Such execution, delivery and performance do not violate or conflict with any law applicable to it, any provision of its constitutional documents, any order or judgment of any court or other agency of government applicable to it or any of its assets or any contractual restriction binding on or affecting it or any of its assets;

(iv)   *Consents.* All governmental and other consents that are required to have been obtained by it with respect to this Agreement or any Credit Support Document to which it is a party have been obtained and are in full force and effect and all conditions of any such consents have been complied with; and

(v)   *Obligations Binding.* Its obligations under this Agreement and any Credit Support Document to which it is a party constitute its legal, valid and binding obligations, enforceable in accordance with their respective terms (subject to applicable bankruptcy, reorganisation, insolvency, moratorium or similar laws affecting creditors' rights generally and subject, as to enforceability, to equitable principles of general application (regardless of whether enforcement is sought in a proceeding in equity or at law)).

(b)   *Absence of Certain Events.* No Event of Default or Potential Event of Default or, to its knowledge, Termination Event with respect to it has occurred and is continuing and no such event or circumstance would occur as a result of its entering into or performing its obligations under this Agreement or any Credit Support Document to which it is a party.

(c)   *Absence of Litigation.* There is not pending or, to its knowledge, threatened against it or any of its Affiliates any action, suit or proceeding at law or in equity or before any court, tribunal, governmental body, agency or official or any arbitrator that purports to draw into question, or is likely to affect, the legality, validity or enforceability against it of this Agreement or any Credit Support Document to which it is a party or its ability to perform its obligations under this Agreement or such Credit Support Document.

(d)   *Accuracy of Specified Information.* All applicable information that is furnished in writing by or on behalf of it to the other party and is identified for the purpose of this Section 3(d) in paragraph 2 of Part 3 of the Schedule is, as of the date of the information, true, accurate and complete in every material respect.

(e)   *Payer Tax Representation.* Each representation specified in Part 2 of the Schedule as being made by it for the purpose of this Section 3(e) is accurate and true.

(f)   *Payee Tax Representations.* Each representation specified in Part 2 of the Schedule as being made by it for the purpose of this Section 3(f) is accurate and true.

4. Agreements

Each party agrees with the other that, so long as it has or may have any obligation under this Agreement or under any Credit Support Document to which it is a party:–

ISDA 1987

(a)   *Furnish Specified Information.* It will deliver to the other party:–

　(i)   any forms, documents or certificates relating to taxation specified in Part 3 of the Schedule or any Confirmation; and

　(ii)   any other documents specified in Part 3 of the Schedule or any Confirmation,

by the date specified in Part 3 of the Schedule or such Confirmation or, if none is specified, as soon as practicable.

(b)   *Maintain Authorisations.* It will use all reasonable efforts to maintain in full force and effect all consents of any governmental or other authority that are required to be obtained by it with respect to this Agreement or any Credit Support Document to which it is a party and will use all reasonable efforts to obtain any that may become necessary in the future.

(c)   *Comply with Laws.* It will comply in all material respects with all applicable laws and orders to which it may be subject if failure so to comply would materially impair its ability to perform its obligations under this Agreement or any Credit Support Document to which it is a party.

(d)   *Tax Agreement.* It will give notice of any failure of a representation made by it under Section 3(f) to be accurate and true promptly upon learning of such failure.

(e)   *Payment of Stamp Tax.* It will pay any Stamp Tax levied or imposed upon it or in respect of its execution or performance of this Agreement by a jurisdiction in which it is incorporated, organised, managed and controlled, or considered to have its seat, or in which a branch or office through which it is acting for the purpose of this Agreement is located ("Stamp Tax Jurisdiction") and will indemnify the other party against any Stamp Tax levied or imposed upon the other party or in respect of the other party's execution or performance of this Agreement by any such Stamp Tax Jurisdiction which is not also a Stamp Tax Jurisdiction with respect to the other party.

5.   Events of Default and Termination Events

(a)   *Events of Default.* The occurrence at any time with respect to a party or, if applicable, any Specified Entity of such party, of any of the following events constitutes an event of default (an "Event of Default") with respect to such party:–

　(i)   *Failure to Pay.* Failure by the party to pay, when due, any amount required to be paid by it under this Agreement if such failure is not remedied on or before the third Business Day after notice of such failure to pay is given to the party;

　(ii)   *Breach of Agreement.* Failure by the party to comply with or perform any agreement or obligation (other than an obligation to pay any amount required to be paid by it under this Agreement or to give notice of a Termination Event or any agreement or obligation under Section 4(a)(i) or 4(d)) to be complied with or performed by the party in accordance with this Agreement if such failure is not remedied on or before the thirtieth day after notice of such failure is given to the party;

　(iii)   *Credit Support Default.*

　　(1)   Failure by the party or any applicable Specified Entity to comply with or perform any agreement or obligation to be complied with or performed by the party or such Specified Entity in accordance with any Credit Support Document if such failure is continuing after any applicable grace period has elapsed;

　　(2)   the expiration or termination of such Credit Support Document, or the ceasing of such Credit Support Document to be in full force and effect, prior to the final Scheduled Payment Date of each Swap Transaction to which such Credit Support Document relates without the written consent of the other party; or

　　(3)   the party or such Specified Entity repudiates, or challenges the validity of, such Credit Support Document;

　(iv)   *Misrepresentation.* A representation (other than a representation under Section 3(e) or (f)) made or repeated or deemed to have been made or repeated by the party or any applicable Specified Entity in this Agreement or any Credit Support Document relating to this Agreement proves to have been incorrect or misleading in any material respect when made or repeated or deemed to have been made or repeated;

　(v)   *Default under Specified Swaps.* The occurrence of an event of default in respect of the party or any applicable Specified Entity under a Specified Swap which, following the giving of any

ISDA 1987

applicable notice or the lapse of any applicable grace period, has resulted in the designation or occurrence of an early termination date in respect of such Specified Swap;

(vi) *Cross Default*. If "Cross Default" is specified in Part 1 of the Schedule as applying to the party, (1) the occurrence or existence of an event or condition in respect of such party or any applicable Specified Entity under one or more agreements or instruments relating to Specified Indebtedness of such party or any such Specified Entity in an aggregate amount of not less than the Threshold Amount (as specified in Part 1 of the Schedule) which has resulted in such Specified Indebtedness becoming, or becoming capable at such time of being declared, due and payable under such agreements or instruments, before it would otherwise have been due and payable or (2) the failure by such party or any such Specified Entity to make one or more payments at maturity in an aggregate amount of not less than the Threshold Amount under such agreements or instruments (after giving effect to any applicable grace period);

(vii) *Bankruptcy*. The party or any applicable Specified Entity:—

(1) is dissolved; (2) becomes insolvent or fails or is unable or admits in writing its inability generally to pay its debts as they become due; (3) makes a general assignment, arrangement or composition with or for the benefit of its creditors; (4) institutes or has instituted against it a proceeding seeking a judgment of insolvency or bankruptcy or any other relief under any bankruptcy or insolvency law or other similar law affecting creditors' rights, or a petition is presented for the winding-up or liquidation of the party or any such Specified Entity, and, in the case of any such proceeding or petition instituted or presented against it, such proceeding or petition (A) results in a judgment of insolvency or bankruptcy or the entry of an order for relief or the making of an order for the winding-up or liquidation of the party or such Specified Entity or (B) is not dismissed, discharged, stayed or restrained in each case within 30 days of the institution or presentation thereof; (5) has a resolution passed for its winding-up or liquidation; (6) seeks or becomes subject to the appointment of an administrator, receiver, trustee, custodian or other similar official for it or for all or substantially all its assets (regardless of how brief such appointment may be, or whether any obligations are promptly assumed by another entity or whether any other event described in this clause (6) has occurred and is continuing); (7) any event occurs with respect to the party or any such Specified Entity which, under the applicable laws of any jurisdiction, has an analogous effect to any of the events specified in clauses (1) to (6) (inclusive); or (8) takes any action in furtherance of, or indicating its consent to, approval of, or acquiescence in, any of the foregoing acts;

other than in the case of clause (1) or (5) or, to the extent it relates to those clauses, clause (8), for the purpose of a consolidation, amalgamation or merger which would not constitute an event described in (viii) below; or

(viii) *Merger Without Assumption*. The party consolidates or amalgamates with, or merges into, or transfers all or substantially all its assets to, another entity and, at the time of such consolidation, amalgamation, merger or transfer:—

(1) the resulting, surviving or transferee entity fails to assume all the obligations of such party under this Agreement by operation of law or pursuant to an agreement reasonably satisfactory to the other party to this Agreement; or

(2) the benefits of any Credit Support Document relating to this Agreement fail to extend (without the consent of the other party) to the performance by such resulting, surviving or transferee entity of its obligations under this Agreement.

(b) *Termination Events*. The occurrence at any time with respect to a party or, if applicable, any Specified Entity of such party of any event specified below constitutes an Illegality if the event is specified in (i) below, a Tax Event if the event is specified in (ii) below, a Tax Event Upon Merger if the event is specified in (iii) below or a Credit Event Upon Merger if the event is specified in (iv) below:—

(i) *Illegality*. Due to the adoption of, or any change in, any applicable law after the date on which such Swap Transaction is entered into, or due to the promulgation of, or any change in, the interpretation by any court, tribunal or regulatory authority with competent jurisdiction of any applicable law after such date, it becomes unlawful (other than as a result of a breach by the party of Section 4(b)) for such party (which will be the Affected Party):—

ISDA 1987

(1) to perform any absolute or contingent obligation to make a payment or to receive a payment in respect of such Swap Transaction or to comply with any other material provision of this Agreement relating to such Swap Transaction; or

(2) to perform, or for any applicable Specified Entity to perform, any contingent or other obligation which the party (or such Specified Entity) has under any Credit Support Document relating to such Swap Transaction;

(ii) **Tax Event.**

(1) The party (which will be the Affected Party) will be required on the next succeeding Scheduled Payment Date to pay to the other party an additional amount in respect of an Indemnifiable Tax under Section 2(d)(i)(4) (except in respect of interest under Section 2 (e)) as a result of a Change in Tax Law; or

(2) there is a substantial likelihood that the party (which will be the Affected Party) will be required on the next succeeding Scheduled Payment Date to pay to the other party an additional amount in respect of an Indemnifiable Tax under Section 2(d)(i)(4) (except in respect of interest under Section 2(e)) and such substantial likelihood results from an action taken by a taxing authority, or brought in a court of competent jurisdiction, on or after the date on which such Swap Transaction was entered into (regardless of whether such action was taken or brought with respect to a party to this Agreement);

(iii) **Tax Event Upon Merger.** The party (the "Burdened Party") on the next succeeding Scheduled Payment Date will either (1) be required to pay an additional amount in respect of an Indemnifiable Tax under Section 2(d)(i)(4) (except in respect of interest under Section 2(e)) or (2) receive a payment from which an amount has been deducted or withheld for or on account of any Indemnifiable Tax in respect of which the other party is not required to pay an additional amount, in either case as a result of a party consolidating or amalgamating with, or merging into, or transferring all or substantially all its assets to, another entity (which will be the Affected Party) where such action does not constitute an event described in Section 5(a)(viii); or

(iv) **Credit Event Upon Merger.** If "Credit Event Upon Merger" is specified in Part 1 of the Schedule as applying to the party, such party ("X") consolidates or amalgamates with, or merges into, or transfers all or substantially all its assets to, another entity and such action does not constitute an event described in Section 5(a)(viii) but the creditworthiness of the resulting, surviving or transferee entity (which will be the Affected Party) is materially weaker than that of X immediately prior to such action.

(c) **Event of Default and Illegality.** If an event or circumstance which would otherwise constitute or give rise to an Event of Default also constitutes an Illegality, it will be treated as an Illegality and will not constitute an Event of Default.

6. Early Termination

(a) **Right to Terminate Following Event of Default.** If at any time an Event of Default with respect to a party (the "Defaulting Party") has occurred and is then continuing, the other party may, by not more than 20 days notice to the Defaulting Party specifying the relevant Event of Default, designate a day not earlier than the day such notice is effective as an Early Termination Date in respect of all outstanding Swap Transactions. However, an Early Termination Date will be deemed to have occurred in respect of all Swap Transactions immediately upon the occurrence of any Event of Default specified in Section 5(a)(vii)(1), (2), (3), (5), (6), (7) or (8) and as of the time immediately preceding the institution of the relevant proceeding or the presentation of the relevant petition upon the occurrence of any Event of Default specified in Section 5(a)(vii)(4).

(b) **Right to Terminate Following Termination Event.**

(i) **Notice.** Upon the occurrence of a Termination Event, an Affected Party will, promptly upon becoming aware of the same, notify the other party thereof, specifying the nature of such Termination Event and the Affected Transactions relating thereto. The Affected Party will also give such other information to the other party with regard to such Termination Event as the other party may reasonably require.

(ii) **Transfer to Avoid Termination Event.** If either an Illegality under Section 5(b)(i)(1) or a Tax Event occurs and there is only one Affected Party, or if a Tax Event Upon Merger occurs and the Burdened Party is the Affected Party, the Affected Party will as a condition to its right to designate an Early Termination Date under Section 6(b)(iv) use all reasonable efforts (which will not require such party to incur a loss, excluding immaterial, incidental expenses) to transfer within 20 days after it gives notice under Section 6(b)(i) all its rights and obligations under this Agreement in respect of the Affected Transactions to another of its offices, branches or Affiliates so that such Termination Event ceases to exist.

If the Affected Party is not able to make such a transfer it will give notice to the other party to that effect within such 20 day period, whereupon the other party may effect such a transfer within 30 days after the notice is given under Section 6(b)(i).

Any such transfer by a party under this Section 6(b)(ii) will be subject to and conditional upon the prior written consent of the other party, which consent will not be withheld if such other party's policies in effect at such time would permit it to enter into swap transactions with the transferee on the terms proposed.

(iii) *Two Affected Parties.* If an Illegality under Section 5(b)(i)(1) or a Tax Event occurs and there are two Affected Parties, each party will use all reasonable efforts to reach agreement within 30 days after notice thereof is given under Section 6(b)(i) on action that would cause such Termination Event to cease to exist.

(iv) *Right to Terminate.* If:–

(1) a transfer under Section 6(b)(ii) or an agreement under Section 6(b)(iii), as the case may be, has not been effected with respect to all Affected Transactions within 30 days after an Affected Party gives notice under Section 6(b)(i); or

(2) an Illegality under Section 5(b)(i)(2) or a Credit Event Upon Merger occurs, or a Tax Event Upon Merger occurs and the Burdened Party is not the Affected Party,

either party in the case of an Illegality, the Burdened Party in the case of a Tax Event Upon Merger, any Affected Party in the case of a Tax Event, or the party which is not the Affected Party in the case of a Credit Event Upon Merger, may, by not more than 20 days notice to the other party and provided that the relevant Termination Event is then continuing, designate a day not earlier than the day such notice is effective as an Early Termination Date in respect of all Affected Transactions.

(c) *Effect of Designation.*

(i) If notice designating an Early Termination Date is given under Section 6(a) or (b), the Early Termination Date will occur on the date so designated, whether or not the relevant Event of Default or Termination Event is continuing on the relevant Early Termination Date.

(ii) Upon the effectiveness of notice designating an Early Termination Date (or the deemed occurrence of an Early Termination Date), the obligations of the parties to make any further payments under Section 2(a)(i) in respect of the Terminated Transactions will terminate, but without prejudice to the other provisions of this Agreement.

(d) *Calculations.*

(i) *Statement.* Following the occurrence of an Early Termination Date, each party will make the calculations (including calculation of applicable interest rates) on its part contemplated by Section 6(e) and will provide to the other party a statement (1) showing, in reasonable detail, such calculations (including all relevant quotations) and (2) giving details of the relevant account to which any payment due to it under Section 6(e) is to be made. In the absence of written confirmation of a quotation obtained in determining a Market Quotation from the source providing such quotation, the records of the party obtaining such quotation will be conclusive evidence of the existence and accuracy of such quotation.

(ii) *Due Date.* The amount calculated as being payable under Section 6(e) will be due on the day that notice of the amount payable is effective (in the case of an Early Termination Date which is designated or deemed to occur as a result of an Event of Default) and not later than the day which is two Business Days after the day on which notice of the amount payable is effective (in the case of an Early Termination Date which is designated as a result of a Termination Event). Such amount will be paid together with (to the extent permitted under applicable law) interest thereon in the Termination Currency from (and including) the relevant Early Termination Date to (but excluding) the relevant due date, calculated as follows:–

(1) if notice is given designating an Early Termination Date or if an Early Termination Date is deemed to occur, in either case as a result of an Event of Default, at the Default Rate; or

(2) if notice is given designating an Early Termination Date as a result of a Termination Event, at the Default Rate minus 1% per annum.

Such interest will be calculated on the basis of daily compounding and the actual number of days elapsed.

(e) *Payments on Early Termination.*

(i) *Defaulting Party or One Affected Party.* If notice is given designating an Early Termination Date or if an Early Termination Date is deemed to occur and there is a Defaulting Party or only one Affected Party, the other party will determine the Settlement Amount in respect of the Terminated Transactions and:–

(1) if there is a Defaulting Party, the Defaulting Party will pay to the other party the excess, if a positive number, of (A) the sum of such Settlement Amount and the Termination Currency Equivalent of the Unpaid Amounts owing to the other party over (B) the Termination Currency Equivalent of the Unpaid Amounts owing to the Defaulting Party; and

(2) if there is an Affected Party, the payment to be made will be equal to (A) the sum of such Settlement Amount and the Termination Currency Equivalent of the Unpaid Amounts owing to the party determining the Settlement Amount ("X") less (B) the Termination Currency Equivalent of the Unpaid Amounts owing to the party not determining the Settlement Amount ("Y").

(ii) *Two Affected Parties.* If notice is given of an Early Termination Date and there are two Affected Parties, each party will determine a Settlement Amount in respect of the Terminated Transactions and the payment to be made will be equal to (1) the sum of (A) one-half of the difference between the Settlement Amount of the party with the higher Settlement Amount ("X") and the Settlement Amount of the party with the lower Settlement Amount ("Y") and (B) the Termination Currency Equivalent of the Unpaid Amounts owing to X less (2) the Termination Currency Equivalent of the Unpaid Amounts owing to Y.

(iii) *Party Owing.* If the amount calculated under Section 6(e)(i)(2) or (ii) is a positive number, Y will pay such amount to X; if such amount is a negative number, X will pay the absolute value of such amount to Y.

(iv) *Adjustment for Bankruptcy.* In circumstances where an Early Termination Date is deemed to occur, the amount determined under Section 6(e)(i) will be subject to such adjustments as are appropriate and permitted by law to reflect any payments made by one party to the other under this Agreement (and retained by such other party) during the period from the relevant Early Termination Date to the date for payment determined under Section 6(d)(ii).

(v) *Pre-Estimate of Loss.* The parties agree that the amounts recoverable under this Section 6(e) are a reasonable pre-estimate of loss and not a penalty. Such amounts are payable for the loss of bargain and the loss of protection against future risks and except as otherwise provided in this Agreement neither party will be entitled to recover any additional damages as a consequence of such losses.

7. Transfer

Subject to Section 6(b) and to any exception provided in the Schedule, neither this Agreement nor any interest or obligation in or under this Agreement may be transferred by either party without the prior written consent of the other party (other than pursuant to a consolidation or amalgamation with, or merger into, or transfer of all or substantially all its assets to, another entity) and any purported transfer without such consent will be void.

8. Contractual Currency

(a) *Payment in the Contractual Currency.* Each payment under this Agreement will be made in the relevant currency specified in this Agreement for that payment (the "Contractual Currency"). To the extent permitted by applicable law, any obligation to make payments under this Agreement in the Contractual Currency will not be discharged or satisfied by any tender in any currency other than the Contractual Currency, except to the extent such tender results in the actual receipt by the party to which payment is owed, acting in a reasonable manner and in good faith in converting the currency so tendered into the Contractual Currency, of the full amount in the Contractual Currency of all amounts due in respect of this Agreement. If for any reason the amount in the Contractual Currency so received falls short of the amount in the Contractual Currency due in respect of this Agreement, the party required to make the payment will, to the extent permitted by applicable law, immediately pay such additional amount in the Contractual Currency as may be necessary to compensate for the shortfall. If for any reason the amount in the Contractual Currency so received exceeds the amount in the Contractual Currency due in respect of this Agreement, the party receiving the payment will refund promptly the amount of such excess.

(b)   *Judgments.* To the extent permitted by applicable law, if any judgment or order expressed in a currency other than the Contractual Currency is rendered (i) for the payment of any amount owing in respect of this Agreement, (ii) for the payment of any amount relating to any early termination in respect of this Agreement or (iii) in respect of a judgment or order of another court for the payment of any amount described in (i) or (ii) above, the party seeking recovery, after recovery in full of the aggregate amount to which such party is entitled pursuant to the judgment or order, will be entitled to receive immediately from the other party the amount of any shortfall of the Contractual Currency received by such party as a consequence of sums paid in such other currency and will refund promptly to the other party any excess of the Contractual Currency received by such party as a consequence of sums paid in such other currency if such shortfall or such excess arises or results from any variation between the rate of exchange at which the Contractual Currency is converted into the currency of the judgment or order for the purposes of such judgment or order and the rate of exchange at which such party is able, acting in a reasonable manner and in good faith in converting the currency received into the Contractual Currency, to purchase the Contractual Currency with the amount of the currency of the judgment or order actually received by such party. The term "rate of exchange" includes, without limitation, any premiums and costs of exchange payable in connection with the purchase of or conversion into the Contractual Currency.

(c)   *Separate Indemnities.* To the extent permitted by applicable law, these indemnities constitute separate and independent obligations from the other obligations in this Agreement, will be enforceable as separate and independent causes of action, will apply notwithstanding any indulgence granted by the party to which any payment is owed and will not be affected by judgment being obtained or claim or proof being made for any other sums due in respect of this Agreement.

(d)   *Evidence of Loss.* For the purpose of this Section 8, it will be sufficient for a party to demonstrate that it would have suffered a loss had an actual exchange or purchase been made.

9.   **Miscellaneous**

(a)   *Entire Agreement.* This Agreement constitutes the entire agreement and understanding of the parties with respect to its subject matter and supersedes all oral communication and prior writings with respect thereto.

(b)   *Amendments.* No amendment, modification or waiver in respect of this Agreement will be effective unless in writing and executed by each of the parties or confirmed by an exchange of telexes.

(c)   *Survival of Obligations.* Except as provided in Section 6(c)(ii), the obligations of the parties under this Agreement will survive the termination of any Swap Transaction.

(d)   *Remedies Cumulative.* Except as provided in this Agreement, the rights, powers, remedies and privileges provided in this Agreement are cumulative and not exclusive of any rights, powers, remedies and privileges provided by law.

(e)   *Counterparts and Confirmations.*
        (i)   This Agreement may be executed in counterparts, each of which will be deemed an original.
        (ii)   A Confirmation may be executed in counterparts or be created by an exchange of telexes, which in either case will be sufficient for all purposes to evidence a binding supplement to this Agreement. Any such counterpart or telex will specify that it constitutes a Confirmation.

(f)   *No Waiver of Rights.* A failure or delay in exercising any right, power or privilege in respect of this Agreement will not be presumed to operate as a waiver, and a single or partial exercise of any right, power or privilege will not be presumed to preclude any subsequent or further exercise of that right, power or privilege or the exercise of any other right, power or privilege.

(g)   *Headings.* The headings used in this Agreement are for convenience of reference only and are not to affect the construction of or to be taken into consideration in interpreting this Agreement.

10. Multibranch Parties

If a party is specified as a Multibranch Party in Part 4 of the Schedule, such Multibranch Party may make and receive payments under any Swap Transaction through any of its branches or offices listed in the Schedule (each an "Office"). The Office through which it so makes and receives payments for the purpose of any Swap Transaction will be specified in the relevant Confirmation and any change of Office for such purpose requires the prior written consent of the other party. Each Multibranch Party represents to the other party that, notwithstanding the place of payment, the obligations of each Office are for all purposes under this Agreement the obligations of such Multibranch Party. This representation will be deemed to be repeated by such Multibranch Party on each date on which a Swap Transaction is entered into.

11. Expenses

A Defaulting Party will, on demand, indemnify and hold harmless the other party for and against all reasonable out-of-pocket expenses, including legal fees and Stamp Tax, incurred by such other party by reason of the enforcement and protection of its rights under this Agreement or by reason of the early termination of any Swap Transaction, including, but not limited to, costs of collection.

12. Notices

(a)   *Effectiveness.* Any notice or communication in respect of this Agreement will be sufficiently given to a party if in writing and delivered in person, sent by certified or registered mail (airmail, if overseas) or the equivalent (with return receipt requested) or by overnight courier or given by telex (with answerback received) at the address or telex number specified in Part 4 of the Schedule. A notice or communication will be effective:–

  (i)   if delivered by hand or sent by overnight courier, on the day it is delivered (or if that day is not a day on which commercial banks are open for business in the city specified in the address for notice provided by the recipient (a "Local Banking Day"), or if delivered after the close of business on a Local Banking Day, on the first following day that is a Local Banking Day);

  (ii)   if sent by telex, on the day the recipient's answerback is received (or if that day is not a Local Banking Day, or if after the close of business on a Local Banking Day, on the first following day that is a Local Banking Day); or

  (iii)   if sent by certified or registered mail (airmail, if overseas) or the equivalent (return receipt requested), three Local Banking Days after despatch if the recipient's address for notice is in the same country as the place of despatch and otherwise seven Local Banking Days after despatch.

(b)   *Change of Addresses.* Either party may by notice to the other change the address or telex number at which notices or communications are to be given to it.

13. Governing Law and Jurisdiction

(a)   *Governing Law.* This Agreement will be governed by and construed in accordance with the law specified in Part 4 of the Schedule.

(b)   *Jurisdiction.* With respect to any suit, action or proceedings relating to this Agreement ("Proceedings"), each party irrevocably:–

  (i)   submits to the jurisdiction of the English courts, if this Agreement is expressed to be governed by English law, or to the non-exclusive jurisdiction of the courts of the State of New York and the United States District Court located in the Borough of Manhattan in New York City, if this Agreement is expressed to be governed by the laws of the State of New York; and

  (ii)   waives any objection which it may have at any time to the laying of venue of any Proceedings brought in any such court, waives any claim that such Proceedings have been brought in an inconvenient forum and further waives the right to object, with respect to such Proceedings, that such court does not have jurisdiction over such party.

Nothing in this Agreement precludes either party from bringing Proceedings in any other jurisdiction (outside, if this Agreement is expressed to be governed by English law, the Contracting States, as defined in Section 1(3) of the Civil Jurisdiction and Judgments Act 1982 or any modification, extension or re-enactment thereof for the time being in force) nor will the bringing of Proceedings in any one or more jurisdictions preclude the bringing of Proceedings in any other jurisdiction.

(c)   *Service of Process.* Each party irrevocably appoints the Process Agent (if any) specified opposite its name in Part 4 of the Schedule to receive, for it and on its behalf, service of process in any Proceedings. If for any reason any party's Process Agent is unable to act as such, such party will promptly notify the other party and within 30 days appoint a substitute process agent acceptable to the other party. The parties irrevocably consent to service of process given in the manner provided for notices in Section 12. Nothing in this Agreement will affect the right of either party to serve process in any other manner permitted by law.

(d)   *Waiver of Immunities.* Each party irrevocably waives, to the fullest extent permitted by applicable law, with respect to itself and its revenues and assets (irrespective of their use or intended use), all immunity on the grounds of sovereignty or other similiar grounds from (i) suit, (ii) jurisdiction of any court, (iii) relief by way of injunction, order for specific performance or for recovery of property, (iv) attachment of its assets (whether before or after judgment) and (v) execution or enforcement of any judgment to which it or its revenues or assets might otherwise be entitled in any Proceedings in the courts of any jurisdiction and irrevocably agrees, to the extent permitted by applicable law, that it will not claim any such immunity in any Proceedings.

14.   Definitions

As used in this Agreement:–

"Affected Party" has the meaning specified in Section 5(b).

"Affected Transactions" means (a) with respect to any Termination Event consisting of an Illegality, Tax Event or Tax Event Upon Merger, all Swap Transactions affected by the occurrence of such Termination Event and (b) with respect to any other Termination Event, all Swap Transactions.

"Affiliate" means, subject to Part 4 of the Schedule, in relation to any person, any entity controlled, directly or indirectly, by the person, any entity that controls, directly or indirectly, the person or any entity under common control with the person. For this purpose, "control" of any entity or person means ownership of a majority of the voting power of the entity or person.

"Burdened Party" has the meaning specified in Section 5(b).

"Business Day" means (a) in relation to any payment due under Section 2(a)(i), a day on which commercial banks and foreign exchange markets are open for business in the place(s) specified in the relevant Confirmation and (b) in relation to any other payment, a day on which commercial banks and foreign exchange markets are open for business in the place where the relevant account is located and, if different, in the principal financial centre of the currency of such payment.

"Change in Tax Law" means the enactment, promulgation, execution or ratification of, or any change in or amendment to, any law (or in the application or official interpretation of any law) that occurs on or after the date on which the relevant Swap Transaction is entered into.

"consent" includes a consent, approval, action, authorisation, exemption, notice, filing, registration or exchange control consent.

"Credit Event Upon Merger" has the meaning specified in Section 5(b).

"Credit Support Document" means any agreement or instrument which is specified as such in this Agreement.

"Default Rate" means a rate per annum equal to the cost (without proof or evidence of any actual cost) to the relevant payee (as certified by it) of funding the relevant amount plus 1% per annum.

"Defaulting Party" has the meaning specified in Section 6(a).

"Early Termination Date" means the date specified as such in a notice given under Section 6(a) or 6(b)(iv).

"Event of Default" has the meaning specified in Section 5(a).

"Illegality" has the meaning specified in Section 5(b).

"Indemnifiable Tax" means any Tax other than a Tax that would not be imposed in respect of a payment under this Agreement but for a present or former connection between the jurisdiction of the government or taxation authority imposing such Tax and the recipient of such payment or a person related to such recipient (including, without limitation, a connection arising from such recipient or related person being or having been a citizen or resident of such jurisdiction, or being or having been organised, present or engaged in a trade or business in such jurisdiction, or having or having had a permanent establishment or fixed place of business in such jurisdiction, but excluding a connection arising solely from such recipient or related person having executed, delivered, performed its obligations or received a payment

under, or enforced, this Agreement or a Credit Support Document).

"law" includes any treaty, law, rule or regulation (as modified, in the case of tax matters, by the practice of any relevant governmental revenue authority) and *"lawful"* and *"unlawful"* will be construed accordingly.

"Loss" means, with respect to a Terminated Transaction and a party, an amount equal to the total amount (expressed as a positive amount) required, as determined as of the relevant Early Termination Date (or, if an Early Termination Date is deemed to occur, as of a time as soon thereafter as practicable) by the party in good faith, to compensate it for any losses and costs (including loss of bargain and costs of funding but excluding legal fees and other out-of-pocket expenses) that it may incur as a result of the early termination of the obligations of the parties in respect of such Terminated Transaction. If a party determines that it would gain or benefit from such early termination, such party's Loss will be an amount (expressed as a negative amount) equal to the amount of the gain or benefit as determined by such party.

"Market Quotation" means, with respect to a Terminated Transaction and a party to such Terminated Transaction making the determination, an amount (which may be negative) determined on the basis of quotations from Reference Market-makers for the amount that would be or would have been payable on the relevant Early Termination Date, either by the party to the Terminated Transaction making the determination (to be expressed as a positive amount) or to such party (to be expressed as a negative amount), in consideration of an agreement between such party and the quoting Reference Market-maker and subject to such documentation as they may in good faith agree, with the relevant Early Termination Date as the date of commencement of such agreement (or, if later, the date specified as the effective date of such Terminated Transaction in the relevant Confirmation), that would have the effect of preserving for such party the economic equivalent of the payment obligations of the parties under Section 2(a)(i) in respect of such Terminated Transaction that would, but for the occurrence of the relevant Early Termination Date, fall due after such Early Termination Date (excluding any Unpaid Amounts in respect of such Terminated Transaction but including, without limitation, any amounts that would, but for the occurrence of the relevant Early Termination Date, have been payable (assuming each applicable condition precedent had been satisfied) after such Early Termination Date by reference to any period in which such Early Termination Date occurs). The party making the determination (or its agent) will request each Reference Market-maker to provide its quotation to the extent practicable as of the same time (without regard to different time zones) on the relevant Early Termination Date (or, if an Early Termination Date is deemed to occur, as of a time as soon thereafter as practicable). The time as of which such quotations are to be obtained will, if only one party is obliged to make a determination under Section 6(e), be selected in good faith by that party and otherwise will be agreed by the parties. If more than three such quotations are provided, the Market Quotation will be the arithmetic mean of the Termination Currency Equivalent of the quotations, without regard to the quotations having the highest and lowest values. If exactly three such quotations are provided, the Market Quotation will be the quotation remaining after disregarding the quotations having the highest and lowest values. If fewer than three quotations are provided, it will be deemed that the Market Quotation in respect of such Terminated Transaction cannot be determined.

"Office" has the meaning specified in Section 10.

"Potential Event of Default" means any event which, with the giving of notice or the lapse of time or both, would constitute an Event of Default.

"Reference Market-makers" means four leading dealers in the relevant swap market selected by the party determining a Market Quotation in good faith (a) from among dealers of the highest credit standing which satisfy all the criteria that such party applies generally at the time in deciding whether to offer or to make an extension of credit and (b) to the extent practicable, from among such dealers having an office in the same city.

"Relevant Jurisdiction" means, with respect to a party, the jurisdictions (a) in which the party is incorporated, organised, managed and controlled or considered to have its seat, (b) where a branch or office through which the party is acting for purposes of this Agreement is located, (c) in which the party executes this Agreement and (d) in relation to any payment, from or through which such payment is made.

"Scheduled Payment Date" means a date on which a payment is due under Section 2(a)(i) with respect to a Swap Transaction.

"Settlement Amount" means, with respect to a party and any Early Termination Date, the sum of:–

(a) the Termination Currency Equivalent of the Market Quotations (whether positive or negative) for each Terminated Transaction for which a Market Quotation is determined; and

(b) for each Terminated Transaction for which a Market Quotation is not, or cannot be, determined, the Termination Currency Equivalent of such party's Loss (whether positive or negative);

provided that if the parties agree that an amount may be payable under Section 6(e) to a Defaulting Party by the other party, no account shall be taken of a Settlement Amount expressed as a negative number.

"Specified Entity" has the meaning specified in Part 1 of the Schedule.

"Specified Indebtedness" means, subject to Part 1 of the Schedule, any obligation (whether present or future, contingent or otherwise, as principal or surety or otherwise) in respect of borrowed money.

"Specified Swap" means, subject to Part 1 of the Schedule, any rate swap or currency exchange transaction now existing or hereafter entered into between one party to this Agreement (or any applicable Specified Entity) and the other party to this Agreement (or any applicable Specified Entity).

"Stamp Tax" means any stamp, registration, documentation or similar tax.

"Tax" means any present or future tax, levy, impost, duty, charge, assessment or fee of any nature (including interest, penalties and additions thereto) that is imposed by any government or other taxing authority in respect of any payment under this Agreement other than a stamp, registration, documentation or similar tax.

"Tax Event" has the meaning specified in Section 5(b).

"Tax Event Upon Merger" has the meaning specified in Section 5(b).

"Terminated Transactions" means (a) with respect to any Early Termination Date occurring as a result of a Termination Event, all Affected Transactions and (b) with respect to any Early Termination Date occurring as a result of an Event of Default, all Swap Transactions, which in either case are in effect as of the time immediately preceding the effectiveness of the notice designating such Early Termination Date (or, in the case of an Event of Default specified in Section 5(a)(vii), in effect as of the time immediately preceding such Early Termination Date).

"Termination Currency" has the meaning specified in Part 1 of the Schedule.

"Termination Currency Equivalent" means, in respect of any amount denominated in the Termination Currency, such Termination Currency amount and, in respect of any amount denominated in a currency other than the Termination Currency (the ''Other Currency''), the amount in the Termination Currency determined by the party making the relevant determination as being required to purchase such amount of such Other Currency as at the relevant Early Termination Date with the Termination Currency at the rate equal to the spot exchange rate of the foreign exchange agent (selected as provided below) for the purchase of such Other Currency with the Termination Currency at or about 11.00 a.m. (in the city in which such foreign exchange agent is located) on such date as would be customary for the determination of such a rate for the purchase of such Other Currency for value the relevant Early Termination Date. The foreign exchange agent will, if only one party is obliged to make a determination under Section 6(e), be selected in good faith by that party and otherwise will be agreed by the parties.

"Termination Event" means an Illegality, a Tax Event, a Tax Event Upon Merger or a Credit Event Upon Merger.

"Unpaid Amounts" owing to any party means, with respect to any Early Termination Date, the aggregate of the amounts that became due and payable (or that would have become due and payable but for Section 2(a)(iii) or the designation or occurrence of such Early Termination Date) to such party under Section 2(a)(i) in respect of all Terminated Transactions by reference to all periods ended on or prior to such Early Termination Date and which remain unpaid as at such Early Termination Date, together with (to the extent permitted under applicable law and in lieu of any interest calculated under Section 2(e)) interest thereon, in the currency of such amounts, from (and including) the date such amounts became due and payable or would have become due and payable to (but excluding) such Early Termination Date, calculated as follows:–

(a) in the case of notice of an Early Termination Date given as a result of an Event of Default:–

(i) interest on such amounts due and payable by a Defaulting Party will be calculated at the Default Rate; and

(ii) interest on such amounts due and payable by the other party will be calculated at a rate per annum equal to the cost to such other party (as certified by it) if it were to fund such amounts (without proof or evidence of any actual cost); and

(b) in the case of notice of an Early Termination Date given as a result of a Termination Event, interest on such amounts due and payable by either party will be calculated at a rate per annum equal to the arithmetic mean of the cost (without proof or evidence of any actual cost) to each party (as certified by such party and regardless of whether due and payable by such party) if it were to fund or of funding such amounts.

Such amounts of interest will be calculated on the basis of daily compounding and the actual number of days elapsed.

IN WITNESS WHEREOF the parties have executed this document as of the date specified on the first page of this document.

....
        (Name of party)   (Name of party)

By: ....   By: ....

Name: Name:

Title: Title:

SCHEDULE
to the
Interest Rate and Currency Exchange Agreement

dated as of ....

between .... and ....
          ("Party A")   ("Party B")

Part 1
Termination Provisions

In this Agreement:–

(1)   *"Specified Entity"* means in relation to Party A for the purpose of:–

      Section 5(a)(iii) and (iv) and Section 5(b)(i), ...

      Section 5(a)(v), ...

      Section 5(a)(vi), ...

      Section 5(a)(vii), ...

in relation to Party B for the purpose of:–

      Section 5(a)(iii) and (iv) and Section 5(b)(i), ...

      Section 5(a)(v), ...

      Section 5(a)(vi), ...

      Section 5(a)(vii), ...

(2)   *"Specified Swap"* will have the meaning specified in Section 14 unless another meaning is specified here...

....

....

(3)   The *"Cross Default"* provisions of Section 5(a)(vi) will/will not* apply to Party A
                                         will/will not* apply to Party B

If such provisions apply:–

"Specified Indebtedness" will have the meaning specified in Section 14 unless another meaning is specified here ....

....

"Threshold Amount" means ....

....

(4)   *"Termination Currency"* means .... , if such currency is specified and freely available, and otherwise United States Dollars.

(5)   The *"Credit Event Upon Merger"* provisions of Section 5(b)(iv) will/will not* apply to Party A
                                         will/will not* apply to Party B

*Delete as applicable   15   ISDA 1987

Part 2

Tax Representations

Representations of Party A

(1) *Payer Tax Representation.* For the purpose of Section 3(e), Party A will/will not* make the following representation:–

It is not required by any applicable law, as modified by the practice of any relevant governmental revenue authority, of any Relevant Jurisdiction to make any deduction or withholding for or on account of any Tax from any payment (other than interest under Section 2 (e)) to be made by it to the other party under this Agreement. In making this representation, it may rely on:–

(i)   the accuracy of any representation made by the other party pursuant to Section 3(f);

(ii)   the satisfaction of the agreement of the other party contained in Section 4(a)(i) and the accuracy and effectiveness of any document provided by the other party pursuant to Section 4(a)(i); and

(iii)   the satisfaction of the agreement of the other party contained in Section 4(d).

(2) *Payee Tax Representations.* For the purpose of Section 3(f), Party A makes the representation(s) specified below:–

(a)   The following representation will/will not* apply:–

It is fully eligible for the benefits of the "Business Profits" or "Industrial and Commercial Profits" provision, as the case may be, the "Interest" provision or the "Other Income" provision (if any) of the Specified Treaty with respect to any payment described in such provisions and received or to be received by it in connection with this Agreement and no such payment is attributable to a trade or business carried on by it through a permanent establishment in the Specified Jurisdiction.

If such representation applies, then:–

"Specified Treaty" means ....

"Specified Jurisdiction" means ....

(b)   The following representation will/will not* apply:–

Each payment received or to be received by it in connection with this Agreement relates to the regular business operations of the party (and not to an investment of the party).

(c)   The following representation will/will not* apply:–

Each payment received or to be received by it in connection with this Agreement will be effectively connected with its conduct of a trade or business in the Specified Jurisdiction.

If such representation applies, then *"Specified Jurisdiction"* means ....

(d)   The following representation will/will not* apply:–

It is a bank recognised by the United Kingdom Inland Revenue as carrying on a bona fide banking business in the United Kingdom, is entering into this Agreement in the ordinary course of such business and will bring into account payments made and received under this Agreement in computing its income for United Kingdom tax purposes.

(e)   Other representations:– ....

....

....

....

N.B. The above representations may need modification if either party is a Multibranch Party.

*Delete as applicable   16   ISDA 1987

Representations of Party B

(1) *Payer Tax Representation.* For the purpose of Section 3(e), Party B will/will not* make the following representation:–

It is not required by any applicable law, as modified by the practice of any relevant governmental revenue authority, of any Relevant Jurisdiction to make any deduction or withholding for or on account of any Tax from any payment (other than interest under Section 2 (e)) to be made by it to the other party under this Agreement. In making this representation, it may rely on:–

(i) the accuracy of any representation made by the other party pursuant to Section 3(f);

(ii) the satisfaction of the agreement of the other party contained in Section 4(a)(i) and the accuracy and effectiveness of any document provided by the other party pursuant to Section 4(a)(i); and

(iii) the satisfaction of the agreement of the other party contained in Section 4(d).

(2) *Payee Tax Representations.* For the purpose of Section 3(f), Party B makes the representation(s) specified below:–

(a) The following representation will/will not* apply:–

It is fully eligible for the benefits of the ''Business Profits'' or ''Industrial and Commercial Profits'' provision, as the case may be, the ''Interest'' provision or the ''Other Income'' provision (if any) of the Specified Treaty with respect to any payment described in such provisions and received or to be received by it in connection with this Agreement and no such payment is attributable to a trade or business carried on by it through a permanent establishment in the Specified Jurisdiction.

If such representation applies, then:–

''Specified Treaty'' means ....

''Specified Jurisdiction'' means ....

(b) The following representation will/will not* apply:–

Each payment received or to be received by it in connection with this Agreement relates to the regular business operations of the party (and not to an investment of the party).

(c) The following representation will/will not* apply:–

Each payment received or to be received by it in connection with this Agreement will be effectively connected with its conduct of a trade or business in the Specified Jurisdiction.

If such representation applies, then *''Specified Jurisdiction''* means ....

(d) The following representation will/will not* apply:–

It is a bank recognised by the United Kingdom Inland Revenue as carrying on a bona fide banking business in the United Kingdom, is entering into this Agreement in the ordinary course of such business and will bring into account payments made and received under this Agreement in computing its income for United Kingdom tax purposes.

(e) Other representations:– ....

....

....

....

N.B. The above representations may need modification if either party is a Multibranch Party.

Part 3
Documents to be delivered

For the purpose of Section 4(a):–

(1) Tax forms, documents or certificates to be delivered are:–

Party required to deliver document	Form/Document/ Certificate	Date by which to be delivered
....	....	....
....	....	....
....	....	....
....	....	....
....	....	....

(2) Other documents to be delivered are:–

Party required to deliver document	Form/Document/ Certificate	Date by which to be delivered	Covered by Section 3(d) Representation
....	....	....	Yes/No*
....	....	....	Yes/No*
....	....	....	Yes/No*
....	....	....	Yes/No*
....	....	....	Yes/No*

Part 4
Miscellaneous

(1) *Governing Law*. This Agreement will be governed by and construed in accordance with English law/the laws of the State of New York without reference to choice of law doctrine*.

(2) *Process Agent*. For the purpose of Section 13(c):–

Party A appoints as its Process Agent ....

....

....

Party B appoints as its Process Agent ....

....

....

(3) *"Affiliate"* will have the meaning specified in Section 14 unless another meaning is specified here

....

....

* Delete as applicable   18   ISDA 1987

(4) **Multibranch Party.** For the purpose of Section 10:–

Party A is/is not* a Multibranch Party and, if so, may act through the following Offices:–

....

....

Party B is/is not* a Multibranch Party and, if so, may act through the following Offices:–

....

....

(5) **Addresses for Notices.** For the purpose of Section 12(a):–

Address for notices or communications to Party A:–

Address: ....

Attention: ....

Telex No: .... Answerback: ....

(For all purposes/only with respect to Swap Transactions through that Office*.)

Address for notices or communications to Party B:–

Address: ....

Attention: ....

Telex No: .... Answerback: ....

(For all purposes/only with respect to Swap Transactions through that Office*.)

(6) **Credit Support Document.** Details of any Credit Support Document:–

....

....

....

....

(7) **Netting of Payments.** If indicated here, "Net Payments – Corresponding Payment Dates" will apply for the purpose of Section 2(c) with effect from the date of this Agreement:– _____**

Part 5

Other Provisions

Printed by Financial Print & Communications Ltd [FPC]   6083

ISDA 1987

CHAPTER 6

STRUCTURAL VARIATIONS IN CURRENCY SWAPS

Raj E. S. Venkatesh
Chase Manhattan Bank, N. A.
New York

Vijaya E. Venkatesh
Credit Lyonnais Bank
New York

Ravi E. Dattatreya
Sumitomo Bank Capital Markets, Inc.
New York

INTRODUCTION

A *cross currency swap,* often called simply a *currency swap,* is a privately negotiated contract between two parties to exchange certain cash flows involving usually two (but sometimes more) currencies. As such, the structure of the cash flows in a swap can be designed to satisfy the needs of the parties to the contract. Consequently, we find wide variations of structures in currency swaps. The currently prevalent cash flow valuation models based on robust theoretical principles have provided significant flexibility in the design of swap structures. However, the counterbalancing need for liquidity, in the event that a swap transaction must be unwound, encourages swap structures to gravitate toward a few selected formats. Market liquidity, aided by sophisticated valuation models, also increases the ability of swap providers to hedge swaps, in turn resulting in a better price for the end user. In cases where liquidity is not a concern, from the view of both end user and provider, swaps can be engineered with almost limitless variety.

STRUCTURAL VARIATIONS

All the variations available in interest rate swaps are present in currency swaps, with the currency of the cash flows as an additional variable. In this chapter we will examine some of the more common variants. Most examples that have been employed to illustrate the structural variations use the yen and the dollar as the currencies, but they are equally applicable to all currencies.

Standard Currency Swaps

An interest rate swap consists of the exchange of only the interest payments on a given notional principal. The principal amounts are not exchanged. In contrast, a currency swap consists of the exchange of interest payments as well as principal amounts. An interest rate swap involves the exchange of floating- and fixed-rate payments. In a currency swap, the addition of the currency component adds a new basic dimension. For the yen/dollar combination, we thus have the following types of swaps: (1) fixed yen versus fixed dollar, (2) fixed yen versus floating dollar, (3) floating yen versus floating dollar, and (4) floating yen versus fixed dollar. Among these four variations, the fixed yen for floating dollar swap is currently the most common and most widely quoted. In other currencies, one of the other structures might be more popular. For example, among the four basic varieties of sterling swaps, the floating sterling versus floating dollar swap is the most common.

In what follows, a number of simple case studies, or "situations," have been employed to illustrate each particular variation of basic currency swaps.

Situation—Achieving Funding Cost Target

ZYX, a Japanese corporation, is seeking ¥3.5 billion of funding for 10 years on a fixed-rate basis. It finds that its interest rate cost of 8.05 percent for domestic yen borrowing is slightly higher than its target rate of 7.90 percent. It can raise floating dollar funds in the Eurobond market at LIBOR flat.

ZYX can achieve its fixed yen funding target by raising $25 million of floating-rate funds in the Euromarket and swapping into fixed yen, as in Exhibit 1. Under the swap, ZYX pays yen interest at the fixed rate of 7.89 percent on ¥3.5 billion and receives dollar LIBOR on $25 million. At maturity, ZYX will pay ¥3.5 billion and receive $25 million. In effect, ZYX will have a 10-year funding at a fixed rate of 7.89 percent on ¥3.5 billion.

Coupon-Only Swaps

Currency swaps usually involve the exchange of principal amounts at maturity. Only by including this exchange can a borrowing (or asset) in one currency be converted effectively into a borrowing (or asset) in another currency. However, there are situations in which it is advantageous to eliminate the exchange of principal amounts and swap only the interest payments, as in an interest rate swap. This is called a *coupon-only swap*, or an *annuity swap*.

EXHIBIT 1
Achieving Funding Cost Target

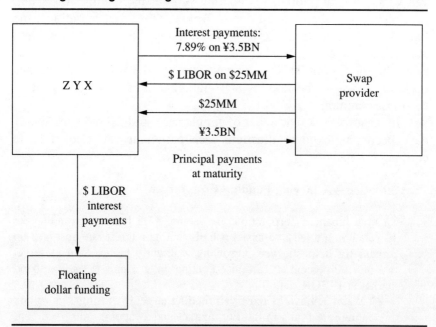

Situation—Hedging a Dual-Currency Bond

Uco, a U.S. multinational, is interested in raising cheap dollar funds for five years. Finding that investors in Europe pay a premium for instruments that offer opportunities to benefit from changes in the currency exchange rates, Uco is considering a dual-currency bond. The bond is set up such that periodic interest payments are made annually in yen on a given notional amount but the principal is paid in dollars.

Uco can swap the dual-currency bond into a dollar liability by means of a coupon-only swap. Under the swap, as shown in Exhibit 2, Uco will pay dollars and receive yen to cover the interest payments on the bond. Since the principal on the bond is already in dollars, there is no need to include it under the swap agreement.

After Uco uses the swap to hedge, the funding is effectively in dollars, so Uco is indifferent to the yen/dollar exchange rate. The premium paid by the investors for the dual-currency bond translates into a lower net interest rate cost for Uco. On the other hand, the investors have an opportunity to benefit significantly if the exchange rate between the dollar and the yen changes. Investors seeking dollars will benefit via the yen coupon payments if the yen gets stronger.

EXHIBIT 2
Hedging a Dual-Currency Bond

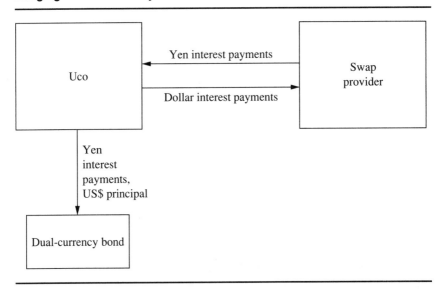

Investors seeking yen will benefit if the dollar gets stronger against the yen because the dollar principal payment will be worth more in yen.

Off-Market Swaps

Currency swaps are usually initiated such that their initial value is zero. That is, the present value of the cash flows to be paid equals the present value of the cash flows to be received. Any change in the market rates (i.e., interest rates in the two currencies or the exchange rate between the currencies, or just the passage of time) can cause a deviation in the value of the swap. A currency swap with nonzero value is called an *off-market swap*. If a new swap is off-market (i.e., has nonzero value), a compensating up-front payment from one party to the other will be required to bring the net value to zero. The adjustment may also be made with a lower-than-market coupon.

Situation—Hedging an Ex-Warrant Bond

JLC, a Japanese leasing company, has just issued a four-year, dollar-denominated bond in the Euromarket with attached equity warrants. JLC would like to convert the bond cash flows into yen.

The coupon on the bond is most likely to be below market, given that the bond has attached warrants. Therefore, JLC would enter into an off-market yen-dollar currency swap. JLC would receive cash up front from the swap provider or (more likely) would enjoy a lower-than-market dollar coupon.

Off-market swaps are generally used to unwind or reverse out of older currency swaps in which the interest rates or currency exchange rates have moved since the inception of the swap. They are also used in cases (see the discussion of asset swaps below) in which a given cash flow needs to be matched exactly. They can also be used to create discount or premium assets or liabilities in conjunction with a change in currency, as demonstrated in the following discussion of zero-coupon swaps.

Zero-Coupon Swap

A *zero-coupon swap* is an extreme case of an off-market swap in which one of the counterparties makes a lump sum payment instead of periodic payments over time.

Situation–Creating a Zero-Coupon Liability

JTC, a Japanese trading company, has just issued a fixed-rate, five-year, dollar-denominated bond in the Eurobond market. It is considering swapping the bond into a yen liability. However, because it would like to conserve cash as much as possible for operational reasons, it would prefer a zero-coupon funding.

JTC can achieve its goal by means of a zero-coupon currency swap. Under the swap, JTC will receive fixed-rate dollar cash flows for five years and the dollar principal payment at maturity. These cash flows will exactly service the outstanding Eurobond. As part of the swap contract, JTC will make a lump sum payment in yen at maturity. This payment is the effective zero-coupon liability for JTC.

Other variations of the zero-coupon swap are possible. The lump sum payment can occur at any time, up front, at maturity, or during the life of the swap.

Basis Swap

A *basis swap* entails two floating-rate indexes, one in each currency. An example is a swap of yen LIBOR interest payments against dollar LIBOR interest payments on the same notional principal amount. A basis swap can be a full currency swap—that is, including the exchange of principal amounts at maturity—or it can be a coupon-only swap.

Situation—Asset-Liability Matching

JFC, a Japanese finance company, has an active Euroyen commercial paper (CP) program. It has just purchased $25 million of a LIBOR-based dollar asset. It would like to convert the commercial paper liability into floating-rate dollars tied to LIBOR in order to match the floating-rate dollar asset.

To effect this conversion, JFC enters into a basis swap, as in Exhibit 3, paying dollar LIBOR and receiving yen LIBOR. Using an exchange rate of 140 yen to the dollar, JFC will exchange $25 million for ¥3.5 billion at maturity. Note that JFC retains the exposure to the difference between yen LIBOR and Euroyen commercial paper rate, the reason being that it can obtain a better price for the LIBOR/LIBOR swap than for a CP/LIBOR swap. Another exposure that remains is the difference between dollar LIBOR and the returns from the floating-rate dollar asset.

EXHIBIT 3
Asset-Liability Matching

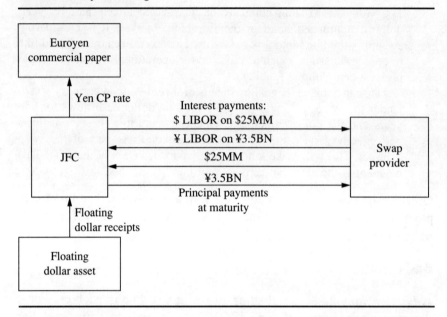

In some currencies, the basis swap is the more common transaction than the fixed-for-fixed or even the fixed-for-floating swap. For example, the swap of sterling LIBOR for dollar LIBOR is a very popular transaction.

Asset Swap—Synthetic Securities

Swaps are used not only for managing liabilities, but also for engineering the cash flows from assets into desired formats. For example, a yen asset can be converted into a synthetic dollar asset using a currency swap.

Situation—Creating a Synthetic Dollar Asset

JI, a Japanese investor, has just acquired a fixed-rate yen bond at an attractive yield. He would like to convert the bond into a dollar LIBOR asset.

JI can achieve its goal by entering into an asset swap. Under the swap contract, JI will essentially pay all the yen cash flow received from the asset, including the yen principal to the swap counterparty. It will receive dollar LIBOR payments periodically and a dollar balloon payment (representing the principal) at maturity. Note that the currency swap entered into may be an off-market swap so as to match the cash flows from the yen bond exactly. Also, the swap counterparty might require that the yen asset be pledged as collateral, depending on the credit rating of JI.

Synthetic assets can provide attractive returns relative to conventional securities. It should be remembered, however, that synthetic assets in general have lower liquidity and are appropriate only when they are expected to be held to maturity.

Forward Swap

A *forward swap* is one in which there is a significant delay between the date on which the swap is executed or committed to and the settlement or effective date of the swap.

Situation—Avoiding Exchange-Rate Risk

MWCo is a Midwestern manufacturing company that is planning to raise dollar funds in the near future, three months from now. It has determined that the optimal strategy would be to issue fixed-rate yen bonds in Europe and swap them into fixed-rate dollars. Clearly, the company is subject to the risk that interest rates might change in the interim. This risk is acceptable to MWCo, but the company does not want to take any exchange-rate risk between now and the actual funding date in the future. This concern is natural since the effect of variations in exchange rates can often dwarf the effect of interest rate changes.

MWCo can eliminate the currency exposure by entering into a forward currency swap immediately. The swap will settle, or become effective, three months from today, coinciding with the planned bond issue. Under the swap, MWCo will pay fixed-rate dollars and receive fixed-rate yen. The swap is entered into now so that its pricing is based on current market conditions. The effective rate is thus locked in for MWCo, independent of future exchange rates.

Forward swaps can be used similarly in conjunction with planned future asset acquisitions.

Swaps with Variable Notional Principal

Usually, the notional principal of a swap is held constant throughout the life of the swap. However, situations might arise in which there is a need for varying the notional principal. There are several common varieties of variable notional principal swaps.

In *amortizing swaps,* the notional principal starts at a high level and gradually decreases. An amortizing swap is suitable when the asset or liability being hedged is itself amortizing. It is possible to analyze and price an amortizing swap as a combination of smaller swaps of different maturities. A *step-down swap* is a similar to an amortizing swap. Its notional principal falls in one or more steps over time.

An *accreting swap* is one in which the notional principal starts low and slowly increases over the life of the swap.

Situation—Hedging a Construction Loan, I

JCC is a Japanese construction company. It has secured a yen loan for a construction project in the United States. It intends to draw down on the loan as the construction progresses. Also, it wishes to convert the liability into dollars now because it finds the current exchange rate to be attractive.

One alternative for JCC is to enter into a series of currency swaps, receiving yen and paying dollars, as the loan is drawn down. In addition to the inconvenience of a potentially large number of small-sized transactions, this option also exposes JCC to changes in future exchange rates. An acceptable alternative is to enter into an accreting currency swap with the notional principal increasing in step with the planned drawdown of the loan. The swap would be priced on the basis of current market conditions, thus providing protection to JCC from future changes in exchange rates.

Two observations are notable in the context of this example. First JCC assumes the small risk that the actual drawdowns may not exactly match the planned drawdowns, on which the swap is based. In most real-world situations, it is best to retain this type of small, unquantifiable risk rather than hedge it out to the last penny by introducing option-like features into the currency swap. It is simply a matter of economics. The incremental cost of the optional features would probably not be justified in view of the small size of the risk. One reason for this is that any option incorporated into a swap is priced according to the potential movement of interest rates, whereas the drawdowns on the loan may not be so strongly correlated with interest rate levels. Thus, buying optional features for the risk could be an over-hedge. One simple principle to follow is to hedge *generic* risks in the market through derivatives and retain *specific* risks. This way, it is possible to apportion the task of hedging among different players optimally. In this example, JCC is far better equipped to handle the specific risk than is any swap dealer. On the other hand, the swap dealer can easily hedge the market risk.

Secondly, notice that JCC could also achieve its goals by entering into a number of forward swaps, each corresponding to a planned drawdown. This illustrates the point that, conceptually, an accreting swap is simply a combination of forward swaps.

A *step-up swap* is similar to an accreting swap: its notional principal increases in usually one, but sometimes more than one, step over the life of the swap.

A *roller-coaster swap* combines the properties of step-up and step-down swaps, with its notional principal increasing and decreasing at different times. Such a swap is used to engineer, in detail, cash flows to a specific need. They are relatively uncommon in practice.

Situation—Hedging a Construction Loan, II

JCC is a Japanese construction company. It has secured a yen loan for a construction project in the United States. The terms of the loan require JCC to draw down the funds as the project progresses. The terms also require gradual repayment as soon as the project is completed and begins to produce income. The expenses and income from the project are in U.S. dollars.

JCC can hedge the currency risk inherent in this project and its funding by means of a roller-coaster currency swap. The notional principal of the swap is set to increase in step with the projected drawdown schedule of the loan. Once the loan has been completely drawn down, the notional amount is set to decrease according to the projected cash flow to be received from the project.

As before, note that JCC retains the residual risk that the actual drawdowns and the actual cash flow from the project may not be exactly the same as the projected amounts. We believe that it is prudent on the part of JCC to accept this risk.

Callable and Putable Swaps

Each of the currency swap variations discussed can be further enhanced by incorporating option features. Since a call option on one currency acts like a put option on another, it is difficult to force a specific terminology for such swaps. Broadly, we can call an option to terminate a swap a put and, correspondingly, an option to initiate a swap a call.

Situation—Hedging Contingent Liabilities

CEC, a U.S. civil engineering company, is bidding on a construction project in Japan. The bidding process is expected to take about three months. CEC is bidding on a fixed-cost basis and is uncomfortable about the foreign-currency exposure inherent in the bid given the long processing time. CEC would like to fix the dollar cost of its bid.

CEC can consider entering into a currency swap, converting its yen expenses to dollars. However, if CEC does not win the bid, then it will have to unwind or terminate the swap contract. Thus, a simple currency swap will still expose CEC to currency risk.

An acceptable alternative is for CEC to purchase a call option on a yen/dollar currency swap. This option gives CEC the right to enter into a swap paying dollars and receiving yen at prescribed terms. If CEC wins the bid, it will enter into the swap, either at the market or via the exercise of the option, whichever gives it the lower dollar cost. If CEC does not win the bid, it will not enter into any swap. It will simply cash in the value, if any, of the option.

Swaps with option features are used to hedge risks of a contingent nature. In any such usage, we should remember not to over-hedge, that is, not to hedge specific risk with a generic product. Always consider retaining part of the risk as long as it is prudent.

Situation—Hedging a Callable Bond

WB is an international bank that has issued a 10-year bond in the Euroyen market. The bond is callable in 7 years. WB is seeking to convert this bond into a dollar liability.

As far as WB is concerned, neither a 7-year nor a 10-year straight currency swap will achieve the full flexibility of the callable bond. It therefore enters into a 10-year currency swap, paying dollars and receiving yen, which is putable in years 7 through 10. If and when the bond is called, WB plans to exercise its option to terminate the swap as well.

Note that there is no requirement that WB exercise the call option on the bond and the put option on the swap simultaneously. If the swap market and the bond market spreads diverge significantly, it might be advantageous for WB to exercise one and not the other. WB, of course, retains the flexibility to profit from this advantage.

SUMMARY AND CONCLUSION

We have examined several variations of the basic structure of currency swaps. Since a swap is a privately negotiated contract between two parties, it can be sculpted to meet the needs of the situation. This flexibility is enhanced when advanced and sophisticated valuation and hedging models are available to the swap provider. However, we recommend moderation in complicating a transaction, unless otherwise warranted. Undue complexity always extracts its price. Similarly, if option features of swaps are involved, we recommend hedging generic risks rather than specific risks, unless the situation demands otherwise.

This discussion of currency swap variations is by no means exhaustive. We have touched upon just the major varieties. There are other, less common, varieties, a natural evolution of privately negotiated contracts. It is possible that some of these obscure structures might become tomorrow's standards. The direction in which the structural variations will develop in the future is perhaps the incorporation of option features into the basic formats. As the industry gains more confidence in the newly acquired valuation and hedging techniques of options, we can expect them to become more prevalent in the future, both to create added value and to meet the varying needs of the market participants.

PART 2

APPLICATIONS OF SWAPS

CHAPTER 7

CAPITAL MARKET APPLICATIONS OF CROSS CURRENCY SWAPS

Peter L. Harnik
Union Bank of Switzerland
Tokyo

INTRODUCTION

Although the forerunner of currency swaps as we know them today was the blocked currency swap, it has been in the capital markets that the application has grown and reached maturity. Issuers have gradually learned that the choice of market, type of instrument, and currency in which debt is raised can be totally divorced from the type of liability they ultimately wish to assume. This has in large part been made possible by the development of a variety of new financial products such as currency swaps, currency options, Eurocurrency interest rate futures, and options on swaps ("swaptions"). These have been used alone and in combination with more traditional risk management products such as foreign exchange to allow borrowers to float debt in many different forms. Thus the underlying debt issue increasingly provides little if any clue to the final liability assumed by the issuer. For example, a five-year Swiss franc issue callable after three years might actually be used to raise fixed-rate yen for five years; a U.S. dollar floating-rate issue might be converted to fixed-rate positions in several different currencies.

As is common to all swaps, currency swaps in the capital markets are based on arbitrage principles by which market inefficiencies are exploited. At the simplest level, this reflects the diverse and essentially balkanized capital markets of different countries with viable bond markets. The significance of currency swaps in the capital markets is the way these markets have been linked through the medium of the currency swap.

In this chapter we shall briefly review how currency swaps and capital markets first became linked, and how they have evolved to the present. We will also attempt to gain an appreciation of what conditions are particularly favorable to the use of currency swap–linked capital market transactions. We will then examine some practical aspects of how the currency swap, sometimes in combination with other risk management products, is used to reduce the cost of debt at the time of issuance. As we shall see, many of these techniques are true examples of arbitrage in the sense that the underlying liability is transformed at the time of launch into an instrument with totally different character. This means that there is little, if any, residual sensitivity to the liability that actually appears on financial accounts. Other transactions, however, are predicated on the issuer's willingness to retain some interest or exchange rate sensitivity in order to obtain the most advantageous cost of funding. Finally, we shall examine the characteristics of selected capital markets and their applicability to currency swaps.

A HISTORICAL PERSPECTIVE

As noted earlier, the precursor to today's currency swap was the blocked currency swap. Sometimes structured as a series of foreign exchange contracts or as a parallel loan agreement, blocked currency swaps had as a central theme the idea of allowing companies otherwise constrained from free remittance of dividends or profits to exchange some or all of those cash flows with another company under mutually agreeable conditions.

Similarly, the first currency swaps linked to capital market transactions came about when currency swaps were created out of an exchange of cash flows from bond issues launched simultaneously in different markets. That is, a company might agree to issue a bond in one market on the condition that another company meet all the associated cash flows from the issue. In turn the first company would meet all the payments under an issue launched by the second company. Like the blocked currency exchange, the timing of all payments, from principal payment and coupon payment dates to redemption, was exactly matched. That way, all settlement risks for the counterparties were extinguished. The deal that is generally credited with providing legitimacy to the market involved a Swiss franc issue by IBM Corporation and a U.S. dollar issue by the International Bank for Reconstruction and Development (the "World Bank").

This requirement for absolute synchronization, which typified the market's early days, was a major constraint. It effectively limited swap opportunities to occasions when the markets moved into the right constellation and stayed there long enough to achieve the launch of both the issues while simultaneously meeting the borrowing targets of both issuers. It also meant that only borrowers with frequent need to tap the capital markets were likely to be in a position to take advantage of the "window of opportunity" when it occurred.

As the concept of currency swaps became more popular, the next step in its evolution was the insertion of large international commercial banks as central conduits for the cash flows between issuers, which were typically sovereign or corporate entities, often in different countries. As an intermediary, the bank performed a credit function and served effectively as a guarantor that funds from XYZ Corporation would be paid on time to the Treasury of the Kingdom of ABC and vice versa. Each debt issuer, therefore, could expect the intermediary bank to cover the payment on its debt and did not need to concern itself with the ability of the other debt issuer to perform its obligation under all circumstances. For this guarantor function, the bank would typically be paid a fee at the deal's inception or be compensated with a deduction from each fixed payment it made under the exchange.

Gradually, however, two factors emerged that changed the market dramatically. First was the development and popularization of new financial products, such as financial futures on Eurocurrency deposits and bonds. These products, together with foreign exchange, allowed issuers more latitude in managing the currency and interest sensitivity risks generated in the transactions. Second, the banks themselves became popular with investors as issuers of debt. The commercial and investment banks were active users of the new financial products for their own and customers' accounts, and they soon saw that they could profitably employ their own capital by taking on and managing mismatched risk positions in addition to fulfilling the intermediary or guarantor's role. Although the window of opportunity still prevailed, the banks' willingness to add flexibility gave the market liquidity and allowed a much larger number of issuers to access markets on terms tailored to meet their needs.

As of this writing there are many counterparties making markets in currency swaps and swaptions and other derivative products through branches and subsidiaries in major market centers. As counterparties have become experienced in the use of these products, liquidity has even been generated in centers where capital markets were essentially nonexistent, notably Scandinavia, the Iberian Peninsula, and Hong Kong.

CAPITAL MARKET ARBITRAGE: WHERE ARE THE OPPORTUNITIES FOUND?

The first ingredient in a successful capital market–linked currency swap is a bond issue at terms favorable to the issuer. This also means that the investment must be attractive to investors. In general, if one or more of the following conditions apply, a fertile environment can be said to exist:

1. Investor familiarity with the issuer.
2. High ratings/class of issuer.
3. Market depth (or lack thereof).
4. Scarcity value of an issuer's debt.
5. Willingness to invest in hybrid instruments.

Investors in bonds, who are by nature or charter conservative, are inclined to pay higher prices for bonds floated by issuers familiar to them. Such issuers consequently benefit from lower yields or issuing cost. In European bond markets for international issuers, for example, "household" corporate names such as IBM, Unilever, Johnson & Johnson, and Toyota all benefit from name recognition owing to product or brand familiarity among investors. As a result, they have frequently achieved issuing terms equal to or better than those achieved by top-rated sovereign issuers. Similarly, a provincial bank may achieve relatively exceptional terms in a fixed-rate market simply because the bond investors have become comfortable with the bank's name by seeing its branches on nearby street corners. Although this type of opportunity is not new, the issuer's options have changed. In the past the issuer had a simple choice: Either issue to the demand and accept the underlying liability or forego the opportunity if it did not suit the issuer's present funding needs. With the advent of the currency swap, a Belgian bank faced with demand from customers for fixed-rate deposit instruments did not need to wait for a funding need for a long-term asset to issue fixed-rate debt. The bank could now offer a fixed-rate bond in Canadian dollars with its exposure swapped back to a sub-LIBOR spread in Deutschemarks, U.S. dollars, or Belgian francs, or even a mixture of the three.

Ratings are important in that portfolio managers generally have strict guidelines as to how much they may hold in lower-rated instruments. Many central banks are proscribed from holding any bonds rated less than AAA. Although it is not surprising that the highest-rated issuers achieve the best terms, at times they may achieve particularly exceptional terms simply because investors are starved of other alternatives for this class of investment and so are prepared to pay a special premium. This situation again provides the basis for a currency swap–linked bond issue if the issuer has no need to raise the liability directly in the debt issue.

Market depth, or the capacity of a capital market to absorb the incremental issuer's debt at the same price, also plays a role in creating arbitrage opportunities. Perhaps the best single historical example of this is that of the World Bank in the Swiss franc market.

The Bank conducts its lending activities in a variety of currencies and has relatively huge capital needs, and was therefore a frequent issuer in various international markets, including Switzerland. Furthermore, its currency weighting models called for a significant liability exposure to Swiss francs, so representatives made frequent trips to borrow in Switzerland. Despite its unquestioned AAA rating, in time the Bank's bonds had to be priced to yield some 20 basis points higher than those of equivalent issuers to find favor with investors. It was this situation that led the Bank to use IBM's name, which was attractive in Switzerland, as a proxy for its own and then exchange the liabilities via a currency swap. The World Bank/IBM deal was made possible by the fortuitous combination of three of the abovementioned conditions conducive to swap-linked capital market transactions: first, investor familiarity with IBM's name; second, the oversupply of World Bank debt relative to the lack of market depth in the Swiss franc market; and third, the high value of the World Bank's AAA-rated debt in the much deeper Eurodollar market.

Scarcity value is effectively the other side of the same coin. An issuer that rarely issues debt in a particular market or, even better, rarely offers debt at all, can frequently obtain outstanding terms. Interestingly, this can occur even when the entity's debt has been unrated, as is true for certain European multinationals. Here again, the market is driven by the possibility that low-cost but unneeded liability positions can be created and traded through a currency swap for a desirable position.

Finally, the willingness to invest in hybrid instruments also helps to create arbitrage opportunities. These instruments range from simple ones, like bonds with attached warrants for equity, debt, or commodities, to bonds where the interest and principal are payable in different currencies, to even more complicated ones involving option-linked formulas for redemption. These instruments normally derive their appeal by giving investors access to an investment opportunity they might not otherwise have or exposure to an instrument in a size or maturity they might not be able to otherwise obtain. As we shall see, however, it is occasionally the issuer's capacity or desire to take measured risk that helps provide the window of opportunity.

CAPITAL MARKET CURRENCY SWAP APPLICATION

Let us now turn to an example of how a capital market–linked currency swap works in practice. The most common scenario is for an issuer of fixed-rate debt in one currency to swap for a floating-rate debt position in another currency. By fulfilling several of the conditions outlined in the previous section, certain European banks, benefiting from Eurobond investor familiarity and enjoying high ratings, are well received as issuers of fixed-rate debt. Though they have little need for fixed-rate funding, as commercial banks they have a continuing need to fund floating-rate assets. Furthermore, because they possess large balance sheets, these banks have the flexibility to quickly absorb attractive window-of-opportunity positions when their floating-rate targets are met.

This situation can be contrasted with that of the unrated Canadian subsidiary of a multinational corporation, which can fund itself by borrowing at a floating rate from local banks but has virtually no chance to obtain fixed-rate funding in the capital markets on its own. If we assume that the bank can obtain five-year fixed-rate funds at the rate of Canadian Treasuries plus 80 basis points, a swap beneficial to both sides can be arranged along the following lines:

ABC Bank pays:	C$ Treasuries + 80 in the bond
ABC Bank receives:	C$ Treasuries + 100 in the swap
ABC Bank pays:	US$ LIBOR in the swap
ABC Bank's net position:	US$ LIBOR − 20 bp (in C$)

This compares favorably with the bank's alternative cost of discretionary funding, which is by definition the bid side of the interbank deposit market, or LIBOR − 0.125 percent. Furthermore, the bank has improved its liquidity position by locking up the funds for five years. By using an indirect method of obtaining this funding, it has also preserved its capacity for further direct borrowings in the interbank market. For its part, the subsidiary has obtained fixed-rate Canadian dollar funding for 100 basis points plus the spread it pays on the floating-rate borrowings.

The Effect of Underwriting Commissions

In the actual execution of the currency swap–linked capital market issue, an important point that must be established is the amount of currency the issuer wishes to borrow after the swap. The issuer's willingness to tolerate residual foreign exchange and interest rate risk is also significant.

Most issuers want the synthetic liability to be nearly the same size after conversion to the second currency as the amount underwritten in the first. Because currency swaps are generally based on the actual exchange of notional principal at the same nominal foreign exchange rate at start and maturity, the net proceeds received from the underwriting syndicate are quite important. We illustrate this with an example.

If we assume a par-priced issue of A$100 million and fees of 2 percent, the issuer will actually receive only A$98 million from the underwriters. If it wishes to have use of A$100 million in Japanese yen, the normal currency swap will require them to pay A$100 million over to the swap counterparty in order to obtain the yen countervalue. Thus there is a potential A$2 million shortfall that either the issuer or the counterparty must absorb. If the counterparty absorbs the shortfall, the rate the issuer must pay on the yen amount will be sufficiently increased to allow the counterparty to amortize the shortfall over the life of the currency swap. This is one reason that Eurobond issues are frequently priced at premiums nearly equal to the underwriting commissions. In the above example, instead of being priced at par or 100 percent, the issue might be priced at 101.875 percent so that the differential is reduced to 0.125 percent.

Another matter that relates to residual foreign exchange and interest rate risk is the treatment of the underlying issues' coupon payments. Returning to our initial example of the Canadian dollar bond for which the issuer could achieve C$ Treasuries + 80 and swap it at C$ Treasuries + 100, two possibilities emerge:

	Alternative I		Alternative II	
Underlying	Bank Receives	Bank Pays	Bank Receives	Bank Pays
C$ T + 80	C$ T + 100	US$ LIBOR	C$ T + 80	US$ LIBOR − X

In the first case, the issuer is tacitly accepting a foreign exchange risk, because it has created a 20-basis-point surplus in Canadian dollars but now has a liability in U.S. dollars. In the second case, the counterparty takes on the differential and passes it back through the swap mechanism, receiving a sub-LIBOR (LIBOR − X) payment in exchange. In practice the second alternative is much more commonly used. The first approach is used when the issuer has large multicurrency asset and liability exposures; examples include the World Bank, national export financing organizations, and certain multinational corporations. By using a generic, or "plain vanilla," swap structure against US$ LIBOR with no spread (the basis on which deals are transacted between dealers in the interbank swap market), these issuers greatly enlarge the universe of potential swap counterparties. In this way they can achieve a better price, although they also assume an additional level of risk. For these issuers, however, the incremental risk taken on may in fact be offset or minimized by other positions already in their books.

Recurring Fees in Capital Market Issues

Other details that must be addressed include whether or not recurring fees such as payment commissions, agency fees, and any bank guarantee fees, which are normally denominated in the currency of the capital market issue, need to be included in the swap. Though they typically amount to only a few basis points (except for the guarantee fee, which may be much more), the resulting foreign exchange exposure can be quite material if the issue is large or if the currency of the issue is not one in which the issuer has routine business exposure. The conservative approach is to include them in the currency swap.

Another consideration is the necessity of timing the fixed swap payments to coincide with the coupon payments under the capital market issue. For example, coupon-paying agency agreements may require the issuer to furnish funds one day before the coupon payment or principal is due. For this reason, most issue-related swaps will have the calendar date immediately preceding the coupon payment date specified as the swap payment date; for example, if the coupon payment date is March 15 each year, the swap payments will be exchanged on the 14th. To compensate for the effect of holidays and weekends, the "preceding business day" convention will be elected. This means that any swap payment that would otherwise fall on a weekend or holiday will be moved to the first business day before the swap payment date. In the example above, if March 14 were to fall on a Sunday, the swap payment date that year would in fact be March 12.

FLOATING-RATE NOTES AND CAPITAL MARKET SWAPS

In times of rising interest rates, either markets are not receptive to fixed-rate issues or investors only want to purchase short-duration instruments. In such times, the floating-rate note (FRN) can be a useful tool for creating a liability position in another currency.

For example, assume an issuer desires funding in fixed-rate Swiss francs, but the market is effectively closed to the issuer because the high coupon necessary to attract investors is well above the issuer's target. In this case, the issuer could take advantage of the steady appetite for U.S. dollar–denominated FRNs from commercial banks in London and then swap the proceeds for fixed Swiss francs.

Let us see how this works in practice. Since the banks investing in FRNs can generally fund themselves around the "bid" or buy side of the interbank market (also called LIBID) or, at worst, at the offered side or LIBOR, a spread of 0.125 to 0.25 percent above LIBOR, depending on credit quality, will usually look attractive to the investor. Assuming that our issuer can issue to this demand and that a foreign subsidiary of a Swiss company is in need of LIBOR-based funds, an interesting swap arbitrage can occur. This is because the same investors who will demand a large premium to invest in a foreign issuer's notes in the Swiss franc market will actually bid aggressively for paper from a major Swiss multinational's subsidiary. This differential, a good example of the effect of investor familiarity combined with scarcity value, can range anywhere from 50 basis points to 1 percent or more and will be present even in the absence of a rating or if the subsidiary's issue is not guaranteed by the parent. Thus, fixed-rate funding in Swiss francs could be raised as follows:

	Instrument	*Cash Flow*
Capital Market Issue		
Issuer	FRN	US$ LIBOR + 25 bp
Subsidiary	Swiss franc private placement	7.25
Swap		
Issuer		Pays 7.50%
Subsidiary		Pays US$ LIBOR
Result		
Issuer	Synthetic Swiss francs	Pays 7.75%
Subsidiary	Floating U.S. dollars	Pays U.S.$ LIBOR − 25

If we assume the foreign issuer would have had to pay at least 8.25 percent for the direct issue, the savings approaches 50 basis points.

A similar result could be accomplished if, instead of the FRN, the issuer simply relied on periodic issuance of short-term debt, such as commercial paper or revolving bank loans, for its funding. The economic result in terms of the fixed rate could even be better, though not strictly comparable due to liquidity risk, because the FRN is outstanding for the full five years, while the revolving loan facility could be canceled or renegotiated at terms unfavorable to the issuer. Similarly, the commercial paper terms could change radically because of market developments or poor corporate performance by the issuer. This liquidity premium has concrete value and should be considered when making comparisons of different fund raising alternatives.

STRUCTURING CAPITAL MARKET TRANSACTIONS FOR GREATER VALUE

There are many techniques used in the execution of capital market issues to improve the final economic picture. The most common strategies take advantage of the shape of the yield curve. Let us briefly examine some opportunities offered in different environments.

The Positive Yield Curve

With a positive yield curve, where short-term interest rates are well below long-term interest rates, the idea is to somehow extend the issue to take advantage of *positive carry.* Positive carry occurs when a long-term investment at a higher rate can be funded short-term at a lower cost such that the investor enjoys a positive differential. In the context of the capital market swap, we will look at the differential between a currency swap matched to the issue and a generic swap.

In a capital market issue in the Euromarkets, the payout date is normally four to five weeks after launch. By agreeing to pay the fixed rate on behalf of the issuer for a future start, the swap counterparty is immediately subject to a loss in the event that rates fall between the time of launch and the payout of the issue. To hedge this risk, the swap counterparty either enters into a swap to receive a fixed rate for the full period (e.g., five years and one month for a five-year issue), or purchases a liquid government security denominated in the currency of the issue. In either case, the issuer will enjoy a positive spread on the position: in the first case, the fixed rate received will be well above LIBOR, and in the second case, the bond coupon will be higher than the cost of financing it.

Let us look at a practical example. We assume the following rates:

Overnight	6.0%
6-mo./7-mo. LIBOR	6.5%
5-year bond yield	6.75%
5-year swap	7.25%

Our swap provider stands to gain about 75 basis points per annum between the time of launch and the start of the swap, because it does not have to start paying under the issue-related swap until the payout date, but it enjoys the positive spread from the hedge for the intervening period. Amortized over the full five years, this means an additional 2 basis points are gained by delaying the swap's start. Though that may not sound like much, it equals about $20,000 a year on a $100 million issue.

Some portion of this benefit is usually passed back to the issuer in the form of a slightly improved cost in the target liability. This means that as long as the issue terms (price and coupon) are unchanged, the farther ahead the payout date, the better the result after swap.

Another way of achieving the same effect is the so-called partial pay structure. In this case the bond offered to investors allows them to, in effect, make installment payments to purchase the bond. For example, a quarter of the proceeds might be due on the initial payout date with the balance due three months later. This structure may be attractive to the investor if the investment currency is expected to weaken in relation to the investor's base currency in the interim. From the capital market swap perspective, however, the effect is to simply delay the payout date. This is because the coupon on the bond, and therefore on the swap, will be fixed as of the launch date. In other words, the weighted average payout date has been extended to a date between the first and final payout dates, allowing the effect of additional positive carry to be captured.

The Inverted Yield Curve

Techniques for enhancement of results in a negative yield environment, where short-term rates are much higher than long-term rates, are effectively the reverse of those used where a positive yield curve exists. The objective is to shorten the bond's maturity, move up the payout date, and perhaps delay the start of the swap.

A simple example from the Swiss franc bond market will help illustrate. For the bond we will assume a seven-year private placement with an all-in cost of 7.80 percent and a long first coupon of 15 months. Assuming a swap rate of 8 percent against LIBOR flat for seven years, the issue generates around LIBOR − 20 basis points (7.8 − 8.0% = −0.20%). Suppose, however, that three-month Swiss franc rates are 9.375 percent and that the issuer is indifferent as to when the offsetting liability swap starts as long as there is no economic exposure to Swiss francs. In this case, one could arrange to start the swap into the synthetic liability with a four-month delay and put the issue proceeds on deposit on the customer's behalf for three months (assuming payout is one month after launch). The earnings on the deposit of about 2.37 percent (9.375 × 91/360) can then be passed back in the form of a better sub-LIBOR spread.

Callable Issues in the Capital Markets

Yield curves can also be maximized with the use of callable issues and capital market swaps. Unlike the cases of positive and negative yield curve exploitation described above, this application centers on the different valuation of calls embodied in bonds by investors and technical traders.

Assume that bonds can be sold to investors for both five and seven years at identical terms, including coupon and price. This implies that a seven-year issue callable at par in five years should probably achieve similar pricing. A callable swap or swaption can be used to good advantage if we assume the issuer is indifferent as to whether his liability terminates after five years or runs to the full seven years.

Let us say the callable issue creates an all-in yen cost of 7 percent, whereas a seven-year swap to US$ LIBOR can be concluded at 7.25 percent. Furthermore, a counterparty would pay 50 basis points up front for an option on the right to receive 7.25 percent against US$ LIBOR starting in five years' time for two years. From the swap and bond issue alone, a cost of LIBOR − 25 basis points is achieved (7.0 − 7.25% = −.25%). If we add the "call swaption" (so called because it resembles a call option on a bond in exercise characteristics), our issuer can be said to have locked in about LIBOR − 37 basis points for five years, and possibly LIBOR − 25 basis points for the remaining two years. This is because by selling the call swaption, the firm is selling the rights to a 7.25 percent fixed cash flow in yen, which exactly matches the remainder of the cash flow from the original seven-year swap. If the swaption is exercised, the issuer will have two obligations to pay fixed-rate yen—the bond issue of 7 percent and the new swap at 7.25 percent—and so will presumably call the bond to eliminate the extra exposure.

A chart will illustrate the results under the different interest rate levels that may prevail in five years' time:

Interest Rate	Swap Option	Issuer's Action	Issuer's Result
Above 7.25%	Not exercised	None	US$ LIBOR − 25
Below 7.25%	Exercised	Calls issue	Refunds in lower interest rate environment

The same effect could be achieved through a callable swap, a swap where the fixed-rate payer has the right to simply terminate its payment of 7.25 percent in five years' time or continue for the full seven years. In the above example, then, the swap counterparty might agree to pay the 7 percent cost on the issue in exchange for LIBOR − 33 basis points (7% − 7.25% − 50 bp amortized over seven years, or about 8 bp p.a.). The exercise characteristics are identical to the swaption outlined above. Since this benefit (i.e., paying the fixed rate in exchange for a sub-LIBOR payment in return) is commonly built into the swap, care must be used to see that the remaining premium is recaptured in the event of exercise, because in this structure, the last two years worth of sub-LIBOR benefit are foregone. Therefore, an arrangement must be made to recapture the remaining 15 basis points of unamortized value. Alternatively, the issuer could enter into a swap in exchange for LIBOR − 25 basis points and receive the full 50 basis points as a separate premium at the outset.

Using the Foreign Exchange Market

Another tool for enhancing the value of capital market–linked transactions is the foreign exchange market. One structure that has been particularly popular with Japanese corporate issuers is to fund in a foreign currency with a low nominal interest rate and hedge the position sometime between launch and maturity. Also common are structures that take advantage of premiums or discounts available in the foreign exchange forward and option markets.

Issue with an Unhedged FX Position

An issuer will leave its FX position unhedged if it believes that the value of the currency in which the liability is denominated will be stable or, ideally, depreciate against the synthetic borrowing currency. Also, the currency of the issue almost always has a lower coupon than the target currency. The rationale is that the lower current cost via the low coupon is partial compensation for the additional foreign exchange risk.

An example will illustrate. A Japanese company can raise SF100 million at 6 percent through a Swiss franc issue or at 7.5 percent in Japanese yen for five years. The company undertakes the Swiss franc financing and converts the net proceeds of SF98 million, at an exchange rate of 100, to ¥9.8 billion. It now has use of the yen and is exposed to making a series of 6 percent coupon payments and returning the Swiss franc principal. After exactly one year, the yen has strengthened to 90 against the Swiss franc, and the company decides to hedge with a currency swap in order to eliminate the residual exposure. Assuming interest rate levels are unchanged, this yields the following:

	Swiss Franc Issue (98,000,000)	Yen Cash Flow 9,800,000,000
Year 1	6,000,000	(540,000,000)*
Year 2	6,000,000	(675,000,000)**
Year 3	6,000,000	(675,000,000)
Year 4	6,000,000	(675,000,000)
Year 5	6,000,000	(675,000,000)
Principal	100,000,000	(9,000,000,000)

Internal rate of return (IRR) = 5.11%

* SF6 million × 90
** ¥9 billion × 7.5%

Assuming that the overall level of rates has not changed, the issuer has substantially improved on its marginal borrowing cost of 7.5 percent by taking on the exchange risk. Obviously, this approach is not without risk, as the yen could have weakened instead of strengthening against the Swiss franc. In cases where inflation differentials between countries are narrow and not expected to widen, however, the risks are not untenable.

ARBITRAGING THE FORWARD MARKET

Now let us turn to two examples in which the difference between the spot and forward rates of a currency can be used to create an attractive issuing opportunity. Unlike the previous example, these constitute true arbitrage, as the positions are immediately offset when created. The first involves a dual currency bond and the second, a hybrid bond combining the characteristics of a fixed-rate bond with an FRN.

Dual-Currency Bonds

The dual-currency bond was created to let investors speculate on the value of the redemption amount. The bond would be issued in one currency with redemption specified as being a certain amount of a second currency. This created a synthetic foreign exchange contract since the investors were effectively selling their original investment currency for another at a predetermined rate in the future.

The driving force behind these bonds was an arbitrage of perceptions. The foreign exchange rate for conversion was a substantial discount from the spot rate and far below historical lows for the currency, on one hand, but still well above the theoretical forward rate derived from borrowing/reinvestment rates. To gain a higher current yield, investors were thus prepared to bet that their fundamental view was more correct than the technical view described by the interest differentials.

As an example, let us look at the ¥25 billion 8 percent Euroyen issue by the Student Loan Marketing Association (Sallie Mae), for which redemption was set at US$136 million (¥183), the spot yen rate at the time of launch in September 1985 was ¥215, and the outright ten-year rate was around ¥157. This meant that though Sallie Mae paid an 8 percent coupon (compared with a market level of about 7.25 percent for a plain bond from a similar issuer), either Sallie Mae or its swap arranger could actually buy the US$136 million for ¥21.3 billion. On an IRR basis, therefore, Sallie Mae's borrowing cost was actually about 6.95 percent

in yen, which in turn was swapped to lower cost U.S. dollars—
either LIBOR − 30 (6.95 − 7.25 = −.30), a lower spread to U.S.
Treasuries, or, in Sallie Mae's case, probably a spread to Treasury
Bills.

A slightly more complicated example of the same arbitrage centers on a hybrid bond from a sovereign issuer that offers a fixed rate
in Deutschemarks for two years and then converts to a U.S. dollar–
based FRN-paying LIBOR flat for the remaining two years. The key
to this bond is that, similar to the dual currency issue described above,
it provides for conversion to a specific amount in U.S. dollars after
two years at a rate different from that implied in the foreign exchange
market. The positive benefit of this differential is used to reduce the
cost of issuing and also to provide coupon enhancement for the investor (e.g., an FRN coupon of LIBOR versus the typical level for
this borrower of LIBOR − 15 bp).

The arbitrage can be most easily seen if we focus on the actual
principal flows over the life of the transaction, as shown in Figure 1.
Though the issuer is provided with US$100 million at the outset of
the transaction through the currency swap in exchange for Deutsche-

FIGURE 1

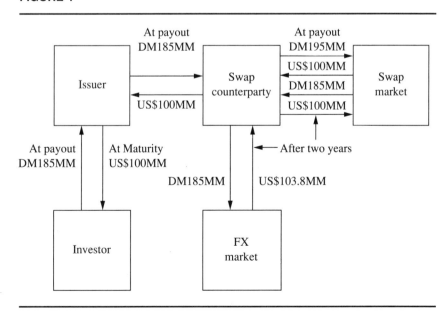

marks, the bond's structure obligates it to pay U.S. dollars, not Deutschemarks, to investors at maturity. Thus there is no need for the issuer to repay Deutschemarks through a final exchange in the swap. The swap counterparty, in turn, will have a surplus of DM185 million in two years' time and a countervailing shortage of US$100 million. Therefore, the swap counterparty hedges the incoming DM185 million from the swap market by selling it forward in the foreign exchange market at the two-year forward rate of DM1.7825/US$, to generate US$103,786,816.30 (DM185 million ÷ 1.7825). Since the counterparty is only obligated to pay US$100 million in exchange for the Deutschemarks, it is able to capture the difference of about 3.15 percent, which is used to enhance the investor's coupons and lower the issuer's cost.

While we have seen mechanically how the arbitrage described can be exploited, the question remains of why it arises. Simply put, the cause is the investor's willingness to buy U.S. dollars forward at a price different from that found in the interbank forward market. Theoretically, each investor could invest for two years in Deutschemarks, then sell the proceeds to generate U.S. dollars, and so jointly generate an aggregate of US$103.7 million in principal to invest in FRNs. Two points should be made here, however. First, individual investors likely could not arrange long-term forward foreign exchange contracts in amounts corresponding to their investment amounts. Second, some of the benefit is actually being recaptured through the enhanced coupons they receive.

Embedded Currency Options and Capital Market Issues

Earlier we saw how call options embedded in capital market issues could enhance synthetic funding opportunities. Similarly, currency options combined with the redemption formulas for bonds provide an opportunity for investors and sometimes issuers to achieve superior results when they hold a particular fundamental view.

A bond's redemption value is often linked to a formula that puts a one-sided boundary on the final proceeds, usually along the following lines:

$$\text{The lower of } 100\%, \text{ or } 1 - \left[\frac{FX_s - FX_m}{FX_s} \times k \right]$$

where FX_s = Strike exchange rate (usually between the spot ex-
change rate and the implied forward rate)
FX_m = Exchange rate at maturity
k = Gearing coefficient

(This is an example of an embedded call option. Reversing the positions of FXs and FXm in the numerator will change it into a put option.)

From option theory, we know that the value of any option consists of two parts: its *intrinsic value,* or the amount it is in the money, and its *extrinsic value,* or the time value to expiration. If the strike price is deliberately set between the spot and the forward values, an option with tangible value is created. This in turn can be sold to an investor or corporation seeking a hedge for assets or a long-term cash flow. The premium thus created can be used to lower the issuer's cost and augment the coupon for the investors.

One example of this structure in practice is the Long Term Credit Bank's 10-year US$120 million 11.5 percent Eurodollar issue, which matures in October 1995. In this case, the strike rate was set at ¥169.00, which meant that the bond included an "in the money" call option on yen. As we saw in the Sallie Mae issue launched at about the same time, the ten-year forward yen was around ¥157.00, so the option had an intrinsic value of at least ¥12 or about 5.6 percent of the issue amount ([¥12 × US$120 million ÷ [US$120 million × ¥215]). This alone equates to about 1 percent p.a. for 10 years at the then-prevailing rate of 11 percent. In fact, the actual value was probably higher, as we could expect a reasonably large extrinsic or time value for such a long-term option.

In this case, the bond was driven by the investor's willingness to accept a lower redemption amount in the event the yen strengthened beyond the embedded option's strike rate of ¥169.00. The arbitrage of this fundamental view, together with a high current return, allowed the issuer to obtain superior issuing terms.

It should also be emphasized that this sort of arbitrage need not be limited to an investor's perceptions of the future trends in rates. For example, a multinational resources company with production in oil or coal might well be willing to base the redemption amount of a bond it issues on the future price of one of those commodities or its relative foreign exchange value. In turn, the company would enjoy a substantial reduction in the cost of the synthetic liability coming from the premium received when the forward or option component is sold.

SWAP WINDOWS IN DIFFERENT MARKETS

Early in this chapter, we identified several conditions that are particularly conducive to the application of currency swaps in the capital markets. In this final section we will look briefly at some of the major markets to see where those window opportunities can be expected to occur. In each case we will look at the markets from the perspective of the investor as well as from that of the issuer or swap provider.

U.S. Dollar Markets

The two major U.S. dollar markets are the U.S. domestic and Eurodollar markets. The more germane for currency swaps is the Eurodollar market. This market is most often driven by investors' views on the strength of the U.S. dollar, and also by interest rate views. Since it has tended to feature a higher coupon level than the strong European currencies such as the Swiss franc and the Deutschemark, investors become aggressive purchasers when either the dollar is stable and interest rates are expected to fall or the dollar is expected to appreciate. The market is also typically sensitive to the level of the coupon. So an optically interesting coupon (e.g., 10 percent can frequently enable an issue to be launched at a lower all-in cost or spread to Treasuries than a coupon in the 9-percent range. Issuers also benefit from the Eurodollar's position as a major reserve currency as central banking institutions worldwide are active purchasers when their rating requirements are satisfied.

From the issuer's standpoint, the U.S. dollar market affords greater depth than any other market. Thus it is not uncommon to see very large issues floated that are in fact swapped into synthetic liability positions in several currencies.

The Swiss Franc Market

The Swiss franc market for international borrowers is an interesting market for several reasons. From the investor perspective it is foremost a "buy and hold to maturity" market. In contrast with other markets, prices on the secondary market often do not reflect the current yield curve and, in fact, the Swiss franc swap market is generally considered to represent the "real" yield curve. The practical meaning of this is that the price buyers will pay at any time for an issue is the main determinant of proper value. As a result, factors such as scarcity of paper and investor familiarity with the issuer play a far more important role in creating opportunities for swap-linked issues. Furthermore, when investor perceptions diverge from theoretical levels as implied by the swap market, interesting arbitrages can be created. The Swiss franc market has also been willing to accept nonstandard structures such as dual currency and commodity-linked bonds, though the vast majority of issues are still routine fixed-rate issues.

The Swiss franc market has been popular among issuers for its low coupon levels relative to other currencies and for its name recognition factor. The low coupon levels also result in steady demand from willing swap participants who want to pay fixed Swiss francs but are unable to create enough liabilities by directly accessing the market. In addition to the World Bank, institutions in European countries such as Austria and Germany are particularly evident. This is primarily because their currencies have been positively correlated with the Swiss franc so the incremental foreign exchange risk is judged to be small.

High-Coupon Markets: A$, C$, and NZ$

The Australian, Canadian, and New Zealand dollar markets are examples of smaller Eurocurrency markets that provide good swap opportunities from time to time. In general, off-shore investors are attracted to the high interest differentials between the Eurocurrency and their home currency. This is frequently done unhedged at the expense of theoretically high foreign exchange risk, as the inflation differentials are also typically wide. This also means that investor interest dries up when foreign exchange rates drop sharply.

From the issuer's side, the favored firms are "household" corporate names and commercial banks in Europe, particularly in Germany, that enjoy familiarity with the typical high-coupon market investor. These borrowers can sometimes achieve exceptional results as investors' opportunities for this kind of paper are normally limited and the potential for aggressive bond pricing is high. The swap markets in these currencies are normally hedge-driven, allowing firms without access to the capital markets or banks with structural asset/liability management needs to cover their positions.

The Eurosterling Market

While the Eurosterling market has also featured high coupons, its characteristics are slightly different than the high-coupon dollar markets discussed above. The first bonds date from 1972; however, until the lifting of exchange controls in 1979, little sustained volume was seen because residents of the United Kingdom were effectively barred from investing.

This market has been characterized by periods of heavy volume followed by periods of inactivity. Like the U.S. dollar market, it is largely exchange rate– and interest rate–sensitive. Periods of market expansion have occurred when the currency has been strong or expected to strengthen, while coupon rates have been high. The market is also noted for the relatively long maturities that have been available; issues of 15 to 20 years are not uncommon and 30- to 40-year bonds have been underwritten. It has also derived strength from the gradual shrinking of the U.K. "gilt" (government bond) market as fiscal surpluses have allowed the government to gradually redeem outstanding issues. Since the major demand from investors has come as a replacement for government debt, high-rated issuers, preferably AAA, have been favored.

From the swap perspective, volatile interest rates have encouraged active participation by corporations and building societies (savings banks) that seek to hedge their exposure to long-term rates. Municipal entities (local authorities) have also been active and natural users of this market, as they are funded on a floating-rate basis from the Exchequer. Recently, however, the authorities' participation has been somewhat curtailed since the Hammersmith & Fulham affair* has cast shadows over their use as off-balance-sheet hedging mechanisms.

---

*The local authority Hammersmith & Fulham apparently engaged in a series of interest rate option transactions for speculative rather than hedging purposes. These, together with Hammersmith & Fulham's interest rate swap transactions, were declared illegal, thereby threatening the ability of all local authorities to engage in this sort of transaction.

CONCLUSION

In this chapter, we explored some of the ways currency swaps can be linked to capital market issues. The emphasis has been on understanding how arbitrage opportunities between markets occur and how these can be exploited in ways beneficial to both issuers and investors.

As we saw, there are five factors that tend to create fertile ground for international capital market–linked currency swaps. These include investor familiarity with the issuer, disproportionate preference for high ratings, market depth, scarcity value of an issuer's debt, and investor willingness to invest in hybrid instruments.

By using currency swaps, these opportunities can be exploited singly or in combination in order to achieve optimum results. More importantly, we have seen that the underlying liability, in terms of currency or interest rate, need have nothing to do with the issuer's ultimate objective. The borrower can target the market that offers the best relative reception and then use the currency swap mechanism to move its exposure into a more desirable market. In fact, issuers may even do this in several stages, by issuing and first swapping to a short-duration liability such as U.S. dollar LIBOR; when interest rate or foreign exchange targets are met, they can complete the process through other interest rate and currency swaps.

Issuers can also use options embedded in issues to good effect. Calls in issues can be sold via swaptions or callable swaps to reduce the cost of issuance. Similarly, foreign exchange forwards and long-term options embedded in bonds can provide both investors with opportunities otherwise not available to them and issuers with lower-cost funding.

Finally, we have seen that most capital market currency swap applications are fully covered arbitrage exercises—that is, the liability is fully covered at the outset. Sometimes, however, an issuer's natural capacity for taking risk, either through the natural economic exposure of its business or its rate views, can be exploited to substantially improve the resulting synthetic liability.

Through the flexibility of the currency swap, the barriers that previously limited an issuer's horizons have largely been dismantled. Firms in the future will make even more active use of this dynamic mechanism to alter the nature of their exposure to best suit their changing business needs and views.

CHAPTER 8

ASSET-BASED CROSS CURRENCY SWAPS

Suresh E. Krishnan
Merrill Lynch
New York

INTRODUCTION

Cross currency swaps were almost exclusively used as liability management tools in the early days of their development. In the early 1980s, the focus on cross currency swaps as an appendage to new issues of debt limited their flexibility. However, with the market's increase in size, liquidity, and knowledge, the cross currency swap has become commonplace as an asset management tool.

The possible permutations and combinations of synthetic assets using cross currency swaps are extensive. The variety of assets available in the global markets is truly enormous, and the synthetic securities that can be created from them are also fairly unlimited. The most common form of asset swap involves the transformation of cash flows in the same currency. In contrast, cross currency asset swaps can be used to change cash flows from one currency to another. A single-currency asset swap is necessarily less complicated than a cross currency asset swap. In designing asset swap strategies involving two different currencies, various complicating factors such as foreign exchange rate and interest rate movements, differential regulations, taxes, accounting practices, and political risk have to be considered.

In the companion volume, *Interest Rate Swaps,* we discuss the use of interest rate swaps in creating synthetic assets. In this chapter, we discuss asset-based swaps in a multicurrency context: we focus on the role of cross currency swaps in creating synthetic assets denominated in currencies other than the currency of denomination of the underlying security.

DEFINITIONS

An *interest rate swap* is defined as a contract between two parties to exchange a series of fixed interest payments for a series of floating interest payments. These interest payments are based on a notional principal amount agreed on by the two parties; the interest rate swap does not involve the actual exchange of principal between the swap counterparties.

A *cross currency swap* is defined as a contract between two parties to exchange a series of payments in one currency for a series of payments in another currency. These cash flows are based on a notional principal amount that is mutually agreed on by the parties at the outset. Unlike the interest rate swap, the cross currency swap involves the exchange of principal between the two counterparties at the outset and at maturity.

An asset-based swap, sometimes simply referred to as an asset swap, is the combination of an asset and a swap. An interest rate swap can be used to change the complexion of an asset's cash flows. It can be used to transform a conventional fixed-rate security that produces a stream of fixed interest flows into a synthetic floating-rate security that produces a stream of floating interest flows. It can be used with equal flexibility to transform a conventional floating-rate instrument into a synthetic fixed-rate instrument.

In a similar fashion, a cross currency swap can be used to effectively change the currency of denomination of an asset and its related cash flows. For example, it can be used to transform a conventional fixed-rate security denominated in pounds sterling into a synthetic fixed-rate or floating-rate security denominated in U.S. dollars. It can also be used for transforming a conventional floating-rate security denominated in pounds sterling into a synthetic fixed-rate or floating-rate security denominated in U.S. dollars. Exhibit 1 shows the possible combinations of conventional pound sterling securities and cross currency swaps in the creation of synthetic U.S. dollar securities.

The list in the exhibit is by no means exhaustive. Various types of securities are available other than just fixed- or floating-rate securities. For example, a security with sinking fund features or call features has to be dealt with in a fashion different from that presented in this chapter. Those features and the appropriate swap structures to be used in such cases are discussed elsewhere in this book.

EXHIBIT 1
Creating Synthetic Assets Using Cross Currency Swaps

| Underlying Asset | Cross Currency Swap | | Synthetic Asset |
	Pay	Receive	
Pound fixed	Pound fixed	Dollar fixed	Dollar fixed
Pound fixed	Pound fixed	Dollar floating	Dollar floating
Pound floating	Pound floating	Dollar fixed	Dollar fixed
Pound floating	Pound floating	Dollar floating	Dollar floating

RATIONALES FOR CREATING SYNTHETIC SECURITIES WITH CROSS CURRENCY SWAPS

There are many reasons for using cross currency swaps to create synthetic securities. We will attempt to classify them into separate categories.

Incomplete Markets

Conventional securities of the type the investor is looking for may not exist in the marketplace. For example, the investor may be interested in a security issued by a particular entity in a particular currency. If the issuer has issued securities only in U.S. dollars and the investor wishes to invest in a Japanese yen security by the same issuer, the cross currency swap provides a viable way of achieving this. The incomplete nature of markets is thus an important reason for the creation of synthetic securities using cross currency swaps.

Another example is the investor that wishes to obtain a floating-rate security denominated in French francs issued by a U.S. entity. If the U.S. entity has issued fixed-rate bonds denominated in Deutschemarks, a cross currency swap can be constructed in such a manner that not only allows the currency of denomination to be changed from Deutschemarks to French francs, but also allows the nature of coupon payments to be converted from fixed to floating rates.

Restrictions on Institutional Investors

Major institutional investors, such as pension funds and insurance companies, usually have restrictions on the type of securities in which they may invest. Restrictions come in many forms, including those imposed by government authorities and those imposed for internal financial control purposes. Some of the most common forms of restrictions include minimum credit quality requirements and percentage limits on foreign currency–denominated securities. These restrictions may to some degree be circumvented by the creative use of synthetic securities.

Diversification of Credit Risk

Diversification of credit risk is another major reason for entering into asset swaps. By creating a synthetic security with acceptable credit risk and cash flow characteristics not currently available in the market, the investor is able to enlarge the pool of securities available and thus effect improved portfolio diversification.

Traditionally, banks have accounted for the majority of floating-rate securities issued. With the well-publicized problems of banks in general and U.S. and Japanese banks in particular, investors may have a preference for high-quality nonbank issues. Investors looking for floating-rate securities issued by creditworthy entities have found such issues not readily available in the market. This gap provided the incentive to create synthetically a high-quality floating-rate asset by buying a fixed-rate security of acceptable quality and then combining it with an interest rate swap.

In many instances, firms with acceptable credit quality may not have securities denominated in a currency desirable to the investor. In such cases, diversification across national boundaries can be achieved by buying bonds issued by foreign entities in their home currency and swapping them into the desired currency. In this way, the investor may increase geographic diversification not only in terms of domicile of the issuer, but also in terms of the currency mix of the portfolio.

Changing Currency Allocations in a Portfolio

Often investors desire to change the cash flow patterns—both interest rate and currency composition—of their asset portfolios without selling the underlying securities. Asset swaps allow the investor to obtain the desired cash flow patterns without having to dispose of assets from the portfolio. Interest rate flows can be changed from floating to fixed and vice versa quite easily by the use of an interest rate swap without the need to buy and sell securities from the portfolio. The currency composition of the portfolio can be changed to the desired allocation without the investor incurring transaction costs associated with selling existing securities and buying others; this is achieved by the use of a cross currency swap.

Arbitrage Opportunities

The creation of synthetic securities also helps in the arbitrage process. In the early days of the asset swap market, substantial arbitrage opportunities existed. If synthetic securities have yields higher than those of similar conventional securities, investors could benefit from creating synthetic securities. If the process of arbitrage is taken to its logical conclusion, the creation of synthetic securities will cease only when the yield differential becomes negligible.

Windows of opportunity are available from time to time that allow such arbitrage between a synthetic security and a conventional security. These opportunities are usually very short-lived and require careful monitoring of markets.

Market Dislocations

In other instances, substantial market dislocations tend to keep certain securities undervalued and illiquid for long periods of time. Investors with long-term investment horizons can profit from these opportunities by buying such securities cheap and holding them to maturity.

The collapse of the perpetual floating-rate note (FRN) market in the mid-1980s after a period of rapid growth, and the lack of faith in the FRN market that ensued, made FRNs exceptionally cheap in 1986 and 1987. Many FRNs became undervalued and illiquid, and for those investors willing to take advantage of the situation, substantial yield pickup opportunities were available through the use of interest rate swaps and cross currency swaps.

Japanese companies saturated the market for equity warrant issues in the 1980s as the Japanese stock market moved to record highs. The attached securities carried extremely low coupons to compensate the issuer for issuing the warrants. Japanese companies were thus able to obtain considerable savings in their cost of borrowing. The global stock market crash of 1987 practically decimated the market for such issues. Some of these bonds were stripped of their warrants, and the resulting low-coupon bonds were then asset-swapped into attractive floating-rate instruments, many into other currencies. The equity warrant market picked up again as the Japanese stock market recovered and reached record highs in 1989. The collapse of the Japanese stock market in 1990 has again created similar asset swap opportunities.

Withholding Taxes

Withholding taxes tend to play a significant role in cross-border investments. Many investors prefer to deal in securities that are free from withholding taxes, namely, Eurobonds. In theory, the foreign withholding tax may be applied as a tax credit in the investor's home country if the two countries have a tax treaty. Frequently, such arrangements are time-consuming and onerous. Investors in general prefer to invest in bonds free of withholding taxes and are therefore willing to accept lower pretax yields on them than on similar bonds subject to withholding taxes. However, on an after-tax basis, the yields on Eurobonds may be higher than yields on domestic bonds subject to withholding taxes.

Swap payments in general are not subject to withholding taxes. For those investors who can take a full tax credit for any withholding tax paid to foreign countries, this creates an opportunity to pick up yield. By buying bonds in a country with high withholding taxes and swapping those bonds into a desired currency, the investor may be able to obtain more attractive yields compared with buying bonds not subject to withholding taxes.

EXAMPLES

Earlier we outlined some of the transformations from conventional securities to synthetic securities that are possible through cross currency swaps. Since it is not feasible to go into the infinite number of variations, we shall illustrate two basic combinations here. We assume that the swaps are done at par to simplify the illustration. Later we describe the adjustments necessary to account for nonpar swaps.

Creating a Synthetic Fixed-Rate Security Denominated in U.S. Dollars from a Conventional Floating-Rate Note Denominated in Pounds Sterling

An investor who wishes to own a security paying a fixed rate of interest in U.S. dollars may, of course, purchase a conventional U.S. dollar fixed-rate security outright. Alternatively, the investor could create a synthetic U.S. dollar fixed-rate security by buying either a fixed-rate or a floating-rate instrument in another currency and combining it with a cross currency swap. We illustrate the case of buying a conventional sterling floating-rate security and transforming it into a synthetic U.S. dollar fixed-rate security. The transformation is expressed in the following equation, and the mechanics are illustrated in Exhibits 2 and 3.

Conventional sterling floating-rate security

plus

Cross currency swap
(receive U.S. dollar fixed/pay sterling floating)

equals

Synthetic U.S. dollar fixed-rate security

Essentially, the investor will receive sterling interest payments from his floating-rate asset; these cash inflows are based on a given spread over (under) the London Interbank Offered Rate for sterling (sterling LIBOR). LIBOR is reset on a semiannual basis. On the semiannual coupon payment dates, the investor makes sterling LIBOR payments to the swap counterparty; in return, the investor receives fixed interest payments in U.S. dollars. The investor, in effect, now owns a synthetic security that provides a fixed stream of interest receipts denominated in U.S. dollars.

If we assume that the conventional fixed-rate security and the synthetic fixed-rate security have the same credit risk, and that the credit risk on the cross currency swap is negligible, then the decision to invest in the straight bond or the synthetic fixed-rate bond is mainly dependent on their respective rates of return. The investor should undertake the asset swap (i.e., invest in the synthetic security) if

EXHIBIT 2
Creating a Synthetic U.S. Dollar Fixed-Rate Security from a Conventional Foreign-Currency Floating-Rate Note (cash flows)

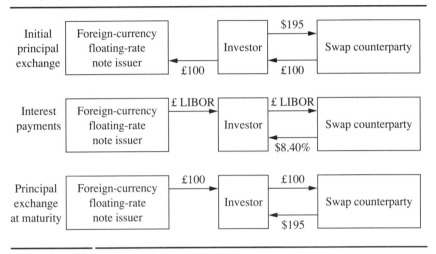

the return on the synthetic U.S. dollar fixed-rate security exceeds the return available on the conventional U.S. dollar straight bond. In some instances, the investor's objective may be simply to create the synthetic security because the conventional security is nonexistent. In such cases, it is impossible to calculate the yield pickup.

In the example, the three-year sterling FRN is priced at par and pays 6-month sterling LIBOR flat. A conventional three-year U.S. dollar fixed-rate bond by the same issuer has a yield of 8.20 percent. The investor receives 8.40 percent U.S. dollar payments from the fixed side of the swap and pays sterling LIBOR to the swap counterparty on a semiannual basis.

The cash flows from the perspective of the investor are given in Exhibit 3. The investor's sterling floating-rate cash flows cancel each other, leaving only the U.S. dollar fixed-rate cash inflows from the swap. These are received semiannually and give an internal rate of return of 8.40 percent, assuming semiannual compounding. The 20–basis point yield pickup available on the synthetic fixed-rate security may or may not be sufficient to induce the investor to undertake the asset swap. Note, however, that the investor has to factor in the

EXHIBIT 3

Example of a Synthetic U.S. Dollar Fixed-Rate Security: Cash Flows from the Investor's Perspective

Time Period	Conventional Sterling FRN (a)	Currency Swap		Synthetic U.S. Dollar Fixed-Rate Security (d = a + b + c)
		Pounds (b)	Dollars (c)	
0	−100	+100	−195	−195
1	+0.5L_0	−0.5L_0	+8.19	+8.19
2	+0.5L_1	−0.5L_1	+8.19	+8.19
3	+0.5L_2	−0.5L_2	+8.19	+8.19
4	+0.5L_3	−0.5L_3	+8.19	+8.19
5	+0.5L_4	−0.5L_4	+8.19	+8.19
6	+(0.5L_5 + 100)	−(0.5L_5 + 100)	+(8.19 + 195)	+(8.19 + 195)
Return	+£ LIBOR flat	−£ LIBOR flat	+8.40%	+8.40%

Note: Time periods 0 and 1 refer to the start and end of the first six-month period, respectively. LIBOR (L) for each period is determined at the start of the period and paid at the end of the period.

additional credit risk on the cross currency swap, however small it may be.

Creating a Synthetic Floating-Rate Security Denominated in U.S. Dollars from a Conventional Fixed-Rate Security Denominated in Pounds Sterling

An investor who wishes to own a security paying a floating rate of interest in U.S. dollars, in lieu of purchasing such a security outright, can create a synthetic security by buying a conventional fixed-rate instrument denominated in a foreign currency and combining it with a cross currency swap. Such a transformation is shown in the following equation:

Conventional sterling fixed-rate security

plus

Cross currency swap
(pay sterling fixed/receive U.S. dollar floating)

equals

Synthetic U.S. dollar floating-rate security

The decision to invest in a conventional FRN or a synthetic FRN depends on their relative rates of return. The investor should undertake the asset swap (i.e., invest in the synthetic security) only if the return on the synthetic security exceeds the return available on the conventional U.S. dollar FRN. Note again that such comparison is appropriate only when the credit risks on the conventional and synthetic floating-rate securities are substantially similar and when the credit risk on the swap is quite small.

The mechanics of such a swap are illustrated in Exhibits 4 and 5. The yield on a conventional three-year U.S. dollar floating-rate security is six-month U.S. dollar LIBOR flat. The yield on a conventional three-year sterling fixed-rate security is 12 percent. The investor will receive 12 percent semiannually from the fixed-rate security and pay 12 percent semiannually to the swap counterparty. The investor will also receive U.S. dollar LIBOR plus 10 basis points from the swap

EXHIBIT 4
Creating a Synthetic U.S. Dollar Floating-Rate Note from a Conventional Foreign-Currency Fixed-Rate Security (cash flows)

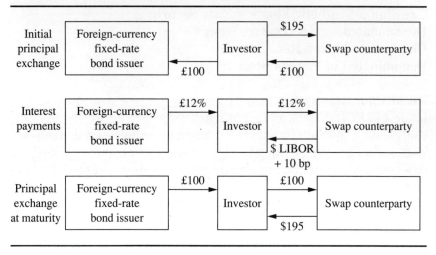

counterparty. The net result is that the investor will obtain U.S. dollar LIBOR + 10 basis points for the synthetic FRN. As far as the investor is concerned, he now owns a synthetic security that provides a floating stream of interest receipts in U.S. dollars. This 10–basis point pickup makes the synthetic FRN preferable to the conventional FRN, all other things equal.

ADJUSTMENT SWAPS (OFF-MARKET SWAPS)

The discussion so far has been on creating synthetic securities that are valued at par. However, the underlying asset to be swapped is seldom available at the par price. Frequently, the fact that a security is trading at a big discount to its par value—due to market dislocations or illiquidity—increases its attractiveness as raw material for an asset swap. In this section, we briefly outline some of the methods to

EXHIBIT 5
Example of a Synthetic U.S. Dollar Floating-Rate Security: Cash Flows from the Investor's Perspective

Time Period	Conventional Sterling Fixed-Rate Security (a)	Currency Swap Pounds (b)	Currency Swap Dollars (c)	Synthetic U.S. Dollar Floating-Rate Security (d = a+b+c)
0	-100	+100	-195	-195
1	+6	-6	$+0.5L_0 + 0.05$	$+0.5L_0 + 0.05$
2	+6	-6	$+0.5L_1 + 0.05$	$+0.5L_1 + 0.05$
3	+6	-6	$+0.5L_2 + 0.05$	$+0.5L_2 + 0.05$
4	+6	-6	$+0.5L_3 + 0.05$	$+0.5L_3 + 0.05$
5	+6	-6	$+0.5L_4 + 0.05$	$+0.5L_4 + 0.05$
6	+(6 + 100)	-(6 + 100)	$+(0.5L_5 + 0.05 + 195)$	$+(0.5L_5 + 0.05 + 195)$
Return	+12%	-12%	$ LIBOR + 10 bp	$ LIBOR + 10 bp

Note: Time periods 0 and 1 refer to the start and end of the first six-month period, respectively. LIBOR (L) for each period is determined at the start of the period and paid at the end of the period.

evaluate swaps when the underlying asset is trading at a discount or premium to its par value.

If the underlying asset is trading at a discount (premium) to par value, this implies that the coupon rate of that bond is less (more) than the coupon rate currently available in the market for bonds of comparable credit risk. The notional principal amount of a cross currency swap is usually based on the par value of the bond. Since a cross currency swap involves an up-front exchange of principal between the investor and the swap counterparty, complications may arise due to the inequality between the price paid for the security and the notional principal exchanged at the outset.

We illustrate this with a three-year sterling 10% coupon bond with a yield to maturity of 12 percent and price of £95.08. Assume that the current fixed-rate sterling/U.S. dollar LIBOR cross currency swap rate is 12 percent. Also assume that the notional principal is £10 million and the spot exchange rate is £1.95/dollar. Under these assumptions, the investor will receive £10 million from the swap counterparty and will make a payment of $19.5 million to the counterparty at the outset. The £10 million received by the investor is in excess of the £9.5 million paid for the sterling bond. However, over the course of the three-year period, the investor will receive only £0.5 million from the sterling asset and pay £0.6 million to the counterparty semiannually. There is a mismatch between the sterling cash flows of the underlying asset and the swap as far as the investor is concerned. There are two ways to take care of this problem.

One method is simply to adjust the sterling interest payments from the investor to the counterparty downward so that they equal the interest payments received on the sterling bond. In effect, the investor will receive £0.5 million from the underlying sterling asset and pay £0.5 million to the counterparty. In exchange for accepting a £0.5 million payment, rather than the market rate of £0.6 million, semiannually from the investor, the swap counterparty will make a downward adjustment to the up-front payment to the investor. That adjustment will equal the present value of the difference between the £0.5 million received from the investor and the market rate of £0.6 million that the counterparty should have received. In this example, the counterparty will provide a £9.5 million payment to the investor rather than the current swap market payment of £10 million. Note that in this case the sterling cash flows of the investor completely offset each other.

Another method is to keep the up-front and final principal payments exactly equal to the par swap and to make adjustments to both the intermediate sterling payments and dollar payments. The investor again pays £0.5 million to the swap counterparty, which is lower than the par swap payment of £0.6 million. In exchange for this, the investor will receive sub–U.S. dollar LIBOR payments from the swap counterparty.

These illustrations are applicable to premium bonds as well, with the appropriate modifications.

DEFAULT RISK AND CREDIT RISK CONSIDERATIONS

When making an investment in a synthetic security, the investor bears the entire risk of default by the issuer of the underlying security. Therefore, it is imperative that the investor be satisfied with the creditworthiness of the underlying security. A default by the issuer will deprive the investor of the cash flows from the bond. When a swap is used to create a synthetic security, the investor is obligated to make payments to the swap counterparty regardless of what happens to the cash flows of the bond. This aspect is particularly crucial for synthetic securities based on cross currency swaps because of the principal exchange at maturity. Unwinding the swap before maturity may involve substantial foreign exchange gains or losses for the investor.

The swap also carries with it the credit risk that the counterparty may default on its obligations. The investor is exposed to the risk that the swap dealer may default, while the swap dealer is exposed to the risk that the investor may default. In the case of an interest rate swap, this risk is minimal because the parties are exposed only to the net difference between the fixed and the floating payments of the swap; the risk is therefore only on a small percentage of the notional principal. In the case of a cross currency swap, the credit risk may be considerably higher because of the principal exchange at maturity. A default by one party is likely to subject the other to losses as the latter is forced to offset the exposure at unfavorable exchange rates. The credit risk issue is to some degree handled by keeping the exposure to any one counterparty at a tolerable level.

LIQUIDITY

Lack of liquidity is a major drawback of asset swaps. Asset swaps tend to have maturities of less than five years and, in general, are held until maturity. Since these swaps are built mostly around assets with very little liquidity to start out with, this feature should not be surprising. In addition, disposing of an asset swap involves not only the selling the underlying asset, but also unwinding the attached swap. Thus, asset swaps tend to be less liquid than the underlying bond itself. However, the higher return available on the synthetic security takes into account the liquidity differential between the synthetic security and the conventional security.

Several methods have been devised to overcome the perception of lower liquidity in asset-based cross currency swaps. In one method, underlying assets and attached swaps are offered as packages by the arranging financial institutions. Thus, the resulting synthetic security itself may be bought and sold before maturity without unwinding the swap. Liquidity thus increases somewhat but is still dependent on the arranger's willingness to create a market in the synthetic instrument. A second approach is for the financial intermediary to launch a special-purpose vehicle to improve the liquidity of the synthetic security. This vehicle invests in conventional securities and, through the use of swaps, converts them to synthetic securities. Liquidity is enhanced because the repackaged paper is backed by this special legal entity, and secondary market activity is in turn supported by the arranging financial intermediary.

IMPACT OF ASSET SWAPS

Asset swaps help to broaden the investor base for the primary market for debt instruments. For example, banks have traditionally confined their investments to floating-rate instruments to match their assets and liabilities. By making fixed-rate instruments available to bank investors and at the same time meeting their floating-rate cash flow requirement, asset swaps are able to find a whole new class of investors. With the use of cross currency swaps the investor base is broadened further by making securities denominated in foreign currencies available to investors with a domestic currency orientation.

In the same manner, asset swaps facilitate the issuance of fixed-rate bonds by lower rated issuers, who were traditionally excluded from that market. Since investors can asset-swap these lower-rated fixed-rate bonds into floating-rate securities at attractive margins over LIBOR, such bonds can be placed with investors more readily than in the past. Those bonds can also be swapped into other currencies at attractive rates.

In addition, asset swaps effectively define the levels below which the price of the new issue may not fall. If prices were to fall beyond a certain level, new issues would be likely to be asset-swapped, thus creating a demand for poorly performing new issues and keeping their prices above the floor. As a result, the asset swap market has some effect on the pricing of new bond issues.

The fact that asset swaps are usually held until maturity contributes to the locking up of securities for fairly long periods of time. Although this can be viewed as contributing to illiquidity in the secondary market for the underlying bonds, the truth is that asset swaps are most beneficial when they are based on illiquid and under-priced bonds. Rather than hindering secondary market liquidity, asset swaps should be viewed as broadening the demand for fairly illiquid bonds.

The traditional orientation of the swap market as a liability management tool associated with new bond issues is likely to continue to be the predominant influence on swap spreads. Since the asset swap market is still a fraction of the liability swap market, its effect on swap spreads has been fairly limited. However, if the size of the asset swap market increases in relation to the liability swap market, it is likely to exert more influence on the determination of swap spreads.

CONCLUSION

The asset swap market is an extremely valuable medium for investors to effect structural changes in their portfolios, whether they are related to the nature of floating or fixed cash flows or the currency of denomination of these cash flows. By using interest rate swaps and cross currency swaps, investors can create a multitude of synthetic securities that would not be available otherwise. Therefore, swaps provide an opportunity to change certain characteristics of a portfolio without unduly altering other, desirable characteristics. Ever-changing market conditions continually provide new opportunities for creating new, higher-yielding synthetic instruments. In this chapter, we have outlined the rationale for using asset-based cross currency swaps and the associated advantages and disadvantages.

CHAPTER 9

FORWARD CURRENCY SWAPS: AN INSTRUMENT FOR MANAGING INTEREST RATE AND CURRENCY EXPOSURE

Janet L. Showers
Salomon Brothers Inc
New York

Sovereign and corporate managers must evaluate numerous markets and financing alternatives. In addition to the decision of where and how to fund, issuers must confront questions of rescheduling outstanding liabilities in various currencies and managing exposure to changes in interest and currency rates. Interest rate swaps and capital market–related currency swaps are important elements of strategies for effectively managing funding costs. This chapter will help issuers become more familiar with the forward currency swap as a hedging technique.

Many strategies for hedging interest rate exposure in U.S. dollars have been developed over the past decade. The range of techniques includes hedging with U.S. Treasury securities (forward sale or purchase), options on those securities, the futures markets, and U.S. dollar interest rate swaps. Although some of these techniques may be available in other currencies, a forward currency swap transaction is one of the few alternatives for hedging interest rates in most nondollar currencies. Currency swap strategies have the following attributes:

- A forward currency swap can be used to lock in a future fixed-rate cost of funds in a nondollar currency.

The author wishes to thank Bruce Brittain and Philip Tremmel of Salomon Brothers Inc for their contributions to this chapter.

- A forward currency swap can create a forward liability without limiting the market of issuance to the same currency. This allows the issuer to maintain maximum access to favorable markets.
- As is true of more traditional uses of currency swaps, these strategies allow the issuer the possibility of arbitrage across different markets. This could result in a lower-hedged interest cost.
- In hedging the interest cost for a future need for funds with a forward currency swap, actual debt issuance does not have to occur until the future date when funds are needed.
- Forward currency swaps can be used to manage currency exposure while hedging interest rate risk on the underlying funding.
- Forward currency swaps can be used to hedge the currency exposure of existing assets or liabilities without requiring any additional funding.

STRUCTURE OF FORWARD CURRENCY SWAP TRANSACTIONS

A currency swap is an agreement between two counterparties to exchange specified amounts of two currencies today and reexchange them at a future date. Periodic interest payments are also exchanged between the two counterparties throughout the life of the swap. The interest payments in either currency may be based on a fixed rate set at the beginning of the swap or on a floating-rate index that will be reset throughout the swap.

A forward currency swap is a currency swap that is agreed to today but that has an effective date in the future. No payments occur until the effective date, at which time interest payments start to accrue. The trade date is the date on which the counterparties commit to the swap. All of the terms of the swap, including effective date, principal amounts, implicit exchange rates, interest rates, payment amounts, and payment dates are agreed to on the trade date. The typical forward currency swap involves the exchange of principal on the effective date, exchange of periodic interest payments between the effective date and maturity, and reexchange of principal at maturity.

Forward currency swaps can be structured as fixed rate for floating rate or as fixed rate for fixed rate, depending on the application.

For hedging interest rate expense in nondollar currencies, the basic form of transaction involves a forward currency swap between floating-rate U.S. dollars and fixed-rate nondollars. This is a forward cross currency interest rate swap. Fixed-rate for floating-rate forward swaps with all payments denominated in the same currency are labeled forward interest rate swaps.

Although forward currency swaps are usually structured to have an exchange of principal on the effective date as well as at maturity, the swap can be structured to have no exchange of principal on the effective date. In this case, the agreement is only for the exchange of interest payments and principal at maturity.

Forward currency swaps can be either funded or unfunded. A funded swap is one in which the company raises new cash on the effective date and uses the swap to convert the liability to another currency. The unfunded swap may simply be used as the hedge of a nondollar asset or liability, much like a foreign currency forward exchange contract. The unfunded swap may also be used to convert an existing liability of another currency.

THE ROLE OF FORWARD CURRENCY SWAPS IN MANAGING CURRENCY AND INTEREST RATE EXPOSURE

Forward currency swaps can be used as part of an overall liability management program to manage interest cost as well as currency risk. Corporations undertake interest rate hedging strategies to reduce risk and to separate the time of the funding from the pricing of those funds. Similarly, corporations undertake currency hedging strategies to protect the value of foreign investments and to reduce exchange risk in foreign currency costs and revenues. Forward currency swaps give the issuer more control over the interest rate and currency dimensions of its assets and liabilities.

Hedging Interest Rate Risk

Forward currency swaps can be used to hedge the interest rate for an issuer's future non–U.S. dollar liabilities. In the same way that a forward U.S. dollar interest rate swap can be used to hedge interest rate exposure in U.S. dollars, a forward cross currency interest rate swap between fixed-rate nondollars and floating-rate U.S. dollars will fix the borrowing rate for a specified amount of nondollar principal. Example 1 discusses the details of such a transaction.

Some of the situations in which forward currency swaps have application for managing interest rate risk follow:

- *Lock in interest rate for future financing.* Forward currency swaps can be used to lock in a fixed interest rate for a future nondollar financing, whether to produce new funds or to roll over existing nondollar debt.
- *Advanced refunding.* Forward currency swaps can be used to plan for the refunding of an existing bond that is not currently callable but will be in the future. By entering into a forward currency swap today, a company can protect the current value in the call option of an existing nondollar bond. An alternative to this advanced refunding strategy is to repurchase the bonds today via either a tender or an open-market repurchase. However, with some bonds, as a consequence of either the distribution of the bonds or the fact that the bonds are issued in bearer form, these alternatives are not practical because they do not result in the retirement of a large number of bonds. Particularly in these situations, forward currency swaps are an attractive strategy for rescheduling nondollar liabilities. This application is discussed in Example 2.
- *Hedge interest rate for delayed financing.* Forward currency swaps can be used to lock in current interest rate levels (to reduce risk or capture attractive rate levels, depending on the issuer's economic views) for a planned financing that is delayed because of legal, regulatory, or other constraints.

Managing Currency Exposure

Forward currency swaps allow a company to manage its exposure to fluctuations in exchange rates. The company can create a foreign currency liability to match against a foreign currency asset or to hedge a foreign currency stream of revenues. Alternatively, a company can use a forward currency swap to develop funding strategies that incorporate a company's views on exchange rates.

One characteristic of a forward currency swap structured with an exchange of principal on the effective date is that exchange rate movements will not affect the market value of the forward swap until the initial principal exchange. Until that time, any movement in the exchange rate will cause a change in the market value of the initial principal. However, this will be offset by the change in value of the principal reexchange at maturity. Thus, until the effective date, the company has a long and a short position in each of the swap currencies. Therefore, by using a forward currency swap with initial exchange of principal, a company can plan for hedging the currency risk of a future investment that will create foreign currency exposure and yet not create any reverse foreign currency exposure prior to the acquisition of the foreign currency asset.

However, a forward currency swap structured to have no initial exchange of principal will create exposure to exchange rate movements starting on the trade date. In this case, the company has a short position in one currency and a long position in the other currency, beginning on the trade date. A company may wish to take advantage of this if it believes that the short currency will depreciate against the long currency. For example, suppose the company undertakes a forward swap to pay fixed-rate nondollars and receive floating-rate U.S. dollars, and the company funds the swap on the effective date. If the currency does depreciate against the U.S. dollar, the company will receive a larger amount of nondollar proceeds when the U.S. dollar floating-rate principal is exchanged at the spot rate compared with the amount of nondollar principal that the company will have to repay at maturity under the terms of the swap.

Some situations in which forward currency swaps have application in managing currency exposures follow:

- *Roll over hedge of foreign investment.* A company that has hedged an investment in a foreign subsidiary by issuing non-dollar debt and that wishes to roll over the hedge at maturity or call date can use a forward currency swap to maintain the nondollar hedge and also capture attractive interest rates in a given environment.
- *Plan for future nondollar investment.* A company that plans a nondollar future investment can use a forward currency swap to plan for the funding of that asset, choosing the nondol-lar currency to match the currency of the asset. The forward currency swap would hedge the value of the investment, hedge

the dollars required to invest, and also fix the interest expense on the funding.

* *Active management of funding costs.* A company that believes that the interest rate in a nondollar currency has reached a cyclical low can use a forward currency swap to lock in that rate and structure the swap with or without exchange of principal to develop a strategy incorporating its view on the near-term direction of the expected change in the nondollar exchange rate against the U.S. dollar. Example 3 discusses this strategy.

EXAMPLES

The following three examples illustrate the structure of forward currency swap transactions and show how the costs of forward currency swap strategies can be evaluated. For simplicity, underwriting fees and expenses and taxes have been ignored. In an actual transaction, the swap structure and analysis can be adjusted for these items.

Example 1.
Hedging a Future Financing
with a Forward Currency Swap

Situation
A company has committed to acquire a Deutschemark asset one year from today and desires to lock in a fixed interest rate for the funds used to purchase the asset. To hedge its exchange rate exposure, the company plans to undertake a five-year DM100 million liability in one year.

Solution
To achieve both of these objectives, the company enters into a forward currency swap agreement today with a counterparty to pay fixed-rate Deutschemarks and receive in exchange U.S. dollars with interest payments based on a U.S. dollar floating-rate index. The effective date of the swap coincides with the date that funds are needed to acquire the asset. On the effective date, the company will fund the swap by issuing U.S. dollar floating-rate funds. The transaction would be executed as follows.

Step 1. Enter into the Swap Agreement Today
- The company enters into an agreement with the counterparty to undertake a five-year, cross currency interest rate swap starting one year from today. All terms of the swap are set today and include an initial exchange of principal.

Step 2. Exchange Proceeds on the Effective Date of the Swap
- The company issues a U.S. dollar floating-rate note with a maturity of five years. The face amount of the floating-rate note equals the U.S. dollar principal amount of the swap.
- The company uses the proceeds of the floating-rate issue to pay the counterparty the U.S. dollar amount specified in the swap agreement.
- The counterparty pays the company the Deutschemark amount specified in the swap agreement. The company uses the Deutschemark amount to acquire the Deutschemark asset.

The funding of the swap and the initial exchange of proceeds are illustrated in Figure 1.

Step 3. Exchange of Interest Payments Over the Life of the Swap
- The company uses the U.S. dollar interest payments received from the counterparty under the swap to pay the interest on its U.S. dollar floating-rate liability.
- The company pays the counterparty the Deutschemark fixed-rate interest payment specified in the swap agreement.

Step 4. Exchange of Principal Amounts at Maturity
- The company uses the U.S. dollar principal received from the counterparty under the swap to repay the principal amount of its U.S. dollar floating-rate liability.
- The company pays to the counterparty the Deutschemark principal amount specified in the swap agreement.

Figure 2 shows the exchange of interest payments over the life of the swap and the reexchange of principal amounts at maturity. The net result of this transaction is that the company has created a five-year Deutschemark liability starting one year forward at a fixed interest rate that is set today. All payments on the company's underlying U.S.

FIGURE 1

Hedge of Future Financing with a Forward Currency Swap: Steps 1 and 2

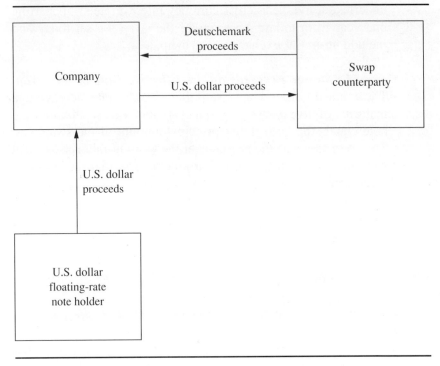

dollar liability are offset by the U.S. dollar payments that the company receives under the swap terms. The effective structure created by the swap is shown in Figure 3.

Cash Flow Analysis

Illustrative cash flows for this transactions are shown in Figure 4. Under the forward swap agreement, the company will make 6.296 percent annual fixed-rate Deutschemark interest payments in return for receiving semiannual U.S. dollar interest payments set at six-month LIBOR flat. Interest on the swap starts accruing one year from today and continues for five years. Initial and final principal amounts are to be exchanged at the one-year forward rate of DM1.9985/U.S. dollar. At this exchange rate, the currency swap interest payments are based on principal amounts of DM100 million and US$50.038 million. The

FIGURE 2
Hedge of Future Financing with a Forward Currency Swap: Steps 3 and 4

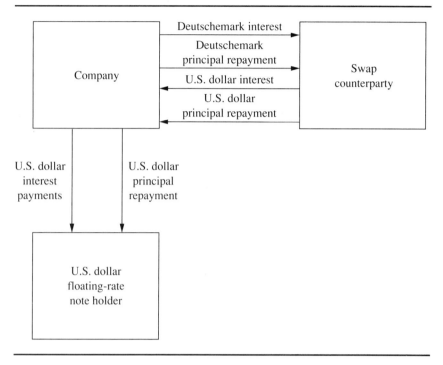

FIGURE 3
Hedge of Future Financing with a Forward Currency Swap: Resulting Deutschemark Liability

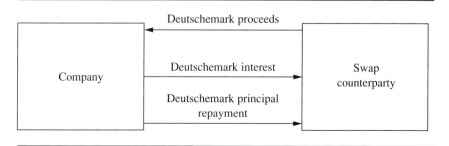

FIGURE 4
Hedge of Future Financing with a Forward Currency Swap: Cash Flow Analysis (Dollars and Deutschemarks in Thousands)

Years from Trade Date	Currency Swap							
	U.S. Dollar Floating Rate Note		U.S. Dollar Cash Flows		Deutschemark Cash Flows		Net Deutschemark Liability	
	Principal	Interest[a]	Principal	Interest[a]	Principal	Interest	Principal	Interest
Trade date 0.0								
0.5								
Effective date 1.0	$50,038		$(50,038)		DM100,000		DM100,000	
1.5		$(1,459)		$1,459				
2.0		(1,459)		1,459		DM(6,296)		DM(6,296)
2.5		(1,459)		1,459				
3.0		(1,459)		1,459		(6,296)		(6,296)
3.5		(1,459)		1,459				
4.0		(1,459)		1,459		(6,296)		(6,296)
4.5		(1,459)		1,459				
5.0		(1,459)		1,459		(6,296)		(6,296)
5.5		(1,459)		1,459				
Maturity date 6.0	(50,038)	(1,459)	50,038	1,459	(100,000)	(6,296)	(100,000)	(6,296)
					Deutschemark financing cost (from effective date to maturity)			6.296%

[a] Actual interest will be based on six-month LIBOR as of reset dates. In this example, six-month LIBOR is assumed to be 5.75 percent for the term of the swap.

company funds the swap by issuing, one year from today, a U.S. dollar floating-rate note and paying interest at six-month LIBOR flat. The transaction is structured so that the currency swap offsets the exact cash flows of this debt issuance. As such, the floating-rate note will have a face amount of US$50.038 million.

The financing cost achieved by the forward swap is 6.296 percent compounded annually. The analysis assumes that the company funds at six-month LIBOR flat. Should the company be able to come to market at a more favorable spread to the floating-rate index, the Deutschemark financing cost will be correspondingly decreased.

Benchmarks for Comparison

In evaluating the cost of this forward currency swap strategy, there are two obvious alternatives for comparison. One strategy is to take no action today, wait to finance until funds are needed, and obtain the current market interest rates at that time. A second strategy, prefunding, is to raise funds today, thereby capturing current rates, and invest the proceeds until needed.

The desirability of locking in an interest rate today depends on the level of interest rates on the effective date. The forward swap strategy is attractive if interest rates rise significantly. If rates remain stable or decline, the unhedged borrower will have a lower cost of funds. The effective-date interest rate level at which the unhedged and forward currency swap strategies will result in the same financing cost can be determined. In this example, again assuming no issuing expenses, the breakeven future financing rate occurs when the company can issue a fixed-rate Deutschemark bond with an annual coupon of 6.296 percent. This represents a 54.6–basis point increase above the company's five-year annual coupon at that time of 5.75 percent.

Prefunding is the most direct way for a borrower to lock in a rate on nondollar funds needed in the future. Usually, the interest rate earned on the short-term nondollar investment will be less than the interest rate paid on the nondollar liability. The difference between these rates will increase the borrower's effective cost of funds. In this example, assuming that the company can issue a six-year, fixed-rate Deutschemark debt today with an annual coupon of 5.75 percent, and that the Deutschemark proceeds can be invested for one year at the 4.50 percent Deutschemark Eurodeposit rate, the company would lock in an all-in cost of funds of 6.032 percent for five years, one year forward. Although prefunding produces a financing cost that is 26.4 basis points lower than the forward swap, it has the disadvantage of raising funds before they are needed.

Eliminating Floating-Rate Spread Risk

Because the company's floating-rate note new issuance spread may vary over time, waiting to fund the forward currency swap until the effective date will create some uncertainty in the actual funding cost achieved. Alternatively, should the company choose to raise funds via the commercial paper or other short-term market, the spread to the swap floating-rate index may vary over the term of the swap.

If the Deutschemark borrower wishes to lock in its currency floating-rate new-issue spread, the borrower could issue today the floating-rate U.S. dollar note that funds the swap and reinvest the proceeds in a short-term U.S. dollar floating-rate security until the funds are needed. Although eliminating exposure to changes in the floating-rate new issuance spread, this strategy has the disadvantage of requiring that the company raise funds in advance of actual financing needs.

Example 2.
Advanced Refunding of
High-Coupon Debt Using a
Forward Currency Swap

Situation

A company has an existing high-coupon Deutschemark liability that is callable in one year. The existing issue has an 8.50 percent coupon, has six years left to maturity, and is callable in one year at 102.5 percent of par. The company wishes to lock in today's favorable interest rates for refunding the existing issue on the call date.

Solution

To capture the current value of the call provision on outstanding high-coupon nondollar debt, the company uses a forward currency swap to fix the interest rate on a five-year Deutschemark liability one year forward, as in Example 1. The effective date of the swap would be the call date of the outstanding bond. At that time, the swap will be funded by raising cash in the U.S. dollar floating-rate market. The proceeds of the floating-rate note, exchanged for Deutschemarks via the swap, will be used to retire the outstanding high-coupon bond. To implement this advanced refunding strategy, the company would proceed as follows and as illustrated in Figures 5 and 6.

Step 1. Enter into the Swap Agreement

Step 2. Exchange Proceeds on the Effective Date of the Swap
- The company issues a U.S. dollar floating-rate note and uses the proceeds to pay the counterparty the U.S. dollar amount specified in the swap agreement.
- The company uses the Deutschemark amount received from the counterparty under the swap to call the outstanding high-coupon Deutschemark debt.

Step 3. Exchange of Interest Payments over the Life of the Swap
- The company uses the U.S. dollar interest payments received from the counterparty under the swap to pay the interest on its U.S. dollar floating-rate liability.
- The company pays the counterparty the Deutschemark fixed-rate interest payments specified under the swap.

Step 4. Exchange of Principal Amounts at Maturity
- The company uses the U.S. dollar principal received from the counterparty under the swap to repay the principal amount of its U.S. dollar floating-rate liability.
- The company pays the counterparty the Deutschemark principal amount specified in the swap agreement.

By entering into this transaction, the company has extinguished its outstanding high-coupon debt as of the call date and replaced it with a fixed-rate Deutschemark liability at a substantially lower financing rate than the original issue.

Cash Flow Analysis
Cash flows for the use of the forward currency swap in this advanced refunding situation are shown in Figure 7. As in Example 1, the company enters into a forward currency swap in which it receives six-month U.S. dollar LIBOR interest payments and pays 6.296 percent annual fixed-rate Deutschemark interest payments for five

FIGURE 5
Advanced Refunding with a Forward Currency Swap: Steps 1 and 2

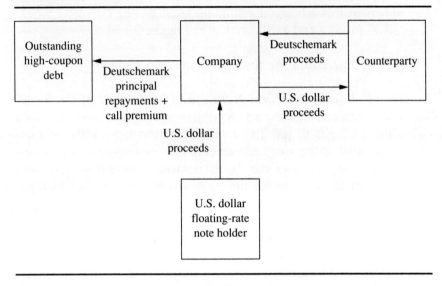

FIGURE 6
Advanced Refunding with a Forward Currency Swap: Steps 3 and 4

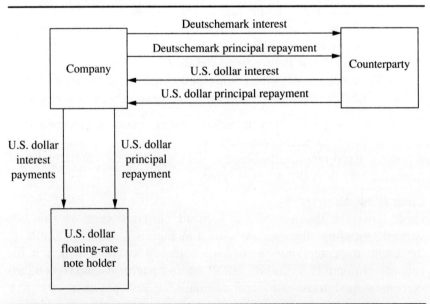

years beginning one year from today. Initial and final principal amounts are to be exchanged at the one-year forward exchange rate of DM1.9985/U.S. dollar. The company will need DM102.5 million to call the outstanding bond on the call date. Given the swap contract exchange rate, swap principal amounts are DM102.5 million and US$51.288 million. On the call date, the company issues a U.S. dollar floating-rate note at par paying interest at six-month LIBOR flat, with a face amount of US$51.288 million. This amount, swapped for Deutschemarks at the specified exchange rate, is used to call in the outstanding issue.

The Deutschemark refinancing cost achieved by the swap transaction is 6.296 percent compounded annually, as in the previous example. This analysis assumes that the company funds at six-month LIBOR flat. Any deviation in the company's U.S. dollar floating-rate funding spread to the six-month LIBOR swap index will correspondingly increase or decrease the company's all-in refinancing cost.

Benchmarks for Comparison

In addition to the alternative funding strategies discussed with Example 1, a useful comparison for evaluating advanced refunding via a forward swap is to compute the savings that result from refinancing with the forward swap versus leaving the existing bond outstanding to its maturity. On a present-value basis, this forward swap transaction locks in savings of 6.42 percent of the par amount retired versus the debt service cost of leaving the bonds outstanding to maturity.

Example 3.
Use of Forward Currency Swaps
in the Active Management of Funding Costs

Situation

This example discusses an application of forward currency swaps by an issuer that actively manages its liability portfolio. The company is not risk-averse and takes views on currency exchange rates and interest rates. The company borrows in a variety of currencies, looking for low interest rates, and its mix of currencies is weighted toward those expected to depreciate. Forward currency swaps can be helpful in reflecting economic views in a company's liability portfolio.

Assume that the company must raise cash today. The company is bearish about current West German interest rates, believing that the

FIGURE 7
Advanced Refunding with a Forward Currency Swap: Cash Flow Analysis (Dollars and Deutschemarks in Thousands)

| | U.S. Dollar Floating Rate Note | | Currency Swap | | | | Net Deutschemark Liability | |
| | | | U.S. Dollar Cash Flows | | Deutschemark Cash Flows | | | |
Years from Trade Date	Principal	Interest[a]	Principal	Interest[a]	Principal	Interest	Principal	Interest
0.0								
0.5								
1.0	$51,288		$(51,288)		DM102,500		DM102,500	
1.5		$(1,495)		$1,495				
2.0		(1,495)		1,495		DM(6,453)		DM(6,453)
2.5		(1,495)		1,495				
3.0		(1,495)		1,495		(6,453)		(6,453)
3.5		(1,495)		1,495				
4.0		(1,495)		1,495		(6,453)		(6,453)
4.5		(1,495)		1,495				
5.0		(1,495)		1,495		(6,453)		(6,453)
5.5		(1,495)		1,495				
6.0	(51,288)	(1,495)	51,288	1,495	(102,500)	(6,453)	(102,500)	(6,453)

Trade date — 0.0

Effective date — 1.0

Maturity date — 6.0

Deutschemark financing cost (from effective date to maturity) = 6.296%

	Years from Trade Date	Cash flows of Outstanding Bond until Called		Net Deutschemark Cash Flows for Outstanding Bond until Call and Refinancing		Deutschemark Cash Flows for Existing Bond if Left Outstanding to Maturity	
		Principal	Interest	Principal	Interest	Principal	Interest
Trade date	0.0						
	0.5						
Effective date	1.0	DM(102,500)	DM(8,500)		DM(8,500)		DM(8,500)
	1.5						
	2.0				(6,453)		(8,500)
	2.5						
	3.0				(6,453)		(8,500)
	3.5						
	4.0				(6,453)		(8,500)
	4.5						
	5.0				(6,453)		(8,500)
	5.5						
Maturity date	6.0			DM(102,500)	(6,453)	DM(100,000)	(8,500)
Present-value cost of funds as a percentage of par (from trade date to maturity)[b]					107.21%		113.63%

[a] Actual interest will be based on six-month LIBOR as of reset dates. In this example, six-month LIBOR is assumed to be 5.75 percent for the term of the swap.
[b] Discount at 5.75 percent, the assumed all-in six-year Deutschemark cost of funds.

Deutschemark interest rate has reached a cyclical low and is likely to rise. However, the company believes that the Deutschemark is likely to appreciate against the U.S. dollar over the next year and then begin a period of stability or depreciation.

Solution

The company can implement a strategy based on these views by raising cash today via a U.S. dollar floating-rate note and entering into a Deutschemark forward cross currency interest rate swap to swap into fixed-rate Deutschemarks one year forward. The forward swap would have an effective date one year from now and would be structured to have an initial exchange of principal so as not to expose the company to the appreciation of the Deutschemark over the next year. We assume that the company needs funds for six years, that the company's base currency is U.S. dollars, and that the company has no Deutschemark asset that it is hedging. The transaction is illustrated in Figures 8, 9, and 10.

Step 1. Enter into the Swap Agreement and Fund Today

- The company enters into an agreement with a counterparty to undertake a five-year cross currency interest rate swap starting one year from today.
- The company issues a U.S. dollar floating-rate note with a maturity of six years. The proceeds are used immediately for general corporate purposes.

Step 2. The Company Makes Interest Payments on the U.S. Dollar Floating-Rate Note Prior to and on the Effective Date

Step 3. Exchange of Proceeds on the Effective Date of the Swap

- The company pays to the counterparty the U.S. dollar principal amount specified in the forward swap agreement.
- The company exchanges the Deutschemark principal amount received from the counterparty under the swap agreement for U.S. dollars in the spot market.

Step 4. Exchange of Interest Payments over the Life of the Swap

- The company uses the U.S. dollar interest payments received from the counterparty under the swap to pay the interest on its U.S. dollar floating-rate liability.

FIGURE 8
Active Management of Funding Costs with a Forward Currency Swap:
Steps 1 and 2

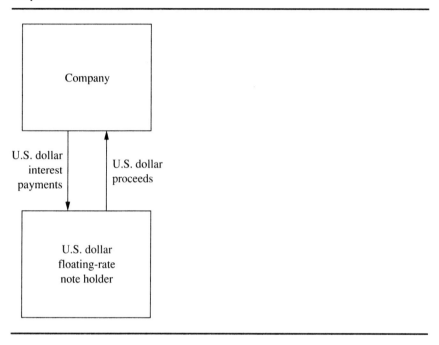

FIGURE 9
Active Management of Funding Costs with a Forward Currency Swap:
Step 3

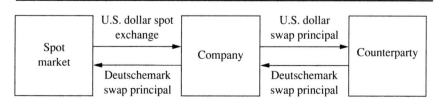

FIGURE 10
Active Management of Funding Costs with a Forward Currency Swap:
Steps 4 and 5

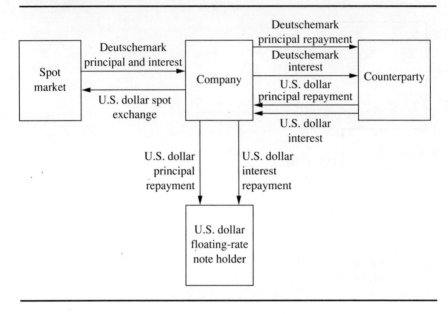

- The company exchanges U.S. dollars for Deutschemarks in the spot market to pay the counterparty the Deutschemark fixed-rate interest payments specified in the swap.

Step 5. Exchange of Principal Amounts at Maturity
- The company uses the U.S. dollar principal received from the counterparty under the swap to repay the principal amounts of its U.S. dollar floating-rate liability.
- The company exchanges U.S. dollars for Deutschemarks in the spot market to obtain the Deutschemarks necessary to pay the counterparty the principal amount specified in the swap agreement.

Cash Flow Analysis
To illustrate the cash flows for this strategy, we assume that the company issues a US$100 million floating-rate note today at par, with a maturity of six years and paying interest at six-month LIBOR flat. Under the terms of the forward currency swap, the company receives six-

month U.S. dollar LIBOR and pays 6.296 percent fixed-rate Deutschemarks annually for five years, beginning one year from to-day. Initial and final principal amounts are to be exchanged at today's one-year forward exchange rate of DM1.9985/U.S. dollar. With a U.S. dollar principal amount of US$100 million, the principal amount is DM199.85 million. We assume that by the end of the first year, the Deutschemark has appreciated to DM1.95/U.S. dollar and that the Deutschemark/dollar exchange rate stays at that level for the re-maining five years. The cash flows for this transaction are shown in Figure 11. The U.S. dollar financing cost achieved by this strategy for six years is 6.22 percent annually. This cost assumes that six-month LIBOR remains constant at 5.75 percent for the first year.

Benchmarks for Comparison

We can compare this strategy with two others: entering into a current settlement cross currency interest rate swap (or otherwise creating a fixed-rate Deutschemark liability today), or waiting until one year from today to enter into the cross currency interest rate swap. The first alternative will lock in today's favorable West German interest rate but expose the company to the appreciation of the Deutschemark over the coming year. This strategy produces an all-in U.S. dollar financing cost of 6.76 percent, 54 basis points higher than the for-ward swap strategy. The second alternative protects the company from appreciation of the Deutschemark but exposes it to changes in West German interest rate.

Figure 11

Active Management of Funding Costs with a Forward Currency Swap: Cash Flow Analysis (U.S. Dollars and Deutschemarks in Thousands)

	Years from Trade Date	U.S. Dollar Floating-Rate Note		Currency Swap			
				U.S. Dollar Cash Flows		Deutschemark Cash Flows	
		Principal	Interest[a]	Principal	Interest[a]	Princial	Interest
Trade date	0.0	$100,000					
	0.5		$(2,915)				
Effective date	1.0		(2,915)	$(100,000)		DM199,850	
	1.5		(2,915)		$2,915		
	2.0		(2,915)		2,915		DM(12,583)
	2.5		(2,915)		2,915		
	3.0		(2,915)		2,915		(12,583)
	3.5		(2,915)		2,915		
	4.0		(2,915)		2,915		(12,583)
	4.5		(2,915)		2,915		
	5.0		(2,915)		2,915		(12,583)
	5.5		(2,915)	100,000	2,915		
Maturity date	6.0	(100,000)	(2,915)		2,915	(199,850)	(12,583)

216

Net Cash Flows

Years from Trade Date	U.S. Dollar		Deutschemark		Exchange Rate (DM/US$)	Net U.S. Dollar Flows	
	Principal	Interest[a]	Principal	Interest		Principal	Interest
Trade date							
0.0	$100,000		DM199,850		DM2.0285[b]	$100,000	$(2,915)
0.5		$(2,915)					(2,915)
Effective date							
1.0	(100,000)	(2,915)			1.950	2,487	(6,453)
1.5		0					(6,453)
2.0		0		DM(12,583)	1.950		(6,453)
2.5		0					(6,453)
3.0		0		(12,583)	1.950		(6,453)
3.5		0					(6,453)
4.0		0		(12,583)	1.950		
4.5		0					
5.0		0		(12,583)	1.950		
5.5		0					
Maturity date							
6.0		0	(199,850)	(12,583)	1.950	(102,487)	(6,453)
U.S. dollar financing cost (from trade date to maturity)							6.225%

[a] Actual interest will be based on six-month LIBOR as of reset dates. In this example, six-month LIBOR is assumed to be 5.75 percent for the term of the swap.

[b] Refers to the spot rate on the trade date.

CHAPTER 10

CROSS CURRENCY SWAPTIONS

Vincent J. Cirulli
Citibank
New York

INTRODUCTION

The growth of the interest rate and cross currency swap market in the 1980s allowed corporate issuers to arbitrage the world's capital markets in search of the lowest cost of capital. The swap market (a derivative market in that the value of a swap depends on the value of another, underlying financial instrument) is an efficient means of exchanging, eliminating, or accepting different interest rate and currency risks. A corporation can exchange one rate of interest, whether fixed or floating, for another type of fixed or floating rate. The two rates exchanged can be either in the same or in different currencies.

After the growth of the interest rate and cross currency swap markets in the mid-1980s, a logical step in the evolution of the derivatives market was the appearance of swaptions. Swaptions represent the next level of derivative products in that their value depends, not only on another financial instrument, but on another derivative product: the interest rate or cross currency swap. Swaptions are options, giving the buyer the right, but not the obligation, to enter into a swap or to cancel an already existing swap.

This chapter will begin with a discussion of single-currency interest rate swaptions and will then move on to cross currency swaptions.

TERMS AND CONVENTIONS

The following definitions will be helpful in explaining the many terms and conventions used in the swaptions market.

Put swaption (payer's swaption): The buyer of a put swaption has the right to pay a fixed rate of interest on a notional principal amount in one currency and to simultaneously receive a floating rate on the same notional amount. A put swaption would be exercised by its holder if interest rates rise above the strike rate. This is because the owner of a put swaption will pay a lower fixed rate of interest over the term of the underlying swap by exercising the swaption than by going into the market and paying the current rate of interest.

Call swaption (receiver's swaption): The buyer of a call swaption has the right to receive a fixed rate of interest and to simultaneously pay a floating rate. A call swaption will be exercised by its holder if interest rates fall. This is because the holder of a call swaption will receive a higher rate of fixed interest over the term of the underlying swap by exercising the call swaption than by going into the market and receiving the prevailing interest rate.

Strike rate: The fixed rate to which the option holder is entitled if the swaption is exercised.

Fixed/floating (interest rate) swap: A transaction in which a counterparty swaps a fixed rate of interest for a floating rate in the same currency. For example, a corporation borrowing fixed-rate sterling at 12.64 percent for 10 years may want to switch to a borrowing rate based on floating six-month sterling LIBOR. This is accomplished by entering into a sterling interest rate swap in which the borrower receives fixed sterling for 10 years at 12.64 percent and agrees to pay six-month sterling LIBOR for the 10-year period. Thus, the corporation swaps its floating rate for a fixed rate for 10 years. This is illustrated in Exhibit 1, where corporation XYZ has issued a sterling bond at par with a semiannual coupon of 12.64 percent. XYZ decided to swap this fixed borrowing rate for one based on a short-term rate, such as six-month sterling LIBOR.

Fixed/fixed swap (cross currency swap): A swap in which a counterparty swaps a fixed rate of interest in one currency for a fixed

EXHIBIT 1
Interest Rate Swap

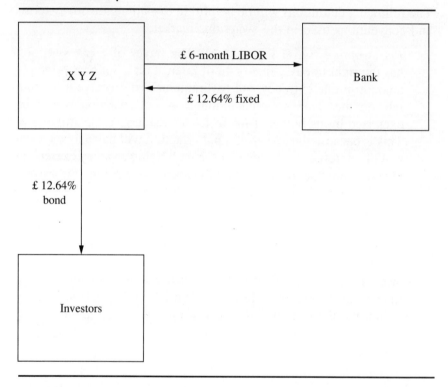

rate of interest in another currency. For example, a corporation that is currently paying fixed sterling at 12.64 percent for 10 years may wish instead to pay fixed U.S. dollars for 10 years. This is illustrated in Exhibit 2, which shows that XYZ has entered into a (fixed/fixed) cross currency swap in which it receives fixed sterling interest rates at 12.64 percent and agrees to pay U.S. dollar interest rates at 9.51 percent for 10 years. Sterling and dollar principal exchanges are made at the beginning and end of the swap. The illustrative sterling/U.S. dollar exchange rate is 1.9450.

Single-currency basis swap (floating/floating swap): A swap in which a counterparty exchanges one floating rate of interest for another. For example, a financial institution may wish to swap interest payments based on floating six-month LIBOR for interest payments based on three-month commercial paper.

EXHIBIT 2
Cross Currency Swap

Initial principal flows

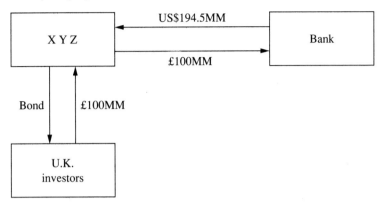

Interim interest flows

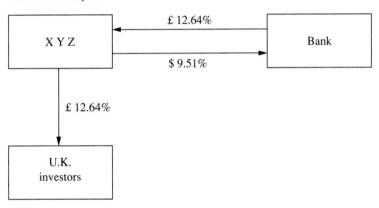

Final principal exchange

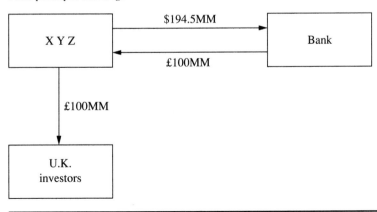

Cross currency basis swap: A swap in which floating interest payments in one currency are exchanged for a floating rate of interest in another currency. One example is the exchange of six-month Deutschemark LIBOR for six-month yen LIBOR.

Forward rate: The current market rate on a deferred start swap, such as a fixed/floating swap beginning 5 years from today and maturing 10 years from today. The rate on this forward swap will depend on current 5- and 10-year rates and will be priced in such a way that there is no arbitrage opportunity among the three rates. The forward rate is an underlying rate in a swaption and thus is a critical parameter for pricing swaptions. The next section will describe this relationship in greater detail.

In-the-money swaption: This swaption has intrinsic value. This means that the swaption holder has the right either to pay a rate that is lower than the current underlying forward rate or to receive a fixed rate that is higher than the forward rate. The intrinsic value is quantified as the net present value of the difference between the strike and the forward rate.

Out-of-the-money swaption: Here the swaption holder has the right to pay a fixed rate that is higher than the current forward rate or to receive a fixed rate that is lower than the forward rate. There is no intrinsic value in an out-of-the-money swaption, but it may have time value if some potential exists for the swaption to go in the money by the exercise date.

At-the-money swaption: A swaption held in which the strike rate equals the forward rate.

Volatility: The expected volatility of an underlying forward swap over the life of the swaption is expressed as an annualized standard deviation of the daily percent changes in interest rates and is an input in the modified Black-Scholes option-pricing model. Volatility is the most difficult parameter to estimate.

Swap maturity/option maturity: This concept is best illustrated by an example. A "10-5" swaption is one with a final swap maturity of 10 years from today where the option is exercisable in 5 years into a 5-year swap. A "7-3" swaption has an option maturity of 3 years, at which time it is exercisable into a 4-year swap, for a total of 7 years from today.

THE FORWARD RATE

The forward rate is a breakeven interest rate that extends from the date of possible option exercise until the defined swap maturity date. For example, in a 10-5 swaption the forward rate is the interest rate that one can lock into on day 1 for the period beginning 5 years from today and ending 10 years from today. A forward borrowing rate can be created by borrowing at a fixed rate of interest for 10 years and simultaneously lending at a fixed rate for 5 years. After 5 years, there is still a 5-year borrowing remaining at the original fixed rate. The breakeven forward rate then can be calculated as the original 10-year coupon plus or minus the carrying cost for the first 5 years.

The forward swap rate is critical in the pricing of a swaption and in structuring swaps with embedded swaptions. This is so because, although a 10-5 swaption gives the holder the right to enter into a swap beginning in 5 years and lasting for the remaining 5 years, the forward rate is the interest rate that can actually be guaranteed today for that latter period. The relationship between the strike rate on a swaption and the forward rate for the same underlying period determines how close the swaption will be to its intrinsic value and the likelihood of its being in the money at maturity.

As indicated in the preceding discussion, the forward rate is derived from two rates obtained from the yield curve. In the example of a 10-5 swaption, the forward rate in 5 years for the following 5 years is derived from the current 10-year rate and the current 5-year rate. If the curve is normally shaped, the forward rate will be higher than the 10-year rate. This is because the forward rate is a breakeven rate that must factor in the negative carrying costs of borrowing money for 10 years at the 10-year rate and lending the money for the first 5 years at the lower 5-year rate. Conversely, if the yield curve is inverted, the forward rate will be below the 10-year rate. This is illustrated in Exhibit 3, where the sterling yield curve is shown along with the 5-year forward rate beginning in 5 years.

This relatively low forward rate increases the price of call swaptions relative to put swaptions when the strike rate is chosen along the yield curve. The reverse is true for a situation involving a normal yield curve.

EXHIBIT 3
Sterling Yield Curve and Forward Swap

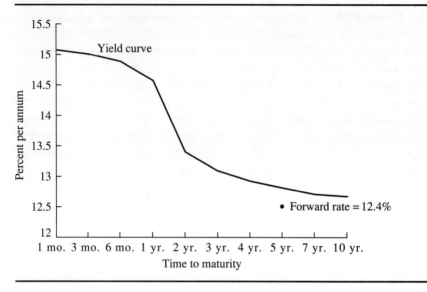

CALLABLE BOND ISSUES

Exhibit 1 presented an example where a borrower swapped a fixed rate of interest for a floating rate in the same currency. This transaction would be suitable for an underlying bond issue with no call provision. For a bond containing a call provision, however, the hedge would become more complicated. The borrower would want to call the bond if interest rates were to fall. This can be illustrated by describing a few basic strategies designed around the call feature of a bond. However, it is first necessary to describe how the call premium affects the equilibrium exercise of a bond's call option and, in turn, the implied strike rate of a swaption.

Since the borrower must pay a premium above par to call a bond from an investor, this additional cost must be factored into the remaining life of the bond to determine its per-annum cost. For a 10-year bond callable in 5 years at 101 percent, the 1 percent premium represents a per-annum cost of about 0.26 percent over each of the last

5 years. Thus, for a bond issued at 12.64 percent, interest rates must fall below 12.38 percent (12.64 − 0.26) before it would become economical to call the bond. If the borrower wished to sell an offsetting call swaption to the interbank market, it should sell the swaption with a strike rate of 12.38 percent.

BASIC SWAPTION STRATEGIES

Call Swaption Strategy

The preceding example assumed that rates fell over the five years. If interest rates were to rise instead, the corporation would not call the bond, and the swap would remain in place for the full 10 years, as originally contracted. Bond investors demand a higher rate of interest for the risk of the bond being called away—a higher cost to the issuer for a feature that it may never use. This is where the swaption comes into play. By issuing a callable bond to investors, the corporation is in effect buying a call from the investors, who in turn are compensated through a higher rate of interest on the bond. Until the swaption market developed, a corporate issuer had no choice but to hold on to the call until interest rates fell, at which time the call provision would be exercised. Under these conditions the borrower would receive full benefit from a sharp decline in interest rates. If rates did not fall, the borrower would have paid for a feature that it did not need.

Exhibit 4 illustrates this concept. The graph shows the borrowing cost for company XYZ for the last 5 years of a 10-year bond that is callable in 5 years. If 5-year interest rates, shown along the x-axis, are at or above 12.38 percent at call date, the company would not call the bond, and its borrowing cost would remain fixed at 12.64 percent. However, if rates were to fall below 12.38 percent, XYZ would call the bond and receive full benefit from the rate decline. The disadvantage here is the wide range of uncertainty with regard to borrowing costs in the last 5 years.

With the development of the swaption market, the issuer can sell the call swaption to the interbank market, monetize the value of the option, and lower its cost of capital in the process. If the interbank market valued the call at a price higher than that at which corporate bond investors valued the call, the issuer could stand in between the

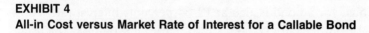

EXHIBIT 4
All-in Cost versus Market Rate of Interest for a Callable Bond

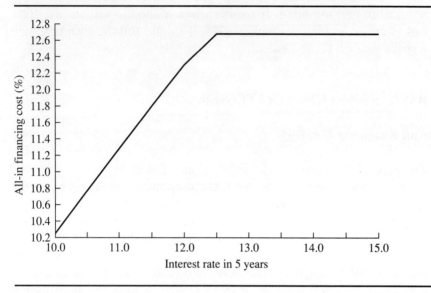

two counterparties and earn the difference by arbitraging. Selling the equivalent of the bond call in the form of a swaption would enable the borrower to benefit regardless of whether rates rise or fall. This is demonstrated in Exhibit 5. Here the same 10-year sterling bond is sold to investors at par with a 5-year call feature at 101 percent. Assume that the market price for the swaption is 1.93 percent up front. This 1.93 percent up-front swaption value is equivalent to 3.56 percent at a point 5 years from today. This in turn is equivalent to 0.98 percent per annum over the final 5 years of the financing. Exhibit 5 shows the company's cost of borrowing under the two scenarios. If rates are above 12.38 percent on the exercise date or below 12.38 percent, in either scenario the company's cost of borrowing is constant at 11.66 percent after the benefit of the up-front swaption premium is factored in.

It is possible, therefore, for a corporation to lower its cost of capital and simultaneously reduce the uncertainty of its financing costs past the call date. There is a cost for these advantages, however, in that the issuer has sold away its upside potential in the event interest

EXHIBIT 5
Callable Strategy Outcomes If Rates Vary About 12.38 Percent

On financing date

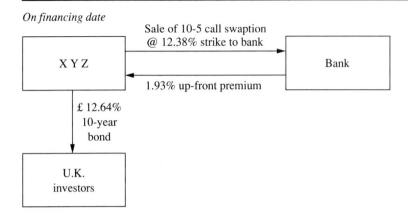

If rates fall below 12.38%
• Bond is called from U.K. investors
• Bank exercises its call swaption

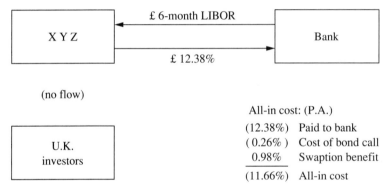

All-in cost: (P.A.)

(12.38%)	Paid to bank
(0.26%)	Cost of bond call
0.98%	Swaption benefit
(11.66%)	All-in cost

If rates rise above 12.38%
• Bank's swaption expires worthless
• X Y Z continues to pay U.K. bond investors

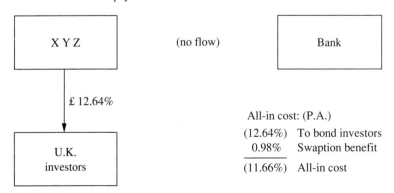

All-in cost: (P.A.)

(12.64%)	To bond investors
0.98%	Swaption benefit
(11.66%)	All-in cost

rates fall dramatically by the call date. This possibility is, after all, what the swaption buyer is paying for. The interbank market accepts potentially large but risky future benefits in exchange for a certain up-front premium.

Putable Strategy

A second financing strategy utilizes a "putable" swaption. In this example, the corporation would still issue a callable bond but instead of selling an offsetting call swaption to the interbank market, it would sell a put swaption. This strategy is illustrated in Exhibit 6. In this scenario the issuer would pay a fixed rate of interest for the first five years. In the fifth year either the call in the bond or the put in the swaption would be exercised, depending on whether rates rose or fell. If interest rates fell, the bond call would be exercised by the borrower. At the same time the put that was originally sold to the bank would become worthless and expire unexercised. If interest rates rose, the call would become worthless. However, the put swaption that was originally sold to the interbank market would have value and would be exercised by the bank. Upon exercise, the bank would pay the issuer a fixed rate of interest in exchange for receiving a floating rate in the swaption. This rate would offset the fixed rate still being paid to investors on the original bond issue. The corporation would earn the difference between the rate paid to investors and the rate received on the swap due to the exercise. In addition, it would receive the put premium. This scenario results in a reduced cost of capital over the life of the financing. The difference between this put swaption strategy and a callable strategy is that with the putable strategy, it is unknown whether the last five years will entail a fixed or floating rate of interest; however, it is still possible for the borrower to swap from a floating rate to a fixed rate in the last five years, if desired.

These examples demonstrate a few ways in which swaptions can be used by issuers to tailor risk/return trade-offs that would not be possible without option-based instruments.

Building the Swaption Premium into the Swap

Rather than paying the swaption premium up front, issuers sometimes wish to have the cost built into the interest rate swap itself. The

EXHIBIT 6
Putable Strategy

Initial financing

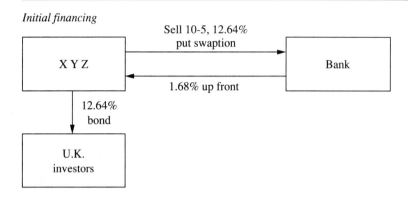

If interest rates fall to 10.00%
- 12.64% bond is called
- 10.00% bond is issued
- Call premium of 1% is paid to investors
- Put swaption expires worthless

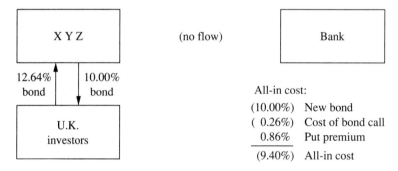

All-in cost:

(10.00%)	New bond
(0.26%)	Cost of bond call
0.86%	Put premium
(9.40%)	All-in cost

If rates rise to 14.00%
- The call in the bond expires worthless
- The bank exercises the put
- Fixed rate from bank offsets
  fixed rate to investors

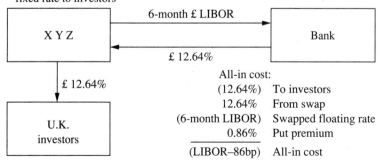

All-in cost:

(12.64%)	To investors
12.64%	From swap
(6-month LIBOR)	Swapped floating rate
0.86%	Put premium
(LIBOR–86bp)	All-in cost

following example shows how the sale of a swaption can be structured into an interest rate swap. The process of determining where the value of the swap and the value of the swaption are balanced is an interactive process.

Assume a bond financing that is swapped into a floating rate of interest. The issuer may be indifferent between a fixed versus a floating rate of interest after five years, so it sells a call swaption to a swap counterparty. It decides to receive the premium for the call swaption over time by accepting a higher fixed coupon for 10 years on the swap rather than receiving an up-front fee for the call swaption. The up-front premium of 1.93 percent that it would receive translates into 35 basis points per annum, payable semiannually. If this amount is added to the current market coupon on the swap of 12.64 percent, the new coupon would become 12.99 percent. However, this would change the strike rate on the swaption since the swap counterparty now would have the right to cancel the swap by paying 12.99 percent fixed instead of paying 12.64 percent. There is a higher-up front value to this strike rate, 2.34 percent. Once again, this must be translated into a per-annum payment, now 42 basis points, which adds up to a new swap of 13.06 percent. Ultimately, the process converges at 13.08 percent.

PRICING SWAPTIONS

The parameters used to price swaptions are:

- Maturity of the option.
- Maturity of the underlying swap.
- Details of the underlying swap, such as whether the fixed rate is paid annually or semiannually.
- Put or call.
- American- or European-style option.
- Interest rate swap volatility.
- Strike level of the swaption.

For the purposes of this chapter, we will consider only the pricing of European-style options.

Suppose that the following sterling yield curve exists:

1 mo.	15.06%
3 mo.	15.00
6 mo.	14.88
1 yr.	14.56
2 yr.	13.35
3 yr.	13.03
4 yr.	12.86
5 yr.	12.76
7 yr.	12.66
10 yr.	12.64

The following European swaption can then be priced using these parameters.

Option maturity	5 years
Swap maturity	5 years from date of option expiration
Fixed rate	12.64% annually
Floating rate	6-month Sterling LIBOR
Volatility	8% p.a.
Option type	Call
Underlying swap rate	12.40% (forward rate)

Based on the given parameters, the price of the swaption would be calculated as 1.93 percent of the notional amount up front using a European option-pricing model.

It is interesting to see how the price of the swaption varies depending on its underlying assumptions. Exhibit 7 shows how the up-front price of a 10-5 call swaption varies depending on the strike rate assumed. Exhibit 8 shows a series of prices for different swaptions all priced at the money to remove the effects of intrinsic value, and all with a final swap maturity in 10 years. The key difference is the combination of option length and swap length. The first price is a 10-1 swaption, where the option length is very small compared with that of the underlying swap. The final swaption is a 10-9 swaption, a very long option maturity combined with a relatively short swap. Note that after an initial rise in price, the value of the swaption drops dramatically. There are two forces at work on the swaption price as we move from a 10-1 to a 10-9 swaption. Increasing time to option maturity tends to make the option more expensive, but decreasing the tenor of the un-

EXHIBIT 7
Option Price versus Strike Price (10-5 Call Swaption)

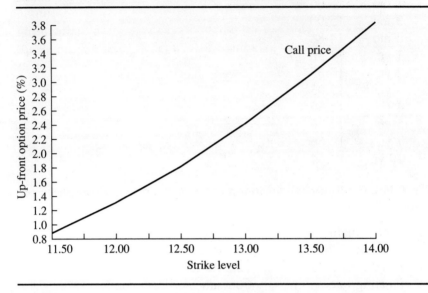

EXHIBIT 8
Option Price versus Tenor of Option/Swap (10-year Total Maturity, at the Money)

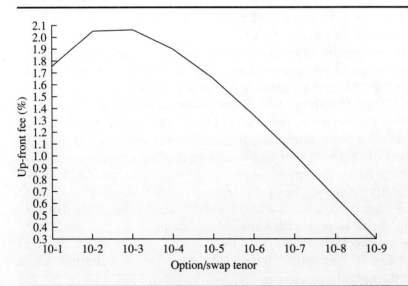

derlying swap tends to reduce the value of the swaption. On the left side of the graph, increasing time to option maturity exerts the dominant effect, but this is quickly surpassed by the effect of the declining swap tenor. A borrower can minimize financing costs by structuring the option/swap tenor to maximize the up-front value of the swaption.

CROSS CURRENCY SWAPTIONS

The existence of initial and final principal exchanges complicates the issue of pricing cross currency swaptions. If both initial and final flows were included in the swaption, the value of the swaption would depend upon the level of the fixed rate of interest in the swap, just as for a single-currency interest rate swaption. For example, a 7-3 swaption in which the buyer has the right to pay fixed yen at 7.88 percent and receive floating U.S. dollars has the same value as a swaption to pay fixed yen at 7.88 percent and receive floating yen. This is so because the ongoing value of a basis swap, in theory, is at or very close to par, and if the swaption were exercised, it could be used to swap back into floating yen. If both principal exchanges were included in the swaption, the value would theoretically be equal to that of a single-currency interest rate swaption. If the final principal exchange were removed, the swaption's value would be affected by the potential exchange rate at the termination of the underlying swap. Removing the final principal exchange from an option on a cross currency basis swap, for example, would effectively create a foreign exchange option. This occurs because movements in interest rates alone would not affect exercise of the option.

In a cross currency fixed/floating swaption, removal of the final principal exchange also adds a foreign exchange component, but exercise of the swaption would depend on a combination of the value of its exchange rate and interest rate components. This is illustrated in Exhibit 9, where the final yen/dollar exchange rate is unknown. It is possible for the exchange rate to have positive value relative to market rates at the time of exercise and for the fixed coupon rate simultaneously to have negative value. Since it is not possible to exercise the foreign exchange component of the swaption without also exercising the interest rate component, the holder of the option would be subject to both risks. Valuing such a swaption therefore depends

EXHIBIT 9
Cross Currency Swaption: No Final Principal Exchange

- Assume XYZ sells a 7-3 put swaption
- Strike = ¥ 7.88% vs. 6 mo. dollar LIBOR
- Assume foreign exchange rate is ¥132/dollar

If we remove final principal exchange, assume at year 3
option is exercised:

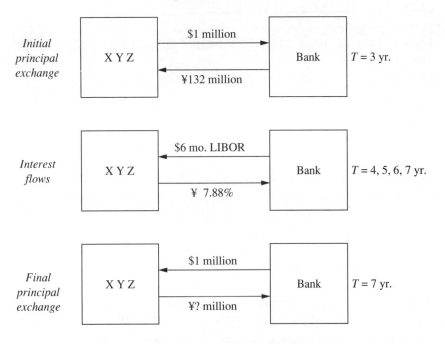

At exercise, the value of this swap would depend on
the value of a four-year yen interest rate swap, and
the cost of a four-year yen/dollar basis swap, at the
yen/dollar exchange rate in year 3.

on the degree of correlation between the underlying interest and exchange rates. In this example, a high positive correlation between yen interest rates and the value of the yen versus the dollar would result in a high swaption value. This is so because the underlying value of the fixed interest rate component and the yen exposure would either increase or decrease simultaneously, resulting in a volatile underlying instrument. Conversely, a high negative correlation would result in a situation where the interest and exchange rate movements offset each other, resulting in a low-volatility instrument, which would have little option value. If the two risks are uncorrelated, the swaption's value would fall somewhere in between.

In the case of cross currency fixed/fixed swaptions, even when both initial and final principal exchanges are included, the value of an option on two fixed interest rates would be determined by the correlation between the two interest rates. This occurs because the holder of the option cannot choose to exercise one fixed rate and leave the other side unexercised. Upon exercise, the holder of a fixed/fixed swaption must agree to simultaneously pay a fixed rate of interest in one currency and receive a fixed rate of interest in another currency. One rate may be advantageous compared to current market level, while the other may be at a disadvantageous level. The decision to exercise would depend on whether the net present value of the combined fixed-rate sides were positive. If the final principal exchange were left out in this structure, the decision of whether to exercise the swaption would be based on the combined values of three variables: the two market rates of interest and the final foreign exchange value. The valuation of this option on the trade date would need to take into account the cross correlations among all three variables.

The important point for the borrower to consider is that cross currency swaptions enable a company to take advantage of these trade-offs in exchange rates and interest rates in order to obtain a lowering of its borrowing costs. A borrower indifferent to funding in either of two currencies may wish to sell a cross currency swaption allowing the holder to transfer the company out of one currency financing into another in exchange for a high up-front premium.

SPREADTIONS

A spreadtion is an option on a spread between two commodities or financial instruments. The strike price would be expressed in terms of the price spread or rate spread between the two instruments, as opposed to the absolute levels of these instruments. A spreadtion on the difference between two interest rates is another form of a fixed/fixed cross currency swaption. One example is an option on the

EXHIBIT 10
Interest Rate Spread Opportunities

	Sterling	U.S. Dollar	Difference
Current 5-year	12.76	9.10	3.66
Current 10-year	12.64	9.51	3.13
5-year in 5 years	12.40	10.14	2.26

spread between five-year fixed sterling and five-year U.S. dollar rates (see Exhibit 10).

Notice that the difference between current five-year sterling and dollar rates is 3.66 percent, whereas the difference between the two forward rates is 2.26 percent. Thus, the shapes of the two individual yield curves imply a narrowing of the difference between the two rates. The U.S. dollar yield curve, which is normally shaped, implies a higher five-year rate in the future than in the current swap market. Conversely, the negatively sloped sterling yield curve implies a lower five-year swap rate in five years compared with the rate that exists currently.

One could take a position on a narrowing of the spread between the two rates in the future by either (1) receiving the forward sterling rate and paying the forward U.S. dollar rate or (2) buying a 10-5 put spreadtion with a strike price of 2.66 percent (at the money). In either case one would benefit if five-year sterling rates were less than 2.66 percent over five-year dollar rates in five years.

The pricing of interest rate spreadtions will vary across currencies depending on the correlation of interest rates in the different

EXHIBIT 11
Cross Correlation of 10-Year Interest Rate Swaps

	DM	SF	Yen	Stg	A$	C$	DFI	ECU	US$
DM		.58	.30	.38	.13	.24	.77	.69	(.02)
SF			.43	.38	.06	.12	.61	.53	.16
Yen				.31	.09	.18	.38	.35	.40
Stg					.07	.11	.30	.38	.11
A$						.22	.18	.20	.19
C$							.15	.24	.48
DFI								.70	.06
ECU									.19

currencies. Exhibit 11 shows historical cross-correlation coefficients for 10-year interest rate swaps.

The correlation between two interest rates helps to determine the volatility of the interest rate spread between the two rates. If two interest rates have a high positive correlation, the spread between them will not be as variable as the spread between two interest rates that are not as positively correlated.

CONCLUSION

Cross currency swaptions give a borrower a high degree of financing flexibility. This tool can be used to take advantage of one or more yield curve arbitrage opportunities, fixed/floating strategies, and cross currency interest rate and exchange rate differentials. The borrower has the task of identifying its sensitivity to each of these parameters. Once this is known, hedge protection can be purchased for those risks that are unacceptable, or additional premiums can be earned for accepting risks to which the borrower is indifferent.

CHAPTER 11

GOVERNMENT USE OF CROSS CURRENCY SWAPS

Kari Nars
Finland
Ministry of Finance, Finland
Helsinki

James R. Ramsey
Office of Financial Management and Economic Analysis
Commonwealth of Kentucky

Carl R. Beidleman
Lehigh University
Bethlehem, Pennsylvania

INTRODUCTION

Interest rate differentials arise between countries due to differing economic and political conditions and to market inefficiencies. When such interest rate differentials exist, it can be advantageous for public or private borrowers to raise capital in those markets with the lowest interest rates. Such practices are particularly common for multinational corporations operating in the international economy. However, public entities also have frequently entered the foreign markets to borrow funds.

Taking advantage of lower interest rates available in another country exposes the borrower to currency exchange risk. Such currency risk exists because principal and interest payments are paid in the future in the currency in which the debt is denominated. For example, a Samurai bond (i.e., one publicly issued in Japan by a non-Japanese private firm, bank, or public entity) will require future repayment of principal and interest in yen. Movements in exchange rates for the yen in terms of the borrower's home currency over the life of the debt will influence the final cost of borrowing.

The total cost of a Samurai bond issue will increase for a U.S. issuer, for example, as the value of the dollar falls. Suppose that at the time of issuance the initial exchange rate is ¥125/dollar and the annual interest payments are ¥100,000, or $800, at the initial exchange rate. If the exchange rate falls to ¥100/dollar, the dollar payment increases to $1,000. If the lower exchange rate continues throughout the life of the debt, the total cost of borrowing will be higher than the original coupon interest rate on the debt, and the borrowing savings that initially existed between the countries may disappear or become negative if the currency exchange risk is not managed.

Much has been written in this volume and elsewhere about the role of cross currency (and interest rate) swaps as hedging, arbitrage, and speculative instruments. In general, these applications of swaps have been confined to the corporate and financial sectors of the economy. Currency swaps have been used by finance managers of industrial and financial firms to hedge exchange-rate risk or to obtain a lower all-in cost of funds. They have also been used by portfolio managers to realize higher all-in rates of return on investment strategies than would be immediately available in a direct investment process. These applications of financial swaps in the private sector have become very well accepted and understood by potential users of swaps.

Similar applications also exist in the public sector; however, governmental units have been a bit more deliberate in deploying swaps, for a number of reasons. In this chapter we present case studies of two widely different applications of cross currency swaps undertaken by public bodies. The first case centers on macro problems of financing a country while maintaining currency stability. The second focuses on a municipal approach to obtain efficient financing that establishes a desired presence.

SOVEREIGN DEBT MANAGEMENT

Swaps may be regarded as the most important invention within the financial world during the last 20 to 30 years. The swap technique means that no loan decision need be final. Loan currencies and interest rate modes can be exchanged with ease.

The government of Finland has become an active user of swaps in its international liability management. During the period 1987 to 1990, the Finnish government's liability management team, located within the Ministry of Finance and assisted by the state Treasury Office, entered into about 50 different international currency and interest rate swaps, US$50–200 million at a time. The average size of the government's swaps was equivalent to US$50 million per transaction in any one currency.

Of the government's total outstanding foreign debt of some US$6 billion by the end of June 1990, 30 percent, or the equivalent of almost US$2 billion, was swapped. Most of the Finnish government's swaps have related to newly issued loans.

The Finland government's swap policy objectives have been:

- To achieve immediate cost savings through the effective use of swaps.
- To bring about the desired liability currency structure as one way of hedging foreign exchange risks.

High Credit Ratings Support Swaps

The government of Finland has enjoyed high credit ratings by both Moody's and Standard & Poor's. Finland is one of the few highly rated sovereign governments actively borrowing in the international capital markets. Hence, it has been able to obtain financing on very favorable terms. Other such active AAA/AAA or AAA/AA borrowers include the governments of Sweden, Austria, and Canada and supranational banks such as the World Bank, the European Investment Bank, and the Nordic Investment Bank. For instance, the $550 million Eurobond issue launched by the government of Finland in 1989 has been trading at about the same spreads to U.S. Treasury issues as similar loans of the World Bank.

The use of swaps relies on the concept of exchanging relative advantages. A high credit rating is a definite advantage in using currency and interest rate swaps to achieve desired objectives. By issuing fixed-interest-rate bonds in the international markets on the strength of its high credit rating, subsequently swapping these into floating-rate dollars, and then further swapping to one or several target currencies, the government has been able to achieve substantially reduced financing costs. This is due to the fact that the government's swap counterparties, generally large international banks and corporations, cannot easily achieve the same favorable all-in costs in the fixed-rate bond markets as the low-risk AAA/AA-rated government of Finland.

Measuring the Impact of Swaps

The financing strength of a borrower can be measured in terms of the sub-LIBOR levels that it can achieve in swapping from fixed to floating rates of interest. These sub-LIBOR levels are determined primarily by:

- The relative strength of the borrower.
- The prevailing market situation.
- The type of loan ("plain vanilla" or some more risky version, including options or other variations).

At certain times (1985–86) it was possible for the Finnish government to achieve levels of over 100 basis points below LIBOR using five-year plain vanilla loans. In 1990, the levels that could be achieved by the government were drastically reduced to some 30–50 basis points below LIBOR due to deteriorating markets. During this period, the relative difference between the financing costs of top-rated sovereign borrowers such as the government of Finland and banks and corporations had not decreased. Actually, the spread had increased due to the higher risk aversion of large institutional investors in the wake of international debt problems and their growing inclination to prefer AAA- or AA-rated sovereigns and supranational banks, coupled with the weaker results of many commercial banks and new uncertainties in the markets.

Sub-LIBOR levels for plain vanilla loan swaps should not be compared with those achievable for risky types of loans such as some warrants and options. If the borrower were willing to take added risks, the sub-LIBOR levels could be more attractive.

Swaps can generally also be used to change the interest-rate risk position of borrowers depending on the current interest rate outlook. Typically, a borrower with fixed-rate loans would reduce the debt's maturity and switch to floating-rate financing if interest rates were expected to fall. In this way, the borrower could ride down with the wave and benefit from falling interest rates.

Compared with normal borrowings, swaps do not increase the borrower's net indebtedness, because a swap involves both a liability and an asset of the same magnitude. The borrower obviously does not receive any funds into its cash reserves, as in the case of a drawdown of a normal loan.

Swaps and Currency Gains

One major objective of the Finnish government's external financing policies is to configure the currency of its foreign liabilities in the direction of the country's official currency basket, to which the Finnish mark is pegged. The currency basket has been designed to approximately match the mix of currencies of the countries with whom Finland trades. By pegging the mark to this basket of currencies, the Bank of Finland can stabilize the average (effective) external value of the Finnish mark and significantly reduce the exchange-rate risk faced by Finnish corporates. By distributing the currencies of the government's external debt roughly according to this currency basket, it is possible to even out the exchange-rate risk of the external obligations.

The use of offshore debt markets has been helpful in reducing the effective cost of debt from what would have been incurred had the Ministry of Finance funded the government in domestic markets. External markets are far deeper, and some of them provide low nominal interest rates. Thus, the use of an optimal mix of foreign-currency debt instruments to source the debt, coupled with the use of cross currency swaps to translate the currency of the debt portfolio to the desired mix in the Finnish currency basket, has enabled the Ministry of Finance to obtain a lower effective cost of debt. These differences are illustrated in Exhibits 1 and 2, which clearly reflect the lower effective cost of foreign debt. This is further illustrated by comparing the market interest rates of 7–9 percent in the yen, Deutschemark, and U.S dollar markets with the 12–14 percent rate in the Finnish mark market.

By balancing the government's foreign debt according to this basket (whose weighting is based on import and export weights), fluctuations in the exchange rates of the international currencies represented in the government's foreign debt portfolio will not, over time, change the domestic value of the government's debt. Since the average (effective) value of the Finnish mark is kept stable, an appreciation of one currency is compensated by depreciation in other currencies.

Using this strategy, the ministry's foreign debt team has even been able to outperform the currency index to which the Finnish mark is pegged. The annual currency gains (realized and unrealized) on the government's foreign debt have exceeded the recent appreciation of the Finnish mark (which has reduced the debt as measured in local currency). Exhibit 3 shows the situation. In 1989 alone, the "excess"

EXHIBIT 1
Republic of Finland: Effective Cost of Domestic Debt

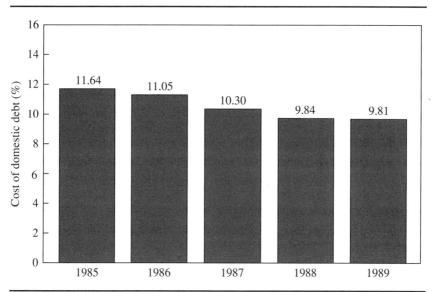

foreign exchange gains (beyond that associated with a strengthening of the mark) were estimated at some US$40 million (some Fmk150 million) compared with total currency gains of some Fmk900 million (about US$225 million), due largely to the decline in the value of the debt currencies in relation to the strong Finnish mark.

The relatively favorable currency results were due to the fact that although the major objective is to align the foreign debt structure with the official currency basket, it is not possible to achieve a 100 percent alignment. Market circumstances may be difficult, and some of the currencies in the currency basket may not be readily available for borrowing operations (due to administration hindrances in the country concerned). Therefore, in its management of the currency composition of its external debt, the government's foreign debt team has utilized certain intervals around the major currency shares in the foreign debt. The widths of these intervals have partly been determined on the basis of the outlook for the currencies in question.

The substantial changes in the government's debt composition achieved through swaps is illustrated by the fact that the actual share of the Japanese yen in the government's external debt in 1989 was

EXHIBIT 2
Republic of Finland: Effective Cost of Foreign Debt

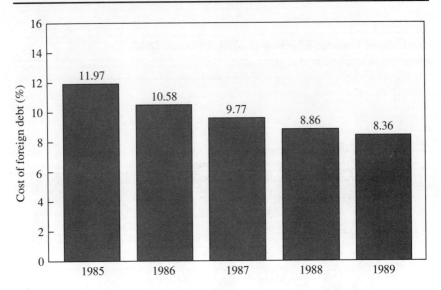

Note: The effective cost includes payments of interest and other fees, as well as realized and unrealized foreign exchange gains or losses on the debt during the year.

EXHIBIT 3
Republic of Finland: Foreign Debt Currency Gains (+) or Losses (−)
(Realized and unrealized FX/gains or losses on the government's foreign debt during the year)

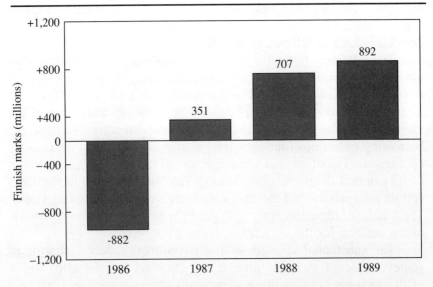

Note: Includes realized and unrealized FX gains or losses on the government's foreign debt during the year.

23 percent. However, cross currency swaps were used to reduce this exposure to only 12 percent in 1989 and to 5 percent in 1990.

Government Swap Case

Exhibit 4 provides an illustrative case study of how a sovereign swap works. The starting point was a US$70 million fixed-rate 10-year-bullet-maturity Eurobond issued by the government of Finland. The fixed-rate coupon of the issue was 8.375 percent p.a. The net proceeds of the loan were swapped to floating U.S. dollars and then to the desired end currency, in this case fixed-rate ECU debt. This denomination was chosen because additional ECU-denominated debt fit well with the desired debt currency mix at the time.

The end result was that the fixed-rate ECU debt had an all-in cost of 7.33 percent p.a. This was 0.5 percent p.a. below the cost

EXHIBIT 4
Sovereign Swap Example

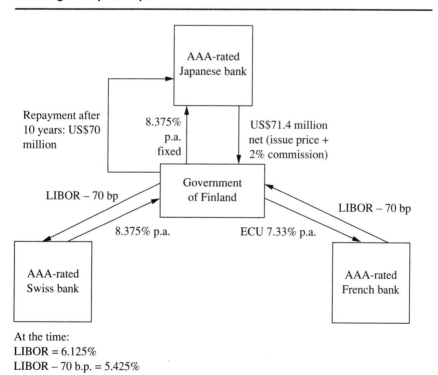

At the time:
LIBOR = 6.125%
LIBOR − 70 b.p. = 5.425%

of a similar straight debt issue in the fixed-rate ECU markets. The savings made possible by the swap during the 10-year loan period (compared with direct borrowing in the international capital markets) were equivalent to US$4.4 million.

Institutional Framework

In Finland, Parliament has to approve annually the general borrowing authorization for the government. On this basis, the Council of State (i.e., the cabinet) is entitled to authorize the Ministry of Finance to borrow domestically and abroad in different currencies.

The exact choice of currencies, the amounts borrowed (within the covered framework), and the timing of the loans and swaps are determined by the Ministry of Finance. This procedure provides flexibility in the financing operations, since the best opportunities in the markets often appear suddenly and remain in place for only a short time. The ministry's debt team must be able to respond very rapidly to the numerous loan and swap offers conveyed to it almost daily by major international banks. The composition of foreign debt by currency (after swaps) is shown in Exhibit 5. The exhibit also compares the currency composition with the currency index.

As indicated in the exhibit, the foreign debt share of the "DM bloc" of currencies, as well as those of the yen and the pound, were quite close to the currency index weights. The overrepresentation of the U.S. dollar was partly compensated for by the fact that the dollar has a high weight in two other basket currencies in which it was not possible to borrow: the Swedish krona and the Norwegian krone. If these indirect weights of the dollar were added to the dollar weight in the currency index, the discrepancy would be much smaller.

Swap Risks

Swaps frequently involve the assumption of risks. The Finnish government has established a structured policy to reduce swap risks. These risks arise primarily if the swap counterparty is unable to fulfill its payment obligations. Swap agreements generally include a cancellation clause in case the counterparty is in default on its repayments,

EXHIBIT 5
Republic of Finland Foreign Debt by Currency Compared with Bank of Finland Currency Index July 30, 1989

Currency	Foreign Debt (%)		Currency Index Weight (%)	
U.S. dollar	22.7		8.8	
Pound sterling	11.5		13.1	
Swedish krona	—		19.0	
Norwegian krone	—		3.8	
Danish krone	3.7		4.4	
Deutsche mark	18.2		19.0	
Dutch guilder	6.2		4.8	
Belgian franc	8.3	DM block	3.1	DM block
Swiss franc	7.6	50.3%	2.4	47.1%
French franc	6.3		6.7	
Italian lira	—		5.1	
Austrian schilling	—		1.6	
Peseta	—		2.0	
Yen	4.8		6.2	
ECU	8.9		—	
Other	1.8		—	
	100.0		100.0	

but since most bonds tend to be bullet-type loans, the repayment obligation arises only at expiration of the loan period.

The Finnish government has adhered to a very risk-averse policy. Acceptable counterparties are generally large financial firms (international banks or insurance corporations) rated AAA or AA, or creditworthy sovereigns and supranational banks. Even large and well-known corporates are not acceptable. The government has also established certain limits for its various counterparties so as not to run up too large an exposure on any single institution. Needless to say, the general economic situation of each of the government's various counterparties is continuously monitored.

The currency and interest-rate risks relating to swaps are not in principle different from the risks attached to straight loans. As an example, the currency of the swap asset or claim may appreciate (depreciate) while that of the liability or debt may depreciate (appreciate), leading to a mismatch in terms of domestic currency. For this reason, swaps are generally monitored on a mark-to-market basis, with the fluctuations in the values of the assets and liabilities taken into account.

The risks are obviously larger for currency swaps, where the exchange rate of the underlying currency may change, than for interest rate swaps, where only interest rate streams may be affected and not the whole loan capital.

Since swaps involve both an asset and a claim, the issue of *netting* has risen to the forefront in recent years. Netting means that if, for example, the Finnish government has both a swap claim and a swap liability toward the same large international bank, then the net exposure position is not affected provided that currency values have not changed. The netting principle is now generally approved in all major markets in case there are defaults.

MUNICIPAL DEBT MANAGEMENT

The purpose of this case study is to: (1) review the issues involved in managing currency risk in the issuing of municipal bonds in foreign markets, and (2) present a discussion of the hedging techniques used by the Kentucky Development Finance Authority (KDFA) to protect against changes in the yen/dollar relationship on a recent Samurai bond issue sold by KDFA. The discussion also addresses the interest rate hedging strategy utilized by KDFA to protect against nonorigination of loans in the event that interest rates decline and the loanable funds of KDFA were to be no longer attractive vis-à-vis alternative capital sources.

Currency and Interest Rate Hedging: The KDFA Example

In March 1989, the Commonwealth of Kentucky became the first state to issue bonds in the Japanese Samurai bond market. The state chose to borrow funds in this market due to the extremely low interest rates that could be achieved relative to the domestic U.S. taxable market, and to further enhance the commonwealth's economic development programs and its attractiveness to Japanese investors.

It was determined that KDFA could borrow ¥10 billion for 10 years in the Samurai market at approximately 5 to 5.5 percent per annum and an equivalent amount in the domestic U.S. taxable market at 10.5 to 11 percent; a 550–basis point differential. However, the Samurai bond issue would leave KDFA initially exposed to exchange-rate risk since the interest payments due over the life of the issue and the repayment of principal must be made in yen. As a matter of public policy, it was determined that *any* exposure to such risk was unacceptable.

To protect against this risk, KDFA analyzed the forward exchange market, the futures market, and the swap market. Since the forward exchange market is essentially limited to transactions shorter in life than the proposed KDFA bond issue, hedging KDFA's currency risk in this market was not practical. Also, since the futures market is highly structured, it did not provide KDFA with the flexibility necessary from the bond issuance perspective. Therefore, KDFA elected to manage its risk in the swap market. The main considerations in structuring KDFA's swaps were: (1) minimizing KDFA's currency exchange-rate risk, and (2) eliminating interest-rate risk due to uncertain loan origination dates.

The yen financing was undertaken, and a series of swaps was constructed by KDFA involving the following steps:

1. KDFA issued ¥10 billion of Samurai bonds at a yen fixed rate of 5.4 percent (see Exhibit 6).

2. KDFA entered into a 10-year liability cross currency swap agreement with the Industrial Bank of Japan (IBJ), an AAA-rated bank, whereby KDFA initially swapped the bond proceeds of ¥10.13 billion for US$77,674,418.60. At maturity, IBJ agreed to provide KDFA with ¥10.02 billion—the principal amount needed to pay the bondholders and the 0.2 percent principal repayment fee. KDFA will provide IBJ with $77,674,418.60. In addition, a second currency swap was transacted in which KDFA exchanged its 5.4 percent yen semiannual interest payments on the bonds and its 0.3 percent interest payment fee (¥270.81 million each payment period) with IBJ for a semiannual interest rate of six-month U.S. dollar LIBOR + 18.5 basis points on $77,674,418.60. IBJ effectively pays KDFA's semiannual yen payments, and KDFA provides IBJ with semiannual dollar interest payments. Therefore, KDFA effectively has a floating dollar liability of six-month U.S. dollar LIBOR + 18.5 basis points (see Exhibit 7).

3. To ensure that KDFA's assets earn an income stream matching KDFA's liability stream, a set of asset swaps were transacted. The dollar proceeds that KDFA received from the bond issue were used to purchase AAA- and AA-rated securities paying dollar-denominated

EXHIBIT 6
Samurai Bond Cash Flows: Step 1

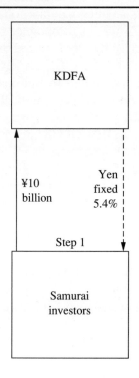

— Initial flow
−− Interim flow

interest flows (see Exhibit 8). The specific assets purchased, their initial prices, and par values are shown in columns 1, 2, and 3 in Exhibit 9.

4. KDFA then swapped these dollar interest flows with the asset swap counterparty, Bankers Trust, for an interest income stream of six-month U.S. dollar LIBOR − 10 basis points. Essentially, KDFA's net asset stream is now six-month U.S. dollar LIBOR − 10 basis points (see Exhibit 10).

KDFA's assets and liabilities were then matched in terms of interest rate, with the exception of the negative arbitrage cost of 28.5 basis points. This negative arbitrage cost of carry would have been present regardless of whether the money was raised domestically or in a foreign market. Further, a comparison of the all-in borrowing costs from this structure and that available in the domestic taxable markets indicated

EXHIBIT 7
Currency Swap Transaction

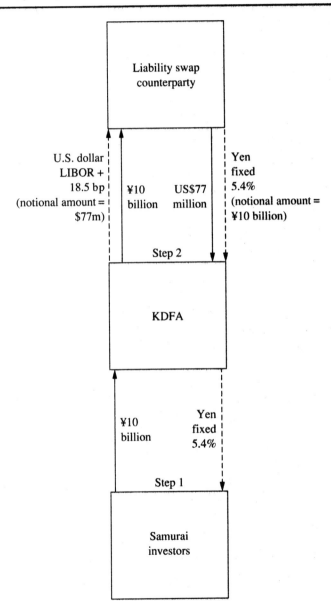

— Initial flow
-- Interim flow

EXHIBIT 8
Investment of Dollar Swap Proceeds

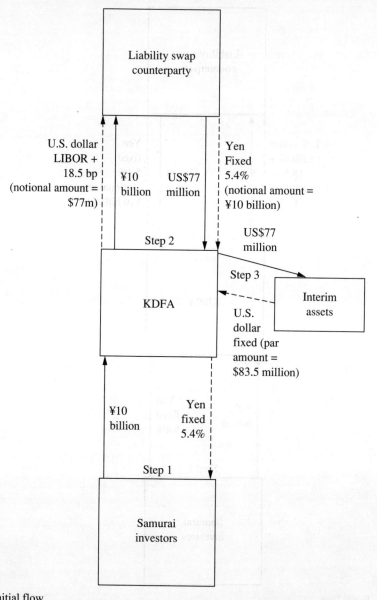

— Initial flow
-- Interim flow

EXHIBIT 9
Bids on Swap Unwind/Reassignment

Security	Initial Price* at Purchase	Par Value**	Accrued Interest	Best*** Bid Purchase Price	Current Market Price	Net Gain on Sale	Reassign (Unwind) Cost	Net Cost to KDFA	Cost per Notional Dollar
					FIRM A				
Dresdner	$36,500,000	$36,500,000	$120,652.77	99.93	$36,474,450	$ 95,103	$ (376,000)	$(280,897)	$(0.0077)
Footworks	10,406,614	12,000,000	209,625.00	89.92	10,790,400	593,411	(740,000)	(146,589)	(0.0141)
Furukawa	15,236,517	18,000,000	422,812.50	89.83	16,169,400	1,355,696	(1,555,000)	(199,305)	(0.0131)
Nakanagumi	8,531,288	10,000,000	215,000.00	90.15	9,015,000	698,712	(790,000)	(91,288)	(0.0107)
					FIRM B				
Dresdner	$36,500,000	$36,500,000	$120,652.77	99.93	$36,474,450	$ 95,103	$ (393,801)	$(298,698)	$(0.0082)
Footworks	10,406,614	12,000,000	209,625.00	89.92	10,790,400	593,411	(741,020)	(147,609)	(0.0142)
Furukawa	15,236,517	18,000,000	422,812.50	89.83	16,169,400	1,355,696	(1,568,939)	(213,244)	(0.0140)
Nakanagumi	8,531,288	10,000,000	215,000.00	90.15	9,015,000	698,712	(837,207)	(138,494)	(0.0162)
					FIRM C				
Dresdner	$36,500,000	$36,500,000	$120,652.77	99.93	$36,474,450	$ 95,103	No bid	No bid	No bid
Footworks	10,406,614	12,000,000	209,625.00	89.92	10,790,400	593,411	$ (715,000)	$(121,589)	$(0.0117)
Furukawa	15,236,517	18,000,000	422,812.50	89.83	16,169,400	1,355,696	(1,530,000)	(174,305)	(0.0114)
Nakanagumi	8,531,288	10,000,000	215,000.00	90.15	9,015,000	698,712	(800,000)	(101,288)	(0.0119)

*This is the notional amount used to calculate the original asset swap counterparty's interest payments to KDFA.
**This is the notional amount used to calculate KDFA's interest payments to asset swap counterparty.
***Bids were independently taken to determine the best sell price for the securities, and then the best bid was used to determine the most effective unwind/reassignment alternative.

EXHIBIT 10
Asset Swap Cash Flow

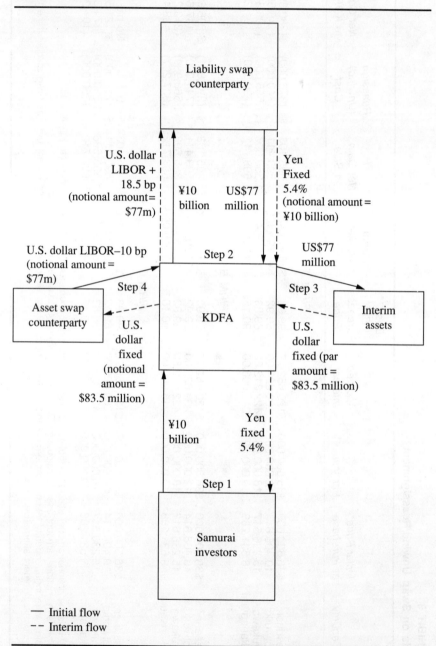

that KDFA was able to borrow funds at a savings of approximately 30 basis points under the costs of funds in the domestic market.

Loan Origination and Second-Generation Hedging

KDFA is the primary economic development agency of the Commonwealth of Kentucky. Its purpose is to provide capital to existing businesses in the state and to those companies looking to locate in Kentucky. The proceeds of the Samurai bond transaction were designed to be an additional source of capital to complement KDFA's existing loan programs. KDFA, utilizing the currency and interest rate structure outlined, was initially perfectly hedged to protect itself against changes in the yen/dollar exchange rate and changes in interest rates. In addition, this structure provided KDFA with the ability to make eight yen- or dollar-denominated loans at fixed or variable rates. The use of the bond proceeds to originate fixed-rate loans required that second-generation hedges be constructed to maintain KDFA's risk management program.

As economic development loans were made, securities, as outlined in step 3, were replaced by loans. Since the income stream from the securities were swapped in step 4 of the outline, the original asset swap needed to be unwound and a portion of the securities liquidated in order to fund the new loan. Conceptually, the existence of efficient markets would ensure that the value of a swap and the value of the underlying security move in opposite directions, at approximately the same magnitude. For example, if interest rates went down following the initial swap transaction, the counterparty receiving the fixed interest rate had value in the swap. Therefore, the fixed-rate payer (KDFA) would have had to pay the fixed-rate receiver a premium to "unwind" the initial transaction. However, the fixed-rate payer (i.e., the holder of the underlying security yielding a fixed coupon) saw the value of that security appreciate. Conceptually, the increased security value should offset the unwind cost on the swap. However, markets are not fully efficient, and the unwind cost may exceed the gain on the security.

March 1990 was the second interest payment date with respect to the KDFA Samurai bonds. KDFA was prepared to make $8.5 million in loans: a $6 million fixed-rate loan and a $2.5 million floating-rate loan. Therefore, KDFA was faced with a dual decision: which asset to sell and how to eliminate the corresponding asset swap liability.

Two options were available for eliminating the asset swap liability constructed in step 4. KDFA could unwind, that is, directly eliminate its contractual agreement with its asset swap counterparty, or it could reassign the asset swap to another institution desiring to assume KDFA's position. KDFA had to then liquidate a security, or a portion thereof, to provide the loan funds. Exhibit 9 outlines the bid information that KDFA utilized to analyze this dual decision. Three institutions bid on the purchase of the securities. Based on these bids, the best price for each security was selected (column 5) and any subsequent gain or loss on the sale of the securities was calculated (column 7).

Two of the institutions' "reassign" bid prices were compared with the actual unwind cost bid. The difference between the reassign/unwind costs and the gain on the security sale was subsequently calculated per dollar of notional swap principal to make the necessary comparisons. These calculations are also shown in Exhibit 9. The reassign cost bid by firm A on the Dresdner securities was the most competitive, and in fact, firm A had also provided the best bid for the purchase of these bonds. Therefore, KDFA (1) sold $8.5 million of its Dresdner bonds and (2) reassigned its corresponding portion of the asset swap to firm A. The net cost to KDFA to eliminate this swap liability was $65,450 ($8,500,000 @ $0.0077 per dollar of notional principal).

Since the $2.5 million loan was at a variable rate, KDFA's assets and liabilities were effectively matched. The $6 million fixed-rate loan required an additional transaction to become a LIBOR-bearing asset matched to the original liability swap. Therefore, as in step 4, KDFA swapped this fixed-interest cash flow for a LIBOR-based cash flow, thus rehedging the portfolio. Exhibit 11 portrays graphically all the transactions required for making a fixed-rate loan.

SUMMARY

In this chapter we have attempted to overcome the aversion of public bodies to the use of currency swaps by presenting case studies of two widely different applications that were undertaken by governmental units. The first case focused on an application of hedging currency risk to fund a national treasury in the most active capital markets in the world and, at the same time, to realize a significantly lower cost of funds. This was done by the ministry of finance of a progressive

EXHIBIT 11
Making a KDFA Fixed-Rate Loan

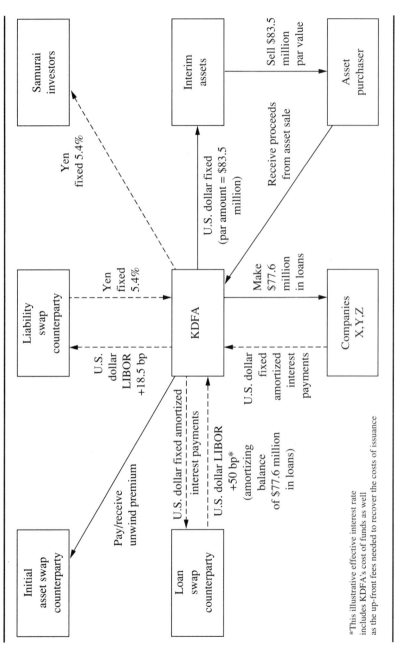

*This illustrative effective interest rate includes KDFA's cost of funds as well as the up-front fees needed to recover the costs of issuance

257

democracy. The second case parallels many commercial applications in the private sector in that it secures funds for a governmental endeavor in a foreign capital market to obtain a lower funding cost and increase the goodwill associated with international foreign direct investment in the borrower's region. These cases are of interest primarily because of the extension of swaps to the public sector, but also because of some of the underlying subtleties. They reflect the significant role of swaps in accomplishing both direct and indirect objectives in finance.

CHAPTER 12

HEDGING ECONOMIC RISKS USING CURRENCY SWAPS

Vembar K. Ranganathan
Security Pacific National Bank
New York

INTRODUCTION

Despite the emergence of a wide range of hedging tools to protect the long-term cash flows of a multinational firm from the vagaries of the exchange markets, many corporate treasury departments continue to focus primarily on the accounting aspects of exchange-rate fluctuations. Following the 1971 collapse of the Bretton Woods arrangement, which ended the linkage of the dollar to gold, the accounting profession responded to corporate treasury demands by establishing uniform standards with the Statement of Financial Accounting Standards No. 8 (FASB 8). This allowed for the translation of transactions of multinational firms according to their underlying measurement basis, current or historical. This was superseded in 1982 with the adoption of FASB 52, which improved the rules by permitting translation gains and losses to be presented under a separate equity account on the parent's balance sheet. Although FASB 52 is undoubtedly a significant improvement over FASB 8, it is clear that these statements are simply the accounting profession's responses to the demands arising from a corporation's need to present to the public its quarterly financial statements.

The Financial Accounting Standards Board's responses so far have been *static,* inasmuch as they ignore the dynamic nature of exchange-rate exposures and their long-term economic consequences to the firm. Essentially, the role of a corporate treasurer continues to be one of minimizing the risks arising from currency fluctuations on the cash flows of the firm. This accounting approach obviously ignores the economic exposure or the impact on the net worth of the firm arising from changes to future cash flows attributable to the volatility of exchange rates.

ECONOMIC EXPOSURE

Economic exposure is the risk to the present value of future cash flows of a firm, traceable to unanticipated changes in exchange rates. The market invariably discounts available information. Changes that are expected to occur are already discounted and included in the spot exchange rates. It is unanticipated changes that create risk, and these are random phenomena. Exposure represents the sensitivity of the value of the firm to exchange rate randomness.

Adler and Dumas (1984) have attempted to present economic exposure as the regression coefficient or, if there are many currencies, the vector of partial regression coefficients, when an asset's dollar value is regressed on exchange rates. The regression technique attempts to quantify the extent to which changes in the cash flows of the firm are correlated with changes in the spot exchange rate of the dollar vis-à-vis currencies in which initial cash flows are denominated. In a simple regression model, cash flows arising from, say, Germany could be converted to dollar values, and from the time series built from the monthly or quarterly data, we could regress dollar cash flows as a function of Deutschemark/dollar exchange rates:

$$CF_t = A + B(DM/\$)_t$$

where CF_t is the dollar equivalent of cash flows in period t and $(DM/\$)_t$ is the actual exchange rate of the Deutschemark per dollar for the same period t. The coefficient B measures the sensitivity of dollar cash flows to changes in exchange rate.

The t-statistic of this regression will show the statistical significance of the B coefficient. The t-statistic is a measure of the unlikelihood that there is no relationship between the dependent variable, CF, and the independent variable, DM/$. Thus, a high t-statistic means that it is very unlikely that the noted relationship is just a fluke or chance.

In a multiple regression model, cash flows of a multinational corporation arising from various geographic locations could be regressed on all the relevant exchange rates. Thus, a firm with operations in Germany, France, Japan, and Hong Kong could consider a model such as the following:

$$CF_t = A + B(DM/\$)_t + C(FF/\$)_t + D(¥/\$)_t + E(HK\$/\$)_t$$

In a regression model, the key statistic is the R^2 value. It measures the explanatory power of the model, or the variability of cash flows explained by variations in exchange rate. An R^2 value of .3 implies that 30 percent of the changes in cash flows are explained by changes in the exchange rate. If the R^2 value is very low, then the firm need not allocate significant resources to foreign exchange risk management, even if the coefficients are large and statistically significant.

As changes in exchange rates impact cash flows for several periods ahead, the regression model could be modified as follows:

$$CF_t = A + B(DM/\$)_t + C(DM/\$)_{t-1} + \cdots + Z(DM\$/\$)_{t-n}$$

where $(DM/\$)_{t-n}$ is the exchange rate in period $t - n$. This model attempts to capture the lagged impact of exchange rate changes on current cash flows. It is likely that the R^2 value could improve as a result. Because prices often adjust to offset exchange-rate changes over a period of one year, it seems sufficient to use the average exchange rates for the previous four quarters.

There are obvious limitations in determining the sensitivity of cash flows to exchange-rate changes via a regression coefficient. This procedure assumes that the *future* sensitivity of cash flows to such changes will be the same as in the past. In addition, the cash flows of a firm and the exchange rates may be simultaneously affected by other forces, such as monetary factors. It is pertinent to note that in such cases even purely domestic firms, such as public utilities, may be affected by exchange-rate movements through effects on aggregate demand or on the cost of traded inputs. Thus, real assets will be affected in value by exchange-rate movements, whatever their location. A cross-sectional study by Phillipe Jorion (1990) reveals significant differences among U.S. multinational firms in the relationship between the value of a firm and exchange-rate movements. Jorion's study of 40 multinational firms shows that the exposure, or the relationship between the value of the firm and the exchange rate, was positively correlated with the firm's degree of foreign involvement. Conversely, exposure did not appear to differ across domestic firms (i.e., those without foreign operations). Given that the value of the dollar is one of the factors differentially affecting U.S. firms, it could affect their cost of capital via foreign currency borrowing and hedging.

PRICE LEVELS AND EXCHANGE RATES

A firm's cash flows will remain unaffected if nominal exchange-rate fluctuations are fully offset by changes in the general price level. Thus, a U.S. exporter to Germany will find its dollar cash flows unaltered if a dollar depreciation of 10 percent from DM1.54/US$1 to DM1.39/US$1 during 1991 is accompanied by a 10 percent inflation rate in the United States and 0 percent inflation in Germany. A 10 percent increase in U.S. price levels will be offset by a 10 percent depreciation of the dollar vis-à-vis the Deutschemark, with the real exchange rate and cash flows kept constant. In determining economic exposure, it is essential to consider real exchange-rate changes derived from relative price differentials rather than nominal exchange-rate changes.

Real rates are in reality purchasing power parities (PPPs) or equilibrium exchange rates. The PPP theory has been one of the most controversial in economic literature. The "absolute" version of the theory states that the exchange rate is the ratio of domestic prices to foreign prices. The "relative" version of the PPP theory states that changes in spot exchange rates should be equal to the inflation differential between the two countries. The PPP theory is rooted in the "law of one price." In the absence of transport costs and trade restrictions, and subject to other basic assumptions of perfect competition, perfect commodity arbitrage would ensure that each good is uniformly priced, supporting the law of one price throughout the world. In reality, as Peter Isard (1977) pointed out, the law of one price has been flagrantly and systematically violated in the past. This, however, is due to the fact that manufactured goods across national borders do not have near-perfect substitutes. Lawrence Rosenberg (1977) has shown that the relative dollar prices of traded goods that are near-perfect substitutes, such as steel plates from Europe, Japan, and the United States, were fairly constant over time and were not affected by exchange-rate realignments.

Frenkel (1978) examined the causality between prices and exchange rates during the 1920s and concluded that key exchange rates covering the flexible-exchange-rate period of this decade moved in a way that fully offset divergent trends in national price levels. However, his further research (1981) showed that simple versions of PPP collapsed in the 1970s. Frenkel observed that exchange rates, like the prices of financial instruments such as bonds and equities, are much more sensitive to expectations concerning future events than are national price levels. Therefore, deviations from PPP are more the rule than the exception. Hakkio's (1984) cross-sectional analysis established that PPP is a long-run proposition, although it permits short-run deviations. Rush and Husted (1985) also found support for the long-run PPP interpretation for the Canadian dollar, Japanese yen, and some European currencies. Meher Manzur (1990), using a new approach based on Divisia index numbers to test PPP, concluded that long-run data, implying a five-year horizon, are quite well correlated with the PPP hypothesis. Despite the controversies surrounding PPP and its postulate, in its strictest version, that exchange rates are determined by relative price differentials, a multinational firm can ignore the message of PPP only at its peril. A firm operating in a country with a high inflation rate relative to the rest of the world is likely to be exposed to rising costs of production, a potential reduction in its net assets located in the inflation-prone country, and high export revenues traceable to long-run depreciations of the local currency.

OPERATING EXPOSURE

It is clear that real operating exposure is the result of changes in exchange rate as well as price levels in countries where a firm operates. Changes in exchange rates and price levels may not fully cancel each other, and this could impact the operating cash flows of the firm. When real exchange rates and relative prices are affected, so are a firm's long-run cash flows. The sharp increase in the value of yen from ¥240/$US$1 in 1985 to ¥136/$US$1 in 1990 should have depressed the demand for Japanese products. However, Japanese manufacturers exercised the painful option of keeping the dollar prices constant in an effort to retain market share. This imposed an enormous strain on the Japanese manufacturers, as the domestic cost of production in Japan has been rising in several product categories. Happily for Japan, an appreciation of the yen generally implies lower import costs, as most of its raw materials are imported. To some extent, this enabled Japan to offset yen appreciation with marginal yen price reductions so as to keep nominal dollar prices unchanged.

It is interesting to note that both the domestic and international operations of an American firm will be affected by a change in the value of the dollar. On the domestic front, an appreciation of the dollar will affect cash flows depending on the price elasticity of demand for the product. A case in point is the U.S. auto industry. An American automobile manufacturing unit, which primarily produces and sells in the United States, employs primarily domestic labor and material, and has little accounting exposure to changes in exchange rates, is still very much affected by exchange-rate fluctuations due to competition from foreign manufacturers. Likewise, a Japanese corporation producing cars in the United States for the American market is also exposed to yen/dollar exchange-rate fluctuations, as its yen outlays will be matched by dollar revenues.

It is quite possible that domestic demand will remain unchanged despite increased foreign competition arising from lower-priced foreign imports, if the products are highly differentiated. Product differentiation can also work to protect the export market despite unfavorable exchange-rate movements. Despite the strong appreciation of the Japanese yen and the Deutschemark, automobiles from Japan and Germany have been able to retain an excellent market in the United States, as they have established a reputation for trouble-free performance. The technological component of these products is perceived to be superior, and they therefore enjoy a relative monopoly status. The Japanese yen, in particular, can be regarded as a techno-currency in the sense that the higher price of a Japanese product arising from a stronger yen may not necessarily lead to a sharp decline in the demand for Japanese products. The products of the U.S. defense industry are highly differentiated from corresponding products of other countries, and export demand for them is likely to remain unchanged despite an appreciation of the dollar. Although such product differentiation could offer some immunity from global competition and exchange-rate volatility and thus protect a firm's long-term cash flows, the monopoly status of such commodities is likely to be eroded over time. Even where such immunity is available, proactive treasury managers who employ currency swaps and similar derivative products to manage their multicurrency portfolios are likely to enhance the long-term cash flows of their respective firms, compared with passive treasury managers.

CURRENCY SWAPS AS A MEANS OF HEDGING ECONOMIC EXPOSURE

Currency swaps offer an efficient and quick means of creating hedges to offset economic exposures. This is illustrated in the following examples.

Case 1

XYZ Co., a U.S. multinational firm specializing in the manufacture of electronic control systems, opened manufacturing operations in Japan at a total cost of $100 million (¥14 billion, assuming an exchange rate of ¥140/US$1), primarily for sales in Japan and the Far East. Despite its several operations abroad, XYZ has never issued debt in the international capital markets. The ease, speed, and cost-efficient manner in which it has been able to issue debt in the U.S. capital market has been partially responsible for its indifference toward tapping international capital markets. XYZ funded its long-term investment in Japan by drawing on its committed five-year bank revolver line, priced at six-month U.S. dollar LIBOR flat. This created a currency exposure, with net yen assets standing at ¥14 billion funded with XYZ's $100 million revolver drawdown.

XYZ could eliminate the currency exposure by executing a currency swap, whereby its dollar debt is converted into yen debt, which in turn could be serviced by yen revenues generated from XYZ's Japan operations. The notional amount of the currency swap should generally be equal to the net asset position of XYZ in yen. Exhibit 1 shows the cash flows arising from XYZ's investment in Japan as well as from the currency swap serving as an economic hedge. In the example, XYZ is shown to swap floating yen LIBOR for floating U.S.

EXHIBIT I
Hedging Economic Exposure with a Currency Swap

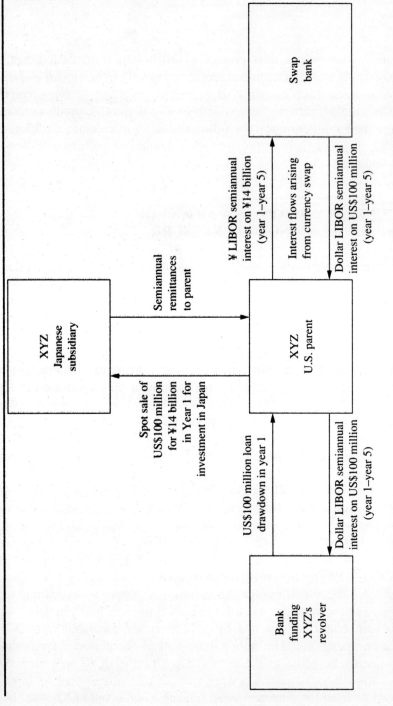

dollar LIBOR. These floating interest rates can easily be converted to fixed interest rates, resulting in the periodic exchange of fixed dollar interest receipts for fixed yen interest payments.

A currency swap is generally preceded by an exchange of principal at the beginning of the contract. The initial exchange of principal is as follows:

With the initial exchange at the prevailing spot exchange rate of ¥140/US$1, XYZ can obtain $100 million from its loan drawdown under the revolver and transfer it to the swapping bank. Simultaneously, it will transfer ¥14 billion received from the swapping bank to its Japanese subsidiary. By mutual agreement, XYZ and the swapping bank can also decide not to have an initial exchange of principal. Nevertheless, a book entry will have to be created showing an asset of $100 million with a matching liability of ¥14 billion in XYZ's books.

One of the significant contributions of FASB 52 is that it permits gains or losses arising from a foreign currency transaction that has been designated as an economic hedge of a net investment abroad to be shown as a separate component of shareholders' equity. In the example used here, the gain or loss arising from exchange-rate fluctuations attributable to the net asset position of ¥14 billion will bypass XYZ's income statement but will be shown in shareholders' equity under "cumulative translation adjustments." The currency swap would be designated as a hedge of XYZ's net investment in Japan. It is assumed that the Japanese subsidiary's *functional currency* is yen, in contrast to the *reporting currency* of the parent, which happens to be the U.S. dollar.

Whether or not there is an initial exchange of principal in a currency swap, at the end of the swap contract there is generally a reexchange of principal at the spot exchange rate at which the contract was initiated. Thus, at the maturity of the swap, XYZ will be required to pay the swapping bank ¥14 billion in exchange for $100 million:

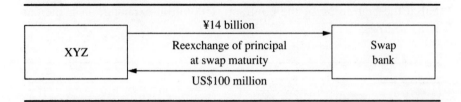

XYZ will pay off its revolver debt with the principal receipts from the swapping bank. Repayment of ¥14 billion to the swapping bank will be met out of cash flows from XYZ's Japanese subsidiary.

Coupon Swaps

Currency swap techniques have become increasingly sophisticated in recent years, permitting the elimination of exchange of principals. These have come to be known as "coupon swaps," involving simply the exchange of interest payments in two different currencies. The coupons are adjusted in a manner that will reflect the potential long-term appreciation or depreciation of the currencies at swap maturity. The differential in interest rates between two currencies for term borrowings are employed to derive the forward exchange rates. The resulting currency discount/premium is incorporated into the swap coupons, eliminating the need for a principal exchange at swap maturity.

**EXCHANGE RATE–INDUCED
CHANGES IN CASH FLOWS**

It is clear that nominal exchange rate changes per se many not have a significant impact on the cash flows of a firm, as these nominal changes are often offset by inflation rate differentials. Thus, for a U.S. subsidiary operating in Spain, a devaluation of the Spanish peseta will produce a net reduction in cash flows expressed in U.S. dollar terms, provided devaluation does not result in any changes in Spanish prices, costs, and sales volume. However, a devaluation is generally accompanied by rising local prices and costs. Over time, devaluation will also generate increased demand for products of Spain. A depreciation of the peseta could actually result in an increase in dollar cash flows as a result of price and sales volume growth. Net changes in dollar cash flows from the Spanish operation will depend on the price elasticity of demand, the ability of the Spanish subsidiary to adjust its mix of inputs relative to cost changes, and its capacity to economize on its working capital.

The economic exposure of the firm will not be significantly affected as long as changes in exchange rates result in a movement toward an equilibrium rate or purchasing power parity. Where a change in the *real* exchange rate occurs, resulting in changes in the relative prices of the firm's inputs or outputs, cash flows of the firm will indeed be impacted. The general response of a multinational firm to wide swings in relative prices and real exchange rates should be directed at changing its marketing and production strategies. For example, there have been significant changes in the relative prices of products of Japan through most of the 1970s and 1980s, largely due to the low inflation rate of Japan relative to global, notably U.S., inflation rates. This triggered a shift in the real exchange rate of yen, with nominal exchange rates catching up over time. A real appreciation of Japanese yen has to be matched by an increase in the foreign-currency prices of Japanese products, in some cases at the expense of some export volume. A change in the real rate that is perceived to be permanent may lead a multinational firm to shift production facilities abroad. The phenomenal strength of the U.S. dollar during the early 1970s led many U.S. corporations to shift production facilities to Europe, the Far East, and Latin America. Likewise, the relative weakness of the dollar against the yen and the ongoing criticism of Japan's burgeoning trade surpluses vis-à-vis the United States has led several Japanese auto manufacturers to open production facilities in the United States. Although shifts in marketing and production strategies are appropriate for managing economic exposures arising from long-lasting changes in relative price levels, currency swaps could offer a simple solution for retaining cash flows in the backdrop of tumultuous exchange rate changes.

Case 2

Let us suppose that a Japanese auto manufacturer with a large export market in the United States is exposed to declining cash flows as a result of steady appreciation of the yen. An increase in dollar prices is out of the question due to stiff price competition from U.S. auto manufacturers. The Japanese auto manufacturer can mitigate the dollar cash flow declines partially by converting yen debt into dollar debt as follows. It is assumed that the Japanese firm invests ¥14 billion in Japan, specifically targeting its production for final sales in the United States. The firm expects to recoup the investment in 10 years. It is further assumed that there is no initial exchange of principal arising from the currency swap. However, there is a final exchange of principal, as shown in Exhibit 2. The swap bank will deliver ¥14 billion

EXHIBIT 2
Managing Economic Exposure of a Japanese Auto Maker

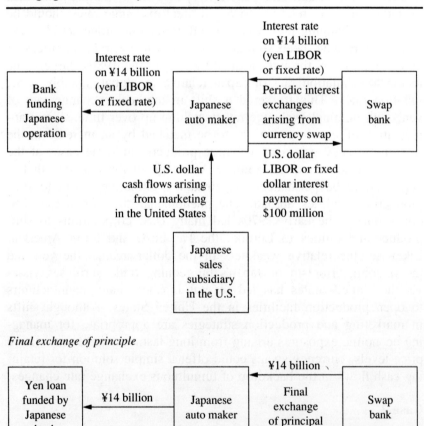

Final exchange of principle

at the maturity of swap after 10 years. The Japanese auto manufacturer will repay its 10-year yen debt to the Japanese bank funding the production facility. Simultaneously, the firm will be required to repay $100 million in the final exchange of principal. If the Japanese yen appreciates from the initial spot rate of ¥140/US$1 to ¥100/US$1 at maturity, the firm would still be required to pay only $100 million instead of $140 million (the new market rate) under the currency swap. This example further underscores a basic premise of borrowing by a multinational, namely, that it should generally borrow in currencies that are candidates for depreciation. The Japanese firm stands to benefit by repaying the principal in terms of depreciated dollars.

Case 3

The wild gyrations in the exchange markets witnessed since the inception of the floating-rate regime in 1973 has generated economic exposures of significant magnitude for several global corporations. The problems of the German auto maker Porsche AG during the 1980s arising from exchange-rate fluctuations[1] are illustrative of unhedged economic exposures disrupting the marketing plans of an otherwise successful firm. Porsche had traditionally exported 50 percent of its production to the United States. In early 1981, it decided on a strategy of widening its U.S. market at considerable effort and expense, and it scaled up its distribution network. The steady rise of the dollar from a low of DM1.7/US$1 during 1980 to a high of DM3.4/US$1 in 1986 led to rising U.S. sales and a sharp growth in cash flows traceable to a weak Deutschemark. This changed rather precipitously after 1987, when the dollar began a decline from its 1986 peak to about DM1.65 in 1988. The strong appreciation by almost 50 percent of the Deutschemark against the dollar during these years, together with the stock market crash in October 1987, led to a sizable decline in the demand for Porsche cars in the United States. Porsche could not raise its U.S. prices fast enough to compensate for the depreciation of the dollar. Porsche's overall profits declined to DM50 million in fiscal 1987 from DM75 million in the previous year. The aggressive marketing strategies of Porsche, which were well suited to a rising dollar scenario, ran afoul with a declining dollar.

---

[1]See *The Wall Street Journal,* December 17, 1988.

Porsche could have partially immunized itself against economic exposures in the United States by simply converting its Deutschemark debt (funding its manufacturing and marketing activities tailored to the U.S. market) into dollar debt via a currency swap. Porsche's Deutschemark manufacturing expenditures would have been matched by annual Deutschemark cash inflows from a currency swap. Its U.S. dollar interest obligations arising from a currency swap could have been serviced by U.S. dollar cash flows generated from its U.S. marketing activity. Although such a swap would have prevented the extraordinary growth in Porsche's cash flows arising from the upsurge in the dollar vis-à-vis the Deutschemark during the early 1980s, it would have also sheltered Porsche from falling sales and profit margins traceable to a weakening dollar against the Deutschemark. A proactive debt management on the part of Porsche would have put in place a currency swap in 1987–88, when it was becoming increasingly clear that the dollar was rising above its equilibrium value.

Porsche's unhedged economic exposure is depicted in Exhibit 3, where U.S. dollar cash inflows from U.S. sales efforts are matched by Deutschemark cash outflows attributable to manufacturing operations in Germany, funded by German banks in Deutschemarks. In the early 1980s, a weak Deutschemark obviously helped Porsche to fortify and expand its sales activity in the United States, besides simultaneously generating improved Deutschemark cash inflows traceable to the strength of the dollar.

Had Porsche followed a proactive treasury management policy, it would have perceived the overvaluation of the dollar during 1986–87 against the backdrop of relative dollar/Deutschemark inflation differentials, and it would have put in place hedges to protect its U.S.

EXHIBIT 3
Porsche's Unhedged Cash Flows

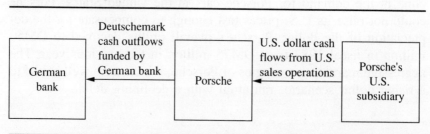

markets against a potential decline of the dollar. A simple currency swap converting its Deutschemark debt into dollar debt would have sheltered Porsche against the loss of markets arising from the falling dollar. Exhibit 4 assumes an initial five-year debt of DM300 million, an exchange rate of DM3/US$1 in 1985 at the time of the swap, and a swap tenor of five years. It further assumes that Porsche skips initial exchange of principal.

At the maturity of the swap in 1990, the cash flows shown in Exhibit 5 would occur, and it is assumed that the exchange rate maturity was DM1.45/US$1.

Besides providing an economic hedge and protecting future cash flows from foreign operations, a currency swap can enable a firm to benefit from spot exchange rate movements. Thus, at maturity, Porsche would have exchanged $100 million for DM300 million, generating an exchange gain of $106.9 million. (At a spot rate of DM1.45/US$1, Porsche would pay the swap bank only $100 million instead of $206.9 million for an exchange of DM300 million.) This underscores the basic premise that a multinational firm should fund itself, other things being equal, in currencies that are potential can-

EXHIBIT 4
Porsche's Hedged Cash Flows

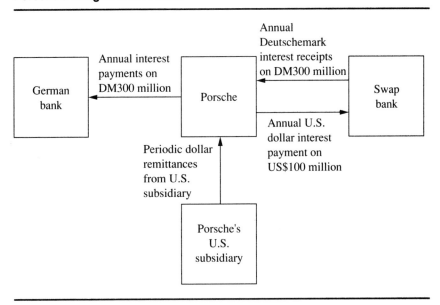

EXHIBIT 5
Porsche's Cash Flows at Swap Maturity

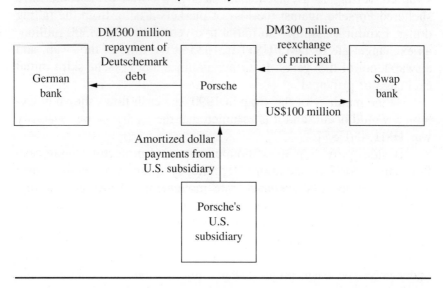

didates for depreciation. The actual and anticipated inflation rates, as could be gleaned from the monetary policies of the respective governments, should provide an ample warning of impending long-run appreciation or depreciation of respective currencies.

SUMMARY

In the context of the heightened volatility of exchange markets arising from the floating of exchange rates in 1973, economic exposures of multinational firms have increased markedly. Although production, marketing, and pricing strategies can help firms manage these risks, currency swaps offer an excellent mechanism for protecting the long-term cash flows of multinational firms from the vagaries of exchange markets. Current financial accounting standards are somewhat restrictive and tend to treat several of these hedges as speculative, unless the hedge can be identified as applying to a net asset or liability position held abroad. Despite these constraints, dynamic treasury managers at several corporations have begun to employ currency swaps and derivative products to hedge economic risks.

REFERENCES

Adler, M., and Dumas, B. 1984. "Exposure to Currency Risk: Definition and Measurement," *Financial Management,* Summer, pp. 41–50.

Frenkel, J. A. 1978. "Purchasing Power Parity: Doctrinal Perspectives and Evidence from the 1920s," *Journal of International Economics,* vol. 8, pp. 169–191.

Frenkel, J. A. 1981. "The Collapse of the Purchasing Power Parity During the 1970s," *European Economic Review,* vol. 16, pp. 145–165.

Hakkio, C. S. 1984. "A Re-examination of Purchasing Power Parity," *Journal of International Economics,* vol. 17, pp. 265–277.

Isard, P. 1977. "How Far Can We Push the Law of One Price?" *American Economic Review,* vol. 67, pp. 942–948.

Jorion, P. 1990. "The Exchange-Rate Exposure of U.S. Multinationals," *Journal of Business,* vol. 63, no. 3, pp. 331–345.

Manzur, M. 1990. "An International Comparison of Prices and Exchange Rates: A New Test of Purchasing Power Parity," *Journal of International Money and Finance,* vol. 9, pp. 75–91.

Rush, M., and S. Husted. 1985. "Purchasing Power Parity in the Long Run," *Canadian Journal of Economics,* vol. 1, pp. 137–245.

CHAPTER 13

EQUITY-LINKED CROSS CURRENCY SWAPS

David F. DeRosa
Philip G. Nehro
Alliance Capital Management L.P.
New York

THE SWAP AGREEMENT
AND EQUITY MARKETS

Institutional investors have recently begun to use the financial swap agreement concept to take on exposure to equity markets. The vehicle is called an *equity index–linked swap* or sometimes a *cross currency equity-linked swap*. In some circles, these agreements have been called *synthetic or derivative equity,* and some practitioners have looked to this new market as the second phase of the derivative revolution, following index futures and index options.

The appeal of the equity index–linked swap is that equity index returns can be earned without incurring basis risk or margin requirements. There are transparent savings in transactions and custodial costs, and there is the possibility of significant return enhancement. Market makers now routinely quote equity index swaps for S&P 500 (United States), the FTSE 100 (United Kingdom), the Nikkei and Topix (Japan), CAC 40 (France), and DAX (Germany). Other country indexes appear from time to time, such as the TSE (Canada), the All Ordinaries (Australia), and the Hang Seng (Hong Kong). Usually, the investor can choose between accepting the index return in the local currency of the market or in his or her own domestic currency. Also, macro index swaps have now appeared. These swaps feature EAFE, MSCI World, and FT Actuaries composite indexes as the basis for floating rate payments.

Although two-sided bid-offer quotes on equity-linked swaps have begun to appear in the marketplace, swaps are not nearly as liquid as the cash, index futures, or index futures options markets. Most institutional investors take on long-term strategic exposure to markets; hence the sparse liquidity of the equity swap market may not be too large a concern compared to the apparent benefits. Although it might be difficult or costly to liquidate or to unwind a swap, it is not difficult to neutralize the resultant exposure to an equity market. If there are derivative instruments, all that is necessary is for an opposite position to be established with index futures or options.

THE MECHANICS OF AN EQUITY INDEX SWAP

An equity index–linked swap is a contractual agreement between an investor and a counterparty whereby the counterparty pays the investor the index total return and receives from the investor a predetermined floating rate (usually LIBOR) interest payment. The LIBOR term—three or six months—matches the swap reset frequency. Exhibit 1 contains a sample summary term sheet for an S&P 500 swap.

Equity index–linked swaps are based on the notional amount of principal that is not exchanged with the counterparty. The principal is invested in what is called an *operant portfolio,* which is held by the investor's custodian bank or trust company (see Exhibits 2 and 3). In addition to negotiating and administering the swap, the investor's investment manager is charged with managing the operant portfolio.

The date at which the exchange of funds takes place is called the *reset date*. Most swaps are reset quarterly or semiannually, but monthly or annual resets are possible as well. The notional amount of the swap is usually adjusted on the reset date to reflect the change in the index.

Swaps are quoted in terms of basis points under or above the LIBOR payment, stated as LIBOR less or plus. For example, a swap to pay the total return (capital gains and dividends) on the S&P 500 might be quoted as "LIBOR less 15." Assuming semiannual reset, the investor and the counterparty would exchange the net difference between the total return on the S&P 500 and the LIBOR rate that prevailed at the beginning of the period less 15 basis points. Sometimes

EXHIBIT 1
Summary Term Sheet for an S&P 500 Swap

Investment objective	Produce an index total return (i.e., S&P 500) plus a proforma projected enhancement over the index.
Minimum investment	$25 million
Contractual period	1 to 5 years
Client investor investments	High-quality fixed income assets with an average maturity of 12 months or less (A-rated or better securities or sovereign credits) generating substantial returns over LIBOR.
Linkage mechanism index-linked swap	A contractual agreement between the client investor and a third party whereby the third party is obligated to pay the investor the index total return and receives from the investor a predetermined LIBOR interest payment. These rates are negotiated by the investment manager on behalf of the client.
Applicable index swap market indexes	Many well-known indexes can be applied including equity, fixed income, U.S. and international (i.e., S&P, Topix, FTSE 100, DAX, CAC, EAFE, Salomon BIG, Salomon WGB, etc.).
Major advantage	The total return and desired exposure to the various domestic and international markets are acquired without some of the drawbacks caused by investing cash in those markets.
Additional advantages	No direct purchase of stock Index total return Meaningful and generally predictable outperformance of the index No index-tracking error No portfolio rebalancing Reduced transaction cost Reduced custody cost No dividend withholding (offshore investors) Potential country tax benefits, interest income versus capital gains Administrative simplicity
Considerations	Credit Reduced liquidity
Manager and investment advisor (QPAM*)	The investment manager will manage assets and negotiate terms on behalf of the client investor

* A QPAM is a Qualified Professional Asset Manager designated to act on behalf of ERISA clients in negotiating, executing, and managing index-linked or interest rate swaps.

EXHIBIT 2
The Structure of an Index-Linked Swap on the S&P 500 Index

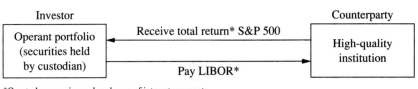

*Quarterly or semiannual exchange of interest payments

a swap is quoted as an enhancement over an index, such as "S&P 500 plus 50 basis points."

In the example in Exhibit 4, if the swap were quoted at six-month LIBOR "flat," the semiannual S&P total return were 5 percent, and the beginning LIBOR rate were 8 percent, then the semiannual exchange of funds on a $100 million swap would be:

S&P Total Return

$$\$100 \text{ million} \times 5\% = \$5.0 \text{ million}$$

Less LIBOR

$$\$100 \text{ million} \times (180/360) \times (8\%) = \$4.0 \text{ million}$$

Net Payment to Investor = $1.0 Million

EXHIBIT 3
Some Examples of Index-Linked Swaps

Macro Indexes	**Country Indexes**
EAFE—Asia	S&P 500
EAFE—Europe	Nikkei 225
MSCI World	DAX
FT Actuaries	CAC
Salomon World Government Bond	FTSE
Morgan World Bond	
Customized Index	

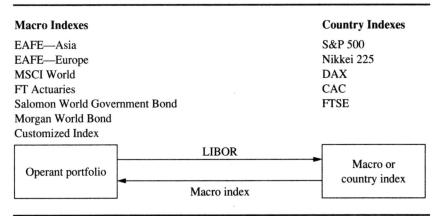

EXHIBIT 4

Hypothetical Example of an Index-Linked Swap with a $100 Million Notional Amount and Semiannual Reset

New client portfolio $105,075,000	Begin new period	New notional amount $105,000,000

S&P index total return plus 15 basis points
(semiannual) $2,537,500

$100 million notional swap

$5,000,000 S&P index		
+ 75,000 15 basis points	S&P nominal (5%)**	High-quality financial institution
$5,075,000	$5,000,000	
$75,000 (15 basis points)	Semiannual LIBOR (8%)	
$4,000,000 (LIBOR)	$4,000,000	
Investment manager		

LIBOR (8%) + 15 basis points
$4,075,000

Operant portfolio

*Value added: The investment manager manages the portfolio and index-linked swap to provide S&P 500 index return plus excess return over a two- to five-year period. The swap is quoted at LIBOR flat.
**Credit exposure is limited to the differential between interest payments exchanged.

SWAP PERFORMANCE AND THE OPERANT PORTFOLIO

The most common operant portfolio is composed of floating rate notes (FRNs), which are a natural for index-linked swaps because they also have periodic reset dates when their coupons are adjusted to market LIBOR conditions plus an FRN discount margin.

To the extent that the operant portfolio does better than LIBOR (i.e., plus or minus the FRN discount margin), the swap will outperform the index, thereby achieving an enhanced return. Therefore, the goal of the operant portfolio manager is to outperform LIBOR without exceeding the client's acceptable level of risk.

In Exhibit 4, the operant portfolio is assumed to have outperformed LIBOR by 15 basis points (annualized) in a given semiannual period. Since LIBOR was 8 percent, the total cash return on the operant portfolio is:

$100 million $\times$ (180/360) $\times$ (8% + 0.15%) = $4.075 million

The full set of cash flow on reset date can be summarized as follows.

S&P total return payment	$5,000,000
Less: LIBOR payment to counterparty	($4,000,000)
Return from operant portfolio	$4,075,000
Net	$5,075,000

In effect, the swap program has outperformed the index by the 15 basis points (equal to $75,000 over the semiannual period as applied to $100 million of notional principal) by which the operant portfolio outperformed LIBOR. Of course, had the swap been negotiated at a sub-LIBOR rate, this also would have been translated into further enhancement of the S&P index.

In the Exhibit 4 example, the swap notional amount would be reset to $105,000,000 (which does not include the performance of the operant portfolio above LIBOR). The notional value must be reset, otherwise the swap program would deviate widely from the index performance. Imagine the hypothetical case of the S&P 500 doubling in one reset period—if the notional amount were not doubled, the swap program would be 50 percent underexposed to whatever returns would be produced on the S&P 500 in the next reset period.

THE COUNTERPARTY

Swap counterparties are typically investment banks, commercial banks, or quality fronting industrial or financial institutions. Traders and arbitrageurs at investment and commercial banks are natural counterparties to equity-linked swaps because swaps often fit the needs of their proprietary trading activities. By selling a swap, the trader establishes a long-term short position in an index, something that might be expensive to create in the cash market and difficult to maintain in the futures market because of the need to roll maturing contracts.

The legal mechanics of the swap transaction are well established. Usually, the counterparty and the investor begin with general legal forms that have been adopted by the International Swap Dealers Association (ISDA). The ISDA language has functioned as the legal template for trillions of dollars worth of interest rate and currency swaps. A small modification is needed to make the swap contract applicable to an equity index–linked swap. Other changes might also be needed to meet the specific requirements of the investor and the counterparty. A thorough review by each party's legal counsel is typically done to ensure the feasibility of the swap agreement contract.

The ability of the counterparty to perform on the swap contract is also a pertinent issue. Understandably, many investors have become cautious of entering into large transactions with financial institutions because of credit concerns. Although this is an essential consideration, it is important to remember that the actual credit exposure in a swap transaction is relatively small compared to the notional amount. First, the notional amount of principal is not exchanged with the counterparty; rather, it is held by the investor's custodian to form the operant portfolio. Second, the actual credit exposure is limited to the net exchange of cash flow at the next reset date. In most cases, the exchange of cash will be small because the payment to the counterparty, based on LIBOR (less or plus), will balance a good portion of the payment due from the counterparty for the performance of the equity index. Furthermore, steps can always be taken to manage the size of the credit exposure. Reset dates can be set with greater frequency (e.g., quarterly or even monthly), and the swap credit can be collateralized by having the counterparty deposit securities with the investor's custodian bank.

ALTERNATIVE OPERANT PORTFOLIOS

Although FRNs are the most basic and most frequently used operant portfolio, any investment can be put into an operant portfolio. However, if the investment fails to produce LIBOR or other related liability return, the operant portfolio may have to be invaded to meet the cash flow obligation of the swap. For this reason, operant portfolios that have low volatility are preferred. Some examples of innovative alternative operant portfolios are active fixed income, global fixed income, and market neutral equity.

Active Fixed Income Operant Portfolios

Active fixed income management adds the dimensions of duration (interest rate risk), yield curve uncertainty, and possibly credit risk to the problem of managing the operant portfolio. In return for bearing these risks, however, there is the possibility of serious overperformance compared to LIBOR. Some managers have been successful in using fixed income securities (e.g., mortgage-backed securities) in combination with derivative instruments (e.g., bond options and futures) to limit the size of the possible fluctuations in their portfolio returns. This practice increases their ability to meet the swap cash flow requirements.

Global Fixed Income Operant Portfolios

Very-short-duration global fixed income portfolios are sometimes used for operant portfolios. Because of the need to produce a fairly steady stream of returns to meet the swap cash flow requirements, global fixed income strategies that attend to currency risk are good candidates for the operant portfolio. One technique of currency risk management, called *cross hedging,* achieves risk arbitrage within the European Monetary System Exchange Rate Mechanism currencies by taking exposure to nondollar cross exchange rates.

Market-Neutral Equity Operant Portfolios

Operant portfolios also can be constructed with equity securities. A method that seems to merge well with index-linked swaps and that can provide for the necessary swap cash flow needs is called the *market-neutral* (or *long-short*) method. In a market-neutral equity portfolio, the investment manager assumes both long and short equity positions, thereby adding value from both positions, usually in weighted proportions so that the whole portfolio has no net exposure to the market (i.e., zero beta) nor to any particular sectors or industries. An important feature of the market-neutral strategy is that investors can be eligible for a rebate on a substantial portion of the interest on the proceeds of the short sales.

Initially, the absolute values of the long and short portfolios are set equal to each other. The net return on the total market-neutral portfolio is then equal to the rebated interest on the short sales plus the net difference between the returns on the long and short portfolios. Except in cases where the investment manager grossly misjudges the choice of which securities to go long and which to go short, market-neutral portfolio returns will be positive. This stability is reinforced by the presence of the interest rebate, which acts as a cushion, and by the fact that the overall portfolio is not exposed to general market movements or industry or sector biases.

Using market-neutral equity as the operant portfolio, the investor can achieve the return on the DAX index, for example, through a swap, which can be enhanced through security selection in the U.S. equity operant portfolio.

COMPLEX EQUITY INDEX–LINKED SWAPS

At least three complex equity index–linked swaps also have appeared in the marketplace. The first is called the cross-index swap (see Exhibit 5). In this case, the investor would agree to pay the total return on one index in exchange for receiving the total return on some other equity index. This may be hedged or unhedged in the case of a foreign stock index. In Exhibit 5, the investor is long in the S&P 500. This position might consist of a cash index fund, a futures position, or an S&P 500 index-linked swap. The cross-index swap allows the investor to exchange one index total return for the return of some other index. The other index, typically a foreign stock market index, may be paid in dollars or a foreign currency, as the investor chooses.

EXHIBIT 5
Cross-index Swap

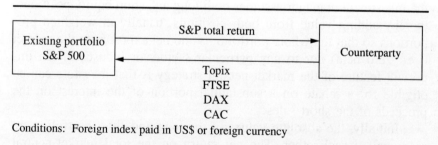

Conditions: Foreign index paid in US$ or foreign currency

Depending on the other index, there might be an adjustment, positive or negative, on the index return that the counterparty must pay to the investor. The ability to effectively exchange one index return for another, or to do *synthetic index shuttling* as it has become known, is a major benefit and advantage for index-linked swap users.

For example, consider the following cross-index swap between S&P 500 and DAX:

Investor pays	S&P 500 total return
Counterparty pays	DAX total return + 50 basis points
Notional amount	$100 million
Reset	Semiannual
Currency	U.S. dollars

This example uses a single currency, the U.S. dollar; multicurrency swaps are discussed in the next section. If during the semiannual period, the total returns on the S&P 500 and DAX are 10 percent and 12 percent, respectively, the exchange of funds would be:

Investor pays	
10% × $100 million	($10.0 million)
Investor receives	
(12% + .50%) × $100 million	$12.5 million
Net	$ 2.5 million

The second complex swap is the multi-index swap (see Exhibit 6). This swap can afford investors an enhanced global portfolio return. A single operant portfolio sustains a number of separate index-linked swaps, each on a different stock market and each paying in foreign currency or the investor's own currency. Some dealers have quoted this swap with a special feature that allows the exposure to the various markets to be adjusted up to some maximum level or down to some minimum level on reset days. This allows the investor to do a limited but relatively inexpensive form of international asset allocation.

The third complex equity index–linked swap contains embedded options. The purpose of the option is to establish a minimum floor return on the exposure to the equity market. Floors, which are essentially put options, have option premiums that are usually quoted as a percentage of the notional amount of principal. In a typical arrange-

EXHIBIT 6
Multi-index Swap

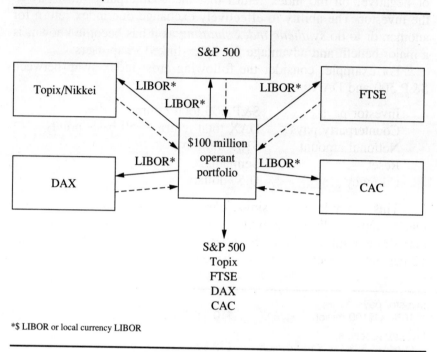

*$ LIBOR or local currency LIBOR

ment, a one-year floor might be set at 95 percent. This means that the total return after one year cannot be less than negative 5 percent; at lower levels, the floor comes into play to ensure the return to the investor.

Unfortunately, ever since the October 1987 market crash, the price of equity index put options, and consequently equity swap floors, has been high. This has led some investors to a more complex option transaction called a *collar,* a *range forward,* or a *fence.* In the collar, the cost of the put floor is offset by the investor selling (or "writing") a call option. This is sometimes called a *cap.* The call is usually struck well above the floor. For instance, the cost of the 95 percent floor might be covered in full by the acceptance of a 110 percent cap. If the market goes up, the maximum total return that the investor could enjoy is 10 percent. Because the cost of the floor and the cap are equal in this example, the transaction is referred to as a *zero premium collar.* In effect, the collar investor would have sold off the change of a very large gain to subsidize the cost of the floor "insurance."

Exhibit 7 shows the application of a multicurrency operant portfolio with embedded three-year European options struck at 95 percent and 100 percent to create a floor (puts) and a collar (puts and calls).

EXHIBIT 7
A Case Study of Enhanced Index Strategy with Embedded Options

---

Step 1. Invest funds in a separate operant portfolio using the multicurrency operant portfolio strategy.

- Characteristics of a global, short-duration, high-return, stable asset value portfolio

  Average maturity: 12 months or less
  Credit quality: AA or better (mostly sovereign credits)
  Currency impact: managed down through cross-hedging
  Asset stability: 1/5 or less the volatility of the U.S. dollar
  Liquidity: less than 30 days

- Historical annualized 18-month return as of September 30, 1990

	Historical	*Projected Risk Adjusted*
Annualized return	13.99%	11.00%
LIBOR	9.16%	8.25%
Excess over LIBOR	4.83%	2.75%

Step 2. Arrange an index-linked swap (one to five years) with a counterparty to pay them LIBOR out of the multicurrency operant portfolio (keeping the projected excess of 2.75%) in order to receive from them the S&P 500 index total return on a quarterly basis.

- Mechanics

Multicurrency Operant Portfolio Projected Return		*Counterparty*
+11.00%	Total return	
− 8.25%	LIBOR	8.25% received from portfolio
+ 2.75%	(Retain)	
+S&P 500	T. R. receipt	S&P 500 total return paid
S&P 500	T. R. + 2.75% enhancement result	

- Advantages
  Low transaction cost
  Low custody fees
  Simple administration
  Reduced or no handling of physical equity securities
  Tax advantages

EXHIBIT 7 (continued)

Step 3. Alternative downside risk protection using portfolio enhancement. Examples assume 3-year European option (costs as of October 31, 1990).

* Floor alternative on the S&P 500 index total return

	Annual		*Annual*
Cost 100% for initial index	2.31% (6.91% 3-year total)	Cost 95% for initial index	1.84% (5.51% 3-year total)
Portfolio enhancement over S&P	2.75%	Portfolio enhancement over S&P	2.75%
Net S&P enhancement	0.44% annual	Net S&P enhancement	0.91% annual

* Advantages

  Downside risk protection
  Cost potentially covered by operant portfolio
  Potential net enhancement even with cost of floor
  Monitoring of and continued value added to floor level

* Disadvantage

  Option cost

* Collar alternative on the S&P 500 (3-year)

Index Floor	*Index Cap*	*Annual Premium*	*Annualized Return at Cap*	*Annualized Cap Return with Portfolio*
100*	143.0	–0–	12.7%	15.45%
95*	149.5	–0–	14.2%	16.95%

*Floors effectively enhanced with portfolio 2.75% projected excess (100 increased to 109; 95 increased to 104)

* Advantages

  Downside risk protection
  No out-of-pocket cash outlay
  Floor and cap increased by portfolio
  Monitoring of and continued value added to collar

* Disadvantages

  Option cost
  Upside limitation

EQUITY-LINKED CROSS CURRENCY SWAPS

An equity-linked swap can be affected in various ways by foreign currency. For example, from a Canadian investor's perspective, some conditional variations could include the following for someone who has an operant portfolio in Canadian or U.S. dollars and an equity-linked S&P 500 swap (see Exhibit 8):

- A U.S. dollar S&P 500 return for a U.S. dollar LIBOR payment.
- A U.S. dollar S&P 500 return for a Canadian dollar LIBOR (BAs*) payment.
- The S&P 500 return paid in Canadian dollars for a U.S. dollar LIBOR payment.
- The S&P 500 return paid in Canadian dollars for a Canadian dollar LIBOR (BAs) payment.

These conditional variations may be currency hedged or unhedged as to principal only or interest only or both. Generally, if the index swap payment and LIBOR payment are unhedged and in the same currency, the cost of the index-linked swap is unchanged. However, if a Canadian investor wishes to pay LIBOR in U.S. dollars and in return receive the return on the S&P 500 in Canadian dollars, and if, in addition, the investor wishes the counterparty to hedge the risk of the exchange rate, there will be an additional adjustment, up or down, to the cost of the swap. The adjustment depends on whether the investor's local currency is a higher or lower interest rate currency. A higher interest rate currency is a *discount currency* and a lower

EXHIBIT 8
Equity-Linked Cross Currency Swap

Canadian investor's operant portfolio	S&P index hedged or unhedged US$ LIBOR	Counterparty

---

*In reality, there is no Canadian dollar LIBOR; however, an acceptable floating rate alternative that is sometimes used is Canadian Bankers Acceptances (hence the acronym BA).

interest rate currency is a *premium currency*. Basically, a high interest currency investor who wants to receive currency-hedged returns in terms of a lower currency would obtain a better price on the index-linked swap. This is a function of the interest rate differential between the two currencies and of the maturity along the swap curve. The pricing benefit is determined in part by the present value of the yield drop between the two currencies. The investor's counterparty would hedge the currency exposure at each reset date. The reverse case—that is, a low-interest currency investor seeking to take payments in a high-interest currency—would add to the cost of the swap.

Cross Currency Hedged S&P 500 Index Swap

Investor Pays	US$ LIBOR plus 170 basis points
Counterparty pays	S&P 500 index total return in C$ hedged
Notional amount	US$100 million
Reset	Semiannual
Currency	U.S. Dollars
Swap maturity	3 years
Exchange rate	Fixed at beginning of swap (1.1503)

If at the beginning of the semiannual period, the US$ LIBOR was 8 percent and, if during the period, the semiannual return on the S&P 500 was 5 percent and the return on the operant portfolio was 8 percent annualized, then the exchange of cash flow at reset would be:

Investor pays	
(8% + 1.70%) × (180/360) × $100 million	($4.850 million)
Investor receives	
(5%) × $100 million × C$1.1503 fixed	
equals C$5.752, which is equivalent to	$5.000 million
Net	$0.150 million
Return from operant portfolio	$4.000 million
Total	$4.150 million

The cost of the hedge is the base price consisting of LIBOR less 15 basis points (based on the market quote from the prior example), plus the increment of 170 basis points, for a total cost of 185 basis points. At the end of the period, steps must be taken to prepare for the required calculations for the next period. The S&P index is reset; the notional amount of the swap is adjusted to $105 million, as was detailed previously; and a new LIBOR is set.

Since foreign currency is hedged out of the swap, the currency contribution to total return is not a factor (i.e., all S&P 500 returns are converted at the initial spot rate fixed at C$1.1503).

Cross Currency Unhedged S&P 500 Index Swap

Currency is a factor in this example of a Canadian investor who elects to receive the S&P 500 index return unhedged in U.S. dollars.

Investor pays	US$ LIBOR less 15 basis points
Counterparty pays	S&P 500 index total return C$
Notional amount	US$100 million
Reset	Semiannual
Currency	U.S. dollars and Canadian dollars
Swap maturity	3 years
Exchange rate	Spot rate at each reset

If at the beginning of the semiannual period, US$ LIBOR was 8 percent and, if during the period, the semiannual return on the S&P 500 was 5 percent and the return on the operant portfolio was 8 percent annualized, then the exchange of cash flow at reset would be the same as in the previous example with the additional adjustment for changes in the exchange rate. Assume that the spot rate of exchange at the end of the reset period is C$1.1503.

Investor pays
    (8% − .15%) × (180/360) × $100 million
    (US$3.925 million) × 1.1503   (C$4.514 million)

Investor receives
    (5%) × $100 million × $1.1503   C$5.751 million
      Net   C$1.236 million

Return from operant portfolio
    US$4.0 million × 1.1503   C$4.601 million
      Total   C$5.837 million

Again, at the end of the period, steps must be taken to prepare for the required calculations for the next period. The S&P index is reset; the Canadian dollar notional amount of the swap is adjusted to $105 million times the exchange rate 1.1503, or C$120.78; and a new LIBOR is set.

At end of the next period, the S&P 500 index return in Canadian dollar terms will be computed as follows:

Beginning C$ notional amount − [(US$ notional swap amount)
    × (S&P 500 return for period) × (C$ spot exchange rate)]

SUMMARY

Index-linked swaps are a new vehicle for taking on market exposure; they are cost efficient and offer the possibility of return enhancement. In the simple case, the investor receives the total return on a stock market index in exchange for agreeing to make a floating interest rate payment on the nominal value of the investment principal. Other more complex swaps allow synthetic shuttling between stock market indexes; for example, an investor can exchange the return on the S&P 500 for the return on a foreign index. Also, index-linked swaps can have imbedded put and call options that create floor protection and collars. When coupled with currency swaps, the index-linked swap investor can choose not only among stock market index but also among currencies.

CHAPTER 14

THE FUNCTION OF TOKYO IN THE CROSS CURRENCY SWAP MARKET

Alicja K. Malecka
Deutsche Bank Capital Corp.
New York

INTRODUCTION

Since the breakdown of the Bretton Woods system and the elimination of the gold standard—or, more specifically, since the Smithsonian agreement of 1971—the threat of currency risk has become a continuous, rather than a discrete, issue faced by financial managers. Following the agreement, individual governments could no longer issue unilateral decrees to adjust the value of one currency against another. This surprised few of the interested parties, who, for the most part, had sufficient political savvy or advance information based on solid economic forecasts. They were able to protect themselves by converting their assets into another currency in advance. Others suffered the often devastating consequences of a devaluation.

Since that time the market forces have taken over the role of currency value regulators. Fortunes were made and lost in the initial period due to wide and often illogical currency swings. The dollar at first looked as if it had lost its supremacy as it quickly lost much of its strength. Ultimately, however, the dollar has retained its position as the linchpin of the foreign exchange markets, as all tradable currencies continue to fluctuate primarily against the dollar. Exhibit 1, for example, illustrates the recent fluctuation of the yen/U.S. dollar exchange rate along with the U.S.–Japan real yield spread.

EXHIBIT 1
U.S.–Japan Real Yield Spread and the Yen/Dollar Exchange Rate

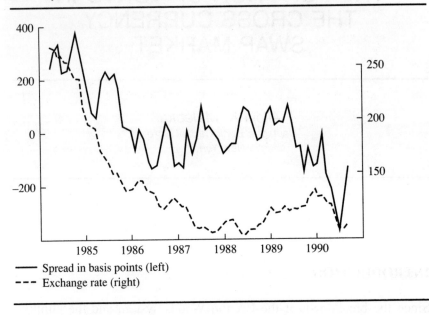

— Spread in basis points (left)
--- Exchange rate (right)

The fluctuation of major currencies gave rise to the need for currency hedging. This is turn led to creation of the currency forward and futures markets, fashioned after the commodities futures, where one can buy currencies forward or sell them short. Currencies became commodities. But the forward markets were not always sufficient in depth and size to accommodate all transactional needs. In particular, they proved inadequate in the face of a variety of national capital controls imposed by many countries in the 1970s, largely aimed at containing capital outflows and stabilizing currency values. As a means to overcome this inadequacy, American banks developed the cross currency swap structure out of its corporate predecessor—the parallel loan. Individually negotiated currency swaps have been transacted since the late 1970s in Swiss francs, Deutschemarks, and sterling, each against the U.S. dollar. Initially, they resulted from the need to hedge low-interest-rate borrowings in a currency of reasonable liquidity (i.e., Swiss francs) by foreign borrowers and as a means for U.S. companies to create funding in local currencies for their European subsidiaries where local controls prohibited capital imports.

Despite their increasing popularity in Europe, currency swaps were slow to develop in Japan. The two prerequisite financial characteristics, low interest rates and high liquidity, were absent from the Japanese market, which led to the lag in development of yen-related swaps. Japanese interest rates were very high due to high inflation levels, and the Japanese financial markets were highly regulated, rigid, and not open to creativity until the first in a series of changes was made in the foreign exchange law in 1980.

SIZE OF THE YEN CROSS CURRENCY SWAP MARKET

Cross currency yen/dollar swaps preceded the domestic yen interest rate swap market, and the average size of individual transactions remained larger until the first half of 1989, when it declined sharply from US$29 million to US$18 million. As shown in Exhibit 2, the total volume of cross currency yen swaps reached $42 billion in the first half of 1990, rising 22 percent over the same period in the preceding year, and accounted for roughly 40 percent of all cross currency swaps. By comparison, the yen interest rate swap volume soared from $29 billion in the first half of 1989 to $67 billion in the same period of 1990. For the purpose of analyzing the origins of yen cross currency swaps, it is worth noting that 66 percent, or $28 billion, were transacted with the end users, over half of which were Asian entities. The remainder involved professional interbank trading (see Exhibit 3).

THE JAPANESE BACKGROUND OF CROSS CURRENCY SWAPS

Changing Financial Environment

Although overall financial regulations were relaxed in the early 1980s, many regulatory relics remained, which in the climate of growing yen internationalization provided the impetus to capital market–driven arbitrage. In the face of growing demand for capital, swaps offered the flexibility to circumvent the regulatory constraints, and the development of a liquid Eurodeposit market for yen provided the necessary

EXHIBIT 2

Yen Cross Currency Swap Growth: Notional Principal by Currency
(In Billions of U.S. Dollars, Representing All Sides of Each Transaction)

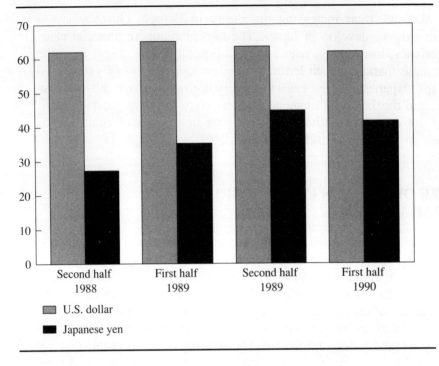

EXHIBIT 3

End Users of Yen Cross Currency Swaps (Principal Amounts, in Billions of Yen)

Location	Corporates	Financial Institutions	Governments & Supras	International Banks	Total
United States	133	152	14	—	300
Canada	66	78	11	—	155
Europe	208	812	356	—	1,429
Asia	1,330	844	73	—	2,284
Australia/ New Zealand	61	44	46	—	151
Global	15	54	20	2,200	2,289
	1,814	1,980	520	2,200	6,608
	(27.5%)	(30.0%)	(7.09%)	(33%)	

Note: Numbers rounded up
Asian counterparties = 35%

Source: 1990 ISDA Review.

296

floating-rate reference index in the form of LIBOR. This confluence of factors contributed to the rapid development of yen-related cross currency swaps in the 1980s.

Yen Swaps and the Domestic Banking

A brief view of the Japanese financial markets will set the stage for understanding the conditions under which swap transactions became important to the Japanese banks and corporations and how they led to the development of the domestic swap markets.

The banking system in Japan consists of three main groups of participants: city banks (commercial banks), long-term banks, and trust banks. Only the long-term banks, of which there are three—Industrial Bank of Japan, Long-Term Credit Bank, and Nippon Credit Bank—along with a handful of specialty banks, such as BOT, Shoko-chukin, and Norinchukin, are allowed to raise yen long-term funds by issuing domestic debentures. The debenture rate is used by Bank of Japan as a base for its monthly setting of the long-term prime rate (LTPR), which is the benchmark for the fixed corporate lending rate (see Exhibit 4). The LTPR, however, in practice is adjusted very

EXHIBIT 4
Structure of Japanese Interest Rates

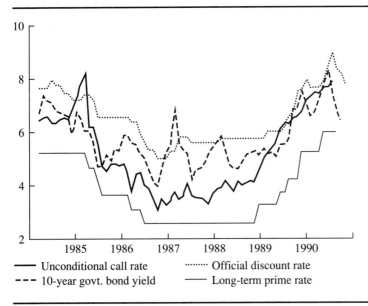

Unconditional call rate ⋯⋯⋯ Official discount rate
--- 10-year govt. bond yield —— Long-term prime rate

infrequently. As a result, the long-term banks have constituted the only natural source of *fixed-rate receivers* in the swap market when they want to convert their fixed-rate funds to floating-rate.

The city banks and the trust banks traditionally had no access to domestic long-term funding. Therefore, in the early 1980s they adopted the swap technique to manage their foreign–sourced, U.S. dollar–denominated borrowings and, later, their investments. Initially, there was neither the technology nor the need for yen interest rate swaps as long as domestic rates remained low and stable. Under these conditions, corporations were happy to borrow on a short-term basis via the common mechanism, the bill discount rate, and the rather arbitrary short-term prime. But with rapid economic expansion, the perception grew that the interest rates might be more volatile in the face of higher foreign rates, and borrowers began demanding more fixed-rate funding. For city banks and trust banks, domestic sources of funds were expanding, and they began to look for ways of fixing rates on their assets.

The opportunity to provide the means was seized by the foreign (Gaijin[1]) banks. American banks were first to adapt their expertise in managing U.S. dollar interest rate swap books in creating and managing yen interest rate swaps, thus offering to the city banks and trust banks, as well as to the adventurous corporate customers, a synthetic fixed rate. Other foreign banks followed.

It is no coincidence that foreign banks led the development of yen interest and currency swaps. Earlier on, foreign banks were the only providers of foreign funds to Japanese corporations, the so-called impact loans, which were named to reflect the impact they had on the country's balance of payments. Foreign banks had limited access to yen funds without a significant local deposit base and, hence, limited opportunity to expand yen assets. Consequently, they took advantage of the inability of city banks to provide foreign currency loans under the Ministry of Finance (MOF) foreign exchange laws.

However, by the early 1980s, the lending opportunities of foreign banks were seriously impaired by the revision of the Foreign Exchange Act, which abolished restrictions on Japanese banks' offering impact loans and on the conversion of foreign currencies into yen in general. Although the old impact loans were sometimes hedged through the

---

[1] A common Japanese term for an outsider or foreigner.

long-term foreign exchange market, they were often left totally unhedged by the corporate borrowers. By the early 1980s, this was no longer sufficient. The large-scale involvement of the Japanese banks and corporations in the Euromarket necessitated the development of a more structured instrument to hedge against daunting foreign exchange risks resulting from massive volumes of traded currencies, increased foreign exchange volatility, and the growing need to clearly define the cost of funds in yen terms.

THE TECHNOLOGY OF YEN SWAPS

To facilitate understanding of these relationships, it is necessary to define a yen currency swap and its standard terms and to compare it with the older hedging tool, the long-term foreign exchange contract.

In yen, as in other currencies, a currency swap is defined as an agreement between two parties to effectively assume each other's assets or liabilities in two different currencies for an agreed period of time and to reexchange them at maturity at the same exchange rate. As in other currencies, the market convention in a yen/U.S. dollar swap is to quote a fixed yen rate against U.S. dollar six-month LIBOR for all maturities, which are normally in the 2- to 10-year range.

Because of its close linkage with Euromarket bond issuance activities, the yen currency swap market developed in an erratic pattern and experienced periods of very low liquidity. Its technical parameters have also been more difficult to establish than for swaps of other currencies. As mentioned earlier, the floating index for the swap transactions was offered by the liquid Euroyen deposit market, or yen LIBOR.

In accordance with the domestic interest rate market, yen rates are calculated on an actual/365 semiannual basis, rather than a bond basis (30/360), as is customary in other currencies. The exchange rate for a currency swap is usually set at the basis of the prevailing spot rate.

The yen fixed-rate index is more interesting, if only because of its somewhat convoluted background. The reference for the long end of the Japanese financial markets has been represented by three relevant rates: the long-term debenture rate, the resulting long-term prime rate, and the Japanese government bond (JGB) rate. While the LTPR has been determined by the Bank of Japan in consultation with long-term banks and MOF and consequently has always moved in a stepwise fashion, the JGB rate has been continuously volatile as a result of the often extreme bond buying and selling activities by the major securities houses.

In practice, only the 10-year maturity of JGB has traded on a liquid basis. Shorter-term maturities have been illiquid and have not gained the benchmark status. This offered a dilemma to setting rates for yen swaps of various maturities. In the absence of a relevant JGB yield curve, the swap yield curve developed as a moving hybrid of the various long-term rates in the yen market, including long-term debentures, Eurobonds, and fixed-rate domestic lending rates. Swap rates were also very sensitive to supply and demand factors. Exhibit 5 shows the relative movement of swap and JGB rates. For these reasons, yen swap rates have always remained very volatile and more difficult to forecast than swap rates in other currencies. In the absence of hedging instruments, such as underlying Treasury securities, the management of yen swap books has been a complicated art. The increased risk undertaken by "book runners" added to the volatility of the swap rates as well as to the volume growth, since to hedge new swaps a combination of offsetting swaps has had to be transacted.

EXHIBIT 5
JGB Rate versus Swap Rate

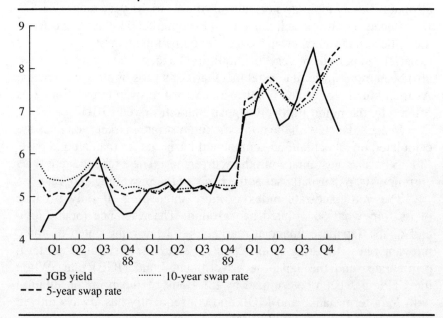

SWAP VERSUS FOREIGN EXCHANGE

Before discussion continues on the evolutionary application of yen cross currency swaps, the technical differences between swaps and foreign exchange contracts should be examined to facilitate understanding of some of the financial structures.

A typical yen/U.S. dollar swap can be expressed through a simple diagram as shown in Exhibit 6, which assumes that a U.S. dollar–based borrower (party A) converts his funding to yen basis.

EXHIBIT 6
Cross Currency Swap

Principal dollar amount:	US$50,000,000
Foreign exchange rate:	¥140/US$1
Principal yen amount:	¥7,000,000,000
Yen fixed rate:	6.50%
U. S. dollar fixed rate:	9.00%
Maturity:	5 years

Initial exchange

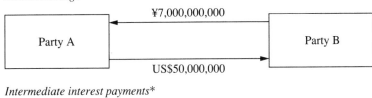

*Intermediate interest payments**

Final exchange

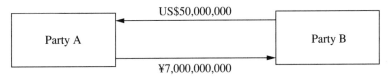

* Five equal annual payments

A currency swap is a simpler solution than a foreign exchange contract when assets and liabilities with steady cash flows are involved. Hence, it has improved applicability for hedging such instruments as bonds and loans, which are balance sheet–, rather than income statement–, related items.

In addition, the availability of long-term foreign exchange contracts for long-term maturities and in large volumes has always been limited, resulting in very wide bid/offer spreads. This naturally contributes to higher costs. Using long-term foreign exchange, party A would have to undertake the steps indicated in Exhibit 7 to hedge its yen exposure.

As illustrated, long-term foreign exchange contracts have different rates associated with each forward period, which causes uneven cash flows and reinvestment/funding risks. In our example, party A knows that its yen fixed rate is 6.50 percent throughout the transaction if a swap is used to convert funding from dollars into yen. If long-term foreign exchange contracts are used, yen coupon payments will differ in each period, and less yen will be collected at maturity for principal repayment than was originally taken in. To determine what yen interest rate the borrower would be paying, one has to calculate the internal rate of return (IRR), which is not a comfortable cost measure for many borrowers and results in complex accounting implications.

EXHIBIT 7
Long-Term Foreign Exchange

Step 1. Convert US$50,000,000 into yen at the spot rate of ¥140/US$1.
Step 2. Buy yen forward for the equivalent of US$4,500,000 (coupon payment) for the five future interest payment dates. Forward yen are purchased at the current forward rate, which includes a forward premium.
Step 3. Buy the US$50,000,000 five years forward for yen.

Period	U.S. Dollar	¥/US$	Yen Amounts
0	50.0	140.00	7,000.00
1	(4.5)	138.50	(623.25)
2	(4.5)	135.00	(607.50)
3	(4.5)	134.00	(603.00)
4	(4.5)	133.00	(598.50)
5	(4.5)	132.00	(594.00)
	(50.0)	131.00	(6,550.00)
	IRR = 6.52% p.a.		

ASSETS AND LIABILITIES
BEHIND YEN CURRENCY SWAPS

Types of Financial Transactions

Yen currency swaps originated largely in conjunction with the following capital market–related currency conversions:

- Swapping U.S. dollar loans into yen by Japanese borrowers.
- Swapping U.S. dollar Eurobonds into yen by Japanese issuers.
- Swapping yen Eurobond issues into U.S. dollars by non-Japanese issuers.

Later on, as Japan became a major exporter of capital, other investment-related sources developed, such as conversions of:

- Yen loans into U.S. dollars by non-Japanese borrowers.
- U.S. dollar bonds into Japanese yen by Japanese investors.

On balance, listed in declining order of importance, there are four market forces driving the yen currency swap market:

1. Shortage of domestic liquidity—until 1986.
2. Excess of domestic liquidity—after 1986.
3. Credit and derivative product arbitrage.
4. Hedging of commercial exposure.

Later on we will expand on the intricacies of the relationship of a swap transaction with each of the listed capital market sources.

Funding Japan with Foreign Currencies

Considering the issues reviewed so far, a Japanese borrower of dollars who needed yen funding would typically adopt a yen/U.S. dollar currency swap for that purpose. As with all cross currency swaps, the convention is that a fixed-rate yen is swapped against the floating (LIBOR) U.S. dollar rate. Consequently, a company that borrowed U.S. dollar fixed-rate funds would swap it first into U.S. dollar LIBOR before swapping into yen. For the sake of simplicity, this step was ignored in Exhibit 6. Furthermore, a borrower that needs floating-rate yen funds would enter into a yen/yen interest rate swap in addition to a cross currency swap. This would be the case for impact loans as well as Eurodollar bond issues and other foreign-currency loans.

Impact Loans

As previously mentioned, U.S. banks originally used the yen swap business to facilitate hedging of the so-called impact loans, extended in U.S. dollars to Japanese customers. These were very popular in the 1970s, when liquidity in Japan was very tight. The loans were typically extended for five years at a floating rate. In the majority of the cases, the foreign exchange exposure was left open, with the Japanese corporation taking full risk on the yen/dollar rate.

The original impact loan turned out to be more the inspiration for than the user of swaps, because the 1980 ministry of finance (MOF) ruling, which permitted the Japanese banks to lend foreign currencies, eliminated the foreigners' monopoly on the market. On the other hand, the rule expanded exponentially the demand for cross currency swaps and necessitated their standardization, as Japanese banks became large-scale users of the instrument. The size of the market exploded.

Euromarket Contribution

The growth of cross currency swaps has paralleled that of the Euro-market bond issuance activities. In the case of yen, Japanese banks

EXHIBIT 8
U.S. Dollar Bond Issues by Japanese Borrowers (in millions of dollars)

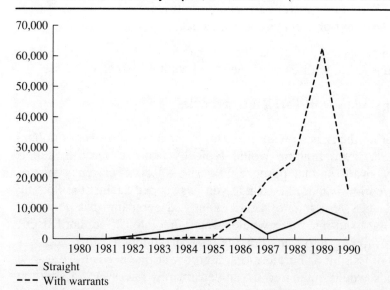

——— Straight
- - - With warrants

began to issue U.S. dollar straight bonds to fund customers in the early 1980s (see Exhibit 8). This phenomenon precipitated the rapid growth in demand for U.S. dollar interest swaps by Japanese issuers and the expansion of the U.S. dollar interest rate swap (IRS) market in Tokyo in 1982–1985.

As mentioned earlier, IRSs were used as the first leg of the currency swap. It is fair to say that the explosion of the U.S. dollar issue market was swap-driven. An example of this process is illustrated in Exhibit 9.

EXHIBIT 9
A Two-Step Swap Structure for a Dollar Eurobond

1. *U.S. dollar interest rate swap*
   - Payment to bondholders: US$ annual bond coupon of 9%
   - Receive US$ fixed 9%
   - Pay LIBOR – 20 bp in swap: 20 bp arbitrage against US$ swap market

2. *Yen cross currency swap (see Exibit 6)*
   - Initial exchange: US$50 million for ¥7.00 billion
   - Future cash flows: US$ LIBOR interest rate for yen swap
                                 fixed rate, 6.5%
   - Final Exchange: ¥$7.00 billion for US$50 million

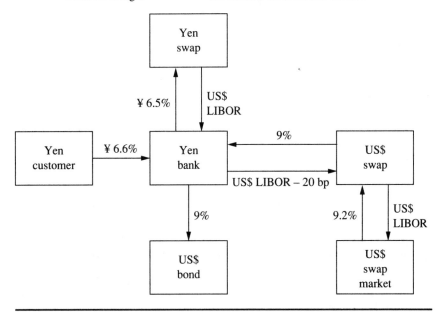

In this example, the Japanese bank is the U.S. dollar bond issuer. The bank's objective is to lend yen to a domestic customer. To do so, the bank will first swap the bond proceeds to dollar floating rate; that is, it will *receive* the fixed rate with which it will service the bond coupon, and it will *pay* floating LIBOR. Due to the arbitrage opportunity that existed between the U.S. dollar swap market (9.2 percent) and the Eurobond rates (9.0 percent), the Japanese bank could earn 20 basis points through the dollar swap.

Progression of Steps

1. Japanese bank issues $100 million Eurobond for a five-year maturity with a coupon of 9 percent.
2. Japanese bank uses the funds to make loans to Japanese customer.
   a. Japanese bank swaps all its bond proceeds into U.S. floating dollars, at LIBOR −20 basis points.
   b. Japanese bank swaps all its floating dollar proceeds into fixed yen at 6.5 percent and lends yen to the customer at 6.6 percent.
   c. Japanese bank earns 30 basis points: 20 on the U.S. dollar interest rate swap and 10 on the difference between the yen swap and the loan rate.

In 1984, Tokyo was reported as the fastest-growing swap market in the world. This was largely attributable to the hedging and speculative activities in the U.S. dollar interest rate swap market. The dollar bond issuance by Japanese borrowers accounted for the lion's share of these activities; these were swapped into floating dollars and subsequently converted to fixed yen funds via forward FX or cross currency swaps.

The Equity Warrant Bond

The primary issue–driven swap market grew further as the value of issuing U.S. dollar bonds with warrants attached became more apparent. The booming Tokyo equity market, which moved up from 19,000 on the Nikkei index in 1985 to 38,000 by December 1989 (see Exhibit 10), was a major driving force behind equity warrant issues. Not only has the number of issuers expanded exponentially, but the size of individual deals has also increased significantly.

EXHIBIT 10
Performance of Major Equity Markets Expressed in Yen
(First Week 1986 = 100)

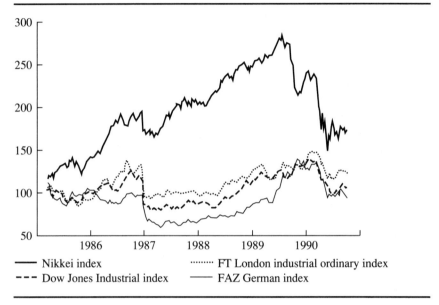

Nikkei index

Dow Jones Industrial index

FT London industrial ordinary index

FAZ German index

In the summer of 1988, Toyota issued the famous $1 billion bond with warrants attached. The market was driven by the insatiable appetite of Japanese investors for:

- U.S. dollar–denominated assets issued by strong Japanese credits. (In view of the historically low Japanese interest rates and strong U.S. dollar cash flows, the cash, generated by exporters and the booming domestic growth, sought relatively high yields elsewhere.)
- Detached equity warrants that promised multiple returns over those of conventional investment vehicles.
- Equity warrant instruments that generated zero or subzero funding costs in yen.
- Strong demand for floating-rate synthetic investments produced from the deeply discounted ex-warrant assets used for *Zeitech*,[2]

---

[2]*Zeitech* means "financial engineering," which refers to an arbitrage technique whereby a spread above LIBOR is locked in for the life of an investment, and funded at sub-LIBOR rates achieved through structured borrowing.

whereby companies borrowed on sub-LIBOR terms and invested in above-LIBOR assets.

The warrant mania created a number of circular activities, and U.S. dollar straight bonds with warrants attached (see Exhibit 11) have developed as a variation on the straight U.S. dollar Eurobond issues. The major characteristic of this instrument is the warrant, which the investor can exercise for a specified number of shares of the issuing company at a predetermined price before the maturity of the bond.

The warrant itself has a market value, which allows the coupon on the bond to be reduced accordingly. Thus, the return to the investor from such a bond with an equity warrant attached consists of two components:

1. The bond yield.
2. The warrant market value.

By offering the investor an additional return opportunity with the warrant, the issuer (Japanese borrower) could pay a below-market interest rate coupon.

The mechanics of valuing such transactions are quite complicated and beyond the scope of this chapter. However, to demonstrate how these transactions generated swap opportunities, it is necessary to explain their impact on both borrowers and investors.

The issuer (borrower) would end up paying a U.S. dollar fixed rate of interest, lower than the coupon, on a straight dollar issue (e.g., 6 percent instead of 10 percent). The price the issuer had to pay for the cheap coupon was a promise of giving up, at a future date, a portion of its equity through issuing more stock to satisfy warrant exercise. In the era of a booming stock market, this risk was extremely real.

The primary investor, the buyer of the bond with a warrant, received a below-market yield on its investment. This shortfall, however, was offset by the right to exercise the warrant for shares of stock of the issuing company when such stock price exceeded the strike price of the warrant. The investor thus took a gamble on the rising stock market values. Typically, the primary investor would want to monetize this risk by detaching the warrant from the bond and selling it in the open market.

EXHIBIT 11
A Eurodollar Bond Issue with Warrant Attached

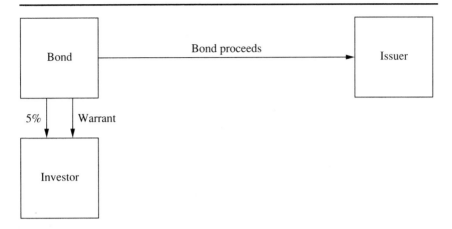

Step 1: Issuer (borrower) swaps (ex) warrant bond into floating U.S. dollar

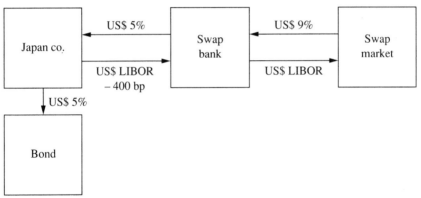

Issuer obtains funding at LIBOR – 400 bp.

Step 2: Issuer swaps U.S. dollar sub-LIBOR funding into fixed yen

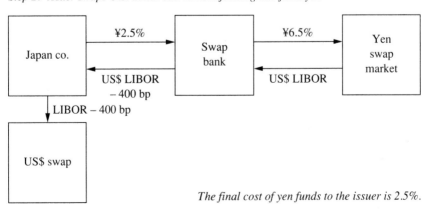

The final cost of yen funds to the issuer is 2.5%.

During 1985–1989, the warrant market was extremely active, and with the frenzy of speculative activity, the detached warrants would command premiums in multiples of their intrinsic value. Thus, the final yield to the investor in a warrant-related bond could be extremely lucrative.

Zero-Cost Funding through the Use of Warrants Our earlier example will now be expanded to consider a more favorable case for the issuer. Recall that the U.S. dollar bond was issued with a 5 percent coupon. The warrant, or right to purchase stock, represented no initial cost in dollars; thus, it was disregarded in calculating the cost of funding. The issuer would then swap the 5 percent bond into Japanese yen for use in domestic investment activities.

To accomplish this, the issue was first swapped into floating dollars at the prevailing market rate (see Exhibit 12). Often, issuers took advantage of the market when the U.S. dollar rate/yen rate spread was particularly high. As a result of swapping first into U.S. dollar LIBOR, the borrower would receive from the swap market a premium, or a spread equal to the differential between the swap market rate and the rate needed to service the low-coupon bond. This spread would be translated to a floating-rate subsidy, resulting in final funding cost considerably below the U.S. dollar LIBOR rate (LIBOR − 625 basis points in this example).

In the second step, the issuer (borrower) would swap the U.S. dollar floating funds into fixed Japanese yen via a cross currency swap. Since one leg in such a swap is U.S. dollar LIBOR flat and the other leg is a "market"-determined yen fixed rate, which reflected the general level of Japanese long-term rates, the transaction would result in a yen fixed rate equal to zero. This technique has so far been the best practical manifestation of "streets paved with gold."

This example has been deliberately simplified by ignoring conversion factors and daycount fraction calculations, which would modify the rates by 10–20 basis points, but it illustrates in principle how the interest rate arbitrage worked for Japanese borrowers.

In many instances, a negative cost of funds resulted. The issuer could achieve paying only a 5 percent coupon when U.S. dollar swap rates were over 11 percent because of the anticipatory, very rich valuation of the detached warrant. The warrant, by definition, was highly leveraged, which in times of a soaring stock market multiplied its

EXHIBIT 12
Zero-Cost Funding

Step 1: Interest rate swap

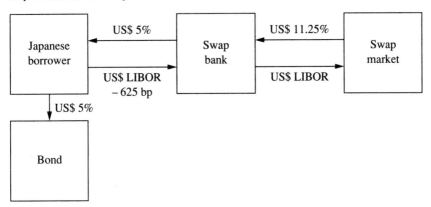

Step 2: Cross currency swap

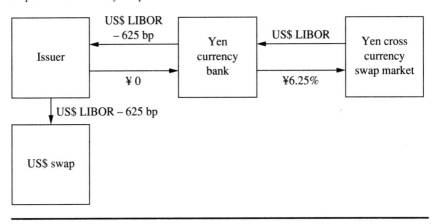

initial cost by a factor of 2 or 3. As a result, the warrant market expanded dramatically between 1987 and 1989 during the booming Japanese stock market (see Exhibit 10).

The key factors that facilitated this arbitrage were:

• Generous market valuation of the warrants, enabling a significant reduction in the coupon paid on the bond.
• A large differential between Japanese and U.S. interest rates in favor of the dollar.

- Often, additional arbitrage available in the U.S. dollar interest rate swap vis-à-vis the U.S. dollar Eurobond rate by top-credit borrowers.

Benefits for Investors The primary investor, as mentioned earlier, would strip the bond of its warrant and sell the detached warrant in the open market, often for more than its intrinsic value in the bond-plus-warrant structure.

After the stripping, the investor would be left with an ex-warrant bond, the par value of which would be discounted to reflect the interest rate differential between the bond's coupon and market rates. The discounted value of such a bond could be 75–85 percent of par, depending on the quality of the issuer. It could then be swapped into a U.S. dollar synthetic floating-rate asset with a yield of LIBOR plus spread. The spread would be achieved by distributing the bond discount over the floating leg of the swap. Asset swaps of the type needed to accomplish this are covered in Chapter 8. Our discussion of ex-warrant-related assets at this juncture is primarily to show how the strong demand for assets contributed to the evolution of yen currency swaps.

Japanese Foreign Investments

We have discussed yen cross currency swaps originating from U.S. dollar financing transactions, whereby the swap participant converted dollar funding into yen funding. In swap language, the participant was the *fixed-funds yen payer* and the *floating U.S. dollar receiver.* The other side of the market, however, has developed very rapidly with the expansion of yen domestic liquidity in the mid-1980s and concurrent yen capital export growth.

Once the Japanese pension funds, banks, and insurance companies began to accept foreign risks for portfolio diversification purposes, the export of yen capital was accomplished by the following forms of yen-based assets:

- Direct yen loans to corporations and sovereign entities by Japanese banks.
- Direct private placements of yen by Japanese investors to foreign financial institutions, sovereign agencies, and select corporates.

- Purchases by Japanese investors of U.S. dollar Eurobonds and Shogun bonds issued by Japanese borrowers.

These investments resulted in, or were explicitly driven by, yen currency swaps in which the Japanese investor ultimately preferred to receive a yen return. Consequently, in these types of swap transactions, the Japanese counterparty became the receiver of fixed-rate yen and the payer of floating U.S. dollars, if their investments were made in dollars. Alternatively, the non-Japanese borrower became the receiver of yen in the swap, if the Japanese investor made the investment in yen. In either case, the asset- or investment-related swap transactions have been receiver-driven, as compared with the U.S. dollar debt or liability conversions into yen, which have been payer-driven.

Yen Lending to Foreigners
Overseas yen lending has been done primarily in three forms:

1. Loans to Asian corporate entities by banks and leasing companies, usually using amortized structures.
2. Loans to corporate entities through concessionary funds from the Japan Export-Import Bank, using amortized or balloon structures.
3. Loans/private placements by Japanese insurance companies to foreign financial institutions, sovereign entities, and select corporations.

Typically, the foreign borrower needed to convert the yen loan proceeds into U.S. dollars in order to employ them in that currency or further convert them to their functional currency. In most cases the investor would want to hedge the interest payments throughout the life of the loan and the principal repayment at maturity.

By entering into a cross currency yen/dollar swap transaction, the borrower would receive through the initial exchange the dollar funds converted at the spot rate and would undertake to pay a U.S. dollar floating rate (LIBOR) throughout the interest period, in accordance with a specified schedule. In return, the borrower would receive a fixed yen rate based on the current swap market, which would be used to meet the obligations to the Japanese lender.

Normally, loans to foreign customers provided by banks, leasing companies, or smaller regional banks would be priced at market rates and, depending on the swap conditions, would result in an all-in floating cost of funds of U.S. dollar LIBOR flat or U.S. dollar LIBOR plus a spread.

An ordinary bank loan to a foreign corporate borrower would be made at an all-in yen rate usually exceeding the fixed rate in the cross currency swap market. Exhibit 13 illustrates the whole transaction.

EXHIBIT 13
Hedged Yen Financing

Loan amount:	¥5,000,000,000
Maturity:	5 years
Loan rate:	7.00%
Market swap rate:	6.50%
Exchange rate:	¥145/US$1
US$ amount:	US$34,500,000

Initial exchange

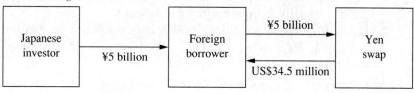

Interim interest payments

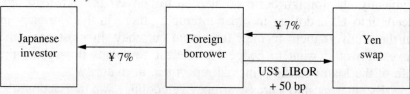

Final exchange

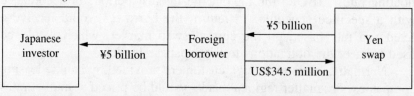

The resulting cost of funding, in U.S. dollars, to the borrower was LIBOR + 50 basis points, with the spread over LIBOR usually lower than that obtainable by borrowing dollars directly. This cost reduction was achieved by arbitraging the cheaper cost of funds in Japan through a swap transaction.

Subsidized Yen Loans

The final U.S. dollar cost of funds in the preceding example would have been significantly different if subsidized or concessionary funds were loaned, as in the case of the Export/Import (EXIM) Bank's loans or through a special subsidy offered by city and trust banks for certain projects. Such rates have generally been lower than the prevailing yen swap rate. Therefore, a typical subsidized or low-cost loan with a swap would yield the dollar results to the borrower indicated in Exhibit 14.

To reflect the differential between the yen swap market rate and the loan rate, the fixed rate on the cross currency swap would be adjusted to meet the borrower's interest payment obligation. The difference would be translated into a 100-basis-point subsidy on the U.S. dollar LIBOR, or floating, side of the swap.

This structure, which originated from the EXIM Bank loans to developing countries and was followed by other subsidized commercial funding, gave rise to a *U.S. dollar sub-LIBOR* or otherwise attractive funding trend prior to 1990. The major contributors to this trend have been Japanese trust banks and insurance companies. The ability to provide attractively priced dollar funds by Japanese investors met with great demand overseas and stemmed from a combination of factors, similar to those accompanying the origins of swaps. Examples include the regulatory constraints surrounding the insurance industry, Japan's largest investor group, and the market's creative ability to adjust to the new demands by creating special tools.

Insurance Companies:
The Excess Liquidity Syndrome

As a matter of background, it should be mentioned that the rapid growth of capital exports in the 1985–1990 period reflected the fast growth of the Japanese economy, creative efforts of insurance companies to accommodate the ballooning savings of the population, and, in 1986, the increase by the Ministry of Finance in the insurance companies' foreign investment ceiling. Under this rule, the insurers

EXHIBIT 14
Subsidized Yen Loan

- Yen loan rate 5.5%
- Other terms as shown in Exhibit 13

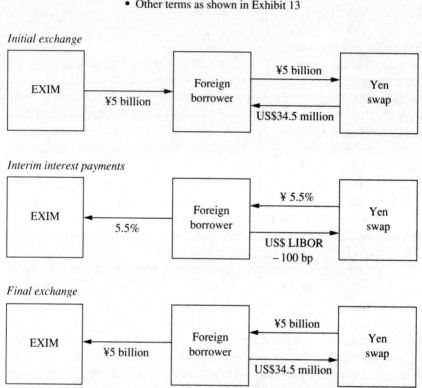

Initial exchange

Interim interest payments

Final exchange

were permitted to invest up to 30 percent of their investable assets in non–yen denominated instruments, as opposed to only 10 percent before that time. This regulatory change resulted in an explosion of foreign-oriented investments, as shown in Exhibit 15.

A relevant regulatory constraint facing the insurers was the requirement to pay dividends from income rather than capital gains. This generated a need to invest in high-yielding assets, often by deliberately accepting significant foreign exchange, commodity, and other financial risks. These risks have been transferred to operating departments and either managed/hedged or absorbed in the overall accounts, and the collected risk premiums from attached derivative products were

EXHIBIT 15
Yen Foreign Investments, Six-Month Moving Average (in Billions
of U.S. dollars)

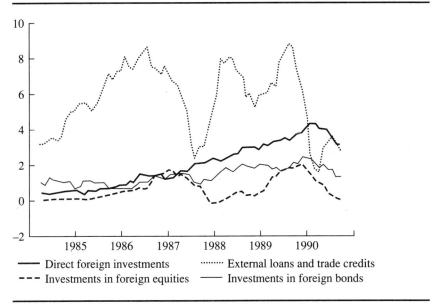

—— Direct foreign investments   ········· External loans and trade credits
- - - Investments in foreign equities   —— Investments in foreign bonds

used to enhance the current yield. This risk-transfer trade-off gave
rise to the creation of new instruments.

To the extent that these investors ultimately needed yen-deno-
minated returns, they lent the funds in yen. However, the relevant
investment instruments would be swapped into U.S. dollars for the
benefit of the borrower. The typical instruments have been direct yen
loans, Eurobonds, and private placements. Although the categories
differ greatly in size, legal definition, and means of execution, from
the perspective of this discussion they can be treated as a group with
common characteristics in terms of overall structure and resulting cash
flows.

Use of Swaptions
Under the guidance of the Japanese Ministry of Finance, the yield
on these investments should be based on the prevailing long-term
prime rate (LTPR); however, discounts have been known to be made.
Therefore, in a structured transaction, the objective would be to ensure

a yen return equal to the LTPR, and a U.S. dollar cost of funds to the foreign borrower with an acceptable sub-LIBOR spread.

The first step is the use of a cross currency yen/U.S. dollar swap. However, during periods when the yen swap rate was lower than the LTPR, which have predominated in the last few years (see Exhibit 16), an additional "enhancement" would be created if the rates were linked. The "yield enhancement" could be obtained through the investor's taking a risk on the investment's maturity (swaption structure) or a monetary risk on the cash value of the investment—its principal or interest. Such risk-driven structures have been very popular with Japanese investors in the past few years.

An example of a swaption is shown in Exhibit 17. The borrower obtained funds at U.S. dollar LIBOR − 10 basis points, and the investor received interest based on LTPR. However, the swap counterparty had an option to cancel (call) the swap after three years if the swap market rate exceeded the call strike rate of 6.0 percent. By agreement, the borrower had the right to call the loan if his swap was canceled. Consequently, the investor was subject to the risk that the in-

EXHIBIT 16
Yen Five-Year Swap Rate versus LTPR

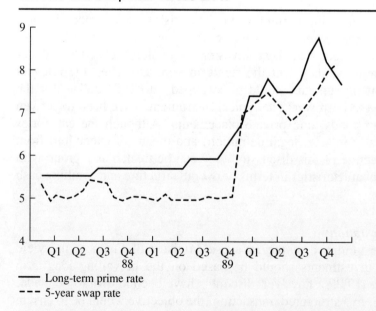

——— Long-term prime rate
- - - 5-year swap rate

EXHIBIT 17
Loan with a Call Option: Swaption

Loan principal amount:	¥5,000,000,000
LTPR:	6.80%
Yen swap rate:	6.60%
Maturity:	7 years
Enhancement:	Swap call option: 30 bp
Call maturity:	3 years

Interest rate cash flows

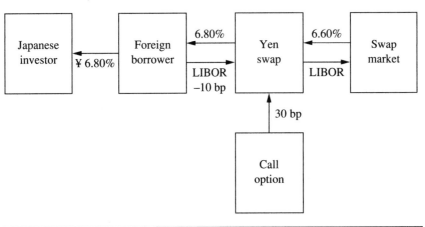

vestment would be terminated long before the intended maturity. This is a risk the insurance company can accept, known as maturity risk.

The original investment had to be written for a longer maturity to meet investment policy objectives. More importantly, it required a 10-year maturity at the time for the combination of a 7-year cross currency swap and a 3-year call option (swaption) to produce the needed results. Depending on market conditions, such combinations might involve swaps of 5 to 10 years and swaptions of 2 to 5 years, whichever carried the greatest premium in the market at the time. The success of such transactions depends on an intricate confluence of factors in the markets. Therefore, its execution is often time-consuming and complicated.

In terms of market participants, investors have usually been life insurance companies lending up to ¥5 billion per transaction, as per the Ministry of Finance limit, mostly to foreign financial institutions for routine funding operations. Larger transactions have been done through the Euromarkets, involving a syndication of a few insurance companies put together by a Japanese trust or city bank.

Monetary Risk: Dual-Currency and Reverse Dual-Currency Structures

Dual-Currency Instruments Other yield enhancement-producing instruments involve the investor's taking a monetary risk, such as foreign exchange risk. One example of such a transaction, which was very popular in 1985–1988, was a dual-currency bond or a dual-currency loan. The concept of dual-currency structure evolved differently for bonds and loans.

The dual-currency Eurobond issues, which were popular in 1985 and 1986, were driven by the Japanese investor's need to earn a high coupon. Consequently, the borrower issued a yen straight bond that paid a yen coupon at an above-market rate. The redemption of principal, however, was determined in U.S. dollars at a prespecified exchange rate different from the issue rate and yielded a dollar amount different from the initial issue proceeds. Thus, the investor ultimately received either a predefined dollar amount or its yen equivalent at the future spot rate. In either case, the issuer bore an open currency risk on the principal investment.

The borrower's risk on the yen coupon was hedged through the long-term foreign exchange market to convert it to a fixed dollar coupon, which was then swapped into a floating rate. The ultimate benefit was a below-market cost of funding, usually U.S. dollar LIBOR$-x$, and no risk on the principal. Exhibit 18 illustrates the structure of both sides.

The value of this transaction was derived from a particular relationship between yen and dollar interest rates. The key rate was the redemption FX rate of 145, which was derived in calculations as a breakeven rate to the borrower, based on a 7.5 percent yen coupon, the prevailing U.S. dollar swap fixed rate, and the long-term foreign exchange costs.

The foreign exchange hedge of the yen coupon gave rise to the development of a special swap structure known as the *coupon swap,* which will be explained in the next section.

In the preceding example, the borrower received yen bond proceeds from the investor and converted these proceeds into

EXHIBIT 18
Dual-Currency Bond Structure

Initial exchange

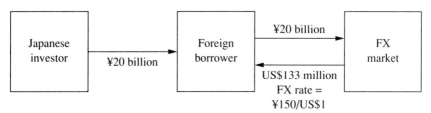

Interest payments

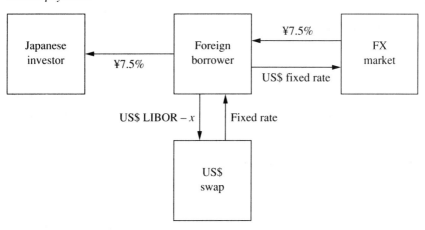

Final exchange

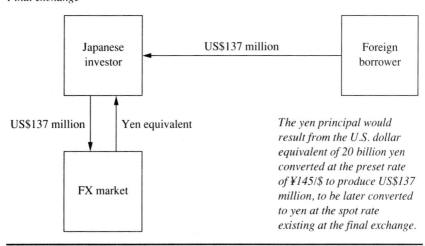

The yen principal would result from the U.S. dollar equivalent of 20 billion yen converted at the preset rate of ¥145/$ to produce US$137 million, to be later converted to yen at the spot rate existing at the final exchange.

U.S. dollars at a spot foreign exchange rate of ¥150/US$1 realizing US$133 million. At maturity, the borrower had to repay a higher amount, US$137 million, but did not have to worry about currency risk on the principal. The dollar difference was generated from the exchange of yen/dollar coupons.

The investor received an attractive yen coupon of 7.5 percent compared with the market rate of about 6.5 percent, but had an open currency risk on the principal. This risk has usually been managed by the foreign exchange department of the investing insurance company. The resulting gains and losses would be charged back only if they exceeded 15 percent per annum, which was yet another accounting loophole supporting investment creativity.

The dual-currency loan used the concept of the bond structure but was driven by the Japanese borrower who accepted the risk of principal repayment, based on a foreign currency-linked formula, in exchange for paying a below-market yen interest rate. The lender was usually a Japanese or foreign bank, which covered foreign exchange risk through a complex series of cross currency and interest rate swaps. Exhibit 19, a rough diagram of an actual transaction arranged by a money center bank for a customer, illustrates this type of structure.

Reverse Dual-Currency Instruments   A variation on the dual-currency structure that has been employed very extensively is the so-called reverse dual-currency (RDC) instruments: loans and, more recently, Samurai bonds. The reverse dual-currency loans were popular with small borrowers in 1989, particularly in the domestic market, and were known as "Koala" loans due to their Australian dollar coupon, which the borrower could convert through a coupon swap into an attractive yen interest rate. On the other side of the market, big investors used the structure to enhance the investment yield, taking on monetary risk on their interest receipts.

The most interesting feature of a RDC structure is the coupon swap concept. Similar to a dual-currency structure, the investor accepts the foreign exchange risk, usually on an exotic currency which naturally bears a high coupon. The RDC instruments have had their principal denominated in yen, with a 100 percent yen principal redemption but with the interest payments in a high-yielding currency at

EXHIBIT 19
Dual-Currency Loan

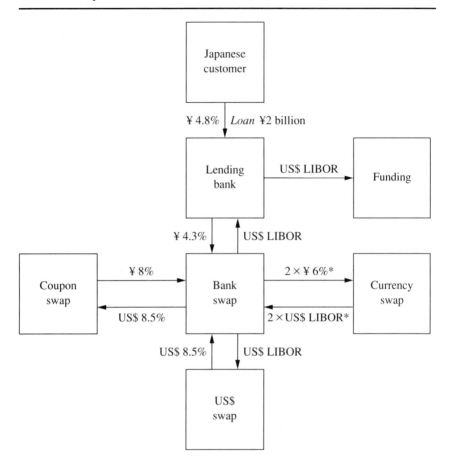

Repayment Formula:

$$x = ¥4 \text{ billion} - (US\$14 \text{ billion} \times \text{spot FX})$$

If spot FX is lower than ¥143/US$1, the customer would pay more than he borrowed.

If spot FX is higher than ¥143/US$1, the customer would pay less than he borrowed.

*Note that in this swap hedge the principle amounts of both yen and corresponding dollars are doubled.

a below-market rate (i.e., Australian dollars, Canadian dollars, and, sporadically, Spanish pesetas).

Although RDC loans have been in the Japanese domestic market since 1988 and have grown dramatically, they did not acquire international status until September 1990, through a series of Samurai bond issues (foreign issues in the domestic yen market) with the RDC features. There were approximately ¥475 billion of these issues, mostly by foreign financial institutions placed with small Japanese banks. They represented yet another unique way to circumvent accounting rules on the books of the banks.[3] Exhibit 20 illustrates the cash flows and relative benefits of the RDC structure.

The new swap instrument developed for this purpose was the coupon swap, a direct descendant of the long-term foreign exchange forward. A coupon swap is a hybrid instrument that differs from a cross currency swap in the following ways:

1. It carries no principal exchange at inception.
2. It carries no principal exchange at maturity.
3. Interest rates are fixed in both currencies.
4. Interest rates are set independently of the swap rates; the high-coupon currency rate is derived from the cost of hedging a given base currency (yen) interest rate.
5. The high currency coupon is at a below-market rate.

With this investment instrument, the investor takes an open currency risk on his interest receipts, which will fluctuate in line with the value of the high-coupon currency vis-à-vis the yen. Again, in a strictly monetary sense, the transaction is speculative, but it is satisfied by the need for higher coupon. The swap counterparty has to use a combination of foreign exchange, currency deposits, and yen LIBOR/U.S. dollar LIBOR swaps to cover the risk and to generate the needed foreign-currency (Australian dollar) rate.

Other Arbitrage and Niche Products
The limits of financial innovation in the Tokyo market have been greatly stretched to accommodate its unique needs and highly speculative appetite for the *Zeitech* of the 1980s. There has been a full

---

[3] *International Financial Review*, "Japanese Finance: The dual purpose of reverse dual currency Samurai bonds," Sept. 29, 1990, p. 6.

EXHIBIT 20
Reverse Dual-Currency Bond Structure

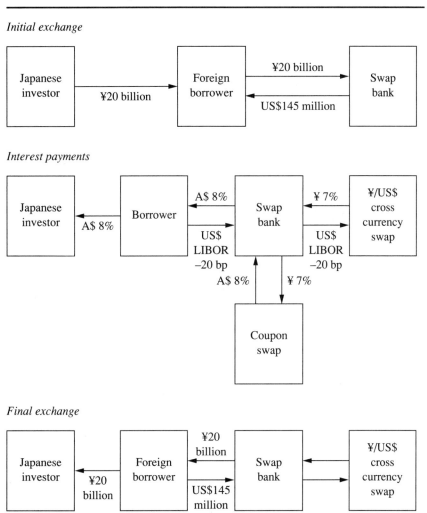

Initial exchange

Interest payments

Final exchange

menu of financial structures relating to lease financing and other investments that have been swap-driven and have contributed to the expansion of the yen swap market.

Although it is not possible to cover it in depth here, the principle of *Zeitech* is an arbitrage involving investments of borrowed funds,

EXHIBIT 21
Japanese Corporate Liquidity (Two-Quarter Moving Average)

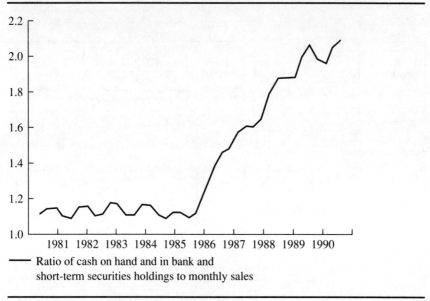

─── Ratio of cash on hand and in bank and
short-term securities holdings to monthly sales

usually at below-market cost, in financial assets on a fully matched basis with a positive spread locked in.

In the cases of banks and insurance companies, some low-cost funds were obtained in the course of conducting their primary business. This was aided by financial regulations that kept a ceiling on deposit rates. Other market participants, such as manufacturing companies, raised funds specifically for financial investments, through equity warrants or structured loans and bonds.

Consequently, the structured investments with swaps attached expanded foreign investments far beyond the volume of domestic investment sources available and included some very nontraditional investors. An indication of the rapid growth in the corporate liquidity that accommodated these transactions is illustrated in Exhibit 21.

THE FUTURE OF THE YEN SWAP MARKET

In absolute terms, the yen cross currency swap volume peaked in the second half of 1989 at about US$42 billion and represented 40 percent of all U.S. dollar–based cross currency swaps. The market is quite mature, and it will have to grow more slowly in the future. Moreover, many factors indicate that the volume will decline in outright terms.

The Japanese banks are in the process of rationalizing their asset expansion and revising profitability targets. Capital adequacy requirements of the Bank for International Settlements, coupled with the dramatic drop in the equity markets, have exerted pressure on banks to increase their returns. Still, the banks will continue to lend while reducing existing assets through sales or securitization. They will also continue to raise funds through the Eurodollar market, although perhaps at a slower pace. Following a temporary reduction due to greater domestic opportunities and a squeeze on funds resulting from aggregated bond redemptions in 1990, the insurance industry should continue to direct up to 30 percent of its investments overseas. These activities will continue to rely heavily on cross currency swaps.

The cooling of speculative activities and a broad volume decline in equity-related bond issues, for as long as the Japanese stock market remains uncertain, would suggest that the growth in the swap volume will be equally restrained. Yen currency swaps will probably give up some of their share in the industry to European currencies but are likely to remain the second largest currency block in the industry for the near future.

PART 3

VALUATION OF SWAPS

CHAPTER 15

CURRENCY SWAP PRICING AND VALUATION

Cal Johnson
Salomon Brothers Inc
New York

Janet L. Showers
Salomon Brothers Inc
New York

INTRODUCTION

Early currency swaps, generally arranged by an intermediary as agent, were motivated by a "capital markets arbitrage"—the ability of issuers to obtain a cheaper cost of funds. Today the currency swap market in the major currencies functions much like the interest rate swap market,[1] to which it is closely linked. It is a separate principals' market, dealing in generic swaps that do not need to be linked to specific capital market transactions and that are hedged using a variety of techniques. As the market has developed, so have new applications that are not necessarily motivated by arbitrage or capital markets activity.

After providing a brief history of the currency swap market, we will establish the structure of a generic currency swap and describe the variety of swap structures that have been developed to address specific applications and hedging needs. For a full understanding of the possibilities of the currency swap market, an understanding of the pricing and valuation of currency swaps is useful. Pricing and

---

The authors wish to acknowledge their colleagues, Vince Balducci, Kumar Doraiswami, and Ali Satrap, who provided research assistance and helpful comments.
[1] Fixed rate versus floating rate in a single currency.

valuation are discussed in the balance of this chapter. The appendixes provide a more detailed discussion of the theory on which the principles of pricing are based, define the terms of a generic swap, summarize swap market conventions, and report the current availability of swaps in various currencies.

The Development of the Currency Swap Market

A currency swap in its original form occurred when a domestic issuer sold a foreign-currency bond in a foreign bond market, a foreign issuer sold a domestic-currency bond in the domestic bond market, and the two issuers swapped all cash flows, including initial proceeds, coupon payments and redemption of principal. Because this apparently is equivalent to each issuer selling in his own market, why should they go to the trouble of arranging a swap? The answer, of course, is that the two issuers may be received differently in the markets they enter. If each has an advantage—that is, can borrow at a lower rate—in the other's market, then a swap will be in their mutual interest. In fact, an advantage enjoyed by one party in the other's market may be large enough to make a swap work even when the counterparty enjoys no such advantage; all that is required is a net, or "relative," advantage.

In the first currency swaps, each party directly accepted the risk that its counterparty would not perform its obligations under the swap. Then intermediaries began to be used in "brokered" swaps to protect each of the counterparties from the credit risk of the other. This opened the market to lower-quality participants. Market makers soon realized that they could hedge their positions and thus were willing to position one side of the swap until the opposite side was found; simultaneous debt issues were no longer necessary. This was a major factor in the growth of the currency swap market.

Capital markets arbitrage continued to be a driving force in the market. A wave of new-issue yen swaps in 1985 and 1986, for example, was driven by an arbitrage that existed between the so-called sushi bond market, where Japanese borrowers could issue U.S. dollar–denominated bonds on favorable terms, and the Euroyen market, where certain high-quality, non-Japanese issuers received favorable terms.

Initially, currency swaps were used to create attractively priced domestic currency debt. More recently, as cross-border acquisition activity has increased, certain issuers in need of foreign-currency funding have found it cheaper to issue domestically and swap, thus reversing the traditional arbitrage by using currency swaps to create "synthetic" foreign debt. Today's nondollar markets, for example, in which investors are reluctant to accept "event" risk, are not receptive to many U.S. corporations. These corporations therefore use currency swaps to create nondollar funding, in contrast to the early U.S. users of currency swaps, who issued nondollar debt and swapped to dollars.

The marketplace has been expanded by the use of currency swaps in realms beyond the raising of new funds in the public or private debt markets. The currency swap, for example, to a large extent has supplanted the long-dated forward currency contract as a hedging vehicle, primarily because of the superior liquidity of the swap market.

The Currency Swap Structures

As the currency swap market has developed, a large variety of swap structures have emerged, to the point where the term *currency swap* can be used in its broadest sense to describe any exchange between two counterparties of two cash flow streams, each denominated in a different currency. To begin our discussion of swap structures, we describe the generic currency swap, which is the structure most often seen in the marketplace. We then discuss some of its most common variations. The swaps we describe are "at-the-market" swaps, that is, currency swaps in which flows reflect current market rates and no net exchange of principal is required at the outset.[2]

Generic Currency Swaps
A generic currency swap is a contract between two parties to exchange currencies at the current spot exchange rate at a future date (the maturity date) and to make periodic payments reflecting current market interest rates in the two currencies. This is in contrast to the traditional forward currency contract, which calls for no such periodic

---

[2]Throughout this chapter we speak of long-dated (longer than 12–18 months) currency swaps. The term *swap* is also used to describe a transaction in which a party simultaneously agrees to buy one currency (for example, yen) and sell another (for example, U.S. dollars) on a near date, and then to sell that same currency (that is, yen) and buy the other (that is, U.S. dollars) on a later date. These transactions are known as "foreign exchange swaps."

payments and instead incorporates the interest rate differential into the forward exchange rate in the form of a premium or discount applied to the spot exchange rate. Generic currency swaps are fixed-rate in one currency and either fixed-rate or floating-rate in the other. Although most early swaps were fixed-for-fixed, a structure that matched the cash flows of two fixed-rate bonds, fixed-for-floating currency swaps have become common. Figure D-1 in Appendix D defines the terms of a generic fixed-for-floating swap. In generic swaps, the cash flows match those of standard bullet maturity bonds[3] in the same currency. Figures D-2 and D-3 in Appendix D show the conventions for fixed-rate and floating-rate payments for generic swaps in the major currencies.

Currency swaps may or may not have an initial exchange of principal payments on the effective date of the swap. When an initial exchange occurs, the direction of currency flows is opposite to that of the remaining flows. In Deutschemark/U.S. dollar swap, for example, the Deutschemark payer would pay U.S. dollars and receive Deutschemarks in the initial exchange. The Deutschemark flows represent the cash flows on a Deutschemark loan, and the Deutschemarks received at the initiation represent the loan proceeds; the U.S. dollar flows represent the cash flows of a U.S. dollar asset, and the dollars paid at initiation represent the investment. In a generic Deutschemark/U.S. dollar swap, the periodic cash flows in each currency are at current market interest rate levels, the Deutschemarks received at initiation equal the Deutschemarks repaid at maturity, and the Deutschemark principal equals the U.S. dollar principal at the spot exchange rate. In the generic swap, the Deutschemarks received at initiation equal the U.S. dollars paid at initiation (at the current spot exchange rate). Therefore, the value of the swap is the same whether or not the initial exchange occurs, and its inclusion in the swap contract is a matter of convenience to the swap parties. If an exchange of cash from one currency to the other is desired for a particular application, the initial exchange is included. This usually is the case when swaps are used in conjunction with new borrowings.

Figure 1 is a diagram of the contractual cash flows associated with a generic fixed-for-fixed Deutschemark/U.S. dollar currency swap when the five-year Deutschemark swap rate is 8.00 percent annually, the five-year U.S. dollar swap rate is 9.00 percent semiannually, and

---

[3] Bullet maturity bonds are bonds that pay only interest prior to maturity, with all principal repaid at maturity.

the spot exchange rate is DM2.0/US$1; the swap has market coupons and principal amounts, US$100 million versus DM200 million, that are equal at the market spot exchange rate. Because the present value of the Deutschemark side (DM200 million) equals the present value of the U.S. dollar side (US$100 million) at the current exchange rate, an exchange of payments at initiation is not necessary. However, an at-the-market swap undertaken simultaneously with a bond issue is likely to call for an initial exchange of principal, because there are proceeds from the issuance that the issuer may want exchanged.[4]

FIGURE 1
Cash Flows for a Generic Fixed-for-Fixed Currency Swap (with No Initial Exchange of Principal)

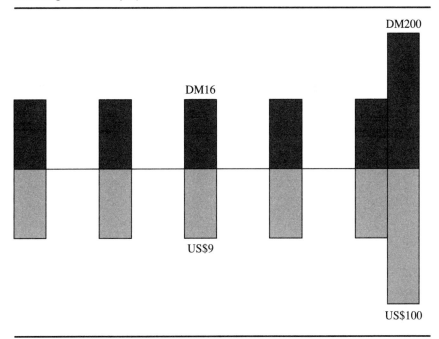

Note: For simplicity, the diagram shows U.S. dollar payments as annual, although they are actually semiannual payments.

---

[4]When a currency swap is entered into simultaneously with a bond issue, the swap usually is structured to match all of the cash flows associated with the bond issue. This may include new-issue premiums or discounts from par, underwriting fees and expenses, and paying agent fees, if any, in addition to the actual coupon and principal payments on the bond. As a result, swaps with new issue bonds may not be exact generic swaps, but they will be close.

Comparison with Interest Rate Swaps

Currency swaps share many features with interest rate swaps. Each is an exchange of payments between two counterparties, and in both cases, generic swaps take their structure from securities in the bond market. With an interest rate swap, the two principal amounts at maturity, like the two initial principal amounts, always offset each other, and no actual exchange occurs. In a currency swap, however, the principal repayments at maturity are actually exchanged under the terms of the swap, because these payments likely will not be equal and offsetting. When a swap involves principal in two different currencies, the contractual exchange rate may not coincide with the market exchange rate at termination; thus, the swap calls for a terminal exchange of principal. For this reason, *there is more counterparty credit exposure in a currency swap than in an ordinary interest rate swap.*[5]

A currency swap, like an interest rate swap, can be thought of as a matched asset and liability. The U.S. dollar payer in the currency swap of Figure 1, for example, has purchased a five-year Deutschemark asset and funded that purchase with a five-year U.S. dollar borrowing. This is analogous to an interest rate swap, where the fixed-rate payer has purchased a floating-rate asset with a fixed-rate liability.

Currency Swap Variations

Variations on the generic currency swap structure occur when the cash flow patterns of the asset and liability are altered from the typical bullet bond structure in a way that leaves their net present value equal to zero. There are many ways in which the cash flows can be altered. Common variations follow.

- *Annuity swaps.* Figure 2 shows an annuity swap in which level cash flow streams are matched, with no exchange of principal at the end.[6] The level DM17.73 million cash flow stream has the same present value, at the spot exchange rate, as the US$9 million stream. Note the contrast with Figure 1, where

---

[5] In a generic interest rate swap, both sides of the swap—the fixed rate and the floating rate—have equal value at initiation and at maturity. Although the swap may not have a value of zero in between because of interest rate changes, the fact that the value must return to zero at maturity serves as a "limiting" factor on the possible credit risk.

[6] The principal associated with an annuity is amortized over its lifetime. Like a mortgage, which is an annuity, the level payments contain an increasing proportion of principal and a decreasing proportion of interest.

FIGURE 2
Cash Flows for an Annuity Swap

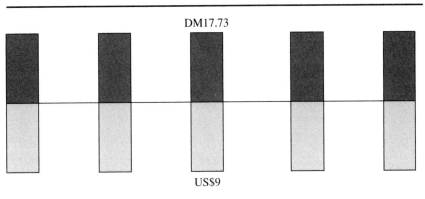

DM17.73

US$9

Note: For simplicity, the diagram shows U.S. dollar payments as annual, although they are actually semiannual payments.

the 8.00 percent Deutschemark rate gave a level coupon stream of DM16 million; because the principal amounts in Figure 1 do not have the same present value, the annuities obtained by removing them cannot have the same present value. To compute annuity swap levels correctly, same-maturity swap rates are generally insufficient, and annuity swap rates are required (see Example 3 later in this chapter).

- *Zero-coupon swaps.* Figure 3 shows a zero-coupon swap, in which the periodic payments (representing "coupon" payments) are removed and incorporated into the terminal amounts. This swap is equivalent to a long-dated forward contract. The US$105.78 million has the same present value as the DM200 million. These amounts reflect a five-year forward exchange rate of DM1.891/US$1, in contrast to Figure 1, in which the US$100 million versus DM200 million reflects the spot exchange rate. As with Figure 2, same-maturity swap rates are generally insufficient for pricing. In this case, zero-coupon rates are required (see Example 4).
- *Amortizing currency swaps.* A currency swap can be customized to incorporate virtually any pattern of cash flows in the two currencies, but the common structures are relatively bond-like. An amortizing currency swap is structured with a

FIGURE 3
Cash Flows for a Zero-Coupon Swap

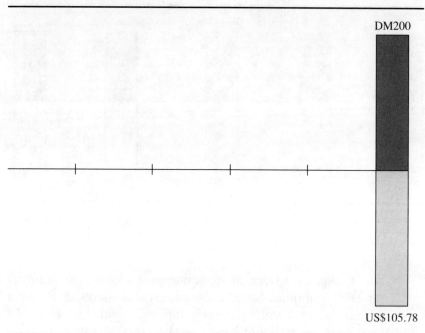

declining principal schedule, usually designed to match that of an amortizing asset or liability.[7] A typical application is project-financing loans, where the debt is paid down over a series of years as the project begins to generate cash.

- *Forward currency swaps.* A forward currency swap has the structure of a bond with forward settlement and may be used to hedge the interest rate and currency risk of a future foreign-currency borrowing. A forward swap has all terms set today but has an effective date in the future. On the effective date, the initial exchange of principal (if any) occurs, and interest

---

[7]An annuity swap is not, in general, an amortizing swap, although the two are similar. The principal repayment schedule of an annuity, like that of an ordinary mortgage, is a function of the interest rate at which it is priced. Thus, if the two sides of an annuity swap are priced at different interest rates, the two implicit principal repayment schedules cannot be the same, as they would be in an amortizing swap.

begins to accrue. Whether or not an exchange of principal oc-curs on the effective date will significantly affect the currency exposure of a forward swap.[8]

- *Basis swaps.* Floating-for-floating currency swaps with an ex-change of principal at the end are sometimes called basis swaps. They are used primarily to convert interest rate swaps to currency swaps and to link currency swaps quoted as fixed-for-U.S. dollar LIBOR (London Interbank Offered Rate) to floating rates in other currencies. The term *basis swap* is ap-plied more often to floating-for-floating swaps—one floating index for another—in a single currency.

Once an at-the-market swap has been entered into, its market value—the present value of the asset cash flows minus the present value of the liability cash flows—likely will not remain at zero and may become either positive or negative. The market value of a cur-rency swap is sensitive to the exchange rate and the asset and liability interest rates.[9] The interest rate exposure of a fixed-for-fixed currency swap is primarily to the interest rate *differential;*[10] thus, if the two interest rates move in the same direction, the exposure is mostly to the exchange rate. If the two interest rates move in opposite directions, however, it is possible for the interest rate impact on a fixed-for-fixed swap to dominate the exchange rate impact. The dynamics of currency swap value are discussed in more detail in the next section.

CURRENCY SWAP PRICING AND VALUATION

In this section, we use simple numerical examples to illustrate: (1) how the pricing of a currency swap is determined by market rates in three different markets—two interest rate swap markets and a for-eign exchange market; (2) how the interaction of these market rates determines the value of an off-market swap; and (3) how the results

---

[8]For a more detailed discussion of forward currency swaps, see Chapter 9, "Forward Cur-rency Swaps: An Instrument for Managing Interest Rate and Currency Exposure."

[9]Note the contrast with an interest rate swap, where the exposure is to a single interest rate.

[10]The interest rate exposure of a fixed-for-floating currency swap is to the fixed rate only.

of this interaction can be interpreted in an asset/liability framework. Certain aspects of the valuation process[11]—those related to the "term structure" of a given swap curve—are sufficiently technical that we have relegated them to the appendixes.

Currency swaps in all of their varied forms can be valued using one basic principle: The value of a swap equals the value of the asset component of the swap minus the value of the liability component. Mathematically, this principle is expressed by the equation

$$V = S \cdot Q^* \cdot P^* - Q \cdot P$$

where V = Value of the swap in domestic-currency units,

S = Spot price of the foreign currency (in domestic-currency units per foreign-currency unit),

Q^* = Amount of foreign bond (in foreign-currency units),

P^* = Price of foreign bond as a percentage of the amount Q^*,

Q = Amount of domestic bond (in domestic-currency units), and

P = Price of domestic bond as a percentage of the amount Q.

The term *bond* in these definitions refers to all of the payments in a single currency, and these may take the form of any fixed-income security, including annuities and floating-rate notes.[12] (When applied to annuities, the amounts Q and Q^* are the annual payments, and the prices P and P^* are the annuity factors described later.) Although the equation views the foreign bond as the asset and the domestic bond as the liability, this could be reversed by a change of sign. The prices P and P^* are computed using the relevant daycount/compounding conventions and *include accrued interest*.[13]

When this formula is used for pricing, S, P^*, and P are determined using market rates, and the amounts Q and Q^* are chosen to

---

[11] Namely, the relationships among annuity, zero-coupon, and par swap rates.

[12] Swap market convention assumes that a floating-rate note "flat"—no spread over or under the index—has a price of par on coupon reset dates.

[13] In the examples to be considered, which use the U.S. dollar and the Deutschemark as the two currencies, all pricing is on coupon dates; thus, there is no accrued interest.

make the value V equal to zero. This is the definition of an at-the-market swap. When the formula is used to compute the value of an off-market swap, the amounts Q and Q^* already are known, and the market prices P and P^* are used to compute the value V.

The use of the valuation formula will be illustrated with several examples, all of which are based on the simplified data given in Figure 4. However, before we look at the examples, there is an important question that must be answered.

What Discount Rate Should I Use?

The asset and liability components of a currency swap are valued separately. Each of these valuations involves the discounting of cash flows, and unless the yield curves are flat or an approximate swap value will do, one must take care that the proper discount rates are used. The examples considered here will ignore bid/offer spreads, but in practice, the components of a swap must be priced at the appropriate side of the market. Both currency and interest rate swaps represent financing costs for borrowers in the interbank market. The most readily available source of discount rates for valuing currency

FIGURE 4
Data for the Pricing and Valuation Examples

	Domestic	Foreign
Currency	U.S. dollar	Deutschemark
Two Years Ago		
Exchange rate	US$0.40 / DM1	DM2.50 / US$1
Seven-year swap rate	10.00% semiannual	7.00% annual
Today		
Exchange rate	US$0.50 / DM1	DM2 / US$1
Five-year swap rate	9.00% semiannual	8.00% annual
Five-year zero-coupon rate	9.50% semiannual	8.50% annual
Five-year annuity factor	4.125 semiannual	4.187 annual

swaps usually are the current interest rate swap levels. Because an at-the-market interest rate swap is a par bond matched with a floating-rate note of the same currency priced, by convention, at par, *current inter-est rate swap levels should be viewed as par bond coupons (and hence par bond yields) in both the interest rate swap and currency swap markets.* Premium (high-coupon) and discount (low-coupon) bonds are not traded at the par yield to maturity, because that would ignore the shape of the yield curve and misprice, for example, zero-coupon bonds. Instead, a premium or discount bond is viewed as a par bond plus or minus a level annuity consisting of the differential coupon. Pricing the asset and liability bonds of an off-market swap (finding P and P^* in the valuation formula) thus amounts to pricing the annu-ities that are to be added to or subtracted from par. To the extent that the shape of the yield curve makes it inaccurate to price zero-coupon bonds using par yields, it also is inaccurate to price these annuities using par yields.

Annuity Factors

Our method of pricing an annuity will be to use an "annuity factor" that can be thought of as either the price of a "unit" annuity—US$1 per annum[14] or DM1 per annum, for example—in the relevant cur-rency, or more properly, the price of an annuity expressed as a per-centage of its per-annum payment. A 10-year annuity factor of 6.50 (or 650 percent), for example, would mean that a 10-year annuity paying US$2 million per annum has a price of US$13 million. An-nuity factors (beyond one year and for nonastronomical interest rates) are greater than 1 (100%), just as zero-coupon bond prices are less than 1 (100%).

The five-year annuity factors to be used in Examples 2 and 3 are given as part of the simplified data in Figure 4. In fact, they can be derived from the five-year swap rates and the five-year zero-coupon rates given there, and they correspond to five-year "annuity rates" of 7.32 percent semiannual for the dollar and 6.22 percent annual for the Deutschemark. These computations, together with some further discussion, appear in Appendix A.

---

[14]If dollar rates are compounded semiannually, the unit US$1 annuity is paid in semiannual installments of US$0.50 each.

Example 1. At-the-Market Swap

Two years ago a U.S. corporation created a synthetic U.S. dollar liability by issuing a Deutschemark bond and swapping it into dollars with a seven-year currency swap. It agreed to receive fixed-rate Deutschemarks at 7.00 percent annually on DM250 million and pay fixed-rate dollars at 10.00 percent semiannually on US$100 million.[15] The swap, consisting of a DM250 asset (a 7.00 percent par bond) matched—at the then-current exchange rate—with a US$100 liability (a 10.00 percent par bond), was an at-the-market swap. Its value V was zero, as given by the valuation formula using $S = \text{US\$0.40/DM1}$, $Q^* = \text{DM250}$, $P^* = 1$ (100 percent), $Q = \text{US\$100}$, and $P = 1$ (100 percent):

$$
\begin{aligned}
V &= S \cdot Q^* \cdot P^* - Q \cdot P \\
&= 0.4 \cdot \text{DM250} \cdot 100\% - \text{US\$100} \cdot 100\% \\
&= \text{US\$100} - \text{US\$100} \\
&= 0
\end{aligned}
$$

Example 2. Off-Market Swap

Today, the issuer in Example 1 wishes to close out the swap. The exchange rate has moved and—through a combination of interest rate moves and aging[16]—today's five-year rates are different from yesterday's seven-year rates. As a result, the swap is now off-market and no longer has a value of zero. We first show how its new value is computed and then take a closer look at the factors that contribute to its change in value. Finally, we show how the value of an off-market swap can be interpreted when it takes the form of an up-front payment made or received upon entering the swap.

Valuation
To compute the value V of the swap in Example 1, we use the valuation formula with $Q^* = \text{DM250}$ and $Q = \text{US\$100}$, as before,

---

[15] For the remainder of this example and for the following three examples, all Deutschemark and U.S. dollar amounts are in millions.

[16] The asset and liability bonds in this example have "rolled down" positively sloped yield curves.

and S = US\$0.50/DM1, today's exchange rate. The bond prices P^* and P require a little more work. They must be computed as in the interest rate swap market, using par bonds and annuities.

P^* is now the price of a foreign five-year bond having a 7.00 percent coupon when the five-year par coupon is 8.00 percent—a discount bond. To price a discount (premium) bond, we view it as a par bond minus (plus) an annuity consisting of the coupon differential. Applying the five-year Deutschemark annuity factor of 4.187 to the 1.00 percent coupon differential of this example gives a value of $0.01 \cdot 4.187 = 0.04187$ (4.187 percent). The price of this discount bond—the price of the par bond minus the price of the annuity—is thus $P^* = 1 - 0.04187 = 0.95813$ (95.813 percent).

Similarly, P is the price of a domestic five-year bond having a 10.00 percent semiannual coupon when the five-year par coupon is 9.00 percent—a premium bond. Applying the five-year dollar annuity factor of 4.125 to the 1.00 percent coupon differential gives it a value of $0.01 \cdot 4.125 = 0.04125$ (4.125 percent). The price of this premium bond—the price of the par bond plus the price of the annuity—is now $P = 1 + 0.04125 = 1.04125$ (104.125 percent).

Putting everything together enables us to calculate the value of the swap:

$$
\begin{aligned}
V &= S \cdot Q^* \cdot P^* - Q \cdot P \\
&= 0.5 \cdot \text{DM250} \cdot 95.813\% - \text{US\$100} \cdot 104.125\% \\
&= \text{US\$119.77} - \text{US\$104.13} \\
&= \text{US\$15.64}
\end{aligned}
$$

All we have done here is price the 7.00 percent Deutschemark bond in its current 8.00 percent environment, price the 10.00 percent dollar bond in its current 9.00 percent environment, and net the two bond values at the spot exchange rate. Because the yield curves were not flat, we could not simply price the two bonds at 8.00 percent and 9.00 percent, which are *par* yields. If we had done so, the bond prices P^* and P would have been calculated incorrectly to be 96.007 percent and 103.956 percent, respectively, giving an incorrect swap value of US\$16.05.

Comparison of this computation with that in Example 1 should clarify how this swap has acquired a positive market value. The Deutschemark asset bond has lost value in its local currency. The U.S.

dollar liability bond has increased in value, causing the short U.S. dollar position to show a loss. However, the foreign currency in which the asset bond is denominated has increased in value by 25 percent, going from US$0.40/DM1 to US$0.50/DM1. *This currency gain dominates the interest rate losses on the bonds, leaving the net position with a positive market value.*

Dynamics of the Change in Swap Value

It is useful to decompose the change in value of a currency swap—in this case, the change from zero to US$15.64—into three components showing the contributions of the three factors affecting its value, namely, the exchange rate, the foreign interest rate, and the domestic interest rate. One possible decomposition is given by the following formula, where the symbol Δ is used to denote "change":

$$\Delta V = \Delta S \cdot Q^* \cdot P^*_{old} + S_{new} \cdot Q^* \cdot \Delta P^* - Q \cdot \Delta P$$

This rather imposing formula has three terms, one for each changing factor, and we examine them one at a time.

Suppose that the only factor that changes is the exchange rate. Its impact on the swap's value is called the *exchange rate effect,* and this is measured by the first term in the formula for ΔV.

$$\begin{aligned}
\text{Exchange rate effect} &= \Delta S \cdot Q^* \cdot P^*_{old} \\
&= (S_{new} - S_{old}) \cdot Q^* \cdot P^*_{old} \\
&= (0.5 - 0.4) \cdot \text{DM250} \cdot 100\% \\
&= \text{US\$25}
\end{aligned}$$

Now suppose that, after the exchange rate has moved, the asset interest rate (the Deutschemark interest rate) changes. The incremental impact of this change, *the asset interest rate effect,* is measured by the second term in the formula:[17]

---

[17]The asset interest rate effect, as defined here, includes a "second-order" exchange rate effect, because it incorporates the new exchange rate. To separate out a "pure" asset interest rate effect, we would have to introduce a "cross-product" term, $\Delta S \cdot Q^* \cdot \Delta P^*$, to the decomposition, which we have chosen not to do; it would add confusion if included and sacrifice exactness if excluded. Our decomposition, which is exact, is intended merely to illustrate the dynamics, not to create "official" definitions.

$$\text{Asset interest rate effect} = S_{\text{new}} \cdot Q^* \cdot \Delta P^*$$
$$= S_{\text{new}} \cdot Q^* \cdot (P^*_{\text{new}} - P^*_{\text{old}})$$
$$= 0.5 \cdot \text{DM250} \cdot (95.813\% - 100\%)$$
$$= 0.5 \cdot (-\text{DM}10.47)$$
$$= -\text{US\$}5.23$$

The third component of our decomposition is the impact of the liability interest rate move. This *liability interest rate effect* is measured by the third term in the formula:

$$\text{Liability interest rate effect} = -Q \cdot \Delta P$$
$$= -Q \cdot (P_{\text{new}} - P_{\text{old}})$$
$$= -\text{US\$}100 \cdot (104.125\% - 100\%)$$
$$= -\text{US\$}4.13$$

Adding all three effects gives the total change in value, US\$25 − US\$5.23 − US\$4.13 = US\$15.64, which we computed earlier. Notice how the combined interest rate effects (−US\$5.23 − US\$4.13 = −US\$9.36) have served to partially offset the exchange rate effect. If the exchange rate move had been smaller—or the durations[18] of the bonds greater—the total interest rate effect might have fully offset or even dominated the exchange rate effect.

The combined asset and liability interest rate effects on a fixed-for-fixed currency swap can be viewed as a single *interest rate differential effect*. The preceding example illustrates how changes in the interest rate differential affect the value of such a swap. The dollar/Deutschemark interest rate differential that affects this swap decreased by 200 basis points, from 3.00 percent two years ago (10.00 percent for U.S. dollars versus 7.00 percent for Deutschemarks) to 1.00 percent today (9.00 percent for U.S. dollars versus 8.00 percent for Deutschemarks), creating a negative total interest rate effect. If this interest rate differential had not changed, there would have been little net interest rate effect. If it had increased significantly, the total interest rate effect would have been positive.

---

[18]The (modified) duration of a bond is a measure of its price sensitivity to yield changes. Duration can be interpreted as the approximate percentage price change that accompanies a 100–basis point change in interest rates.

The change in value of a fixed-for-fixed currency swap thus can be viewed as the net result of only two effects—the exchange rate effect and the interest rate differential effect—and, barring strong views on possible correlations among the interest and exchange rates, these two effects may be considered independent. *As a rough "rule of thumb," the interest rate differential effect can be estimated by using the average duration*[19] *of the asset and liability bonds.* If, in the preceding example, we estimate the duration of a five-year bond at about four, the adverse interest rate differential move of 200 basis points means a loss of about 8 percent. Together with the 25 percent gain on the foreign currency, this gives an estimated net gain of about 17 percent, or US$17.[20] (The correct answer, as we have seen, is US$15.64.)

Off-Market Swap Value as an Up-Front Payment

The US$15.64 value of this off-market swap represents a payment that will be received by the issuer of Examples 1 and 2 when the swap is closed out. From the point of view of a U.S. dollar payer entering such a swap, it represents an *up-front payment* that must be made to the Deutschemark payer. The decomposition of the change in swap value given earlier can provide a useful way to view this payment. What is it for, and how does it look in a framework of matched assets and liabilities?

In a framework of matched assets and liabilities, an at-the-market swap has no up-front payment, and the value of the asset equals the value of the liability. In a swap with an up-front payment, the value of the asset differs from the value of the liability. The payment is made as compensation to the party that is receiving an asset whose value is less than that of the liability that it is taking on.

Using the decomposition of swap value as a guide, we can decompose the cash flows of the asset and liability sides of a swap into

---

[19]The relevant sensitivity measure in this context—100 times the "price value of a coupon basis point" for a par bond—turns out to be the annuity factor. With a flat yield curve, the annuity factor also is equal to 100 times the "price value of a (yield) basis point" for a par bond, which, in turn, is equal to the (modified) duration of the par bond.

[20]From the Deutschemark payer's point of view, the interest rate differential move is a gain of about 8 percent, and the investment in U.S. dollars is a loss of 20 percent, for an estimated net loss equal to roughly 12 percent of the DM250 principal amount, or DM30.

several assets and liabilities. First, as illustrated in Figure 5, we identify the annuities that represent the differentials between the coupon payments on the existing swap and the current market interest rates for a Deutschemark/U.S. dollar currency swap. The Deutschemark side decomposes into a DM250 par bond worth US$125 less a DM2.5 annuity worth US$5.23. The dollar side decomposes into a US$100 par bond plus a US$1 annuity worth US$4.13.

Next, we recognize that, at the current exchange rate, the two par bonds no longer constitute an at-the-market currency swap. As illustrated in Figure 6, by matching DM200 of the DM250 par bond with the US$100 par bond, we create an at-the-market currency swap (with a net value of zero) and leave an unmatched DM50 par bond worth US$25.

FIGURE 5
Decomposition of Off-Market Swap Into Annuities and Par Bonds

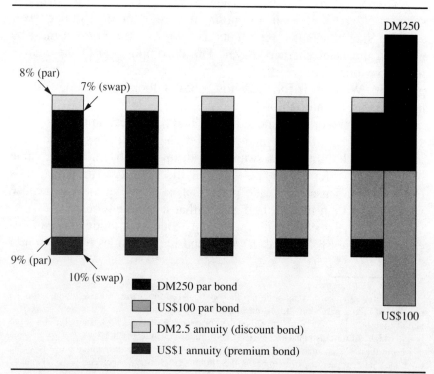

Note: The bars are not drawn to scale.

FIGURE 6
Decomposition of Par Bonds into an At-the-Market Swap Plus
an Additional Par Bond

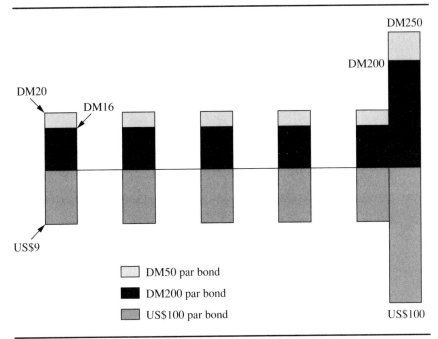

DM250

DM200

DM20

DM16

US$9

DM50 par bond

DM200 par bond

US$100 par bond

US$100

Note: The bars are not drawn to scale.

The up-front payment of US$15.64 thus consists of the values of three pieces: a DM50 par bond worth US$25, a DM2.5 annuity worth US$5.23, and a US$1 annuity worth US$4.13. Notice that the prices of these three pieces correspond to the exchange rate effect, asset interest rate effect, and liability interest rate effect, respectively. The two interest rate effects are represented by annuities (the difference between swap and market coupons), and the exchange rate effect is represented by a par bond.[21]

From the point of view of a dollar payer who pays US$15.64 to enter this swap, the swap is economically equivalent to the following

---

[21]When this decomposition method is applied to an interest rate swap, the entire up-front payment (excluding accrued interest) represents the value of an annuity, the difference between the swap's coupon and the current market coupon.

set of asset and liability transactions: (1) funding the purchase of an 8.00 percent DM200 asset with a 9.00 percent US$100 liability—a par swap with zero value, (2) receiving a US$5.23 loan repayable as a DM2.5 annuity, (3) receiving a US$4.13 loan repayable as a US$1 annuity, and (4) purchasing an 8.00 percent DM50 bond for US$25. The dollar payer, who receives assets worth US$25 and takes on liabilities worth only US$9.36, must pay the difference, US$15.64, to the Deutschemark payer. Another way to view the payment is that the dollar payer has purchased several assets, funded most of them with liabilities of matching value, and purchased one of them—US$15.64 of the 8.00 percent Deutschemark bond—for cash.

From the point of view of a Deutschemark payer who receives US$15.64 for entering this swap, it is economically equivalent to the following transactions: (1) funding the purchase of a 9.00 percent US$100 asset with an 8.00 percent DM200 liability—a par swap with zero value, (2) receiving a US$25 loan repayable as an 8.00 percent DM50 bond, (3) purchasing a DM2.5 annuity asset for US$5.23, and (4) purchasing a US$1 annuity asset for US$4.13. The Deutschemark payer, who receives assets worth only US$9.23 while taking on liabilities worth US$25, receives the difference in a compensating up-front payment. Alternatively, the Deutschemark payer has purchased several assets, funded all of them with liabilities of matching value, and received a cash loan of US$15.64, repayable as an 8.00 percent Deutschemark bond.

Example 3. Annuity Swap

Suppose that a U.S. corporation has sold a Deutschemark asset on an installment-sale basis and will receive five annual installments of DM20 each. It wishes to swap this five-year Deutschemark annuity into a five-year U.S. dollar annuity with semiannual payments. What is the amount (the per-annum payment) of the dollar annuity? The answer, US$10.15, can be computed either by reasoning from first principles or by formally applying the valuation formula.

Using first principles, we reason as follows: The five-year Deutschemark annuity factor is 4.187, which makes the DM20 annuity worth DM20 · 4.187 = DM83.74, or US$41.87 at today's exchange rate of US$0.50/DM1. With a five-year dollar annuity factor of 4.125, US$41.87 will purchase an annuity of US$41.87/4.125 = US$10.15, paid semiannually.

Alternatively, we can apply the valuation formula by setting $V = 0$, solving for Q, and "plugging in" $Q^* = DM20, P^* = 4.187, S = US\$0.50/DM1$, and $P = 4.125$. The formula becomes

$$0 = S \cdot Q^* \cdot P^* - Q \cdot P$$
$$Q = [S \cdot Q^* \cdot P^*]/P$$
$$= [0.5 \cdot DM20 \cdot 4.187]/4.125$$
$$= US\$41.87/4.125$$
$$= US\$10.15$$

As an additional example of a cross currency annuity calculation, we revisit Figure 2, where a five-year US\$9 annuity was converted to a Deutschemark annuity. Again, we can either reason from first principles or use the valuation formula, this time solving it for Q^*:

$$Q^* = [(1/S) \cdot Q \cdot P]/P^*$$
$$= [2.0 \cdot US\$9 \cdot 4.125]/4.187$$
$$= DM74.25/4.187$$
$$= DM17.73$$

Notice that, having worked out the first example, we could have simplified the second by reasoning (correctly) that if the US\$10.15 annuity is equivalent to DM20 annually, then a US\$9 annuity must be equivalent to $(9/10.15) \cdot DM20 = DM17.73$ annually.

Example 4. Long-Dated Forward

Suppose that a U.S corporation will need DM200 five years from now, perhaps for a large-scale purchase of equipment from a German manufacturer. Concerned about exchange rate exposure, it wishes to convert the DM200 liability to U.S. dollars. What is the dollar cost of DM200 five years forward?

Analytically, the corporation is swapping the DM200 face amount of a Deutschemark five-year zero-coupon bond for an unknown face amount Q of a U.S. dollar five-year zero-coupon bond.[22]

---

[22]The zero-coupon rates relevant to the pricing of long-dated forwards in the swap market can be computed using swap market annuity factors (or annuity rates), if these are available. See Appendix A for details.

Once again, we apply the valuation formula with $V = 0$, this time to zero-coupon bonds. Using the five-year Deutschemark zero-coupon rate (8.50 percent annual), we find that $P^* = 1/(1.085)^5 = 0.66505$ (66.505 percent). The five-year U.S. dollar zero-coupon rate (9.50 percent semiannual) gives $P = 1/(1.0475)^{10} = 0.62872$ (62.872 percent). Because we know $Q^* = DM200$ and $S = US\$0.50/DM1$, the valuation formula gives

$$Q = [S \cdot Q^* \cdot P^*]/P$$
$$= [0.5 \cdot DM200 \cdot 66.505\%]/62.872\%$$
$$= US\$105.78$$

Notice that pricing this zero-coupon swap is equivalent to computing a forward exchange rate: a dealer selling DM200 five years forward would hedge by purchasing an 8.50 percent five-year DM200 zero-coupon bond for $DM200/(1.085)^5 = DM133.01$, or US\$66.505 at the spot exchange rate.[23] It would be financed in dollars with a five-year 9.50 percent zero-coupon borrowing. The amount needed to repay this loan, $US\$66.505 \cdot (1.0475)^{10} = US\$105.78$, would be the forward price of the DM200, and any price significantly different could be arbitraged. The five-year forward exchange rate would thus be $US\$105.78/DM200 = US\$0.5289/DM1$, or DM1.891/US\$1.

Because the face amounts of zero-coupon bonds in Example 4 reflect the five-year forward exchange rate, we can focus on the forward exchange rate computation for its own sake. We find that

$$Q/Q^* = S \cdot P^*/P$$
$$= 0.5 \cdot (1.0475)^{10}/(1.085)^5$$
$$= 0.5 \cdot (1 + 0.095/2)^{2.5}/(1.085)^5$$
$$= US\$0.5289/DM1$$

The general formula for computing forward exchange rates is given in Appendix C.

---

[23]The hedging technique described here is somewhat idealized when applied to long-dated forwards. Techniques used in practice, however, are economically equivalent to the one described.

SUMMARY

A currency swap in its most general form is a fixed-income asset denominated in one currency, together with a fixed-income liability denominated in a second currency. In the most common swap structures, assets and liabilities are par coupon bonds or floating-rate notes, with liability and asset par amounts that are equal at the spot exchange rate. Many variations are possible. In two common ones, par bonds are replaced with level-pay annuities (annuity swaps) or zero-coupon bonds (long-dated forwards).

The value of a currency swap equals the value of the asset minus the value of the liability. The individual asset and liability securities are valued using the interest rates and conventions appropriate to each, and the asset value is converted to the liability currency (or vice versa) using the spot exchange rate. When a swap is initiated, the asset and liability are generally matched, that is, chosen to make the value of the swap equal to zero. As a swap ages, the individual asset and liability values are affected by interest rates in their respective currencies. The spot exchange rate, at which these values are netted, may also change. As a result, the swap becomes "off-market" and has a nonzero value that may be either positive or negative. The gain or loss represented by this value becomes realized if the swap is closed out prior to maturity.

APPENDIX A

PRICING ANNUITIES

An annuity can be viewed as a portfolio of zero-coupon bonds with different maturities, so it could be priced by discounting each of its cash flows individually at the appropriate zero-coupon rates. This method can require substantial amounts of computation and additional information, namely, all the necessary zero-coupon rates. Because zero-coupon rates are used to price swaps with irregular cash flows, dealers and other swap market participants often have software to convert a par swap curve to a set of zero-coupon rates; these computations cannot be done on the back of an envelope (see Appendix B). When annuities need to be priced "by hand," some shortcuts are available.

Annuity Rates

When a par swap curve is converted to a set of zero-coupon rates, it is easy to obtain a set of "annuity rates," one for each maturity.[24] These rates, if available, can be used to price annuities. An annuity rate is a single discount rate that is applied to all of the cash flows of an annuity to compute its price, generally using a financial calculator. If the price of an annuity is known, the corresponding annuity rate can be computed by finding the internal rate of return (IRR) of the annuity.

Annuity Factors

An annuity factor is defined as the price of a "unit" annuity—US$1 per annum or DM1 per annum, for example—in the relevant currency or, more properly, the price of an annuity expressed as a percentage of its per-annum payment. A 10-year annuity factor of 6.50 (or 650 percent), for example, would mean that a 10-year annuity paying US$2 million per annum has a price of US$13 million. The use of annuity factors to price annuities is illustrated in Examples 2 and 3. There are two easy ways to compute the annuity factors themselves.[25]

If the annuity rate is known, the annuity factor is readily computed with a financial calculator; one simply uses the annuity rate to find the price of the unit annuity. A 10-year annuity rate of 8.71 percent with annual compounding, for example, produces a 10-year annuity factor of 6.50: US$1 per year for 10 years paid annually and discounted at 8.71 percent annually has a present value of US$6.50. If the 8.71 percent is a semiannual rate, the annuity factor is 6.59: US$1 per year for 10 years *paid semiannually* and discounted at 8.71 percent semiannually has a present value of US$6.59.

If the annuity rate is not known, the annuity factor can be computed using the par and zero-coupon rates for the appropriate maturity. We use this approach to compute two five-year annuity factors, one for Deutschemarks and one for U.S. dollars, using the data from Figure 4.[26] The corresponding Deutschemark and dollar annuity rates— 6.22 percent annual and 7.32 percent semiannual, respectively—can

---

[24]See Appendix B.

[25]Each of these ways, however, requires a piece of information—an annuity rate or a zero-coupon rate—that, in practice, is obtained by converting a par swap curve to a zero-coupon curve, as outlined in Appendix B.

[26]Five-year swap rates: Deutschemarks 8.00 percent annual, U.S. dollars 9.00 percent semi-annual. Five-year zero-coupon rates: Deutschemarks 8.50 percent annual, U.S. dollars 9.50 percent semiannual.

be computed with a financial calculator; simply find the IRR of each unit annuity after setting its price equal to the annuity factor.

1. A five-year Deutschemark swap rate of 8.00 percent means that a five-year par bond (the fixed side of an at-the-market interest rate swap) has an 8.00 percent coupon. Using the five-year Deutschemark zero-coupon rate of 8.50 percent to compute the present value of the principal gives $1/(1.085)^5 = 0.66505$ (66.505 percent). That leaves $1 - 0.66505 = 0.33495$ (33.495 percent) as the present value of the coupons, an 8.00 percent annuity. To find the price of a "unit" annuity, we now divide by the per-annum coupon rate, arriving at a five-year Deutschemark annuity factor of $0.33495/0.08 = 4.187$ (418.7 percent).

2. Computation of the five-year U.S. dollar annuity factor is similar, except for the fact that compounding is semiannual. The principal of a five-year par bond, discounted at the five-year zero-coupon rate of 9.50 percent, has a present value of $1/(1.0475)^{10} = 0.62872$ (62.872 percent). The 9.00 percent coupons of the par bond have a present value of $1 - 0.62872 = 0.37128$ (37.128 percent). Dividing by the per-annum par coupon rate results in a five-year dollar annuity factor of $0.37128/0.09 = 4.125$ (412.5 percent).

Because the 9.00 percent U.S. dollar coupon is paid semiannually, the dollar annuity factor we have just computed should be applied to annuities whose per-annum payment is made semiannually. For example, the price of a five-year annuity paying US$1 per year in 10 semiannual installments of US$0.50 each is US$4.125.

Converting Annuity Rates to Zero-Coupon Rates

If the annuity rate and the par coupon for a given maturity are known, the zero-coupon rate for that maturity can be found by simply reversing the calculation that we have just performed: use the annuity rate or annuity factor to find the present value of the par coupons, and subtract this from par to get the present value of the principal. A glance at the last set of equations in Appendix B may help to clarify the relationship.

APPENDIX B

ZERO-COUPON BOND MATH

To show how a par yield curve can be converted to a set of zero-coupon rates and a corresponding set of annuity rates, we will assume annual compounding and a yield curve out to only three years. This may seem like a gross over-simplification, but it makes the mathematical notation less abstract and cumbersome with no real loss of generality, because the generalizations are so obvious. We also will view percentages of par as decimal numbers (100 percent is 1, for example, and 8.00 percent is 0.08) to avoid cluttering the equations.

Assume that a par yield curve is given, and denote the one-, two-, and three-year par coupons as c_1, c_2, and c_3, respectively. We want to find one-, two-, and three-year zero-coupon rates r_1, r_2, and r_3. Instead, we will concentrate on finding the zero-coupon bond *prices* Z_1, Z_2, and Z_3. If successful in computing the Zs, we can find the rs because we know that

$$Z_1 = 1/(1 + r_1)$$
$$Z_2 = 1/(1 + r_2)^2$$
$$Z_3 = 1/(1 + r_3)^3$$

Because coupon bonds are portfolios of zero-coupon bonds, we can write the one-, two-, and three-year par bond prices as

$$1 = (1 + c_1) \cdot Z_1$$
$$1 = c_2 \cdot Z_1 + (1 + c_2) \cdot Z_2$$
$$1 = c_3 \cdot Z_1 + c_3 \cdot Z_2 + (1 + c_3) \cdot Z_3$$

These are linear equations and are easy to solve for the unknowns Z_1, Z_2, and Z_3. You can see how a computer program (or matrix inversion routine) might go: Solve the first equation for Z_1, then use it to solve the second equation for Z_2, and use them both to solve the third equation for Z_3. That's it.

Once the Zs are found, the annuity factors A_1, A_2, and A_3 can be found either from their definitions,[27]

$$A_1 = Z_1$$
$$A_2 = Z_1 + Z_2$$
$$A_3 = Z_1 + Z_2 + Z_3$$

or by solving the par bond equations, rewritten as

$$1 = c_1 \cdot A_1 + Z_1$$
$$1 = c_2 \cdot A_2 + Z_2$$
$$1 = c_3 \cdot A_3 + Z_3$$

---

[27]With nonannual compounding, these definitions would incorporate the compounding frequency. With semiannual compounding, for example, the three-period annuity factor would be defined as *one-half* the sum of three zero-coupon bond prices, and the three-year (that is, six-period) annuity factor would be one-half the sum of six zero-coupon bond prices.

Notice this relationship among the three fundamental "building blocks"—par bonds, zero-coupon bonds, and annuities.[28]

If annuity rates a_1, a_2, and a_3 are needed, an IRR routine or other iterative approximating procedure (which has not been required up to this point) must be used to solve equations like the one defining a_3:

$$A_3 = 1/(1 + a_3) + 1/(1 + a_3)^2 + 1/(1 + a_3)^3$$

APPENDIX C

COMPUTING FORWARD EXCHANGE RATES

A general formula for computing forward exchange rates is given by

$$F = S \cdot (1 + r_d)^n / (1 + r_f)^n$$

where F = n-year forward price of the foreign currency (in domestic-currency units per foreign-currency unit),

S = Spot price of the foreign currency (in domestic-currency units per foreign-currency unit),

r_d = Domestic n-year zero-coupon interest rate, *compounded annually,* and

r_f = Foreign n-year zero-coupon interest rate, *compounded annually.*

If either of the interest rates has a nonannual compounding frequency, the appropriate substitution must be made in this formula. If the domestic rate is compounded semiannually, for example, then $(1 + r_d)^n$ must be replaced in the formula by $(1 + r_d/2)^{2n}$. *If the interest rates are money market rates*—as they would be for an ordinary short-dated forward contract, where n is a fraction of a year— they must be converted, if necessary, from discount rates to simple interest (or CD-equivalent) rates. Each $(1+r)^n$ term in the formula must then be replaced by a $(1 + r \cdot n)$ term, with the fraction n expressed using the appropriate daycount convention.

An attempt to incorporate every possible daycount/compounding convention into one grand formula leads to more notational trouble than it is worth. If any confusion should arise, the guiding principle is that the formula

---

[28]Examples illustrating the use of these par bond equations to compute annuity factors appear in Appendix A.

is derived from *prices*; interest rate conventions are useful—but ultimately arbitrary—ways of expressing them. The "grand formula" is as follows:

$$F = S \cdot Z_f / Z_d$$

where F = n-year forward price of the foreign currency (in domestic-currency units per foreign-currency unit),

S = Spot price of the foreign currency (in domestic-currency units per foreign-currency unit),

Z_f = Price of a foreign n-year zero-coupon bond as a percentage of the face amount, and

Z_d = Price of a domestic n-year zero-coupon bond as a percentage of the face amount.

Z_f and Z_d (which may be discount money market instruments when n is a fraction less than 1) now are priced using any appropriate market convention. Each Z is simply the present value of $1 (or other currency unit) paid n years from now, where n might be a fraction (such as 2 1/2) and might be less than 1.

There is a form of the "grand formula" favored by academics that explicitly shows the effect of the interest rate *differential* ($r_d - r_f$) on the forward price. We include it here for its elegance and because it is sometimes encountered in using option models. It employs *continuously compounded* interest rates and time τ in (possibly fractional) years:

$$F = S \cdot e^{r_d \tau} / e^{r_f \tau} = S \cdot e^{(r_d - r_f)\tau}$$

where F = τ-year forward price of the foreign currency (in domestic-currency units per foreign-currency unit),

S = Spot price of the foreign currency (in domestic-currency units per foreign-currency unit),

r_d = Domestic τ-year zero-coupon interest rate, *continuously compounded*, and

r_f = Foreign τ-year zero-coupon interest rate, *continuously compounded*.

There is a useful rule-of-thumb approximation that can be used when $(r_d - r_f)\tau$ is small:

$$F \approx S \cdot [1 + (r_d - r_f)\tau]$$

This approximation also can be used when r_d and r_f are not continuously compounded, provided that their compounding frequencies are not too different. As an example, we apply this approximation to the five-year forward exchange rate computed in Example 4. (This forward exchange rate was US$0.5289/DM1, or DM1.891/US$1, based on five-year zero-coupon rates of 9.50 percent semiannual for dollars and 8.50 percent annual for Deutschemarks.)

Viewing Deutschemarks as the foreign currency and U.S. dollars as the domestic currency, we approximate the five-year forward dollar/Deutschemark exchange rate, US\$0.5289/DM1, as follows:

$$0.5289 \approx 0.5 \cdot [1 + (0.095 - 0.085) \cdot 5]$$
$$= 0.5 \cdot (1 + 0.05)$$
$$= 0.5250$$

Alternatively, we could view the dollar as the foreign currency and the Deutschemark as the domestic currency, approximating the five-year forward Deutschemark/dollar exchange rate, DM1.891/US\$1, as follows:

$$1.891 \approx 2.0 \cdot [1 + (0.085 - 0.095) \cdot 5]$$
$$= 2.0 \cdot (1 - 0.05)$$
$$= 1.900$$

Whether or not the errors introduced—less than 1% in the example—are acceptable depends on the context, but this approximation can only be pushed so far. It is a good idea to experiment with realistic rates and time horizons before using the rule-of-thumb formula in a real-life situation.

Forward price formulas that highlight the interest rate differential should demonstrate, for the uninitiated, why the terms *high-coupon currency* and *discount currency* are synonymous, as are the terms *low-coupon currency* and *premium currency*.

APPENDIX D

MARKET CONVENTIONS

FIGURE D-1
Terms of a Generic Currency Swap (Fixed Non–U.S. Dollar vs. U.S. Dollar LIBOR)

Terms	Definitions
Maturity	Two to 10 years
Effective date	Two business days from trade date. The effective date is such that the first payment period for both counterparties is a full coupon period (that is, no long or short first coupons).
Settlement date	Effective date
Contractual exchange rate	Spot exchange rate
	Fixed Payment[a]
Currency	Non–U.S. dollar currency
Notional principal	Contractual exchange rate × U.S. dollar notional principal
Fixed coupon	Current Market rate in nondollar currency
Payment frequency	Either semiannually or annually
Daycount	Either 30/360 or actual/365
Pricing date	Trade date
	Floating Payment[b]
Currency	U.S. dollar
Floating index	U.S. dollar LIBOR
Spread	None
Determination source	Some publicly quoted source, for example, Reuters page LIBO
Payment frequency	The term of the floating index itself (i.e., six months for six-month LIBOR)
Daycount	Actual/360
Reset frequency	The term of the floating index itself
First coupon	Current U.S. dollar LIBOR
Up-front payment	None

[a] For details on fixed-payment standards for individual currencies, see Figure D-2.
[b] For details on floating-payment standards for individual currencies, see Figure D-3.

FIGURE D-2
Fixed-Rate Payment Standards for Currency Swaps

Currency	Payment Frequency	Daycount
Australian dollar	Semiannual	Actual/365
British pound	Semiannual	Actual/365
Canadian dollar	Semiannual	Actual/365
Danish krone	Annual	30/360
Deutschemark	Annual	30/360
Dutch guilder	Annual	30/360
European currency unit (ECU)	Annual	30/360
French franc	Annual	30/360
Italian lira	Annual	30/360
Japanese yen	Semiannual	Actual/365
New Zealand dollar	Semiannual	Actual/365
Swiss franc	Annual	30/360
U.S. dollar	Semiannual	30/360

Note: As a rule of thumb, the coupon payment standard for Japan and British Commonwealth member countries is semiannual (actual/365). In other countries, however, coupons are paid annually on a 30/360 basis, except in the United States, where coupons are paid semiannually on a 30/360 basis.

FIGURE D-3
Floating-Rate Payment Standards for Currency Swaps

Currency	Floating Index	Daycount	Cash Market Quotation Basis
Australian dollar	A$ BBR[a]	Actual/365	Discount
	A$ LIBOR	Actual/365	CD
British pound	£ LIBOR	Actual/365	CD
Canadian dollar	C$ BA[b]	Actual/365	Discount
	C$ TBILL[c]	Actual/365	Discount
Deutschemark	DM LIBOR	Actual/360	CD
	DM FIBOR[d]	Actual/360	CD
Dutch guilder	Dfl AIBOR[e]	Actual/360	CD
European currency unit (ECU)	ECU LIBOR	Actual/360	CD
	ECU PIBOR[f]	Actual/360	CD
French franc	FF PIBOR[g]	Actual/360	CD
Italian lira	Lit LIBOR	Actual/360	CD
Japanese yen	¥ LIBOR	Actual/365	CD
New Zealand dollar	NZ$ BBR[h]	Actual/365	Discount
Swiss franc	SF LIBOR	Actual/360	CD
U.S. dollar	US$ LIBOR	Actual/360	CD
	US$ prime	Actual/360	CD
	US$ Treasury bill	Actual/Actual	Discount
	US$ CD	Actual/360	CD
	US$ commercial paper	Actual/360	Discount
	US$ federal funds	Actual/360	CD
	US$ BA[i]	Actual/360	CD
	US$ TIBOR[j]	Actual/360	CD

[a] Australian dollar bills
[b] Canadian dollar Bankers' Acceptances
[c] Canadian Treasury bills
[d] Deutschemark Frankfurt Interbank Offered Rate
[e] Dutch guilder Amsterdam Interbank Offered Rate
[f] European currency unit Paris Interbank Offered Rate
[g] French franc Paris Interbank Offered Rate
[h] New Zealand dollar bills
[i] U.S. dollar Bankers' Acceptances
[j] U.S. dollar Tokyo Interbank Offered Rate

APPENDIX E

TABLE OF AVAILABILITY

FIGURE E-1
Availability of Currency Swaps

Currency	Size US$ (millions)	Maturity (years)	Secondary Liquidity
Australian dollar	50	10	Fair
British pound	100	10	Good
Canadian dollar	75	10	Fair
Deutschemark	100	10	Good
Dutch guilder	10	5–10	Fair
European currency unit (ECU)	75	10	Good
French franc	100	10	Good
Italian lira	10	3–5	Fair
Japanese yen	100	10	Good
New Zealand dollar	25	5	Fair
Swiss franc	50	10	Fair

Note: Indication is given only of the maximum size and maturity that could be executed on a "normal" trading day. Larger sizes and maturities can be executed, depending on market conditions.

CHAPTER 16

THE ROLE OF CURRENCY SWAPS IN INTEGRATING WORLD CAPITAL MARKETS

Donna J. Fletcher
Carl R. Beidleman
Lehigh University
Bethlehem, Pennsylvania

INTRODUCTION

During the 1980s the technological explosion transformed the nature of international financial markets. Enhanced computing power enabled intermediaries to provide investors with new products devised to manage the increasingly fluctuating interest and exchange rates. According to market participants and the financial press,[1] some of these products failed to provide the promised services (portfolio insurance is one example), whereas others have had profound impacts on world capital markets. This chapter examines the pervasive belief that interest rate and currency swaps have increased the integration of international capital markets. Specifically, the role of currency swaps in binding once-discrete national financial markets into a global whole is evaluated.

CAPITAL MARKET INTEGRATION

The Meaning of Integration

According to Akhtar and Weiller (1987), capital market integration, in general, refers to movements of assets between countries in response

---

[1]See, for example, the July 21, 190, issue of *The Economist*.

to actual or expected rates of return and other economic factors, given the existing regulations, market structures, and institutions. The degree of integration of a given set of markets lies somewhere between 0 and 100 percent, the latter denoted as perfect capital mobility. Researchers indicate that perfect capital mobility assumes the following:[2]

1. Instantaneous adjustment to portfolio equilibrium.
2. Perfect substitutability between foreign and domestic assets (e.g., no exchange rate or political risk).
3. No significant transactions costs.
4. No capital controls or other institutional impediments to capital flows.
5. Ex ante purchasing power parity.

Relaxing assumption 5 implies perfect financial integration, in which the interest rate on a domestic asset is equal to that on a similar (in terms of maturity and risk class) foreign financial asset adjusted for the expected change in the exchange rate. Thus, when financial markets are perfectly integrated, it is assumed that an investor can set asset prices or returns to conform to his or her expected values.[3]

Perfect financial market integration, although not implausible, precludes government intervention on the exchange rate and requires informationally efficient prices, rational expectations, and frictionless markets. Given the reality of transactions costs and differential information, the degree of financial integration of world capital markets is less than perfect, yet participants feel that the level has increased dramatically over the last decade.[4] To examine the reasoning behind this belief, we now focus on the recent dissipation of factors that have traditionally segmented capital markets, as well as the recent increase in factors that integrate.

Factors that Segment World Capital Markets

Capital markets are segmented when the price and/or return of a given asset differs in different markets, that is, the "law of one price"

---

[2] See Oxelheim (1990), Akhtar and Weiller (1987), Niehans (1984b), and Kohlhagen (1983).
[3] Levich (1985, p. 1027).
[4] See, for example, Handjinicolaou (1990), Lucas et al. (1987), and Cooper (1986).

does not hold.[5] Prices differ due to market anomalies or because of capital controls that do not permit universal access to specific investment/borrowing needs. Segmentation of financial markets can therefore occur due to government controls, regulatory dissimilarities, differential taxation, differential information, differential borrowing costs, and market saturation.

As Handjinicolaou (1990) argued, technically there is no single market that is freely accessible to all investors, yet the above-mentioned factors that segment international capital markets have diminished—either directly, as in the case of deregulation of capital controls, or indirectly through arbitrage. Beidleman (1985, p. 45) states that arbitrage involves the simultaneous purchase and sale of an identical (similar) asset in different markets, risklessly profiting from the market anomalies causing the price differences. Normally, arbitrage transactions operate to eliminate their own incentive, yet until the advent of the financial swap facility,[6] certain market inefficiencies had not been fully exploited.

One market anomaly exploited by interest rate and currency swaps is differential credit risk premiums (or borrowing costs) between currency markets. Table 1 illustrates an example of this anomaly arising from a credit risk premium in U.S. dollars of 1.5 percent as opposed to a 0.5 percent credit risk premium in Swiss francs between counterparty A, the better-quality borrower, and counterparty B. Table 2 shows calculation of the gain resulting from this market anomaly. The total gain is equal to the difference between the price of the credit differential in the Swiss franc market as compared to the U.S. dollar market and is shared by both counterparties and the intermediary.[7]

---

[5]Kohlhagen (1983, p. 114) noted that if there is evidence that market participants are bearing diversifiable risk on some financial assets (i.e., when the risk-adjusted rate of return on such assets is lower than on assets with no such risk), the markets are segmented.

[6]Handjinicolaou (1990) stated that the volatility of interest and exchange rates in a financial environment of deregulation prompted the exploitation of these market anomalies beginning with the introduction of swaps in 1981. It is also important to note that the technological and communication explosion contributed to the advent of the swap facility, which enabled arbitrage of previously unexploited market anomalies.

[7]Cooper (1986, p. 5) provided the example that is the basis of the tables.

TABLE 1
Capital Market Credit Risk Premium

		Fixed five-year borrowing rates		
		SF	US$	Net
A		7.00	15.00	
B		7.50	16.50	
	Difference	0.50	1.50	1.00

Handjinicolaou (1990) and Beidleman (1985) noted that this anomaly is an indication of informational inefficiency, which provides one source of market segmentation that can be exploited by currency swaps: name arbitrage. If capital markets were perfectly integrated in the sense that every agent within each market possessed the same information, corporations would be evaluated identically and thus be able to raise funds at the same credit risk premium. A number of large, well-known firms, however, use their names to achieve lower costs of funding than are available in their domestic capital markets. The spread compression that results from this anomaly is exploited through currency swaps, interest rate swaps, and a combination of the two (cross currency swaps). As is inherent in the process of arbitrage, the cost saving resulting from the use of financial swaps has been significantly reduced, indicating that differential borrowing costs no longer effectively segment the fixed-rate currency markets.

TABLE 2
Net Gains from the Swap

	Direct Borrowing Cost	Cost with Swap	Gain
A	7.00	6.50	0.50
B	16.50	16.25	0.25
Bank			0.25
Total			1.00

Other market inefficiencies that can be exploited by financial swaps include differential tax rates[8] and regulatory dissimilarities.[9] Again, the arbitrage profits (and hence factors that segment international capital markets) have narrowed, yet the use of swaps continues to grow. Smith, Smithson, and Wakeman (1986) claim that the reason for the continued growth of the swap market is that swaps contribute to market completeness by filling gaps left by missing markets. For example, currency and interest rate swaps have been used to create a synthetic Swiss Treasury bill market. Thus, international capital markets have become more integrated through this financial innovation. A more detailed discussion of financial innovation, as well as other factors that contribute to the recent increase in capital market integration, follows.

Factors that Integrate World Capital Markets

Harries (1987) noted that financial innovation has increased significantly in the last three decades, representing a long-term trend rather than a cyclical development that will recede in the near future. During the 1960s, rapid economic growth and increasing capital mobility in the industrialized countries spurred many governments to implement capital controls in defense of the fixed exchange rate system. Banks quickly circumvented these and other regulatory constraints, introducing such financial innovations as Eurodollars, Eurobonds, and parallel loans. The decade of the 1970s, in contrast, was characterized by increased instability and volatility of exchange rates, interest rates, and inflation rates, and produced innovations to cope with exchange and interest rate risks.[10]

Financial innovation in the 1980s and beyond has been stimulated by the continued volatility of interest and exchange rates, as well as the following factors, which will be shown to have also increased the integration of international capital markets:

---

[8]Lucas et al. (1987) and Smith, Smithson, and Wakeman (1986) gave examples of tax arbitrage achieved through cross currency and interest rate swaps.

[9]Kasman and Pigott (1988), Akhtar and Weiller (1987), and Lucas et al. (1987) discuss the circumvention of regulatory constraints enabled by financial swaps.

[10]Dufey and Giddy (1981).

1. Computer/telecommunication capability and other technological advances.
2. Competition among financial intermediaries.
3. Concomitant user sophistication.

Technological change appears to be the most inexorable of these factors, as the electronic revolution and real-time communication have significantly reduced transactions costs. Cooper (1986) and Lucas et al. (1987) argued also that technological advances have led to user sophistication, augmenting the already fierce competition among financial intermediaries.

Each of these factors stimulating financial innovation has reduced spreads (or transactions costs) on conventional transactions to the breakeven point. Niehans (1984a) noted that where transactions costs are low, the yields for comparable securities in terms of risk and maturity must be virtually equal, and markets approach full integration. Moreover, according to Handjinicolaou (1990), Kasman and Pigott (1988), and Taylor (1988), financial innovation in response to the need to manage and transfer risk helps to integrate capital markets by allowing investors and borrowers access to markets previously denied to them. Thus, financial innovation increases the level of capital market integration, reduces transactions costs, and encourages still more financial innovation and subsequent integration.

Given the linkage between financial innovations and capital market integration, attention is now focused on the role of the currency swap.

EVOLUTION OF CURRENCY SWAPS AND LINKAGES TO OTHER SWAP MARKETS

As Clinton (1988, p. 359) points out, the swap facility existed in foreign exchange long before the recent upsurge in commercial swaps. The so-called exchange market swap is a facility in the short-dated forward exchange markets whereby banks quote a bid/ask price for spot and forward exchange, known as the swap rate. This swap rate quote is equivalent to the forward premium or discount on the relevant exchange rate.

The recent phenomenon of financial swaps began with a longer-dated version of the exchange market swap. It was originally called a currency swap, denoted here as a fixed-rate currency swap. As with its longer-dated predecessor, the parallel loan, under the fixed-rate currency swap structure, principal and interest denominated in one currency are swapped for principal and interest in another. Following the period of fixed exchange rates, many early participants sought low funding rates in low-interest-rate currencies to protect themselves from changes in exchange rates. These participants searched for currency cover utilizing parallel loans, back-to-back loans, and subsequently currency swaps. Intermediaries arranged these swaps on a tailored basis, matching counterparties by currency and principal amounts desired.[11] This hedging application of swaps was soon supplemented by capital market arbitrage applications. As demonstrated in Tables 1 and 2, borrowing rate differentials for higher-quality credits versus lower-quality credits between the two currencies enabled a cost savings for both participants and the intermediary arranging the swap.

The arbitraging of market anomalies between currencies soon led to similar activity within the same currency through utilization of the "plain vanilla" interest rate swap, wherein floating-rate interest payments are exchanged for fixed-rate payments. Next a combination of the fixed-rate currency swap and the interest rate swap appeared, denoted as a cross currency swap. Here the interest rate in one currency is fixed and the rate in the other is floating. Market pricing convention today is to quote cross currency swap rates and interest rate swap rates, rather than directly quoting fixed currency swap rates as such.[12] Batlin (1991) notes that the implication of the current pricing convention is that the exposure created by a standard cross currency swap is the sum of the exposures of a U.S. dollar interest rate swap and a fixed-rate currency swap.

The decomposition of the cross currency swap into its component swaps became important in identifying arbitrage opportunities within the swap market itself. Financial engineering afforded the opportunity to combine swaps in forming variations of the basic swap instrument

---

[11]Smith, Smithson, and Wakeman (1986).

[12]According to Smith, Smithson, and Wakeman (1986), matching of counterparties was not as difficult in the U.S. dollar interest rate swap market as in the fixed-rate currency swap market. Moreover, the product became homogeneous, and the demand for matched deals dissipated. Consequently, directly quoting fixed-for-fixed currency swap rates was no longer necessary because these swaps could be synthesized by a combination of swaps of foreign fixed-rate versus dollar LIBOR, where the LIBOR flows offset each other.

or disaggregating complex swaps into their component parts. Examples of variations to the basic swaps include forward swaps, amortized swaps, roller coaster swaps, swaptions, caps, floors, and collars, which are discussed more fully in Chapter 6.

Thus, the swap market grew out of the arbitrage process, enabling further integration through continued arbitrage. Practitioners agree that the result of the use of financial swaps in international finance is increased integration of capital markets. As demonstrated in Figure 1, Handjinicolaou (1990) noted that the interest rate swap markets are integrally linked to the local money and capital markets, and at the same time, these markets are linked with the currency swap sectors, composing an international web of satellite markets. Changes in one of the satellite markets are transmitted through swaps to the other markets in the web.

Despite the intermarket linkages, there has been no published empirical work to date to verify the theoretical premise of integration

FIGURE 1
The Fixed- and Floating-Rate Financial Swaps Markets

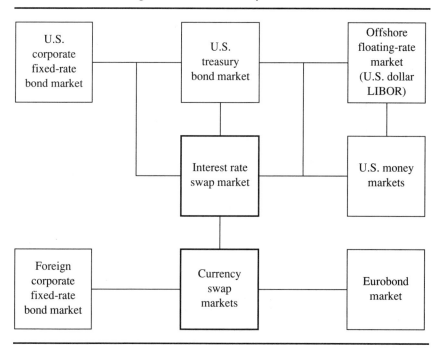

among the long-dated capital markets. Both Clinton (1988) and Mahajan and Mehta (1986) tested for evidence of capital market integration using the short-dated exchange market swap. Their respective works evaluated the covered interest parity (CIP) and uncovered interest parity (UIP) conditions. These measures of capital market integration and the model chosen to test for evidence of world capital market integration brought about by currency swaps are presented in the next section.

MEASURES OF INTEGRATION

Interest Differential Models in General

Oxelheim (1990, p. 6) suggested that there are three alternative approaches for evaluating financial integration:

1. Study the interest sensitivity of capital flows, through either covered or uncovered interest differentials.
2. Measure the reflow of capital.
3. Analyze the relationship among interest rates in different countries, again using covered or uncovered interest differentials.

Given the difficulty of obtaining a consistent measure across countries for the size of capital flows, the last approach has been chosen for this empirical study.

It is important to understand the degree of financial integration assumed under the UIP and CIP conditions. Empirical studies of perfect financial integration evaluate the UIP condition, which links the interest rate differential to the expected change in the future spot exchange rate. These studies have been unable to establish conclusive evidence of perfect financial integration.[13] It has been conjectured that

---

[13] See Akhtar and Weiller (1987), Levich (1985), Loopesko (1984), and Kohlhagen (1983) for summaries of UIP studies. Fama (1984) found evidence of a risk premium that varies over time, as well as variation in the expected future spot rate component of forward rates. Loopesko found some evidence of imperfect asset substitutability and inefficient use of the information set by rational investors. Leddin (1988) found evidence of a risk premium and determined that UIP does not hold.

these tests failed due to the use of ex post data in testing ex ante theory (especially as proxies for unobservable expectational variables), rather than because capital markets are less than perfectly integrated. Akhtar and Weiller (1987) argue that if capital markets are not perfectly integrated, the failure of UIP may be attributable to imperfect asset substitution (the presence of a risk premium) or to other sources of market inefficiency. In either case, it can be safely stated that perfect financial market integration has not been established.

Covered Interest Parity Models of Capital Market Integration

Evidence of less-than-perfect financial market integration, denoted here as (covered) capital market integration, has been established empirically. CIP theory maintains that, in equilibrium, the premium (or discount) on a forward contract for foreign exchange is equal to the interest differential between the two currencies. The pair of domestic and foreign assets should be identical in all respects (maturity, risk class, etc.) except for the currency of denomination.[14] When the covered interest rate parity relationship is not upheld, it may be possible to undertake covered interest arbitrage to extract a risk-free profit from the market inefficiency that caused the parity relationship to break down.

Empirical studies of the degree of capital market integration using CIP models have focused on the short-dated offshore Eurocurrency markets primarily, and also on the short-dated domestic capital markets.[15] Although all of these studies find deviations from covered interest parity, the profit opportunities are quite small and short-lived when account is made of the following factors that cause market inefficiencies:

1. Transactions costs.
2. Differential political risk.
3. Less-than-infinite elasticities of demand and supply of foreign exchange and securities.
4. Differential taxes.

---

[14]Reinhart and Weiller (1987, p. 125).

[15]See, for example, Maasoumi and Pippenger (1989), Clinton (1988), Bahmani-Oskooee and Das (1985), Hilley et al. (1979), Frenkel and Levich (1975, 1977), and Aliber (1973).

The presence of market inefficiencies precludes complete capital market integration, establishing a band around covered interest parity expectations, the width of which is determined by the impact of these anomalies. Moreover, as noted by Hilley et al. (1979) and Levich (1985), these inefficiencies are interrelated. For example, "during a speculative crisis, deviations of the forward rate from the parity rate may be due to both higher transactions costs and heavy speculative pressure, causing the supply of arbitrage funds to become inelastic."[16]

It is important to distinguish financial market efficiency and equilibrium within the context of the covered interest parity condition. Oxelheim (1990, p. 4) presented the consensus of the majority of researchers in stating that "if the differential in expected risk-adjusted returns is greater than zero but less than or the same as transactions cost, we can say that markets are disintegrated, but nonetheless efficient." Yet transactions costs inhibit trades, and caution is warranted in relating the absence of profit opportunities from covered interest parity that do not exceed transactions costs to financial market efficiency.[17] Rather, it can be stated that (1) the CIP equilibrium condition is maintained when deviations from parity are less than or equal to transactions costs, and (2) the larger the transactions costs of trading in particular markets, the less efficient are such markets.

Beyond the theoretical efficiency issue, limitations of empirical testing of capital market integration using CIP models include a lack of consistency, both in methodology and in proxies for transaction costs; the absence of testing of the longer-dated securities markets;[18] and lack of evidence of integration through time. The empirical study presented in this chapter addresses the latter two issues.

To test for CIP, it is necessary that a forward exchange market exist in order to cover the exchange rate risk. Up until 1981, with the advent of currency swaps, the longer-dated forward currency quotations were in short supply and contained exceedingly high transactions costs, reflecting market makers' reluctance to carry substantial credit risks and tie up capital for more than three years.[19] The recent devel-

---

[16]Hilley et al. (1979, p. 4).
[17]See Clinton (1988) and LeRoy (1989) for further arguments along this line.
[18]The working paper by Popper (1987) is a noted exception.
[19]Hilley et al. (1979).

opment of the currency swap market now provides the requisite cover and enables empirical evaluation of capital market integration in the longer-dated maturities. Development of the theoretical and empirical model that employs currency swaps as an arbitrage instrument in testing covered interest arbitrage is presented next.

Theoretical Models

The proposed model is based on the theory that covered interest parity suggests that a foreign return that is covered for exchange rate risk through a fixed-rate currency swap should be equal to the domestic return (for securities of the same risk class and maturity). This relationship can be seen in equation (1):

$$i_{t,T}^e - i_{t,T}^{SW} = i_{t,T}^{*e} - i_{t,T}^{*SW} \tag{1}$$

where $i_{t,T}^e$ = Domestic Eurobond interest rate

$i_{t,T}^{SW}$ = Currency swap fixed interest rate on the domestic currency

$i_{t,T}^{*e}$ = Foreign Eurobond interest rate

$i_{t,T}^{*SW}$ = Currency swap fixed interest rate on the foreign currency

All rates are given at time t for maturity at T. Rearranging terms so as to focus on deviations from covered interest parity results in equation (2), which can be utilized for empirical testing.

$$(i_{t,T}^e - i_{t,T}^{SW}) - (i_{t,T}^{*e} - i_{t,T}^{*SW}) = \alpha + \epsilon_t \tag{2}$$

where ϵ_t is a disturbance term.

Equation (2) posits an equilibrium condition, which may not be upheld in empirical testing for the following reason. Covered interest parity may not hold in the currency swap market due to the presence of some market imperfection (e.g., less-than-infinite elasticities in the securities and exchange markets, or differential political risk). Tests of equation (2) simultaneously test for the existence of covered interest arbitrage and the degree of capital market integration brought about by currency swaps.

In frictionless markets with comparable degrees of political risk, the conditional mean of the differential between "swap" covered nominal interest rates should be zero. This suggests that the expected value of the coefficient α would be zero:

$$E[\alpha] = 0$$

However, transactions costs are present in the long-dated securities markets. Therefore, they must be accounted for in the revised empirical model, as shown in equation (3):

$$|Y| = (i_{t,T}^{e} - i_{t,T}^{SW}) - (i_{t,T}^{*e} - i_{t,T}^{*SW}) = \alpha + \beta_1 TC_t + \epsilon_t \qquad (3)$$

where TC_t = Transactions costs
$|Y|$ = Absolute value of deviations from CIP

In equilibrium, transactions costs should account for all of the deviations from CIP. Thus, the expected value of the coefficient β_1 would equal 1:

$$E[\beta_1] = 1$$

Econometric Considerations

Limited-Dependent-Variable Models
Maasoumi and Pippenger (1989), in response to an article by Bahmani-Oskooee and Das (1985), argue that an ordinary-least-squares (OLS) regression of $|Y|$ on TC does not indicate how much (or how little) TC will account for seemingly unexploited covered interest arbitrage opportunities. As illustrated in Figure 2, all of the deviations from CIP, $|Y|$, are less than TC. Thus, transaction costs provide a simple economic explanation for all the deviations from CIP, yet an OLS specification of equation (3) would indicate no discernible correlation between the deviations from covered interest arbitrage and transactions costs.[20]

These researchers imply that it is important to segregate the CIP conditions into two regimes:

---

[20]Maenning and Tease (1987) also note that (OLS) regression analysis alone may lead to incorrect conclusions in the presence of transactions costs.

FIGURE 2
Equilibrium Condition under CIP: |Y| ≤ TC

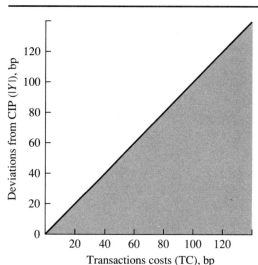

1. *Equilibrium:* All of $|Y|$ is within a band defined by TC. There are no profitable trading opportunities in excess of TC. Thus, $|Y| - \text{TC} \leq 0$.
2. *Disequilibrium:* Profitable trading opportunities through CIP exist in excess of transactions costs. Thus, $|Y| - \text{TC} > 0$.

Because there are two regimes, Maasoumi and Pippenger suggest, but fail to demonstrate, that the inconsistency and bias resulting from an OLS specification can be eliminated by a type of endogenous switching equilibrium/disequilibrium regression model. Maddala (1983) and Quandt (1978) note that such modeling requires knowledge of the distribution of the disturbance term, ϵ_t, with respect to either when equilibrium "switches" to disequilibrium or the behavior of the disturbance term under both regimes.

As can be seen in Figure 2, it can be argued that transactions costs represent an upper bound on the absolute value of deviations from CIP. Consequently, equation (3) will be estimated through a limited-dependent-variable model, adjusting for the equilibrium/disequilibrium switching point at the level $|Y| - TC = 0$. One type of limited-dependent-variable model is a Tobit, or censored regression, model. This specification has been chosen because a priori knowledge of the switching point is not available.[21] The data are "censored" by setting those deviations from parity that are less than or equal to transactions costs equal to zero.

Because equilibrium observations have been censored (set equal to zero), the actual value of these net deviations is no longer known. Thus, the equilibrium condition under CIP is latent, or unobserved. Yet the Tobit specification utilizes all observations of deviations from CIP, both those that are at the limit of $|Y| - TC \leq 0$ (or in equilibrium) and those that are greater than TC (or in disequilibrium), by incorporating the probability that a given observation of $|Y|$ falls within the equilibrium or disequilibrium regime. Thus, estimation of equation (3)[22] measures the expected value of net deviations from parity, whether the capital markets are in equilibrium or disequilibrium. If there are no profit opportunities in excess of transactions costs from CIP in using fixed-rate currency swaps to cover the exchange rate risk, the expected values of α and β_1 should be as follows:

$$E[\alpha] \leq 0$$

$$E[\beta_1] \leq 0$$

Figure 3 delineates the two regimes, equilibrium and disequilibrium, captured by the Tobit specification. If the CIP condition exists in the longer-dated securities markets tested, then as transactions costs rise, net deviations from parity in excess of transactions costs $(|Y| - TC)$ should fall, and the capital markets tested can be considered in equilibrium. A sign of disequilibrium would be a positive relationship between TC and $(|Y| - TC)$, indicating some market anomalies/imperfections remain and total (covered) capital market integration has not been accomplished through the use of currency swaps.

---

[21] Admittedly, a better specification of the switching mechanism would include proxies of the market anomalies that account for unexploited covered interest arbitrage profit opportunities. The difficulty of obtaining such proxies as well as the absence of a priori knowledge regarding which market anomalies are present preclude modeling of the switching mechanism beyond $|Y| - TC = 0$. Also, some information is lost by manually censoring the data, yet the Tobit does capture both the equilibrium and disequilibrium regimes and provides consistent parameter estimation.

[22] The actual Tobit specification is not presented in this chapter. Please refer to Fletcher (1991) for details of the Tobit or censored regression.

FIGURE 3
Disequilibrium and Equilibrium Regimes of Covered Interest Parity

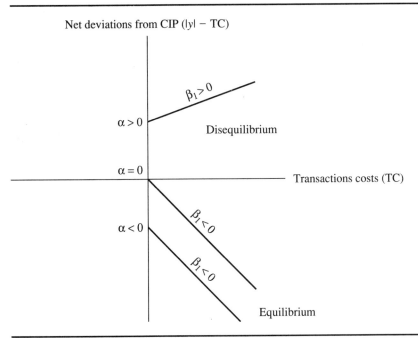

Thus, β_1 would be positive, and TC would be a proxy for market inefficiencies in excess of ($|Y| - $ TC) yet related to transactions costs, such as differential information or political risk.[23] Moreover, a positive value for α would also indicate a market imperfection that is constant over time, such as brokerage fees.

Autoregressive Disturbance Term
Given the fact that the data to be tested are drawn from a series of weekly observations of the fixed-rate currency swap rates and Eurobond and foreign bond interest rates, there is reason to suspect serial correlation in the disturbance term, ϵ_t. Because the data are censored,

---

[23]As discussed in the following section, foreign bond interest rates were used for the Swiss franc and Japanese securities. Consequently, the presence of political risk is possible in these onshore markets.

it is not possible to determine the order of the autoregressive correlation. Therefore, lagged values for both the dependent and independent variables were included in the model specification. For example, it was necessary to use one lag length to eliminate the serial correlation displayed by the data in the British pound–U.S. dollar five-year market. Thus, equation (3) for this market was estimated using the following single-lag specification:

$$|Y| = \alpha + \beta_1 TC + \beta_2 |Y|_{t-1} + \beta_3 TC_{t-1}$$

The particular lag structure was determined by using successive lag lengths until the serial correlation was eliminated.

Specification of Data

The domestic currency is herein represented by the U.S. dollar (US$), and the foreign currencies include the Canadian dollar (C$), the West German Deutschemark (DM), the Japanese yen (¥), the British pound (£), and the Swiss franc (SF). Regulations in the Swiss capital markets do not permit Eurobond trading. Moreover, Japanese Eurobonds were not extensively traded before the latter part of 1986. Consequently, the Swiss franc and yen uncovered yields were represented by onshore markets: the foreign market in Swiss franc–denominated securities and the Japanese Samauri market, respectively.

Data on the Eurobond and onshore market yields were provided by Salomon Brothers Inc.'s bond market research publication, *International Market Roundup*. These interest rates represent average yields on a sample of prime issues, quoted at 2:00 P.M., London time. Cross currency swap data and interest rate swap data also came from this source and were supplemented by data obtained from Security Pacific Hoare Govette Ltd.

The overall time period tested covered weekly observations on consecutive Thursdays from October 3, 1985, to March 2, 1989. Covered interest parity conditions were evaluated for the five-year maturity securities over the entire period. The seven-year maturity spectrum was evaluated from October 3, 1985, to September 24, 1987; the test period for the 10-year maturity securities began on October 1, 1987, and ended on March 2, 1989.

Following Clinton (1988), measurement error must be taken into account. Point estimates of deviations from CIP calculated from posted bid and ask quotations will not in general be equal to the actual deviations on either side of the bid or ask price because the quotations define only a range within which trades may take place. Thus, all of the interest rates used in this study were midrates, halfway in between the posted bid and ask quotations.

Moreover, Clinton (1988) found that the bounds on measured deviations from parity (or the size of transactions costs) were given by the lower of the sum of the bid/ask spreads on the two Eurocurrencies, or the spread on the swap. Bid/ask spreads on the Eurobond and onshore securities markets were not available; hence, transactions costs were represented by the sum of the bid/ask spreads of the interest rate swap (the spread between U.S. dollar LIBOR and LIBID) and the cross currency swap quotations.

As noted earlier, financial swap market convention is to provide quotations for cross currency swaps and interest rates swaps rather than to directly quote fixed-rate currency swap rates. Moreover, interest rate swaps are quoted as a spread in basis points (bp) over term U.S. Treasury bonds against U.S. dollar (3 mo.) LIBOR flat. Further, cross currency swap rates provide a fixed foreign currency rate for AA-rated counterparties against U.S. dollar (6 mo.) LIBOR. The following example details the conversion of this interest rate and cross currency swap rate data into fixed-rate currency swap interest rates needed for the study.

	5-Year US$ Interest Rate Swap			5-Year DM/US$ Cross Currency Swap	
(1) Basis Points above Treasury Rate	(2) Treasury Rate	(3) 3-Month LIBOR	(4) US& Swap Rate[1]	(5) DM Swap Rate[2]	(6) 6-Month LIBOR
61	9.76	8.13	10.49	6.625	8.25

[1] i^{SW}, US$ Fixed-Rate Currency Swap Rate: (4) = (1) + (2) − (3) + (6)
[2] i^{*SW}, DM Fixed-Rate Currency Swap Rate: (5)

FINDINGS

The Tobit model has been estimated for all of the currency pairs in the 5-, 7-, and 10-year maturities. The regression results appear in

Tables 3, 4, and 5. The results suggest that covered financial integration exists and has increased in the long-date international capital markets through the use of currency swaps. The goodness-of-fit measure, as represented by the term R^2, is a summary statistic that indicates the accuracy with which the model approximates the observed data. Given that the sample is cross-sectional, an R^2 within the range of approximately 15 percent to 50 percent would be acceptable. Twelve of the 13 bilateral currency markets tested exhibit R^2 within this range. Consequently all of the regression equations can be considered good approximations of the data, except for the C$-US$ ten-year maturity.

As discussed, there is reason to suspect serial correlation in the data. Prior research using CIP models have assumed a first-order autocorrelation scheme, wherein the disturbance term in one period is a proportion of the disturbance of the previous time period.[24] Because weekly data were used in this study, it was possible that deviations from CIP in one period were correlated with deviations from CIP in prior periods beyond the previous period. Tables 3, 4, and 5 indicate the lags of the dependent and transactions costs variables that were included in the model specification of equation (3) for each of the markets tested. The DM-US$ five-year maturity data exhibited a fourth-order autocorrelation scheme, as up to four lags of the dependent and independent variables were necessary to eliminate the serial correlation. Data in the ¥-US$ five- and seven-year maturities exhibited the next highest order of serial correlation (three lags), whereas all of the other currency pairs tested did not exceed a second-order autocorrelation process. It is interesting to note that (1) the data in 6 of the 13 markets tested revealed a first-order autocorrelation scheme, and (2) 3 of these 6 markets included the SF-US$ currency pair in the 5-, 7-, and 10-year maturity spectrums. According to Oxelheim (1990), since it takes time for integration (or price convergence) to occur, it is possible that the lag lengths indicate the length of time necessary for price convergence to take effect. Thus, it would appear that, on average, a time period of one week was necessary for price

---

[24]The popularity of a first-order autocorrelation scheme is due to the ease in adjusting the estimation of the equations for this form of serial correlation.

TABLE 3
Five-Year Maturity Equation (3) Results

Currency Pair	Constant	TC	Lags of Dependent Variable				Lags of Transactions Costs			
			1	2	3	4	1	2	3	4
C$-US$	-13.2 (-1.54)	-0.99 (-2.62)[a]	0.56 (3.17)	0.27 (1.55)			-0.31 (-0.82)	0.99 (3.02)		
R²: 15.1%										
DM-US$	0.53 (1.01)	-0.02 (-0.09)	1.03 (5.93)	0.14 (0.67)	-0.21 (-0.95)	0.37 (2.09)	0.27 (1.19)	0.09 (0.48)	-0.36 (-1.76)	-0.42 (-1.97)
R²: 39.7%										
£-US$	-41.25 (-2.52)[b]	-0.54 (-1.15)	1.07 (4.63)				0.56 (1.29)			
R²: 15.0%										
SF-US$	-5.67 (-0.94)	-0.2 (-1.03)	1.17 (7.14)				-0.12 (-0.61)			
R²: 30.0%										
¥-US$	-21.1 (-3.64)[a]	0.11 (0.50)	0.88 (4.93)	0.22 (1.11)	0.32 (1.76)		0.18 (0.71)	-0.59 (-2.3)	0.39 (1.74)	
R²: 30.0%										

Notes:
T-statistics appear in parentheses.
[a] Significantly different from zero at the 1% level.
[b] Significantly different from zero at the 2% level.

TABLE 4
Seven-Year Maturity Equation (3) Results

Currency Pair	Constant	TC	Lags of Dependent Variable				Lags of Transactions Costs			
			1	2	3	4	1	2	3	4
DM-US$	−25.77 (−2.62)[a]	−1.54 (−2.08)[b]	0.46 (1.90)	0.58 (2.55)			0.5 (1.83)	0.35 (1.38)		
R^2: 36.1%										
SF-US$	−14.06 (−0.78)	−0.31 (−0.74)	0.82 (1.70)				−0.04 (−0.33)			
R^2: 16.8%										
¥-US$	−30.93 (−1.81)[c]	−0.09 (−0.20)	1.05 (3.15)	−0.03 (−0.07)	0.81 (2.54)		0.26 (0.58)	−0.57 (−1.13)	0.19 (0.43)	
R^2: 50.1%										

Notes:
T-Statistics appear in parentheses.
[a] Significantly different from zero at the 1% level.
[b] Significantly different from zero at the 2% level.
[c] Significantly different from zero at the 10% level.

TABLE 5
Ten-Year Maturity Equation (3) Results

Currency Pair	Constant	TC	Lags of Dependent Variable				Lags of Transactions Costs			
			1	2	3	4	1	2	3	4
C$-US$	4.94 (0.19)	-0.51 (-0.71)	-0.15 (-0.34)				-0.54 (-0.68)			
R^2: 2.3%										
DM-US$	-14.26 (-0.63)	-0.92 (-1.22)[a]	0.46 (2.13)				0.74 (0.98)			
R^2: 23.9%										
£-US$	-25.07 (-1.57)[a]	-0.06 (-0.14)	0.43 (2.72)	0.46 (3.06)			0.61 (1.52)	0.06 (0.13)		
R^2: 46.4%										
SF-US$	-15.23 (-0.66)	-0.33 (-0.52)	1.11 (3.50)				-0.15 (-0.28)			
R^2: 20.1%										
¥-US$	10.35 (7.2)	-0.39 (-0.91)	0.42 (3.03)	-0.42 (3.04)			0.36 (0.85)	-0.45 (-1.03)		
R^2: 50.1%										

Notes:
T-Statistics appear in parentheses.
[a] Significantly different from zero at the 10% level.

convergence between domestic and foreign covered yields in almost 50 percent (6 out of 13) of the markets tested.

Moreover, because currency swaps enable users to take advantage of previously unexploited profitable arbitrage opportunities, convergence should occur, over time, with respect to price differences of securities of equal risk and maturity yet different currency denominations. However, given the technological advances and information explosion during the last decade, as well as the increase in financial innovation, transactions costs should have declined over this time. The implication of the advance in technology and the increase in financial innovation is that both gross deviations from parity, $|Y|$, and transactions costs, TC, should exhibit downward trends due to the numerous financial innovations available, including currency swaps. A general discussion of the degree of efficiency brought about by currency swaps, as evidenced through the absolute size of transactions costs, is warranted. The implications of our empirical findings in each market tested follows that discussion.

Transactions Costs

Currency swaps are a financial innovation that should have contributed to the overall decline in transactions costs. Prior to the advent of currency swaps, empirical evaluation of covered interest parity conditions in the long-dated securities markets suffered from excessively wide long-date forward currency bid/ask quotations. In fact, these quotations were only indications of transactions prices and ran as high as 192 basis points in the five-year maturity spectrum.[25] To show the behavior of current transactions costs, a comparison of transactions costs over the sample period for currency swaps for each maturity spectrum is presented in Figures 4 through 7.[26]

All three maturity spectrums exhibit an overall downward trend in the transactions costs incurred in covered interest arbitrage strategies

---

[25]Hilley et al. (1981, p. 100).

[26]Some measurement error was discovered in calculation of transactions costs for the period March 1988 to September 1988, resulting in abnormally low bid/ask spreads on the U.S. dollar interest rate swap. However, the overall trend in transactions costs is downward until this time period and drops again during the end of the sample period. Please see Fletcher (1991) for further details.

FIGURE 4
**Pattern of Transactions Costs: Five-Year Maturity Spectrum—
Offshore Markets**

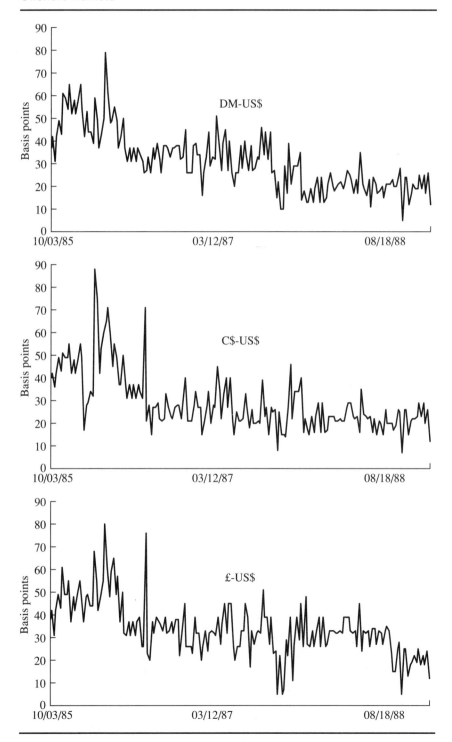

FIGURE 5
Pattern of Transactions Costs: Five-Year Maturity Spectrum—
Onshore Markets

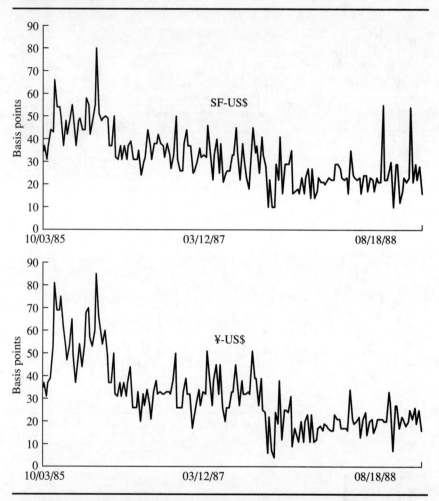

using fixed-rate currency swaps. The five markets composing the five-year maturity spectrum are shown in Figures 4 (the offshore markets) and 5 (the onshore markets). These markets display a large degree of comovement over time, as compared to the 7- and 10-year maturity spectrums, whose individual markets are less compact and more volatile. Moreover, the width of the transactions costs band is largest in the shorter-dated maturities (from an average low of 15 basis

FIGURE 6
Pattern of Transactions Costs: Seven-Year Maturity Spectrum

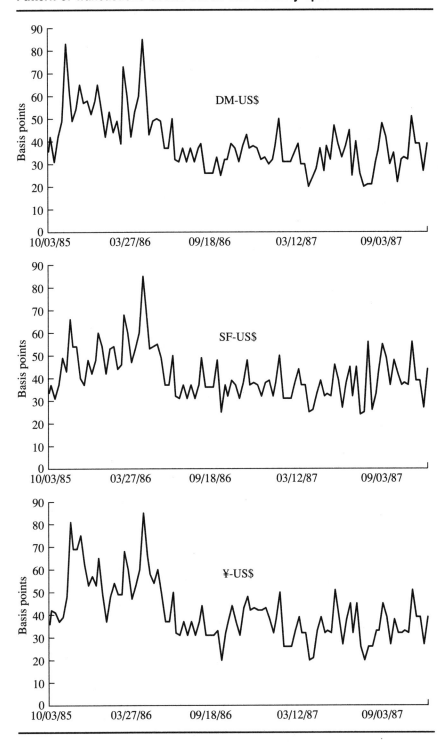

FIGURE 7
Pattern of Transactions Costs: 10-Year Maturity Spectrum

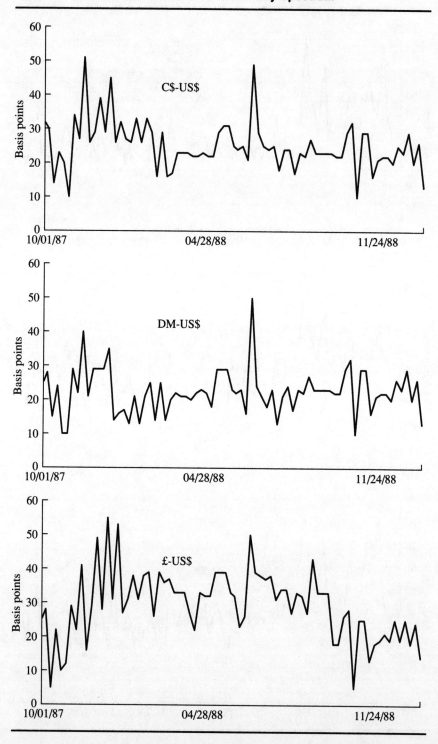

FIGURE 7 *(continued)*
Pattern of Transactions Costs: 10-Year Maturity Spectrum

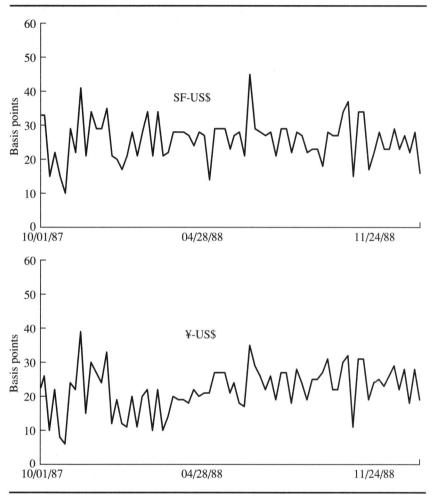

points to an individual high of 87 basis points). Transactions costs for the 7-year maturity spectrum ranged from approximately 85 basis points to 43 basis points, whereas transactions costs for the 10-year maturity spectrum ranged from less than 10 basis points to almost 60 basis points. It is interesting to note that the width of the transactions costs band in the 10-year maturity spectrum is smaller than in either the 7- or 5-year securities markets. This apparent paradox may be explained, perhaps, by the fact that the sample period for the 10-year maturity spectrum began on October 1, 1987, as opposed to October 3, 1985, which was the beginning of the sample period for both the 5- and 7-year maturities. Consequently, the process of arbitrage had already begun to reduce the costs of transactions prior to the beginning of the 10-year maturity sample period.

In general, visual inspection of transactions costs over time provides evidence of increasing capital market integration through financial innovations, including currency swaps. A more detailed analysis of the individual markets tested is presented in the next section.

Net Deviations from Covered Interest Parity: Summary of Findings

There was no significant evidence of unexploited covered interest arbitrage opportunities in any of the long-dated security markets tested. Hence, this study found empirical evidence of long-date capital market integration brought about primarily by currency swaps. This high degree of market integration must be attributable to currency swaps because prior to their inception, there was no convenient way to hedge long-date foreign exchange risk, and market inefficiencies remained unchecked. Table 6 details the mean or expected value of net deviations from CIP in each of the markets tested, as well as the average lag length involved in price convergence between the domestic and foreign (swap) covered yields. The expected values of the net deviations include both actual deviations from CIP in excess of transactions costs and (unobserved) equilibrium values.

It must be emphasized that the desirable quality of the Tobit specification is that it captures the probability of both the disequilibrium and equilibrium regimes of the CIP condition. The mean net deviation from CIP for 11 of the 13 markets tested is negative, indicating that, on average, there were no profitable trading opportunities from covered interest arbitrage in excess of transactions costs. The expected value of net deviations from parity over the sample period for both the £-US$ and ¥-US$ 10-year maturities are positive, indicating disequilibrium values. However, these mean deviations are small (approximately 21 and 6 basis points, respectively).

Table 6 also indicates those markets in which the coefficient of the transactions cost variable and/or the constant term were signifi-

TABLE 6
Summary of Net Deviation from Parity

Currency Pair	Number of Lags[a]	Expected Value of Net Deviations from CIP (in basis points)
5-Year Maturity		
C\$-US\$[b]	2	−3.79
DM-US\$	4	−7.79
£-US\$[b]	1	−33.11
SF-US\$	1	−9.58
¥-US\$[b]	3	−8.53
7-Year Maturity		
DM-US\$[b]	2	−7.36
SF-US\$	1	−29.04
¥-US\$[b]	3	−23.96
10-Year Maturity		
C\$-US\$	1	−22.16
DM-US\$[b]	1	−15.7
£-US\$[b]	2	6.31
SF-US\$	1	−22.93
¥-US\$	2	20.55

[a] Average number of weeks until price convergence is attained.
[b] Equilibrium regime of CIP dominates in these markets.

cantly different from zero and negative. Such findings indicate that net deviations from parity can be characterized as predominantly in equilibrium (within the transactions costs band) over the sample period in the C\$-US\$, £-US\$, and ¥-US\$ markets in the 5-year maturity spectrum, the DM-US\$ and ¥-US\$ markets in the 7-year maturity spectrum, and the DM-US\$ and £-US\$ markets in the 10-year maturity spectrum. Table 7 indicates the percentage of the observations in four of these markets that were in the disequilibrium regime of the CIP condition. The percentage of observations outside of the transactions costs band ranged from 23.07 percent in the £-US\$ five-year market to 44.0 percent in the ¥-US\$ five-year market. Also, Table 7 details

TABLE 7
Markets Predominantly in Equilibrium/
Summary of Disequilibrium Values

Currency Pair	Percentages of Observations In Disequilibrium	Mean Value (in basis points)
	5-Year Maturity	
C$-US$	28.77	18.80
£-US$	23.07	25.18
¥-US$	34.46	13.99
	7-Year Maturity	
DM-US$	44.00	5.92

the average size of these disequilibrium values: the largest average value is 25.18 basis points, in the £-US$ five-year maturity market; the smallest average value is 5.92 basis points, in the DM-US$ seven-year market. These findings suggest that currency swaps have contributed to international integration in that roughly 66.5 percent of the observations in these markets upheld covered interest parity. Yet the data also suggest that although profitable covered interest arbitrage opportunities were small in size, they were not rare.

Figures 8, 9, 10, and 11 display the pattern of net deviations from parity in these markets. The equilibrium values of net deviations from CIP are represented by zeros in these figures. As shown in Figure 8, the size of the disequilibrium values, or deviations from parity in excess of transactions costs, ranged from a low of approximately 2 basis points to a high of 90 basis points in the C$-US$ five-year maturity market. The £-US$ five-year market, shown in Figure 9, displayed a range of 1 to 70 basis points in the size of these net deviations; the size of the disequilibrium values in the ¥-US$ five-year securities (Figure 10) and the DM-US$ seven-year securities (Figure 11) fluctuated between approximately 0.5 basis points and 50 basis points. Further, both the ¥-US$ and £-US$ five-year maturity spectrums did not show any evidence of disequilibrium at the end of the sample period.

FIGURE 8
Net Deviations from CIP: C$-US$ 5-Year Censored Data

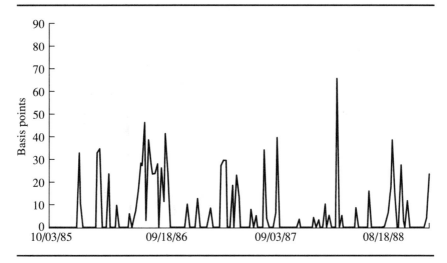

FIGURE 9
Net Deviations from CIP: £-US$ Five-Year Censored Data

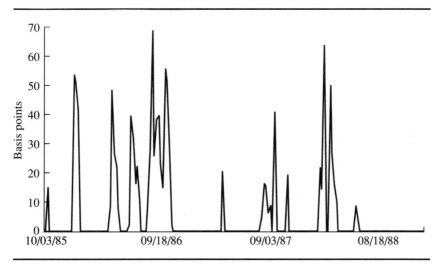

FIGURE 10
Net Deviations from CIP: ¥-US$ Five-Year Censored Data

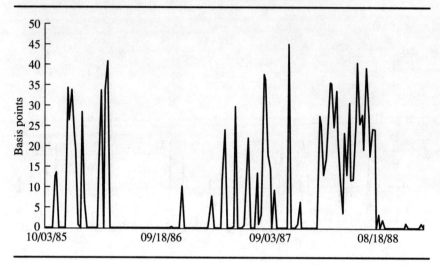

FIGURE 11
Net Deviations from CIP: DM-US$ Seven-Year Censored Data

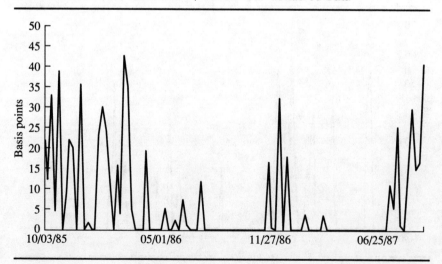

SUMMARY

This chapter has examined the pervasive belief that interest rate and currency swaps have increased the integration of world capital markets. The results of the empirical study presented here lend support to this belief, indicating that (covered) capital market integration is both possible and present through the use of currency swaps in the long-dated maturity spectrum. Moreover, the study provided evidence of decreasing transactions costs over the period studied, which indicates increasing capital market integration, prompted by the technological and communication explosion of the recent decade, and the growth of financial innovations, including currency swaps. Thus, the use of currency swaps has led to increased integration of international financial markets.

REFERENCES

Abdullah, F. A. 1988. "At Last, a Swaps Primer," *Financial Executive* (July/August): 53–7.

Akhtar, M., and K. Weiller. 1987. "Developments in International Capital Mobility: A Perspective on the Underlying Forces and the Empirical Literature." Research Paper, Federal Reserve Bank of New York, *International Integration of Financial Markets and U.S. Monetary Policy* (December): 13–70.

Aliber, R. Z. 1973. "The Interest Rate Parity Theorem: A Reinterpretation," *Journal of Political Economy* (December): 1451–9.

Bahmani-Oskooee, M., and S. Das. 1985. "Transaction Costs and the Interest Parity Theorem," *Journal of Political Economy* (August): 793–9.

Batlin, C. A. 1991. "Relationships between Interest Rate Swaps and Cross Currency Swaps," Chapter 19 in this volume.

Beidleman, C. R. 1985. *Financial Swaps: New Strategies in Currency and Coupon Risk Management.* Homewood, Ill.: Dow Jones-Irwin.

Bicksler, J., and A. H. Chen. 1986. "An Economic Analysis of Interest Rate Swaps," *Journal of Finance* (July): 645–55.

Broaddus, A. 1985. "Financial Innovation in the United States— Background, Current Status, and Prospects," *Economic Review* (January/February): 2–22.

Clinton, K. 1988. "Transactions Costs and Covered Interest Arbitrage: Theory and Evidence," *Journal of Political Economy* (April): 358–70.

Cooper, I. 1986. "Innovations: New Market Instruments," *Oxford Review of Economic Policy* (Winter): 1–17.

Dufey, G., and I. H. Giddy. 1981. "Innovation in the International Financial Markets," *Journal of International Business Studies* (Fall): 33–51.

Engle, R. "Estimates of the Variance of U.S. Inflation Based upon the ARCH Model," *Journal of Money, Credit, and Banking* (August): 286–301.

Fama, E. 1984. "Forward and Spot Exchange Rates," *Journal of Monetary Economics* (April): 319–38.

Fletcher, D. 1991. "The Impact of Currency Swaps on Capital Market Integration." Dissertation (February), Lehigh University.

Frenkel, J. A., and R. M. Levich. 1975. "Covered Interest Arbitrage: Unexploited Profits?" *Journal of Political Economy* (April): 325–38.

— — —.1977. "Transaction Costs and Interest Arbitrage: Tranquil versus Turbulent Periods," *Journal of Political Economy* (December): 1209–26.

Handjinicolaou, G. 1990. "The Place of Interest Rate Swaps in Financial Markets." In *Interest Rate Swaps,* ed. C. R. Beidleman. Homewood, Ill.: Business One Irwin, 25–60.

Harries, J. R. 1987. "New Financial Instruments: Some Aspects of the Cross Report," *Canadian Banker* (April): 40–44.

Hilley, J. L., C. R. Beidleman, and J. A. Greenleaf. 1979. "Does Covered Interest Arbitrage Dominate in Foreign Exchange Markets?" *Columbia Journal of World Business* (Winter): 2–20.

— — —.1981. "Why There Is No Long Forward Market in Foreign Exchange," *Euromoney* (January): 94–103.

Kasman, B., and C. Pigott. 1988. "Interest Rate Divergences among the Major Industrial Nations," *FRBNY Quarterly Review* (August): 28–44.

Kmenta, J. 1986. *Elements of Econometrics,* 2nd ed. New York: Macmillan.

Kohlhagen, S. 1983. "Overlapping National Investment Portfolios: Evidence and Implications of International Integration of Secondary Markets for Financial Assets." In *Research in International Business and Finance,* Vol. 3: *The Internationalization of Finance Markets and National Economic Policy,* ed. R. G. Hawkins, R. M. Levich, and G. C. Wihlborg. Greenwich, Conn., and London: JAI Press, 113–37.

Lamfalussy, A. 1983a. "The Changing Environment of Central Bank Policy," *American Economic Review* (May): 409–13.

Leddin, A. 1988. "Interest and Price Parity and Foreign Exchange Market Efficiency: The Irish Experience in the European Monetary System," *Economic and Social Review* (April): 215–31.

LeRoy, S. "Efficient Capital Markets and Martingales," *Journal of Economic Literature* (December): 1583–1621.

Levich, R. 1985. "Empirical Studies of Exchange Rates." In *Handbook of International Economics,* vol. 2, ed. R. W. Jones and P. B. Kenen. Amsterdam, New York, and Oxford: Elsevier Publisher B.V., 1025–35.

Loopesko, B. E. 1984. "Relationships among Exchange Rates, Intervention, and Interest Rates," *Journal of International Money and Finance* (December): 257–77.

Lucas, C., A. Hook, R. Aderhold, M. Alvarez, S. Fogel, A. Harwood, and B. Lancaster. 1987. "Recent Trends in Innovations and International Capital Markets." Unpublished paper. International Capital Markets Staff, Federal Reserve Bank of New York.

Maasoumi, E., and J. Pippenger. 1989. "Transaction Costs and the Interest Rate Parity Theorem: Comment," *Journal of Political Economy* (February): 236–43.

Maddala, G. S. 1983. *Limited-Dependent and Qualitative Variables in Econometrics.* Cambridge, N.Y.: Cambridge University Press.

Maenning, W. C., and W. Tease. 1987. "Covered Interest Parity in Non-Dollar Euromarkets," *Weltwirtschaftisches Archiv.* (August): 606–17.

Mahajan, A., and D. Mehta. 1986. "Swaps, Expectations, and Exchange Rates," *Journal of Banking and Finance* (October): 7–20.

Niehans, J. 1984a. "Forward Exchange." In *International Monetary Economics,* 2nd ed., ed. J. Niehans. Baltimore: Johns Hopkins University Press, 172–4.

―――. 1984b. "National Monetary Policy in an International Capital Market," *Kobe Economic and Business Review* (annual report): 1–10.

Oxelheim, L. 1990. *International Financial Integration.* Berlin, New York: Springer-Verlag.

Popper, H. 1987. "Long-Term Covered Interest Parity: Two Tests Using Currency Swaps." Unpublished paper. University of California at Berkeley.

Quandt, R. E. 1978. "Tests of Equilibrium vs. Disequilibrium Hypothesis," *International Economic Review* (June): 435–52.

Radecki, L. J., and V. Reinhart. "The Globalization of Financial Markets and the Effectiveness of Monetary Policy Instruments," *Federal Reserve Bank of New York Quarterly Review* (Autumn): 18–27.

Reinhart, V., and K. Weiller. 1987. "What Does Covered Interest Parity Reveal About Capital Mobility?" Research Paper No. 8713, Federal Reserve Bank of New York: *International Integration of Financial Markets and U.S. Monetary Policy* (December): 119–58

Smith, C. W., C. W. Smithson, and L. M. Wakeman. 1986. "The Evolving Market for Swaps," *Midland Corporate Finance* (Winter): 20–32.

Taylor, A. R. 1988. "The Swap Market and Financial Risk," *World of Banking* (September/October): 22–4.

CHAPTER 17

THE ROLE OF COVERED INTEREST ARBITRAGE IN THE PRICING OF CROSS CURRENCY SWAPS

Benjamin Iben
General Re Financial Products Corporation
New York

INTRODUCTION

Over the last decade, the currency swap market has played a major role in the increased integration of international capital markets by providing asset/liability managers with unprecedented flexibility in managing both their currency and interest rate exposures. Investors and issuers can use currency swaps to tailor their cash flow receipts/payments with precision without incurring large transaction costs. The usefulness of this capability is reflected in the size of the currency swap market, which, in 1989, exceeded US$400 billion in new issue volume.[1]

The flexibility of the currency swap as an asset/liability management tool is greatly enhanced by the wide variety of structures available in the market. The many structures traded in the market can, however, be grouped into the following four major categories:

1. Floating/floating currency swap (i.e., floating rate in Currency A vs. floating rate in Currency B).
2. Fixed/floating currency swap (i.e., fixed rate in Currency A vs. floating rate in Currency B).

---

[1] The International Swap Dealers Association, Inc. is the source of all volume estimates.

3. Fixed/fixed currency swap (i.e., fixed rate in Currency A vs. fixed rate in Currency B).
4. Zero-coupon or principal-only swaps.

One signficant challenge to currency swap market players is how to consistently value all of these structures and their many variants. Since the two sides of a currency swap are denominated in different currencies, currency swap valuation is dependent not only on two different interest rate markets but also on the exchange rate market. There are two different but consistent approaches to addressing this valuation problem. The first is the zero-coupon approach first developed for interest rate swaps.[2] The second approach is to synthetically recreate each currency swap with a combination of instruments whose prices are already known. This second approach relies heavily on covered interest arbitrage concepts.

In this chapter we introduce the concepts of zero-coupon valuation and covered interest arbitrage. We then demonstrate how to value each of the major currency swap structures using both these approaches. In the process, we illustrate how the foreign exchange market impacts currency swap valuation and also how the currency swap market impacts foreign exchange valuation.

THE ZERO-COUPON APPROACH

A zero-coupon rate is literally the yield to maturity of a zero-coupon bond. More generally, a zero-coupon rate is the discount rate appropriate for calculating the present value of a single cash flow to be received at a future date. For example, the present value (P) of US $1 to be received t periods in the future is:

$$P = \frac{US\$1}{(1 + z[t])^t} \tag{1}$$

where $z[t] = t$-year zero-coupon rate

The key attribute of a zero-coupon rate is that, once calculated, it is the correct discount rate for any flow to be received on that particular

---

[2]See B. Iben, "Interest Rate Swap Valuation," Chapter 12 of *Interest Rate Swaps,* C.R. Beidleman, ed., Richard D. Irwin, Homewood, IL., 1990.

date, regardless of the structure to which the flow is attached. Since zero-coupon rates correctly value individual flows, the present value of a swap with very complicated cash flow streams can easily be calculated, given the appropriate zero-coupon rates, as the sum of the values of its component cash flows.

Table 1 contains an example of the zero-coupon valuation of the fixed side of a three-year fixed/floating U.S. dollar swap with a notional principal of US$10 million and 10 percent annual interest payments. We calculate the present value of each cash flow in Table 1 using Formula (1) and the assumed zero-coupon rates. For example, the present value of the first cash flow is

$$US\$917,431 = 10\% \times \frac{US\$10,000,000}{1.09}$$

The present value of the fixed side of the swap is equal to the sum of the present values of the three cash flows, US $9,573,460.

The floating side of the swap can, in turn, be viewed as a floating-rate bond. If the swap's floating side is set at LIBOR flat, then the present value of the floating side of the swap will be par, or US$10 million, because the zero-coupon rates are consistent with LIBOR deposit rates. The net present value of the swap to the counterparty receiving the fixed side and paying the floating side is equal to the sum of the present values of the two sides, namely, $-\$426,540$.

As the above example indicates, valuation of interest rate swaps, given the relevant zero-coupon rates, is straightforward. The calculation of zero-coupon rates, however, is somewhat more complicated. There are a number of methods available for calculating zero-coupon

TABLE 1
Zero-Coupon Valuation of an Interest Rate Swap

Year	Zero-Coupon Rate (%)	Cash Flow (US$)	Present Value of Cash Flow (US$)
1	9	1,000,000	917,431
2	10	1,000,000	826,446
3	12	11,000,000	7,829,583
Present value of swap fixed side			US$9,573,460

Note: The cash flow at the end of the third year includes a coupon of US$1 million and a principal payment of US$10 million.

rates. One way is to back out the zero-coupon rates of zero-coupon bonds. Another is to calculate a series of implied zero-coupon rates, or a zero-coupon curve, from a series of generic interest rate swap rates. Appendix A demonstrates this procedure.

The procedure used to value currency swaps using zero-coupon rates closely follows the interest rate swap valuation methodology. The swap is split into its two sides, and each side is valued independently. Each cash flow is valued using the appropriate zero-coupon rate. However, currency swaps, unlike interest rate swaps, require two zero-coupon curves, one for each currency.

COVERED INTEREST ARBITRAGE

Covered interest arbitrage can be summarized in the following formula, which we will refer to as the *interest rate parity formula,* linking the interest rate deposit and foreign exchange markets:

$$F = S \times \frac{(1 + z_{FC})^t}{(1 + z_{US})^t} \tag{2}$$

where F = forward exchange rate (in units of foreign currency per dollar) at time 0 for delivery at time t

S = spot exchange rate (in units of foreign currency per dollar) at time 0

z_{FC} = zero-coupon rate from time 0 to time t implied by foreign currency deposit market

z_{US} = zero-coupon rate from time 0 to time t implied by U.S. dollar deposit market

t = number of days from time 0 to time t divided by 360

Quadrangle arbitrage is the means through which the market ensures that this formula holds. The basic idea behind quadrangle arbitrage, as for other types of arbitrage, is that two portfolios with the same payoffs must have the same value, or an arbitrageur can earn riskless profits. In the case of quadrangle arbitrage, the following instruments are involved:

1. Spot foreign exchange.
2. Forward foreign exchange.
3. Domestic deposit/loan.
4. Foreign deposit/loan.

Any three of the above instruments can be used to replicate the fourth. As a result, if the value of any one of the assets does not equal that of its replicating portfolio, an arbitrageur can earn riskless profits by buying the cheap portfolio and selling the expensive one. Table 2 contains the market rates relevant to completing a quadrangle arbitrage involving the six-month deposit and forward exchange markets, the implied zero-coupon rates, and a sample arbitrage transaction.

Both the loan and the investment expire in 180 days, and the interest payments are calculated using the following formula:

$$\text{Payment} = \text{Principal} \times \text{Rate} \times {}^{180}\!/_{360}$$

Using the interest rate parity formula (Formula 2), the arbitrage-free six-month forward exchange rate would be

$$1.95238 = 2 \times \frac{(1 + 0.050625)^{180/360}}{(1 + 0.1025)^{180/360}}$$

Since the actual forward is 1.953, the forward Deutschemark is undervalued. The arbitrage transaction contained in Table 2 exploits

TABLE 2
Quadrangle Arbitrage

Currency	Market Rates: Interest Rate (LIBOR,%)	Zero-Coupon Rate(%)	Foreign Exchange Rates Spot (DM/US$)	Forward (DM/US$)
U.S. dollar	10	10.25	2.00	1.953
Deutschemark	5	5.06		

	Cash Flows (millions)			
	Initial		Terminal	
Transaction	US$	DM	US$	DM
Borrow DM 200 million at 5%		200.00		−205.00
Buy US$100 million spot	100.00	−200.00		
Invest US$100 million at 10%	−100.00		105.00	
Buy DM 205 million forward			−104.97	205.00
Net cash flows	0.00	0.00	0.03	0.00

this. The arbitrageur would purchase the undervalued asset (forward Deutschemarks) and sell the overvalued replicating portfolio. In this case, the arbitrage involves borrowing DM200 million for six months at 5 percent. The DM200 million borrowed would then be exchanged for US$100 million, which would be invested at 10 percent. In order to pay back the loan plus interest, the arbitrageur would have to buy DM205 million six months forward. At the market exchange rate of 1.953, this would require him to pay US$104.97 million. Since he would receive US$105 million from his loan, he would make a profit of approximately US$28,600 (the present value of US$30,000 to be received in six months, when discounted at the market rate of 10 percent).

The example in Table 2 is a simplification in that it ignores transaction costs. In the foreign exchange and interest rate markets, transaction costs take the form of a bid/ask spread. In the case of the interest rate markets, the bid/ask spread is the differential between the borrowing and lending rate, usually 0.125 percent. Assuming the rates in Table 1 are actually midmarket rates, the rate at which the arbitrageur would have been able to borrow Deutschemarks would really be 5.06 percent, and the rate at which he could lend out his U.S. dollars would be 9.94 percent. Given these rates, the entire arbitrage profit of US$28 thousand would be consumed by transaction costs.

In a world with transaction costs, covered interest rate arbitrage can only be profitably executed if market FX (foreign exchange) forward rates fall outside a band around the rate implied by the interest rate parity formula. The width of the band depends on the size of the transaction costs incurred in the three replicating transactions. Generally, market FX forward rates remain within these bands, and arbitrage profits are difficult to earn.

FLOATING/FLOATING CURRENCY SWAP

The floating/floating currency swap market represents approximately 10 percent of the overall currency swap market volume. However, floating/floating currency swaps play an important role in completing the link between the interest rate and currency swap markets. Valuing a floating/floating currency swap is relatively straightforward, because the arbitrage bounds on its value are easily determined. In fact, a single-period floating/floating currency swap can be combined with FX spot and forward contracts to replicate the four transactions involved in quadrangle arbitrage.

The swap takes the place of the two transactions in the deposit market. In order to replicate the example in Table 2, the arbitrageur would need to receive US$ LIBOR and pay DM LIBOR. Currency swaps, unlike interest rate swaps, involve actual principal exchanges; therefore, the cash flow payments on a currency swap are identical to those incurred by borrowing US$100 million at US$ LIBOR and lending out DM200 million to the same counterparty at DM LIBOR.

If the FX market and the currency swap markets were perfectly integrated, then the arbitrage transactions would result in zero profits. If, for example, the forward exchange rate at the beginning of period 1 for delivery at the end of period 1 were 1.95238 (i.e., consistent with the interest rate parity formula) then the present value of the swap calculated with the FX market and the six-month U.S. dollar zero-coupon rate would be zero. That is, the present value of the Deutschemark side of the swap would equal

$$\frac{\$200,000,000}{2} - \frac{\left(\dfrac{205,000,000}{1.95238}\right)}{1.1025^{0.5}} = 0$$

and the present value of the U.S. dollar side would equal

$$-\$100,000,000 + \left(\frac{105,000,000}{1.1025^{0.5}}\right) = 0$$

In short, when interest rate parity holds, we obtain the same U.S. dollar present value for a future foreign currency cash flow whether we discount the cash flow using the appropriate foreign currency zero-coupon rate and convert the result to U.S. dollars at the spot rate, or convert the cash flow first to U.S. dollars at the forward rate and then discount it using the U.S. dollar zero-coupon rate.

The quadrangle arbitrage can be executed for multiperiod floating/floating currency swaps in much the same way as for a single-period swap. The two-period arbitrage is somewhat more complicated because at the end of the first period, the forward FX hedge must be adjusted. Table 3 demonstrates the extension of the quadrangle ar-

TABLE 3

Cash Flows from Covered Arbitrage Executed with Floating/ Floating Currency Swap

	Market Rates at End of Period 1			
	Market Rates		Foreign Exchange Rates	
Currency	LIBOR (%)	Zero-Coupon Rate (%)	Spot (DM/US$)	Forward (DM/US$)
U.S. dollar	9.0	9.2025	1.7500	1.725
Deutschemark	6.0	6.09		

	Cash Flows (millions)					
	Start of Period 1		End of Period 1		End of Period 2	
	US$	DM	US$	DM	US$	DM
Swap	−100.00	200.00	5.00	−5.00	104.50	−206.00
Forward	0.00	0.00	−104.97	205.00	−119.42	206.00
Spot	100.00	−200.00	114.29	−200.00	0.00	0.00
Period 1 net Reinvested	0.00	0.00	0.00	0.00	14.96	0.00
Net	0.00	0.00	14.32	0.00	0.04	0.00

bitrage to a two-period swap, using the market rates in Table 2 for the first period of the swap and the market rates from period 2 for the second period of the swap. The two-period swap is identical to the single-period swap described above, except it has two six-month payment periods and matures in one year instead of six months. The first-period cash flows come from the swap and the FX forward hedge executed at the beginning of period 1.

At the beginning of period 1, the forward FX transaction executed would be identical to that used to hedge the single-period swap. The cash flows at the end of period 1 would differ, however, because the notional principal repayment of the two-period swap does not occur until the end of the second period. The net positive cash flow at the end of the first period, US$14.32 million, reflects the fact that the gain of the forward FX contract would be realized at that time, whereas the offsetting loss on the swap would not be realized until the end of the second period. The spot FX transaction would be executed at the end of period 1 in order to net out the Deutschemark flows at that time. The US$14.32 million cash inflow is invested over period 2 at 9 percent.

At the end of period 1, a new FX forward transaction must be executed to hedge the Deutschemark cash flows to be made at the end of period 2. In order to purchase DM206 million forward to cover the Deutschemark interest and principal payment, the arbitrageur would have to sell US$119.42 million forward, since the forward exchange rate at the end of period 1 for delivery at the end of period 2 is 1.725 DM/US$. The U.S. dollar cash inflow from the swap at the end of period 2 would be US$104.5 million, representing the principal and interest payments. Thus, the net cash outflow from the swap and the second-period FX forward transaction would be US$14.92 million. This cash outflow is due to the realization of the foreign exchange loss on the swap that occurred in the first period. The cash outflow is, in turn, offset by the US$14.96 million received at the end of period 2 from investing the first-period profit of US$14.32 million at 9 percent (i.e., LIBOR) for the second period.

The net profit on the series of transactions to be realized at the end of period 2 is US$40,000. The US$10,000 incremental profit of the two-period arbitrage transaction over the single-period transaction is due principally to the fact that the second forward rate was not equal to the rate consistent with interest rate parity, 1.72488DM/US$.

If financial institutions could always borrow and lend at LIBOR, and interest rate parity always held, then floating/floating currency swaps would be priced at LIBOR flat. Any spread over or under LIBOR would represent an arbitrage profit opportunity. The spread between the rate at which major banks borrow and lend is generally 0.125 percent. Thus, spreads of at least 0.125 percent around LIBOR can persist in the floating/floating currency swap market without creating arbitrage opportunities. The spreads in the floating/floating currency swap market are, in fact, usually within 0.125 percent.

FIXED/FLOATING CURRENCY SWAP

Fixed/floating currency swaps alone account for roughly half of the volume of the entire currency swap market. As with floating/floating currency swaps, we can utilize an arbitrage relationship to value fixed/floating currency swaps; in this case, however, the arbitrage replication is with a fixed/floating interest rate swap and a floating/floating currency swap. Exhibit 1 demonstrates how to replicate a fixed Deutschemark/floating U.S. dollar swap with a Deutschemark interest rate swap and a floating U.S. dollar/floating Deutschemark swap.

Exhibit 1 illustrates how a financial institution can replicate the cash flows of a swap executed with firm A by executing offsetting swaps with firms B and C. As long as floating/floating currency swaps are priced at LIBOR flat, the fixed rate appropriate for valuing fixed/floating currency swaps is the same as that used in the interest swap market; otherwise, arbitrage profit opportunities would exist. Exhibit 1 shows how this arbitrage works. The fixed rate that the bank receives from firm A is 7.10 percent, and the fixed rate that it pays to firm B is 7.00 percent. The notional principal receipts (payments) on the two currency swaps offset each other exactly. If, for example, the notional principals on the two currency swaps are DM150 million and US$100 million, at the start of the swap the financial institution pays DM150 million to firm A and in return receives US$100 million, and

EXHIBIT 1
Fixed/Floating Currency Swap Replication

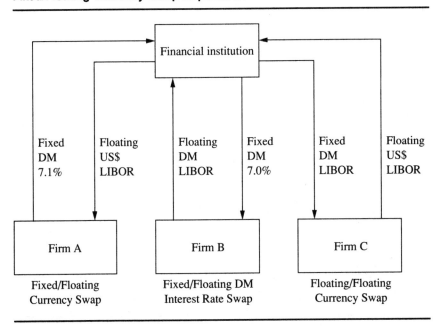

it receives DM150 million from firm C and in return pays US$100 million. Thus, the financial intermediary is left with a 10–basis point arbitrage profit after executing the three swaps.

Fixed/floating currency swaps are generally priced so that there is no arbitrage opportunity between the interest rate and the currency swap markets. That is, when the floating/floating currency swap rates diverge from LIBOR, the divergence will be reflected in the difference between the fixed rate on fixed/floating currency swaps and the Deutschemark interest rate swap rate. If, for example, the floating Deutschemark/floating U.S. dollar swap market rate were US$ LIBOR flat versus DM LIBOR minus 0.125 percent, the arbitrage-free fixed rate on a fixed Deutschemark/floating U.S. dollar would be 0.125 percent below the Deutschemark fixed/floating interest rate swap rate of the same maturity.

Exhibit 2 contains an example of an arbitrage-free fixed/floating currency swap. The fixed rate on the Deutschemark interest rate swap is 7.125 percent, and the fixed rate on a fixed Deutschemark/floating

EXHIBIT 2
Arbitrage-Free Fixed/Floating Currency Swap Pricing

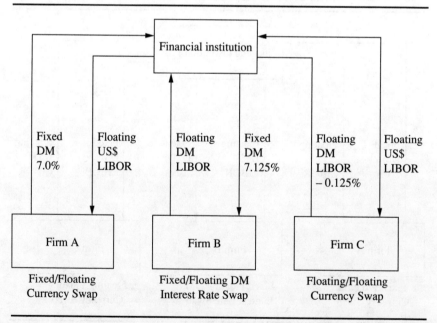

U.S. dollar swap is 7 percent. Thus, the financial institution would have a 12.5–basis point spread on the fixed rate that it receives and the fixed rate that it pays. The 12.5–basis point spread on the fixed rates is, however, exactly offset by the 0.125 percent spread on its floating receipts. Thus, the financial institution has zero net flows on the entire transaction.

FIXED/FIXED CURRENCY SWAP

The third major currency swap structure commonly traded is the fixed/fixed currency swap. Fixed/fixed currency swaps (including zero-coupon currency swaps) account for approximately 40 percent of all currency swap volume. Fixed/fixed currency swaps can be replicated with a fixed/floating currency swap combined with a fixed/floating interest rate swap. Exhibit 3 contains an example of a fixed Deutschemark/fixed U.S. dollar currency swap replicated exactly with a fixed U.S. dollar/floating Deutschemark currency swap

EXHIBIT 3
Synthetic Fixed/Fixed Currency Swap

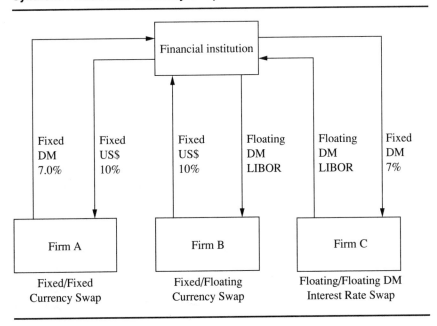

and a Deutschemark fixed/floating interest rate swap. The notional principals on which the currency swap interest payments are made are US$100 million and DM150 million. These notional principals are consistent with a spot exchange rate of 1.5 DM/US$ when the transaction is initiated. The notional principal on the Deutschemark interest rate swap is DM150 million. All three deals have the same maturity.

In the example shown in Exhibit 3, the financial institution's principal receipts (payments) from (to) firm A are exactly offset by its payments (receipts) to (from) firm B. For example, at the initiation of the fixed/fixed currency swap, the financial institution receives US$100 million in return for payment of DM150 million; at the initiation of the fixed/floating currency swap, the financial institution receives DM150 million in return for payment of US$100 million. The financial institution's interest receipts (payments) from (to) firm A are, in turn, exactly offset by its combined payments (receipts) to (from) firms B and C. In this example, as is generally true in the market, no arbitrage profits can be made by replicating a fixed/fixed currency swap with a fixed/floating currency swap and a fixed/floating interest rate swap.

ZERO-COUPON CURRENCY SWAPS AND SYNTHETIC LONG-DATED CURRENCY FORWARDS

Interest rate parity concepts have traditionally been used to link the deposit and FX markets. Deposit market activity is concentrated in maturities of one year or less. As a result, the arbitrage bands on forward contracts that mature in more than one year have tended to be quite wide. Activity in the currency swap market is, however, concentrated in maturities greater than one year.

Early in the development of the swap market, market participants were aware of the potential for arbitraging the FX markets with fixed/fixed currency swaps. Table 4 contains an example of a typical arbitrage transaction between the Deutschemark/U.S. dollar swap and FX markets. In this example the fixed Deutschemark/fixed U.S. dollar swap rates for all maturities are 7.5 percent and 10 percent, respectively. Since the swap yield curve is flat, the Deutschemark/U.S.

TABLE 4
Fixed/Fixed Currency Swap/FX Forward Arbitrage

Time	FX Rates (DM/US$)	Swap Flows US$	Swap Flows DM	FX Rates US$	FX Rates DM	Net Flows (US$)	PV Net Flows (US$)
0	2.00	−100.00	200.00	100.00	−200.00	0	0
1	1.95	10.00	−15.00	−7.69	15.00	2.31	2.10
2	1.91	10.00	−15.00	−7.85	15.00	2.15	1.78
3	1.87	10.00	−15.00	−8.02	15.00	1.98	1.49
4	1.82	10.00	−15.00	−8.24	15.00	1.76	1.20
5	1.79	110.00	−215.00	−120.11	215.00	−10.11	−6.28
Net present value							0.29

Note: All cash flows are in millions.

dollar zero-coupon rates consistent with this yield curve are also 7.5 percent and 10 percent, respectively, for all maturities. The notional principal of the swap is DM200 million/US$100 million. Table 4 contains the FX rates at which all Deutschemark cash flows are exchanged for dollars.

The arbitrage transaction detailed in Table 4 involves a five-year currency swap and a series of Deutschemark/U.S. dollar forwards. The purpose of the FX forward portion of these arbitrage transactions is to convert all cash flows into U.S. dollars. That is, the swap generates net Deutschemark outflows at the end of periods 1 through 5; these cash flows are exactly offset by the series of forward purchases, so the net Deutschemark flow in each period is zero.

The net U.S. dollar flows are converted to a present value using a discount rate of 10 percent. If this particular transaction were executed, the profit would be US$290,000. However, this profit would be subject to dollar interest rate risk, since the net U.S. dollar flows would only be realized over five years. For example, if swap rates rose to 11 percent, the profit on the transaction would increase to US$430,000. The profit on the transaction increases (decreases) when rates rise (fall), because the large cash payment at the end of five years is more sensitive to interest rate movements than the series of smaller cash receipts in prior years.

The fixed/fixed currency swap/FX arbitrage transactions have two drawbacks. First, the arbitrage requires execution of a whole series of forward FX transactions, because all the coupons on the currency swap have to be converted to U.S. dollars. Second, the interest rate risk of an uneven stream of net U.S. dollar flows would have to be hedged in order to lock in the profit.

The cash flows of a zero-coupon currency swap closely approximate those of a single FX swap, the generic transaction in FX forward market. In the FX market, a swap refers to a forward exchange of one currency for another, combined with an offsetting spot exchange. Table 5 presents an FX swap and a replicating zero-coupon currency swap. The FX swap involves an exchange (both spot and forward) of DM300 million for the equivalent U.S. dollar amounts. The spot and forward exchange rates used are 2 and 1.79 DM/US$, respectively. In the case of the FX swap, an equal number of Deutschemarks are exchanged spot and forward. In the case of the zero-coupon currency swap, however, the forward exchange is larger than the spot exchange, because the forward exchange includes five years' interest at an annual rate of 7.5 percent on the initial notional principal.

Since the initial Deutschemark flows on the zero-coupon swap do not equal those of the FX swap, we need to enter into a third transaction, referred to as a *spot hedge,* in order to eliminate any FX risk. This third transaction is a purchase of DM91 million spot (the exact opposite of the net exposure from the zero-coupon swap and the FX swap).

The only unmatched cash flow of this arbitrage, if it were executed, would be the profit on the transaction of US$700,000. Since this profit would not be realized for five years, it would be subject to U.S. dollar interest rate risk, which could be easily hedged.

TABLE 5
Zero-Coupon Currency Swap/FX Swap Arbitrage

Time	Zero-Coupon Swap		FX Swap		Spot Hedge		Net Flows	
	US$	DM	US$	DM	US$	DM	US$	DM
0	−104.5	209.0	150.0	−300.0	−45.5	91.0	0	0
5	168.3	−300.0	−167.6	300.0	0.0	0	0.7	0

Note: All cash flows are in millions.

The zero-coupon currency swap/FX swap arbitrage only involves three transactions, whereas the fixed/fixed currency swap FX arbitrage involves a whole series of forward transactions. Consequently, the zero-coupon swap currency/FX swap arbitrage is easier to execute and involves lower transaction costs.

SUMMARY

In this chapter we extend the zero-coupon valuation methodology to the valuation of currency swaps. The strength of the zero-coupon methodology is that it provides a direct means of consistently valuing a wide range of products, including all interest rate and currency swaps. This consistency of valuation across products is important because it enables swap market makers to value complicated products efficiently and accurately.

The application of the zero-coupon pricing approach to the valuation of currency swaps is based on covered interest arbitrage concepts. Therefore, its accuracy is dependent on the ease with which the arbitrage transactions can be executed and on the transaction costs involved in doing so. For example, the transaction costs involved in replicating floating/floating currency swaps through the FX forward market enable a 0.125 percent spread to persist in the market's valuation of floating/floating currency swaps. Since a floating/floating currency swap is the most direct link between the interest rate and currency swap markets, this spread in the floating/floating currency swap market enables spreads of at least 0.125 percent to persist between the fixed/floating interest rate swap market and the fixed/floating currency swap market.

As the currency swap market has grown, arbitrage activity between the swap and FX markets has become more common. This has, in turn, reduced both the frequency and profitability of arbitrage opportunities involving generic currency swaps and FX forward contracts. Arbitrageurs have consequently turned to more complicated arbitrage transactions in which risk is limited but not eliminated. This strategy requires relatively sophisticated pricing and hedging capabilities, of which the zero-coupon valuation approach is only a small part.

APPENDIX A
ZERO-COUPON CALCULATION

A series of zero-coupon rates or a zero-coupon curve can be calculated from generic swap rates through a procedure called *bootstrapping*. The first step in this procedure is to calculate the one-year zero rate ($z[1]$) using the one-year swap rate ($c[1]$). Given an annual payment frequency, the one-year zero rate can be calculated as follows:

$$P = \frac{1 + c[1]}{1 + z[1]}$$

Since the generic swap will be priced at par (in this case, 1), the one-year zero rate is equal to the one-year swap rate. The one-year zero rate and the two-year swap rate ($c[2]$) are then used to calculate the two-year zero rate ($z[2]$) using the following relationship:

$$1 = \frac{c[2]}{1 + z[1]} + \frac{1 + c[2]}{(1 + z[2])^2}$$

This procedure may then be continued to calculate an entire zero rate curve. The general formula for calculating the *n*-year zero rate ($z[n]$), given the zero rates for all preceding years and the *n*-year swap rate ($c[n]$), is:

$$z[n] = \left[\frac{1 + c[n]}{1 - c[n] \sum_{i=1}^{n-1} \left(\frac{1}{1 + z[i]} \right)^i} \right]^{\frac{1}{n}} - 1$$

where $z[i]$ = *i*th-year zero rate

PART 4

CONCEPTUAL RELATIONSHIPS

CHAPTER 18

RISK MANAGEMENT OF A SWAP PORTFOLIO

David E. Lawrence
Citicorp Investment Bank Ltd.
London

INTRODUCTION

The objective of this chapter is to prescribe a simple framework for the management of price risk in a cross currency swap portfolio. This framework must allow the user to measure the risk, to analyze the risk, and to control or limit the risk.

In establishing the conceptual framework, two major considerations should be taken into account:

1. A set of simple and flexible price risk monitoring and control procedures is needed. These procedures must provide the trader with an exact measure of the current level of risk and be completely compatible with the way the trader actively manages that risk.

2. A mechanism is also needed to limit losses. This is done by setting equivalent limits on positions that will contain losses within acceptable bounds without imposing undue restraints on the trader.

To meet these objectives, it is necessary to establish two sets of limits—one on performance and one on positions. We are primarily concerned with the position limits in this chapter.

MEASUREMENT OF PRICE RISK: MARK-TO-MARKET VALUATION

The first important objective of the analysis is to identify the exact value of the swap portfolio. As swap contracts do not have directly quoted market prices, an accurate valuation model is required. Such a model simulates the orderly liquidation of the price risk position by closing out each swap with an opposite swap. This will require extra interest payments to be made or received whenever the original swap is no longer at current market rates. The model must calculate the present value of these extra interest payments, given the current term structure of interest rates (TSIR) and spot foreign exchange rates.

This calculation might appear to be a complicated one. However, it can be shown that the change in the value of the swap, as measured by the present value of these extra interest payments, is the same as the change in value of a bond with the same (notional) principal and the same fixed coupon as the swap. This greatly simplifies the valuation model.

The market data required as input to the model consists of the appropriate yield curves and spot foreign exchange rates. A TSIR is required for each currency and usually comprises three separate yield curves—the government, money market, and swap yield curves. The government and money market yield curves are not needed to value the swap portfolio itself, but they are needed to value instruments that are used to hedge the swap portfolio, such as treasuries and forward rate agreements.

The first step in the valuation process is to convert the quoted market yields to a common basis, namely, zero-coupon rates, from an annual money market rate or a semiannual bond rate. For longer tenors, the rate is quoted on the assumption that intermediate coupons will be paid regularly throughout the life of the instrument, that is, on the basis of yield to maturity $Y(t)$, where t is the time to maturity. These yields are converted to zero-coupon yields or to zero-coupon discount factors $F(t)$, using the following formulas:

For values of t up to one year:

$$F(t) = \frac{1}{1 + t \times Y(t)}$$

For currencies with annual interest payments:

$$F(t) = \frac{1 - Y(t) \times \sum\limits_{n=1}^{t-1} F(n)}{1 + Y(t)}$$

For currencies with semiannual interest payments:

$$F(t) = \frac{1 - 0.5 \times Y(t) \times \sum\limits_{n=0.5}^{t-0.5} F(n)}{1 + 0.5 \times Y(t)}$$

The preceding transformations must be performed at all points on the maturity grid—those tenors for which yield curve data have been input. If a zero-coupon discount factor is needed for a point that is not on the maturity grid, it is interpolated by exponential interpolation, as follows.

Let an arbitrary date, D, lie between times $T(n-1)$ and $T(n)$ on the maturity grid, where $T(n)$ is the time, in years, to point n. Then the fractional period p from $T(n-1)$ to D is

$$p = \frac{D - T(n-1)}{T(n) - T(n-1)}$$

The interpolated discount factor F for date D is then

$$F = F(n-1)^{1-p} \times F(n)^{p}$$

The present value V of a future cash flow C is then

$$V = C \times F$$

The total present value of the swap portfolio is obtained by summing the present values of all its future cash flows. These include fixed and floating interest payments as well as the final exchange of the (notional) principal. Each cash flow is converted to its present value using the zero-coupon discount factors for its own currency. The total of all these present values is obtained in each currency. In the final evaluation of the swap portfolio, these aggregate present values are then converted to the base currency using the current spot exchange rates.

Formal valuation models are also necessary to value hedge instruments, even though those instruments have quoted market prices.

The quoted market price is used for accounting purposes, whereas the valuation model is used to calculate exactly which instruments are needed to hedge the portfolio accurately.

Among the hedge instruments that are needed are long-term foreign exchange (LTFX) contracts. As an LTFX contract consists of two future cash flows—one in each currency—it can be valued using exactly the same zero-coupon discount method as just described, except that the money-market yield curve is used rather than the swap yield curve.

ANALYSIS OF PRICE RISK

Factor Sensitivity

The mark-to-market value of a cross-currency swap portfolio is obtained by using the valuation model described. This value depends upon a number of market factors, namely, the swap TSIR in each currency and the spot foreign exchange rates.

We define the portfolio's factor sensitivity to a given market factor as the change in the value of the portfolio for a one-unit change in the given market factor, holding all other market factors constant. Thus, there are as many factor sensitivities as there are market factors, and the market factors are assumed to be independent variables.

Change in portfolio		Factor		Unit
value due to change	=	sensitivity	×	change in
in market factor Y		to factor Y		factor Y

Mathematically,

$$dV = \frac{dV}{dy} \times dy$$

That is, the factor sensitivity is the partial derivative of the value with respect to the appropriate market factor.

The unit change in the independent market factor is selected according to the nature of the market factor. If the market factor is spot foreign exchange, then the unit change reflects a 1 percent relative change. If the market factor is the term structure of interest rates, the unit change reflects a 1-basis-point absolute change.

Factor sensitivities to a given market factor of exposure can be simply aggregated across portfolios of different instruments. For example, the factor sensitivity of a money-market deposit can be added to the factor sensitivity of a forward rate agreement (FRA), as they are both valued using the money-market TSIR. It does not matter exactly which instrument has been used; the exposure is to a change in the money-market TSIR regardless of the instrument.

Aggregation of factor sensitivities cannot be done across different market factors of exposure, as a sensitivity to an exchange rate is quite different from a sensitivity to an interest rate.

A most important property of factor sensitivities for a swap portfolio is that they are fairly insensitive to errors in the market factors used to determine the value of the portfolio. This is because the value of the swap is almost a linear function of the market factors—the yield curves. However, the factor sensitivities are very sensitive to the cash flows of the transactions that make up the portfolio. This means that they are an effective tool for managing risk, even in cases where the market factors are not well defined or the valuation model is not perfect.

Potential Loss Amount

The potential loss amount is the amount of loss that could occur during the time it takes to close out a position. It depends upon the amount of market risk to which the portfolio is currently exposed, which is quantified by factor sensitivities, and the possible changes in the market that could occur before the position is closed out. Thus, the potential loss amount depends on the action time required to close out the position (a function of market size and liquidity) and the current volatility of the market factors of exposure. For a swap portfolio, which contains liquid instruments or instruments that can be suitably hedged with liquid instruments, the time to close out the position is assumed to be one day.

The factor sensitivity formula can be modified slightly and used to calculate the potential loss amount:

$$
\begin{array}{lll}
\text{Potential} & \text{Factor} & \text{Potential} \\
\text{loss} & = \text{sensitivity} & \times \text{change in} \\
\text{amount} & \text{to factor } Y & \text{factor } Y
\end{array}
$$

The potential loss amount always assumes an adverse movement in the market factor and is always quoted as an absolute number.

The potential change in the market factor is usually estimated on a two-standard-deviation basis, which means that there is a 5 percent probability that the change during the period will be greater than the estimate; the probability that the change will be greater than the estimate in the wrong direction is therefore only 2.5 percent.

For a single-currency swap portfolio, the potential loss amount is the product of the TSIR factor sensitivity and the potential daily change in the TSIR for swaps. For a cross currency swap portfolio, whose value depends on several market factors, the potential loss amounts could be added, as they are expressed in compatible terms. However, this addition assumes that all market factors can simultaneously move in the wrong direction by two standard deviations and that there is no correlation between the various market factors. The interpretation of such a total PLA must therefore be made with considerable caution.

CONTROL OF PRICE RISK

Factor Sensitivity Limits

If we are to limit overall losses, we must limit the potential loss amount. As stated earlier, the amount that a portfolio gains or loses is the product of two quantities: the factor sensitivity of the portfolio (within the control of the trader) and the change in the market factor (beyond the control of the trader). To put a limit on the potential loss amount itself is not a sensible solution, since the changes in the market factors are outside the control of the trader. A preferable way is to place limits on the factor sensitivities.

The potential loss amount must be compatible with the expected revenues. The limit on each particular factor sensitivity is then set to be compatible with the potential loss amount. In addition, various qualitative factors such as the experience and skill of the trader, the market environment and liquidity, and current expectations of market movements must be taken into account. With multiple factor sensitivities, some account must also be taken of the possible correlations between the market factors.

Let us take a simple example in which the maximum potential loss amount has been set at $1,000,000 and there is only one market factor, namely, the TSIR, with a two-standard-deviation movement of 20 basis points. This means that the factor sensitivity limit would be $50,000 per basis point ($1,000,000/20 bp). Such a limit could be used to hold a relatively larger portfolio of shorter-term interest rate–sensitive instruments or a relatively smaller portfolio of longer-term interest rate–sensitive instruments. For example, a $191 million holding of three-year 8 percent bonds and a $126 million holding of five-year 9 percent bonds each have a factor sensitivity of $50,000. The choice between these alternatives would be determined by other considerations, such as factor sensitivities at different points along the yield curve (yield curve shape risk).

The advantage of this system is that generic risks (exposure to a given market factor) can be grouped together, and holdings of related instruments can be easily substituted for each other without changing limits. Factor sensitivities can also be aggregated upward to permit a reallocation of limits between different trading units, if this is needed. However, at the lowest level, factor sensitivities will be calculated in more detail to enable the correct hedging decisions to be made.

Other Sensitivity Limits

The concept of factor sensitivity limits can be extended to limit or control other risks of the trader, which can be far more significant. A yield curve contains a number of points, and each point could be regarded as a separate market factor. A swap portfolio could be hedged with treasuries and forward rate agreements, which means that there are three yield curves to deal with.

The limits that a trader might be given are described in the following list, and an example is given in the next section.

Net sensitivity limit: The net sensitivity limit is the limit on the factor sensitivity of the whole portfolio to a 1-basis-point parallel movement in the term structure of all three yield curves. It assumes that movements in all three yield curves are perfectly correlated.

Yield curve sensitivity limits: In addition to parallel movements in the term structure of interest rates, the total portfolio can show a loss if the three yield curves change shape, by steepening, flattening, or twisting. To limit such losses, there are also factor sensitivity limits at each point down the yield curve. These yield curve sensitivity limits cover yield curve reshaping risk, assuming that all three yield curves change shape in the same manner.

Basis risk sensitivity limit: Because a treasury instrument is used to hedge a swap, there could be a loss if the two yield curves move apart. Therefore, limits are placed on the factor sensitivities to each yield curve. These limits on the three factor sensitivities are the basis risk sensitivity limits.

These individual yield curve point sensitivities are continually used by the trader to manage the portfolio. Frequently, the risk from changes in the shape of the yield curve is far greater than the risk from parallel movements.

Yield curve sensitivity limits can also be placed on each yield curve individually, if an even stricter degree of control is required.

MANAGEMENT OF PRICE RISK

Sample Analysis

The analysis needed to verify that these limits have not been exceeded is the same as that needed to manage and to hedge the swap warehouse. This is best illustrated by an example.

A representative warehouse of fixed/fixed cross currency swaps between pounds sterling and U.S. dollars has been hedged with gilts, treasuries, FRAs, and LTFX contracts. This is the total portfolio, which is then analyzed one currency at a time. The results for pounds sterling are presented in Table 1.

The three yield curves used to revalue the three different instruments are shown. The numbers in the column labeled "swap," for example, give the pound change in the value of the portfolio if the corresponding point on the swap yield curve is increased by 1 basis point.

For example, an increase in the government 10-year yield from 14.80 percent to 14.81 percent will decrease the portfolio value by £17,957; an increase in the swap 10-year yield from 15.50 percent

TABLE 1
Portfolio Sensitivity Analysis

| | Pounds Sterling Warehouse | | Date: 10990 | Values in Pounds Sterling | | | |
| | Yield Curves (%) | | | Portfolio Revaluation at +1 Basis Point | | | |
Number of Months	Govt.	Swap	Money Mkt.	Govt.	Swap	Money Mkt.	Net
1	14.00	14.50	14.15	0	0	0	0
2	14.00	14.50	14.20	0	0	0	0
3	14.00	14.50	14.25	0	-17	0	-17
6	14.10	14.60	14.30	-5	23	-2	15
9	14.15	14.65	14.40	-1	-42	0	-43
12	14.20	14.70	14.50	-10	-231	35	-206
18	14.25	14.75	14.55	146	-879	83	-650
24	14.30	14.80	14.60	2,321	-1,224	440	1,537
36	14.40	14.95	14.70	640	-45	-456	140
48	14.50	15.10	14.80	-22	606	-1,832	-1,248
60	14.60	15.25	14.80	7,228	-8,563	2,441	1,107
84	14.70	15.40	14.80	-842	391	431	-19
120	14.80	15.50	14.80	-17,957	19,390	-1,903	-469
Entire yield curve				-8,498	9,406	-762	147
Spot FX 1% sensitivity (in US$), pounds sterling @ 1.900				-24,163	16,814	3,700	-3,649

to 15.51 percent will increase the portfolio value by £19,390; an increase in the money market 10-year yield from 14.80 percent to 14.81 percent will decrease the portfolio value by £1,903. Thus, if all 10-year yields move by 1 basis point, the value of the portfolio will decrease by only £469. This is because the holding of 10-year gilts was adjusted so that it would have approximately equal and opposite sensitivity to the holding of the 10-year swap, with a small contribution from the LTFX contract covering a final exchange of principal. The same is then done at all points on the yield curve.

If all three yield curves move up by 1 basis point, there will be a loss of £8,498 on the gilts, a gain of £9,406 on the swaps, and a loss of £762 on LTFX, for a total gain of £147.

The net sensitivity limit applies to the number 147; the basis risk sensitivity limit applies to the numbers −8,498, 9,406 and −762; the yield curve sensitivity limit applies to numbers in the "net" column from −17 to −469. These limits could be, for example, 5,000, 20,000 and 10,000, respectively.

The spot FX factor sensitivity is also shown. It shows that the value of the total portfolio will decrease by $3,649 if the British pound were to increase in value by 1 percent against the U.S. dollar. Thus, we must be net short $364,900 worth of British pounds. In other words, the swap portfolio has been made almost completely insensitive to changes in the foreign exchange rate as well as changes in the overall level of sterling interest rates.

The results of the analysis for U.S. dollars are presented in Table 2. The portfolio has been made insensitive to changes in U.S. dollar interest rates. The spot FX sensitivity is trying show the effect of the U.S. dollar appreciating against all other currencies, with the results measured in U.S. dollars, which clearly has no meaning when the currency is the base currency—in this case, U.S. dollars. However, it does show the net position of the portfolio to be short 100 times $77,180, or $7.718 million.

Hedging

A number of other conclusions can be drawn from an inspection of the preceding British pound analysis.

The swap factor sensitivity at 10 years is £19,390. This is a positive number, which means that there is a short position in the 10-year maturity and that some long swaps (receiving fixed-rate payments)

TABLE 2
Portfolio Sensitivity Analysis

U.S. Dollars Warehouse   Date: 10990

	Yield Curves (%)			Portfolio Revaluation at +1 Basis Point Values in U.S. Dollars			
Number of Months	Govt.	Swap	Money Mkt.	Govt.	Swap	Money Mkt.	Net
1	7.53	8.56	8.25	0	0	77	77
2	7.53	8.56	8.37	0	−1	0	−1
3	7.53	8.56	8.50	3	12	0	16
6	7.89	8.93	8.87	−8	8	−14	−14
9	8.08	9.06	9.00	9	33	−10	32
12	8.28	9.19	9.12	−1	443	−794	−352
18	8.48	9.31	9.27	−150	1,614	−405	1,059
24	8.68	9.43	9.43	−2,165	1,955	−873	−1,084
36	8.78	9.57	9.57	−558	−365	995	73
48	8.86	9.64	9.64	−2,081	−1,540	3,893	272
60	8.94	9.70	9.64	−12,109	17,635	−5,567	−41
84	9.10	9.86	9.64	2,089	−1,273	−676	140
120	9.22	9.98	9.64	40,857	−45,612	4,623	−132
Entire yield curve				25,877	−27,080	1,248	45
Spot FX 1% sensitivity (in US$), U.S. dollars @ 1.000				−151,612	76,438	−2,006	−77,180

429

would be needed to bring the book back into balance. To do this, the first step would be to adjust the quoted bid and offer prices to encourage long 10-year swaps and discourage short 10-year swaps. The reverse situation applies for 5-year maturities.

The factor sensitivity of a £1 million 10-year swap at 15.5 percent is simple to calculate. The present value of the 20 semiannual coupon payments and the final principal discounted at 15.5 percent semiannual is obviously £1,000,000. The present value discounted at 15.51 percent semiannual is £999,500, which gives a factor sensitivity of £500.

Given that the swap factor sensitivity at 10 years is £19,390 and the factor sensitivity of a £1,000,000 swap is £500, it is easy to calculate that swaps with a nominal value of some £38,780,000 are needed to balance the book at 10 years.

The factor sensitivities at other maturities can be calculated by the same method, and the results are indicated in Table 3. Given these results, it is fairly straightforward to calculate exactly what swaps are needed to bring the portfolio into balance.

Whenever a swap is added to or deleted from the portfolio, the hedge will have to be adjusted. The effectiveness of the hedge must also be monitored every day, since the exact amount of the required hedge changes slowly with the passage of time. This will eventually require that an adjustment be made to the hedge. If a new swap is added to the portfolio, it would normally be hedged with a gilt of the same maturity. However, if there is a need to adjust the hedge because of the passage of time, it may make sense to buy or sell a gilt at a different maturity.

TABLE 3
Factor Sensitivities
(per 1 million face)

Maturity	Yield	Factor Sensitivity
24	14.80	168
36	14.95	235
48	15.01	292
60	15.25	341
84	15.40	419
120	15.50	500

Positioning

Given the information in the factor sensitivity analysis, a trader can calculate the effect of a change in the yield curve on the aggregate value of the warehouse portfolio. This could be done to calculate the effect of changes that have already occurred in the yield curve during the day, so that the formal overnight revaluation does not produce any unexpected results. This could also be done using hypothetical yield curve changes, thereby allowing the trader to position the portfolio to profit if expected changes actually do occur, whether these are changes in overall yield levels, yield curve shape, or basis spread.

SUMMARY

The problem of risk management of a swap portfolio can be tackled using a general approach involving the following steps.

First the market factors of exposure are identified; these are the market factors that are required as input to a suitable mark-to-market valuation model. Next the factor sensitivities are calculated; these are the changes in the value of the portfolio arising from unit changes in the market factors. Finally, limits are placed on these factor sensitivities to minimize the losses caused by adverse changes in the market factors.

The same factor sensitivities can also be used to manage the warehouse—to hedge it correctly and to position it to take advantage of expected changes while minimizing the effect of other, unexpected changes.

It is this multiplicity of uses that makes the use of factor sensitivities such a powerful technique for the risk management of a cross currency swap portfolio.

CHAPTER 19

RELATIONSHIPS BETWEEN CROSS CURRENCY SWAPS AND INTEREST RATE SWAPS

Carl A. Batlin
Manufacturers Hanover Trust Company
New York

INTRODUCTION

In a cross currency swap, two parties agree to exchange cash flow streams, usually representing periodic interest payments and the return of a notional principal amount at maturity, denominated in different currencies. An interest rate swap, on the other hand, is an agreement to exchange periodic interest payments denominated in the same currency. From these definitions, it is apparent that cross currency swaps are more complex than interest rate swaps. In the first place, denominating the two sides of the swap in different currencies permits three possible structures—fixed-rate vs. fixed-rate, fixed-rate vs. floating-rate, and floating-rate vs. floating-rate—in contrast to the solitary fixed-rate vs. floating-rate structure of an interest rate swap.[1] In addition, three variables are needed to characterize the terms of a cross currency swap (i.e., the fixed interest rate or floating-rate index on each side and the spot foreign exchange rate that equalizes the two notional principal amounts), whereas only the value of the fixed rate is needed to "price" an interest rate swap.

---

[1] Strictly speaking, there can exist floating/floating interest rate swaps, where the two sides are based on different interest rate indexes (e.g., commercial paper vs. LIBOR). In terms of the standard floating-rate index (LIBOR), however, there can be only one possible interest rate swap structure.

In spite of their additional complexity, cross currency swaps are used for the same generic purposes as interest rate swaps. Since both types of swaps create gains or losses for the two parties as interest rates and/or exchange rates change, either type can be combined with an underlying balance sheet position to reduce the existing exposure to rate movements (hedging), to increase the existing exposure (speculation), or to take advantage of price differences between the swap market and the markets in which the underlying assets or liabilities are priced (asset yield enhancement or borrowing cost reduction).

To explore how cross currency swaps and interest rate swaps are used for these purposes, we shall analyze the case of a U.S. dollar (USD)–based firm that can borrow either USD- or foreign currency (FC)–denominated funds to invest in either a USD- or a FC-denominated interest-earning asset at an initial time 0. We denote as N the firm's per-period USD net income per dollar of investment, R_I as its investment yield, and R_B as its borrowing rate. In addition, any funds borrowed or invested in the foreign currency are exposed to appreciation or depreciation over the accrual period by the amount of the gross change in the spot exchange rate, measured as S_t/S_0—the ratio of the spot exchange rate (expressed as the number of U.S. dollars per unit of the foreign currency) at the end of the period to its value when the asset or liability is created. We can reflect this additional exposure of FC assets and liabilities by multiplying each interest rate, R_I and R_B, by its corresponding "currency factor"—denoted C_I and C_B, respectively, which equals S_T/S_0 in the case of FC assets or liabilities and which takes a value of 1 for USD borrowed or invested funds.[2] Accordingly, the firm's net income per dollar of investment is stated as

$$N = R_I C_I - R_B C_B \qquad (1)$$

---

[2]The currency factors emerge from the fact that an initial USD amount is converted into a FC amount by dividing it by the initial exchange rate S_0. Then, after that FC amount accrues the FC interest rate between time 0 and time T, it is reconverted to U.S. dollars by multiplying principal plus interest by the current exchange rate S_T. Then, with both sides now expressed in a common currency (U.S. dollars), the revenue and cost can be netted to obtain the net income. In the case where the investment yield or borrowing rate is a USD rate already, the currency factor is 1, because the initial exchange rate S_0 and the current exchange rate S_T both equal 1.

Similarly, we shall denote as P the firm's periodic swap payment (measured in U.S. dollars) per dollar of notional principal, R_R as the interest rate received, R_p as the interest rate paid, and C_R and C_p as the currency factors corresponding to these two interest rates. The net per-period swap payment received per dollar of notional principal is therefore[3]

$$P = R_R C_R - R_P C_P \qquad (2)$$

and the total combined cash flow per dollar of notional principal each period, calculated as the sum of equations (1) and (2), is

$$N + P = (R_I C_I - R_P C_P) + (R_R C_R - R_B C_B) \qquad (3)$$

We shall use the general framework of equations (1)–(3) to compare how interest rate swaps and cross currency swaps accomplish the purposes of hedging, speculation, and yield enhancement or cost reduction.

INTEREST RATE SWAPS

When the currency factors C_I and C_B in equation (1) are the same (i.e., $C_I = C_B = 1$ or $C_I = C_B = S_T/S_0$), the appropriate type of contract with which to combine the firm's net income is an interest rate swap. When both currency factors equal 1, the asset and liability are both denominated in U.S. dollars, and the firm can modify its exposure or profitability with a USD interest rate swap. When both currency factors equal S_T/S_0, on the other hand, the asset and liability are both denominated in the foreign currency, so that net income modifications are achievable with a foreign-currency interest rate swap.

At the outset, the asset and the liability can be priced on either a fixed-rate or a floating-rate basis. The fixed borrowing rate is denoted

---

[3]In all but the final payment period, the swap payment is calculated by multiplying each side's interest rate by its notional principal (which is the same on both sides in an interest rate swap) and netting the two sides. In the final period, the principal and interest are exchanged. In an interest rate swap, the principals on the two sides always cancel each other, but in a cross currency swap, they will be different, and the principal reexchange will generally constitute an important part of the swap.

R_F, and the fixed investment yield is defined axiomatically as the spread e_F above that. The floating borrowing rate is LIBOR, denoted R_L, and the floating investment yield is defined as the spread e_L above LIBOR. Thus, the investment yield R_I in equation (1) can equal either $(R_F + e_F)$, if it is a fixed interest rate, or $(R_L + e_L)$, if it is a floating rate, while the borrowing rate can equal either R_F or R_L. In the case of the swap, one side pays or receives the fixed swap rate, denoted as R_S, while the other side reciprocates with LIBOR. Either interest rate, R_R or R_p, in the swap can therefore equal R_S or R_L. The following analysis assumes the case of USD assets and liabilities, so that all currency factors are set equal to 1, but the FC asset and liability case emerges if all results are simply multiplied by the factor S_T / S_0.[4]

Short-Funding

Consider first the case of a fixed-rate asset funded by LIBOR. The exposure inherent in this position is that net income is inversely impacted by short-term interest rate movements: it will increase if interest rates fall, and it will decrease if interest rates rise. To reduce this exposure, the firm needs to lengthen its liability from a floating-rate to a fixed-rate basis or shorten its asset from a fixed-rate to a floating-rate basis; either is achieved by paying the fixed rate and receiving the floating rate in an interest rate swap. The LIBOR receipts from the swap will then offset the floating-rate debt payments, so that the combined cash flow is

$$N + P = R_F + e_F - R_S \qquad (4)$$

which is independent of subsequent LIBOR changes.

Hedging the inherent exposure in a firm's balance sheet is a major application of swaps. Alternatively, the firm might be able to match-

---

[4]Thus, when net income is expressed in USD terms (i.e., for a U.S.-based firm), all positions that are exposed to gains or losses from changes in foreign-currency interest rates automatically generate foreign exchange risk, because those gains or losses must then be translated back into U.S. dollars. The magnitude of this type of foreign exchange risk—created by net income that is generated in a foreign currency—is much smaller than the type of foreign exchange exposure created by having assets and liabilities denominated in different currencies. The latter risk is what is addressed by cross currency swaps.

fund the asset when it is acquired. If so, the exposure-free net income available to it by match-funding the asset with the liability directly in the cash market would be either e_L (for a matched floating-rate asset and liability) or e_F (for a matched fixed-rate pair). From equation (4), it is clear that the indirect strategy of short-funding the asset in the cash market and paying the fixed rate on the swap is more profitable than the direct approach of funding a fixed-rate asset with fixed-rate debt if the swap rate R_s is lower than the fixed borrowing rate R_F. Under that condition, the firm can reduce its borrowing cost by creating a synthetic fixed-rate liability in the swap market.

Long-Funding

The other type of position that is exposed to interest rate risk is a floating-rate asset financed by a fixed-rate liability. Net income generated by this position is positively affected by short-term interest rate changes: it increases when interest rates rise and decreases when they fall. If the firm wants to enter into a swap to hedge this exposure, it should receive the fixed rate and pay the floating rate in the swap, which will have the effect of lengthening the asset to a fixed-rate basis or shortening the liability to a floating-rate basis. Since the LIBOR-based receipts from the investment cover the LIBOR payments in the swap, the resulting combined net income plus swap payment would be

$$N + P = e_L + R_S - R_F \tag{5}$$

which does not depend on subsequent values of LIBOR.

It is also possible that the firm might create a long-funded asset expressly for the purpose of swapping it into a match-funded position, because this indirect procedure could be more profitable than the direct approach of funding a fixed-rate (or floating-rate) asset with a fixed-rate (or floating-rate) liability. From equation (5), it is clear that the condition that enhances the yield of a synthetically created match-funded asset above that of a floating-rate asset directly match-funded in the cash market is that the fixed swap rate exceeds the fixed borrowing rate in the cash market. When the fixed swap rate is higher, it is profitable to receive it in the swap.

Interest Rate Speculation

The discussion of interest rate swaps so far has considered an underlying mismatched balance sheet position that is exposed to interest rate risk and that can be immunized from the effect of changes in interest rates by the addition of an interest rate swap. The motivation behind this reduction in the underlying balance sheet's exposure varies: sometimes it is the simple hedging of the interest rate risk, while in other instances, it is the indirect creation of a hedged synthetic position whose profitability exceeds that of the comparable position directly available in the cash market.

It is possible, of course, regardless of the underlying balance sheet exposure, to enter into an interest rate swap for purposes of increasing the underlying exposure to changes in interest rates. If, for instance, the firm expects interest rates to rise, it could profit by receiving the floating interest rate and paying the fixed interest rate in an interest rate swap. This might be a less expensive way (in terms of transaction costs) to create the exposure than long-funding a floating-rate asset in the cash market. Similarly, expectations of falling short-term interest rates can be capitalized on by receiving the fixed interest rate and paying the floating interest rate in a swap. Moreover, such a speculative position might be cheaper to initiate and eventually to unwind than the direct approach of short-funding a fixed-rate asset in the cash market. In either case, the extent to which such a position is ultimately profitable depends on the degree to which the firm's expectations about future interest rates are realized.

FIXED/FIXED CROSS CURRENCY SWAPS

If the currency factors C_I and C_B in equation (1) have different values, a cross currency swap is the appropriate vehicle for the firm to use to alter its risk exposure or improve its profitability. When one of these currency factors equals 1 and the other equals S_T/S_0, the implication is that the relevant asset and liability are denominated in different currencies, as is commonly the case for multinational corporations. Accordingly, one of the two cash flows—either the investment revenue or the borrowing cost—must be converted from the foreign currency back into U.S. dollars, and as a result, net income is exposed to gains or losses from movements in the foreign exchange rate.

The simplest way to analyze the use of cross currency swaps for hedging, speculating, and yield enhancement or cost reduction purposes is to explore the case where both the investment yield and the borrowing rate are fixed interest rates. We will distinguish the USD fixed interest rate (R_F^{US} for the borrowing rate and e_F^{US} for the additional spread incorporated in the investment yield) from the FC fixed interest rate (analogously, R_F^{FC} and e_F^{FC}) and also set the currency factor for the USD asset or liability equal to 1 and that for the FC asset or liability equal to S_T/S_0. As a result, the investment revenue in equation (1), $R_I C_I$, can equal either $(R_F^{US} + e_F^{US})$ or $(R_F^{FC} + e_F^{FC})S_T/S_0$, and the borrowing cost, $R_B C_B$, can equal either R_F^{US} or $R_F^{FC}S_T/S_0$, provided the two cash flows are not both denominated in U.S. dollars or in the foreign currency. In the swap, the receiving side, $R_R C_R$, and the paying side, $R_p C_p$, can equal either a fixed USD swap rate, R_s^{US}, or a fixed foreign-currency swap rate, $R_s^{FC}S_T/S_0$. How the underlying balance sheet position and the swap are combined to achieve the prescribed purposes depends on whether it is the asset or the liability that is denominated in the foreign currency.

U.S. Dollar Funding

First consider the case of a foreign-currency fixed-rate asset funded by a USD fixed-rate liability. Applying these conditions to equation (1) suggests that net income per dollar of investment is expressed as

$$N = (R_F^{FC} + e_F^{FC})S_T/S_0 - R_F^{US} \qquad (6)$$

Equation (6) implies that, unlike the single-currency case, net income is not affected by changes in short-term interest rates. It is, however, positively impacted by exchange rate changes, in that net income increases when the foreign currency strengthens (the U.S. dollar weakens) and declines when the foreign currency weakens (the U.S. dollar strengthens). To mitigate this exposure, the firm should transform its liability into the foreign currency (out of U.S. dollars) or convert its asset out of the foreign currency (into U.S. dollars). Both these goals are accomplished by receiving the USD interest rate and paying the

FC interest rate in a fixed/fixed cross currency swap. The combined net income plus swap payment per dollar of notional principal, using equation (3), would equal

$$N + P = (R_S^{US} - R_F^{US}) + (R_F^{FC} + e_F^{FC} - R_S^{FC})S_T/S_0 \qquad (7)$$

The hedged net income in equation (7) could still contain foreign exchange risk since, like the unhedged net income in equation (6), it is composed of two parts, only one of which is influenced by exchange rate movements. There is, however, a significant difference between equations (6) and (7): in equation (6), net income is characterized as the difference between two interest rate levels that always have opposite signs, while in equation (7), the combined cash flow is expressed as the sum of two interest rate spreads, which may have the same sign. Since exchange rate changes merely affect the scale of one term relative to the other, so long as both spreads are positive, foreign exchange rate movements cannot affect the overall sign of the combined cash flow (i.e., they cannot turn a gain into a loss). Moreover, even if one spread is positive and one is negative, since both spreads are small relative to the two interest rate levels in equation (6), the impact of foreign exchange rate movements will also be relatively small. As a result, the existing level of foreign exchange risk in equation (6) is certainly reduced by the addition of a cross currency swap in equation (7).

Beyond the goal of hedging, equation (7) also sheds light on the conditions under which the creation of a synthetic U.S. dollar or foreign-currency asset or liability might be more profitable than the direct funding of a fixed-rate asset with a fixed-rate liability in the same currency. In this case, if a fixed-rate FC asset had been financed with a fixed-rate FC liability, the resulting net income would have been $e_F^{FC}S_T/S_0$. From equation (7), it is apparent that the indirect approach of funding a foreign-currency asset with a USD liability, and then swapping the liability into the foreign currency or swapping the asset out of the foreign currency into U.S. dollars, could improve the profitability of the transaction in either of two ways: (1) If the foreign-currency swap rate, R_S^{FC}, is less than the foreign-currency borrowing rate available in the cash market, R_F^{FC}, the borrowing cost would be reduced by paying the fixed foreign-currency interest rate in the swap. (2) If the USD swap rate, R_S^{US}, exceeds the fixed interest rate available in the USD cash market, R_F^{US}, investment revenue would be enhanced by receiving the fixed USD rate in the swap. Any combination of these two circumstances that produces a value of the combined cash flow in equation (7) greater than the matched fixed-rate foreign-currency spread, $e_F^{FC} S_T / S_0$, would make the indirect approach worthwhile.

Foreign Currency Funding

The other case in which a fixed/fixed cross currency swap can be useful is that of a fixed-rate U.S. dollar asset financed with a fixed-rate foreign-currency liability. From equation (1), the net income per dollar of investment from this position is

$$N = R_F^{US} + e_F^{US} - R_F^{FC} S_T / S_0 \tag{8}$$

It is apparent that although this expression is not affected by changes in short-term interest rates, it is inversely related to exchange rate movements: net income is reduced by a strengthening of the foreign currency (a weakening of the U.S. dollar) and enhanced by a weakening of the foreign currency (a strengthening of the U.S. dollar). To hedge this exposure, the firm should receive the foreign-currency interest rate and pay the U.S. dollar interest rate in a fixed/fixed cross currency swap, swapping out of the foreign-currency liability (into U.S. dollars) or into a foreign-currency asset (out of U.S. dollars). The hedged net income per dollar of notional principal from the combined position is

$$N + P = R_F^{US} - R_S^{US} + e_F^{US} + (R_S^{FC} - R_F^{FC}) S_T / S_0 \tag{9}$$

Since the spread between the fixed swap rate and the fixed interest rate available in the FC cash market is relatively small, the exposure of the combined position in equation (9) to exchange rate changes is much smaller than the exposure of the unhedged net income in equation (8).

Equation (9) elucidates the conditions under which the profitability of borrowing FC funds to finance a USD asset and then swapping into a USD liability or into a FC asset exceeds the profitability of a USD asset match-funded with a USD liability (i.e., e_F^{US}). Either (1) the FC swap rate that the firm receives must exceed the fixed interest rate available in the FC cash market, or (2) the USD swap rate that the firm pays must be less than the fixed interest rate available in the USD cash market. Of the two conditions, the latter is preferable, since whether or not the value of equation (9) exceeds the fixed interest rate spread e_F^{US} in the former case depends on future exchange rate movements.

Exchange Rate Speculation

As with interest rate swaps, cross currency swaps may also be used for speculative purposes. Independent of its underlying balance sheet position, a firm can enter into a fixed/fixed cross currency swap to attempt to profit from its expectations about the future value of the exchange rate.

Specifically, an open position to receive the fixed USD interest rate and pay the fixed FC interest rate creates a swap payment per dollar of notional principal equal to

$$P = R_S^{US} - R_S^{FC} S_T / S_0 \qquad (10)$$

This payment is inversely related to movements in the exchange rate: it increases when the foreign currency weakens (the U.S. dollar strengthens) and decreases when the foreign currency strengthens (the U.S. dollar weakens). Since this position is equivalent to the foreign-currency funding of a USD asset, the implication is that the firm gains from borrowing in the foreign currency and lending in U.S. dollars when the foreign currency weakens (the U.S. dollar strengthens) and loses from this strategy when the exchange rate moves in the opposite direction.

In contrast, the swap payment resulting from an open position to pay the fixed USD interest rate and receive the fixed FC interest rate is the negative of equation (10) and therefore creates the same exposure as borrowing in U.S. dollars and investing in the foreign currency. Such a position benefits from a strengthening of the foreign currency (a weakening of the U.S. dollar) and loses from a weakening of the foreign currency (a strengthening of the U.S. dollar). The implication of these two cases taken together is that it is beneficial to invest in currencies that subsequently strengthen (i.e., that are currently under-valued) and to borrow in currencies which subsequently weaken (i.e., that are currently overvalued).

FIXED/FLOATING CROSS CURRENCY SWAPS

A common variation on the previous situation, in which a firm finances a fixed-rate asset in one currency with a fixed-rate liability in another, occurs when one of the two interest rates (almost always the USD rate) is a floating rate that resets every period (e.g., six-month LIBOR). Substituting this rate, denoted R_L^{US}, for the corresponding fixed interest rate in the cash market, R_F^{US}, and in the swap market, R_S^{US}, changes equations (6) through (10) somewhat. The net income from the USD-funded FC asset in equation (6) is now inversely affected by changes in short-term USD interest rates, as well as being positively impacted by changes in the value of the foreign currency. To hedge this two-pronged exposure, the firm must pay the fixed FC interest rate and receive USD LIBOR in the swap, in order to lengthen the maturity of its liability and simultaneously swap it into the foreign currency, or shorten the maturity of its asset and swap it into U.S. dollars. As a result, its hedged net income per dollar of notional principal in equation (7) becomes

$$N + P = (R_F^{FC} + e_F^{FC} - R_S^{FC})S_T/S_0 \qquad (11)$$

From equation (11), the only source of improved profitability is the case in which the FC swap rate is lower than the fixed borrowing rate available in the FC cash market.[5]

In the case of a USD asset financed by a FC liability, the net income in equation (8) would be improved by increases in USD LIBOR and reduced by decreases in LIBOR. Moreover, net income would still be adversely affected by changes in the value of the foreign currency.

---

[5]Moreover, the residual foreign exchange risk left in the combined balance sheet plus swap position is less than in the fixed/fixed cross currency swap case, since all remaining elements of the cash flow are equally affected by movements in the exchange rate.

The appropriate swap position to hedge these exposures would be to receive USD LIBOR and pay the fixed FC interest rate, the effect of which would be to lengthen the maturity of the asset and simultaneously swap it into the foreign currency, or to shorten the maturity of the liability and swap it into U.S. dollars. The resulting hedged net income per dollar of notional principal in equation (9) would be transformed into

$$N + P = e_L^{US} + (R_S^{FC} - R_F^{FC})S_T/S_0 \qquad (12)$$

where e_L^{US} is the spread above USD LIBOR earned by a floating-rate USD asset. This spread, which can be earned by match-funding a floating-rate USD investment with USD LIBOR, can—from equation (12)—be improved upon synthetically only if the fixed FC swap rate exceeds the fixed interest rate available in the FC cash market.

Speculative positions in fixed/floating cross currency swaps capitalize on the characteristic that such swaps combine the interest rate exposure of a USD interest rate swap with the exchange rate exposure of a fixed/fixed cross currency swap. The suitably modified version of equation (10)—with R_L^{US} in place of R_S^{US}—would imply that the receiver of USD LIBOR and the payer of the fixed FC interest rate would benefit from rising short-term USD interest rates and a weakening of the foreign currency (a strengthening of the U.S. dollar) and be harmed by the reverse conditions. The fortunes of a payer of USD LIBOR and receiver of the fixed FC interest rate in the swap would rise/fall under the opposite set of circumstances.

FLOATING/FLOATING CROSS CURRENCY SWAPS

The third cross currency exposure that a multinational firm might face occurs when the interest rates of both the asset and the liability not only are denominated in different currencies, but are both reset based on a floating-rate index every period as well. The implication of this situation for equations (6) through (10) is that foreign-currency LIBOR, R_L^{FC}, as well as USD LIBOR, is substituted for the fixed interest rates in the cash market and in the swap market, changing the nature of the exposures from those of the two previous cross currency swap cases. For the USD-funded foreign-currency asset, the net income expression in equation (6) and its equivalent created by the swap—the negative of equation (10)—would now be positively affected by changes in foreign currency short-term interest rates, inversely affected by changes in short-term USD interest rates, and positively affected by movements in the value of the foreign currency. The foreign currency–funded USD asset, on the other hand, whose net income is formalized in equation (8) and whose swap equivalent is given by equation (10), would have the opposite three exposures.

The hedged net income per dollar of notional principal in equation (7)—after the owner of the USD-funded foreign-currency asset hedged the position by paying FC LIBOR and receiving USD LIBOR in the swap—would become

$$N + P = e_L^{FC} S_T / S_0 \qquad (13)$$

where e_L^{FC} is the match-funded spread available in the floating-rate FC cash market. From equation (13), it is notable that the floating/floating cross currency swap market offers no opportunity for investment yield enhancement or borrowing cost reduction through the creation of synthetic assets or liabilities. The hedged net income for the opposite position (the FC-funded USD asset presented in equation (9)), on the other hand, is simply the match-funded floating-rate USD spread e_L^{US}. This, then, is the only cross currency exposure case in which the addition of a cross currency swap permits the total elimination of foreign exchange rate risk.

RELATIONSHIPS AMONG INSTRUMENTS

In comparing the different ways in which interest rate swaps and the three varieties of cross currency swaps are used for purposes of hedging, speculation, and profitability improvement through investment yield enhancement or borrowing cost reduction, several conclusions can be reached:

1. Interest rate swaps enable firms to manage pure interest rate risk.

2. Fixed/fixed cross currency swaps produce exposures that are influenced only by movements in foreign exchange rates.
3. Other types of cross currency swaps appear to be hybrids of these two instruments.

These results can now be combined with the fact that another instrument—the foreign exchange forward contract—also exists for the management of foreign exchange rate risk. This information suggests the existence of four relationships involving interest rate swaps, cross currency swaps, and foreign exchange forwards, which form the basis for all arbitrage and hedging activities using these instruments, independent of underlying balance sheet positions.

I. Strip of Forwards = Fixed/Fixed Cross Currency Swap

A foreign exchange forward contract is an agreement to exchange a specified quantity of one currency for another at a specified future date at today's forward exchange rate. The forward contract creates a gain or loss for both parties if the future spot exchange rate on the maturity date differs from the agreed-upon forward rate. The buyer of the foreign-currency forward (seller of U.S. dollars forward) gains if the future spot rate exceeds the forward rate (expressed as the USD value of one FC unit) and loses if the future spot rate is lower. The seller of the foreign-currency forward (buyer of U.S. dollars forward) is in the reverse situation.

In general, the forward exchange rate differs from the spot exchange rate prevailing at the same time. The reason is that the market value of the forward rate must be set so as to prevent firms from conducting profitable arbitrage transactions of interest rate differentials between currencies. Stated formally, the Interest Rate Parity Theorem requires that the forward exchange rate satisfy the following relationship:

$$F_{0,t} = S_0(1 + R^{US})^t / (1 + R^{FC})^t \tag{14}$$

where $F_{0,t}$ is the forward exchange rate at time 0 for currencies to be exchanged at time t, S_0 is the spot exchange rate at time 0, and R^{US} and R^{FC} are the relevant U.S. dollar and foreign-currency interest rates for borrowing or lending between time 0 and time t (often determined in the swap market).[6]

Since a fixed/fixed cross currency swap requires the initial equalization of two notional principal amounts in different currencies at the prevailing spot rate S_0 and the periodic exchange of interest payments determined by fixed interest rates on each side of the swap, its structure suggests that such a swap is related to a collection of forward exchange contracts. The specific type of collection is called a strip, which is characterized by all forward exchange contracts being initiated at the same start date, but each having a different maturity date corresponding to the payment dates in the swap. The following analysis implies that, in economic terms, a strip of foreign exchange forwards is exactly equal to a fixed/fixed cross currency swap.

First, consider the cash flows per U.S. dollar of notional principal of the USD side of the swap. For an investment of \$1 (n.b., the swap is begun at par) the investor receives R_S^{US} per period except in the final period (period T), where an additional \$1 is received in the form of principal repayment. The yield on this stream of cash flows is the discount rate Y_S^{US} that equates the present value of the benefits of this stream of cash flows to its initial \$1 cost. Schematically,

$$1 = \frac{R_S^{US}}{1 + Y_S^{US}} + \frac{R_S^{US}}{(1 + Y_S^{US})^2} + \cdots + \frac{1 + R_S^{US}}{(1 + Y_S^{US})^T} \qquad (15)$$

Since the value of the cash flow stream is at par, the yield Y_S^{US} simply equals the coupon rate R_S^{US}, so that the investor earns the USD fixed swap rate from the USD side of the swap.

The yield on the foreign-currency side of the swap, Y_S^{FC}, can be calculated in the same way. The cash flows, however, are expressed in foreign-currency units, so the initial investment becomes $1/S_0$ units of foreign currency, and the future cash flows are all converted into the

---

[6]Strictly speaking, the interest rates in equation (14) should be zero-coupon rates, or rates of return for investments made at time 0 that deliver a single liquidating payment at time t. The text blurs, for the sake of convenience in the exposition, the distinction between these zero-coupon rates and the yields on multiple-payment swap transactions. The two concepts are exactly equivalent only in a flat-yield-curve environment.

foreign currency by dividing their present values by S_0. As a result, Y_s^{FC} is determined by solving the equation

$$1/S_0 = \frac{R_S^{FC}/S_0}{1 + Y_S^{FC}} + \frac{R_S^{FC}/S_0}{(1 + Y_S^{FC})^2} + \cdots + \frac{(1 + R_S^{FC})/S_0}{(1 + Y_S^{FC})^T} \qquad (16)$$

By multiplying both sides of equation (16) by S_0, it becomes clear that since the foreign-currency side of the swap also begins at par, the yield Y_S^{FC} earned on the investment on that side of the swap is the coupon rate R_S^{FC}.

A strip of foreign exchange forwards would be equivalent to a fixed/fixed cross currency swap in economic terms if, when the cash flows on the U.S. dollar side of the swap in equation (15) are converted into the foreign currency at the appropriate forward exchange rates, the yield of the resulting set of cash flows is identical to the yield that would have been earned on the foreign-currency side of the swap (i.e., R_S^{FC}). To express the initial investment of \$1 in equation (15) in foreign-currency units, it is necessary only to divide it by the initial spot exchange rate S_0. Subsequent cash flows, however, must be converted at their forward exchange rates: the first coupon must be divided by $F_{0,1}$, the second by $F_{0,2}$, and so on. Denoting the yield of this stream of cash flows corresponding to the strip of foreign exchange forwards as Y_F, we have

$$1/S_0 = \frac{R_S^{US}/F_{0,1}}{1 + Y_F} + \frac{R_S^{US}/F_{0,2}}{(1 + Y_F)^2} + \cdots + \frac{(1 + R_S^{US})/F_{0,T}}{(1 + Y_F)^T} \qquad (17)$$

The solution to equation (17) is easier to see by substituting the interest rate parity equivalent of each forward exchange rate from equation (14) to obtain

$$1/S_0 = \frac{R_S^{US}(1 + R_S^{FC})}{S_0(1 + R_S^{US})(1 + Y_F)} + \frac{R_S^{US}(1 + R_S^{FC})^2}{S_0(1 + R_S^{US})^2(1 + Y_F)^2} +$$

$$\cdots + \frac{(1 + R_S^{US})(1 + R_S^{FC})^T}{S_0(1 + R_S^{US})^T(1 + Y_F)^T} \qquad (18)$$

Now, after multiplying both sides of equation (18) by S_0, it can be seen that if $Y_F = R_S^{FC}$, the right-hand side of equation (18) reduces to an expression that can be verified as being the par bond identity from equation (15). The implication is that whether the foreign-currency investor (borrower) receives (pays) the foreign-currency side of the swap or buys (sells) the strip of forward foreign exchange contracts for the USD swap amounts, the yield will be the same. Accordingly, the fixed/fixed cross currency swap and the strip of foreign exchange forwards are equivalent instruments for managing the foreign exchange exposure of underlying balance sheet items.

II. Fixed/Fixed Cross Currency Swap = USD Interest Rate Swap + Fixed/Floating Cross Currency Swap

A fixed/fixed cross currency swap can also be expressed as the amalgamation of two other swaps. This can be seen from the cash flow for the receiver of fixed U.S. dollars and payer of the fixed foreign currency in equation (10). By adding and subtracting USD LIBOR to equation (10), this equation becomes

$$R_S^{US} - R_S^{FC} S_T / S_0 = (R_S^{US} - R_L^{US}) + (R_L^{US} - R_S^{FC} S_T / S_0) \qquad (19)$$

Equation (19) shows that the cash flow for this swap is equivalent to the sum of the cash flows from (1) receiving the fixed USD interest rate and paying USD LIBOR in a USD interest rate swap and (2) receiving USD LIBOR and paying the fixed FC interest rate in a fixed/floating cross currency swap. Correspondingly, the payer of the fixed USD interest rate and receiver of the fixed FC interest rate, who would receive the negative of equation (10), has the cash flows associated with (1) receiving USD LIBOR and paying the fixed USD interest rate and (2) receiving the fixed FC interest rate and paying USD LIBOR. The fixed/fixed cross-currency swap is therefore equivalent in economic terms to a portfolio containing a USD interest rate swap and a fixed/floating cross currency swap.

III. Fixed/Floating Cross Currency Swap = Floating/Floating Cross Currency Swap + FC Interest Rate Swap

In a similar fashion, a fixed/floating cross currency swap can be decomposed into two other swaps. The cash flow for the receiver of

USD LIBOR and payer of the fixed FC interest rate can be transformed into the sum of the cash flows from the two other swaps by adding and subtracting foreign-currency LIBOR to obtain

$$R_L^{US} - R_S^{FC} S_T / S_0 = (R_L^{US} - R_L^{FC} S_T / S_0) + (R_L^{FC} - R_S^{FC}) S_T / S_0 \quad (20)$$

The first term on the right-hand side of equation (20) is the cash flow from receiving USD LIBOR and paying FC LIBOR in a floating/floating cross currency swap. The second term is the cash flow from receiving FC LIBOR and paying the fixed FC interest rate in a FC interest rate swap. Moreover, the FC LIBOR payer's cash flow in a fixed/floating cross currency swap is the same as the negative of either side of equation (20). The implication is that a fixed/floating cross currency swap is equivalent in economic terms to the combination of a floating/floating cross currency swap and a foreign-currency interest rate swap.

IV. Floating/Floating Cross Currency Swap = Rolling Forwards

The final relationship to be shown is that the payment stream from a floating/floating cross currency swap, properly adjusted, can be replicated by the cash flows from another collection of foreign exchange forward contracts, namely, a program of rolling forwards. Rolling forwards are a series of constant-maturity foreign exchange forwards that are initiated sequentially at different dates. For instance, a program of rolling six-month forwards would begin with the purchase or sale of the first amount today at the current forward rate; six months later, as the first contract matured, the second six-month forward would be bought or sold at the forward rate prevailing at that time. The process would then continue in similar fashion until the termination of the program.

The structural similarity between a floating/floating cross currency swap and a program of rolling forwards stems from the fact that the interest rates on both sides of the swap are reset each period. The main difference between the two instruments is that the swap payments are based on the swap's initial spot exchange rate, whereas the rolling forwards incorporate, because of the Interest Rate Parity Theorem, new spot exchange rates at every maturity, or roll, date.

Once this difference, known as "spot drift," is corrected for by adjusting the notional principal to be bought or sold forward each period by the gross change in the spot exchange rate since time 0, however, the two instruments are equivalent in economic terms.

To demonstrate this equivalence, consider that at time $t - 1$, the interest rates that determine the interest payments of the swap at time t become known. As of time $t - 1$, then, the known principal plus interest payment of the U.S. dollar side of the swap per dollar of notional principal is $1 + R_L^{US}$, and that of the foreign-currency side is $(1 + R_L^{FC})/S_0$. If, instead, the spot-adjusted principal plus interest of the USD side, $(1 + R_L^{US})S_{t-1}/S_0$, were bought or sold forward at the prevailing forward rate $F_{t-1,t}$, the result, using the Interest Rate Parity Theorem in equation (14), would be

$$\frac{(1 + R_L^{US})S_{t-1}/S_0}{F_{t-1,t}} = \frac{(1 + R_L^{US})S_{t-1}/S_0}{S_{t-1}(1 + R_L^{US})/(1 + R_L^{FC})} = \frac{1 + R_L^{FC}}{S_0} \quad (21)$$

which is precisely the same as the cash flow from the foreign-currency side of the swap. In other words, an investor would be indifferent between (1) buying (or selling) the spot-adjusted principal plus interest of the U.S. dollar side of the swap forward on a rolling basis and (2) receiving (or paying) the foreign-currency side of the floating/floating cross currency swap. In economic terms, the two instruments are equivalent, since they produce the same cash flow streams.

Implications for Arbitrage and Hedging

The significance of these four relationships linking interest rate swaps, cross currency swaps, and foreign exchange forward contracts is that they suggest possible applications of these instruments beyond their conventional uses of modifying balance sheet exposures. In this regard, the earlier discussion of balance sheet–related uses of swaps might be a more appropriate description of how corporate and financial institution end-user firms might employ these instruments, while the current discussion might be more relevant for professional swap dealers and intermediaries.

The most immediate application of these four relationships is that arbitrage opportunities occur in instances when they are violated. In particular, it is possible to calculate the yield on a strip of foreign exchange forwards from, for example, six months to five years in six-month increments; if this yield deviates significantly from the foreign currency interest rate on a five-year fixed/fixed cross currency swap with semiannual payments, it would be profitable to sell the lower-yielding instrument and buy the higher-yielding one. This swap-forward arbitrage may be feasible because of the relative illiquidity of the foreign exchange forward market in maturities beyond one year. The arbitrage operation may be performed by an outside user of the forward foreign exchange market, who simply matches offsetting swaps and mispriced forward foreign exchange strips to gain arbitrage profits on a deal-by-deal basis. Alternatively, it may be implemented by a swap dealer with a large inventory of cross currency swaps that creates forward foreign exchange positions synthetically and is able to price them more aggressively than more traditional forward foreign exchange dealers.

The other relationships have useful implications for the way swap dealers might hedge themselves. In particular, the four relationships together, summarized in Figure 1, imply that a swap dealer can enter into any type of cross currency transaction and transform the risk into pure interest rate risk; that is, the swap dealer need never be exposed to changes in foreign exchange rates.

Consider, for instance, a dealer who uses relationship I to perform an arbitrage between a strip of foreign exchange forwards and a fixed/fixed cross currency swap. As a result, the dealer becomes a principal in a fixed/fixed cross currency swap with another firm, exposing it to foreign exchange rate risk. To hedge this position, the firm first uses relationship II to transform this swap into its equivalent combination of a USD interest rate swap and a fixed/floating cross currency swap. The USD interest rate swap is then managed with other USD interest rate instruments (i.e., either other offsetting interest rate swaps or temporary hedges, such as Treasury notes or interest rate futures contracts). The remaining fixed/floating cross currency swap is then transformed, through relationship III, into a foreign currency interest rate swap, whose interest rate risk is hedged with other foreign currency interest rate swaps or fixed-income instru-

FIGURE 1

Arbitrage and Hedging Relationships among Interest Rate Swaps, Cross Currency Swaps, and Foreign Exchange Forward Contracts

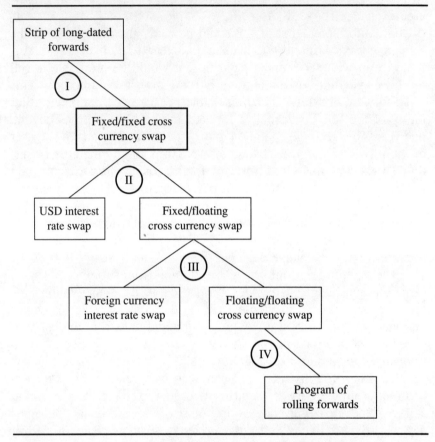

ments, and a floating/floating cross currency swap. The latter swap is then hedged, through relationship IV, by a program of rolling forwards. Thus, through these relationships, a potentially dangerous exposure to foreign exchange rate movements can be transformed into two manageable interest rate risks.

CHAPTER 20

USING FINANCIAL ENGINEERING TO CREATE LONG-DATE FORWARD FOREIGN EXCHANGE (LDFX) TRANSACTIONS, CROSS CURRENCY ANNUITY SWAPS, AND CURRENCY SWAPS WITH NOTIONAL PRINCIPALS

Ian Mordue
Australia and New Zealand Banking Group Limited
Melbourne

With the evolution of the global financial market, sufficient liquidity now exists in certain Treasury instruments—interest rate swaps and currency swaps in particular—to "financially engineer" new Treasury products. *Financial engineering* in this regard may be defined as packaging Treasury instruments to satisfy asset/liability requirements associated with capital market and treasury activities that would otherwise not be directly obtainable. Financial engineering can be used not only to create new instruments, but also to arbitrage markets that may traditionally have been traded based on theoretical prices.

This chapter will first look at a traditional market instrument, long-date forward foreign exchange transactions, to show how such an instrument may be financially engineered and will then cover some previously unobtainable instruments that may also be financially engineered.

LONG-DATE FOREIGN EXCHANGE (LDFX) OUTRIGHT TRANSACTIONS

Background

Long-date forward foreign exchange (LDFX) outright transactions developed out of a desire on the part of exporters and importers to know in advance what, in their home currency, they would receive or have to pay for goods sold or purchased in a foreign currency at some date in the future. If two equal and opposite requirements could be identified at a particular point in time, a deal could be struck directly between the two parties. More often, a bank would accommodate one party's requirements, hedging this position until the opposing requirements became available to offset. Either way, there was a need to determine a fair price for the transaction. Various theoretical models have been used that were based on interest rates available for comparable investments of appropriate maturity in the two currencies.[1]

A Conceptual Approach to Pricing LDFX

If one is normally a holder of Australian-dollar (A$) Australian Government Bonds, then one may be indifferent to holding U.S.–dollar (US$) U.S. Treasuries of the same maturity, if one could exchange the US$ at the end for A$. On maturity the holder of U.S. Treasury Bond would in theory be prepared to exchange the US$ principal plus cumulative interest payments after reinvestment for the A$ principal plus cumulative interest after reinvestment from the equivalent A$ Australian Government Bond.

The major difficulty in determining precisely the future value of the US$ Treasury Bond or the A$ Government security plus cumulative interest was that interest rates for reinvestment of the interest received from the government securities could not be known or fixed in advance. Assumptions had to be made regarding the reinvestment rates for both A$ and US$ over the life of the government securities. The future values of the A$ and US$ principals plus cumulative interest after reinvestment became the basis for the forward LDFX

---

[1] See Boris Antl, "Pricing the Hedge to Cut the Cost," *Euromoney,* May 1983, pp. 230–233.

exchange rate only after participants in the market had made their assumptions about reinvestment rates.

Financial Engineering of an LDFX Using Currency Swaps and Interest Rate Swaps

The advent of interest rate swaps made it possible to "lock in," or fix, the reinvestment rate for the interest received from the government securities. Thus, the major difficulty in precise determination of future values was overcome.

Alternatives to government securities were also opened up for fixed-rate investment, and the swap yields became the norm as the basis for determining the theoretical forward LDFX exchange rate.

Currency swaps, with their principal exchanges at maturity, made it possible to determine not only the theoretical LDFX rate but also the actual rate.

Methodology
In the following example we will financially engineer an LDFX outright; that is, we will determine the fixed amount of one currency (x) to be exchanged for a fixed amount of another currency (y) for a point of time n in the future, using a set of currency and interest rate swaps.

The currency swaps used in the example will be fixed rate in one currency (x) and floating rate the other (y). Principal exchanges at the start are not necessary, as one could sell the currency received to obtain the currency to pay at the start via the spot foreign exchange (FX) market. Principal exchange at maturity is one of the key components in constructing the LDFX.

The first step in the construction will be a currency swap with the same maturity, n, as the LDFX to give the fixed amount at maturity (principal plus final fixed-interest payment) required for currency x in the LDFX. Step 2 is to add another swap to convert the floating interest in currency y to fixed interest. Steps 3, 4, and 5 use further swaps to eliminate the fixed interest flows at time period $(n - 1)$ resulting from the swaps of maturity n in steps 1 and 2. Steps 6, 7, and 8 eliminate the net fixed-interest flows at time period $(n - 2)$ resulting from the swaps of maturity n in steps 1 and 2 and from the swaps of maturity $(n - 1)$ in steps 3, 4, and 5. The process is continued to time period 1.

When net interest flows are eliminated for currency x, there will be a surplus or a deficit of currency y that is invested or borrowed at a fixed rate of interest until maturity, n, when it will be taken into account to specify the LDFX. The investing or borrowing until maturity may be achieved with a combination of two swaps: one paying fixed interest and the other receiving fixed interest for the same principal amount but different maturities.

The effect of entering all the currency and interest rate swaps, plus any investment or borrowing, is to produce a net cash-flow position of zero (fixed and floating) at each point in time until maturity n.

Example: A Three-Year A$/US$ LDFX

At maturity the receiver of A$ interest in a three-year A$ fixed/US$ LIBOR currency swap will receive not only the A$ interest but also the A$ principal in the exchange of principals at maturity inherent in a currency swap.

For an A$10MM (10 million) three-year A$/US$ LDFX, our starting point is an A$ fixed/US$ LIBOR currency swap. In the example, the three-year A$ interest rate is 15 percent annual, and the A$/US$ exchange rate is 0.7740 at the time of calculating the LDFX.

Steps 1 and 2 are swaps to create the A$ in three years and the resultant US$ position.

Step 1. The principal required for the A$ fixed/US$ LIBOR three-year currency swap to give A$10MM (principal plus interest) at maturity is A$10MM divided by (1+ interest rate), or A$10MM/1.15 = A$8,695,652.17.

This means the US$ principal for this A$ fixed/US$ LIBOR swap is $8,695,652.17 \times .7740 = $US$6,730,434.78.

Step 2. Because the US$ LIBOR rate is a variable and because we need to determine the total US$ to pay at maturity, we enter a US$ three-year interest rate swap in which we pay fixed interest (e.g., 9% annual) and receive US$ LIBOR. This results in the conversion of all variable interest payments received from the currency swap in Step 1 to fixed interest payments. The total US$ payout at maturity from these two swaps is now determined: US$6,730,434.78 from the exchange of principals at maturity (associated with the A$8,695,652.17 three-year currency swap in step 1) plus interest from this three-year interest rate swap.

US\$6, 730, 434.78 + (US\$6, 730, 434.78 × .09) = US\$7, 336, 173.91

Diagrammatically, we may represent the two swaps we have entered—one an A\$8,695,652.17/US\$ LIBOR currency swap and the other a US\$6,730,434.78 interest rate swap—as shown in Exhibit 1.

We can see that, as a consequence of entering these two swaps, the US\$ LIBOR periodic interest payments will cancel each other but that we are left with receiving A\$ fixed and paying US\$ fixed interest payments that we do not require at the end of years 2 and 1. *Steps 3, 4, and 5 eliminate the A\$ interest payments at the end of year 2 from the currency swap in step 1 and invest the net surplus US\$ to mature at the end of year 3.*

Step 3.   We may consider either the A\$ interest payment at the end of year 2 or the US\$ interest payment at the end of year 2 as the starting point for elimination. To eliminate the A\$ interest, we enter a two-year A\$ fixed/US\$ LIBOR currency swap. Alternatively, to eliminate the US\$ interest, we enter a two-year US\$ fixed/A\$ Bills currency

EXHIBIT 1
Investment Steps 1 and 2

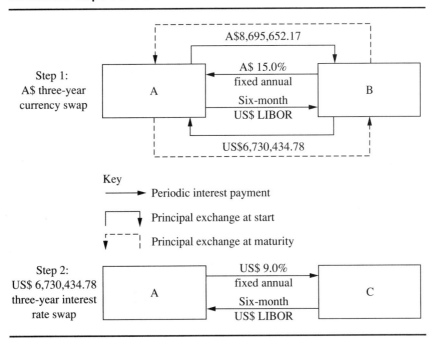

swap. There will be a residual amount of US$ or A$, depending on whether we have entered the A$ fixed/US$ LIBOR currency swap or the US$ fixed/A$ Bills, respectively. Our preference will be determined by the currency we have more dealings with or by where better Treasury instruments exist to handle the reinvestment or borrowings of the residuals.

Because we set out to create an LDFX for A$10MM exactly at the end of three years, we will work to eliminate the A$ interest at the end of year 2 with this example by entering a two-year A$ fixed/US$ LIBOR currency swap. The A$ interest payment at the end of year 2 from this A$8,695,652.17 currency swap at 15 percent annual A$ interest rate is $8,695,652.17 \times .15 = $ A$1,304,347.82. If the two-year A$ fixed/US$ LIBOR swap rate is 15.20 percent, then the currency swap we need to enter to eliminate the interest received in year 2 from the three-year currency swap is $1,304,347.82/1.152 = $ A$1,132,246.38. In this two-year swap we pay A$ interest (note that in step 1 we received A$ interest).

All currency swaps are entered at the same time, and all use the mid rate of the bid/offer spread for the exchange rate setting, which is 0.7740 in this example (although different exchange rates for the various currency swaps are not a problem, we will retain 0.7740 for all swaps for simplicity and since this is normally the case).

Step 4. The US$ principal amount for the A$1,132,246.38 currency swap at an exchange rate of 0.7740 is $1,132,246.38 \times .7740 = $ US$876,358.70. Therefore, to cancel out the US$ LIBOR flows from the two-year A$1,132,246.38 A$/US$ currency swap, we enter a two-year US$ interest rate swap to receive US$ fixed interest on US$876,358.70 and pay six-month US$ LIBOR.

If the current two-year US$ interest rate swap rate is 9.0 percent annual, the US$ interest received from this two-year swap plus the US$ principal received in the exchange of principals at maturity from the two-year A$ currency swap in step 3 is

$$(876,358.70 \times .090) + 876,358.70 = US\$955,230.98$$

Step 5. Because we have entered a US$6,730,434.78 interest rate swap in step 2, where we pay fixed at 9 percent annually, we will be required to pay interest at the end of year 2 of $6,730,434.78 \times .09 = $ US$605,739.13.

The amount of US$ principal and interest received from the two-year swaps in steps 3 and 4 is US$955,230.98. Therefore, we have surplus US$ at the end of year 2 of US$349,491.85 (955,230.98−605,739.13), which we can invest until it is required to help pay the US$ at the end of three years in the three-year A$10MM LDFX.

We can lock in, or fix, the rate of investment for this US$349,491.85 net income in two years by entering into a forward-start US$ interest rate swap, in which we receive fixed interest and pay US$ LIBOR while at the same time investing US$349,491.85 in a US$ LIBOR earning asset. The forward-start interest rate swap required is one in which we receive fixed for one year commencing in two years time. This forward-start interest rate swap may be constructed by receiving fixed for three years and paying fixed for two years. To the extent the two-year swap rate is different from the three-year swap rate, there will be a surplus or a deficit in net fixed interest payments at the end of years 1 and 2, which may be similarly reinvested or borrowed using forward swaps. For simplicity we will assume the two-year pay side is the same rate as the three-year receive side, both 9.0 percent annual. This will result in fixed interest payments, as well as US$ LIBOR interest payments, that are equal and opposite for the first two years, and hence the net cash flows will be zero until the third year.

Diagrammatically, the swaps in steps 3, 4, and 5 may be represented as in Exhibit 2. It can be seen by examining Exhibit 1 and Exhibit 2 that there are two 3-year US$ interest rate swaps: A–C and A–F. These swaps go in opposite directions: in Exhibit 1, A pays fixed for three years, and in Exhibit 2, A receives fixed for three years. These two swaps, A–C and A–F, may therefore be combined into one net swap with A paying fixed for three years. The net effect of all swaps will be shown at the end of the example.

Steps 6, 7, and 8 eliminate the A$ interest payments from swaps in steps 1 and 3 and invest the net surplus US$ to mature at the end of year 3.

Step 6. We have not only A$ and US$ interest flows at the end of year 1 from the original three-year currency swap and three-year US$ interest rate swap, but also interest flows from the two-year swaps in steps 3 and 4.

EXHIBIT 2
Investment Steps 3, 4, and 5

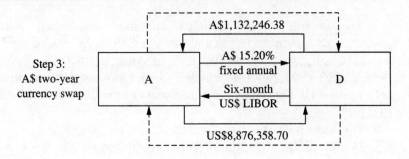

Step 3:
A$ two-year
currency swap

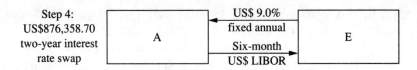

Step 4:
US$876,358.70
two-year interest
rate swap

Step 5:
US$349,491.85
six-month LIBOR
investment and forward-
start swap commencing
end year 2 and maturing
end of year 3

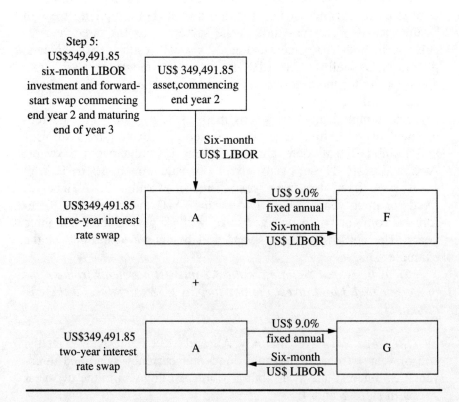

US$349,491.85
three-year interest
rate swap

US$349,491.85
two-year interest
rate swap

The net A$ interest payments at the end of year 1 are

Principal	×	**Interest rate**	=	**Interest (payment) receipt**	
8,695,652.17	×	.15	=	1,304,347.83	(swap A–B)
(1,132,246.38)	×	.152	=	(172,101.45)	(swap A–D)
				1,132,246.38	

Thus, we receive a net of A$1,132,246.38 at the end of year 1.

If the one-year A$ currency swap rate to pay fixed A$ is 15.40 percent annual, we need to enter an A$/US$ currency swap to pay fixed A$ interest on A$1,132,246.38/1.154 = A$981,149.38.

Step 7. The US$ principal amount for the A$981,149.38 currency swap at an exchange rate of 0.7740 is 981, 149.38 × .7740 = US$759, 409.62. Therefore, to cancel out the US$ LIBOR flows from the one-year A$981,149.38 A$/US$ currency swap, we enter a one-year US$ interest rate swap to receive US$ fixed interest on US$759,409.52 and pay US$ LIBOR.

If the current one-year US$ interest rate swap rate is 9.0 percent annual, the US$ interest received from this one-year swap plus the US$ principal received in the exchange of principals at maturity from the one-year $A currency swap in Step 6 is

$$(759, 408.62 \times .090) + 759, 409.62 = US\$827, 756.48$$

Step 8. The US$ interest flows, other than those from Step 7, at the end of year 1 from US$ interest rate swaps pertinent to the cash-flow situation at the end of year 1 are

Notional principal	×	**Interest rate**	=	**Interest (payment) receipt**	
(6,730,434.18)	×	.090	=	(605,739.08)	(swap A–C)
876,358.70	×	.090	=	78,872.28	(swap A–E)
				(526,866.80)	

We may keep the two-year and three-year swaps in Step 5 out of the analysis. It is possible to enter a forward-start swap directly, in which case there would be no interest flows at the end of year 1 from the forward-start swap. Alternatively, if they were to be included, the net end-of-year-1 interest rate effect would be unchanged because the reduction in the notional principal of the three-year swap, which would result in a lesser amount of fixed interest paid at the end of year 1 from the three-year swap, would be matched precisely by an increase in interest paid at the end of year 1 from the two-year swap.

In addition to the US$526,866.80 net interest paid at the end of year 1, there is the US$827,756.48 amount received at the end of year 1 from the one-year currency swap and interest rate swap (see steps 6 and 7). The US$ position at the end of year 1, including receipt of US$ principal from the one-year A$/US$ currency swap and interest flows from the three-year, two-year, and one-year US$ interest rate swaps, is therefore $827,756.48 - 526,866.80 = US\$300,889.68$.

This US$300,889.68 may be invested to mature at the end of year 3 to be used to help pay the US$ required for the three-year A$10MM LDFX.

The interest rate received from the investment may be locked in by entering a forward-start interest rate swap for notional principal US$300,889.68 to receive fixed and pay LIBOR for two years commencing at the end of year 1 and investing the US$300,889.68 in a US$ LIBOR earning asset.

The forward-start interest rate swap to commence at the end of year 1 and run until the end of year 3 may be constructed by entering (a) a three year interest rate swap to receive fixed and pay LIBOR and (b) a one-year interest rate swap to pay fixed and receive LIBOR — both for US$300,889.68.

In addition, as there will be an interest receipt at the end of year 2 from the US$300,889.68 three-year interest rate swap, we will need to enter a forward swap to lock in the interest earned from the end of year 2 to the end of year 3 for $US\$300,889.68 \times .09 = US\$27,080.07$. (For simplicity we have assumed the three-year receive swap rate and the one-year and two-year pay swap rate are all 9.0%.)

Diagrammatically, the currency swap and interest rate swaps in steps 6, 7, and 8 may be represented as in Exhibit 3.

EXHIBIT 3
Investment Steps 6, 7, and 8

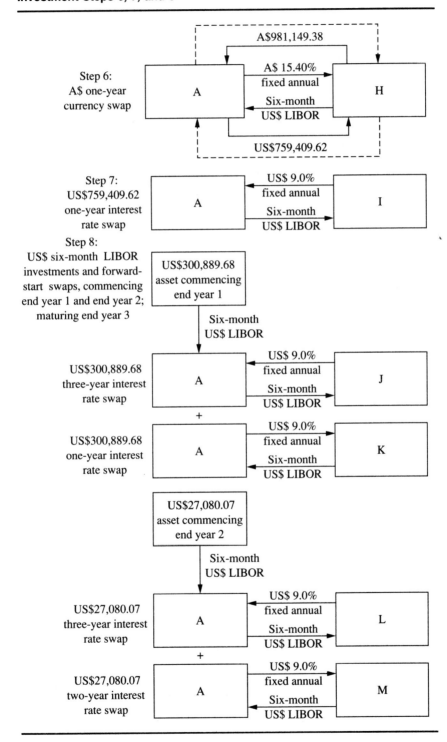

Summary of Net Effect of All Swaps

An examination of Exhibits 1, 2, and 3 shows that there are US$ interest rate swaps that are in the same or opposite directions for like maturities. Note also the effect of entering all these currency swaps and interest rate swaps plus investments in US$ LIBOR earning assets is to have zero net positions all the way through; that is, at 6 months, 12 months, 18 months, 24 months, and 30 months, for fixed and floating interest payments plus principal exchanges, the net effect is zero at each point in time when looked at simply as combined cash flows. We may therefore conclude that by entering the net swap positions and looking solely at the end-of-year-3 effect, we have constructed a synthetic LDFX that is precisely determined.

For this A$10MM A$/US$ three-year LDFX, the following net swaps are required:

three-year currency swap	A$8,695,652.17 three-year A$/US$ currency swap; receive A$ fixed @ 15.0% annual; payUS$ LIBOR exchange rate, 0.7740 (currency swap A–B)
three-year US$ interest rate swap	US$6,052,972.38 three-year interest rate swap; pay fixed US$ @ 9.0% annual; receive US$ LIBOR (swaps A–C, A–F, A–J, and A–L)
two-year currency swap	A$1,132,246.38 two-year A$/US$ currency swap; pay A$ fixed @ 15.20% annual; receive US$ LIBOR (currency swap A–D)
two-year US$ interest rate swap	US$499,786.58 two-year interest rate swap; receive US$ fixed @ 9.0% annual; pay US$ LIBOR (swaps A–E, A–G, A–M)
one-year currency swap	A$981,149.38 one-year A$/US$ currency swap; pay A$ fixed @ 15.40% annual; receive US$ LIBOR (currency swap A–H)
one-year US$ interest rate swap	US$458,519.93 one-year interest rate swap; pay US$ fixed @ 9.0% annual; receive US$ LIBOR (swaps A–I and A–K)

The following investments are required:

US$300,889.68 two-year asset earning 6-month US$ LIBOR, commencing from end year 1

US$376,571.92 (349,491.85 + 27,080.07) one-year asset earning 6-month US$ LIBOR, at the commencing from end year 2

The LDFX position at the end of year 3 is US$6,597,740.69, computed as follows:

US$ principal exchange at maturity from three-year currency swap	US$(6,730,434.78)
US$ interest @ 9.0% on net three-year interest rate swap	(544,767.51)
two-year asset, maturing end year 3	300,889.68
one-year asset, maturing end year 3	376,571.92
	US$(6,597,740.69)

Extension of Synthetic LDFX to Multiple Currencies and Complex Structures —Development of a General Theory

The preceding example of an A$10MM A$/US$ synthetic LDFX showed how one may construct an A$/US$ LDFX out of A$ fixed/US$ LIBOR currency swaps and US$ interest rate swaps. It is also possible to construct, for example, an A$/yen (¥) LDFX the same way, that is, A$ fixed/¥ LIBOR with ¥ interest rate swaps. However, because A$ fixed/¥ LIBOR currency swaps are not readily available, the technique used consists of A$ fixed/US$ LIBOR currency swaps and ¥ fixed/US$ LIBOR currency swaps.

General Theory

From the example of the three-year A$/US$ LDFX, we have seen that one-year, two-year and three-year currency swaps and interest rate swaps are required, as are investments in US$ LIBOR assets at the end of year 1 and year 2 to mature at the end of year 3. For an A$/¥ LDFX it may be shown that we would require one-year, two-year, and three-year A$/US$ LIBOR and ¥/US$ LIBOR currency swaps and no interest rate swaps. There will still be a requirement for investment in US$ LIBOR assets at the ends of year 1 and year 2 to mature at the end of year 3, but there will also be a requirement to use ¥/US$ LIBOR currency swaps to convert these US$ LIBOR floating-rate assets to fixed-rate ¥ investments instead of using interest rate swaps to convert the US$ LIBOR floating assets to fixed-rate US$ investments (see Exhibit 4).

EXHIBIT 4
Diagram of Some Components of an A$/¥ LDFX

Typical Currency Swaps Required to Produce an LDFX in the General Case

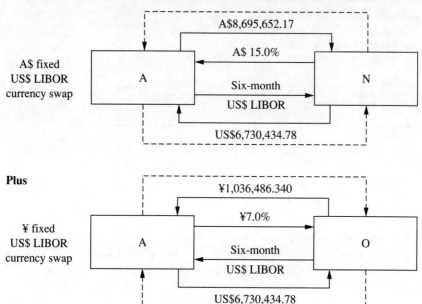

Plus

US$ LIBOR Investment + ¥/US$ LIBOR Currency Swap
(with no exchange of principals at the start)

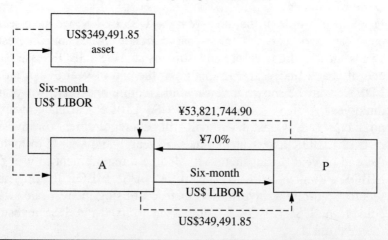

Knowing that we require just three A\$ fixed annual/US\$ LIBOR and three ¥ fixed annual/US\$ LIBOR currency swaps to produce a three-year A\$/¥ LDFX, we examine the combined effect at the end of each year to see what insights might be gained. Note that if currency swaps with semiannual fixed payments are used, we will required six A\$ fixed semiannual/US\$ LIBOR currency swaps with maturities of six months, one year, $1\frac{1}{2}$ year, . . . instead of one year, two years, . . .

A\$/US\$ Currency Swaps Required

End Year 3	A\$10 $= x_3 + .15x_3$	(1)
End Year 2	A\$ 0 $= x_2 + .152x_2 + .15x_3$	(2)
End Year 1	A\$ 0 $= x_1 + .154x_1 + .152x_2 + .15x_3$	(3)

where x_1, x_2, x_3 represent the size in A\$ principals of the A\$/US\$ currency swaps of one-year, two-year, and three-year maturity, respectively, without assigning a sign for direction (pay/receiving).

Yen/US\$ Currency Swaps Required

End Year 3	¥ $x_7 = x_4 + .07x_4$	(4)
End Year 2	¥ 0 $= x_5 + .07x_5 + .07x_4$	(5)
End Year 1	¥ 0 $= x_6 + .07x_6 + .07x_5 + .07x_4$	(6)

where x_4, x_5, and x_6 represent the size in ¥ principals of the ¥/US\$ currency swaps of one-year, two-year, and three-year maturity, respectively (as for A\$), and x_7 is the unknown amount of ¥ at three-year maturity that we are trying to determine for the LDFX.

We thus have six equations in seven unknowns, a system that cannot be solved definitively. The missing link is the unifying equation of the US\$ LIBOR flows for all the A\$ and ¥ currency swaps for years 1, 2, and 3; that is, net US\$ LIBOR flows must be zero.

The currency swaps entered at any step in the construction are such as to eliminate the US\$ LIBOR flows; the sum of all A\$ principals multiplied by the A\$/US\$ exchange rate, 0.774, must therefore equal the sum of all ¥ principals divided by the US\$/¥ exchange rate, 154.0. The seventh equation is therefore

$$(x_1 + x_2 + x_3) \times .774 = (x_4 + x_5 + x_6)/154.0 \qquad (7)$$

Note that this unifying equation contains all principals for years 1, 2, and 3. We saw when developing the A\$/US\$ LDFX that the reinvestment of surplus cash flows (US$ in the example) reduced the principals of certain maturities while adding (the same amount) to others. Therefore, it is not sufficient to look at A$/¥ for any one maturity in isolation; we must look at all maturities combined, as in Equation 7.

The seven equations with seven unknowns may be solved to give the principals of the currency swaps and the ¥ at the end of year 3 for the A$/¥ LDFX.

Because we have developed a general theory, we may apply it to the specific example of the A$10MM/US$ three-year LDFX. The exchange rate for US$ to be used in Equation (7) is 1, that is, the variables on the right-hand side of Equation (7) are divided by 1. The other equations stay the same. Solving these seven equations will give the three A$/US$ currency swaps and the three US$ interest rate swaps as well as the A$/US$ three-year LDFX. The solution to Equations (1 through 7) is (in millions) as follows:

$$
\begin{aligned}
&x_1 = \left.\begin{array}{r} -.981149373 \end{array}\right\} && \text{one-year} \\
&x_2 = \left.-1.132246377\right\} \text{A\$ currency swaps} && \text{two-year} \\
&x_3 = \left.\ \ \ \ 8.695652174\right\} && \text{three-year} \\
&x_4 = \left.\ \ \ \ 6.0529732354\right\} && \text{three-year} \\
&x_5 = \left.-.4997867809\right\} \text{US\$ interest rate swaps} && \text{two-year} \\
&x_6 = \left.-.4585199825\right\} && \text{one-year} \\
&x_7 = \ \ \ \ 6.5977408266 \ \text{US\$ required for A\$10MM at end year 3}
\end{aligned}
$$

This is the same result as in the example worked step by step and represented diagrammatically in Exhibits 1, 2, and 3. The sign associated with the solutions (e.g., -1.132246377) is interpreted as receiving fixed (in this example) or paying fixed, depending on the transaction under consideration; that is, an intelligent application is all that is required.

General Form

The general form of the equations necessary to determine a forward LDFX, outright B for a specified amount A, n years forward, using currency swaps with fixed interest payments annually in arrears, is the system of $(2n + 1)$ equations that follows:

$$A = x_n \quad + i_n x_n$$
$$0 = x_{n-1} + i_{n-1} x_{n-1} + i_n x_n$$

$$\cdot \quad \cdot \qquad \quad \cdot \qquad \cdot$$
$$\cdot \quad \cdot \qquad \quad \cdot \qquad \cdot$$
$$\cdot \quad \cdot \qquad \quad \cdot \qquad \cdot$$

$$0 = x_1 \quad + i_1 x_1 + i_2 x_2 + i_3 x_3 + \cdots + i_n x_n$$
$$B = y_n \quad + j_n y_n$$
$$0 = y_{n-1} + j_{n-1} y_{n-1} + j_n y_n$$

$$\cdot \quad \cdot \qquad \quad \cdot \qquad \cdot$$
$$\cdot \quad \cdot \qquad \quad \cdot \qquad \cdot$$
$$\cdot \quad \cdot \qquad \quad \cdot \qquad \cdot$$

$$0 = y_1 \quad + j_1 y_1 + j_2 y_2 + j_3 y_3 + \cdots + j_n y_n$$

$$(x_1 + x_2 + x_3 + \cdots + x_n)E_A = (y_1 + y_2 + y_3 + \cdots + y_n)E_B$$

where E_A = spot exchange rate, US\$ per unit currency A
E_B = spot exchange rate, US\$ per unit currency B
x_n = the principal amount in currency A for the n-year currency swap required at annual interest rate i_n
y_n = the principal amount in currency B for the n-year currency swap required at annual interest rate j_n

CROSS CURRENCY COUPON SWAPS (ANNUITY SWAPS)

It can be readily seen from the preceding discussion that, as we have $(2n+1)$ equations in $(2n+1)$ unknowns, we may solve for any number of combinations of principal exchanges (i.e., not just B for A at the end of year n), as long as we do not increase the number of unknown variables. An example would be the system with one variable, a, on the left-hand side of each of the first n equations and one variable, b, on the left-hand side of each of the second n equations instead of the two variables A and B in the above. (Of course, one of either a or b must be specified to solve for the other.)

A requirement that meets the condition of not increasing the number of unknown variables emerged in the late 1980s for certain capital markets transactions. This was for *cross currency coupon swaps*, or *annuity swaps*. These annuity swaps may be described as annual exchanges of constant amounts of currency A for constant amounts of currency B each year of the n years of the transaction. By comparison, the LDFX has one exchange of principals at the end of year n. The annuity swap may be represented by $(2n + 1)$ equations consisting of $(2n + 1)$ unknowns.

The $(2n + 1)$ equations for the annuity swaps are as follows:

$$a = x_n \quad + i_n x_n$$
$$a = x_{n-1} + i_{n-1} x_{n-1} + i_n x_n$$

$$\begin{array}{ccccc} \cdot & \cdot & & \cdot & \cdot \\ \cdot & \cdot & & \cdot & \cdot \\ \cdot & \cdot & & \cdot & \cdot \end{array}$$

$$a = x_1 \quad + i_1 x_1 + i_2 x_2 + i_3 x_3 + \cdots + i_n x_n$$
$$b = y_n \quad + j_n y_n$$
$$b = y_{n-1} + j_{n-1} y_{n-1} + j_n y_n$$

$$\begin{array}{ccccc} \cdot & \cdot & & \cdot & \cdot \\ \cdot & \cdot & & \cdot & \cdot \\ \cdot & \cdot & & \cdot & \cdot \end{array}$$

$$b = y_1 \quad + j_1 y_1 + j_2 y_2 + j_3 y_3 + \cdots + j_n y_n$$

$$(x_1 + x_2 + x_3 + \cdots + x_n)E_A = (y_1 + y_2 + y_3 + \cdots + y_n)E_B$$

where a is the constant annual amount of currency A to be exchanged for the constant annual amount b of currency B. Other symbols are the same as for the LDFX general form of equations.

Here is an example of applying these equations to produce a three-year annuity swap. We want to determine the constant annual A$ amounts that equate to constant annual ¥ amounts of ¥700MM for three years given an A$/US$ spot of 0.774; a ¥/US$ spot of 154.0; an A$/US$ annual swap rates of 15%, three years, 15.2%, two years, and 15.4%, one year; and a ¥/US$ annual swap rate of 7%, three years, two years, and one year. The equations are

$$a = x_3 + .15x_3 \tag{1}$$
$$a = x_2 + .152x_2 + .15x_3 \tag{2}$$
$$a = x_1 + .154x_1 + .152s_2 + 15x_3 \tag{3}$$
$$700 = y_3 + .07y_3 \tag{4}$$
$$700 = y_2 + .07y_2 + .07y_3 \tag{5}$$
$$700 = y_1 + .07y_1 + .07y_2 + .07y_3 \tag{6}$$
$$(x_1 + x_2 + x_3) \times .774 = (y_1 + y_2 + y_3)/154.0 \tag{7}$$

Equations such as these may be solved using matrix inversion techniques. A simple Pascal program applying Gaussian elimination to do this has been included in the Appendix to this chapter, which also includes a run using this example as input.

The solution to the equations is interpreted as follows:

a = A\$6.7640104706MM, the equivalent of ¥700MM annually for three years

A\$/US\$ currency swaps pay fixed A\$ annually:
A\$5.8817482353MM for three years @ 15% annual
A\$5.1056842320MM for two years @ 15.2% annual
A\$4.4243364229MM for one year @ 15.4% annual

¥/US\$ currency swaps receive fixed ¥ annually:
¥654.2056074766MM for three years @ 7% annual
¥611.4071097914MM for two years @ 7% annual
¥571.4085138235MM for one year @ 7% annual

Contractual agreements between two counterparties for a transaction such as this may be in the form of three separate LDFX confirmations—one for each of one year, two years, and three years— or as a cross currency coupon swap A\$ fixed/¥ fixed using ISDA documentation and specifying no exchange of principal at maturity.

REVERSE DUAL CURRENCY LOANS

The capital market transactions in the late 1980s that used these A\$/¥ annuity swaps were loans in the Japanese market with interest

EXHIBIT 5
Reverse Dual Currency Swap Structure Using Annuity Swaps

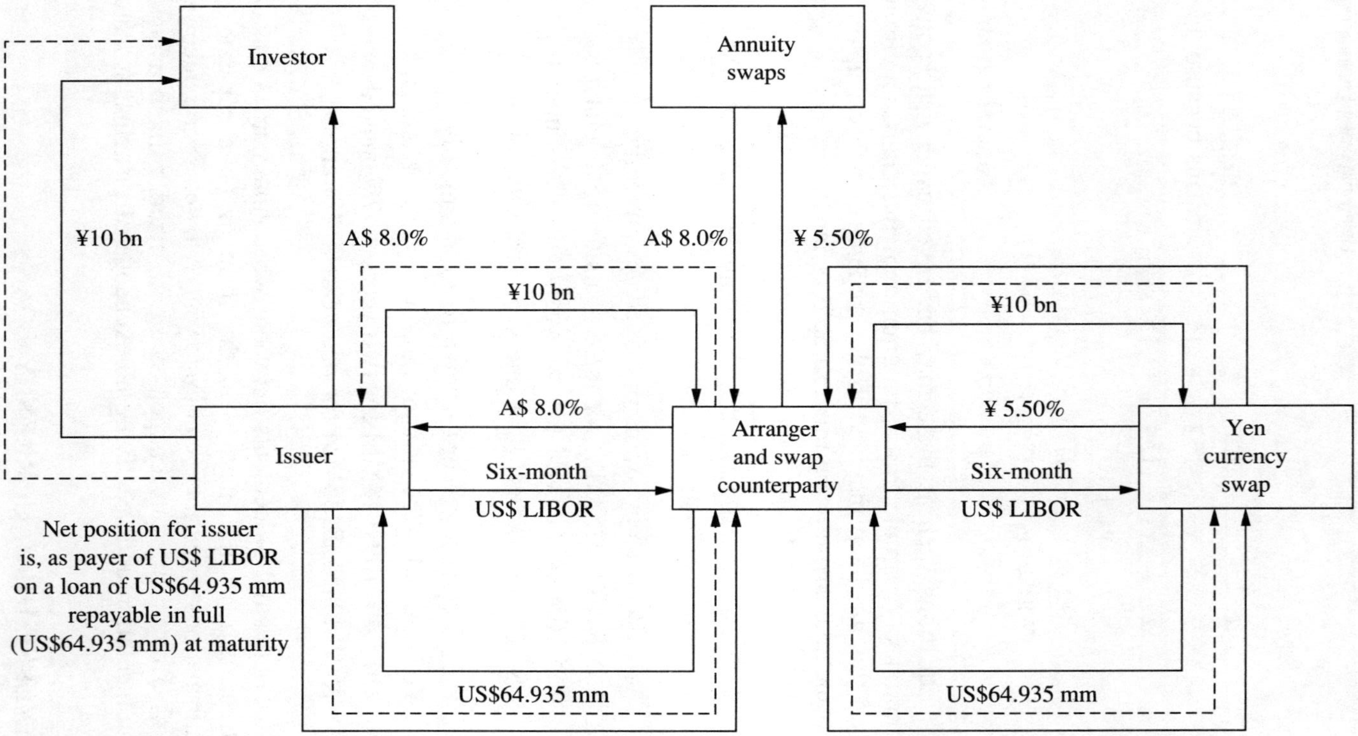

payments in A$ and the loan repaid in ¥. The term *reverse dual currency loans* was coined to describe these loans because they were the "reverse" of their dual currency predecessors in the Swiss market: Swiss coupons and US$ principal at maturity.

These instruments were designed to suit the specific requirements of Japanese investors. Issuers, on the other hand, typically banks raising subordinated debt of 10-year maturity, required a mechanism to convert this A$/¥ reverse dual currency loan into floating-rate US$.

The method employed requires A$/¥ annuity swaps constructed as above, combined with a ¥ fixed/US$ LIBOR currency swap. Exhibit 5 represents diagrammatically a typical structure.

CURRENCY SWAPS WITH
NOTIONAL PRINCIPAL (CSNPs)

We established at the outset that currency swaps must have exchanges of principal at maturity. Having developed annuity swaps, however, we can now create currency swaps with no exchange of principal at maturity (i.e., notional principals).

First, annuity swaps with the annual payments of one currency equal to the periodic swap payments for the required notional principal at the prevailing swap rate are constructed. Then an interest rate swap to replace the fixed annual currency payments of the annuity swap with a variable rate (in the same currency) is added. Exhibit 6 diagrammatically represents examples of the swaps required to construct five-year A$ fixed/US$ LIBOR and three-year A$ fixed/¥ LIBOR currency swaps with notional principals. The fixed interest rates shown are those that would be produced from A$ swaps at about 15% annual, US$ swaps about 9% annual and ¥ swaps about 7% annual.

APPLICATIONS OF CSNPs

Whereas currency swaps are typically used for asset and liability management to change principals as well as interest from one currency to another, CSNPs change only the currency of the interest flows, not the principals.

EXHIBIT 6
Examples of Currency Swaps with Notional Principals (CSNPs)

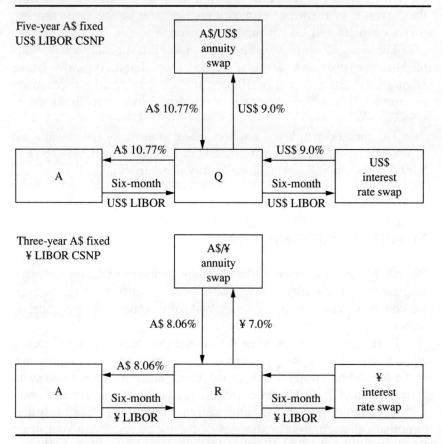

Potential users of these swaps are institutions having portfolios of assets and liabilities that they wish to switch into different currencies and from fixed to floating or floating to fixed for interest payments or receipts. They would be exposed to currency movements on the interest payments but not to the effects of currency movements on the principals.

The swaps are readily reversible in the event one's view of interest rates changes. With currency swaps, reversing means crystallizing on the principals all losses or profits due to the currency movements, but the effect of currency movements with CSNP swaps is limited to the annual fixed interest coupon multiplied by the currency movement for the remaining years.

With all these structures, parties to the swaps should check their particular situation with regards to taxation, accounting, capital adequacy implications, and so on. These may vary from country to country.

SUMMARY

This chapter has shown the important role currency swaps play in financial engineering to synthesize traditional Treasury instruments and to create previously unobtainable ones. The insights gained into the power of financial engineering may provide opportunities for further developments in global financial markets.

APPENDIX TO CHAPTER 20

```pascal
program equations;
uses crt;



{    Author    :  Robert Mordue
     Date      :  23 / 6 / 90

     Purpose   : To solve simultaneous equations using
                                  Gaussian Elimination}

var
   varno, i, j, k, l, m, p  : integer;
   initmatrix               : array [1 .. 51 , 1 .. 50]
                                of real;
   matrix                   : array [1 .. 51 , 1 .. 50]
                                of real;
   temp                     : array [1 .. 51] of real;
   finished                 : boolean;
   dump                     : char;


procedure read_equation;
begin
   write
   ('How many variables are there in the equations? (max 50)');
   readln(varno);
   for i : = 1 to varno do
   begin
     writeln;
     writeln('Equation ',i,'    ');
     for j := 1 to varno do
     begin
       write('X',j,'= ');
       readln(matrix[j,i]);
       initmatrix[j,i] := matrix[j,i];
     end;
     writeln('= ');
     readln(matrix[varno+1,i]);
     initmatrix[varno+1,i] := matrix[varno+1,i];
   end;
end;
```

```
procedure swapline(x, y : integer);
begin

  for m := 1 to varno+1 do
  begin
    temp[m] := matrix[m,x];
    matrix[m,x] := matrix[m,y];
    matrix[m,y] := temp[m];
  end;
end;

procedure addline(scalar : real; x,y : integer);
begin
  for m := 1 to varno+1 do
  begin
    matrix[m,y] := matrix[m,x]*scalar - matrix[m,y];
  end;
end;

procedure scalarmult(scalar : real; x : integer);
begin
  for m := 1 to varno+1 do
  begin
    matrix[m,x] := matrix[m,x]/scalar;
  end;
end;

procedure main;
begin
  repeat
  finished := true;
  for i := 1 to varno-1 do
  begin
    if matrix[i,i] = 0 then
    begin
      for j := i+1 to varno do
      begin
        if matrix[i,j] <> 0 then
        begin
          {This reorders the matrix so that      }
          {there are no zero's along the diagonal}
          swapline(i,j);
          j := varno;
        end;
      end;
      finished := false;
    end;
  end;
  until finished;
```

```
   for j := 1 to varno do
   begin
                     {This makes all the diagonal values    }
                     {equal to one                          }
      scalarmult(matrix[j,j],j);
      for k := j+1 to varno do
      begin
                     {This eliminates all the values under  }
                     {the diagonal                          }
         addline(matrix[j,k],j,k);
      end;
   end;
   for l := varno downto 1 do
   begin
   for p := l-1 downto 1 do
                        {This eliminates all the values above}
                        {the diagonal, leaving a unit matrix }
      begin

         matrix[l,p] := matrix[l,p]*matrix[varno+1,l];
         matrix[varno+1,p] := matrix[varno+1,p] - matrix[l,p];
      end;
   end;
end;

procedure display;
begin
   for i := 1 to varno do
   begin
      write('X',i,' = ',matrix[varno+1,i]:17:10);
      writeln;
   end;
   for j := 1 to varno do
   begin
     if j mod 2 = 0 then
     begin
       repeat until keypressed;
       if keypressed then dump := readkey;
       clrscr;
     end;
     writeln;
     writeln('Equation ',j);
     for i := 1 to varno + 1 do
     begin
       if i < varno + 1 then write('X',i) else write('= ');
       writeln(initmatrix[i,j]:20:10);
     end;
   end;
end;
```

```
begin
  clrscr;
  read_equation;
  clrscr;
  main;
  display;
  repeat until keypressed;
end.
```

OUTPUT FROM PROGRAM

Solutions

```
X1 =        4.4243364229
X2 =        5.1056842320
X3 =        5.8817482353
X4 =      654.2056074766
X5 =      611.4071097914
X6 =      571.4085138235
X7 =        6.7640104706
```

The Input Equations

```
Equation 1
X1        -0.7740000000
X2        -0.7740000000
X3        -0.7740000000
X4         0.0064935064
X5         0.0064935064
X6         0.0064935064
X7         0.0000000000
=          0.0000000000

Equation 2
X1         0.0000000000
X2         0.0000000000
X3         1.1500000000
X4         0.0000000000
X5         0.0000000000
X6         0.0000000000
X7        -1.0000000000
=          0.0000000000
```

```
Equation 3
X1          0.0000000000
X2          1.1520000000
X3          0.1500000000
X4          0.0000000000
X5          0.0000000000
X6          0.0000000000
X7         -1.0000000000
=           0.0000000000

Equation 4
X1          1.1540000000
X2          0.1520000000
X3          0.1500000000
X4          0.0000000000
X5          0.0000000000
X6          0.0000000000
X7         -1.0000000000
=           0.0000000000

Equation 5
X1          0.0000000000
X2          0.0000000000
X3          0.0000000000
X4          1.0700000000
X5          0.0000000000
X6          0.0000000000
X7          0.0000000000
=         700.0000000000

Equation 6
X1          0.0000000000
X2          0.0000000000
X3          0.0000000000
X4          0.0700000000
X5          1.0700000000
X6          0.0000000000
X7          0.0000000000
=         700.0000000000

Equation 7
X1          0.0000000000
X2          0.0000000000
X3          0.0000000000
X4          0.0700000000
X5          0.0700000000
X6          1.0700000000
X7          0.0000000000
=         700.0000000000
```

CHAPTER 21

CONTRASTING SHORT-DATE AND LONG-DATE CROSS CURRENCY SWAP DECISIONS

Samuel C. Weaver
Hershey Foods Corporation
Hershey, Pennsylvania

INTRODUCTION

With the rapid globalization of the world's markets, operating management is pushing the boundaries of business beyond domestic borders. At one time, the only decisions required of a financial manager as the business expanded revolved around issuing domestic debt or equity. If debt was the chosen course, should the debt be short-term debt, intermediate-term notes, or a "plain chocolate," traditional long-term bond? Today the financial manager must also decide if the debt should be issued domestically or in a foreign country.

For decades financial managers were content to match the maturity of debt with the maturity of the underlying asset. Even the corollary — matching the location of the debt with the location of the asset — was widely and blindly practiced. However, throughout the past decade, these principles have come under close scrutiny due to:

- Globalization of business operations.
- Globalization of world debt markets.
- Increased emphasis on debt financing.
- Opportunistic financings for specific borrowers.
- Significantly increased interest rate volatility.
- Significantly increased foreign exchange rate volatility.
- The rapid development and deployment of innovative financial instruments such as interest rate and foreign exchange rate futures, options, and swaps.

- Rapid technological changes that make operating assets functionally valueless within a significantly shorter economic life than originally estimated.
- Marketable portfolios of separable companies acquired in the megamerger market of the 1980s that lead to sometimes unpredictable cash flow generation that could be applied to reduce enormous amounts of debt.

No longer can the financial manager simply follow the matching concepts. No longer can the matching concepts be blindly and irresponsibly applied. A company's debt portfolio demands as much management attention as its asset portfolio.

Although the international investment community is curious about current (historical) levels of inflation, interest rates, and foreign exchange rates, its primary concern lies with the future. Where are interest rates headed? What will the exchange rate be in one year? These are the critical issues that face the international investment community as well as all financial managers. These are the areas that should be considered in deciding on swapping an international interest-bearing instrument. Swaps allow opportunities for financial managers to implement their expectations versus those of the general marketplace.

The purpose of this chapter is to identify the conditions under which a long-date currency swap is equivalent to a strip of short-date swaps and to assess the reasonableness and implicit risks of each course of action. The chapter integrates interest rate expectations theory with interest rate parity theory. The result provides a framework for evaluating the equivalence of a long-date cross currency swap with a sequence or strip of short date forward contracts or swaps. By understanding the market's expectations of future interest rates and foreign exchange rates, the financial manager is able to compare the market's expectations with his or her own views. Potential opportunities based upon these views can lead to improved financial management.

OVERVIEW

Figure 1 portrays two dimensions that will be given careful consideration in this chapter: borrowing maturity and international venue. Position 1A represents a domestic short-term borrower or investor, and 2A represents a domestic long-term borrower or investor. Position 1B

FIGURE 1
Overview of Debt Obligation Position

International Venue	Borrower/Investor	
	Short-term	Long-term
Domestic	1A	2A
Foreign	1B	2B

1A: Domestic short-term debt
1B: Foreign short-term debt
2A: Domestic long-term debt
2B: Foreign long-term debt

represents a foreign short-term borrower or investor, and position 2B indicates a foreign long-term borrower or investor.

Swaps can be implemented along either dimension, involving interest rates or exchange rates. That is to say, an interest rate swap can be accomplished wherein a domestic party swaps a short-term (long-term) investment or borrowing position with a long-term (short-term) domestic investment or borrowing position (i.e., 1A and 2A swap positions). Likewise, a foreign short-term (long-term) investment or borrowing position can be swapped with a long-term (short-term) foreign investment or borrowing position via an interest rate swap (1B and 2B swap positions).

A cross currency swap can be implemented in which a short-term domestic (foreign) borrower or investor swaps positions with a short-term foreign (domestic) borrower or investor (1A and 1B swap positions). Additionally, a long-term domestic (foreign) borrower or investor can swap positions with a long-term foreign (domestic) borrower or investor (2A and 2B swap positions).

Finally, swaps can be implemented across the two dimensions. That is, a combination interest rate swap and currency swap can be executed simultaneously. As an example of this conventional cross currency swap, a domestic (foreign) short-term investor or borrower can swap positions with a foreign (domestic) long-term investor or borrower (1A and 2B swap positions). Additionally, a domestic (foreign) long-term investor or borrower can swap positions with a foreign (domestic) short-term investor or borrower (2A and 1B swap positions).

Interest Rate Swaps

This chapter first examines the conditions that influence the choice of a debt-financing portfolio strategy involving a strip of short-date interest rate swaps versus the alternative strategy involving a long-date swap. Interest rate swaps facilitate the conversion of fixed-rate debt to floating-rate debt or floating-rate to fixed-rate debt. An interest rate swap is a convenient management tool that provides the flexibility to convert debt from one position to the other and is identical to altering the interest payment—fixed-rate to floating-rate and vice versa. An interest rate swap can be implemented at the inception of debt borrowing or throughout the life of an existing borrowing.

It turns out that any rational choice between a series of short-date swaps or forward contracts (i.e., variable-rate financing) and a long-date swap (i.e., fixed-rate financing) necessarily relates to expectations regarding future short-term interest rates. The term-structure theory of interest will be used to develop the market's expectations of future short-term interest rates. This leads to an improved understanding of the assumptions embedded in a given country's yield curve (i.e., the interest rate structure related to increasing maturity of a bond). Parties swapping interest rates can then more fully understand the underlying expectations and analyze their economic decision more effectively.

Cross Currency Swaps

This chapter also examines cross currency swaps and the factors that affect the choice of currency market. A cross currency swap facilitates the conversion of a domestic obligation into an international obligation, and vice versa. A cross currency swap can be implemented either when debt (domestic or international) is issued or throughout the life of an existing borrowing.

Further, any rational choice between one currency and another hinges on expectations of future spot exchange rates. By exploring examples of interest rate parity theory, this chapter will facilitate an understanding of the dynamics involved with the marketplace's future exchange-rate assumptions. Consequently, the financial manager will be able to analyze economic decisions along this dimension as well.

Dual Interest Rate Swap and
Cross Currency Swap

The chapter then integrates the foregoing ideas and provides a framework upon which the efficacy of a combined interest rate swap (i.e., the maturity of a debt obligation) and cross currency swap (i.e., the currency of a debt obligation) can be examined. Ultimately, the application of a dual interest rate and cross currency swap can position the long-term domestic financial manager as a short-term foreign financial manager, and vice versa. The tenets underlying the term-structure theory of interest and interest rate parity theory will be applied in analyzing the dual interest rate swap and cross currency swap.

Equivalence of Swap Positions

Within this framework, if the markets' expectations about future inflation rates, interest rates, and foreign exchange rates come to fruition, net swapped positions provide equivalent costs (or returns). That is, interest rate swaps, cross currency swaps, and dual interest rate–cross currency swaps are all neutral when the expectations of the international investment community are realized. In the final analysis, the appropriate decisions will be revealed to the marketplace, and actual decisions will generate gains or losses to the extent that their underlying expectations are not fulfilled in the marketplace.

The next section explores the interest rate relationships and expectations implicit in an equivalent cost (return) for a short-term rollover strategy versus a long-term bond. The underlying relationships and foreign-currency expectations related to the equivalent cost (return) of a domestic versus a foreign position are then examined. Finally, the developed implications will be applied to examine the equivalence position of a dual interest rate–cross currency swap.

TERM STRUCTURE: THEORY AND
IMPLICATIONS FOR SWAPS

The theory of the term structure of interest rates deals with the relationship between the yield to maturity for identical securities (e.g., same coupon, default risk, tax treatment) and their time to maturity. In this section, the main focus lies in investigating the analytical underpinnings of the term structure.

Implied interest rates, or the market's expectations for forward interest rates, underly the theory of the term structure of interest rates. Said differently, implied interest rates are the forward one-period (e.g., annual) interest rates inherent in an observed multiperiod interest rate. That is, a two-year rate can be separated into a one-year rate and an implied forward "rollover" rate from the end of year 1 to the end of year 2. This concept is necessary for an examination of the relationship between short-date and long-date contracts.

Evaluation of a Short-Date Strategy

To place the concept of implied interest rates in context, suppose that a borrower wants to borrow funds for two years and has numerous alternatives. Keep in mind that this problem is analogous to choosing a long-date swap or a strip of short-date swaps to accomplish a given strategy—hedge, speculation, or arbitrage. Furthermore, this presentation can be extended to its mirror-image transaction (i.e., from the investor's perspective).

Specifically, suppose the borrower narrows the choice to two alternatives: (1) borrow for two years via a zero-coupon instrument that returns an annual interest rate of 8.5 percent (long-term strategy) or (2) borrow the required amount for one year in an 8 percent bank loan and, at the end of the first year, reborrow for the second year at the then-prevailing one-year interest rate. The second alternative is identical to a short-date swap or variable-rate financing.

If the first alternative is accepted, so that $1,000 is financed for two years at 8.5 percent, the borrower will be required to pay $1,177 at the end of the second year based on annual compounding as follows:

$$FV = PV(1 + i)^n \qquad (1)$$

where   FV = Future value at the end of period n
   PV = Present value at the beginning
   i = Stated interest rate
   n = Number of years of investment

or, specifically,

$$\$1,177 = \$1,000(1 + .085)^2$$

On the other hand, rolling the loan over in sequential one-year loans assures the borrower only that the amount of the loan will have increased by 8 percent, to $1,080, at the end of one year (in accordance with the preceding equation). The question facing the borrower is: What will be the annual interest rate from the end of the first year to the end of the second year (denoted as i_{1-2})? To answer this question, equation (1) must be rearranged to allow for differing annual interest rates:

$$FV = PV(1 + i_{0-1})(1 + i_{1-2}) \tag{2}$$

or, specifically,

$$FV = \$1,000(1 + .08)(1 + i_{1-2})$$

The following table presents the results of three different refinancing rates (i_{1-2}) and the associated future costs of the initial $1,000 financing, assuming an 8 percent cost/return in the first year of the two-year debt horizon:

Reinvestment Rate (i_{1-2})	Value at the End of Two Years
8%	$1,166
9	1,177
10	1,188

If the investment community—borrowers and investors—thought the annual interest rate at the end of the first year would be only 8 percent, (1) all borrowers would follow a rollover strategy rather than a two-year investment, and (2) investors with a two-year horizon would choose a two-year investment rather than rolling over a one-year investment at an expected 8 percent reinvestment rate. This situation would put upward pressure on two-year security prices and downward pressure on one-year security prices, altering the stated interest rate relationship of 8 percent for a one-year investment and 8.5 percent for a two-year investment.

Conversely, if the market expected the annual interest rate to increase next year to 10 percent, two-year borrowing would best suit the borrower while the rollover strategy would be more attractive to the investor. Again, the buying and selling pressure would alter the current interest rate relationships until the 10 percent expectation would be fully reflected in the current one-year and two-year interest rates.

Interest Rate Expectations

Clearly, with the given structure of interest rates (one-year, 8 percent; two-year, 8.5 percent), the borrower and investor would be indifferent between an instrument of two years or an instrument for one year at 8 percent that would be reissued for the second year at 9 percent. Given these stated rates, the market expects the second year's one-year interest rate to be 9 percent. Furthermore, as illustrated in the previous example, when the return implied in the rollover strategy (assuming reissuance at the expected interest rate) is equal to long-term financing cost/investment return, there is no immediate market pressure to adjust existing interest rates. This result—the market's expectation, or implied interest rate—can be derived by equating the future values of the two strategies as in equation (3):

Period n financing = Rollover strategy for n periods

$$PV(1 = i)^n = PV(1 + i_{0-1})(1 + i_{1-2}) \cdots (1 + i_{(n-1)-n})$$

$$(1 + i)^n = (1 + i_{0-1})(1 + i_{1-2}) \cdots (1 + i_{(n-1)-n}) \quad (3)$$

Specifically, for the two-year period investment used here:

$$(1 + .085)^2 = (1 + .08)(1 + i_{1-2})$$

$$1.177 = 1.08(1 + i_{1-2})$$

$$1.09 = 1 + i_{1-2}$$

$$.09 = i_{1-2}$$

$$9\% = i_{1-2}$$

This example suggests that by observing consecutive multiple-period interest rates, it is possible to derive the market's expectations for future single-period interest rates. These expected future rates are described as implied rates. The risk that the bond issuer (or investor) faces is that these expectations may not be realized. In the present example, if the actual future one-period interest rate (i_{1-2}) were only 8 percent, the rollover strategy would have been more (less) advantageous to a borrower (investor), providing a total terminal cost (return) of $1,166. On the other hand, if the actual future one-period interest rate (i_{1-2}) were 10 percent, the longer-term strategy of investing for two years at 8.5 percent would have been more (less) advantageous to a borrower (investor), providing a total terminal cost (return) of $1,177, because the cost (return) was "locked in" at 9 percent at the outset.

Multiple-Period Interest Rate Expectations

As demonstrated, the market's implied forward annual interest rate or expected interest rate can be determined from the relationship between the yields to maturity for a one-year bond and a two-year bond. In more general terms, any one-year implicit forward rate can be derived from two long rates with adjacent terms to maturity.

Table 1 illustrates this concept. Given the term structure of interest rates as detailed in the "yield to maturity" column, a one-year implied interest rate for the final year of a three-year rollover strategy can be derived by employing equation (3):

3-year actual yield = (2-year actual yield) (1-year implied yield)

$$(1 + .088)^3 = (1 + .085)^2(1 + i_{2-3})$$

$$1.2879 = 1.1772(1 + i_{2-3})$$

$$.094 = i_{2-3}$$

$$9.4\% = i_{2-3}$$

The implied one-year interest rate from year 2 to year 3 is 9.4 percent. Said differently, a two-year financing with an 8.5 percent yield followed by a one-year rollover with a cost of 9.4 percent is equivalent to a three-year financing with 8.8 percent yield. In both cases the cost is $1,288 in total per $1,000 of principal.

Equation (3) can be rewritten to determine any market expectations for an implied interest rate from any point in the future, such as

TABLE 1
Implied Interest Rates

Year	Yield to Maturity	One-Year Period	Rate	Two-Year Period	Rate	Three-Year Period	Rate	Four-Year Period	Rate
1	8.00%	i_{1-2}	9.00%	i_{1-3}	9.20%	i_{1-4}	9.34%	i_{1-5}	9.38%
2	8.50	i_{2-3}	9.40	i_{2-4}	9.50	i_{2-5}	9.50		
3	8.80	i_{3-4}	9.60	i_{3-5}	9.55				
4	9.00	i_{4-5}	9.50						
5	9.10								

the two-year interest rate one year from now. To solve for this implied rate, equation (3) can be rewritten as:

$$i_{t-n} = \sqrt[(n-t)]{\frac{(1 + i_{0-n})^n}{(1 + i_{0-t})^t}} - 1 \qquad (4)$$

where t = Intermediate time period
     $n - t$ = Implied interest rate term to maturity

Equation (4) is not intuitive, but a simple detailed example will illustrate its use. Based on Table 1, the market's implied or expected two-year interest rate one year from now can be calculated by focusing on the three-year and one-year bonds as follows:

$$
\begin{aligned}
i_{1-3} &= \sqrt[2]{\frac{(1 + .088)^3}{(1 + .080)^1}} - 1 \\
&= \sqrt[2]{\frac{1.2879}{1.08}} - 1 \\
&= \sqrt[2]{1.1925} - 1 \\
&= \quad 1.0920 - 1 \\
&= \quad .0920 \\
&= \quad 9.2\%
\end{aligned}
$$

The column in Table 1 for two-year implied interest rates illustrates the other potential two-year rates that exist within the five-year financing horizon.

Equation (4) can also be employed to develop three-year and four-year expected interest rates. For example, from Table 1, a borrower with a five-year financing horizon is indifferent between a straight five-year debt instrument at 9.10 percent and a one-year borrowing at 8.00 percent with a subsequent reissuance in one year of a 9.38 percent four-year bond.

Table 2 employs intermediate-term actual interest rates with implied interest rates to demonstrate that any possible combination of actual borrowings and rollover strategies is expected to cost the same. For instance, a five-year financing is expected to cost $1,546 whether

TABLE 2
Expected Cost of Financing

Years of Actual	Years of Implied Rates				
Interest Rates	0	1	2	3	4
1	$1,080	$1,177	$1,288	$1,412	$1,546
2	1,177	1,288	1,412	1,546	
3	1,288	1,412	1,546		
4	1,412	1,546			
5	1,546				

Note: The Expected Cost of Financing Indicates that at the Inception of Debt Financing Via Rollover Strategy or Long-Term Placement, the Market's Expectation Is that Any Strategy Will Lead to the Same Cost. For Example, a Straight Four-Year Borrowing (Row 4, Column 0) Will Cost $1,412 for Every $1,000 Borrowed, the Same as a Two-Year Borrowing with a Two-Year Rollover (Row 2, Column 2).

it is done as a five-year borrowing, a one-year financing followed by a four-year financing, or any other combination extracted from Table 2:

Actual	Implied	Cost
i_{0-1}	i_{1-5}	$1,546[a]
i_{0-2}	i_{2-5}	$1,546
i_{0-3}	i_{3-5}	$1,546
i_{0-4}	i_{4-5}	$1,546
i_{0-5}	—	$1,546

[a] Using Equation (2):

$$FV = \$1,000(1 + i_{0-1})(1 + i_{1-5})^4$$
$$= \$1,000(1 + .08)(1 + .0938)^4$$
$$= \$1,546$$

Table 2 illustrates all possible combinations of actual and rollover rates that would lead to the same cost of financing.

Swapped positions are equivalent when the market's expectations (implied interest rates) are realized. Consequently, the financial manager should discern the market's implied interest rates and compare these to his or her own interest rate projections. If the financial manager is in a borrowed (invested) position and expects future interest rates to be below the market's expectation, the proper course of action would be to enter a rollover (long-term) strategy. Said differently, a borrower (investor) who believes future interest rates will be below the market's expectations should swap any long-term debt (short-term investment) into short-term debt (long-term investment). On the other hand, if the financial manager is in a borrowed (invested) position and expects future interest rates to be above the market's expectations, the manager should enter a long-term borrowing (rollover investment) or should swap short-term debt (long-term investment) into long-term debt (short-term investment). The following section derives the same conclusion for cross currency swaps.

EXCHANGE-RATE RISK

This section illustrates exchange-rate risk, discusses a theoretical framework for understanding this risk (i.e., interest rate parity), and develops a method of viewing expected future spot exchange rates. By understanding the expected future spot exchange rates, the financial manager can align personal expectations with the markets and implement an investment or borrowing strategy accordingly.

Interest Rate Parity

The interest rate parity theory addresses the potential exchange-rate risk for an international debt investment. This theory states that future foreign exchange rates will be enhanced by a forward premium or diminished by a forward discount, which is reflective of the difference in national interest rates for securities of similar risk and maturity. The theory can be illustrated by a well-documented market equilibrium situation.

Assume a U.S. investor is looking to purchase a one-year government bond. The investor's first choice is to invest in the United States and earn an 8 percent return, which would lead to a terminal value of $108 for every $100 of investment, assuming both interest and principal are paid at the end of the period. Another alternative would be to invest the funds abroad and perhaps earn a greater rate of return with no additional risk of default by a foreign-government borrower.

For instance, a one-year Canadian government instrument may pay 10 percent interest and offer the same guarantee of a default-free outcome. However, the investor must convert U.S. dollars to Canadian dollars today to buy the bond. At the end of the year, the investor must sell the accumulated Canadian dollars to regain the original currency, U.S. dollars.

If the Canadian dollar currently costs US$0.85, the investor can convert his US$100 to C$117.65, which can be invested in Canada for one year at 10 percent. At the end of that year the investor will have a terminal value of C$129.41 ($117.65 + 10%). The investor is now in a position for an enhanced or diminished return based on the currency exchange rate at the end of the year. The following table illustrates the results for alternative exchange rates at the end of this one-year investment period:

End-of-Year Exchange Rate (US$/C$)	U.S. Value of C$129.41
$0.8000	$103.53
0.8345	108.00
0.8500	110.00
0.9000	116.47

If the exchange rate does not change, the investor would realize a 10 percent return and have a terminal value US$2 greater from the Canadian investment than from the U.S. government bond. Notice that if the exchange rate is greater than $0.8345, the investor will earn a return in excess of the 8 percent U.S. return.

At an exchange rate of US$0.90 one year later, the investor would earn a total return of 16.47 percent. A portion of this is attributed to the foreign interest rate (i.e., 10 percent), and the rest is a direct result of the 5.88 percent appreciation in the value of the Canadian dollar (US$0.85 to US$0.90). In this case, the investor would buy Canadian dollars today to facilitate the foreign investment and at the end of the year would sell the Canadian dollars to return to the home currency. The total return would be:

$$\text{Return} = [(1 + i_{\text{CAN}})(1 + i_x)] - 1 \qquad (5)$$

where i_x is the foreign currency appreciation, or specifically:

$$\text{Return} = [(1 + .10)(1 + .0588)] - 1$$
$$= 1.1647 - 1$$
$$= 16.47\%$$

If the exchange rate is less than $0.8345, the investor would have done better to maintain his investment in the United States. This includes the Canadian investor, who would receive a higher return with a U.S. investment than with a Canadian investment.

At the end of the period, an exchange of $0.8345/Canadian dollar represents an equilibrium, where the investor makes an 8 percent rate of return with a domestic or an international investment. Ultimately, in this international investment strategy, the investor is subject to the risk of changes in the spot exchange rate. This risk can be effectively managed via the forward or futures foreign exchange market.

Forward Foreign Exchange Market

The investor can immediately "lock in" the exchange rate that will apply to the investment's conversion to the home currency one year from now by utilizing the one-year forward or futures foreign exchange market. These markets allow the investor or borrower to buy or sell foreign currency today at an agreed-upon price for delivery and settlement at some point in the future. The use of the forward or futures foreign exchange market eliminates all risks associated with the exchange rate one year later. Interest rate parity theory contends that the equilibrium forward foreign exchange rate should be governed by the interest rate differential between instruments of similar risk and maturity in each of the countries. In our example, this would be US$0.8345. If the one-year forward rate were more than US$0.8345, investors would move to Canada, as illustrated previously. However, with many U.S. investors moving to Canada to take advantage of the price discrepancy, there would be an extraordinary amount of Canadian dollars sold on the forward exchange market. This forward selling (increased supply) would reduce the price of the forward Canadian dollar until all extraordinary investment incentive is removed, and the forward rate becomes the equilibrium rate of US$0.8345 per Canadian dollar.

Conversely, if the forward Canadian dollar rate were at only US$0.80, Canadian investors would maximize their returns by investing in the United States. However, to do this in a risk-free, or hedged, position, the Canadian investor would want to buy forward Canadian dollars (i.e., sell forward U.S. dollars). As Canadians attempted to capture this abnormal return, the price of the forward Canadian dollar would be bid up to the point that all extraordinary investment incentive is removed, that is, to US$0.8345 per Canadian dollar.

This phenomenon would be further compounded by other investors (i.e., non-Canadian and non-American) entering into transactions to capture these extraordinary returns by buying and selling U.S. or Canadian dollar bonds in their portfolios to earn the abnormal returns resulting from the exchange-rate disequilibrium position. This process is called covered interest arbitrage. Its operation eliminates the potential for arbitrage profits.

Interest rate parity theory highlights four variables within the preceding illustration:

- i_{US} = U.S interest rate
- i_{CAN} = Canadian interest rate
- S_t = Spot exchange rate (time t)
- F_{t-n} = Forward exchange rate (time t to time n)

Each of these variables may be partially influenced as the investors move in and out of various holdings to assume a more advantageous position. However, the forward exchange rate may be the variable that is most influenced by investors taking advantage of a profit-producing strategy.

Interest rate parity is delineated as follows:

Equilibrium domestic return = Hedged international return

$$A(1 + i_{US}) = (A/S_t)(1 + i_{CAN})(F_{t-n}) \qquad (6)$$

In this equation, A represents the investment amount in U.S. dollars.

Equilibrium can be illustrated by substituting the specified national interest rates and exchange-rate conditions into equation (6):

$$\$100(1 + .08) = (\$100/\$0.85)(1 + .10)(\$0.8345)$$

$$\$108 = \$108$$

Interest rate parity further holds that the hedged investor who contracts in the forward market will obtain a return equivalent to the domestic rate of return. The forward market provides insight into expectations of future spot exchange rates.

Expected Future Spot Exchange Rate

From another perspective, it can be argued that the current forward exchange rate for period $t-n$ is an unbiased (but not necessarily accurate) estimate of the expected future spot exchange rate at time n. If the forward rate were less (more) than the expected future spot rate, speculators would enter a forward contract to purchase (sell) the foreign exchange with the hopes of reaping a profit in the time n spot exchange-rate market. Arbitrage incentives are dissipated where expectations surrounding the future spot exchange rate equal the current forward exchange rate.

Given that the forward rate is an unbiased estimate of the expected future spot rate (E_n), a substitution can be made in the interest rate parity model as follows:

$$A(1 + i_{\text{US}}) = (A/S_t)(1 + i_{\text{CAN}})(E_n) \qquad (7)$$

The exchange-rate risk to which the unhedged investor is subject is nonrealization of the currently expected future spot exchange rate. However, the forward market alleviates the unhedged position by replacing today's expectation of the future spot rate with the forward rate.

Insight about the international investment community's expected future spot exchange rates can be directly obtained by observing the future markets and indirectly obtained via the intercountry interest rate differentials. By comparing the market's expectations of future spot exchange rates with personal expectations, the financial manager can implement his views. If these views better reflect the eventual spot rate, the financial manager will have enhanced his return.

Short-Date versus Long-Date Currency Contracts

The pricing of a long-date forward contract between U.S. and Canadian dollars was given as equation (6) and is repeated here as equation (8).

$$F_{t-n} = S_t \left(\frac{1 + i_{\text{US}}}{1 + i_{\text{CAN}}} \right)^n \qquad (8)$$

If a U.S. firm wishes to hedge a position for a three-year period and the current spot exchange rate is US$0.85/C$1, where the three-year U.S. and Canadian interest rates are 8.80 percent and 10.60 percent, respectively, it should expect to see a three-year forward rate of approximately US$0.8092/C$1. This calculation is based on equation (8) with substitution of the appropriate values:

$$F_{0-3} = US\$0.85/C\$1\left(\frac{1 + 0.088}{1 + 0.106}\right)^3$$

$$= US\$0.8092/C\$1$$

If markets are in equilibrium, this forward rate could be locked into on day 1 with absolute certainty. The U.S. firm would know that the exchange rate facing it in three years will be US$0.8092/C$1. Capital budgeting decisions, hedged financing operations, or long-range planning processes could be initiated based on this future contractual exchange rate.

The following table provides the results of applying equation (8) to the underlying interest rate relationships:

Year	U.S. Interest Rate	Canadian Interest Rate	Expected Spot Exchange Rate
1	8.00%	10.00%	US$0.8345
2	8.50	10.35	0.8217
3	8.80	10.60	0.8092
4	9.00	10.75	0.7975
5	9.10	10.80	0.7868

Conversely, a financial manager might prefer the added flexibility associated with shorter forward exchange-rate commitments. Recognizing that there is a much more active market in short-date forward contracts, the manager might consider a strategy of hedging positions with five sequential annual forward contracts. In this case, he would enter into a forward contract for one year. At the end of that year, he would roll over the forward contract for another one-year period. This process would continue for n years (five years in this illustration). The determination of each of the five forward exchange rates (F_{t-n}) is summarized below:

$$F_{0-1} = S_0\left(\frac{1 + i_{0-1US}}{1 + i_{0-1CAN}}\right)$$

$$F_{1-2} = S_1\left(\frac{1 + i_{1-2US}}{1 + i_{1-2CAN}}\right)$$

$$F_{2-3} = S_2\left(\frac{1 + i_{2-3US}}{1 + i_{2-3CAN}}\right)$$

$$F_{3-4} = S_3\left(\frac{1 + i_{3-4US}}{1 + i_{3-4CAN}}\right)$$

$$F_{4-5} = S_4\left(\frac{1 + i_{4-5US}}{1 + i_{4-5CAN}}\right)$$

where i_{m-n} = One-year interest rate at the end of year m and the beginning of year n ($n = m + 1$)

S_0 = Spot exchange rate at the end of year 0 and the beginning of year 1

S_m = Expected future spot exchange rate at the end of year m and the beginning of year n

If, at the beginning of a strip of forward contracts, the forward rate for each one-year period is equal to the expected future spot rate at the end of that one-year period (i.e., $F_{0-1} = S_1$, $F_{1-2} = S_2$), substitution and simplification lead to the following:

$$F_{0-3} = S_0\left[\frac{(1 + i_{0-1US})(1 + i_{1-2US})(1 + i_{2-3US})}{(1 + i_{0-1CAN})(1 + i_{1-2CAN})(1 + i_{2-3CAN})}\right] \quad (9)$$

Although the forward rate (F_{0-1}) may not be an accurate predictor of the actual future spot rate (S_1), it is an unbiased predictor of the future spot rate. Numerous studies have shown that, given certain assumptions, the forward rate as calculated in equation (9) does not produce a systematically biased estimate of the future spot rate.[1] The neces-

---

[1] J.L. Hilley, C.R. Beidleman, and J.A. Greenleaf, "Does Covered Interest Arbitrage Dominate in Foreign Exchange Markets?" *Columbia Journal of World Business* (Winter 1979), vol. 14, no. 4, pp. 99–107.

sary assumptions are that purchasing power parity, the Fisher effect, and interest rate parity prevail uniformly throughout the hedge period. If these assumptions are upheld, inflation differentials between countries will be reflected in changes in both foreign exchange rates and differential nominal domestic interest rates; and forward exchange-rate premiums will equate to nominal domestic interest differentials. If the requisite assumptions hold, from equation (9) we see that the future exchange rate obtained using a long-date forward contract (equation (8)) is a function of the expected forward annual interest rates and is exactly the same as a strip of short-date contracts (equation (9)). Specifically, a strip of short-date forward currency contracts would equate to a long-date forward contract if all actual future annual interest rates were equal to implied annual interest rates. This combination of the term-structure theory of interest and the theory of interest rate parity leads to an integrated model of short-date–long-date cross currency swap equivalence.

The following section integrates the interest rate expectation theory with the interest rate parity theory. The result is a framework for evaluating the equivalence of a long-date cross currency swap with a sequence or strip of short-date forward contracts or swaps. By understanding the market's expectations of future interest rates and foreign exchange rates, the financial manager is able to compare the market's expectations with personal views. Potential opportunities based on these views can lead to improved financial management.

INTEGRATED MODEL

Up to this point, two types of risk have been separately identified and illustrated: interest-rate risk (expectations) and exchange-rate risk (expectations). In this section, we integrate these components of risk into a single model. This integration allows for examination of the combined risk experienced by a financial manager faced with the choice of a long-date cross currency swap versus a strip of short-date domestic hedges over a multiperiod time frame.

Implied interest rates can be derived from the Canadian yield curves presented earlier. The following table presents the interest rates and implied annual (one-period) interest rates for the United States and Canada:

Years to Maturity	U.S. Interest Rate		Canadian Interest Rate	
	Actual[a]	Implied[b]	Actual[a]	Implied[b]
1	8.00%	8.00%	10.00%	10.00%
2	8.50	9.00	10.35	10.70
3	8.80	9.40	10.60	11.10
4	9.00	9.60	10.75	11.20
5	9.10	9.50	10.80	11.00

[a] Actual Multiperiod Rate on Day 1.
[b] The Implied Interest Rate Is the One-Year Rate of Interest Implicit in the Interest Rate Structure Determined from Equation (3).

As determined earlier, a two-year investment in the United States would earn 8.50 percent interest, or $117.72 per $100 of investment. A strategy of investin   ne-year instrument at 8.00 percent and rolling over into another one-year instrument at 9.00 percent in the final year would yield the same return, $117.72.

By combining the theories of interest rate expectations and interest rate parity (i.e., similar investments in terms of risk, maturity, etc. throughout the world should yield similar returns), the following equation is derived for a three-period model:

$$\text{U.S. investment} = \text{Canadian investment} \qquad (10)$$

$$A(1 + i_{0-1US})(1 + i_{1-2US})(1 + i_{2-3US})$$
$$= A/S_0(1 + i_{0-1CAN})(1 + i_{1-2CAN})(1 + i_{2-3CAN})F_{0-3}$$

This equation consists of eight variables, including five expected but uncertain variables:

- Domestic interest rate expectations:
  i_{1-2US}
  i_{2-3US}
- Foreign interest rate expectations:
  i_{1-2CAN}
  i_{2-3CAN}

- Future spot exchange rate:
  F_{0-3}

If the financial manager decided to hedge an exposed long-term position with a strip of forwards, the expected spot exchange rate could be calculated by employing equation (8) or by substituting the implied U.S. and Canadian interest rates as follows:

$$F_{0-3} = US\$0.85/C\$1\left[\frac{(1 + .0800)(1 + .0900)(1 + .0940)}{(1 + .1000)(1 + .1070)(1 + .1110)}\right]$$

$$= US\$0.8092$$

Notice that the three-year forward exchange rate calculated in this example using a strip of short-date implied interest rates is the same as the forward exchange rate obtained by using equation (8) to determine the long-term forward exchange rate. Under these conditions, we have a mathematical identity as shown:

$$\left[\frac{(1 + .0880)}{(1 + .1060)}\right]^3 = \left[\frac{(1 + .0800)(1 + .0900)(1 + .0940)}{(1 + .1000)(1 + .1070)(1 + .1110)}\right]$$

At the outset of a hedge decision, it is not at all clear if exchange rate expectations implicit in market interest rates would favor either the long-date forward strategy or a strategy employing a strip of short-term forwards. From the preceding calculations, it appears that the market's expectation is for a US$0.8092/C$1 exchange rate in three years, due to the underlying interest rate relationship. Whether a strip of short-date forwards would actually produce the same ex post three-year exchange rate as a long-date contract depends on whether the actual one-year interest rates turn out to equal the implied annual interest rates.

The problem (the decision) that faces the financial manager arises from the fact that implied interest rates are infrequently realized. Hindsight shows that implied interest rates seldom are accurate predictors of actual future interest rates. Despite the fact that forward exchange rates are unbiased predictors of future spot rates, the same forecasting quality does not apply to interest rates.

Fortunately for the financial manager, the importance of matching implied interest rates to actual future interest rates is mitigated in part by a (perhaps) less onerous requirement. It is not necessary that implied interest rates in each currency be precise predictors of actual future interest rates for a strip of short-date forwards to equate to a long-date forward currency contract. Instead, it is essential only that the interest rate differential between currencies conform to the differential predicted by the implied forward interest rates. However, as indicated in Figure 2, even long-term interest rate differentials tend to fluctuate in contemporary capital markets. The following section analyzes the results of a discrepancy between actual annual interest rates and implied interest rates. By comparing short-date cross currency strategies and long-date cross currency strategies, appropriate generalizations are drawn to assist the financial manager in assessing personal views of interest rate differentials versus the market's expectations of interest rate differentials.

FIGURE 2
Interest Rate Differentials (Canadian Less U.S. 10-Year Government Bonds)

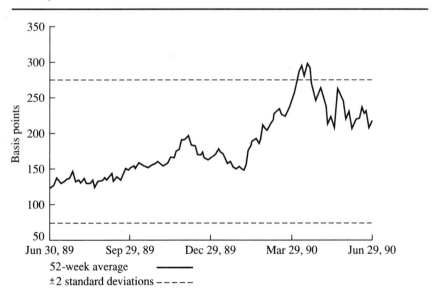

52-week average ⎯⎯⎯
±2 standard deviations − − − − −

Source: Merrill Lynch, Currency and Bond Market Trends, July 5, 1990.

Differences between Actual and Implied Annual Interest Rates and Forward Foreign Exchange Rates

This section considers the effects of movements in interest rates. Specifically, the integrated model is reviewed for narrowing and broadening interest rate differences between the domestic and foreign currencies. However, parallel interest rate movement (i.e., no change in interest rate differentials) is first reviewed.

As previously stated, a strip of short-date forward currency contracts equates to a long-date forward contract if all actual future annual interest rates match implied annual interest rates. Even if future rates differ from implied rates, the future exchange rate derived from a strip of short-term forward currency contracts will equate to the future exchange rate from a long-date swap if the current relationship between foreign and domestic interest rates is maintained. For example, the three-year exchange rate $0.8092/C$1 is maintained even if realized interest rates differ from implied rates, provided that the ratio

$$\frac{1 + \text{Implied U.S. interest rate}}{1 + \text{Implied Canadian interest rate}}$$

is equal to the ratio

$$\frac{1 + \text{Realized U.S. interest rate}}{1 + \text{Realized Canadian interest rate}}$$

In essence, despite differences between implied rates and realized rates, as long as the difference between U.S. and Canadian interest rates remains constant, the three-year exchange rate in a strip of short-date forward contracts will approximate the three-year forward exchange rate. This is illustrated in Table 3, which presents the implied interest rates of the preceding scenario and a 50-basis-point increase or decrease in the realized annual interest rate of each country over the implied annual interest rate. Using equation (9) and the realized annual interest rates, with the interest rate difference between the countries held constant, the three-year exchange rate turns out to be approximately the same as if realized interest rates equaled implied interest rates. If realized rates were to equal the implied interest rates, the three-year exchange rate, as calculated before, would be

TABLE 3
United States and Canadian Realized and Implied Interest Rates: Constant Interest Rate Differentials

Period	Realized = Implied			Realized < Implied			Realized > Implied		
	U.S.	Canada	Differential	U.S.	Canada	Differential	U.S.	Canada	Differential
0–1	8.00%	10.00%	2.00%	8.00%	10.00%	2.00%	8.00%	10.00%	2.00%
1–2	9.00	10.70	1.70	8.50	10.20	1.70	9.50	11.20	1.70
2–3	9.40	11.10	1.70	8.90	10.60	1.70	9.90	11.60	1.70
Three-year spot exchange rate	US$0.8092/C$1			US$0.8091/C$1			US$0.8093/C$1		

US$0.8092/C$1. If the realized interest rates increase or decrease by 50 basis points in each country with respect to the implied interest rates and the rate difference between countries remained constant, the three-year foreign currency exchange rates would be US$0.8091/C$1 and US$0.8093/C$1, respectively. These rates differ slightly from the US$0.8092/C$1 exchange rate.

Many factors cause realized interest rates to deviate from implied rates. These factors include unexpected changes in:

- Fiscal policy.
- Future inflation rates.
- Monetary policy.
- Money supply.
- Balance of payments.
- Political developments and uncertainties.

Although actual deviations from implied rates may run in parallel between two countries, even the implied interest rate difference is not likely to be fully realized in actual interest rates.

Figure 2 presents the actual interest rate difference or spread between U.S. and Canadian 10-year government bonds. This spread was volatile over the period depicted and, as shown, ranged between 125 and 300 basis points in the year ending June 1990.

If the interest rate difference between the United States and Canada narrows, due to either a decrease in realized U.S. interest rates, an increase in realized Canadian interest rates, or some combination of the two, the spot foreign exchange rate will be greater than the implied US$0.8092/C$1 (the exchange rate that would result in three years if realized annual interest rates are the same as implied annual interest rates). Table 4 presents two scenarios to illustrate this point: (1) realized U.S. interest rates exceed implied interest rates and (2) realized Canadian rates fall short of implied rates (in each case, a narrowing of the interest rate differential or spread by 50 basis points).

The results of these scenarios can be compared with the base case. If the realized annual interest rates equal the implied annual interest rates, a three-year exchange rate of US$0.8092/C$1 would prevail. However, if the spread narrows as shown in Table 4, the realized three-year exchange rate would be approximately US$0.8166/C$1.

Similarly, if the realized interest rate spread increased over the implied interest rate spread, the three-year Canadian dollar would be less expensive. This result is shown in Table 5, where U.S. realized

TABLE 4
United States and Canadian Realized and Implied Interest Rate Differentials

Period	Realized = Implied			U.S. Realized > Implied			Canadian Realized < Implied		
	U.S.	Canada	Differential	U.S.	Canada	Differential	U.S.	Canada	Differential
0–1	8.00%	10.00%	2.00%	8.00%	10.00%	2.00%	8.00%	10.00%	2.00%
1–2	9.00	10.70	1.70	9.50	10.70	1.20	9.00	10.20	1.20
2–3	9.40	11.10	1.70	9.90	11.10	1.20	9.40	10.60	1.20
Three-year spot exchange rate	US$0.8092/C$1			US$0.8166/C$1			US$0.8165/C$1		

TABLE 5
United States and Canadian Realized and Implied Interest Rates: Increasing Interest Rate Differentials

Period	Realized = Implied			U.S. Realized < Implied			Canadian Realized > Implied		
	U.S.	Canada	Differential	U.S.	Canada	Differential	U.S.	Canada	Differential
0–1	8.00%	10.00%	2.00%	8.00%	10.00%	2.00%	8.00%	10.00%	2.00%
1–2	9.00	10.70	1.70	8.50	10.70	2.20	9.00	11.20	2.20
2–3	9.40	11.10	1.70	8.90	11.10	2.20	9.40	11.60	2.20
Three-year spot exchange rate	US$0.8092/C$1			US$0.8018/C$1			US$0.8019/C$1		

interest rates are less than implied interest rates in one case and Canadian realized rates are more than implied rates in another case (i.e., widening of the interest rate differential). In this instance the additional 50-basis-point spread results in a three-year Canadian dollar that would cost approximately US$0.8018.

In summary, if realized annual interest rates in both countries equal implied annual interest rates, or if their ratios are maintained, the future currency exchange rate of a strip of short-date forward contracts will be equivalent to the future currency exchange rate of a long-date forward contract. On the other hand, in the more likely case where realized annual interest rates differ from implied annual rates, the following possibilities exist:

Interest rate spread remains constant between realized and implied interest rates.	Three-year forward currency exchange rate is approximately the same under a strip or a single long-date forward contract.
Interest rate spread narrows between realized and implied interest rates.	Three-year forward currency exchange rate is higher under a strip than a single long-date forward contract.
Interest rate spread widens between realized and implied interest rates.	Three-year forward currency exchange rate is lower under a strip than a single long-date forward contract.

That is, if financial managers have the view that interest differentials will be stable or move in their favor over the duration of their foreign exchange exposure, then a strip of short-date contracts would be the preferred currency hedge.

CONCLUSION

Now that we have seen how forward exchange rates depend on implied interest rates in each of the countries and how implied interest rates depend on term interest rates, what financial managers can accomplish by considering short-date or long-date forward currency cover becomes clearer. Ever since the advent of floating exchange rates, the future course of exchange rates has been extremely difficult to predict. Moreover, bearing the full risk of changes in exchange rates or interest rates may be intolerable for those players who cannot afford the cost of excessive adverse exchange-rate or interest-rate movements.

Since each financial transaction's opportunity, or risk, is attributable to an expected variable—the expected domestic interest rates, the expected foreign interest rates, or the expected future spot exchange rate—the investment or financial manager with a definite opinion as to the future movement of either interest rates or exchange rates can use this analysis to select the best investment or borrowing alternative. By determining the market's perception about future interest or exchange rates, comparing the market's view to his own, and taking an appropriate investment or borrowing position, the manager with strong viewpoints can capitalize on those opinions via a rollover strategy (or strip of short-date contracts) or a long-date contract.

In the case of a domestic investment or borrowing, the financial manager need have only an opinion of subsequent periods' interest rates (equation (3)). If his opinion is that interest rates will be higher or lower than the market's expectation, he can appropriately position his funds for a rollover short-term reinvestment strategy or a locked-in long-term investment strategy, respectively.

If the financial manager is considering a single-period international transaction (borrowing or investment), he can employ equation (6) to determine the market's expectation of the future spot exchange rate, compare this view to his personal expectations, and act accordingly. If the manager holds an opinion that the future spot rate will be higher (lower) than the market's expectation, he will want to assume an international investing (borrowing) position.

The financial manager who wants to make extraordinary gains on a multiple-period international investment or borrowing must have an opinion regarding expected domestic interest rates, expected foreign interest rates, and the expected future spot exchange rate. By inserting his viewpoints into equation (10) (the integrated model) along with the current spot exchange rate, the one-period domestic interest rate, and the one-period international interest rate, the manager can compare his views to those of the market and select the best investment alternative to take a short-date domestic position versus a long-date foreign position or to take a long-date domestic position versus a short-date foreign position.

PART 5

PERIPHERAL ISSUES

CHAPTER 22

CREDIT EXPOSURE, REGULATION, AND CAPITAL REQUIREMENTS

Alan M. Pryor
Deutsche Bank Capital Corporation
New York

INTRODUCTION

Fundamental to the credit risk of a currency swap is the definition and quantification of the credit exposure. Customer credit lines are established by banks in proportion to the potential credit exposure that the bank is willing to undertake on behalf of the customer. Regulatory authorities, in turn, ensure that banks can support their potential credit exposure by requiring a minimum level of capital that must be allocated to each transaction. Therefore, banks must measure their credit exposure realistically or risk a regulatory charge against their capital that may not be covered by adequate earnings from the customer relationship.

Corporate counterparties, in their turn, need to understand the actual and potential credit exposure on a currency swap. Unlike a loan, a currency swap involves an extension of credit to a bank that is the mirror image of the bank's extension of credit to the corporation. Prudent financial management would suggest that a corporation know the magnitude of its exposure.

This chapter will evaluate the actual swap credit exposure and suggest alternative ways to measure the potential swap credit exposure. The impact of capital requirements imposed by major central banks under the guidelines of the Bank for International Settlements (BIS) will also be considered.

DEFINING CURRENCY SWAP CREDIT EXPOSURE: A BUILDING-BLOCK APPROACH

Currency swap credit exposure occurs as a result of a change in interest rates and exchange rates from the date on which the transaction was executed. There is no market risk, apart from a dealer's bid/offer spread, at the moment a swap transaction is agreed upon. However, with the passage of time, the price at which the same transaction would be agreed upon may change. Market risk is equivalent to this replacement cost should a counterparty default. The traditional elements of credit risk are managed by techniques that include the evaluation of creditworthiness, certification of incumbency, representations, and warranties which are thoroughly familiar to the credit departments of financial intermediaries. However, the magnitude of the potential credit risk, which we will call *credit exposure,* results from the market risk. The easiest way to think about the market risk on a currency swap is to realize that it is the sum of the embedded interest rate swap risk plus the foreign exchange risk. Accordingly, we will take a building-block approach to calculating the market risk of a currency swap.

The Interest Rate Swap

Using our building-block approach, we will first consider the simple interest rate swap illustrated in Exhibit 1, in which fixed and floating payments are made on the same date and paid on a net basis. In this exhibit, ABC Corp. pays a fixed rate of 7.5 percent per annum ($ FR$_1$) in return for the six-month Eurodollar rate with an original maturity of seven years. Assume that after three years, ABC's counterparty defaults. ABC must then replace the counterparty in default with a creditworthy successor in order to preserve the economics of the original transaction. The replacement transaction must be executed for the remaining four years at the then-current market interest rate. The new market interest rate is assumed to be 10 percent ($ FR$_2$). Therefore, ABC must make payments at a rate of interest 2.5 percent higher after the default. Its loss is shown in the shaded area. The shaded area is equal to the remaining maturity multiplied by the difference in interest rates. The measure of ABC's damages can be

EXHIBIT 1
ABC Corp. Interest Rate Swap

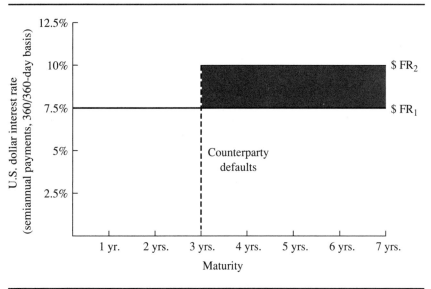

calculated as the present value of the shaded area times the notional principal amount defined as follows:[1]

$$PV = \sum_{d=n}^{m} \frac{P(R_o - R_n)(d/360)}{(1 + R_n/2)^{d/180}}$$

where
PV = present value
P = notional principal
R_o = original rate
R_n = replacement rate
n = time to next payment period
m = time to maturity
d = number of days

---

[1]The actual methodology used by swap dealers tends toward discounting the cash flow for each period by the zero-coupon rate for the associated period, thereby assigning a unique discount rate for each period, rather than using R_n and L_n. The advantage of using the zero-coupon method for marking-to-market is that it is superior for valuing a large portfolio.

In the above example, if the swap default occurred on a date between two payment periods, an additional calculation would be involved. There would be an additional gain or loss associated with any differential in the floating rate for the period until the next payment date. This is determined as follows:

$$PV_{\text{LIBOR STUB}} = \frac{P(L_n - L_o)(d/360)}{(1 + L_n/2)^{d/180}}$$

where L_n = replacement LIBOR
L_o = original LIBOR

Finally, the accrued interest from the last payment date until the default date is calculated as follows:

$$PV_{\text{AI}} = \frac{AI_{\text{fl}} - AI_{\text{fix}}}{(1 + L_n/2)^{d/180}}$$

where AI_{fix} = accrued interest fixed rate
AI_{fl} = accrued interest floating rate

Therefore, the total gain or loss on a simple interest rate swap can be defined as follows:

$$PV = \sum_{d=n}^{m} \frac{P(R_o - R_n)(d/360)}{(1 + R_n/2)^{d/180}} + \frac{P(L_n - L_o)(d/360)}{(1 + L_n/2)^{d/180}}$$
$$+ \frac{AI_{\text{fl}} - AI_{\text{fix}}}{(1 + L_n/2)^{d/180}}$$

Although Exhibit 1 illustrates a loss, had market rates declined below 7.5 percent there would have been a gain.

The Cross Currency Interest Rate Swap

The swap in Exhibit 1 can be changed from an interest rate swap to the standard cross currency interest rate swap shown in Exhibit 2 by substituting a foreign currency Deutschemark (DM) floating rate for the domestic (US$) floating rate. In this transaction, ABC Corp. would pay a fixed rate in U.S. dollars and receive the floating rate in Deutschemarks, as illustrated in Exhibit 2(a). Using a building-block approach to the calculation of replacement cost, the financial

EXHIBIT 2
ABC Corp. Cross Currency Interest Rate Swap

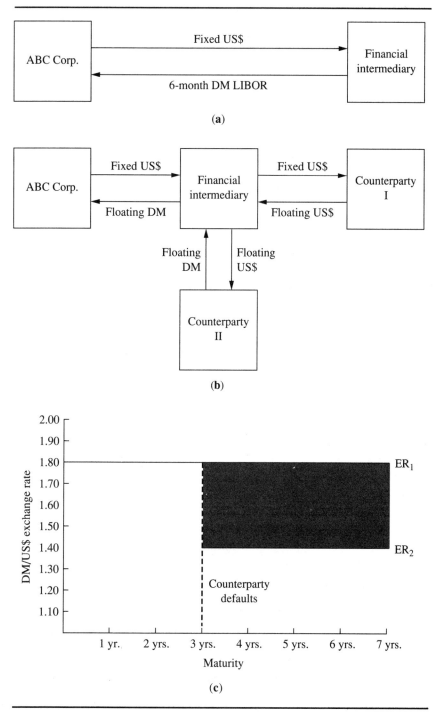

(a)

(b)

(c)

intermediary can eliminate its risk by executing two swaps—a U.S. dollar interest rate swap with Counterparty I and a LIBOR/LIBOR currency swap with Counterparty II, as shown in Exhibit 2(b).[2]

As we can see, a default by the counterparty to ABC Corp. will result in a combined replacement cost for the interest rate swap *and* the LIBOR/LIBOR currency swap. The calculation of the replacement cost for the LIBOR/LIBOR currency swap is illustrated in Exhibit 2(c). Under the contractual terms of the cross currency interest rate swap illustrated, ABC Corp. would deliver Deutschemarks to its counterparty and receive U.S. dollars in return, at a rate of 1.80 DM/US$ (ER_1), at the commencement of the swap. At maturity, this principal exchange would be reversed, with ABC Corp. receiving the original Deutschemark amount and paying the original U.S. dollar amount. Therefore, the final exchange is implicitly at the original foreign exchange rate. If the mark has appreciated against the dollar by 40 pfennig when the counterparty defaults in year 3, ABC Corp. would receive 1.40 DM/US$ under the terms of the replacement swap instead of the original 1.80 DM/US$. Therefore, ABC Corp. would have a dollar loss equal to the present value of 40 pfennig multiplied by the original dollar notional principal amount divided by the current exchange rate. In this example, the credit loss due to the change in the foreign exchange rate would be the present value of 28.57 percent of the notional principal amount.

But an additional exposure needs to be considered as well. If we assume for simplicity that the initial exchange is for US$100 million (DM180 million), a default when the foreign exchange rate has changed to 1.40 DM/US$ would mean that ABC Corp. would receive DM LIBOR on DM140 million instead of DM 180 million upon execution of the replacement swap. In other words, ABC's loss due to the movement in the spot rate between the time of execution (1.80 DM/US$) and the time of default (1.40 DM/US$) would be the present value of a postdefault series of LIBOR payments on DM40 million plus a net payment of DM40 million at maturity. Assuming that ABC can borrow at LIBOR, the present value of these two components is par, or DM40 million.

---

[2] As a practical matter, this is how most dealers will lay off their market risk, although some dealers will roll the LIBOR/LIBOR leg forward in the exchange market until an offsetting swap materializes.

This can be demonstrated by the following expression:

$$PV = \sum_{d=n}^{m} \frac{(L_i)(P_{BR} - P_{BO})(d/360)}{(1 + L_i/2)^{d/180}} + \frac{P_{BR} - P_{BO}}{(1 + L_R/2)^{d/180}} = P_{BR} - P_{BO}$$

where P_{BR} = replacement principal amount (Currency B)
P_{BO} = original principal amount (Currency B)
L_i = LIBOR rate for respective period
L_R = LIBOR rate for last period

This expression demonstrates that the cost of replacement of a basis swap is essentially the sum of additional LIBOR flows for the remaining life of the swap, plus the difference in the principal amounts payable at maturity (i.e., DM40 million). Discounting these cash flows at the respective LIBOR rates would reduce the expression to the difference between the original principal amount and the replacement principal, or US$28,571,429, as illustrated in Exhibit 2(c) and calculated in Appendix B.

From a practical viewpoint, the loss may be locked in at the time of default by the purchase of a LIBOR-bearing instrument (e.g., a CD or an FRN) for a principal amount of DM40 million. If the U.S. dollar is ABC's functional currency, ABC can use the spot foreign exchange market to buy DM40 million at a cost of US$28,571,429 for investment.

In addition to the above, there would be a cost associated with the LIBOR rate differentials for the stub period in the two currencies. This cost is determined as follows:

$$\text{Currency A}_{MTM} = \frac{(P_{AO})(L_{AO} - L_{AR})(d/360)}{(1 + L_{AR}/2)^{d/180}}$$

$$\text{Currency B}_{MTM} = \frac{(P_{BO})(L_{BR} - L_{BO})(d/360)}{(1 + L_{BR}/2)^{d/180}}$$

where P_{AO} = original principal amount (Currency A)
P_{BO} = original principal amount (Currency B)
L_{AO} = original LIBOR rate (Currency A)
L_{BO} = original LIBOR rate (Currency B)
L_{AR} = replacement LIBOR rate (Currency A)
L_{BR} = replacement LIBOR rate (Currency B)
MTM = mark-to-market

Finally, the accrued interest for the LIBOR accruals in both currencies is determined as follows:

$$\text{AI}_{\text{Currency A}} = \frac{(P_{AO})(L_{AO})(d/360)}{(1 + L_{AR}/2)^{d/180}}$$

$$\text{AI}_{\text{Currency B}} = \frac{(P_{BO})(L_{BO})(d/360)}{(1 + L_{BR}/2)^{d/180}}$$

To summarize, the total cost of the basis currency swap is as follows:[3]

$$\text{Total} = \frac{(P_{AO})(L_{AO} - L_{AR})(d/360)}{(1 + L_{AR}/2)^{d/180}} + \frac{(P_{AO})(L_{AO})(d/360)}{(1 + L_{AR}/2)^{d/180}}$$

$$+ \left[(P_{BR} - P_{BO}) + \frac{(P_{BO})(L_{BR} - L_{BO})(d/360)}{(1 + L_{BR}/2)^{d/180}} \right.$$

$$+ \left. \frac{(P_{BO})(L_{BO})(d/360)}{(1 + L_{BR}/2)^{d/180}} \right] (\text{DM}/\text{US\$ spot rate})$$

Therefore, the replacement cost (or gain) for a cross currency interest rate swap is given by the total of (1) the U.S. dollar interest rate swap replacement cost, and (2) the LIBOR/LIBOR basis swap replacement cost.

Replacement Cost Calculation for a Currency Swap

A fixed/fixed currency swap is diagrammed in Exhibit 3. Under the terms of the transaction, ABC Corp. agrees to pay a fixed rate in U.S. dollars in return for a fixed rate in the Deutschemark. ABC Corp. also agrees to exchange a principal amount in Deutschemarks in return for a principal amount in U.S. dollars at the prevailing market rate and to reexchange those same principal amounts at maturity.[4]

---

[3] A LIBOR/LIBOR basis swap may entail an additional cost of 0–12 basis points, reflecting the bank's cost of hedging the position, plus an appropriate return on capital on the swap. This spread has been ignored in the above calculations.

[4] Although the final principal exchange in a currency swap is always mandatory, an initial exchange is optional. Both the initial exchange and the final exchange will entail clean risk (failure to receive payment after disbursing funds) comparable to any exchange transaction.

EXHIBIT 3
ABC Corp. Fixed/Fixed Currency Swap

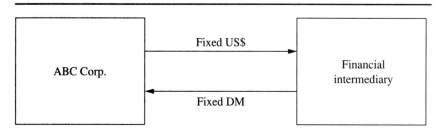

```
┌─────────────┐      Fixed US$      ┌─────────────┐
│             │  ───────────────►   │             │
│  ABC Corp.  │                     │  Financial  │
│             │  ◄───────────────   │ intermediary│
└─────────────┘      Fixed DM       └─────────────┘
```

(a)

```
                    ┌─────────────┐
                    │ Counterparty│
                    │      I      │
                    └─────────────┘
                    Fixed    Floating
                    US$       US$
┌─────────┐  Fixed US$  ┌─────────────┐  Floating US$  ┌─────────────┐
│         │  ─────────► │  Financial  │  ───────────►  │ Counterparty│
│ABC Corp.│             │ intermediary│                │     II      │
│         │  ◄───────── │             │  ◄───────────  │             │
└─────────┘  Fixed DM   └─────────────┘  Floating DM   └─────────────┘
                    Fixed    Floating
                    DM        DM
                    ┌─────────────┐
                    │ Counterparty│
                    │     III     │
                    └─────────────┘
```

(b)

EXHIBIT 3 (continued)
ABC Corp. Fixed/Fixed Currency Swap

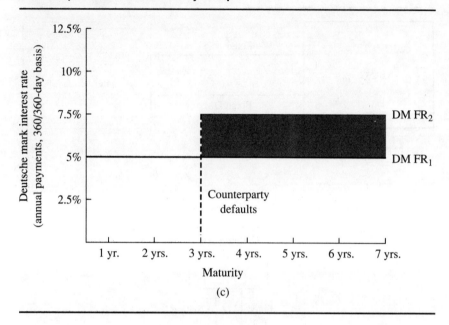

(c)

Using a building-block approach to calculating replacement cost, we can see that there is an additional credit exposure (compared to a cross currency interest rate swap) due to the replacement cost of a second interest rate swap. The replacement cost for Counterparty III, as shown in Exhibit 3(b), is illustrated in Exhibit 3(c) and calculated in Appendix C. In this example, Deutschemark rates are assumed to be 2.5 percent higher when the counterparty defaults at the end of year three. Therefore, substituting a creditworthy successor for the remaining life of the transaction results in a gain on the Deutschemark interest rate swap leg that is equal to the present value of the difference in interest rates over the remaining life of the transaction multiplied by the notional principal amount.[5]

Therefore, the calculation of the credit risk for a fixed vs. fixed currency swap is given by the total of (1) the U.S. dollar interest rate

---

[5]Although the interest differential results in a gain of 2.5 percent for the U.S. dollar leg and a loss of 2.5 percent for the Deutschemark leg, the present value of the gain is greater for the Deutschemark leg due to a lower discount rate.

swap replacement cost, (2) the U.S. dollar/Deutschemark LIBOR/ LIBOR basis swap, and (3) the Deutschemark interest rate swap replacement cost.[6]

MARKET RISK: ESTIMATION AND MEASUREMENT

Financial intermediaries, as well as their corporate counterparties, need to estimate potential market risk before entering into a swap transaction. They also need to monitor that exposure over the remaining life of the transaction. The usual method is to provide for market risk by assigning a fixed percentage of the notional principal amount based on the type of swap and its maturity at the outset of the transaction. This calculation is then monitored and the exposure adjusted over the remaining life by marking to market using the replacement cost methodology. Because the mark-to-market exposure is, by definition, zero at the outset of the transaction, it cannot be relied upon for the calculation of potential credit exposure. Some forecast of the exposure must be made.

Forecasting Potential Credit Exposure

Credit exposure arises as a result of the volatility of interest rates and foreign exchange rates. Institutions typically forecast potential credit exposure by using one or a combination of three approaches to quantifying the volatility:

1. A regression of the historical distribution of price changes over time.
2. Simulation of random price changes over the expected future life of the swap (e.g., Monte Carlo simulation).
3. Adoption of the credit exposure calculation implicit in the BIS capital calculations.

---

[6]In the mark-to-market (MTM) of the cross currency swap, you will observe that the MTM of the LIBOR stub period on the basis swap offsets the MTM of the LIBOR stub period on the interest rate swaps. In other words, the MTM of the U.S. dollar LIBOR stub period is an MTM loss of US$162,235 on the U.S. dollar interest rate swap and is offset by the MTM gain of US$162,235 on the U.S. dollar LIBOR stub period on the basis swap.

A statistical approach that uses a regression to evaluate the probability distribution of past price changes often weights the most recent data more heavily than the earliest observations. This is done under the assumption that, in the future, risk of loss (or gain) due to price change is heavily influenced by the recent past.

Another approach is to recognize that the actual interest rate or foreign exchange rate that will exist in the future cannot be known. However, a large enough sample of random price changes can be generated to create an appropriate number of different scenarios. Statistical techniques can then be applied to a large enough set of scenarios to ensure the estimate of potential credit exposure is reasonably accurate. This statistical technique typically uses a Monte Carlo simulation.[7]

The statistical analysis provided by both these methods was used in establishing the capital guidelines of the BIS. However, the BIS also recognized that the potential credit exposure was not only a function of the market risk but of the basic creditworthiness of the counterparty. Accordingly, the guidelines divide counterparties into classes based on relative creditworthiness. The potential credit exposure can thus be estimated by multiplying the market risk by the risk weight of the class.

Measuring Actual Exposure

A formula used to forecast actual exposures that is based on historical analysis is only a prediction; it may or may not accurately reflect the realized replacement cost as markets change. As a consequence, many institutions supplement the forecast exposure with a mark-to-market valuation, which is in fact required by some central banks. Not only is this a guide as to how accurate forecast exposure proves to be over time, but it will temper the additional extension of credit to counterparties when the credit exposure on a mark-to-market basis exceeds that allowable under the forecast formula. Because marking to market accurately calculates the current credit exposure, many institutions will evaluate credit line usage based on the higher of mark-to-market or forecast exposure.

---

[7]For a more detailed discussion of Monte Carlo simulation, see J. Hull, *Options, Futures, and Other Derivative Securities,* Prentice Hall, Englewood Cliffs, N.J., 1989.

CAPITAL: EXTERNAL REGULATION

Bank regulators mandate minimum capital requirements to support the balance sheet liabilities of the banks that they regulate as well as the contingent claims associated with off-balance-sheet exposure. The framework to be adopted by most regulatory authorities by December 1992 is based on guidelines issued by the Basle Committee of the Bank for International Settlements in 1988.[8] These guidelines mandate that a bank must maintain capital equal to 8 percent of the total of the risk-weighted assets on its balance sheet.

The key term in this context is *risk-weighted assets*. The Basle Committee recognized that credit risk could range from 0 to 100 percent depending upon the nature of the asset. Accordingly, it specified that risk weights of 0, 10, 20, 50, or 100 percent would be applied to specific assets of various risk classes. For example, cash would carry a risk weight of 0 percent, whereas a loan to a corporation would carry a risk weight of 100 percent. This implies that if a bank had US$100 million in capital, it could lend money to corporations in an aggregate amount of US$1,250 million (100/.08). The key issue faced by the Basle Committee was to determine the appropriate risk weights for an interest rate swap and a currency swap. The Committee adopted a two-step approach.

Risk Weight versus Risk Factor

The first step was to assign a risk weight based on the category of the counterparty. For example, the domestic federal government could be given a risk weight of 0 percent, banks 20 percent, and corporations 50 percent. The next step was to adjust the notional principal amount of an interest rate or currency swap by a *risk factor* before applying the risk weight.

The evaluation of the risk factor by the Basle Committee was based upon a consideration of the potential credit exposure for an interest rate or currency swap. The risk factor could be based upon the *original exposure method* or the *current exposure method*.

---

[8]The member countries of the Basle Committee are Belgium, Canada, France, Germany, Italy, Japan, Netherlands, Sweden, Switzerland, the United Kingdom, and the United States.

Exposure Method

Under the original exposure method, credit risk is calculated by a formula over the life of the transaction without any adjustment for its mark-to-market value. The notional principal amount, multiplied by 1 percent per annum, multiplied by the number of years until maturity of the swap, is used as an estimate for interest rate swap market risk. The notional principal amount, multiplied by 3 percent per annum, multiplied by the number of years until swap maturity, is used as an estimate for a currency swap.

The initial credit exposure for an interest rate swap is reduced to reflect its remaining life. This is logical because the shorter the period that is affected by the change in interest rates, the smaller the present value of any loss. This is not true for a currency swap. Foreign exchange rates typically demonstrate greater price volatility than interest rates and dominate the effect of the interest rate replacement cost for a currency swap. As a consequence, the initial exposure is not reduced to reflect the remaining life for a currency swap.

Under the current exposure method, replacement cost is calculated by marking to market in combination with a formula adjustment to ensure that the mark-to-market result doesn't understate the forecast exposure over the remaining life of the transaction. For example, a percentage amount that represents a minimum forecast exposure is established at the outset of a transaction. To the extent that actual exposure on a mark-to-market basis exceeds this minimum, the credit exposure is increased to the mark-to-market level. However, the credit exposure can never fall below the minimum, even if there is no exposure on a mark-to-market basis. Assume, for example, that the forecasted potential credit exposure is 10 percent of the notional principal amount. If, after one year, the actual credit exposure is 15 percent on a mark-to-market basis, there would be an upward adjustment to the forecast exposure. If, after one year, the actual credit exposure is 5 percent, there would be no downward adjustment to the forecast exposure.

Return on Capital and Pricing

Whether capital is computed using the original exposure method or the current exposure method, a required risk weight of 20 percent for banks and 50 percent for corporate counterparties will always result in a greater bank capital charge for the corporate counterparty. Although the impact on interest rate swaps is not substantial, there is a significant impact on currency swaps for corporate counterparties in that the incremental capital requirements imposed on swaps with corporate counterparties reduces the profitability to the bank or increases the return that it must earn on intermediating the swap. International capital market price anomalies, better known as *windows,* are quickly arbitraged by large corporations utilizing cross currency swaps. The effect of the new capital requirements will be that these windows will close sooner than they did in the 1980s, because a greater amount of the price differential will have to be absorbed by bank intermediaries to cover their return on capital. Other things being equal, this will tend to reduce the volume of swap-driven new issues by corporations in a foreign currency, which in turn may have some dampening effect on the globalization of the international capital markets that we witnessed in the 1980s.

Return on Capital and Competition

Regulators must ensure that an adequate discipline exists so that a financial intermediary is not driven to maximize return on capital in the short term by entering into capital-free off-balance-sheet transactions that may endanger capital in the long term. Requiring a minimum amount of capital provides that discipline. Regulators must, however, ensure a level playing field. If one financial intermediary has a lower cost of capital than another, competitive market forces will drive market share to that institution, all other factors being equal. This will occur to the extent that regulatory treatment differs not only within a single country but also between countries. Therefore, regulators must cooperate internationally to ensure that the differences in capital costs between firms that are due to market forces are not distorted by regulatory differences.

SUMMARY AND CONCLUSIONS

Central to the evaluation of credit risk for a currency swap is an understanding and accurate evaluation of the credit exposure due to market risk. A building-block approach has been taken to illustrate the components of a currency swap that, in the aggregate, constitute its market risk. However, it is necessary to supplement a mark-to-market valuation of a currency swap to accurately measure future credit exposure. Three approaches to evaluating this potential credit exposure were discussed. The approaches were based on an analysis of the volatility of price changes in the future. Particular emphasis was placed on the BIS methodology because its use is mandatory for the largest banks in the world.

APPENDIX A

CALCULATION OF REPLACEMENT COST FOR U.S. DOLLAR INTEREST RATE SWAP

Counterparty: ABC Corp.
Notional amount: US$100,000,000
Interest rate paid: 7.50%
Payment frequency: Semiannual
Interest rate received: 6-month LIBOR
Original maturity: 7 years

Swap default at the end of three years, two months

Cost of Fixed Leg of Swap
Current interest rate: 10.00%
Remaining maturity: 3 years, 10 months

Calculation of replacement cost:

$$PV = \sum_{3.17}^{7} \frac{(100,000,000)(\text{Original rate} - \text{Current rate})(d/360)}{(1 + \text{Current rate}/2)^{d/180}}$$

$$= \sum_{3.17}^{7} \frac{(100,000,000)(7.50\% - 10\%)(d/360)}{(1 + 10\%/2)^{d/180}}$$

Yr. 3.5	Yr. 4	Yr. 4.5
= (US$806,664)	(US$1,152,377)	(US$1,097,502)

Yr. 5	Yr. 5.5	Yr. 6
= (US$1,045,240)	(US$995,466)	(US$948,063)

Yr. 6.5	Yr. 7
(US$902,917)	(US$859,921)

= (US$7,808,150)

Cost of Floating Leg of Swap
LIBOR on deal: 8.75%

Current LIBOR rate: 8.25%

No. of days to next pay date: 120

$$PV = \frac{(100,000,000)(\text{Current rate} - \text{Original rate})(120/360)}{(1 + \text{Current rate}/2)^{120/180}}$$

$$= \frac{(100,000,000)(8.25\% - 8.75\%)(120/360)}{(1 + 8.25\%/2)^{120/180}}$$

$$= (US\$162,235)$$

Accrued Interest
LIBOR on deal: 8.75%

Fixed rate on deal: 7.50%

No. of days in accrual period: 60

$$PV = \frac{(100,000,000)(8.75\% - 7.50\%)(60/360)}{(1 + 8.25\%/2)^{120/180}}$$

$$= US\$202,794$$

$$\text{Total PV} = (US\$7,767,592)$$

APPENDIX B

CALCULATION OF REPLACEMENT COST FOR LIBOR/LIBOR SWAP

Counterparty: ABC Corp.

Original exchange rate (DM/US$): 1.8000

Current exchange rate (DM/US$): 1.4000

Notional amount (Currency A): US$100,000,000

Notional amount (Currency B): US$180,000,000

Original LIBOR (Currency A): 8.75%

Original LIBOR (Currency B): 7.75%

Replacement LIBOR (Currency A): 8.25%

Replacement LIBOR (Currency B): 9.25%

No. of days until next pay date: 120

No of days in accrual period: 60

A. LIBOR Mark-to-Market Value

Currency A_{MTM}

$$= \frac{(100,000,000)(\text{Original LIBOR} - \text{Replacement LIBOR})(120/360)}{(1 + 8.25\%/2)^{120/180}}$$

$$= \text{US\$162,235}$$

Currency B_{MTM}

$$= \frac{(180,000,000)(\text{Replacement LIBOR} - \text{Original LIBOR})(120/360)}{(1 + 9.25\%/2)^{120/180}}$$

$$= \text{DM873,277}$$

B. Gain/(Loss) Due to Currency Movements

PV

$$= \frac{\text{Replacement principal (Currency B)} - \text{Original principal (Currency B)}}{\text{Current DM/US\$ spot exchange rate}}$$

$$= \frac{140,000,000 - 180,000,000}{1.4000}$$

$$= (\text{US\$28,571,429})$$

C. Accrued Interest

$$\text{Currency A} = \frac{(100,000,000)(\text{Original LIBOR})(60/360)}{(1 + 8.25\%/2)^{120/180}}$$

$$= (\text{US\$1,419,559})$$

$$\text{Currency B} = \frac{(180,000,000)(\text{Original LIBOR})(60/360)}{(1 + 9.25\%/2)^{120/180}}$$

$$= \text{DM2,255,966}$$

PV(DM flows): 3,129,244
Spot rate: 1.4000
PV (DM flows, in US\$): US\$2,235,174
PV of US\$ flows: (US\$29,828,752)
Total PV of basis swap: (US\$27,593,578)

APPENDIX C

CALCULATION OF REPLACEMENT COST FOR DEUTSCHEMARK INTEREST RATE SWAP

Counterparty: ABC Corp.
Notional amount: 18,000,000
Interest rate paid: 5.00%
Payment frequency: Annual
Interest rate received: 6-month LIBOR
Original maturity: 7 years

Swap default at the end of three years, two months

A. Cost of Fixed Leg of Swap
Current interest rate: 7.50%
Remaining maturity: 3 years, 10 months

Calculation of replacement cost:

$$PV = \sum_{3.17}^{7} \frac{(180,000,000)(\text{Current rate} - \text{Original rate})(d/360)}{(1 + \text{Current rate})^{d/360}}$$

$$= \sum_{3.17}^{7} \frac{(180,000,000)(7.50\% - 5.00\%)(d/360)}{(1 + 7.50\%)^{d/360}}$$

Yr. 4	Yr. 5	Yr. 6	Yr. 7
= 3,530,673	3,941,217	3,666,248	3,410,463

$$= DM14,548,602$$

B. Cost of Floating Leg of Swap
LIBOR rate on deal: 7.75%
Current LIBOR rate: 9.25%
No. of days to next pay date: 120

$$PV = \frac{(180,000,000)(7.75\% - 9.25\%)(120/360)}{(1 + 9.25\%/2)^{120/180}}$$

$$PV = (DM873,277)$$

C. Accrued Interest

LIBOR on deal: 7.75%

Fixed rate on deal: 5.00%

No. of days in fixed period: 60

$$PV = \frac{(180{,}000{,}000)(5.00\% - 7.750\%)(60/360)}{(1 + 9.25\%/2)^{120/180}}$$

$$PV = (DM800{,}504)$$

$$\text{Total PV} = DM12{,}874{,}820$$

$$\text{Total PV in US\$} = US\$9{,}196{,}300$$

Total mark-to-market (MTM) value of currency swap:

MTM of U.S. dollar interest rate swap: (US$7,767,592)

MTM of basis swap: (US$27,593,578)

MTM of Deutschemark interest rate swap: US$9,196,300

Total MTM value of swap: (US$26,164,870)

CHAPTER 23

ARE SWAPS FUTURES?

*Barry W. Taylor**
The First National Bank of Chicago

INTRODUCTION

In 1974, Congress amended the Commodity Exchange Act (CEA) to exempt contracts in foreign currency from the CEA's exchange trading requirement. Sponsored by the U.S. Treasury, the so-called "Treasury amendment" allowed the foreign exchange market to operate among sophisticated and institutional participants as an over-the-counter (OTC) market. Before 1974, the currency of another country could have been classified as a commodity under U.S. commodities laws, and therefore currency transactions arguably were subject to the CEA. Forward exchanges of U.S. dollars for Swiss francs, for example, could have been considered contracts for the purchase and sale of a commodity for future delivery, or "futures," under the CEA.

The CEA bans all futures unless they are executed on a board of trade, or exchange or contract market supervised by the Commodity Futures Trading Commission (CFTC), which administers the CEA. Unless an exemption applies, a violation of the exchange trading requirement is a felony and renders the contract voidable. A primary goal of this requirement is to protect the public from price manipulation and other abuses through CFTC supervision of the market itself. Supervision of the futures market is considered

*Barry W. Taylor is counsel to The First National Bank of Chicago. This chapter is based on a paper entitled "Swaps: Commodities Laws in Transition" that Mr. Taylor presented at the 1990 conference of the Commodities Law Institute, held in Chicago. The author gratefully acknowledges the assistance of Jeffrey S. Lillien in the preparation of this chapter. Views expressed herein are those of the author and not necessarily those of First Chicago.

necessary because the public is permitted to trade directly in this market as speculators and hedgers.

Partly because the Treasury amendment appeared to cover currency swaps, swap market participants largely ignored the commodities laws during the evolution of the OTC financial swaps market in the early 1980s. As currency swaps began to encompass interest rate exchanges and then interest rate swaps evolved, anti-gambling statutes received far more attention. There was some concern that swaps could be viewed as mere bets on the movement of interest rates. But gambling laws were dismissed as wholly inapplicable in a commercial context, especially for hedging and investment activities of this type.

On the surface, financial swaps did not appear to involve contracts for the purchase and sale of a commodity. Even though the CEA encompasses intangible commodities, it was difficult to conceive of bank deposits as commodities underlying LIBOR swaps, for example, or interest rates as their price.

Interest rate swaps and currency swaps involving interest rate exchanges were viewed more as financing contracts, linked to the bank and money markets rather than to the commodities markets. Parties entered into them not to transfer price risk as with futures, but to transfer a funding advantage. In other words, companies with access to cheaper fixed-rate funds could use swaps to "sell" the advantage to others. Further evidence of the financing character of swaps could be found when swap payment frequencies (e.g., fixed and floating amounts) were mismatched between the parties, which resulted in additional credit risk akin to a loan. Besides, the CFTC remained silent as financial swaps mushroomed into a trillion-dollar market. Consequently, swap market participants did not consider the CEA as any real impediment to their swaps business.

This all changed in 1987, when banks and other institutions began entering into commodity swaps. Unlike interest rate swaps, commodity swaps are indexed to tangible commodities, such as the price of crude oil. They were a natural extension of the idea of paying differences on an index. Although these swaps are based on physical commodities, they settle only in cash; there is no right to compel physical delivery of the underlying commodities as there is with futures based on physicals.

In 1987, the CFTC threatened to initiate an enforcement action under the CEA against U.S. commodity swap participants such as

Chase Manhattan Bank, an early entrant in this market. Commodity swaps were viewed as a possible threat to the futures exchanges. The futures exchanges serve to facilitate the transfer of commodity price risk from hedgers to speculators through the trading of fungible (i.e., highly standardized) futures. Banks sought to provide additional commodity price hedges structured to fit their customers' individual needs. Unlike exchange-traded futures, commodity swaps are customized and therefore not suitable for exchange trading. The CFTC wanted to avoid litigation compelling it to enforce the CEA and needed time to study commodity swaps before the market developed.

The CFTC threat cast doubt on the legal status of all swaps involving the payment of rate or price differences, and U.S. banks either refrained from entering into commodity swaps or conducted the business offshore. Domestic commodity swap activity resumed in 1989 after the CFTC issued a policy statement (herein called the Swap Statement), which created a safe harbor for qualifying swaps, whether based on rate or price differences. This safe harbor removed the threat of a CFTC enforcement action, but as a policy statement it could not address concerns about private litigation. Courts could still declare swaps void if they found them to be in violation of the commodities laws.

Swaps had evolved from those strictly based on currencies to those indexed to physical commodities, but the law had yet to evolve to fully accommodate rate or price exchanges. To remove any doubt about the legality of swaps under U.S. commodities laws, market participants recognized that a legislative solution was necessary.

In 1990, legislation was introduced in Congress seeking some form of exemptive relief for swaps. Congress is expected to consider this legislation during 1991. This chapter discussed why a legislative solution became necessary. The root of the problem lies in the CEA, which neither authorizes off-exchange futures nor provides the CFTC with exemptive rulemaking powers to allow commercial parties to engage in futures off-exchange. It also does not preempt state commodities laws that remain applicable to OTC futures. Most of these laws, commonly known as "bucket shop statutes," predate the passage of the federal commodities laws in the 1930s.

After describing the Swap Statement, this chapter examines the state commodities laws and their relationship to federal commodities laws, including the legal test of what a future is. It then analyzes the CFTC's emerging definition of a future in light of a recent judicial decision known as the *Transnor* case and suggests that the Swap Statement, which helped to legitimize off-exchange swaps, bears a strong resemblance to a landmark 1905 Supreme Court case that legitimized certain exchange-traded futures. Finally, this chapter concludes that the legitimacy of swaps will be firmly established under U.S. law once Congress gives the CFTC exemptive and preemptive rulemaking powers to exclude swaps explicitly from the CEA.

THE SWAP SAFE HARBOR

In the Swap Statement, the CFTC said that swaps would qualify under its safe harbor only if they are (1) individually tailored; (2) terminable only by consent without using an exchange-style offset; (3) either unsecured or collateralized without the support of a clearing or maintenance margin system; (4) undertaken in conjunction with each party's line of business; and (5) not marketed to the public.[1] The CFTC recognized that, between commercial and institutional parties, swaps having these characteristics could be distinguished from futures. Accordingly, regulation of qualifying swaps under the CEA would be unnecessary. These criteria are analyzed later in this chapter.

Market participants had asserted that swaps are not futures and therefore fall outside the CFTC's jurisdiction and the exchange trading requirement. Although the CFTC did not agree entirely with this view in its Swap Statement, it conceded that "most swap transactions, although possessing elements of futures or options contracts, are not appropriately regulated as such under the [CEA] and regulations."[2] Implicit in the safe harbor was the CFTC's assertion of potential jurisdiction over swaps not qualifying under one or more of these criteria.

The immediate effect of the Swap Statement was to retract the threat of a CFTC-initiated enforcement action against parties entering into qualifying contracts. Its principal shortcoming was that it was not binding on private litigants. If the CFTC had exempted swaps pursuant to a rulemaking, this would have had the force of law. Unfortunately, the CFTC lacked exemptive rulemaking powers for futures. (Congress delegated exemptive rulemaking powers to the CFTC only for options and leverage contracts.) Therefore, to the extent that swaps could be considered futures, the CFTC was powerless to completely remove the risk that courts could void swaps as illegal off-exchange futures. Nevertheless, the Swap Statement helped to establish the legitimacy of swaps under federal law.

STATE LAW AND PREEMPTION

While the CFTC provided some degree of comfort under federal law, it could do nothing about state laws that also ban OTC futures. Even assuming the CFTC could assert jurisdiction as a matter of law, its decision not to regulate swaps, as reflected in the Swap Statement, probably had no preemptive effect. In 1982, Congress conferred broad jurisdictional authority on the states to regulate or prohibit OTC futures under their police power. The CFTC was left with exclusive jurisdiction over exchange-traded futures.

State commodities laws have the same potential as the CEA to render contracts unenforceable and subject the parties to enforcement actions and criminal penalties. State bucket shop statutes outlaw futures that settle in cash based on commodity price differences. To avoid completely the risk of private litigation, these laws also had to be amended or preempted.

The extent to which the CEA preempts state law is defined in section 12(e) of the CEA, which Congress enacted in 1982 to broaden the enforcement and regulatory powers of states in dealing with off-exchange commodity fraud. This section provides that state statutory law is preempted only for contracts that (1) are conducted on or subject to the rules of a contract market, or (subject to CFTC rule or regulation) any foreign board of trade, exchange or market; or (2) are options or leverage contracts regulated by the CFTC.

Because the exclusive jurisdiction of the CFTC was limited, states could regulate or prohibit OTC contracts falling outside these categories. The CFTC was powerless to preempt state law simply by declining to regulate an OTC contract that failed to qualify as an option or leverage contract.

Bucket Shop Laws

Thus, without federal preemption, state bucket shop laws would still be valid. Section 12(e) resurrected these laws, which states first enacted in the late nineteenth century. New York's bucket shop statute is illustrative. It provides, in pertinent part, that any person shall be guilty of a felony if they:

> ... make or offer to make ... any contract respecting the purchase or sale, either upon credit or margin, of any securities or commodities, including all evidences of debt or property and options for the purchase thereof, shares in any corporation or association, bonds, coupons, scrip, rights, choses in action ... and anything movable that is bought and sold, [i] intending that such contract shall be terminated, closed or settled according to, or upon the basis of the public market quotations of or prices made on any board of trade or exchange or market ... and without intending a bona fide purchase or sale of the same; or ... [ii] intending that such contract shall be deemed terminated, closed and settled when such market quotations ... shall reach a certain figure, without intending a bona fide purchase or sale of the same; or ... [iii] not intending the actual bona fide receipt or delivery of any such securities or commodities, but intending a settlement of such contract based upon the difference in such public market quotations of or such prices at which said securities or commodities are, or are asserted to be bought or sold. ... [3]

Generally, a bucket shop is a speculative enterprise that engages in OTC futures that are incapable of being settled by delivery of the underlying commodity or security, or are intended to be settled only by reference to changes in the market price of commodities or securities. At the turn of the century, bucket shops were notorious scam operations that skipped town before their contracts were due to settle. Even if not perpetrating scams, they assumed price risk without hedging it. When commodity prices moved against them, they filed for bankruptcy or moved to another state, leaving behind uncollectible futures.

States criminalized what courts considered to be unenforceable gambling contracts under common law. Bucket shop laws were also passed in response to populist factions concerned with protecting farmers from commodity price manipulation and speculation, which might occur on unregulated commodities exchanges.

Now that legitimate futures trading is conducted on federally regulated exchanges, state law has less relevance for protecting the public from these evils. Because speculation is necessary for the futures exchanges to function, the moral heritage of bucket shop laws has lost its significance.

Despite being anachronistic, bucket shop laws continue to protect the public from fraud and the financial risks associated with bucket shops and their modern-day counterparts, "boiler rooms," which use high-pressure sales tactics to sell illegal futures or securities to the public. A violation of a bucket shop law is usually a felony and the contract is void. About half of the states still have bucket shop statutes. At the federal level, Congress mandated that all futures be traded exclusively on a regulated exchange to combat the abuses of bucket shops, and to knowingly violate this requirement is also a felony.

Rather than aiming just at fraud, bucket shop statutes outlaw futures altogether—generally without regard to intended use or purpose. A total ban was considered necessary given the difficulty in establishing fraud, the financial risks of allowing unregulated enterprises to trade with the public, and the enforcement problems inherent in policing scam operations. States banned both futures and futures business. The CEA contains a similar ban on the enterprise.

Hedging

Statutes prohibiting futures were construed quite strictly early in this century. As a general rule, futures being used for hedging were still considered illegal. Most courts considered the underlying purpose to be irrelevant. Intent mattered only in ascertaining whether one or both of the parties actually contemplated physical delivery. This delivery requirement still stands as a major obstacle for litigants. Whether the parties expect to settle in cash based upon commodity price differences rather than by physical delivery of commodities is still a major factor in court decisions construing state and federal commodities laws.

Some state courts seemed willing to make concessions when futures were used for hedging purposes, but often found that the contract in question did not satisfy their concept of a hedge. They also did not intimate that hedging would be considered lawful if the contract was not capable of being settled by physical delivery.

In construing state law, federal courts were more inclined to consider futures lawful for hedging purposes. Unlike state courts, however, they often required no proof that the parties were hedging, although there could be no agreement that delivery would not occur. Instead, courts focused more on the method of settlement, especially in cases of exchange-traded futures. Delivery, early close-out, and offset were the only methods recognized as lawful.

In some cases a court would presume that a lawful method was intended and would not void the contract without proof that it would be settled only in cash. For exchange-traded futures, this legal presumption made hedging or speculation practically irrelevant, although futures contracts were sometimes voided when a party had no capacity to deal in physical commodities.

Despite some allowance for hedging under state law, hedging is not a defense under the CEA for violating the exchange trading requirement. Under a prior version of section 4 of the CEA, which outlaws OTC trading, futures were defined as those hedging commodities in interstate commerce; this language now appears in sections of the CEA dealing with fraud and fictitious sales. Thus, OTC trading in these hedging futures was specifically outlawed. Hedging would be a defense only as an exception to the CEA's speculative trading limits and would apply only to exchange-traded contracts.

Business Purpose

Although many state gambling laws contain a *business purpose* exception, state bucket shops laws do not. While this exception might be appropriate under general gambling laws now that speculation for investment has been legitimized, the broad application of this exception could conflict with commodities laws, which serve more specific purposes. No explicit business purpose exception exists under the CEA either, which can also be considered a bucket shop law, albeit a regulatory one.

The CEA was designed to ensure that all legitimate futures would be subject to CFTC regulation or supervision. Congress has made exceptions to the CEA's exchange trading requirement only if (1) regulation of the activity is deemed inappropriate, as in the case of forward contracts involving actual delivery of commodities; (2) the nature of the parties is such that Congress deems regulation to be unnecessary; or (3) the parties or the activity is subject to another regulatory framework such as the securities or banking laws. Although the reason for creating these exceptions might be in the legislative history, the fact remains that the CEA has not been limited to publicly traded contracts nor does it broadly exempt commercial contracts. The CEA's overall design requires exemptions or rulemaking.

Courts therefore might decline to consider whether Congress or a state legislature would have exempted a new form of contract just because relatively sophisticated parties are involved. At the turn of the century, however, the Supreme Court saw its role differently in *Board of Trade v. Christie*,[4] in which it was asked to decide whether the Chicago Board of Trade (CBOT) kept the greatest of all bucket shops. In this landmark 1905 case, the Chicago Board of Trade sued to restrain a bucket shop from using CBOT price quotations. The bucket shop based its defense on antitrust grounds and the "clean hands" doctrine, charging that the CBOT was itself a bucket shop.

Writing for the Court, Justice Holmes upheld exchange trading in the futures pits between member firms despite an apparent violation of the Illinois bucket shop law. He reasoned that its delivery requirement was satisfied by offsetting two or more futures that are deliverable even though one or both parties might not contemplate delivery. By holding that offset is delivery, Justice Holmes approved futures made for "serious business purposes," including hedging. Yet he carefully distinguished between, on the one hand, the offset of an exchange-traded purchase contract against a sales contract and, on the other, a contract that itself is settled by payment of differences between contract and market prices.

Although the legality of futures trading between brokers and their customers would not be established until the CEA was passed, Holmes legitimized the exchanges and futures traded on them by emphasizing the positive side of commercial speculation. Constructive rather than actual delivery would serve important economic goals, according to Holmes, who considered the simple prohibition of a useful economic activity "harmful and vain." *Christie* was viewed in terms of emerging governmental policy toward the exchanges and their role in providing a legitimate mechanism for hedging and speculation.

Notwithstanding the Supreme Court's willingness to consider economic policy at the turn of the century, economic and regulatory complexities have increased. Today courts would have to avoid any conflict with federal law and regulations governing commodities trading, including, to a significant degree, the interests of the commodities exchanges legitimized by Holmes.

Between commercial or institutional parties, cash-settled OTC futures would not necessarily conflict with the goal of protecting the public from speculation unless the public otherwise deals with these institutions as unregulated entities. In the absence of other evils such as fraud and market manipulation, however, an institutional and commercial exclusion still implicates public policy toward the exchanges and their trading franchise.

Today, any judicially created exception would have to depart from old precedents, not so much in terms of the results, but in justifying the means by which a statutory prohibition could be ignored. For exchange-traded futures, the legal fiction of offset has satisfied the delivery requirement. Yet courts have not set a similar precedent for OTC contracts under which neither party has the right to compel delivery. The legitimacy of commercial OTC futures has not been established statutorily or judicially.

Commodity Codes and Blue Sky Laws

A few states have recognized that bucket shop laws are outdated and conflict with the needs of legitimate commodities businesses. Instead they have enacted modern statutes, most of which are based on the Model State Commodity Code.[5] The North American Securities Administrators Association (NASAA) adopted the Model Code in 1985, calling it a modern bucket shop law that states could enact to protect the public from commodity scams.

The Model Code does not attempt to regulate exchange-traded futures and options governed by the CEA. Instead, it bans only OTC commodity contracts entered into primarily for investment or speculation and not for the acquisition or disposition of the underlying commodities. Three major exceptions are discussed below. It also delegates exemptive powers to state administrators for contracts not subject to the exclusive jurisdiction of the CFTC.

First, the Model Code defines commodity contracts as those entered into for speculation or investment purposes and not for the use or consumption by the offeree or purchaser. Therefore, hedging contracts would not appear to be prohibited unless the hedge has an investment purpose.

Second, certain persons are exempt, including CFTC-registered futures commission merchants (FCMs), SEC-registered broker-dealers, affiliates guaranteed by FCMs or broker-dealers, members of CFTC-designated contract markets, and banks, thrifts, and trust companies. The Model Code's preamble states that this exemption is appropriate because the activities of these firms are otherwise regulated. However, NASAA has allowed Congress and the CFTC to control whether this exemption actually takes effect. The exemption for regulated firms does not apply for contracts that are prohibited under the CEA.

Third, the Model Code exempts contracts solely between commodities producers, processors, users, and merchants, as well as any contract under which the offeree or purchaser is one of the regulated firms referred to above, or an insurance or investment company. Because this exemption does not depend on whether the contract violates the CEA, it appears that regulated firms could purchase, or accept offers to enter into, OTC futures. They are restricted only from selling or offering these contracts.

Because these exemptions apply, the Model Code was a significant step forward in the evolution of state bucket shop laws. The Model Code is both an enabling statute and a law aimed at commodity trading abuses.

State "blue-sky" laws might also apply to the extent that any commodity contract involves the sale of securities, or if a particular blue-sky law's definition of a security includes commodity contracts. The unregistered sale of these contracts would be illegal unless an exemption applies.

New York's blue-sky statute serves as an example. When the state legislature amended the Fraudulent Practices (Martin) Act in 1984,[6] it added a registration requirement for commodity broker-dealers, salespersons, and investment advisers. This requirement applies to any nonexempt person who publicly offers commodity contracts for investment or speculative purposes, or provides related advisory services. Failure to file a registration statement constitutes a criminal offense. To some extent, the list of exempt persons resembles the Model Code's list.

When it added this registration requirement to the Martin Act, the New York legislature did not amend the New York bucket shop law. It is unclear whether the Martin Act was intended to encompass futures prohibited under the bucket shop statute or permit registered or exempt persons to enter into these futures.

THE CEA AND STATE LAW

Despite state law issues, broad preemptive relief would be impossible unless the CEA were amended to accommodate OTC futures. The need for such an exemption is not much different under the CEA than it would be under state law, as both prohibit OTC futures.

In contrast with state law, the CEA does not explicitly define futures in terms of how the parties intend to settle the contract. Because the CEA refers to futures as all contracts for future delivery of commodities, it was necessary to exclude contracts that are settled by physical delivery as a matter of course, commonly known as forwards. The CEA exempts forwards, calling them "cash contracts for deferred shipment or delivery" (the forward contract exclusion). The typical state bucket shop statute, on the other hand, does not even encompass forwards.

Courts have defined forwards as contracts in which the parties contemplate the physical delivery of the actual commodity; this resembles the intent test applied under state law. The CFTC has said they are "commercial, merchandising transactions in physical commodities in which delivery actually occurs but is delayed or deferred for commercial purposes."[7]

Only through the process of distinguishing between a future and a forward under the CEA is it possible to ascertain what Congress really intended to prohibit. By exempting forwards that are regularly settled by physical delivery, the CEA could be construed simply to ban off-exchange contracts for future delivery if they are regularly settled in cash by paying differences based on prices or an index (contracts for differences).

While this construction is consistent with how futures are defined under state statutes, which are more forthright than the CEA in what they prohibit, the CEA's relatively obscure meaning can be discerned only by analyzing how the CFTC and courts define a future. This is the focus of the next two sections.

In construing the CEA, courts have considered the method of delivery an important if not overriding factor in distinguishing between futures and forwards. For tangible commodities, both futures and forwards carry with them the right to compel delivery. Unlike forwards, however, futures are typically settled by paying differences; only a small percentage of exchange-traded futures result in physical delivery. Futures on intangibles, however, are not deliverable and must be settled in cash. Among these are stock index futures based on a basket of securities, such as the Standard and Poor's 500 Index.

In addition, the method of delivery seems to be inextricably tied to the economic purpose of futures, which are entered into primarily to shift commodity price risk from one party to another and not for the acquisition or disposition of the underlying commodities. Only if a contract's economic purpose and method of settlement were ignored, or deemed to be secondary considerations, could the forward contract exclusion be considered to apply to intangibles. To avoid swallowing up the CEA, the forward contract exclusion also would have to be read narrowly to confine it to commercial transactions. Otherwise, intangible forwards could be offered to the public. On its face, the CEA does not exempt only commercial forwards.

Were courts to hold that economic purpose and delivery are dispositive in all cases, regardless of policy considerations, the interpretive process would be the same under either federal or state law. Under state bucket shop statutes, courts must ascertain whether the parties intended to settle by physical delivery or by paying only differences, which is not much different from distinguishing, on the basis of delivery, between a forward and a future under the CEA.

Furthermore, failure to meet the delivery requirement could have serious implications for swaps, which are contracts for differences. Unless classified as option, forward, or Treasury amendment contracts, courts could declare swaps illegal under a narrow interpretation of the commodities laws.

In this regard, the fact that swaps are not purchase-and-sale contracts might not make much difference. Courts have recognized that the CEA is ambiguous on its face and therefore could look beyond its plain meaning. For state law purposes, terminology seems to be irrelevant; if neither party intends to settle by physical delivery, no agreement to buy or sell commodities even exists.

In attempting to outlaw fictitious sales, state legislatures used customary futures language in drafting bucket shop laws. They did not refer to simple contracts that are settled in cash against price differences. Under the common law, contracts for differences were already considered gambling because these contracts served no economic purpose considered legitimate at the time.

State legislatures were thus faced with distinguishing legitimate purchase-and-sale contracts involving physical delivery from contracts settled on price differences. Courts were faced with the same problem, which is why they considered absence of an intent to deliver dispositive under state law. In this respect, bucket shop laws were ancillary to gambling laws. To some extent, the CEA merely reflects state statutory language prevalent in the 1930s.

Because courts also consider a contract's economic purpose an important factor, it might be irrelevant that the contract is merely promissory and does not purport to transfer title, potentially or otherwise. Moreover, the *Christie* decision serves as a precedent for substituting the legal equivalent of a statutory requirement. Obviously, the legal consideration arising from an exchange of mutual promises under a swap serves the same function as monetary consideration. In any event, if a boiler room could engage in the activity, the form of statutory language would not be likely to triumph over the substance of legislative intent.

That courts must resort to legal fictions to interpret the commodities laws is evidence of the laws' obscure and anachronistic nature. Adding to the confusion of an obscure statute is the interpretive process. So much attention is focused on distinguishing futures from forwards that it has become unclear whether Congress really intended to prohibit all OTC contracts that are or become contracts for differences, except those specifically exempted.

Moreover, the CFTC has continued to apply characteristics that describe exchange-traded futures in distinguishing between futures and forwards. In doing so, it has sidestepped defining a future strictly in terms of the delivery method.

THE CFTC'S CONCEPT OF A FUTURE

In rendering its *In re Stovall*[8] decision in 1979, the CFTC characterized a future as having four classic elements. Futures are (1) standardized, (2) offered to the public, (3) secured by margin, and (4) entered into primarily to shift commodity price risk without transferring ownership of actual commodities. All of these elements need not be present, according to the CFTC, nor are they exclusive.

These criteria described exchange-traded futures, which illegal enterprises often replicate in peddling OTC futures to the public. However, *Stovall* did not address whether a future could encompass a commercial OTC contract that is privately negotiated, individually tailored, and credit based. Contracts between sophisticated parties would tend to have these characteristics, regardless of the contract's intended use or the delivery method. But unlike state statutes, the CEA does not indicate whether the parties' intent or the delivery method is dispositive.

Stovall also gave the impression that the CEA might be limited to fungible futures. Yet courts have indicated that standardization is relevant because fungible contracts can be offset against each other (i.e., made into contracts for differences). "Fungibility" also enhances a contract's tradeability and marketability, which makes it suitable for exchange trading and a public offering. Thus, standardization eliminates the delivery requirement and makes the contract marketable, thereby allowing anyone—commercial parties and the public—to use futures for hedging and speculation.

A decade after *Stovall,* the CFTC applied three of the four *Stovall* criteria when it released the Swap Statement. It modified them somewhat in identifying safe harbor swaps as those that are individually tailored, unsupported by a clearing or margin system, and used only by commercial parties in their line of business. But the Swap Statement ignored the last of the *Stovall* criteria—whether the parties intended to shift price risk without delivering commodities.

The CFTC had to sidestep this criterion because it describes both futures and commodity swaps. To consider the economic purpose and method of settlement dispositive would have conflicted with the Commission's goal of accommodating commercial interests that do not disrupt exchange trading. The CFTC ignored these two factors in the Swap Statement because it believed that most swaps possess "elements of futurity" (e.g., transfer price risk) but are not appropriately regulated as futures under the CEA.

By ignoring the economic purpose and method of delivery, the CFTC enabled commercial parties to enter into swaps for lawful business purposes without the threat of federal sanctions. There is an interesting parallel between the Swap Statement and Justice Holmes's *Christie* decision. In *Christie,* Holmes cited business purposes to legitimize the exchanges and the contracts traded on them—before Congress enacted the CEA and preempted state law. In the Swap Statement, the CFTC helped to legitimize off-exchange contracts with elements of futurity that are used in a line of business. The CFTC did this before Congress had statutorily carved out a general commercial exemption or given the Commission power to exempt futures by rulemaking.

As one characteristic of a future, posting margin under the *Stovall* test became exchange-style margining under the Swap Statement. In effect, the CFTC prohibited the creation of a clearinghouse or margin system that could compete with the commodities exchanges or undermine their function.

By requiring that material terms be individually tailored, the Swap Statement implicitly recognized that swaps, because they are nonfungible, are not appropriate for exchange trading. Thus, nonfungible swaps posed no immediate threat to the exchanges' fungible business. To the contrary, the exchanges are a direct beneficiary of swaps because swap dealers regularly execute futures on the exchanges to hedge and manage their swap positions. Besides, were they to offer swaps, the exchanges could probably outcompete the swap market because of the efficiencies created by a clearinghouse.

So absent any threat to the exchanges, commercial parties could engage in swaps, including commodity swaps, as long as they observed the safe harbor conditions. In this way, the CFTC successfully balanced the interests of the swaps market and those of the futures market. Just as the *Christie* decision was viewed in terms of emerging governmental policy toward the exchanges, the Swap Statement could be viewed as an existing or emerging federal policy of accommodating commercial interests that do not compete with or disturb the commodities exchanges.

As further evidence of this, the Swap Statement prohibited use of an exchange-style offset. The CFTC explained that this permits only swaps terminable by consent—those entered into with the "expectation of performance" (which sounds a lot like expectation of delivery) and not used for trading purposes. What is interesting about this prohibition is that the CFTC applied it to *contracts for differences*.

Traditionally, offset was viewed as the mechanism by which parties could lawfully extinguish *physical* delivery obligations on an exchange, or unlawfully offset them off-exchange by converting contracts purporting to be forwards into contracts for differences. In closing out swaps, which are already contracts for differences, parties need not acquire equal and opposite contracts to unwind their positions. In contrast, offset is the usual method of closing out exchange-traded futures on intangible commodities such as stock index futures.

In prohibiting the trading of swaps, the CFTC equated offset with assignability and terminability. The Swap Statement explained that an exchange or clearinghouse provides the liquidity for trading to occur. Because the exchange acts as a universal counterparty, consent is unnecessary to offset and liquidate contracts. However, the CFTC did not indicate why commercial parties should be prohibited from trading swaps off-exchange. In transferring or terminating swaps prior to maturity, differences are paid based on the market price of the contract itself, rather than on the price of another kind of instrument to which swaps are indexed, such as bank deposits or U.S. Treasuries. In either case, the contracts are settled in cash based on market rates or prices.

The trading prohibition appears to discourage an active secondary market in swaps and thereby control the extent to which a swap itself can be used as an investment vehicle. The Swap Statement still allows the parties to give their consent and agree to a privately negotiated termination price or formula in advance, which allows some flexibility for investment and hedging strategies. Trading is hampered by the condition that any termination arrangements must be privately negotiated.

As a prohibition against trading, offset has taken on a new meaning as applied to contracts for differences. In this regard, it is worth noting that Justice Holmes used offset to permit exchange trading, whereas the CFTC used it to prohibit off-exchange trading.

To summarize, the CFTC distinguished swaps from futures more in terms of what the parties do with the contract, or what activities are associated with the contract, than in terms of the contract's economic purpose or how the contract is settled. In differentiating swaps from futures, the CFTC has in effect prohibited any public offering, trading, clearing, and margining of swaps—all of which are exchange functions.

Economic Purpose and Delivery Method

The CFTC has permitted institutional participants to facilitate the transfer of commodity price risk alongside the exchanges, provided they adhere to conditions that distinguish them from the exchanges. Courts have yet to abandon the delivery requirement, however, and ignore a contract's underlying purpose in determining whether it is a future.

A federal court cited these two factors in a 1990 case, *Transnor (Bermuda) Ltd. v. BP North American Petroleum*,[9] which held that commercial contracts for the purchase and sale of 15-day Brent crude oil were futures. The plaintiff, Transnor, had alleged that several oil companies had rigged the price of crude oil. Transnor also asserted claims against the oil companies for violation of the CEA.

In addressing the alleged CEA violation, the court reiterated that futures are undertaken primarily to assume or shift price risk without transferring the underlying commodity. In this respect, *Transnor* resembled other state and federal court decisions that have held contracts to be futures.

According to the court's findings, 95 percent of Brent oil contracts are entered into for speculation or hedging—not for the acquisition or disposition of oil. The court concluded that these highly standardized contracts gave the parties an opportunity to offset, and a tacit expectation and common practice of offsetting was sufficient to deem them futures. Thus, the likelihood of avoiding delivery through offset created a "paper market" for hedging and speculation.

Transnor was an important case, not because it set an entirely new precedent (which it did not) or was rightly or wrongly decided. Rather, it served to highlight that the CEA does not explicitly exempt commercial OTC futures and that courts have not yet abandoned the delivery requirement. *Transnor* served notice that commercial parties could still be at risk, despite a CFTC safe harbor. Unless it had rulemaking powers, the CFTC could not exempt OTC futures, at least not as courts define them.

THE POLITICS OF INNOVATION

As swaps evolved from those that are strictly financial to those indexed to tangible commodities, it became apparent that swaps presented a possible conflict between banking and commodities laws. To a great extent, this happened because the commodities laws are more comprehensive, covering all futures trading and concentrating regulation at the exchange level. The public trades directly in the futures markets, which requires government supervision to ensure the fairness, competitiveness, and financial integrity of these markets. In contrast, the banking laws do not purport to regulate the financial markets per se. Instead, regulation is focused on more numerous and dispersed banks. Bank regulators influence the financial markets in other ways, including controlling the money supply and intervening in the foreign exchange markets. Unlike the futures exchanges, banks conduct principally an OTC business.

Until 1990, Congress was not asked to resolve the uncertainty and potential conflict that lay between these two regulatory regimes.

By exempting only certain types of contracts, such as contracts in foreign currency, Congress avoided this broader issue when it passed the Treasury amendment. Also, because of the institutional and sophisticated nature of the financial markets, Congress seems to have assumed that the general public would not have access to these markets. The CEA does not statutorily restrict a public offering of these contracts.

Because swaps came to be based on physical commodities, however, all swaps could no longer be considered an isolated group of financing contracts principally offered by regulated banks to their corporate customers. Consequently, the task of determining the conditions under which institutions would be allowed to facilitate the transfer of price risk off-exchange was forced into the regulatory and political arenas despite the lack of public trading in the swap market.

The Swap Statement and the *Transnor* decision have merely underscored the fact that the CFTC still lacks exemptive rulemaking powers for futures. Without these powers, market participants in effect must seek congressional approval to ensure the integrity of their contracts each time they introduce a new risk-hedging product that has elements of futurity. In dealing with market innovation, the political process is too cumbersome. The markets would be better served through a broad institutional exception or a more expeditious administrative process.

Congress granted the CFTC exemptive rulemaking powers for options and leverage contracts, but the Commission lacks sufficient authority or an explicit congressional mandate to assist the financial markets outside of these areas. The CEA does not adequately deal with market innovation, especially in areas that overlap with banking. This inadequacy has the potential to create market uncertainty, stifle innovation, deprive domestic companies of important financial and hedging products, and make U.S. financial institutions less competitive domestically and abroad.

CONCLUSION

This chapter has suggested that a swaps exemption became necessary for two reasons. First, to issue the swap safe harbor, the CFTC had to ignore economic purpose and settlement method, which have figured prominently in court decisions as key considerations. Second, the

CFTC had no preemptive power to remove the threat to swaps under state commodities law. By affirming the concurrent jurisdiction of states to apply their own laws, Congress removed any possibility of preempting state law through agency proceedings. Consequently, the CFTC could not address the issue of whether swaps are futures under state law.

Accommodating market innovation should be principally a matter of federal rather than state policy. In the final analysis, however, the CEA is no more progressive for commercial interests than state bucket shop laws. To accommodate modern economic needs, the CFTC had no choice but to ignore the delivery requirement and the economic purpose of useful contracts.

In distinguishing between futures and forwards, the federal commodities laws could simply prohibit two deliverable contracts purporting to be OTC forwards from becoming a contract for differences. This prohibition could be deemed to apply across the board or just to those contracts offered to the public. Not even the CFTC, however, was willing to allow commercial parties to enter into contracts for differences unconditionally.

As new financial and hedging instruments emerge, their legality is likely to be a recurring issue. Unless a legislative solution is found, courts could be faced with interpreting a statutory anachronism. To avoid this, Congress must endorse some form of exemptive relief for commercial interests and establish a framework to accommodate off-exchange contracts that are economically useful but not suitable for exchange trading.

NOTES

1. Policy Statement Concerning Swap Transactions, 54 Fed. Reg. 30,694 (July 21, 1989).
2. *Id.*
3. N.Y. Gen. Bus. Law §351, ¶¶1–3.
4. 198 U.S. 236 (1905).
5. NASAA Model State Commodity Code, [1984–1986 Transfer Binder] Comm. Fut. L. Rep. (CCH) ¶22,568, at 30,449 (April 5, 1985).
6. N.Y. Gen. Bus. Law §§352–359.
7. Advance Notice of Proposed Rulemaking Concerning the Regulation of Hybrid and Related Instruments, 52 Fed. Reg. 47,022, at 47,027 (Dec. 11, 1987).

8. [1977–1980 Transfer Binder] Comm. Fut. L. Rep. (CCH) ¶20,941, at 23,775 (1979).

9. 2 Comm. Fut. L. Rep. (CCH) ¶24,829, at 36,893 (April 18, 1990).

SELECTED BIBLIOGRAPHY

Allen, J.M. "Kicking the Bucket Shop: the Model State Commodity Code as the Latest Weapon in the State Administrator's Anti-fraud Arsenal." *Washington & Lee Law Review,* Summer 1985, 889–911.

Committee on Commodities Regulation of the Association of the Bar of the City of New York. "The Forward Contract Exclusion: An Analysis of Off-Exchange Commodity-Based Instruments." *Business Lawyer,* May 1986, 853–906.

Gilberg, D.J. "Regulation of New Financial Instruments under the Federal Securities and Commodities Laws." *Vanderbilt Law Review,* November 1986, 1599–1689.

Hiden, R.B., and D.R. Crawshaw. "Hybrids and the Commodity Exchange Act." *Review of Securities & Commodities Regulation,* December 1989, 233–244.

Hiden, R.B., and D.C. Sullivan. "Swap Transactions Under the Commodity Exchange Act." *Commodities Law Letter,* October 1989, 3–11.

Johnson, P.M., M.S. Sackheim, and T.A. Hale. "Future Rate Agreements: Implications under the Commodity Exchange Act." *Commodities Law Letter,* March 1987, 3–6.

"Legislation Affecting Commodity and Stock Exchanges." *Harvard Law Review,* 1931-1932, 912–925.

Nathan, R.E. "The CFTC's Limited Authority Over Hybrid Instruments." *Commodities Law Letter,* April/May 1988, 2–11.

Patterson, E.W. "Hedging and Wagering on Produce Exchanges." *Yale Law Journal,* April 1931, 843–884.

Stein, W.L. "The Exchange-Trading Requirement of the Commodity Exchange Act." *Vanderbilt Law Review,* April 1988, 473–505.

Taylor, T. "Trading in Commodity Futures—A New Legal Standard of Legality?" *Yale Law Journal,* 1933, 63–106.

Van Wart, K.T. "Preemption and the Commodity Exchange Act." *Chicago Kent Law Review,* 1982, 657–722.

Young, M.D., and W.L. Stein. "Swap Transactions Under the Commodity Exchange Act: Is Congressional Action Needed?" *Georgetown Law Journal,* August 1988, 1917–1946.

CHAPTER 24

ACCOUNTING AND TAXATION FOR CURRENCY SWAPS

Frederick D. S. Choi
New York University

INTRODUCTION

Historically, accounting for debt instruments has been relatively straightforward. Prior to the 1970s, the world's financial markets were largely segmented and macroeconomic conditions less volatile. Under these conditions, debt contracts were typically denominated in a single currency, and contractual interest payments were fixed over the life of the borrowing. Periodic accrual of debt service and the amortization of premiums or discounts associated with instruments sold at more or less than par were sufficient to accommodate most debt transactions.

In recent years, internationalization of the world's financial markets, together with increased volatility in currency values and interest rates, have spurred financial innovations that strain the conventional accounting mold. One such innovation is the financial swap, which enables companies to effectively restructure their assets and liabilities at will to hedge against, or capitalize on, foreign exchange or interest rate movements, lower their all-in funding costs, and/or access markets that were previously not available.

Swaps can be partitioned into two generic types: interest rate swaps and currency swaps. The former is an agreement between two parties to exchange interest payments for a specific period of time on an agreed-upon notional value. It has as its primary objective the conversion of fixed-rate interest coupons to floating-rate payments, or vice versa. The latter basically involves an exchange of debt into another currency until maturity, when repayment is made in the original currency, often at a pre-agreed rate.

This chapter examines some of the accounting and taxation issues associated with currency swaps. Accounting and taxation for interest rate swaps is treated in the companion to this volume.[1] Measurement issues are first examined for currency swaps involving the exchange of principal only. Owing to differences in objectives, a distinction is drawn between financial intermediaries and corporate users of swap products. This is followed by an examination of cross currency swaps, which involve the exchange of fixed for variable interest streams. The taxation of swap cash flows is then described together with a review of tax practices outside the United States. The chapter concludes with a note on current trends in swap disclosure.

CHARACTERISTICS OF SWAPS AND ACCOUNTING TREATMENT

Swap Objectives

Currency swaps offer corporate financial managers a number of advantages in today's volatile financial markets. By enabling managers to change the denomination of an existing asset or liability from one currency to another, currency swaps enable companies to actively manage their currency exposures. They also allow managers to:

- Lower their all-in cost of borrowing or of exchange risk management by enabling counterparties to take advantage of their respective access to specific markets, capitalize on their differential credit rating, or exploit market inefficiencies.[2]
- Circumvent legal restrictions on spot and forward foreign exchange transactions.[3]
- Unbundle the funding decision from the rate decision.[4]
- Access credit markets on a more timely basis by circumventing registration or burdensome disclosure requirements.[5]
- Obtain an off-balance-sheet alternative to refinancing to the extent the swaps are related to an existing debt.[6]
- Access fixed-rate funds from an investor domain that is separate and distinct from public and private markets, thereby preserving the latter for future direct financing.[7]
- Speculate on the future trend in currency and interest rate movements.[8]

Since the inception of currency swaps in the late 1970s, their volume has mushroomed and shows no signs of abatement.[9] However, accounting, taxation, and regulatory provisions have not kept pace with this rapid development. At present, formal guidance for currency swaps is limited. In the United States, guidance for currency swaps is available in *Statement of Financial Accounting Standards No. 52* (SFAS 52).[10] Accountants, however, will find the prescriptions of SFAS 52 of limited help when attempting to account for currency swaps that also take on the features of interest rate swaps. Accordingly, companies, especially those outside the United States, have sought guidance from: (1) existing policies for financial instruments with similar characteristics and (2) fundamental concepts underlying the preparation of conventional financial statements. Concepts that have proved helpful in shaping accounting policy include going concern, accrual, conservatism, consistency, and the general notion that financial accounting should attempt to reflect the economic substance of a transaction.

Nature of Swaps

Understanding the nature of a swap position and its relationship to the financial position and performance of the reporting entity is useful in deciding on an appropriate measurement and reporting posture. Wishon and Chevalier identify several swap categories that are helpful:[11]

1. *Matched swaps*. In a matched swap transaction, there is an underlying interest-bearing liability or asset with terms similar to those of the swap contract. This occurs, for instance, when two counterparties who have each borrowed similar sums swap cash flows to convert a fixed-rate borrowing from one currency to another.
2. *Unmatched swaps*. In the case of an unmatched swap, parties contracting to pay or receive a stream of future cash flows have no liability or asset related to the swap transaction. These one-sided or "naked" positions are motivated by the desire to either hedge an overall risk exposure or speculate on the future trend in interest rates. They may also be undertaken as a temporary measure until a matched hedge can be arranged.
3. *Hedged swaps*. A hedged swap is similar to an unmatched swap in that the exchange agreement bears no relation to an

underlying liability or asset. It differs in that the firm entering the swap arrangement has taken some action to hedge the exchange or interest rate risk (i.e., the potential impact of foreign exchange or interest rate changes on a firm's reported performance).

4. *Offsetting swaps.* In an offsetting swap, an intermediary such as a bank or broker is established between two swap positions that offset one another. Although the intermediary retains the credit risk (i.e., the potential for loss arising from the non-performance of a swap counterparty), it eliminates all of the currency or interest rate risk by arranging the offsetting positions.

Major Accounting Issues

Because swap users are usually reluctant to take on speculative positions, they tend to favor matched swaps. In accounting for currency swaps, fluctuating currency values and interest rates give rise to several issues:

1. To what extent should currency swaps be recognized on the balance sheet? If they are recognized, how should they be valued?
2. What is the nature of revenues and expenses that arise from swap transactions, and how should they be recognized in the income statement?
3. What are the tax implications of swap cash flows for market transactors?

CURRENCY SWAPS

In contrast to an interest rate swap, a currency swap involves an exchange of principal, is effected in different currencies, and may involve an exchange of a fixed-rate obligation for another fixed-rate obligation. A primary objective of a currency swap is to hedge against exchange-rate risk arising from international business operations and/or to enable companies to access a capital market that would not otherwise be accessible at a reasonable cost. Assume, for example, that Alpha Corporation, a U.S.-based multinational, wishes to fund a newly formed Swiss affiliate in Basel, Switzerland, to the extent of US$90,000,000 in local currency to shield its net assets against foreign exchange risk. Alpha, however, is relatively unknown to Swiss investors and would have to pay a premium to obtain Swiss financing. Beta Company, domiciled in Zurich, would like to fund its New York subsidiary with a similar amount of dollar financing. It has a comparable disadvantage in sourcing capital in the United States. Upon advice from its bank, which is aware of Beta Company's mutual circumstance, Alpha Corporation arranges a U.S. dollar/Swiss franc currency swap with Beta.

If both companies have surplus funds, the swap exchange rate is US$0.75/SF1 (both at inception and maturity), the swap term is three years, and interest rates in the United States and Switzerland are 8 percent and 5 percent, respectively, the following cash flow pattern would occur. At inception (let us assume a January 2 transaction date) Alpha Corporation would exchange US$90,000,000 for SF120,000,000 from Beta Company, Ltd. At the end of the three-year swap horizon, each company would reexchange the principal amounts of US$90,000,000 and SF120,000,000. In this sense, the swap contract operates much like a long-dated forward foreign exchange contract, where the forward rate is the current spot rate. Owing to the differential interest rates prevailing in the United States and Switzerland, there would be a corresponding payment from Beta to Alpha (let us assume this payment is made in quarterly installments). This payment compensates Alpha for holding a currency that has a correspondingly higher forward exchange value than the dollar but that will be reexchanged for dollars at the present spot rate. Accordingly, Beta would remit US$675,000 each quarter $\{[(.08 - .05) \times US\$90,000,000]/4\}$ to Alpha. This swap arrangement is depicted in Exhibit 1.

As a result of this swap transaction, both Alpha Corporation and Beta Company are better off. Each has been able to access funds in a market in which it ordinarily would be at a disadvantage, and each has done so without incurring exchange-rate risk.

Accounting Treatment

Currency swaps trace their origin to the parallel loan, which was used extensively during the 1970s. In a parallel loan agreement, two companies enter into equal and opposite agreements in their respective currencies. Their related debt service is denominated in the two dif-

EXHIBIT 1
Currency Swap Cash Flow Pattern

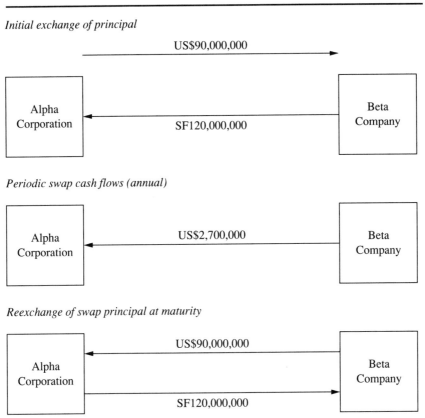

Initial exchange of principal

US$90,000,000 →

Alpha Corporation ← SF120,000,000 — Beta Company

Periodic swap cash flows (annual)

Alpha Corporation ← US$2,700,000 — Beta Company

Reexchange of swap principal at maturity

Alpha Corporation ← US$90,000,000 — Beta Company

Alpha Corporation — SF120,000,000 → Beta Company

ferent currencies. The loans are recognized on the balance sheet and would be accounted for like any other foreign-currency transaction. The currency swap, however, incorporates features that warrant an alternative accounting treatment. If one party defaults on its payments, the counterparty has the right to offset this nonpayment of principal or interest with a comparable nonpayment; that is, the counterparty is automatically relieved of its obligations.[12] Accordingly, a currency swap is not considered a loan in the traditional sense and would therefore not appear as a liability on the balance sheet for accounting and regulatory purposes. Rather, it would be disclosed in an "off-balance-sheet" fashion as a long-term commitment to reexchange currencies in the future.

The off-balance-sheet commitment, in effect, represents a forward exchange transaction. As such, it would be translated to the reporting currency at the spot rate prevailing on the financial statement date and any resultant gains or losses taken to income in most countries.[13] In the United States, SFAS 52 mandates an accounting treatment similar to that prescribed for forward contracts.[14] If the swap is designed to hedge a net investment in a foreign affiliate, gains or losses would be treated as an adjustment to shareholders' equity. If it is used to hedge a foreign-currency transaction, such as a foreign-currency borrowing, any resultant gains or losses on the swap would be taken immediately to income. Similar treatment would be accorded swaps that are intended as foreign-currency speculations. If the currency swap is intended as a hedge of a foreign-currency commitment, including interest on foreign-currency debt, any gains or losses would be deferred and included in the measurement of the foreign-currency transaction.

To illustrate, assume that Alpha Corporation holds the Swiss francs received on January 2 in the form of cash until the start of the second quarter. On April 1 the funds are used to finance its Swiss subsidiary's net asset investment. Hence, during the first three months, the commitment to swap Swiss francs for dollars for three years serves as a hedge of its Swiss franc cash balance. Thereafter, the franc swap commitment acts as a hedge of its net investment in its Swiss affiliate. Spot exchange rates prevailing during the year are as follows:

	US$/SF
January 2	$0.75
March 31	$0.74
June 30	$0.76

The initial exchange of currencies would be recorded as follows:

Jan. 2	Foreign currency (SF)	$90,000,000	
	Cash		$90,000,000

At the same time, the company would record the following off-balance-sheet (contingent) accounts in the notes to its financial statements to disclose the notional amount of the swap facility outstanding:

Contingent receivable (US$)	$90,000,000	
Contingent liability (SF)		$90,000,000

In keeping with SFAS 52, Alpha Corporation would revalue its Swiss franc cash balance at the prevailing spot rate of US$0.74, at the end of its first quarter, and recognize a transaction loss of US$1,200,000:

Mar. 31	Foreign exchange loss	$1,200,000	
	Foreign currency (SF)		$1,200,000

Alpha Corporation would also revalue its SF120,000,000 swap commitment at the spot rate, giving rise to an exchange gain of US$1,200,000. As the commitment may be deemed a hedge of its Swiss franc cash balance, the gain on the commitment offsets the loss on the revaluation of the franc cash balance and would be recognized in current income as well. Hence,

Mar. 31	Contingent Liability (SF)	$1,200,000	
	Foreign exchange gain		$1,200,000

Had Alpha borrowed the dollars to effect its dollar/franc swap, it would have incurred an interest cost of 8 percent. Assuming that the Swiss francs received were initially invested in a Swiss franc deposit at 5 percent, Alpha would have an interest shortfall of 3 percent. Accordingly, the periodic cash receipts from Beta Company to Alpha act as compensation to the latter to maintain interest rate parity. In keeping with the dictates of SFAS 52, these payments would be treated as a reduction of Alpha's interest expense:

Mar. 31	Cash	$675,000	
	Interest expense		$675,000

The following dated entries of April 1 reflect the investment of Alpha's Swiss franc cash balance in its Swiss investment.

Apr. 1	Investment in subsidiary	$88,800,000	
	Foreign currency (SF)		$88,800,000

At the end of the second quarter, Alpha would consolidate the accounts of its Swiss subsidiary with its own. In doing so, it would eliminate the Swiss investment on the parent company's books and combine the net assets of the Swiss affiliate with its own. In turn, the net assets of the Swiss subsidiary would be translated to dollars using the June 30 spot rate in keeping with the current-rate method of translation. Because the Swiss franc has revalued since the last quarter, the company would book a translation gain, which, per SFAS 52, would be deferred in shareholders' equity until the investment in liquidated. The appropriate entries would be:

| June 30 | Investment in subsidiary | $2,400,000 | |
| | Translation gain | | $2,400,000 |

Revaluation of the Swiss franc swap commitment at the prevailing spot rate would give rise to an exchange loss. As the swap commitment can be deemed a hedge of Alpha's net investment in its Swiss subsidiary, the loss would also be deferred and appear as an offset to the translation gain appearing in shareholders' equity. This entry and that needed to record the periodic receipt of the interest rate differential from Beta Company are as follows:

June 30	Foreign exchange loss	$2,400,000	
	Contingent liability (SF)		$2,400,000
	Cash	$675,000	
	Interest Expense		$675,000

Cross Currency Swaps

A hybrid of the currency swap is the cross currency interest rate swap. Better known by its acronym, CIRCUS, this instrument involves an exchange of borrowings whereby two counterparties agree to service each other's obligations, including the exchange of floating-rate interest in one currency for fixed-rate interest in another. What complicates the accounting treatment for this instrument is that its value is affected by both interest rate and foreign-currency fluctuations. How to appropriately separate these two effects is no easy matter, as evidenced by the absence of formal accounting pronouncements that specifically address this reporting dilemma. Until formal guidance is available, policies that seek to reflect the economics of the swap transaction require a logical tack.

Cross currency swaps are generally motivated by considerations of relative cost. Thus, assume that Alpha Corporation wishes to invest in a floating-rate Swiss franc asset but would have to pay an excessive cost to raise francs directly. Beta Company, domiciled in Zurich, wishes to raise fixed-rate dollars but has a comparative advantage in raising floating-rate funds in Switzerland. In this instance, it would be advantageous for both companies to raise funds in their respective home currencies and swap these cash flows over a common time horizon. An illustration follows.

EXHIBIT 2
Cash Flows under a Cross Currency Swap

Initial exchange of principal

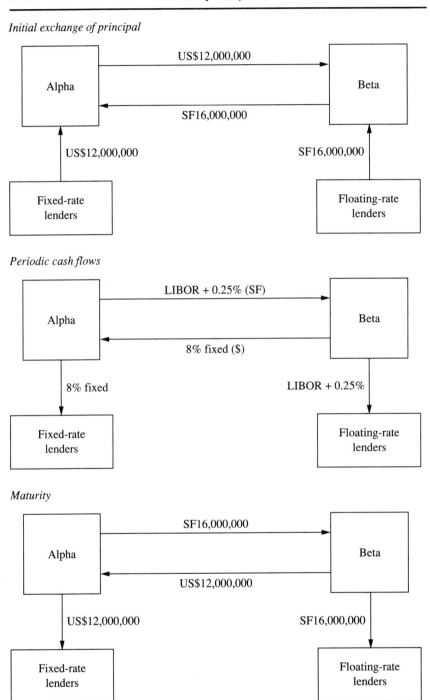

Periodic cash flows

Maturity

On January 2, Alpha borrows $12,000,000 of term debt at a fixed rate of 8 percent for three years. Beta Company borrows an equivalent amount in Swiss francs at LIBOR + 0.25 percent. Under the terms of the cross currency swap, Alpha agrees to service the interest and principal obligations of Beta's Swiss franc borrowing, and vice versa. Alpha immediately invests the swap proceeds in a floating-rate franc asset yielding LIBOR + 1 percent and holds this asset for the term of the borrowing. The exchange and reexchange of currencies between Alpha and Beta are illustrated in Exhibit 2.

Entries to account for the cash flow streams on Alpha's books during the first year of the swap term are based on the following interest and exchange rate patterns. Assume that Alpha closes its books every December 31. Explanatory comments, where appropriate, appear in parentheses following the accounting entry.

	US$/SF	Average LIBOR
December 31, 19X0	$0.80	5.6%
December 31, 19X1	0.76	5.9
December 31, 19X2	0.70	6.4

Initial dollar borrowing from U.S. lender:

1/2/19X0 Cash ($)	$12,000,000	
Note payable ($)		$12,000,000

As Alpha Corporation is legally responsible for servicing its dollar obligation, even though it is being serviced by Beta Company, Alpha would disclose its dollar payable amount in the *long-term liability* section of its balance sheet.

Initial principal swap: Since Alpha's future swap obligation is contingent on the receipt of dollars from Beta Company, the swap obligation and receivable would appear as off-balance-sheet memorandum accounts informing the statement reader of the notional amounts on which interest payments and future exchange of principal are based. Appropriate entries would be:

1/2/19X0	Cash (SF)	$12,000,000	
	Cash ($)		$12,000,000
	Contingent asset ($)	$12,000,000	
	Contingent swap liability (SF)		$12,000,000

(SF16,000,000 × $US0.75 = US$12,000,000)

Alpha's investment of swap proceeds in Swiss franc floating-rate asset:

| 1/2/19X0 | Investment (SF) | $12,000,000 | |
| | Cash (SF) | | $12,000,000 |

(SF16,000,000 × US$0.75)

Accrual of earnings on Alpha's floating-rate Swiss franc asset:

| 12/31/19X0 | Accrued income | $844,800 | |
| | Investment income | | $844,800 |

[SF16,000,000 × (5.6% + 1%) × US$0.80]

Interest payment on dollar borrowing:

| 12/31/19X0 | Interest expense | $960,000 | |
| | Cash | | $960,000 |

(US$12,000,000 × 8%)

Swap payments from Beta Company:

| 12/31/19X0 | Cash | $960,000 | |
| | Interest expense | | $960,000 |

(US$12,000,000 × 8%)

This and the previous set of entries illustrate that the contractual interest Alpha pays on its domestic fixed-rate borrowing is in effect being paid by Beta Company.

Swap payments to Beta Company:

| 12/31/19X0 | Interest expense (SF) | $748,800 | |
| | Cash | | $748,800 |

[SF16,000,000 × (5.6% + 0.25%) × US$0.80]

In this instance, the swap payment to Beta Company is indicative of Alpha's real borrowing costs, as its "on-balance-sheet" dollar obligation, as we have seen, is being serviced by Beta. Moreover, the floating-rate interest that Alpha is remitting to Beta hedges the floating-rate return on Alpha's Swiss franc investment, should interest rates fall in the future.

Per SFAS 52, Alpha would revalue its foreign-currency investment at the year-end spot rate, with any exchange adjustments recognized in current income. Hence,

12/31/19X0	Investment (SF)	$800,000	
	Foreign exchange gain		$800,000

$$[SF16,000,000 \times (US\$0.80 - US\$0.75)]$$

As Alpha's Swiss franc swap commitment may be designated as a hedge of its Swiss franc investment, its commitment would be revalued at the year-end spot rate and any resultant exchange gains or losses recognized in current income as well:

12/31/19X0	Foreign exchange loss	$800,000	
	Contingent swap liability (SF)		$800,000

FINANCIAL INSTITUTIONS

Swap accounting for financial institutions (i.e., banks) is not as clearcut as for industrial corporations. Like a nonfinancial entity, a bank can act as a principal in using currency swaps to hedge foreign exchange risk generated by its own balance sheet position and, in exceptional cases, to earn a trading profit by maintaining an unhedged position. In these instances, accounting issues confronting banks are not unlike those facing nonfinancial corporations. In addition, however, a bank can assume the role of an intermediary between two swap counterparties. Thus, whereas corporations typically engage in matched transactions, financial intermediaries can engage in unmatched and offsetting swaps as well.

In the previous example, Alpha Corporation and Beta Company may have utilized the services of Gamma Bank to arrange their currency swap. In addition to delegating the administrative burden of the swap to Gamma Bank, Alpha and Beta may have chosen to avoid assuming the risk of default by the other. Although, technically, default on the part of swap counterparty B relieves counterparty A of its currency commitment to B, in practice, A would incur the burden of having to find another counterparty and incur the risk that the new swap terms may not be the same as the original agreement with B—hence the need for a reputable financial intermediary.

In our next example, assume that on January 23, 19X0, Gamma Bank, which closes its books monthly, enters into a swap arrangement with Alpha Corporation in which Gamma agrees to pay £10,000,000 in exchange for US$18,000,000. On the same day, Gamma arranges a swap with Beta Company to match the currency swap with Alpha. Interest flows are such that Gamma Bank will receive prime plus 0.125 percent from Beta and remit prime plus 0.0625 percent to Alpha, retaining the interest differential as a swap fee. Gamma, in turn, will receive a fixed 12 percent in sterling from Alpha and remit a fixed 12 percent in sterling to Beta. The relevant swap cash flows are depicted in Exhibit 3.

Gamma Bank's services may include locating and bringing swap counterparties such as Alpha and Beta together, guaranteeing each leg of a swap transaction (i.e., assuming the credit risk of default by Alpha or Beta), acting as a collection and paying agent for swap flows between counterparties, and assuming interest rate risk by warehousing a swap until a couterparty can be located. The primary objective of the intermediary in these instances is to generate fee income. How to account for this income has proved controversial.

EXHIBIT 3
Currency Swap Cash Flows with Bank as Intermediary

Swap cash flows at inception

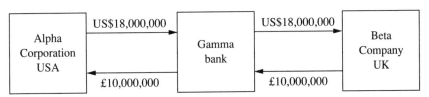

Interest flows

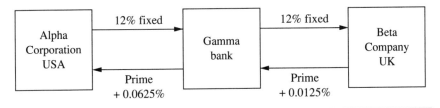

Accounting At Inception

As an intermediary in the offsetting swap transaction, Gamma Bank has not guaranteed the underlying debt obligations of either Alpha or Beta; hence, the notional amounts would not have an impact on Gamma's balance sheet. If Gamma is acting purely as a broker between the counterparties, recognition of the swap contracts would not be appropriate. If Gamma positions itself as a principal between Alpha and Beta, accounting treatments discussed in connection with nonfinancial corporations would hold. In practice, since the swap transaction constitutes a contingent asset and liability from Gamma Bank's perspective, off-balance-sheet treatment by way of footnote disclosure is gaining acceptance.

Accounting During the Swap Term

During the term of the swap, the financial intermediary (Gamma Bank in our example) will accrue both a swap receivable and payable to Alpha and Beta, respectively. Since the right of offset applies here, the receivable from and payable to Alpha would be netted, as would the payable to and receivable from Beta. Only the net amount due from, or due to, each counterparty would be disclosed in Gamma Bank's balance sheet. Fee income over the life of the offsetting swap would be recognized in a fashion that reflects Gamma Bank's role as a swap intermediary. When Gamma Bank acts as a broker with no legal or economic interest in the swap transaction beyond its initial matching services, any fees received would simply be recognized as fee income when the services are performed. In our illustration, this fee income would constitute the interest differential on the variable interest flows between Beta and Gamma and between Gamma and Alpha. Journal entries to accrue the swap income for the month of January, assuming a prime rate of 10 percent, follow.

To record accruals on the swap with Alpha:

Jan. 31	Swap receivable—Alpha	$54,000
	Swap fee income	$54,000

(£10,000,000 × 0.12 × 9/360 × 1.80 exchange rate)

	Swap fee income	$45,281
	Swap payable—Alpha	$45,281

($18,000,000 × 0.100625 × 9/360)

To record accruals on the swap with Beta:

Jan. 31 Swap receivable—Beta $45,562
        Swap fee income $45,562

      ($18,000,000 × 0.10125 × 9/360)

      Swap fee income $54,000
        Swap payable—Beta $54,000

      (£10,000,000 × 0.12 × 9/360 × 1.8)

When Gamma acts as a principal between two counterparties, the issue becomes more complicated. In Exhibit 3, Gamma Bank, in arranging an offsetting matched swap, earned a spread between what it received from one counterparty and what is paid to the other. This differential is designed to compensate Gamma Bank for (1) arranging the swap, (2) administering the swap payments from and to counterparties, and (3) assuming credit risk of default by either Alpha or Beta. But how should Gamma separate these three components, and when should it recognize them in income?

Regarding the former question, some feel that disaggregation of the spread into its relative components is an impossible, or, at the very least, a subjective, process. Hence, no attempt is made to do so. In other cases, reasoned attempts consistently applied over time are undertaken. Tiner and Conneely suggest one approach.[15]

In our example, Gamma Bank earned a spread of 0.0625 percent per annum on the swap arrangement. Its view is that exchange rates or interest rates could increase by 2 percent in a year, and it normally expects a margin of 0.375 percent for standard commercial loans to comparable credit-risk swap counterparties. Using the risk assessment formula

$$P \times dI \times n \times M$$

where P = Notional amount
        dI = Expected annual change in interest/exchange rates
        n = Number of years in the swap agreement
        M = Margin between funding and loan rate applicable to the counterparty risk, for a standard commercial loan transaction

Gamma Bank would break out its interest rate spread as follows:

$$\text{Total swap income} = \$10,000,000 \times 0.000625 \times 3$$
$$= \$18,750$$

$$\text{Credit risk assessment} = \$10,000,000 \times 0.02 \times 3 \times 0.00375$$
$$= \$2,250$$

The total swap income less the income for credit risk less the direct costs of servicing the swap transaction would yield the arrangement fee.

Assuming that allocation procedures such as those presented earlier are feasible, there is still the question of when the various fee components should be recognized. Practice is reportedly varied on this score.[16] Some banks do not recognize any income at the inception of the swap, preferring instead to recognize all income over the swap term. Some recognize, as arrangement fees, the direct costs of arranging the swap and recognize the balance of the swap income over the life of the agreement. Still others estimate the portion of fees that relate to credit risk assumption and ongoing servicing costs and recognize these annually, recognizing the balance as arrangement fee income at inception.

The last practice is not in accord with recent FASB guidelines. SFAS 91 requires that banks defer loan origination fees (origination fees less origination costs) and amortize them over the loan term as yield adjustments. Because swap origination fees are taken to be analogous to loan origination fees, parallel treatment is required.[17] Yet are swap fees similar to loan origination fees? Is deferral of swap arrangement fees consistent with the matching principle, especially when much of the work in arranging a swap occurs up front? Once a swap is arranged, the major risk faced by the intermediary is the risk that a counterparty will default. Does allocation of all income over the life of the swap achieve a proper matching of risk and return? Here current recognition of arrangement fees as fee income, with deferral and amortization of fees for ongoing servicing costs and assumption of credit risk recognized as fee income and as other operating income, respectively, appears more in accord with the substance of the underlying transaction.

Unmatched Swaps
Perhaps the most difficult area of swap accounting for financial institutions relates to unmatched swaps. An unmatched swap might arise

when a financial institution, such as Gamma Bank, enters a swap with Alpha Corporation before locating a counterparty. Until a counterparty is found, Gamma Bank would be exposed to exchange-rate risk unless it were able to hedge this risk in some other fashion (e.g., arrange an internal hedge with another banking affiliate). In this case, the swap position would be considered a speculation, and some form of market value accounting would be called for. One alternative would be to value the swap in accordance with the lower of cost or market rule. The problem here involves determining when an impairment has occurred and whether such impairment is permanent. This is likely to be extremely difficult during periods of volatile exchange rates. Assuming that this treatment is followed, losses, in keeping with the principle of conservatism, would be recognized in current income; gains would be deferred. When a counterparty is eventually secured, income recognition procedures identified for matched swaps, enumerated earlier, would apply.

An alternative is to carry unmatched swaps at market until a counterparty is found. The unmatched swap would be marked to market at stipulated repricing intervals, and associated gains or losses would be recognized in current income. The question is how to obtain market prices that can be used to revalue a swap. Are secondary markets sufficiently developed to offer reliable benchmarks? If not, would discounted cash flow analyses be a reliable surrogate? If the latter question can be answered in the affirmative, what discount rate should be used? Should it reflect an internally generated hurdle rate or a market-determined rate?

As secondary markets for swap instruments continue to evolve, the use of market benchmarks is becoming more feasible. In the meantime, the use of estimated market values based on the discounted present value of swap cash flows using a bank's marginal cost of funds appears to be gaining acceptance.

TAX DIMENSIONS

The tax treatment of currency swaps will vary depending on the means by which economic risk is transferred, the consequent types of payment flows, the underlying motives for entering into a swap transaction, and specific rulings prevailing in differential national tax jurisdictions. Owing to the conditional nature of specific tax treatments and the unsettled state of specific statutory guidelines in this area, the following discussion will necessarily be general in tenor.

Temporary regulations issued by the IRS provide rules for the timing and computation of periodic payments under a currency swap. As a currency swap usually involves an exchange of principal at inception, periodic payments made during the life of the swap are treated as interest streams on a hypothetical borrowing that is denominated in the currency in which the payments are made. Concomitantly, payments received are treated as income on a hypothetical loan denominated in the currency in which the payments are received. Hypothetical interest income and any exchange gains or losses thereon may be subtracted from the hypothetical interest expense and related exchange gains or losses on the hypothetical borrowing to determine the exchange gain or loss on the periodic payments. Up-front fees received by an intermediary would be recognized as ordinary income over the life of the contract.[18]

In contrast to a currency swap, a cross currency swap usually does not involve an exchange of currencies at inception. At maturity, each party settles the other party's principal obligation at the exchange rate prevailing at the inception of the underlying loans. Accordingly, periodic payments under a cross currency swap would receive treatment similar to that of an interest rate swap. Payment of fees would be capitalized and amortized over the life of the swap agreement as fee income or expense.

To elaborate, in an interest rate swap, swap cash flows are not viewed as interest expense or income for U.S. tax purposes. Although an interest rate swap is normally viewed in connection with the underlying debt obligation, the swap and the related debt instrument are regarded as separate transactions, as are the cash flows stemming from each. Accordingly, interest rate differentials received or paid by a swap user during the interim or on final settlement are viewed either as an ordinary gain or loss or as an ordinary business expense deduction.[19] There is a possibility, however, that swap payments may be reflected as adjustments to interest expense or income, provided certain conditions are met—for example, swap payments are made on a net, as opposed to a gross, basis and are related to interest expense on a financial obligation incurred, or interest income on a financial asset held, by the taxpayer. The manner in which swap payments are treated for tax purposes can have a significant effect on a U.S. corporation's foreign tax credit limit.

By way of background, the United States adopts a "worldwide" principle of taxation and thus taxes income arising both within and outside its national boundaries. A direct consequence of this principle is that the foreign earnings of a U.S. multinational company are subject to the full tax levies of at least two countries. To prevent this from occurring, U.S. companies can elect to treat foreign taxes paid as a credit against the parent's U.S. tax liability. Generally, foreign taxes paid are creditable to the extent they do not exceed the foreign tax credit limitation. Foreign-source gains increase the limitation and allow U.S. corporate taxpayers to claim additional credits for foreign taxes paid. Losses attributed to foreign sources reduce it.

Accordingly, swap payments that are treated as adjustments to non–U.S. source interest income increase a U.S. corporation's foreign tax credit limitation. Swap payments treated as adjustments to interest expense as opposed to noninterest treatment also alter a firm's foreign tax credit limitation to the extent it is apportioned between U.S. and non–U.S. source items of income. For example, the interest allocation rules under the U.S. Internal Revenue Code may increase the interest expense allocated and apportioned to foreign-source income if such payments were seen as interest, thus reducing the taxpayer's foreign tax credit limitation. Although swap payments recognized as ordinary gains and losses also affect a U.S. taxpayer's foreign tax credit limitation depending on whether the gain from the swap is treated as U.S. or non–U.S. source, it is more difficult to attribute these to foreign sources. Any gain treated as U.S. source would have no impact on the foreign tax credit limitation.[20]

If the swap were construed as the purchase or sale of foreign currency, likely to be applicable to a cross currency floating to floating interest rate swap, interim swap payments would be viewed as part of the total purchase price and recognized as part of the capital gains or losses attributed to the final exchange of currencies.[21]

An international overview of tax treatments accorded currency swaps and options is provided in Exhibit 4. As can be seen, tax provisions are not uniform among countries, necessitating specialized advice from tax professionals.

EXHIBIT 4

International Tax Overview: Currency Swaps

Currency Swaps	Australia	Belgium	Canada	France	Germany	Japan	Netherlands	Switzerland	United Kingdom	United States
Relief available for swap payments	Y	Y	Y	Y	Y	Y	Y	Y	Y	Y
Swap receipts taxable	Y	Y	Y	Y	Y	Y	Y	Y	Y	Y
Arrangement fees deductible	Y[1]	Y	Y[2]	Y	Y	Y	Y	Y	N[3]	Y[4]
Source of payments where payer is resident or trades	N[5]	N[6]	Y	Y	Y	Y	Y	Y[7]	Y	N[8]
Swap payments subject to withholding tax	N[9]	N[10]	N[11]	N	N	N	N	N	Y[12]	N[13]
Matched swaps accorded matched position for tax purposes	N	Y[14]	Y[15]	N	Y	Y	Y	Y	N[16]	Y

Notes: Y = yes; N = no.

[1] Relief is generally available when fees are paid. Legislation in Australia may determine that the deduction is available on an accruals basis over the swap life. [2] Relief may only be available on an accruals basis. [3] Unless the swap is regarded as a trading item. [4] Fees are deductible on an accruals basis. [5] Source is where the negotiation and execution of the swap is conducted. [6] Source determined by the location of the party receiving the payments. [7] Source is the residence of the debtor or the location where the investment is made. [8] Source is the place of residence of the recipient. [9] Under review. [10] No authoritative guidance available. [11] Provided swap payments are made at the same time and for the same period. [12] Unless the swap payment is made to or by a UK bank or swap dealer in the ordinary case of business. [13] Subject to definitive guidance by the IRS. [14] Provided there is a matching of the accounting treatment and the underlying asset and liability. [15] Problems may arise where the hedged asset is a capital asset. [16] Capital gains rules in the United Kingdom normally distort the matching.

Source: KPMG, *Financial Instruments: An International Tax Survey,* London: Peat Marwick McLintock, 1989.

RELATED DEVELOPMENTS

A major purpose of financial statements is to provide readers with information regarding the performance and risk dimensions of the reporting entity. Owing to the off-balance-sheet nature of currency swaps, there is concern that those who rely on published financial statements receive insufficient information about the risks associated with these instruments and consequently make suboptimal investment, credit, and regulatory decisions.[22]

New Capital Adequacy Guidelines

In the case of financial institutions, concern arises when one of the borrowers in a swap defaults. Under a cross currency swap agreement, for example, a bank agrees to make interest payments on behalf of the defaulted borrower (credit risk). One danger is that the bank will not have the funds to continue making the payments (liquidity risk). Another is that interest rates and/or exchange rates may have changed so dramatically since the swap was initiated that the cost to the financial institution of finding a new counterparty to replace the defaulted company's obligation would be significant (interest-rate and currency risk).

As an example of this concern, banking regulators worry that banks may be undercapitalized, given the risky nature of their assets and obligations. Accordingly, bank regulatory authorities around the world have considered new regulations requiring increased capital levels at banks to reflect the risks of swaps in which banks function as intermediaries. Based on a framework adopted in July 1988 by the Basle Committee on Banking Regulations and Supervisory Practices, which includes supervisory authorities from 12 major industrial countries, the U.S. Federal Reserve Board issued, in January 1989, new capital adequacy guidelines for state member banks and bank holding companies.[23] The guidelines establish a framework that sensitizes regulatory capital requirements to differences in risk profiles among banking organizations by taking off-balance-sheet exposures explicitly into account in assessing capital adequacy. By 1992, banking organizations will be required to have capital equivalent to 8 percent of assets, weighted by their degree of riskiness. Risk weights assigned to off-balance-sheet items are primarily based on credit risk. At present these weights are 50 percent of the credit-equivalent amounts of foreign exchange–related contracts. The risk-adjusted amounts (credit-equivalent amounts), in turn, are based on the following formula:

$$CE = RV + (NV \times ECF)$$

where   CE   = Credit-equivalent amount
         RV   = Replacement value
         NV   = Notional value
         ECF = Exposure conversion factor

The first independent variable represents the cost to the bank of finding a replacement for a defaulted obligation; the second estimates the cost to the bank if exchange rates have changed since the swap's inception. Specifically, the total replacement cost of contracts (RV) is obtained by summing their positive mark-to-market values. This current exposure is added to a measure of future potential increases in credit exposure. The latter is calculated by multiplying the total notional value of contracts (NV) by an exposure conversion factor (ECF) equal to 1.0 percent for contracts with maturities of less than a year and 5.0 percent for exchange-rate contracts with remaining maturities of more than a year.

To illustrate, assume that Gamma Bank is involved with a seven-year cross currency floating/floating interest rate swap with a notional principal of $20,000,000. The currency replacement cost is assumed to be $400,000. The credit-equivalent amount of this interest rate contract would be $1,400,000 ($400,000 + $20,000,000 × 0.05).

Financial Disclosure Initiatives

To afford general-purpose financial statement readers the opportunity to better assess the risks associated with financial innovations, such as currency swaps, more and more accounting standard setters have considered initiatives calling for additional disclosure. At the international level, the International Accounting Standards Committee recently addressed the issue of swap disclosure for banks in its standard IAS 30.[24] Although general in tone, the standard recommends that banks disclose the nature and amounts of contingencies and commitments arising from off-balance-sheet items, including those relating to interest rate– and foreign exchange rate–related items such as swaps, options, and futures. Following the lead of the FASB, IAS 30 also asks that banks disclose an analysis of assets and liabilities in relevant maturity groupings based on the remaining period to the contractual maturity date as of the balance sheet date, and any significant concentrations of off-balance sheet items. Moreover, the Secretariat of the Organization for Economic Cooperation and Development (OECD) has stated:

> To improve the quality of financial statements, as recommended in the *OECD Guidelines for Multinational Enterprises,* it is essential that particulars of off–balance sheet transactions be disclosed in annual (or interim) reports of enterprises. Information should cover the accounting methods used (with particular reference to the treatment of such transactions in the income statement, whether for hedging or trading purposes), the amounts of the different types of commitment and information on the risks incurred on an overall basis and for all financial instruments.[25]

At the national level, the United States has decided to call for disclosures in phases. Focusing on financial instruments with off-balance-sheet risk of accounting loss, the first phase has resulted in the issuance of SFAS 105 in March 1990. Entitled "Disclosure of Information about Financial Instruments with Off–Balance Sheet Risk and Financial Instruments with Concentrations of Credit Risk," the new statement calls for the following information:

1. The face, contract, or notional principal amount and the amount recognized in the statement of financial position.
2. The nature and terms of the financial instruments and a discussion of the credit, market, and liquidity risk and related accounting policies.
3. The loss the entity would incur if any counterparty to the financial instrument failed to perform.
4. The entity's policy for requiring collateral or other security on financial instruments it accepts and a description of collateral on instruments presently held.
5. Disclosure of information about significant concentrations of credit risk in individual counterparties or groups of counterparties engaged in similar activities in the same region.

Some observers of the international financial reporting scene feel that the FASB is asking too much.[26] Along similar lines, it is also felt that enterprises outside the United States are unlikely to be as forthcoming owing to (1) significant differences among countries regarding the amount, nature, and analysis of information required and (2) the absence abroad of similarly extensive disclosure requirements for traditional financial instruments.[27]

Although efforts such as the FASB's may seem overly ambitious, the trend toward more and better disclosure of interest rate products, such as currency swaps, will continue. Banks and nonfinancial institutions, in competing for access to lower-cost funds, will disclose what the market demands as long as doing so does not entail costs that exceed the perceived benefits. Until more definitive disclosure requirements are in place, one should look to practice for guidance. Evidence suggests that reporting entities are beginning to respond to user needs. A good example with regard to swap disclosure is the annual accounts of J.P. Morgan. Footnote 1 of their 1989 annual report, reproduced in Exhibit 5, sets forth Morgan's accounting policy for swap cash flows. Footnote 19, also reproduced in Exhibit 5, provides information regarding swap risk.

CONCLUSION

Currency swaps offer financial managers a number of advantages in a world of currency and interest rate volatility. Major reporting issues associated with this financial innovation relate to balance sheet recognition, income measurement, taxation, and financial disclosure.

Reporting entities, at least in the United States, have generally looked to foreign-currency accounting pronouncements (e.g., SFAS 52) for guidance in accounting for currency swaps. Guidance from the IRS with regard to the taxation of currency swap cash flows has been less definitive, although this situation is beginning to change.[28]

Owing to the different circumstances surrounding the use of currency swaps, it is unlikely that a single accounting treatment will communicate the economic substance of specific swap arrangements equally well. Accordingly, financial disclosures that provide statement readers with sufficient information to formulate reasonable

EXHIBIT 5
Example of Swap Disclosure

Footnote 1. Accounting policies

Interest rate contracts
Interest rate futures, options, caps and floors, and future rate agreements are used as part of J. P. Morgan's trading activities and are also used to hedge certain assets and liabilities, commitments, and anticipated transactions. Gains and losses from trading activities are recognized currently in income. Gains and losses related to contracts that are designated and effective as hedges are generally deferred and recognized over the expected remaining lives of the hedged items.

Interest rate swaps and currency swaps
Revenue or expense associated with interest rate swaps and currency swaps, including all yield-related fees received or paid, is generally recognized over the lives of the agreements.

Footnote 19. Financial instruments

J. P. Morgan uses various off-balance sheet financial instruments to satisfy the financing needs of clients, manage market risks, and conduct trading activities. These instruments generate interest, fees, or trading revenues. The credit, market, and liquidity risks associated with these off-balance sheet financial instruments are generally managed in conjunction with J. P. Morgan's balance sheet activities.

The notional or contractual amounts used to express the volume of these transactions do not necessarily represent the amounts potentially subject to risk. In addition the measurement of the risks associated with these instruments is meaningful only when all related and offsetting transactions are identified. A summary of obligations under these financial instruments at December 31, 1989 and 1988, follows:

In millions	1989	1988
Commitments to purchase foreign currencies and U.S. dollars:		
Spot, less than ten days	$ 32,686	$21,493
Forwards, less than one year	117,967	82,043
Forwards, one year and longer	8,792	6,365
Options	18,399	11,829
Interest rate swaps:		
One year or less	20,907	13,291
More than one year	97,174	60,405
Currency swaps:		
One year or less	4,616	3,148
More than one year	48,000	35,427
Securities, interest rate futures and options, and precious metal contracts:		
Commitments to purchase	25,187	24,068
Commitments to sell	28,093	35,471
Future rate agreements and interest rate caps and floors:		
Future rate agreements sold and interest rate caps written	36,109	17,083
Future rate agreements purchased and interest rate floors written	22,731	11,377

With regard to interest rate swap contracts, the amount at risk approximated $2.7 billion and $1.3 billion at December 31, 1989 and 1988, respectively. These amounts have been calculated by estimating the cost, on a present value basis, of replacing at current market rates all those contracts in a gain position as to which J. P. Morgan would incur a loss in replacing the contract. This calculation does not consider the effect of netting agreements with counterparties. The amount at risk, derived in this way, will increase or decrease during the life of the swap as a function of maturity and market interest rates.

assessments of the performance and risks associated with these off-balance-sheet products are necessary. Some feel that reporting initiatives such as those recently promulgated by the FASB are likely to be resisted, especially by reporting entities domiciled outside the United States, owing to national differences in the amount, nature, and analysis of information required. Although this argument may have some validity, internationalization of the capital markets and the competition for low-cost funds are likely to be compelling forces for voluntary disclosures that exceed the minimum required.

NOTES

1. Carl R. Beidleman, *Interest Rate Swaps,* Homewood, Ill.: Business One Irwin, 1991.
2. David Pritchard, "Swap Financing Techniques," *Euromoney,* May 1984, pp. S4–S7.
3. Y. S. Park, "Currency Swaps as a Long-Term International Financing Technique," *Journal of International Business Studies,* Winter 1984, p. 48.
4. Julian Walmsley, "Interest Rate Swaps: A Review of the Issues," *Economic Review,* November/December 1988, pp. 25–26.
5. Jan G. Loeys, "Interest Rate Swaps: The Hinge between Money and Capital Markets," *The Banker,* April 1985, p. 37.
6. Frederick C. Militello, "Swap Financing: A New Approach to International Transactions," *Financial Executive,* October 1984, p. 34.
7. Anthony J. Gambino, "Cash Management, Interest Rate Swaps, Risk Management Addressed by CPAs in Industry," *Journal of Accountancy,* August 1985, p. 68.
8. Financial Accounting Standards Board, *Discussion Paper on Interest Rate Swaps,* Stamford, Conn.: FASB, January 28, 1985, p. 10.
9. Cyrus Ardalan, "Foreword," in *Inside the Swap Market,* 3d ed. London: IFR Publishing Ltd., 1989, p. 7.
10. Financial Accounting Standards Board, "Foreign Currency Translation," *Statement of Financial Accounting Standards No. 52,* Stamford, Conn.: FASB, December 1981.
11. Keith Wishon and Lorin Chevalier, "Interest Rate Swaps—Your Rate or Mine?" *Journal of Accountancy,* September 1985, p. 74.
12. Bruno Solnik, *International Investments,* Reading, Mass.: Addison-Wesley, 1988, p. 169.

13. Organization for Economic Cooperation and Development, *New Financial Instruments: Disclosure and Accounting,* Paris: OECD, 1988.
14. FASB, "Foreign Currency Translation," op cit., pars. 19–21.
15. John I. Tiner and Joe M. Conneely, *Accounting for Treasury Products,* Cambridge, England: Woodhead-Faulkner Limited, 1989, p. 49.
16. Eugene E. Comiskey, Charles W. Mulford, and Deborah H. Turner, "Bank Accounting and Reporting Practices for Interest Rate Swaps," *Bank Accounting and Finance,* Winter 1987–88, pp. 3–14.
17. Financial Accounting Standards Board, "Accounting for Non-Refundable Fees and Costs Associated With Originating or Acquiring Loans and Initial Costs of Leases," *Statement of Financial Accounting Standards No. 91,* Stamford, Conn.: FASB, December 1986.
18. Michael T. Cartusciello, "Coping With IRS Guidance on Notional Principal Contracts," *Journal of Taxation,* January 1990, pp. 28–29.
19. Christopher D. Spooner, "Foreign Currency Regs Provide Much-Needed Guidance," *Journal of Bank Taxation,* Summer 1990, pp 27–36.
20. See, Martin F. Belmore, "The Tax Treatment of Swaps in the United States," in *Inside the Swap Market,* 3d ed. London: IFR Publishing Ltd., 1989, pp. 187–203. For a parallel discussion of UK treatment of swap cash flows, see Eric Tomsett, "The Taxation of Swaps in the United Kingdom," in the same volume, pp. 181–185.
21. Ibid., pp. 153–54.
22. Financial Accounting Standards Board, "Description of FASB Project on Financial Instruments and Off–Balance Sheet Financing," white paper, June 1986.
23. "Final Guidelines Issued On Risk-Based Capital Requirement," *Federal Reserve Bulletin,* March 1989, pp. 147–148.
24. International Accounting Standards Committee, "Disclosure in the Financial Statements of Banks and Similar Financial Institutions," *International Accounting Standard 30,* London: IASC, August 1990.
25. OECD Secretariat, "Disclosure and Accounting Treatment of New Financial Instruments," in *New Financial Instruments: Disclosure and Accounting,* Paris: OECD, 1988, p. 43.
26. See Malcolm Walley, "Interest Rate and Currency Swaps," in *New Financial Instruments: Disclosure and Accounting,* Paris: OECD, 1988, p. 98.
27. Fédération des Experts-Comptables Européens, "Accounting and Financial Reporting," in *New Financial Instruments: Disclosure and Accounting,* Paris: OECD, 1988, p. 196.
28. For example, see Spooner, op. cit.

CHAPTER 25

INNOVATIONS, NEW DIMENSIONS, AND OUTLOOK FOR CROSS CURRENCY SWAPS

Carl R. Beidleman
Lehigh University
Bethlehem, Pennsylvania

INTRODUCTION

Cross currency swaps were invented in the late 1970s to serve as an effective means to manage long-date foreign exchange risk. If necessity is the mother of invention, it would have to be agreed that the demise of the Bretton Woods fixed-exchange-rate system in the early 1970s was the major event that gave birth to the need for a product like the currency swap. The increased fluctuations in exchange rates that followed the demise of the Bretton Woods arrangements alerted the financial community to the reality of exchange-rate changes and hence the need to hedge the associated exchange-rate risk.

The original instruments designed to facilitate hedging long-date foreign exchange risk were rudimentary by today's standards. Both sides of a transaction needed to be arranged before a deal was done. Documentation was not standardized. Cash flows were not congruent. Credit risk, although not ignored, was relegated to a lesser level of importance. Volume was very modest, and many applications were left unattended.

Nevertheless, the role and function of currency swaps and their ability to arrange and rearrange cash flows became recognized, and the use of swaps became an accepted practice. Cognizant of these new-found capabilities, early financial engineers learned that they could utilize currency swaps to exploit comparative advantages that existed for appropriate participants in alternative national markets for debt securities.

The advent of the arbitrage applications for currency swaps is now well known and is documented throughout this volume. It has, however, led to significant growth in the applications of currency swaps and to the extension of the swap concept to a closely related group of applications that would quickly overshadow currency swaps. The rapid growth of the interest rate swap market provided many collateral benefits to the currency swap in the form of rapid market development, standardized terms and documentation, market and product integration, risk management, and overall market depth and liquidity.

Few today would call interest rate swaps the daughter of currency swaps, but the truth is that the currency swap was the predecessor and conceptual forebear of interest rate swaps. It is interesting to note that the initial applications of interest rate swaps were in the arbitrage of differential credit risk premiums in the fixed-rate and floating-rate markets in a given currency. This was a natural extension of the exciting new arbitrage applications of currency swaps in the late 1970s and very early 1980s. However, it was not long until the full potential of interest rate swaps as an instrument for interest rate risk management became evident, and the volume of transactions began to reflect the need to manage interest rate risk throughout the world.

All of these developments reflect the advances that have been made in the world of finance in the last several decades. Across the entire field of finance, theorists and practitioners have been arduously pushing the discipline into new, exciting, and promising applications and constructions, many of which involve the creation and deployment of new instruments and/or modifications of old ones. Swaps are a striking example of this process. A brief discussion of the process of financial innovation and the impact of swaps will help set the stage for what the future may hold for this promising instrument.

INNOVATIONS IN FINANCE

Improvements and new developments in finance have occurred persistently through the decades but have not followed a regular path. They have evolved at an unsystematic pace, mostly representing attempts to find solutions to impediments to the smooth flow of financing. This sporadic progress has given way to a more continuous flow of innovative processes during the last decade, a period that has been a golden age of financial inventiveness. Evidence of the ongoing flow of innovative output in recent years includes original issue discount bonds; zero-coupon bonds; stripping of coupons from principal; defeasance; partly paid bonds; shelf registrations; mortgage-backed securities; collateralized mortgage obligations (CMOs); interest-only (IO), principal-only (PO) and residual components of mortgage portfolios; CARDS and CARS (credit card, automobile paper, and lease asset-backed securities); futures and options on almost anything, including options on futures; interest rate swaps; cross currency swaps; commodity swaps; dual currency bond issues; adjustable-rate mortgages; adjustable rate preferred stock; mutual funds on nearly any portfolio of assets; high-yield bonds; innovative corporate restructuring offensive and defensive tactics; personal finance initiatives—the list goes on almost inexhaustively.

A common denominator in the burst of new financial products has been the role of computation and modeling on which they are based. This trend is perhaps more significant than the new products themselves because it provides some glimpse of what can be expected in the future. Much has already been said about the concept of financial engineering and its role in rearranging cash flows to suit the purposes of a given application. With the advent of high-speed computer calculations and spreadsheets, multiple simulations can be carried out quickly and accurately.

In this sense, a change in the process of financial innovation has taken place. Training in finance has also become more rigorous, relying more heavily on mathematics, statistics, model building, econometric forecasting, probabilistic outcomes, simulation, and hypothesis testing. This has resulted in new theories of the value of financial assets, many of which have caught on and have influenced the thinking of academics and practitioners alike. Theoretical constructs such as the capital asset pricing theory, arbitrage pricing theory, option pricing theory, and agency theories, among others, have had a marked impact on financial thinking in recent years. Along with current tools of computation and communication, modern technical training has enabled financial engineers to design instruments and methods to satisfy nearly any financial requirement that can be clearly stated.

Financial innovation has followed many of the paths taken by technological innovation earlier in this century. Given these precedents, we should expect that the development characteristics associated with physical design and technological innovation would also be found in financial design and the improved products and services that are the fruits of financial innovation. Financial institutions are well aware of this parallel and have been quick to hire financial "rocket scientists." The process that produces innovation in finance has come to involve task forces including lawyers, traditional bankers, operations specialists, accountants, and tax specialists, as well as conceptual financial designers and product development specialists. These teams have been assembled by a number of financial institutions who also assign market-oriented people to test the relevant markets and devise appropriate means to effectively bring the new products into the marketplace.

Much of the work in this volume is the product of the deployment of such skills. Chapters contained in Part III, "Valuation of Swaps," and Part IV, "Conceptual Relationships," have especially benefited from a careful combination of advanced financial skills, computation and communication, modern theoretical constructs, and astute critical thinking. These chapters demonstrate the intricate relationships among derivative instruments; methods for creating innovative products for risk management; and means for managing the risk of a warehouse portfolio of swaps. There is every reason to expect that the process of financial innovation will continue and accelerate such that in the 1990s our understanding and use of financial products will advance far beyond what we have seen to date. And there is no doubt that the financial swap will be a forerunner in this process.

Innovation Casualties and Staying Power

Development of new products and techniques in response to market needs to improve efficiency or reduce risk is itself a risky process. In their haste to move new concepts toward a market test, product development teams sometimes neglect critical factors or misjudge market reaction to components of the innovation. In other instances, the innovation itself may not fully address its objective, resulting in an inadequate solution; or the innovative treatment may have adverse side effects that seriously thwart its effectiveness. In many cases the avoidance of one type of risk introduces others, some of which may be unacceptable to many market participants. A memorable example is the development of interest-only strips (IOs) of mortgage-backed securities, which were intended to provide a security with negative convexity to help manage interest rate risk. Because of the intense exposure of the IOs to a rather unpredictable prepayment risk, they have been deemed unacceptable instruments for inclusion in bank investment portfolios.

Because of the risk inherent in the innovative process, not all new products and techniques survive. Just a few examples of the casualties of the last few decades include the real estate investment trusts (REITs); IOs, POs, and residuals of stripped mortgage-backed portfolios; multiple-currency bond issues in which the investor has a choice of currency of repayment (in essence an option on foreign exchange flows); certain forms of portfolio insurance; and some varieties of computer-driven trading techniques. And the jury is still out on the long-term survival of high-yield bonds and the concomitant extensive leverage that they entail.

The probation period for most new financial products or techniques is usually quite short, frequently ending within a few years. In some cases repeated attempts by a new product's proponents to underwrite its success may extend the trial period beyond that time, but without bona fide market acceptance and demand, stagnant initiatives seldom survive.

In contrast with the many casualties of financial innovation, cross currency and interest rate swaps have met the test of markets far beyond our most optimistic expectations. Just six years ago when I wrote the final chapter to the first edition of *Financial Swaps,* the market for swaps still relied on a type of arrangement format, where quoted prices took the form of indications rather than firm quotations and counterparties were sought before a deal could be struck. There was little in the way of position taking or warehousing of swaps on the part of intermediaries. And swap documentation was not uniform, adding to the difficulty of enlarging, reducing, or unwinding a swap position as conditions might warrant.

I predicted the evolution of this "shadow market" into a fullfledged market with active market makers taking positions on their own books, offering firm price quotations, cultivating existing applications, and developing new ones. I also foresaw the development of the standardized documentation and quotation mechanisms that were necessary to improve the homogeneity of the swap in its movement toward commodity status. Despite this vision, it must be confessed that I remain happily astonished at the rapid growth and development of the currency swap market. When I boldly estimated a market size of $15 billion in 1983, I had no idea that it would reach $435 billion in 1989. This represents a compound growth rate of more than 75 percent per year. This striking rate of increase was hardly expected—and is hardly repeatable—but it reflects the utility, versatility, and effectiveness of currency swaps and swap-like instruments. This growth is also the result of the creativity and ingenuity of swap providers, swap users, and their analytical teams.

Currency and interest rate swaps have moved out of the shadow market of their early years, and their staying power is assured. They are now the uncontested stars of the financial innovation process of recent years. And like stars of the universe, they do not encounter a finite horizon. Their success is rooted in the need to manage foreign exchange and interest rate risk and to arbitrage inefficiencies in world capital markets. Unless and until exchange rates and interest rates stabilize and world capital markets become fully integrated and perfectly efficient, swaps will retain their prominent place in the galaxy of financial instruments. The prospects for stability in exchange rates and/or interest rates, or fully integrated and perfectly efficient world capital markets, is left to the reader.

Recognizing the current position of financial swaps in the realm of finance, it is helpful to review a bit of recent history to identify how the currency swap markets have developed and attempt to identify certain trends that may be helpful in developing an outlook for the future. In the next section, we focus on recent market data, trends, and perceptions for the future.

CURRENCY SWAPS:
DATA, TRENDS, AND PERCEPTIONS

The International Swap Dealers Association, Inc. (ISDA) was formed in 1985 to foster the development of financial swaps and to coordinate activities of general interest to the swap community. One of its activities is to sponsor an annual market survey of swap transactions and to publish the highlights of the survey. All of the data and trends presented in this section were obtained from the 1989 Market Survey

Highlights as conducted by Arthur Andersen & Co. on behalf of ISDA, using information provided by 64 ISDA members. This survey is believed to be a good representation of global swaps activity during this time. The findings help to clarify recent developments in the market and suggest trends and perceptions for the future.

Table 1 presents a record of outstanding currency swaps by currency at the end of 1989, including a breakdown of currency swap activity based on whether the transaction was conducted with an end user or with another ISDA counterparty. Each currency's share of the total activity (expressed in U.S. dollars) is also shown. Finally, the total currency swap activity of US$869.7 billion is divided by 2 to adjust for the fact that each swap is reported by both sides of the transaction. This results in a net volume of outstanding currency swaps of US$434,869 million at year end 1989.

We can see from the data that slightly over 40 percent of the transactions involved the U.S. dollar as a counterpart. This was followed by the Japanese yen at 23 percent, with the next highest currencies (Swiss francs, Australian dollar, Deutschemark, and European currency unit) each representing 5 to 7 percent of transactions. Subsequent tables will serve to show the trend in these respective market shares. Table 1 also provides information on the split between end-user and ISDA counterparties. In all the currencies represented, more than 70 percent of the swaps were with end users; in some currencies the external activity approached 90 percent. These high levels of end-user activity are significant in that they reflect the degree to which intermarket or secondary transactions have been necessary to effectively support a successful primary market.

Table 2 shows the trend in currency swaps over the past three years and includes the number of survey responses, the number of swap contracts reported, and the average contract size. The growth in swap volume mimics the statistics reported earlier in this chapter and reflects a slight slowdown in outstanding growth in recent years. The increase in the number of swap contracts reflects similar growth, with the average contract size remaining somewhat stable at approximately US$30 million.

Chart 1 shows the U.S. dollar equivalent of all currency and interest rate swaps outstanding at year end for 1987, 1988, and 1989. It also shows the U.S. dollar share of the totals. This chart makes

TABLE 1

Currency Swaps Outstanding as of December 31, 1989

Currency (Rank Order)	US$ Equivalent (Million)	End-User Counterparty	ISDA Counterparty	Currency as percentage of Total
U.S. dollar (US$)	US$354,166	72.78%	27.22%	40.72%
Yen (¥)	201,145	71.83	28.17	23.13
Swiss franc (SF)	64,823	77.42	22.58	7.45
Australian dollar (A$)	61,768	70.77	29.23	7.10
Deutschemark (DM)	53,839	79.93	20.07	6.19
European Currency Unit (ECU)	39,948	83.06	16.94	4.59
Pound Sterling (£)	33,466	74.11	25.89	3.85
Canadian dollar (C$)	32,580	81.72	18.28	3.75
Dutch guilder (NLG)	10,132	82.53	17.47	1.17
French franc (FF)	8,435	88.74	11.26	0.97
New Zealand dollar (NZ$)	5,818	81.90	18.10	0.67
Belgian franc (BF)	2,997	86.89	13.11	0.34
Hong Kong dollar (HK$)	583	90.39	9.61	0.07
Total	US$869,699			
Total/2 (adjusted for reporting of both sides)	US$434,869			

Source: International Swap Dealers Association Confidential Market Survey

TABLE 2
Total Currency Swaps Outstanding 1987 to 1989

Survey Period	Survey Responses	Total Contracts	Total Notional Principal, US$ Equivalent (Millions)/2	Average Contract, US$ Equivalent (Millions)
			End-User	
1987	49	5,173	US$147,304	US$28.47
1988	57	7,724	234,546	30.37
1989	64	11,270	323,758	28.73
			ISDA Member	
1987	49	1,439	US$ 35,503	US$24.67
1988	57	2,547	82,275	32.30
1989	64	4,015	111,091	27.67
			Total	
1987	49	6,612	US$182,807	US$27.65
1988	57	10,271	316,821	30.85
1989	64	15,285	434,849	28.45

Source: International Swap Dealers Association Confidential Market Survey

clear the declining role of the U.S. dollar share of both swap markets and the way in which the growth on interest rate swaps has exceeded the still-rapid growth of the currency swap market. The prodigious growth of the interest rate swap market is caused by the larger volume of interest rate risk that requires management, as well as by the ease with which swap market makers can lay off the risk that they assume in writing a swap with an end user. These data are also useful to compare the growth and size of the respective swap markets in order to place the currency swap market in perspective with its extraordinary offspring.

Chart 2 presents the recent trends of growth in the notional principal of currency swaps for the major currencies. It is notable that while the U.S. dollar still dominates currency swap denomination, its lead is being reduced by the yen, the Australian dollar, and the leading European currencies. Chart 3 breaks down U.S. dollar swaps by the currencies of the counterparties. Here again, the growth in the share of the yen is apparent, primarily at the expense of the Swiss franc.

CHART 1
Interest Rate and Currency Swaps—Total Notional Principal

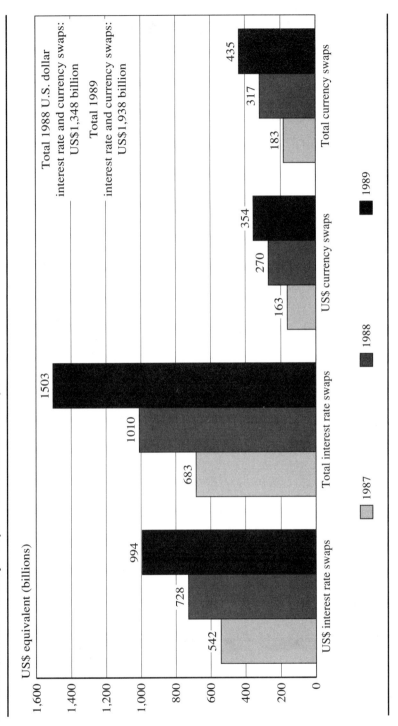

US$ equivalent (billions)

Total 1988 U.S. dollar
interest rate and currency swaps:
US$1,348 billion

Total 1989
interest rate and currency swaps:
US$1,938 billion

US$ interest rate swaps: 994, 728, 542

Total interest rate swaps: 1503, 1010, 683

US$ currency swaps: 354, 270, 163

Total currency swaps: 435, 317, 183

1987 | 1988 | 1989

Source: International Swap Dealers Association, Inc.

CHART 2
Currency Swaps—Notional Principal by Currency

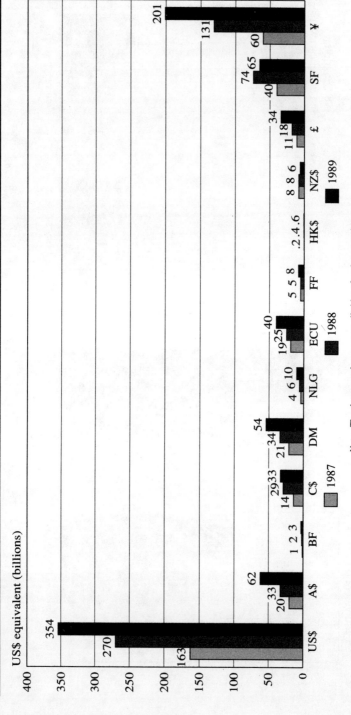

US$ equivalent (billions)

Source: International Swap Dealers Association, Inc.

CHART 3
Currency Swaps—U.S. Dollar vs. Other Currencies

1987	1988	1989

1987 pie chart values: 4.92%, 10.15%, 6.58%, 19.31%, 11.62%, 17.04%, 30.38%

1988 pie chart values: 4.34%, 9.39%, 8.79%, 14.81%, 10.82%, 12.38%, 39.47%

1989 pie chart values: 5.65%, 9.46%, 6.83%, 11.89%, 10.70%, 16.04%, 39.58%

Total US$
notional principle:
US$162.6 billion

Total US$
notional principle:
US$269.5 billion

Total US$
notional principle:
US$354.2 billion

vs. A$ vs. C$ vs. DM   £   vs. SF   vs. ¥   vs. other

Source: International Swap Dealers Association, Inc.

Charts 4 and 5 show the maturity distribution of currency swaps. The marked increase in shorter-term swaps is notable, while longer-maturity currency swaps (with the exception of the six-year maturity) have tended to decline in relative importance. These trends may be related to the trend to finance with shorter maturity debt and/or the ability of the market maker to lay off shorter-term currency risk more easily in related markets.

Chart 6 looks at the trends in currency swap activity by transaction type. It is clear from these results that the fixed/floating combination associated with a cross currency swap dominates (foreign currency fixed versus U.S. dollar floating); however, fixed/fixed swaps (U.S. dollar fixed vs. yen fixed) have also shown significant growth. Floating/floating or basis swaps have also grown but remain a small fraction of total currency swap activity.

In Chart 7 we see an analysis of currency swaps based on end-user business and location. To the surprise of some, these data suggest that U.S. locations do not dominate the currency swap market, representing less than 20 percent of the demand as measured by notional principal. In contrast, more than 40 percent of the traffic originates

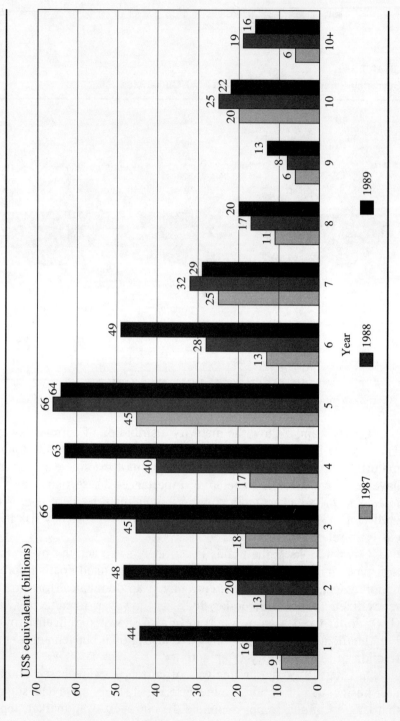

CHART 4
Currency Swaps—Notional Principal by Maturity

US$ equivalent (billions)

Year

■ 1989 ■ 1988 ▨ 1987

Source: International Swap Dealers Association, Inc.

CHART 5
Currency Swaps—Maturity Trend Analysis

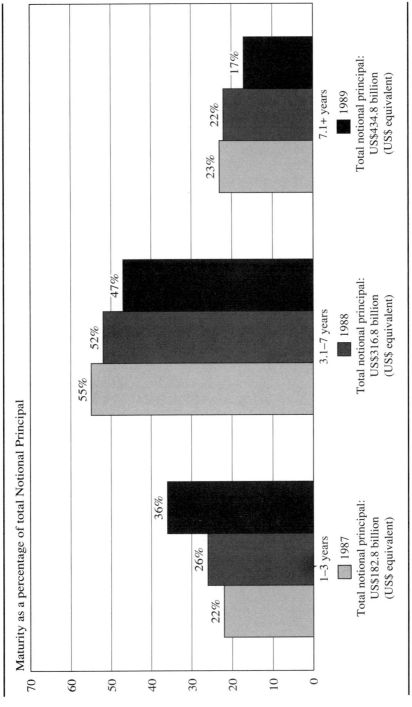

Maturity as a percentage of total Notional Principal

Source: International Swap Dealers Association, Inc.

CHART 6
Currency Swaps—Notional Principal by Transaction Type

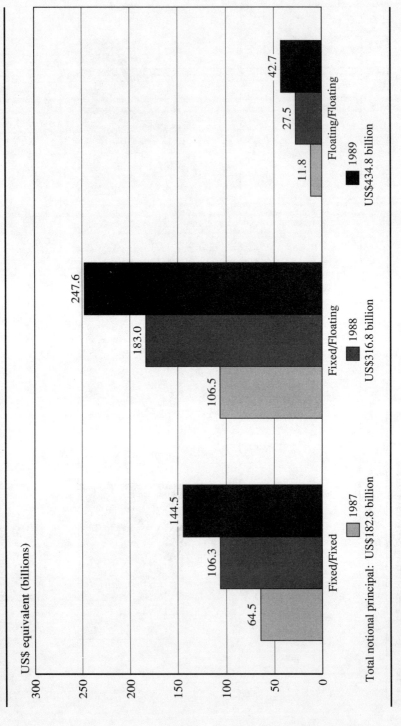

US$ equivalent (billions)

Total notional principal: US$182.8 billion

| 1987 |
| 1988 |
| 1989 |

Source: International Swap Dealers Association, Inc.

CHART 7

Currency Swaps—End-User Business/Location Analysis

Location	1989 Business Type				1989 Total	1988 Total
	Corporation	Financial Institution	Government	Other		
United States	8	7	1	1	17	18
Canada	2	3	2	0	7	6
Europe	9	21	13	1	44	45
Asia	12	9	1	0	22	22
Australia/New Zealand	2	3	2	0	7	7
Other	0	1	1	1	3	1
1989 total	33	44	20	3	100%	
1988 total	31	45	23	1		100%

Note: Data are given as percentages of the total notional principal of currency swaps for each year.

Source: International Swap Dealers Association, Inc.

CHART 8

Currency Swaps—Average Contract Size

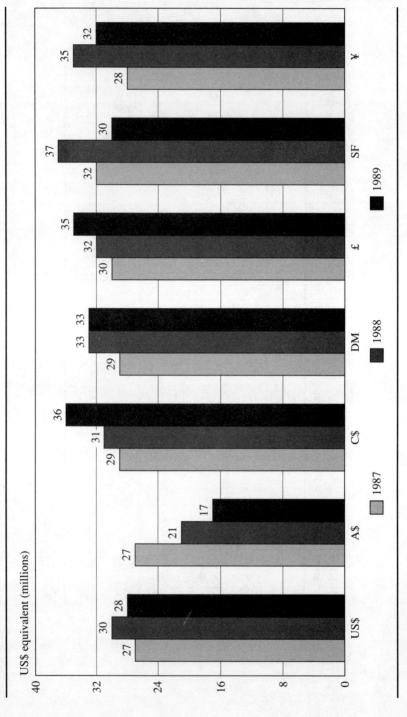

US$ equivalent (millions)

Source: International Swap Dealers Association, Inc.

with European users and more than 20 percent with Asian participants. As might be expected, more than 40 percent of the outstanding notional principal of currency swaps was held by financial institutions, about a third by corporate users, and 20 percent by governments and their agencies.

As mentioned earlier, the average size of currency swap contracts in all currencies from 1987 to 1989 was approximately US$30 million. Chart 8 presents the average contract size for each of the major currencies. The results are not markedly dissimilar from the overall average except for the somewhat larger average size for Canadian dollar and Swiss franc swaps, and the somewhat smaller average size for the Australian and U.S. dollar swaps. Since random forces can affect the size of contracts, little importance can be attached to these extremes. In general, the average contract size of US$25 to 30 million seems to reflect most of the activity in the currency swap market. However, these averages reflect a mix of swaps ranging from less than US$5 million to over US$50 million, with some swaps exceeding US$100 million; hence the averages have little more than nominal significance regarding the forces underway in the individual swap currencies.

The ISDA market survey also contains data on derivative products, such as swaptions. These data show a total of 2061 swaption contracts executed in 1989, with a notional principal of just under US$80 billion. The data do not differentiate between interest rate and currency swaptions; however, if the fraction of currency swaps to total swaps holds at 22.5 percent, the volume of currency swaptions outstanding at year end 1989 would be less than US$18 billion.

LOOKING FORWARD

Our analysis of these historical results and trends provide an interesting perspective upon which to base an outlook for the future of currency swaps. Clearly, the rate of growth in outstanding volume has declined from that of the early years of currency swaps. Nonetheless, the volume has continued to grow and is reflected in recent transactions data for the first half of 1990. The decline in the rate of growth is characteristic of a more mature and stable market, in which participants can catch their breath and evaluate their activity before moving on to identify new applications.

If the past is prologue, it is clear that new applications will be sought and found from time to time. Each new breakthrough will result in a burst of activity, first by the primary innovator and then by the pack of followers who will quickly mimic or imitate each novel discovery.

It is unclear what new uses will be made of currency swaps, or what new spinoffs might appear. Trials have been made on *inflation swaps* and *act-of-God swaps* against natural catastrophes; *commodity swaps* have shown particular promise in hedging the prices of energy, minerals, and certain metals. New arbitrage applications will inevitably arise as market inefficiencies are caused by nonmarket processes. Teams of innovators will continue to examine needs to improve the nature of cash flows and engineer ways to accomplish the needed transformations. As the globe shrinks and international transactions become more widespread, the need to manage currency flows will become more and more routine, and currency swaps will become even more accepted as a tool for streamlining the currency risk management process. The operations aspect of currency swaps themselves will be refined, and this will then allow the swapping process to be applied to heretofore unprofitable applications.

Currency swaps are a product whose staying power is assured. Unless we move to a single world currency or to fixed exchange rates, or world capital markets become perfectly efficient, it is unlikely that the currency swap market will decline. The market is now quite mature; bid-ask spreads are becoming razor thin. Although not yet as competitive as the interest rate swap market, where one basis point can make the difference between success and failure in booking a deal, plain vanilla currency swaps are moving in that direction. In plain vanilla swaps, money is not made on the spread but on the position. This has encouraged larger position taking in the interest rate swap warehouses, and a similar development should take place in the currency swap market as it continues to mature. Cross currency swaps will continue to add value, especially when they are applied to tailored transactions. Currency swaps that have been customized to meet the needs of Japanese investors are excellent examples of this point.

Maturity Trends

Commercial currency swaps were developed to enable users to hedge currency risk for maturities longer than those available in the bank forward market or in the concurrently developing foreign exchange futures markets. In other words, currency swaps originated as a long-date foreign exchange instrument. As we saw in Charts 4 and 5, in recent years the bulk of currency swaps had maturities from three to seven years, with some tendency toward increased volume in the 1- to 3-year and 6-year categories and in maturities longer than 10 years. The rapid growth of foreign currency futures markets has made it considerably easier for market intermediaries to lay off the risk of shorter-dated currency swaps, which has undoubtedly stimulated the growth of these swaps.

Future trends in currency swap maturities are not at all clear. Some analysts see the long-dated swap (10+ years) as a specialized art with little growth prospect. Others foresee flat yield curves, prompting a trend toward shorter maturities. Still others see an increasing call for long-dated swaps related to public and private loans, for project finance, and as means to engineer other long-term enterprise's cash flows or to convert short-term funding in one currency into long-term funding in another without accessing the public market. In contrast with a flat yield curve, a tendency toward a rising yield curve would also prompt an increased interest in longer-dated instruments. Swap maturities in the 15- to 25-year range have already been used in connection with mortgage and leasing projects. Longer maturities also offer more arbitrage opportunities. The upshot of all of this is that the maturity spectrum of currency swaps will probably continue to be distributed somewhat as in the past, with occasional increases in longer-date or shorter-date maturities as market conditions dictate, but with the majority of the transactions remaining in the three- to seven-year range.

Credit Matters

An issue of foremost importance in the swap industry in recent years has been the creditworthiness of counterparties. Not only are strong credit ratings required for swap end users, but they are also a prerequisite for a swap dealer. Swap dealers require a sizable capital investment and a minimum of an "A" credit rating. These constraints serve as a barrier to entry, although others may still participate as arrangers or brokers. Because of the intense emphasis on credit, some dealers, find it necessary to use credit enhancement techniques to improve their own as well as counterparty credit. Recent examples of this trend include the use of change-of-ownership clauses, cash-collateralized transactions, and assignment arrangements in the event of credit downgrades.

Credit concerns are also a primary reason for the decreased attractiveness of U.S. banks as counterparties to foreign names. This reduced appetite for the lower-rated U.S. investment banks is evident in the less attractive terms that they may face (e.g., three basis points under the offer or over the bid on typical quotes). And U.S. commercial banks may also require credit enhancement at times, including termination of the contract if their credit rating is lost.

Marking the swap contract to market as an approach to managing credit risk received considerable attention in the late 1980s, but it has lost some importance following arguments to permit netting of swap transactions in the event of bankruptcy. Moreover, firms do not enjoy taking a loss on a swap that they put on as a hedge, further reducing interest in the mark-to-market concept.

The absence of mark-to-market is a provision that now clearly distinguishes swaps from futures contracts, which *must* mark-to-market. Commodity swaps were once viewed as off-exchange futures transactions and were prohibited in the U.S. by the Commodity Futures Trading Commission (CFTC). This action drove commodity swaps offshore until it was reversed by a policy statement in July 1989. If mark-to-market were to become accepted practice in currency swaps, they might face a similar fate. It is more likely that we will see a dual market in three- to five-year swaps: an over-the-counter (OTC) market regulated by the Federal Reserve and the Securities and Exchange Commission, and an exchange-listed contract (which marks-to-market) regulated by the CFTC.

Credit insurance has also been tried as an alternative to the credit enhancement requirement. For a time, a large European commercial bank offered credit insurance, based on mark-to-market criteria, to the World Bank. However, the program was dropped because of its lack of profitability. In the highly efficient market that now characterizes swap transactions, it is not possible for a credit intermediary to maintain the economics of offering credit insurance. If spreads were wider, the program would be attractive, but the intense competitiveness of the swap market has precluded this form of credit enhancement at this time.

SUMMARY

As indicated earlier, there seems to be some reduction in the U.S. dollar share of the swap markets. This may be due to the impending recession in the U.S. economy or, more likely, to the fact that currency swaps, which were once done mainly with the US$ as a constituent currency, now are more frequently done without a dollar component. This form of catchup is inevitable. It has been offset by significant increases in the yen and D-mark markets reflecting the increased importance of international dealings in these markets.

Product areas that show promise include amortizing currency swaps; low- or zero-coupon currency swaps to convert low- or zero-coupon bonds into fixed- or floating-rate obligations in another currency; option-related products; accreting swaps; annuity swaps; and principal-only or bullet swaps.

These products will be particularly helpful to financial engineers who tackle the growth areas for currency swaps that lie in the intersection of swaps, debt, and traditional international banking activity. Paramount among these are project finance, syndicated lending, long-term trade finance and export credit, real estate projects, and the strong trend toward international initiatives in mergers and acquisitions.

Currency swaps, like interest rate swaps, increase the flexibility of financial managers to deal with rate risks. The flexibility to hedge foreign exchange risk, to exploit advantages that are inherent in market anomalies, or simply to make changes in a balance sheet or investment portfolio in response to revised circumstances, makes currency swaps an extremely useful device that is easily accessible to informed financial managers. Their continued use and phenomenal growth have been largely a function of their acceptance by financial managers. My hope is that this volume and its companion, *Interest Rate Swaps,* will add to the understanding of financial swaps and reduce the fear and apprehension formerly identified with swapping cash flows. If this can be achieved, applications will continue to expand, market liquidity will increase still further, and financial management will be carried out more efficiently and expediently.

INDEX

Abdullah, F. A., 397
Accounting
    CIRCUS swaps, treatment of,
        562–66
    currency swaps, treatment of,
        558–62
    and financial institutions, 566–71
    historical perspective on, 554–55
    swaps, characteristics and treatment of,
        555–57
Accreting swap, 148
Accrued interest, 340
Active fixed income portfolios, 283
Act-of-God swaps, 600
Adjustment swap, 188–91. *See also*
    Off-market swap
Adler, M., 260, 275
Akhtar, M., 364, 365n, 368n, 372n, 373,
    397
Aliber, R. Z., 373n, 397
Allen, J. M., 553
All-in cost of funds, 75, 226
Amortizing currency swap, 148,
    337–38, 371
Annuities
    converting annuity rates to
        zero-coupon rates, 355
    pricing, 353–55
Annuity factors, 342, 346n, 354–56
Annuity swap, 142, 336, 337, 338n,
    350–51, 469–71. *See also*
    Coupon-only swaps; cross
    currency coupon swaps
Antl, B., 71n, 90, 454n
Arbitrage, 31
    and call swaptions, 225–26
    in capital markets, 98, 158–60, 331
    covered interest, 401, 403–5, 407
    cross currency swaps as a tool for, 7, 24,
        47–59
    and the forward market, 170–74

Arbitrage—*Cont.*
    gains in, 50, 52, 53
    and growth of the swap market, 371
    and links between interest rate swaps,
        cross currency swaps, and foreign
        exchange forward contracts, 449–51
    market efficiency and, 59–61
    name, 367
    quadrangle, 403–4, 406
    sources of activity, 54–59
    and synthetic securities, 182
    between U.S. dollar market and
        Eurobond rates, 306
Ardalan, Cyrus, 580
Asset currency swap arbitrage, 53–54, 55
Asset interest rate effect, 345–46
Asset-liability matching, 145–46
Asset swap, 111, 146–47, 179. *See also*
    Synthetic securities
    impact of, 192–93
    liquidity of, 192
    reasons for entering into, 180–83
    single-currency *vs.* cross currency, 178
Asymmetry, 65, 85–88, 89
At-the-market swap, 333, 335, 339, 342,
    343, 347
At-the-money swaption, 222
Autoregressive disturbance term,
    379–80

Back-to-back (BTB) loans, 12, 13–18, 35,
    65–66, 77, 93, 370
    security provisions of, 15–18
Bahmani-Oskooee, M., 373n, 379, 397
Balance of payments, 36, 298
Balducci, Vince, 331n
Bank for International Settlements (BIS),
    327, 513, 524, 525
Bankruptcy, 87, 88, 114, 602
Basis risk sensitivity limit, 426
Basis swap, 6, 145–46, 339

Basle Committee on Banking
　Regulations and Supervisory
　Practices, 525, 527
Batlin, C. A., 370, 397, 432
BBAIRS (British Bankers' Association
　Interest Rate Swaps), 113–14
Beidleman, Carl, 3, 64n, 66n, 90, 238,
　366n, 367, 397, 398, 401n, 499n,
　580, 582
Belmore, Martin, 581
Bicksler, J., 397
Bid-ask spread, 70, 89, 381
Black-Scholes option pricing model, 222
Blocked currency swap, 155
Blue sky laws, 542–43
Board of Trade v. Christie, 541, 546,
　547–48
Bock, David, 94n
Boiler rooms, 539
Bond, defined, 340
Bootstrapping, 415–16
Bretton Woods Agreement, 32, 33, 36,
　37–39, 259, 293, 582
Brittain, Bruce, 195n
Broaddus, A., 397
Brown, Keith, 63, 64n, 75n, 90
Bucket shop laws, 535, 537–42
Building block approach
　cross currency interest rate swap,
　　516–20
　interest rate swap, 514–16
　replacement cost calculation for
　　currency swap, 520–23
Bullet maturity bonds, 334n
Business purpose, 540–41

Callable bonds, 150–51, 224–25
Callable swaps, 150–51
Call swaption, 167, 219, 223, 225–28
Cap, 118, 286, 371
Capital
　and competition, return on, 527
　cost of, 218
　external regulation of, 525
　and pricing, return on, 526–27
　risk weight *vs.* risk factor, 525–26
Capital adequacy requirements, 105–6, 513,
　524, 525, 575–76
Capital costs, 104–6
Capital market arbitrage, 98, 158–60, 331,
　332, 370

Capital market currency swap
　applications of, 160–63
　callable issues, 167–68
　commissions, underwriting, 161–62
　conditions favorable to, 158, 177
　embedded currency options and, 172–74
　floating-rate notes and, 163–65
　historical perspective on, 156–58
　opportunities for arbitrage, 158–60
　recurring fees in, 163
　structuring transactions for greater value,
　　165–70
Capital market integration
　autoregressive disturbance term, 379–80
　covered interest parity models of,
　　373–75
　currency swap market and, 400
　data, specification of, 380–81
　defined, 364–65
　econometric considerations, 376–80
　factors that integrate world capital
　　markets, 368–69
　factors that segment world capital
　　markets, 365–68
　findings, 381–96
　limited-dependent-variable models,
　　376–79
　maturity date, 383–85
　net deviations from covered interest
　　parity, 392–96
　theoretical models, 375–76
　transaction costs, 386–92
Capital markets, purpose of, 55–56
CARDS, 584
CARS, 584
Cartusciello, Michael, 581
Cash flows
　for an annuity swap, 337
　characteristics of, 3–4
　from covered arbitrage, 407
　under a cross currency swap, 5, 6–7, 96,
　　563
　domestic *vs.* nondomestic, 4
　exchange-rate induced changes in,
　　268–74
　finance as a strategy of, 3
　and foreign currency debt placement, 11
　and foreign exchange exposure, 4
　and forward exchange agreement, 21
　for a generic fixed-for-fixed currency
　　swap, 334, 335
　modifying the characteristics of, 4–5

Cash flows—*Cont.*
  for multi-party loans, 13–15, 16
  for old-line currency swaps, 19
  price levels and, 262–63
  sensitivity of, 261–62
  for a zero-coupon swap, 338
Chen, A. H., 397
Chevalier, Lorin, 556, 580
Chicago Board of Trade (CBOT), 541
Chicago Mercantile Exchange, 9
CIRCUS swaps (cross currency interest rate
    swaps), 68n, 100, 562–66
Cirulli, Vincent, 218
Clearinghouse, 104
Clinton, K., 369, 372, 373n, 374n,
    380–81, 397
Cocktail swaps, 98–100
Collar, 118, 286, 371
Collateral, 104, 109
Collateralized mortgage obligation (CMO),
    45, 584
Comiskey, Eugene, 581
Commissions, underwriting, 161–62
Commodity codes, 542–43
Commodity Exchange Act (CEA), 533
  and bucket shop laws, 537–42
  hedging and, 539–40
  preemption of state law, 537–43
  and state law, 543–46
Commodity Futures Trading
    Commission (CFTC), 533
  concept of a future, 546–50
  economic purpose and delivery method,
    549–50
  regulation of swaps by, 533–36,
    602
  rulemaking power of, 551
  Swap Statement, 535, 536–37,
    547–49, 550
Commodity swaps, 584, 600, 602
Comparative advantage, 32, 47, 55
  sources of, 56–58
Competition, 527
Conneely, Joe, 581
Contingent liabilities, 150
Cooke method of risk calculation, 104,
    105n
Cooper, I., 365n, 366n, 369, 398
Counterparties, 13, 29, 64, 65, 75n, 97–98,
    102–3, 281–82, 370n
Coupon-only swaps, 142. *See also*
    Annuity swap

Coupon swaps, 268, 320, 324, 469–71
Covered interest arbitrage, 401, 403–5, 407
Covered interest parity (CIP), 372–73
  disequilibrium and equilibrium regimes
    of, 379
  equilibrium conditions under, 377
  models of, 373–75
  net deviations from, 392–96
Crawshaw, D. R., 553
Credit event upon merger, 116, 117
Credit exposure, 85–88, 282, 336, 513
  building block approach to, 514–23
  estimating and measuring market risk,
    523–27
  and market risk, 514
Credit insurance, 602
Credit ratings, 240, 601–2
Credit risk
  actual, 82–83
  asymmetry in, 65
  on a currency swap, 80–85, 103
  diversification of, 181
  matching, 17
  mitigation of, 108–9
  premium, 366
  specialists in, 17
  and specialization, 107
  in synthetic securities, 191
Cross currency basis swap, 222
Cross currency coupon swaps, 469–71
Cross currency hedged S&P, 500 index
    swap, 290–91
Cross currency interest rate swaps, 28, 97
Cross currency swap market
  and the arbitrage process, 98, 371
  capital market integration in, 400
  counterparties, availability of, 102–3
  credit questions, 103–6
  currency management and, 100, 218
  development of, 332–53
  documentation and definitions, 101
  growth of, 97–100, 588–99
  LIBOR U.S. dollars in, 99–100
  multileg transactions in, 98–100
  outlook for, 109–11
  specialization and, 107–8
  standardization and, 108–9, 117–18
  users, 97–98
  windows in, 174–76, 527
Cross currency swaps, 91, 140, 221, 484,
    485, 562–66. *See also* Swap
    categories

Cross currency swaps—*Cont.*
  as an asset management tool, 178
  basic applications of, 24, 239
  cash flows, 5, 6–7, 96, 563
  creating synthetic securities with, 180–83
  defined, 91, 140, 179
  early documentation, 101, 112–13
  fixed/fixed, 436–41, 444–47
  fixed/floating, 441–42, 447
  floating/floating, 442–43, 447–49
  interest rates and, 110
  vs. interest rate swaps, 443–51
  modern, 23–24
  in the public sector, 239
  structure evolution, 96–97
Cross currency swaptions, 233–35
Cross currency unhedged S&P, 500 index
  swap, 291–92
Cross-default clause, 88, 116, 117
Cross hedging, 283
Cross-index swaps, 284, 285
Cunningham, Daniel, 112
Currency-collateralized loans, 11–13
Currency equity-linked swap, 276, 289–92
Currency exposure
  example of, 8–9
  managing, 198–200
Currency factor, 433
Currency gains, 242–45, 345
Currency hedging, 294
Currency options, 155
Currency risk, 65, 89, 238
Currency swaps, 28, 140, 557–62.
    See also Swap categories
  accounting treatment, 558–62
  applications of, 75–77
  as an arbitrage tool, 7, 24, 47–59
  attributes of, 195–96
  availability of, 363
  average contract size, 598
  basic mechanics of, 69
  capital market element, 35, 77–79, 156,
    160–63
  coupon-only, 142
  credit matters, 601–2
  credit risk on, 80–85, 103
  data, trends, and perceptions,
    587–99
  defined, 28, 196, 554
  development of market, 332–33
  documentation and definitions, 101
  evolution of, 369–72

Currency swaps—*Cont.*
  fixed-rate payment standards for, 361
  flexibility of, 151, 177, 400, 602
  floating-rate payment standards for, 362
  foreign exchange forward market
    interpretation of, 79–80
  vs. forward foreign exchange
    transactions, 91–92, 97
  future of market, 109–11, 599–602
  to hedge economic exposure, 265–68
  historical background and market
    structure, 65–67, 156–58,
    582–83
  implications of, 59–61
  importance of, 30–31
  vs. interest rate swaps, 336, 583
  liquidity of, 102–3
  vs. loans, 19–20
  long-date cover before swaps, 10–24
  maturity trends, 600–601
  origin of the market for, 33–35
  pricing and valuation, 339–53
  quotation conventions, 68–73
  replacement cost calculation for, 520–23
  standard, 141–42
  U.S. dollar *vs.* other currencies, 593, 602
  with variable notational principal, 148–49
  variations, 336–39
Currency swaps with notional principal
    (CSNPs), 473
  applications of, 473–75
  examples of, 474
Current exposure method, 525, 526

Das, S., 373n, 376, 397
Debt obligation position, 483
Debt securities, 5
Decomposition, 345n, 348, 349, 370
Default risk, 104, 191
Default timing option, 65, 86, 87
Defeasance, 584
Delayed financing, 198
Deregulation, financial, 42–44, 98, 366n
Derivative equity, 276
DeRosa, David, 276
Devaluation, 18, 37, 268–69, 293
Differential credit risk premiums,
  366
Discount currency, 289–90, 359
Discount rate, 341–42, 354
Diversification, 58, 181, 312

Documentation
  BBAIRS terms, 113–14
  cancellation clauses, 246–47
  early swap agreements, 112–13
  ISDA Master Agreements, 116
  ISDA, 1985 Code of Standard
    Wording, Assumptions and
    Provisions for Swaps, 114–15
  standardization in, 117–18, 582, 586
  swap master agreements, 115–16
Domestic cash flows, 4
Dordiswami, Kumar, 331n
Dual-currency bond, 143–44, 170–72
Dual-currency Eurobond issues, 320
Dual-currency instruments, 43,
    320–22, 584
Dual-currency loan, 322, 323
Dual interest rate swaps, 485
Dufey, Gunter, 368n
Dumas, B., 260, 275
Duration, 346n

Economic exposure, 260–62
  currency swaps to hedge, 265–68
ECU bonds, 56
Edington, David, 195n
Embedded currency options, 172–74, 177,
    285–86, 287–88
End users, 597
Engle, R., 398
Equity index-linked swap, 276
  appeal of, 276
  complex, 284–88
  counterparties, 281–82
  enhanced index strategy with
    embedded options, 287–88
  examples of, 279, 280
  foreign currency and, 289–92
  hedged S&P 500 Index swap, 174
  liquidity of, 277
  mechanics of, 277–80
  and the operant portfolio, 280–81
  structure of on the S&P 500 Index, 279
  summary term sheet for S&P 500 swap,
    278
  unhedged S&P 500 Index swap, 290–91
Equity warrant bond, 306–10
Eurocurrency interest rate futures, 155
Eurodeposit market, 34, 295
Euro-DM bond market, 43
Eurodollar market, 56, 99, 174

Euromarkets, 36, 42, 43
European currency units (ECUs), 67
Event risk, 333
Exchange-rate risk. *See also* Foreign
    exchange risk
  avoiding, 147
  cash flow induced by changes in,
    268–74
  expected future spot exchange rate, 497
  foreign currency swaps as a management
    tool for, 198–200
  forward foreign exchange market, 495–97
  interest rate parity, 493–95
  short-date *vs.* long-date currency
    contracts, 497–500
  volatility and, 8
Exchange rates. *See also* Bretton Woods
    Agreement
  fluctuations in, 38
  price levels and, 262–63
  volatility of, 33, 37–39
Exchange rate speculation, 441–42
Expertise, 108
Exposure method, 526
Extrinsic value, 173

Factor sensitivity, 422–23
  limits, 424–26
Fama, E., 372n, 398
Federal Reserve Board, 602
Felgren, Steven, 64n, 90
Fence, 286
Financial Accounting Standards Board
    (FASB)
  Statement No. 8, 100, 259
  Statement No. 52, 100, 556, 560, 578
  Statement No. 91, 570
  Statement No. 105, 577–78
Financial disclosure initiatives, 576–78
Financial engineering, 4–5, 66,
    370–71, 453
Financial futures contracts, 41, 45
Financial institutions, 47, 111, 566–71
Financing, expected cost of, 492
First order autocorrelation, 382n
Fixed/fixed cross currency swaps, 83, 92,
    437–42
  exchange rate speculation, 441–42
  foreign currency funding, 440–41
  strip of forwards, 445–48
  U.S. dollar funding, 438–40

Fixed/fixed currency swap, 73–75, 85n, 219, 411–12, 413. *See also* Cross currency swaps
  defined, 87, 219
  synthetic, 411
Fixed/floating cross currency swaps, 442–43, 447
Fixed/floating currency swap, 83, 219, 408–411. *See also* Interest rate swaps
Fixed-funds yen payer, 312
Fixed income securities, 5
Fixed rate receivers, 298, 306
Fletcher, Donna, 364, 378n, 386n, 398
Floating/floating cross currency swaps, 442–44, 447–50
Floating/floating currency swap, 83–84, 220, 405–8. *See also* Single-currency basis swap
Floating/floating interest rate swaps, 432n
Floating-rate notes (FRNs)
  and capital market swaps, 163–65
  defined, 6, 43
  as a financial innovation, 44–45
  market collapse of, 182
Floating rate spread risk, 206
Floating U.S. dollar receiver, 312–15
Floor, 118, 371
Foreign currency debt, 10–11
Foreign exchange contract
  swaps *vs.*, 301–2
Foreign exchange exposure
  and cash flows, 4
Foreign exchange market, 168
Foreign exchange options, 113
Foreign exchange position, unhedged, 169–70
Foreign exchange rates. *See* Exchange rates
Foreign exchange risk, 7–9, 435n, 442n
Foreign exchange swaps, 333n
Forward currency contracts, 20–23, 333–34
Forward currency swap
  in the active management of funding costs, 209–15
  advanced refunding of high-coupon debt using, 206–9
  attributes of, 195–96
  defined, 196, 338–39
  examples of, 200–217
  funded *vs.* unfunded, 197
  hedging a future financing with, 200–206
  in hedging interest rate risk, 197–98

Forward currency swap—*Cont.*
  in managing currency exposure, 198–200
  transactions, structure of, 196–97
Forward discount, 22
Forward exchange agreement (FRA), 21
Forward exchange rate
  computing, 357–58
  negotiating, 20–21
Forward foreign exchange
  arbitrage in, 170–74
  vs. currency swap, 91–92, 97
  defined, 91–92
  long-term, 92–93
  market, 495–97
Forward rate, 222, 223–24
Forward rate agreements (FRAs), 113, 423
Forward swap, 147
Four-party loans, 14, 15, 16, 18
FRABBA (Forward Rate Agreement British Bankers' Association), 113n
Fraudulent Practices (Martin) Act of 1984, 543
Frenkel, J. A., 263, 275, 373n, 398
Functional currency, 267
Funded swap, 197
Fungibility, 547

Gambino, Anthony, 580
Generic currency swaps, 331, 333–35, 360–62
Generic interest rate swaps, 336n
Giddy, Ian H., 368n
Gilberg, D. J., 553
Global fixed income portfolios, 283
Globalization, 30, 46–48, 481–82
Gold standard, 293. *See also* Bretton Woods Agreement
Goodall, Jennifer, 195n
Greenleaf, J. A., 398, 499n

Hakkio, C. S., 263, 275
Hale, T. A., 553
Hammersmith & Fulham, 176n
Handjinicolaou, George, 28, 365n, 366, 367, 369, 371, 398
Harnik, Peter, 155
Hedged swaps, 556–57
Hedging
  callable bonds, 224–25
  under the Commodity Exchange Act, 539–40

Hedging—*Cont.*
  currency, 294
  early techniques for, 195
  and economic exposure, 265–68
  futures and, 539–40
  against interest rate risk, 41, 197–98
  interest rates and, 443–52
  long-date forward, 352n
  and price-risk management, 428, 430
Hiden, R. B., 553
High-coupon currency, 359
Hilley, J. L., 373n, 374, 386n, 398, 499n
Hull, J., 524n
Husted, S., 275
Hybrid instruments, 160

Iben, Benjamin, 400, 401n
IBM/World Bank swap, 28, 66, 67, 93–96, 157, 159
Illiquidity, 182, 188
Immunization, 272
Impact loans, 298, 303, 304
Implied interest rates, 486, 488, 504–9
Incomplete markets, 180
Index-linked swaps. *See* Equity index-linked swap
Inflation swaps, 600
Innovation, financial, 30
  casualties and staying power, 585–87
  developments in, 583–85
  floating rates notes (FRNs) as, 44–45
  politics of, 550–51
  securitization as, 45–46
  stimulation of, 266
In re Stovall, decision, 546–47
Institutional investors, restrictions on, 181
Integration
  covered interest parity models of capital
    market integration,
    373–75
  evaluating, 372
  interest differential models in
    general, 372–73
  meaning of, 364–65
  measures of, 372–81
Interest rate differential, 11, 21, 238, 334, 339, 346–47, 358–59, 372–73, 503, 505, 506, 507–8
Interest rate expectations theory, 482, 488–93

Interest rate parity, 56, 79, 403–5, 406, 412, 449, 482, 493–95, 496–97, 500, 522n
Interest rate risk, 41, 197–98
Interest rates
  vs. forward foreign exchange rates,
    504–9
  implied, 486, 488, 504–9
  volatility of, 39–41
Interest rate speculation, 437
Interest rate spread, 236, 506, 507, 509
Interest rate swaps, 5–6, 28, 220, 434–36, 484
  basis swap, 6
  BBAIRS, 101
  building block approach and, 514–16
  cash flow and, 5–6
  cross currency, 97
  vs. cross currency swaps, 141, 336, 432–34, 443–51
  defined, 28, 179, 554
  dual, 485
  floating/floating, 432n
  generic, 336n
  to hedge against interest rate risk, 41
  interest rate speculation, 437
  ISDA Master Agreements, 101, 116
  long-funding, 436
  plain vanilla, 73, 108, 370
  short-funding, 435–36
  zero-coupon valuation of, 402
Internal rate of return (IRR), 302, 354
International Accounting Standards
    Committee, 576
International Monetary Market, 9
International Swap Dealers Association
    (ISDA), 28
  definition of currency swap, 91
  documentation for cross currency swaps,
    23, 111, 119
  estimates by, 440n
  Interest Rate and Currency Exchange
    Agreement, text of, 120–39
  legal forms for counterparties, 282
  Master Agreements, 101, 116–17
  1985 Code of Standard Wording,
    Assumptions and Provisions for
    Swaps, 114–15
  purpose of, 587
  standardization in Agreements,
    117–18
  surveys by, 28, 64, 67, 588

In-the-money swaption, 222
Intrinsic value, 173, 222
Inverted yield curve, 166–67
Investment premium, 93
Isard, Peter, 262, 275

Japanese government bond (JGB) rate, 299–300
Johnson, Cal, 331
Johnson, P. M., 553
Jorian, Phillipe, 261, 275

Kapner, Kenneth, 64n, 90
Kasman, B., 368n, 369, 398
Kentucky Development Finance Authority (KDFA), 248
currency and interest rate hedging, 248–55
loan origination and second-generation hedging, 255–56, 257
Kmenta, J., 398
Koala loans, 322
Kohlhagen, S., 365n, 366n, 372n, 398
Krishnan, Suresh, 178

Lamfalussy, A., 398
Leddin, A., 372n, 398
LeRoy, S., 374n
Levich, R., 365n, 372n, 373n, 374, 398
Liability currency swap arbitrage, 48–53
Liability interest rate effect, 346
LIBID (London Interbank Bid Rate), 99, 164
LIBOR (London Interbank Offer Rate), 6, 23, 64, 68, 95, 99–100, 114, 161, 164, 184, 277, 432n
Lillien, Jeffrey, 533n
Limited-dependent-variable models, 370–79
Liquidity, 12, 13, 35, 92, 102–103, 107, 140, 192, 277
Loeys, Jan G., 580
London International Financial Futures Exchange, 9
Long-date cover, achieving
currency collateralized loans, 11–13
foreign currency debt and, 10–11
forward currency contracts, 20–23
modern cross currency swaps, 23–24

Long-date cover, achieving—*Cont.*
old-line currency swap, 18–20
parallel and back-to-back loans, 13–18
Long-dated forward, 351–52
Long-date foreign exchange (LDFX) outright transactions
background, 454
conceptual approach to pricing, 454–55
extension of to multiple currencies and complex structures, 465–69
financial engineering of, 455–65
Long-date foreign exchange risk, 7
Long-term foreign exchange (LTFX) contracts, 422
Long-term forward exchange transactions, 92–93
Long-term liability, 564
Long-term prime rate (LTPR), 297–98, 299, 317–18
Loopesko, B. E., 372n, 398
Low-coupon currency, 359
Lucas, C., 365n, 368n, 369, 398

Maasoumi, E., 373n, 376, 377, 399
Macro index swaps, 276
Maddala, G. S., 377, 399
Maenning, W. C., 376n, 399
Mahajan, A., 372, 399
Malecka, Alicja, 293
Manzur, Meher, 263, 275
Market depth, 159
Market dislocations, 182–183, 188
Market inefficiencies, 373–74
Market-neutral equity portfolio, 283
Market risk
forecasting potential credit exposure, 523–24
measuring actual exposure, 524
Mark-to-market valuation, 65, 82, 84, 89, 103–4, 420–22, 523n, 524, 526, 602
Marshall, John, 64n
Martin Act, 543
Matched swaps, 556
Maturity trends, 595, 600–601
Mehta, D., 372, 399
Militello, Frederick, 580
Model State Commodity Code, 542–43

Monetary policy
  as a means to control the money
    supply, 39–41
Monte Carlo simulation, 523, 524
Mordue, Ian, 453
Mulford, Charles, 580
Multi-index swaps, 285, 286
Multileg transactions, 98–100
Multiple regression model, 261
Municipal debt management, 248–56
  currency and interest rate hedging: KDFA
    example, 248–55
  loan origination and
    second-generating hedging,
    255–56
Mutual funds, 584

Name arbitrage, 367
Nars, Kari, 238
Nathan, R. E., 553
Nehro, Philip, 276
Net sensitivity limit, 425, 427
Netting requirement, 88, 106n, 109, 248
Niehans, J., 365n, 369, 399
No-default situation, 117
North American Securities
    Administration Association
    (NASAA), 542
Notional principal, statistics on,
    591–92, 594, 596

Off-market swap, 144, 188–91, 342,
    343–50. *See also* Zero-coupon
    currency swap
Offset, right of, 15–16, 18
Offsetting swaps, 557
Oil crisis, 38
Old-line currency swap, 18–20
One-price, law of, 262, 365–66
Operant portfolio, 277
  active fixed income, 283
  alternative, 282–84
  global fixed income, 283
  market-neutral equity, 283–84
  swap performance and, 280–81
Operating exposure, 263–65
Option price, 232
Options, 41, 45
Ordinary least squares (OLS)
    regression, 376

Organization for Economic Cooperation and
    Development (OECD), 577
Original issue discount bonds, 584
Origination fees, 570
Out-of-the-money swaption, 222
Over-the-counter products, 41, 533
Overvaluation, 87
Oxelheim, L., 365n, 372, 374, 399

Parallel loans, 12, 13–18, 35, 65, 77, 93,
    112, 294, 370, 558
Park, Y. S., 580
Partial pay structure, 166
Par value, 190
Patterson, E. W., 553
Perfect financial market integration, 365
Perfect markets, 56
Petrodollars, 34
Pigott, C., 368n, 369, 398
Pippenger, J., 373n, 376, 377, 399
Plain vanilla currency swap, 64, 68, 85n,
    162, 600
Plain vanilla interest rate swap, 73, 108,
    370
Popper, H., 374n, 399
Portfolio insurance, 364, 586
Positive carry, 165
Positive yield carry, 165–66
Potential loss amount, 423–24, 425
Prefunding, 205
Premium currency, 359
Previous currency, 290
Price levels, 262–63
Price risk
  control of, 424–26
  factor sensitivity, 422–23
  hedging, 428–30
  management of, 426–31
  measurement of, 420–22
  positioning, 431
  potential loss amount, 423–24
  sensitivity analysis, 428–30
Pricing and valuation
  annuities, 353–55
  annuity factors, 342, 347n
  annuity swap, 350–51
  at-the-market, 343
  basic principles of, 339–41, 353
  covered interest arbitrage, 401,
    403–5, 407

Pricing and valuation—*Cont.*
discount rate, 341–42
long-dated forward, 351–52
off-market, 343–50
zero-coupon approach to, 401–3
Pritchard, David, 580
Product differentiation, 264
Profit, 108
Pryor, Alan, 513
Purchasing power parities (PPPs),
262–63, 269, 365
Putable swaps, 150–51, 228, 229
Put swaption, 219, 223, 228, 229

QPAM (Qualified Professional Asset
Manager), 278n
Quadrangle arbitrage, 403–4, 406
Quandt, R. E., 399

Radecki, L. J., 399
Ramsey, James, 238
Ranganathan, Vembar, 259
Range forward, 286
Rawls, S., 63, 90
Real estate investment trusts (REITs), 586
Refunding strategy, 198
Reinhart, V., 373n, 399
Replacement cost, 65, 84, 520–23
calculation of, 520–23, 526
for Deutschemark interest rate swap,
531–32
for LIBOR/LIBOR swap, 529–30
for U.S. dollar interest rate swap, 528–29
Reporting currency, 267
Reset date, 277, 282
Restrictive covenants, 89–90
Reverse dual-currency (RDC)
instruments, 322–24, 325
Reverse dual-currency loans, 471–73
Right of offset, 15–16
Risk
Cooke method of calculating, 104, 105n
credit, 17, 65, 80–85, 89, 103, 107,
108–9, 181, 191
currency, 65, 89, 238
default, 104, 191
differences between actual and
implied annual interest rates
and forward foreign exchange
rates, 504–9
event, 333

Risk—*Cont.*
exchange-rate, 8, 147, 198–200, 268–74,
493–500
floating-rate spread, 206
foreign exchange, 7–9, 435n, 442n
generic/specific, 149
hedging, 107
integrated model of, 500–509
interest rate, 41, 197–98
market, 523–24
price, 420–26, 428, 429, 430
rollover strategy, 103, 485, 488, 493
spread income, 41
swap, 246–48
valuation, 107
Risk factor, 525
Risk management
analysis of price risk, 422–24
control of price risk, 424–26
hedging, 428–30
mark-to-market valuation, 420–22
objectives of, 419
positioning, 431
sample analysis, 426–28, 430
steps in, 431
Risk-weighted assets, 525
Roller-coaster swap, 149
Rolling forwards, 449–50
Rollover hedge, 199
Rollover strategy, 103, 485, 488, 493
Rosenberg, Lawrence, 262, 275
Rush, M., 275

Sackheim, M. S., 553
Samurai bonds, 238–39, 322, 324
the KDFA example, 248–56, 257
S&P, 500 swap
summary term sheet for, 278
Satrap, Ali, 331n
Scarcity value, 160
Schedules, 116–17
Secondary swap markets, 67
Second-order exchange rate effect, 345n
Securities and Exchange Commission
(SEC), 602
Securitization, 45–46, 327
Security value premium, 48
Shelf registrations, 584
Showers, Janet, 195, 331
Single-currency basis swap, 220
Sinking fund, 179

Smith, Clifford W., Jr., 64n, 90, 368, 370n
Smith, Donald, 63, 64n, 75n, 90
Smithson, C., 63, 64n, 90, 368, 370n
Smithsonian agreement, 293
Solnik, Bruno, 580
Sovereign debt management, 239–48
 case study of swaps for, 245–46
 high credit ratings, 240
 institutional framework, 246
 measuring the impact of swaps, 241
 swap risks, 246–48
 swaps and currency gains, 242–45
Specialization, 107–8
Spooner, Christopher, 581
Spot drift, 450
Spot hedge, 414
Spread income risk, 41
Spreadtions, 235–37
Standardization, 108–9
Standby letters of credit, 89
Stein, W. L., 553
Step-down swap, 148
Step-up coupon bond, 80
Step-up swap, 149
Strike rate, 219
Sullivan, D. C., 553
Swap(s)
 accounting issues, 557
 collapse of the Bretton Woods
  Agreement, 37–39
 and currency gains, 242–245
 defined, 28, 333n
 and the economic environment,
  35–37
 equivalence of positions, 485
 factors contributing to emergence of,
  32–33
 factors contributing to the growth and
  development of, 42–47
 financial deregulation, 42–44
 financial innovation, 44–46
 forerunners of, 10–24, 155.
  See also Back-to-back loans;
  parallel loans
 globalization, 46–48
 growth of market for, 28–29
 hedging and, 30
 as instruments for currency risk
  management, 65, 88–89
 measuring the impact of, 241
 nature of, 556–57

Swap(s)—*Cont.*
 with new issue bonds, 335n
 objectives of, 555–56
 with option features, 150–51
 term structure, 485–93
 as tools for currency management, 100
 with variable notional principal, 148–49
 warehousing, 67, 102, 107, 586
Swap agreements. *See* Documentation
Swap categories
 accreting, 148
 adjustment, 188–91
 amortizing currency, 148, 337–38, 371
 annuity, 142, 336, 337, 338n,
  350–51, 469–71
 asset, 111, 146–47, 178–83, 192–93
 at-the-market, 333, 335, 339, 342, 343,
  347
 basis, 6, 68n, 145–46, 339
 BBAIRS, 101, 113–14
 blocked currency, 155
 callable, 150–51
 capital market currency, 156–70, 172–74,
  177
 CIRCUS, 68n, 100, 562–66
 cocktail, 98–100
 commodity, 584, 600, 602
 coupon, 268, 320, 324, 469–71
 coupon-only, 142
 cross currency, 5, 6–7, 91, 96–113, 140,
  172–83, 218, 221, 239, 332–53,
  371, 436–51, 484–85, 562–66,
  599–600
 cross currency basis, 222
 cross currency coupon, 469–71
 cross currency hedged, 290–91
 cross currency interest, 28, 91
 cross currency unhedged, 291–92
 cross-index, 284, 285
 currency, 7, 24, 28, 47–59, 68n, 69,
  75–77, 140, 146–47, 195–96, 363,
  557–62, 598
  with notional principal, 473–75
 currency equity-linked, 276, 289–92
 dual interest rate, 485
 equity index-linked, 276–82, 284–92
 fixed/fixed cross currency, 83, 92,
  436–42, 444–48
 fixed/fixed currency, 73–75, 85n, 87,
  219, 411–12, 413
 fixed/floating cross currency, 441–42, 447

Swap categories—*Cont.*
  fixed/floating currency, 83, 219, 408–11
  floating/floating cross currency,
    442–44, 447–50
  floating/floating currency, 83–84, 220,
    405–8
  floating/floating interest rate, 432n
  foreign exchange, 333n
  forward, 147
  forward currency, 195–215, 338–39
  generic currency, 331, 333–35,
    360–62
  generic interest rate, 336n
  hedged, 556–57
  interest rate, 28, 179, 220, 434–36, 484,
    554
  matched, 556
  off-market, 144, 188–91, 342,
    343–50
  offsetting, 557
  old-line currency, 18–20
  plain vanilla currency, 64, 68, 85n, 162,
    600
  plain vanilla interest rate, 73, 108, 370
  putable, 150–51, 228, 229
  roller-coaster, 149
  single-currency basis, 220
  step-down, 148
  step-up, 149
  unmatched, 556, 570–71
  zero-coupon currency, 144–45,
    412–14
Swap decisions
  evaluation of short-date strategy, 486–88
  and exchange rate risk, 493–500
  interest rate expectations, 488–89
  multiple-period interest rate
    expectations, 489–93
  overview of, 482–85
  term structure of interest rates,
    485–93
Swap groups, 98
Swap intermediation costs, 58
Swap master agreements, 101, 115–16
Swap maturity/option maturity, 222
Swap options, 118, 155
Swap payments
  calculation of, 434n, 441
  estimated volume of outstanding, 31
Swap positions, equivalence of, 485
Swap spreads, 193

Swaption premium, 228, 230
Swaptions, 155, 167, 177, 371
  at-the-money, 222
  basic strategies, 225–30
  call, 167, 219, 223, 225–28
  cross currency, 233–35
  defined, 218
  forward rate and, 223–24
  growth of, 599
  in Japan, 317–20
  in-the-money, 222
  out-of-the-money, 222
  pricing, 223, 230–33
  put, 219, 223, 228, 229
  terms and conventions in, 219–22
Swap windows
  in Eurosterling market, 176
  in high-coupon markets, 175–76
  in Swiss franc market, 174–75
  in U.S. dollar markets, 174
Swap yield curve, 70
Synchronization, 157
Syndicated loans, 36, 53, 94
Synthetic equity, 276
Synthetic index shuttling, 285
Synthetic securities, 146–47, 178, 333. *See
    also* Asset swap
  examples of, 183–88, 189
  rationale for creating, 181–83

Tax considerations, 20, 36, 43, 44, 46, 57,
    113, 114, 115, 118, 183, 571–74
Taylor, A. R., 369, 399
Taylor, Barry, 533
Taylor, T., 553
Tease, W., 376n, 399
Technological change, 369, 482,
    584–85
Term structure of interest rates (TSIR), 340,
    485–93
  evaluation of a short-date strategy,
    486–88
  interest rate expectations, 488–89
  multiple-period interest rate
    expectations, 489–93
Three-party loans, 13, 14
Tiner, John, 581
Tobit model, 377–78, 381
Topping up, 17
Trade date, 196
Trade deficit, 37

Trasnor (Bermuda) Ltd. v. BP North American Petroleum, 549–50
Treasury amendment, 533, 534, 551
Tremmel, Philip, 195n
Turner, Deborah, 581
Two-party loans, 13

Uncovered interest parity (UIP), 372–73
Unfunded swap, 197
Unmatched swaps, 556, 570–71
Up-front payment, 347–50

Valuation. *See* Pricing and valuation
Valuation risk, 107
Van Wart, K. T., 553
Variable notational principal, 148–49
Variable-rate funding, 40
Volatility, 222

Wakeman, L.M., 368, 370n
Walley, Malcolm, 580
Walmsley, Julian, 580
Warrants, 144, 182–83, 306–12
Weaver, Samuel, 481
Weiller, K., 364, 365n, 368n, 372n, 373, 397
Wilford, D. Sykes, 64n, 90
Wishon, Keith, 556, 580
Wood, Michael, 91, 112
World Bank, 58–59, 159, 162, 240, 602. *See also* IBM/World Bank swap

Yen cross currency swap
  arbitrage and niche products, 324–26
  assets and liabilities behind, 303–26
  changing financial environment and, 295–97
  corporate liquidity and, 326
  defined, 299
  and domestic banking, 297–99
  dual-currency/reverse dual-currency structures, 320–24
  end users of, 296
  equity warrant bond, 306–10
  Euromarket contribution, 304–6
  example of, 76

Yen cross currency swap—*Cont.*
  excess liquidity syndrome, 315–26
  financial transactions, types of, 303
  vs. foreign exchange, 301–2
  foreign investments, 317
  funding Japan with foreign currencies, 303–12
  future of market, 326–27
  growth of market, 296, 306
  historical perspective on, 294–95
  impact loans, 298, 303, 304
  Japanese foreign investments, 312–15
  role of foreign banks in development of, 298–99
  size of market, 295
  subsidized yen loans, 315, 316
  technology of, 299–300
  use of swaptions, 317–20
  yen lending to foreigners, 313–15
  zero-cost funding through use of warrants, 310–12
Yield curve
  callable issues and, 167–68
  forward rate and, 223, 224
  inverted, 166–67
  outlook for, 601
  positive, 165–66
  sensitivity limits, 425–26
Yield enhancement, 318, 320
Young, M. D., 553

Zeitech, 324–26
  defined, 307n
Zero-cost funding, 310–12
Zero-coupon bonds, 43, 342, 351–52, 355, 584
  math, 355–57
Zero-coupon currency swap, 92, 144–45, 337, 339, 412–15
Zero-coupon liability, 145
Zero-coupon rates, 351n, 353, 354n, 355, 446n
  advantages of using, 515n
  calculating, 416
  and swap valuation, 401–3
Zero premium collar, 286